Beason
20 Birchcrest Ct.
Durham, NC 27713

# ETHNICITY
# AND
# FAMILY THERAPY

## Second Edition

Edited by
**MONICA McGOLDRICK
JOE GIORDANO
JOHN K. PEARCE**

THE GUILFORD PRESS
New York   London

© 1996 Monica McGoldrick, Joe Giordano, and John K. Pearce
Published by The Guilford Press
A Division of Guilford Publications, Inc.
72 Spring Street, New York, NY 10012

All rights reserved

No part of this book may be reproduced, stored in a retrieval
system, or transmitted in any form or by any means, electronic,
mechanical, photocopying, microfilming, recording, or
otherwise, without written permission from the Publisher.

Printed in the United States of America

This book is printed on acid-free paper.

Last digit is print number:   9   8   7   6   5   4   3   2

**Library of Congress Cataloging-in-Publication Data**
Ethnicity and family therapy / edited by Monica McGoldrick,
   Joe Giordano, John K. Pearce. — 2nd ed.
      p.   cm.
   Includes bibliographical references and index.
   ISBN 0-89862-959-4
      1. Minorities—Mental health services—United States.
   2. Family psychotherapy—United States.   3. Minorities—United
   States—Family relationships.   I. McGoldrick, Monica.
   II. Giordano, Joe.   III. Pearce, John K.
   RC451.5.A2E83   1996
   616.89'156—dc20                                              96-7923
                                                                 CIP

To those who have come before

especially John Spiegel, Fritz Midelfort,
Carolyn Attneave, Joan Taylor, Ruth Levin Sagner,
John Patton, and Randy Gerson

# Contributors

Nuha Abudabbeh, PhD, Naim Foundation, Washington, DC

Rhea Almeida, MSW, DVS, Director, Institute for Family Services, Somerset, New Jersey; Faculty, Family Institute of New Jersey, Metuchen, New Jersey

Leonid Althausen, MSW, Jewish Family and Children's Service, Boston, Massachusetts

Zarita Araújo, MSW, LICSW, President, Cross Cultural Communication Systems, Inc., Winchester, Massachusetts

Guillermo Bernal, PhD, University of Puerto Rico, San Juan, Puerto Rico

Amy Bibb, LCSW, Associate, Family Institute of New Jersey, Metuchen, New Jersey; Senior Social Worker, Jewish Board of Family and Children Services, Bronx, New York

Lascelles Black, MSW, Montefiore Family Health Center, Bronx, New York

James Boehnlein, MD, Psychiatry Department, Oregon Health Sciences University, Portland, Oregon

Nancy Boyd-Franklin, PhD, Faculty, Graduate School of Applied and Professional Psychology, Rutgers University, New Brunswick, New Jersey

Janet Brice-Baker, PhD, Ferkauf Graduate School of Psychology, Yeshiva University, Bronx, New York

Mary Anne Broken Nose, BA, COPSA Institute for Alzheimer's Disease and Related Disorders, University of Medicine and Dentistry of New Jersey, Community Mental Health Center, Piscataway, New Jersey

Georges J. Casimir, MD, Clinical Assistant Professor of Psychiatry, State University of New York Health Sciences Center; Director of Geriatric Service, Kingsboro Psychiatric Center, Brooklyn, New York

Steve Dagirmanjian, PhD, Catskill Family Institute, Kingston, New York

Conrad De Master, LCSW, BCD, Private Practice, Waldwick, New Jersey

Ann Del Vecchio, PhD, Senior Research Associate, Center for Education and Study of Diverse Populations, New Mexico Highlands University, Albuquerque, New Mexico

Mary Anne Dros-Giordano, MSW, Private Practice, New York, New York

Eric Emery, MSW, PhD, Assistant Professor, California State University at Stanislaus, Turlock, California

Beth M. Erickson, PhD, Family Resources Institute, Santa Fe and Albuquerque, New Mexico

Celia Jaes Falicov, PhD, Private Practice, San Diego; Assistant Clinical Professor, Department of Psychiatry, University of California, San Diego, California

v

Irene Feigin, MA, Plymouth Psychiatric Associates, Plymouth Meeting, Pennsylvania

Eva Fogelman, PhD, Senior Research Fellow, Center for Social Research, City University of New York; Codirector of Psychotherapy with Generations of the Holocaust and Related Traumas, Training Institute for Mental Health, New York, New York

John Folwarski, LCSW, Raritan Bay Mental Health Center, Perth Amboy, New Jersey

Nydia Garcia-Preto, MSW, Faculty, Family Institute of New Jersey, Metuchen, New Jersey

Joe Giordano, MSW, Director, Ethnicity and Mental Health Associates, Bronxville, New York

Miguel Hernandez, MSW, Roberto Clemente Family Guidance Center; Ackerman Institute for Family Service, New York, New York

Paulette Moore Hines, PhD, Faculty, Family Institute of New Jersey, Metuchen; Director, Office of Prevention Services, University Mental Health Services at the University of Medicine and Dentistry of New Jersey, Piscataway, New Jersey

Behnaz Jalali, MD, Clinical Professor of Psychiatry, Department of Psychiatry, University of California at Los Angeles School of Medicine, Los Angeles, California

Suzanne Kerr, BA, Graduate Student, University of Pennsylvania, Philadelphia, Pennsylvania

Bok-Lim C. Kim, LCSW, Private Practice, San Diego, California

Eliana Catão Korin, Dipl Psic, Department of Family Medicine, Montefiore Medical Center, Bronx, New York

Jo-Ann Krestan, MA, Consulting Practice, Faculty, Family Institute of Maine; Visiting Faculty, Family Institute of New Jersey, Metuchen, New Jersey

Régis Langelier, PhD, Partner, Langelier and Associates Inc., South Burlington; Clinical Associate Professor, Clinical Psychology Department, Saint Michael's College and College of Education and Social Services, University of Vermont, South Burlington, Vermont

Evelyn Lee, EdD, Associate Clinical Professor, Department of Psychiatry, University of California, San Francisco, California

Paul K. Leung, MD, Psychiatry Department, Oregon Health Sciences University, Portland, Oregon

Catherine D. M. Limansubroto, MS, Assistant Professor of Psychology, Atma Jayaa University, Jakarta, Indonesia

Vanessa Mahmoud, MSW, Psychotherapist, Spelman College, Atlanta, Georgia

Phyllis P. Marganoff, EdD, Faculty, New Jersey Center for Family Studies, Springfield, New Jersey

Wesley Tak Matsui, PhD, New Jersey Center for Family Studies, Springfield, New Jersey

David W. McGill, PsyD, Staff/Family Therapy Supervisor, Cambridge Hospital; Clinical Instructor in Psychology, Department of Psychiatry, Harvard Medical School, Cambridge, Massachusetts

Monica McGoldrick, LCSW, MA, PhD(h.c.), Director, Family Institute of New Jersey, Metuchen; Faculty, University of Medicine and Dentistry of New Jersey, New Brunswick, New Jersey; Visiting Faculty, Fordham University, New York, New York

Lorna McKenzie-Pollock, MSW, Private Practice, International Counseling, Brookline, Massachusetts

**Emeka Nwadiora, MSW, PhD,** Professor, Temple University School of Social Work, Philadelphia; Private Practice, Philadelphia, Pennsylvania

**Spyros D. Orfanos, PhD,** Clinical Supervisor, Psychology Department, Long Island University, Brooklyn; Codirector, Greek-American Research Project, Center for Byzantine and Modern Greek Studies, Queens College, Queens, New York

**John K. Pearce, MD,** Private Practice, Cambridge and Martha's Vineyard, Massachusetts

**Fred Piercy, PhD,** Director, Marriage and Family Therapy Doctoral Program, Department of Child Development and Family Studies, Purdue University, West Lafayette, Indiana

**Elliot J. Rosen, EdD,** Faculty, Family Institute of Westchester, Mount Vernon, New York

**Emilio Santa Rita, EdD,** Department of Counseling and Student Development, Bronx Community College of the City University of New York, Bronx; Senior Staff Therapist, Blanton-Peale Counseling Center, New York, New York

**Ester Shapiro, PhD,** University of Massachusetts, Boston, Massachusetts

**James P. Simon, MEd,** Director of Education and Training, The International Center for the Disabled, New York Hospital–Cornell Medical Center, New York, New York

**Jette Sinkjaer Simon, Clin Psych,** Private Practice, Washington, DC

**Debra Smith, MSW, LCSW,** Private Practice, Hackettstown, New Jersey

**Adriana Soekandar, MS,** Assistant Professor of Psychology, University of Indonesia, Jakarta, Indonesia

**CharlesEtta T. Sutton, MSW,** Faculty, Family Institute of New Jersey, Metuchen; Training Director, Office of Prevention, University of Medicine and Dentistry, Community Mental Health Center, Piscataway, New Jersey

**Nadine Tafoya, MSW,** Private Consultant, Santa Fe, New Mexico

**Sam J. Tsemberis, PhD,** Clinical Assistant Professor, Department of Psychiatry, New York University School of Medicine; Codirector, Greek-American Research Project, Center for Byzantine and Modern Greek Studies, Queens College, Queens, New York

**Susan F. Weltman, LCSW,** Faculty, Family Institute of New Jersey, Metuchen, New Jersey

**Norbert A. Wetzel, PhD,** Princeton Family Institute, Princeton, New Jersey

**Hinda Winawer, MSW,** Faculty, Ackerman Institute for Family Therapy, New York, New York; Cofounder, Princeton Family Institute, Princeton, New Jersey

# Preface

*What would it be like to have not only color vision but culture vision,*
*the ability to see the multiple worlds of others?*
—MARY CATHERINE BATESON (1994, p. 53)

Ethnicity, the story of our connections to our heritage and our ancestors, is always also a story of the evolution of group identities as we migrate, organize, and reorganize ourselves to meet changing historical and geographic circumstances. Ethnicity patterns our thinking, feeling, and behavior in both obvious and subtle ways, although generally we are not aware of it. It plays a major role in determining what we eat and how we work, relate, celebrate holidays and rituals, and feel about life, death, and illness.

Our very definitions of human development are ethnoculturally based. Eastern cultures, for example, tend to define the person as a social being and categorize development by the growth in the human capacity for empathy and connection. By contrast, many Western cultures begin by positing the individual as a psychological being and defining development as growth in the capacity for differentiation. African Americans have a communal sense of identity: "We are, therefore I am," which contrasts deeply with the dominant culture's individualistic "I think, therefore I am." Family therapists have recognized that individual behavior is mediated through family rules and patterns, but we have failed to appreciate that these rules are usually rooted in cultural norms.

Although human behavior results from intrapsychic, interpersonal, familial, socioeconomic, and cultural forces, the mental health field has paid greatest attention to the first of these—the personality factors that shape life experiences and behavior. The study of cultural influences on human emotional functioning has been left primarily to cultural anthropologists. And even they have preferred to explore these influences in distant non-Western cultures, rather than exploring the great ethnic diversity of our assumptions about illness and health, normality and pathology. Andrew Greeley has noted:

> I suspect that the historians of the future will be astonished that . . . (we) could
> stand in the midst of such an astonishing social phenomenon and take it so much

for granted that . . . (we) would not bother to study it. They will find it especially astonishing in light of the fact that ethnic differences, even in the second half of the twentieth century, proved far more important than differences in philosophy or economic system. Men who would not die for a premise or a dogma or a division of labor would more or less cheerfully die for a difference rooted in ethnic origins. (1969, p. 5)

Mental health professionals who have considered culture have often been more absorbed in making international, cross-cultural comparisons than in studying the ethnic groups in our own culture. Our therapeutic models are generally presented as if they were free of cultural biases. Only recently have we begun to consider the underlying cultural assumptions out of which our therapeutic models arise and those that we as therapists bring to each encounter.

What follows is a kind of "road map" for understanding families in relation to their ethnic heritage. The paradigms here are not presented as "truth," but rather as a map to some aspects of the terrain, intended as a guide to the explorer seeking a path. The paradigms draw on historical traits, residues of which linger in the psyche of families many generations after immigration and long after their members have become outwardly "Americanized" and cease to identify with their ethnic background. Although families are changing very rapidly in today's world, our focus here is on the continuities—the ways in which families retain the cultural characteristics of their heritage, often without noticing these patterns. While the suggestions offered here will not, of course, be relevant in every case, they will, we hope, expand readers' ways of thinking about their own clinical assumptions and those of the families with whom they work. Space limitations have made it necessary for us to emphasize characteristics that may be problematic; thus we do not always present families in their best light. We are well aware that this can lead to misunderstandings and feed negative stereotypes. We trust readers to take the information in the spirit in which it is meant, not to limit thinking, but to expand it.

Unfortunately, when discussion of ethnicity has occurred, it has often focused on groups' "otherness" in ways that emphasize their deficits rather than their adaptive strengths or their place in the larger society. The emphasis has also been on how so-called "minorities" relate to the "dominant" societal values of "normality." We have chosen instead to emphasize that ethnicity pertains to everyone and influences everyone's values, not only those marginalized by the dominant society. Thus, everyone's assumptions must be investigated, not just those kept at the periphery of society.

Although stereotyping or generalizing about groups has often reinforced prejudices, one cannot discuss ethnic cultures without such generalizing. The only alternative is to ignore this level of analysis of group patterns, which, in our view, only mystifies and disqualifies our experience, thus perpetuating covert negative stereotyping. Only if we allow ourselves to air our assumptions can we learn about each other's ethnicity. We try to articulate differences among groups in order to sensitize clinicians to the range of values within our multicultural society. Of course, each family is unique. The characterizations made about particular groups are intended to put more questions on the table and help us to broaden our perspectives on values and assumptions that we have long taken for granted.

Family therapy, which was rocked to its foundations by the feminist critique, has been moving toward an awareness of the essential dimension of culture as well as gender. Unfortunately most of the institutions of the field—the major training programs, the publications, and the professional organizations— still view ethnicity as an "add-on" to family therapy, as a "special topic" rather than as basic to any discussion of the subject. Reactions to the recent upsurge in "diversity" presentations at the annual Family Therapy Academy meetings include a frequently articulated longing to "get back to basics." Yet we cannot move "back" to basics. Rather, we must revise the "basics" from more inclusive perspectives, so ethnic and cultural awareness will inform all our work, allowing us to deal empathically with the experience of all our clients.

To many the first edition of *Ethnicity and Family Therapy* provided an "ah hah!" recognition of their own cultural background, or that of a spouse, friends, or clients. Still, when it was written, we were all fairly naive about the meaning of culture in our complex world. Although some feared that our book reinforced cultural stereotypes, we believed then, and believe now, that defining the ethnic paradigms is important to understanding ourselves and our clients.

But it is clearly not enough. In this edition we hope to enrich the paradigms by suggesting how gender, class, race, religion, and politics have influenced families in adapting to American life. The letter of instructions to contributors to this edition read in part as follows:

> Because so much has been happening in the area of cultural diversity in the past few years, we will have to shorten the chapters to make room for new material on groups not included last time. We also have much more awareness of gender, class, and race since the first edition and are asking you to include consideration of these issues in an integrated way in your contribution.
>
> We want to make reference to variations we were unable to include in the last edition, while keeping the liveliness of the cultural descriptions. We urge you to concentrate on conveying relevant and useful details, without allowing people too much room to think that one chapter or one book could possibly provide them with all they need to know to work with those who are culturally different. We are striving to keep the richness of detail about values, patterns, and characteristics, while adding perspectives on the impact of gender, sexual orientation, class, and stigma within the dominant society.
>
> 1. Describe the particular *characteristics and values of the group with some context of history, geography, politics, and economics* as they are pertinent to understand the patterns of the group.

2. Emphasize especially *values and patterns that are relevant for therapy*—those an uninformed therapist might be most likely to misunderstand (i.e., related to problems, help seeking, and what is seen as the "cure" when people are in trouble).
3. Describe *patterns that relate to clinical situations, especially couple relationships; parent–child issues; sibling relationships; three-generational relationships; how families deal with loss, conflict, affection, homosexuality, and intermarriage.*
4. Include relevant information on the impact of *class and class change, religion, gender roles, and migration experience.*

During the past decade, we have become increasingly convinced that we learn about culture primarily not by learning the "facts" of another's culture, but rather by changing our attitude. Our underlying openness to those who are culturally different is the key to expanding our cultural understanding. Thus, cultural paradigms are useful to the extent that they help us recognize patterns we may have only vaguely sensed before. They can challenge our long-held beliefs about "the way things are."

No clinician should feel that, armed with a small chapter about another cultural group, he or she is adequately informed to do effective therapy with them. The chapters that follow are not intended as recipes for relating to other ethnic groups, which is far more influenced by attitude, particularly respect, curiosity, and humility than by "information." As was said about Henry Glassie, a man who has worked closely with people in Bangladesh, Ballymone, Ireland, and Turkey:

> There is a particular magic that blesses some individuals with the gift of breaking down the natural reserve we all feel toward those of another language, another culture, another economic stratum. For Mr. Glassie, this magic apparently developed through years of intimate talk in the quiet cottages of Ballymone and ultimately led in Turkey to a virtual explosion of the boundaries of his life and the angle of focus of this scholarship. (Denny, 1995, p. 9)

David McGill has suggested that the best training for family therapists might be to live in another culture and learn a foreign language. That experience might best help the clinician achieve the humility necessary for respectful cultural interactions, based on more than a one-way hierarchy of normality, truth, and wisdom.

Ethnicity is marked by an ever ongoing cultural evolution. We are all always in a process of changing ethnic identity, from incorporating ancestral influences to forging new and emerging group identities. Group identities emerge in a complex interplay of members' relationships with each other (insiders), and with outsiders. So we must consider a person's ethnicity as both a relationship to whatever groups he or she belongs to (unaware, negative, proud, appreciative), and a sense of his or her relationship to the dominant culture (member, outsider, inferior). In addition, to define one's identity as that of a single ethnic group—for example, "Irish," "Anglo," "African American"—is to greatly oversimplify matters, since no cultural process ever stands still. We are always evolving ethnically.

My (M. M.) Irish ancestors probably had roots in Celtic tribes in what is now Switzerland and in Viking communities in what is now Norway. My husband immigrated from Greece at age 19, his parents having been born in Turkey.

My (J. G.) grandparents came from Italy—Grandpa from Naples and Grandma from Genoa. (Some would say that was a mixed marriage!) I married a Puerto Rican Italian woman. My second wife's mother was Scotch Irish, and her father was born in Holland of a Jewish mother and a Protestant father. I also have three grandchildren whose mother is African American with roots in the Baptist South.

In addition, we consider it important to explore how each generational cohort has a different "culture," as do different geographic regions (e.g., urban areas as opposed to small towns). In addition, we are all increasingly being influenced by the "culture" of television, which is unfortunately replacing family and community relationships for Americans.

So when we ask people to identify themselves ethnically, we are really asking them to oversimplify, to highlight a partial identity, in order to make certain themes of cultural continuity more apparent. We believe that ethnically respectful clinical work helps people evolve a sense of to whom and what they belong. Thus, therapy involves helping people clarify their self-identity in relation to family, community, and their ancestors, while also adapting to changing circumstances as we move on toward our future.

## REFERENCES

Bateson, M. C. (1994). *Peripheral visions.* New York: HarperCollins.

Denny, W. (1994, August 7). Magic carpets [Review of *Turkish Traditional Art Today* by Henry Glassie, Bloomington: Indiana University Press]. *New York Times Book Review.*

Greeley, A. (1969). *Why can't they be like us?* New York: Institute of Human Relations Press.

# Acknowledgments

Many people have supported us in our efforts to produce this second edition of *Ethnicity and Family Therapy*, particularly our publisher, Seymour Weingarten, and all the staff at The Guilford Press. Thanks also to the administrative staff of the Family Institute, especially Meg Tischio and Rene Campbell, for providing assistance, direct and indirect, to make the book come to fruition. Sophocles and John Orfanidis, and Mary Ann Giordano and our (J. G.) nine children and nine grandchildren, made many sacrifices in time and gave their emotional support, which made concentrating on this book possible. Keith Sproul helped us with the technical aspects night and day to get drafts transferred from program to program, so we could work on the editing of the manuscript. David McGill and Rhea Almeida went out of their way to read and comment on others' manuscripts and give personal feedback and to assist various other authors. David Szonyi and Ann Whelan provided editorial help and generosity of time. Betty Carter, friend and soulmate, provided generous emotional support and specific, useful critique, which as always encouraged me (M. M.) to make my best effort. And my (J. G.) soulmate, Irving Levine, whose vision and leadership has helped define the nature of ethinicity in our society, has continued to inspire me and many others over the last three decades. Nollaig Byrne and Imelda McCarthy, loyal friends for many years, gave generously of their time and diplomacy helping me (M. M.) understand the politics of ethnicity in relation to oppression. For his early and honest critique of the first edition of this book, which was formative in pointing my thinking toward the new edition, we thank also Charles Waldergrave, who with the others on the Just Therapy Team of Lower Hutte in New Zealand has had a major impact on our thinking about the effects of the politics of colonialization on cultural identity. Phil Hallen of the Falk Medical Fund and the American Jewish Committee provided financial and organizational support for the first edition, which helped make it a success. We are also grateful to all those who have participated in the Family Institute's annual Cultural Diversity Conference over the past years, our yearly opportunity to connect with friends from around the country who have been working together to push the boundaries of our thinking on culture. Many of these people are contributors to this edition or to its forth-coming companion volume on culture, which will be published by Guilford.

Finally, we thank the authors of the chapters, many of whom worked within a very short time frame and with very tight page constraints to conform to the space limitations of the book, and at the same time infused their creativity and knowledge in their cultural descriptions.

# Contents

1. Overview: Ethnicity and Family Therapy                                  1
   Monica McGoldrick and Joe Giordano

## I. AMERICAN INDIAN FAMILIES

2. American Indian Families: An Overview                                   31
   CharlesEtta T. Sutton and Mary Anne Broken Nose

3. Back to the Future: An Examination
   of the Native American Holocaust                                        45
   Nadine Tafoya and Ann Del Vecchio

## II. FAMILIES OF AFRICAN ORIGIN

4. Families of African Origin: An Overview                                 57
   Lascelles Black

5. African American Families                                               66
   Paulette Moore Hines and Nancy Boyd-Franklin

6. Jamaican Families                                                       85
   Janet Brice-Baker

7. Haitian Families                                                        97
   Amy Bibb and Georges J. Casimir

8. African American Muslim Families                                       112
   Vanessa Mahmoud

9. Nigerian Families                                                      129
   Emeka Nwadiora

## III. LATINO FAMILIES

10. Latino Families: An Overview                                          141
    Nydia Garcia-Preto

11. Cuban Families                                        155
    Guillermo Bernal and Ester Shapiro

12. Mexican Families                                      169
    Celia Jaes Falicov

13. Puerto Rican Families                                 183
    Nydia Garcia-Preto

14. Brazilian Families                                    200
    Eliana Catão Korin

15. Central American Families                             214
    Miguel Hernandez

## IV. ASIAN AMERICAN FAMILIES

16. Asian American Families: An Overview                  227
    Evelyn Lee

17. Chinese Families                                      249
    Evelyn Lee

18. Japanese Families                                     268
    Wesley Tak Matsui

19. Korean Families                                       281
    Bok-Lim C. Kim

20. Vietnamese Families                                   295
    Paul K. Leung and James Boehnlein

21. Cambodian Families                                    307
    Lorna McKenzie-Pollock

22. Indonesian Families                                   316
    Fred Piercy, Adriana Soekandar,
    and Catherine D. M. Limansubroto

23. Pilipino Families                                     324
    Emilio Santa Rita

## V. MIDDLE EASTERN FAMILIES

24. Arab Families                                         333
    Nuha Abudabbeh

25. Iranian Families                                      347
    Behnaz Jalali

26. Lebanese Families                                                 364
    James P. Simon

27. Armenian Families                                                 376
    Steve Dagirmanjian

## VI. ASIAN INDIAN FAMILIES

28. Hindu, Christian, and Muslim Families                             395
    Rhea Almeida

## VII. FAMILIES OF EUROPEAN ORIGIN

29. European Families: An Overview                                    427
    Joe Giordano and Monica McGoldrick

30. Amish Families                                                    442
    Eric Emery

31. American Families with English Ancestors
    from the Colonial Era: Anglo Americans                           451
    David W. McGill and John K. Pearce

32. Dutch Families                                                    467
    Conrad De Master and Mary Ann Dros-Giordano

33. French Canadian Families                                          477
    Régis Langelier

34. German Families                                                   496
    Hinda Winawer and Norbert A. Wetzel

35. Greek Families                                                    517
    Sam J. Tsemberis and Spyros D. Orfanos

36. Hungarian Families                                                530
    Debra Smith

37. Irish Families                                                    544
    Monica McGoldrick

38. Italian Families                                                  567
    Joe Giordano and Monica McGoldrick

39. Portuguese Families                                               583
    Zarita A. Araújo

40. Scandinavian Families: Plain and Simple                           595
    Beth M. Erickson and Jette Sinkjaer Simon

## VIII. JEWISH FAMILIES

41. Jewish Families: An Overview
    Elliot J. Rosen and Susan F. Weltman                    611

42. Soviet Jewish Families
    Irene Feigin                                            631

43. Israeli Families
    Eva Fogelman                                            638

## IX. SLAVIC FAMILIES

44. Slavic Families: An Overview
    Phyllis P. Marganoff and John Folwarski                 649

45. Polish Families
    John Folwarski and Phyllis P. Marganoff                 658

46. Slovak Families
    Suzanne Kerr                                            673

47. Russian Families
    Leonid Althausen                                        680

48. Czech Families
    Jo-Ann Krestan                                          688

    Author Index                                            697

    Subject Index                                           709

CHAPTER 1

# Overview: Ethnicity and Family Therapy

### Monica McGoldrick
### Joe Giordano

*Prejudice is a burden which confuses the past, threatens the future, and
renders the present inaccessible.*
                    —MAYA ANGELOU (1986, p. 155)

*The future of our earth may depend on the ability of all [of us] to
identify and develop new . . . patterns of relating across difference. The
old definitions have not served us, nor the earth that supports us.*
                    —AUDRE LORDE (1995, p. 502)

Ethnicity refers to a common ancestry through which individuals have evolved
shared values and customs. It is deeply tied to the family, through which it is
transmitted. A group's sense of commonality is transmitted over generations
by the family and reinforced by the surrounding community. Ethnicity is a
powerful influence in determining identity. A sense of belonging and of historical continuity are basic psychological needs. We may ignore our ethnicity
or deny it by changing our names and rejecting our families and social backgrounds, but we do so to the detriment of our well-being. The subject of
ethnicity evokes deep feelings, and discussion frequently becomes polarized
or judgmental. According to Greeley (1969), using presumed common origin
to define "we" and "they" seems to touch on something basic and primordial
in the human psyche. Similarly, Levine (personal communication, 1981) has
observed: "Ethnicity can be equated, along with sex and death, as a subject that
touches off deep unconscious feelings in most people."
     The concept of a group's "peoplehood" is based on a combination of race,
religion, and cultural history and is retained, whether or not members realize
their commonalities with one another. The consciousness of ethnic identity

1

varies greatly within groups and from one group to another. Those who have experienced the stigma of prejudice and racism may attempt to "pass" as members of the more valued majority culture. In groups that have experienced prejudice and discrimination, such as Jews and African Americans, family members may absorb the larger society's prejudices and become conflicted about their own identity. Family members may even turn against each other, with some trying to "pass" and others resenting them for doing so. Those who are close enough in appearance to the dominant group's characteristics may experience a sense of choice about what group to identify with, whereas others have no choice because of their skin color or other physical characteristics. Examples of ethnic conflict include some group members' attempts to change their appearance through plastic surgery or other means to obtain "valued" characteristics. Other examples would include an African American accusing another of being "an Oreo," meaning that he or she has "sold out" to the White culture. Families that are not of the dominant culture are always under pressure to give up their values and conform to the norms of the more powerful group. Intrafamily conflicts over the level of accommodation should be viewed not just as family conflicts, but also as reflecting explicit or implicit pressure from the dominant culture.

## FACTORS INFLUENCING ETHNICITY

Ethnicity interacts with economics, race, class, religion, politics, geography, the length of time since migration, a group's specific historical experience, and the degree of discrimination it has experienced. Generally, people move closer to the dominant value system the longer they remain in the United States and the more they rise in social class. Families that remain within an ethnic neighborhood, who work and socialize with members of their group, and those whose religion reinforces ethnic values, will probably maintain their ethnicity longer than those who live in heterogeneous settings.

The impact of war and political oppression can also greatly affect a group's historical traditions, as in Central America, Southeast Asia, and the former Soviet Union. The degree of ethnic intermarriage in the family also plays a role in the evolution of its cultural patterns (McGoldrick & Garcia-Preto, 1984; Crohn, 1995).

Therapists need to be as attuned to migration stresses and ethnic identity conflicts as they are to other stresses of a family's history. Many Americans have experienced the complex stresses of migration; they may be "buried" or forgotten, but they influence the family's outlook, if sometimes subtly, as they try to accommodate to a new situation. Many immigrant groups have been forced to abandon much of their ethnic heritage and thus have lost a part of their identity. Families will be more vulnerable the more they have repressed their past. The effects of this may be all the more powerful for being hidden.

Some families will hold on to their ethnic identification, becoming clannish or prejudiced in response to a perceived threat to their integrity. Others use ethnic identification to push for family loyalty: They might say, "If you do that, you're betraying the Jews." For other groups—for example, Scots, Irish, or French Canadians—such an emotional demand for ethnic loyalty would probably not hold much weight.

Most of us are somewhat ambivalent about our ethnic identification. Even those who appear indifferent to their ethnic background would be proud to be identified with their group in some situations and feel embarrassed or defensive in others. Those most exposed to prejudice and discrimination are most likely to internalize negative feelings about their ethnic identity. Often ethnicity becomes such a toxic issue that people's response is not even to mention it, for fear of sounding prejudiced, although it may be a major factor in their response to a situation.

In the years since the first edition of *Ethnicity and Family Therapy* was published, our awareness of cultural diversity in our society and world has changed profoundly. We have been witnessing some devastating and amazing transformations in ethnic group relationships in South Africa, Northern Ireland, the Middle East, the former Soviet Union, and elsewhere, while the United States is being transformed by rapidly changing demographic realities.

We are experiencing the greatest rise in immigration in 100 years. More than one million legal and undocumented immigrants are arriving annually, most from Asia and the vast Hispanic world ("What Will the U.S. Be Like When Whites Are No Longer the Majority," 1990; "The New Face of America," 1993). With streams of new immigrants expressing their unique cultures, American society has become characterized by unparalleled diversity. Asians, Latin Americans, and other newcomers have become "the new face of America."

Geographic regions vary in the impact of this. In the Pacific region, for example, one-fifth of Americans are foreign born, although in the Midwestern farm belt, this is true of only one person in 50. But overall, during the past decade, African Americans have increased by 13% and now comprise 12% of the population; Latinos have increased by 53% to become 9%; whereas Asians have doubled to become about 3% of the population. Only about 75% of Americans are non-Hispanic Whites (Roberts, 1995).

Asian-born Americans now outnumber European-born ones. In Los Angeles four in 10 residents are foreign born; in New York, three in 10. By the end of the next century, White Americans will be a minority.

Concomitantly, there has been a rapid rise of multicultural consciousness in the United States. The 1990 Census listed 95 racial and ethnic categories and subcategories including White (53 groups), Black, American Indian, Eskimo (or Aleut), and Asian (or Pacific Islander), with 11 Asian and 15 Hispanic subcategories. Indeed, the shift in ethnic identification is so dramatic that more people said they were Cherokee than could possibly have been the case; 1.8 million people said they were Native American, but some claimed they were from "Arabic," "Polish," "Hispanic," or "Haitian" tribes (Roberts, 1995).

The changing ethnic demographics are having a significant impact on all aspects of our society. Of new workers entering the workforce, 80% are women, minorities, or new immigrants. This reality in the context of a growing global economy and the presence of many international corporations helps explain the upsurge in business literature on managing a culturally diverse workforce (Thomas, 1991; Jamieson & O'Mara, 1991; Thiederman, 1991). More than five million children of immigrant parents will enter public schools during the 1990s; about 3.5 million will come from homes where English is not the first language. Today, more than 150 languages are represented in America's schools. Multicultural education, although controversial, is increasingly being included in school curricula (Banks, 1991).

For many decades, large cities were the main places where many different faces of Americans were visible. Today, however, America's suburbs, smaller cities, and even small towns are hardly as homogenous as they once were ("Melting Pot Moves to the Heartland," 1995). Mental health professionals everywhere are being challenged to develop treatment models and services that are more responsive to ethnic, racial and religious identities.

Diversity's impact has become perhaps the major theme of the arts in America today. Writers such as Amy Tan, Richard Rodriguez, Gay Talese, Anne Roiphe, Edwige Denticat, Toni Morrison, Maxine Hong Kinston, Alice Walker, Mary Gordon, Helen Barolini, Eva Hoffman, Thomas King, Lisa See, and Chang-rae Lee are recounting their ethnic roots in growing up in America. Similar ethnic expressions are seen in film, theater, TV, and music.

Concomitantly, there has been a growing realization since this book's first edition that a positive sense of ethnic and racial identity is essential for developing a healthy personal and group identity, and for effective clinical practice. Elaine Pinderhughes's pathbreaking *Understanding Ethnicity, Race, and Power* (1989) has elaborated brilliantly a broad-based, multicultural perspective, clarifying the primary role of power in organizing ethnic and racial relationships. She described the comprehensive model she has developed for mental health training. *The Influence of Race and Racial Identity in Psychotherapy* (Carter, 1995) has elaborated the fact that race is not a "special issue," but rather a pivotal factor in therapy. *The Social and Political Contexts of Family Therapy* (Mirkin, 1993) explores the effects on families of poverty, gender, migration, dislocation, and the threat of nuclear holocaust. *Women in Context* (Mirkin, 1995), a model for family therapy texts, integrates ethnicity, race, class, and sexual orientation into the formulation of every topic. Other important books have laid the groundwork on particular issues or groups, including *Minorities and Family Therapy* (Saba, Karrer, & Hardy, 1989); *Family Therapy with Eth-*

*nic Minorities* (Ho, 1987); *Family Ethnicity* (McAdoo, 1993); *Black Families in Therapy: A Multisystems Approach* (Boyd-Franklin, 1989); *Working with West Indian Families* (Gopaul-McNicol, 1993); *Asian Americans* (Uba, 1994); *Women of Color* (Comas-Díaz & Greene, 1994); *Cultural Perspectives in Family Therapy* (Falicov, 1983); and *Expansions of Feminist Theory through Diversity* (Almeida, 1994). These authors and many others have been contributing to our cultural knowledge. Several more important texts that we know of are due soon, including *Clinical Guide to Working with Asian American Families* (Lee, in press) and *Hispanic Families in Therapy* (Falicov, in press). Yet there has been very little systematic integration of material on ethnicity in any mental health professional training. It remains a "special issue," taught at the periphery of psychotherapy training and rarely written about or recognized as crucial by therapists of the dominant groups. For this perspective to become truly integrated into our work we will need a transformation of our field, which has barely begun (McGoldrick & Green, in press).

## THE CHANGING FACE OF THE UNITED STATES ETHNICALLY

Ethnic identity has always been a central component of American life. Its salience is probably related to the fact that White ethnic groups are slowly becoming a minority of the population in the country. Ethnic distinctions among European Americans are fading, whereas other ethnic groups become more prominent. Indeed, one researcher has suggested that a new ethnic group, Euro Americans, is forming (Alba, 1990). We believe that this eventuality is far off, for ethnicity changes only gradually, in many ways much more slowly than we might think.

Yet our country has been largely defined by those seeking change from their ancestors' cultures. As Tataki (1993) states:

> Indians were already here, while blacks were forcibly transported to America, and Mexicans were initially enclosed by America's expanding border. The other groups came here as immigrants: for them, America represented liminality—a new world where they could pursue extravagant urges to do things they had thought beyond their capabilities. Like the land itself, they found themselves "betwixt and between all fixed points of classification." No longer fastened as fiercely to their old countries, they felt a stirring to become new people in a society still being defined and formed. (p. 6)

The fluidity of cultural identity has always been an American trait. But a conservative backlash against multiculturalism has been developing, illustrated by the rise of White extremist skinheads and neo-Nazi groups that foster racial and ethnic hatred; the increase in racial- and religious-bias crimes, committed primarily by young people; and the new anti-immigrant nativism.

Multiculturalism has been criticized as corrupting our educational institutions (Bloom, 1987; Schleshinger, 1995). They fear that it will destroy national cohesion, that *E Pluribus Unum*—"out of many, one"—is becoming *E Pluribus Plurimus.*

But diversity has always been central to American life; it is embedded in the Founding Fathers' ideology, which provided explicitly for protecting minority views, respecting the persistence of democratic disagreements and minority viewpoints, so that the dominant group does not impose its own culture and values on all other groups (Schwarz, 1995).

Respect for ethnic diversity has flourished during certain periods in American history and been stifled at others. The Founding Fathers, after all, did not include African Americans in their definition of minority, and the Naturalization Law of 1790 restricted citizenship to Whites (Tataki, 1993). Many times, the majority group has asserted its power through an assimilationist "melting pot" ideology, and we have remained ambivalent about the value of ethnic pluralism.

Yet ethnicity remains a major form of group identification and a major determinant of our family patterns and belief systems. The American premise of equality required us to give primary allegiance to our national identity, fostering the myth of the "melting pot," the notion that group distinctions between people should ultimately disappear. The idea that we were all equal led to pressure to see ourselves as all the same. But the melting-pot idea never worked. We have not "melted."

## OUR COMPLEX AND EVOLVING ETHNIC IDENTITIES

Every family's background is multicultural. All marriages are to a degree cultural intermarriages. No two families share exactly the same cultural roots. Understanding the various strands of a family's cultural heritage is essential to understanding its members' lives and the development of the particular individual as well. The multiple parts of our cultural heritage often do not fit easily into a description of any one group.

As family therapists, we work to help clients clarify the various facets of their identity to increase their flexibility to adapt to America's multicultural society. We help them appreciate and value the complex web of connections within which their identities are formed and which cushion them as they move through life.

Our clients' personal contexts are largely shaped by the ethnic cultures in which they live and from which their ancestors have come. As Paolo Friere (1994) has described:

No one goes anywhere alone, least of all into exile—not even those who arrive physically alone, unaccompanied by family, spouse, children, parents, or siblings. No one leaves his or her world without having been transfixed by its roots, or with a vacuum for a soul. We carry with us the memory of many fabrics, a self soaked in our history, our culture; a memory, sometimes scattered, sometimes sharp and clear, of the streets of our childhood. (p. 32)

Of course, each of us belongs to many groups. The sense of belonging is vital to our identity. At the same time the profound differences among us culturally must also be acknowledged. We need to balance validation of the differences among us and appreciation of the common forces of our humanity. It is only when the exclusion of outsiders becomes primary to group identity that one's group identity reflects something dysfunctional—namely a negative identity: defining oneself as part of a group that excludes others.

Those of us born White, who conform to the dominant societal norms, probably grew up believing that "ethnicity" referred to others who were different from us. We were "regular." As Tataki (1993) has pointed out, we have always tended to view Americans as European in ancestry.

We need to develop an open, flexible social system with flexible boundaries—so that people can define themselves by the groupings that relate to their heritages and practices and go beyond labels such as "minorities," "Blacks," "Latinos," or "Americans." Our very language reflects the biases embedded in our society's dominant beliefs. The term "Latino," for example, refers simultaneously to Taino Indians, Cubans of Spanish origin, Chinese who settled in Puerto Rico, families from Africa whose ancestors were brought to Latin America as slaves, and Argentinean Jews, whose ancestors lived in Europe for over 1,000 years until the 1930s or '40s. The term "minority" peripheralizes groups whose heritage is different from the dominant groups. The term "Black" obliterates the ancestry of Americans of African heritage altogether and defines people only by their color. And the fact that there is no term "United Statesan" to describe people of the United States, but only the inaccurate term "American," which makes invisible Canadians, Mexicans, and other Americans, is a serious handicap to our even discussing these issues.

Individuals should not have to suppress parts of themselves in order to "pass" for normal according to someone else's standards. Being "at home" is about people having a sense of being at peace with who they really are, not fitting them into rigidly-defined group identities, which strains their basic loyalties. As family therapists, we believe in helping clients understand their ethnicity as a fluid, ever-changing aspect of who they are. The character Vivian Twostar in *The Crown of Columbus* (Erdrich & Dorris, 1991), describes the complexity this always entails:

I belong to the lost tribe of mixed bloods, that hodgepodge amalgam of hue and cry that defies easy placement. When the DNA of my various ancestors—Irish and Coeur d'Alene and Spanish and Navajo and God knows what else—combined to form me, the result was not some genteel indecipherable puree that comes from a Cuisinart. You know what they say on the side of the Bisquick box, under instructions for pancakes? Mix with fork. Leave lumps. That was me. There are advantages to not being this or that. You have a million stories, one for every occasion, and in a way they're all lies and in another way they're all true. When Indians say to me, "What are you? I know exactly what they're asking and answer Coeur d'Alene. I don't add, "Between a quarter and a half," because that's information they don't require, first off—though it may come later if I screw up and they're looking for reasons why. If one of my Dartmouth colleagues wonders, "Where did you study?" I pick the best place, the hardest one to get into, in order to establish that I belong. If a stranger on the street questions where [my daughter] gets her light brown hair and dark skin, I say the Olde Sodde and let them figure it out. There are times when I control who I'll be, and times when I let other people decide. I'm not all anything, but I'm a little bit of a lot. My roots spread in every direction, and if I water one set of them more often than others, it's because they need it more . . . I've read anthropological papers written about people like me. We're called marginal, as if we exist anywhere but on the center of the page. We're parked on the bleachers looking into the arena, never the main players, but there are bonuses to peripheral vision. Out beyond the normal bounds, you at least know where you're not. You escape the claustrophobia of belonging, and what you lack in security you gain by realizing—as those insiders never do— that security is an illusion. . . "Caught between two worlds," is the way we're often characterized, but I'd put it differently. We are the catch. (pp. 166–167)

Erdrich and Dorris offer a brilliant expression of our multifaceted identities, comprised of complex heritages, judgments about what is possible or preferable in a given context, and other people's projections onto us. They also illustrate what those who belong have to learn from those who are marginalized.

If we look carefully enough, we are all a "hodgepodge." Developing "cultural competence" requires us to explore and question the dominant values and the complexity of cultural identity.

We are all migrants, moving between our ancestors' traditions, the worlds we inhabit, and the world we will leave to those who come after us. For most of us, finding out who we are means putting together a unique internal combination of cultural identities. Maya Angelou (1986), who as an African American naturally found it hard to feel culturally at home in the United States, went to live in Africa. She hoped in some way to be home and found there that who she was could not be encompassed by that important part of her heritage:

If the heart of Africa still remained elusive, my search for it had brought me closer to understanding myself and other human beings. The ache for home lives in all of us, the safe place where we can go as we are and not be questioned. It impels mighty ambitions and dangerous capers . . . We shout in Baptist churches, wear yarmulkes and wigs and argue even the tiniest points in the Torah, or worship the sun and refuse to kill cows for the starving. Hoping that by doing these things, home will find us acceptable or that barring that, we will forget our awful yearning for it. (p. 196)

Those who try to assimilate at the price of forgetting their connections to their heritage are likely to have more problems than those who maintain their heritage.

The work of Klein (1980) with Jews, Cobbs (1972) with Blacks, and Giordano and Riotta-Sirey (1985) with Italians, demonstrates that when people are secure in their identity, they act with greater flexibility and openness to those of other cultural backgrounds. However, if people receive negative or distorted images of their ethnic group, they often develop a sense of inferiority, even self-hate, that can lead to aggressive behavior and discrimination toward outsiders.

## ETHNIC DIFFERENCES IN MENTAL HEALTH

Almost all of us have multiple belief systems to which we turn when we need help. Besides medical or psychotherapeutic systems, we resort to religion, self-help groups, alcohol, yoga, chiropractors, crystals, special foods, and remedies our mothers taught us or those suggested by our friends. Various factors influence which solutions we will rely on at any given time.

Many studies have shown that people differ in the following:

1. Their experience of pain.
2. What they label as a symptom.
3. How they communicate about their pain or symptoms.
4. Their beliefs about its cause.
5. Their attitudes toward helpers (doctors and therapists).
6. The treatment they desire or expect.

Yet a group whose characteristic response to illness is different from the dominant culture is likely to be labeled "abnormal." For example, one researcher found that doctors frequently labeled Italian patients as having psychiatric problems, although no evidence existed that such disorders occurred more frequently among them (Zola, 1966). Another classic study (Zborowski, 1969) found that Italian and Jewish patients complained much more than Irish or Anglo ones, who considered complaining to be "bad form."

A high level of verbal interaction is expected in Jewish, Italian, and Greek families, whereas Anglo, Irish, and Scandinavian families have much less intense interaction and are more likely to deal with problems by distancing.

Therapists need to take these potential differences into account in making an assessment, considering carefully their own biases and their clients' values.

Certain common ethnic traits have been described as typical for families of one or another group. For example, Jewish families are often seen as valuing education, success, family connections, encouragement of children, democratic principles, verbal expression, shared suffering, and having a propensity to guilt and a love for eating. Anglos have been characterized as generally emphasizing control, personal responsibility, independence, individuality, stoicism, keeping up appearances, and moderation in everything. By contrast, Italian American families are generally described as valuing the family more than the individual; considering food a major source of emotional as well as physical nourishment; and having strong traditional male–female roles, with loyalty flowing through personal relationships. African Americans are often described as favoring an informal kinship network and spiritual values. Their strength to survive is a powerful resource, and they tend to have more flexibility in family roles than many other groups. In Hispanic cultures, family togetherness and respect, especially for elders, are valued concepts. People are appreciated more for their character than for merely their vocational success. They may also hold on to traditional notions of a woman's role as the virgin and the sacrificial sainted mother, who tolerates her husband's adventures and absence with forebearance. Chinese families stress harmony and interdependence in relationships, respect for one's place in the line of generations, ancestor worship, saving face, and food as an emotional and spiritual expression. For Asian Indians, purity, sacrifice, passivity, and a spiritual orientation are core values, and death is seen as just one more phase in the life cycle that includes many rebirths.

It would require many volumes to consider any single ethnic group in depth. Indeed, most groups are themselves combinations of multiple cultural groups.

## ETHNICITY AND FAMILIES

The definition of "family" differs greatly from group to group. The dominant American (Anglo) definition focuses on the intact nuclear family, whereas African American families focus on a much wider network of kin and community. For Italians, there is no such thing as the "nuclear" family. To them, family means a strong, tightly knit, third- or fourth-generational network, which also includes godparents and old friends. The Chinese include in "family" all their ancestors and all their descendants, which also reflects a different sense of time than is held in the West.

Studying ethnicity helps one appreciate differences in groups' attitudes toward many core values in the United States. For example, in the world of psychology, the dominant assumption is that talk is good and can heal a person. Therapy has even been referred to as "the talking cure." But consider the different value cultures place on talk.

- In Jewish culture, articulating one's experience may be as important as the experience itself, for important historical reasons. Jews have long valued cognitive clarity. Clarifying and sharing ideas and perceptions helps them find meaning in life. Given the anti-Semitic societies in which Jews have lived for so long, with their rights and experiences so often obliterated, one can understand that they have come to place so much importance on analyzing, understanding, and acknowledging what has happened.
- In Anglo culture, words are used primarily to accomplish one's goals. They are valued mainly for their utilitarian value. As the son says about his brother's death in the movie *Ordinary People*: "What's the point of talking about it? It doesn't change anything."
- In Chinese culture, families may communicate many important issues through food rather than through words. They generally do not accept the dominant American idea of "laying your cards on the table."
- Italians often use words primarily for drama, to convey the emotional intensity of an experience.
- The Irish, perhaps the world's greatest poets, use words to buffer experience—using poetry or humor to somehow make reality more tolerable, not to tell the truth, but perhaps to cover it up or embellish it. The Irish have raised poetry, mystification, double meanings, humorous indirection, and ambiguity to an art form in part, perhaps, because their history of oppression led them to realize that telling the truth could be dangerous.
- In Sioux Indian culture, talking is actually proscribed in certain family relationships. A woman who has never exchanged a single word with her father-in-law may experience deep intimacy with him, a relationship that is almost inconceivable in our pragmatic world. The reduced emphasis on verbal expression seems to free Native American families for other kinds of experience of each other, of nature, and of the spiritual realm.

Cultural groups also vary greatly in the emphasis they place on various life transitions. The Irish and African Americans have always considered death the most important life cycle transition. The Irish place most emphasis on the wake, whereas African Americans spare no expense for a funeral. Italians, Asian Indians, and Poles tend to emphasize weddings, whereas Jews often pay particular attention to the Bar or Bat mitzvah, a transition from childhood that other groups do not mark at all. Families' ways of celebrating these events differ also. The Irish tend to celebrate weddings (and every other occasion) by drinking, the Poles by dancing, the Italians by eating, and the Jews by eating and talking.

Occupational choices, as well, reflect both personal necessity and group values. The Irish are overrepresented in politics and police work; Jews, in small businesses, medicine, and, above all, the mental health field; Germans, in engineering; Greeks and Chinese, in the restaurant business; and Koreans, in food stores.

Ethnic groups' distinctive problems are often the result of cultural traits that are conspicuous strengths in other contexts. For example, British American optimism leads to confidence and flexibility in taking initiative. But the same preference for upbeatness may lead to the inability to cope with tragedy or to engage in mourning. Historically, the British have perhaps had much reason to feel fortunate as a people. But optimism becomes a vulnerability when they must contend with major losses. They have few philosophical or expressive ways to deal with situations in which optimism, rationality, and belief in the efficacy of individuality are insufficient. Thus they may feel lost when dependence on the group is the only way to ensure survival.

Concomitantly, groups vary in what they view as problematic behavior. The English may be concerned about dependency or emotionality; the Irish about "making a scene"; Italians about disloyalty to the family; Greeks about any insult to their pride, or *filotimo*; Chinese about harmony; Jews about their children not being "successful"; Puerto Ricans about their children not showing respect; Arabs about their daughters' virginity; and African Americans about testimony or bearing witness.

Of course, they similarly vary in how they respond to problems. The English see work, reason, and stoicism as the best response, whereas Jews often consult doctors and therapists to gain understanding and insight. Until recently, the Irish responded to problems by going to the priest for confession, "offering up" their suffering in prayers, or, especially for men, seeking solace through drink. Italians may prefer to rely on family support, eating, and expressing themselves. West Indians may see hard work, thrift, or consulting with their elders as the solution, and Norwegians might prefer fresh air or exercise. Asian Indians might focus on sacrifice or purity, and the Chinese, on food or prayer.

Groups also differ in attitudes toward seeking help. In general, Italians rely primarily on the family and turn to an outsider only as a last resort. African Americans have long mistrusted the help they can receive from traditional institutions except the church, the only one that was "theirs." Puerto Ricans and Chinese may somatize when under stress and seek medical rather than mental health services. Norwegians, too, often convert emotional tensions into physical symptoms, which they consider more acceptable—thus, their preference for the doctor to the psychotherapist. Likewise, Iranians may view medication and vitamins as a necessary part of treating symptoms. Many potential patients experience their troubles somatically and strongly doubt the value of psychotherapy. And some groups tend to see their problems as the result of their own sins, actions, or inadequacy (Irish, African Americans, Norwegians) or someone else's (Greeks, Iranians, Puerto Ricans).

Cultures differ also in their attitudes about group boundaries. Puerto Ricans, Italians, and Greeks all have similar rural, peasant backgrounds, yet important ethnic differences exist among these groups. Puerto Ricans tend to have flexible boundaries between the family and the surrounding community, so that informal adoption is a common and accepted practice. Italians have much clearer boundaries within the family and draw rigid boundaries between insiders and outsiders. Greeks have very definite family boundaries, are disinclined to adopt children, and have deep feelings about the "bloodline." They are also strongly nationalistic, a value that relates to a nostalgic vision of ancient Greece and to the country they lost under hundreds of years of Ottoman oppression. By contrast, Italians in the "old country," defined themselves first by family ties, second, by their village, and, third, if at all, by the region of Italy from which they came. Puerto Ricans' group identity has coalesced only within the past century, primarily in reaction to experiences within the United States. Each group's way of relating to therapy will reflect its differing attitudes toward family, group identity, and outsiders, although certain family characteristics, such as male dominance and role complementarity, are similar for all three groups.

## MIGRATION HISTORY

The reasons for migration include what the family was seeking (e.g., adventure or wealth) and what it was leaving behind (e.g., religious or political persecution, or poverty). A family's dreams and fears when immigrating become part of its heritage. Parents' attitudes toward what came before and what lies ahead will have a profound impact on the expressed or tacit messages they transmit to their children.

Families that have already migrated tend to adapt more easily. Those who come as refugees, fleeing political persecution or the trauma of war and who have no possibility of returning to their homeland, may have very different adaptations to American life than those who come seeking economic advancement with the idea of returning to their homeland to retire. In this regard, Coco Fusco's (1987) *English Is Broken Here* gives a remarkable illustration of the particular problems of Cuban immigrants over the past three decades:

> Americans often ask me why Cubans, exiled or at home, are so passionate about Cuba, why our discussions are so polarized, and why our emotions are so raw after thirty-three years. My answer is that we are always fighting with the people we love the most. Our intensity is the result of the tremendous repression and

forced separation that affects all people who are ethnically Cuban, wherever they reside. Official policies on both sides collude to make exchange practically impossible. (p. 3)

Adaptation is also affected by whether one family member migrated alone or whether a large portion of the family, community, or nation came together. Families that migrate alone have usually a greater need to adapt to the new situation, and their losses are often more hidden. Frequently, educated immigrants who come for professional opportunities move to places where there is no one with whom they can speak their native language or share family customs and rituals. When a number of families migrate together, as happened with the Scandinavians who settled in the Midwest, they are often able to preserve much of their traditional heritage.

When a large part of the population or nation came together, as happened in the waves of Irish, Polish, Italian, and Jewish migration, many Americans reacted to these large groups with prejudice and discrimination. The newest immigrants threatened those who came just before, who feared the loss of their tenuous economic security.

Family members vary in how much of their heritage they retain, although clearly the impact of the past diminishes as they have new experiences. They differ in the rate at which they learn English. The language of the country of origin will serve to preserve its culture. It is important to learn what language(s) were spoken while the children in the family were growing up.

The East and West coasts, the entry points for most immigrants, are likely to have greater ethnic diversity and ethnic neighborhoods, and people in these areas are more often aware of ethnic differences (in the East more than the West). The ethnic neighborhood provides a temporary cushion against the stresses of migration that usually surface in the second generation. Those immigrant families who moved to an area where the population was relatively stable, for example, the South, generally had more trouble adjusting or were forced to assimilate very rapidly.

When family members move from an ethnic enclave, even several generations after immigration, the stresses of adaptation are likely to be severe. The therapist should learn about the community's ethnic network and encourage the rebuilding of social and informal connections through family visits or letters or creating new networks.

## RACE AND RACISM

Race is an issue of political oppression, not a cultural or genetic matter. As Ignatiev (1995) puts it: "No biologist has ever been able to provide a satisfactory definition of 'race'—that is, a definition that includes all members of a given race and excludes all others" (p. 1). Clearly, categorizing people by race serves to reduce all members of one group into an undifferentiated social status, beneath that of any member of another group regardless of class (Ignatiev, 1995).

Although racism may be more subtle and covert today, the politics of race continue to be complex and divisive, and, unfortunately, Whites remain generally unaware of the problems our society creates for people of color. Racism and poverty have always dominated the lives of ethnic minorities in the United States. Race has always been a major cultural definer and divider in our society, since those whose skin color marked them as different always suffered more discrimination than others. They could not "pass," as other immigrants might, leaving them with a noticeable "obligatory" ethnic and racial identification.

Racial bigotry and discrimination continue to be a terrible fact of American life, from college campuses to corporate boardrooms. Although conditions have improved from a generation ago, when Blacks were not permitted to drink from the same water fountains as Whites or to attend integrated schools, we still live in an essentially segregated society. The racial divide continues to be a painful chasm, creating a profoundly different consciousness for people of color than for Whites. People find it even more difficult to talk to each other about racism than they do about ethnicity. Each new racial incident ignites feelings and expressions of anger and rage, helplessness and frustration. Exploring our own ethnicity is vital to overcoming our prejudices and expanding our understanding of ourselves in context, but we must also take care in our pursuit of multicultural understanding not to diminish our efforts to overcome racism (Katz, 1978).

The invisible knapsack of privilege (McIntosh, in press) of all White Americans, just by the color of their skin, is something that most White ethnics do not acknowledge. Although there is a rapidly increasing rate of intermarriage among European groups and Whites with people of color, the percentages of the latter is still small. And the level of segregation in the United States between European Americans and people of color, especially African Americans, remains a profound problem in our society, and one that most Whites do not notice.

Thus, most family therapy has been developed and conducted by White Americans for other White Americans, without reference to people of color. Their invisibility in the literature is an issue for therapists that they, for the most part do not realize, just as White families often do not realize their racism unless they are confronted by it if their daughter dates an African American, or if they should have to work closely with a person of color in the workplace. Otherwise, Whites tend to remain oblivious to their hidden relationships with people of color, unaware of the profound ways that minorities support the lives of White families in our society: as housekeepers and nannies, as nursing staff when we are in need of health care, in hotels or other public facilities, where people of color tend to be the invisible, support workforce—those who clean the building, wash the dishes, and so forth. We who are White therapists have a long way to go to expand our consciousness of the way the field itself keeps people of color invisible. Family therapy treats race and ethnicity as a "special issue," not a basic factor. This is a reflection of the problem for White ethnics in recognizing their true relationship to other cultural groups. As patriarchy, class hierarchies, and heterosexist ideologies have been invisible structural definers of all European groups' ethnicity, so have race and racism been invisible definers of European groups' cultural values.

## CLASS

Class increasingly organizes the United States in very insidious ways, including structuring the relationships among ethnic groups, often pitting less powerful groups against each other, or members of a less powerful group against themselves. The distance between the very rich and everyone else has been increasing dramatically in the last two decades. The wealthiest one million people in the United States make as much money as the next 100 million put together. And the share of wealth of the top 1% of the population (40% of the nation's wealth) has doubled since 1970 (Thurow, 1995). Twenty years ago, the typical CEO made 40 times the amount of the typical American worker. Now that ratio has swelled to 190 times as much (Hacker, 1995). Inequalities in earnings between the top 20% of wage earners and the bottom 20% have doubled in the last two decades (Thurow, 1995). Derrick Bell (1993), has suggested that intergroup conflicts, especially racial conflicts, are promoted by those at the top to keep everyone not at the top from realizing their shared interests, because, if they did, it would create a revolution. It is much safer for the dominant group to promulgate the myth that it is the Black man we really have to fear, rather than the power structure that holds our dominant class in place.

Class intersects powerfully with ethnicity and must always be considered when one is trying to understand a family's problems. The influence of class on the status position of groups in the United States is extreme. Of the 1,000 people who have ever appeared on *Forbes* magazine's list of the 400 richest people in America, only five have been Black (Hacker, 1995).

Some maintain that class, more than ethnicity, determines people's values and behavior. Class is important, but not all differences can be ascribed to class alone. Ethnic distinctions generally play a less powerful role among the most educated and upwardly mobile segments of a given group, who tend to dissociate themselves from their ethnic roots. This may create hidden problems in a family, pitting one generation against another, or one segment of a group against another.

Upward mobility is part of the "American dream." While you cannot change your ethnicity, changing class is indeed the expectation of our society.

You may deny your gender or culture, you may not conform to stereotypic patterns of your gender or cultural group, but you cannot change who you are on these dimensions. Yet changes in class, which are among the most profound we experience, are generally not talked about, even within the same family. Silence about class transitions can become quite painful. Parents and children may end up in different socioeconomic groups if the children are either successful or disabled.

Groups also differ in the extent to which they value education or "getting ahead." Family members may feel compelled to make a choice between moving ahead and loyalty to their group, which can be a source of severe identity or intrafamilial conflict. For important historical reasons, certain groups, such as Irish, Italians, Poles, or African Americans, may have a distinct ambivalence or discomfort about moving up in class, while others embrace it wholeheartedly.

## THE FAMILY LIFE CYCLE

Migration is so disruptive that it seems to add an entire extra stage to the life cycle for those who must negotiate it. Adjusting to a new culture is not a single event, but a prolonged developmental process that affects family members differently, depending on their life cycle phase.

When individuals immigrate during the young adult phase, they have the greatest potential for adapting to a new culture in terms of career and marital choice, but they may also be most vulnerable to cutting off their heritage.

Families that migrate with young children are often strengthened by having each other, but they are vulnerable to the reversal of hierarchies. Parents may acculturate more slowly than their children, creating a problematic power inversion. When children interpret the new culture for their parents, parental leadership may be threatened, as children are left without effective adult authority to support them, and without a positive ethnic identity to ease their adaptation to life in this new culture. If the parents are supported in their cultural adjustment, through their workplace or extended family and friends, their children's adjustment will go more easily, since young people generally adapt well to new situations, even when doing so involves learning a new language. But in adolescence, when the children are drawn toward their peer culture, problems may surface. Coaching the younger generation to show respect for their elders' values, even while holding different values themselves, is usually the first step in negotiating such conflicts.

Families migrating with adolescents may have more difficulty, because they will have less time together as a unit before the children move out on their own. The family struggles with multiple transitions and generational conflicts at once. Families' distance from the grandparents in the old country may be particular distressing as they become ill, dependent, or die, and their children may experience guilt or other stress in not being able to fulfill their filial obligations. At times adolescents develop symptoms in reaction to their parents' distress.

Families with young adult children are less likely to migrate seeking a better way of life. More often, if families migrate at this phase, it is because circumstances in the country of origin make remaining there impossible. Migration at this phase may be especially hard, because it is much more difficult for the parents to adapt to a new language, job situation, relationships, and customs. Again, if aging parents are left behind, the stresses of migration will be intensified.

This phase may be more complex if children date or marry individuals from other backgrounds. This is naturally perceived as a threat by many, if not most, parents, since it means a loss of the cultural heritage in the next generation. One cannot underestimate the stress parents experience in their children's intermarriage when they themselves have lost the culture in which they grew up.

Migration in later life can be especially difficult because families are leaving a great deal of their life experience and sociocultural resources behind. Even those who might migrate at a young age have a strong need to reclaim their ethnic roots at this phase, particularly because they are losing other supports. For those who have not mastered English, it can be extremely isolating to be dependent on strangers for health care services when they cannot communicate easily.

When immigrants are older and live in an ethnic neighborhood, acculturation conflicts may be postponed. The next generation, particularly during adolescence, is likely to reject their parents' "ethnic" values and strive to become "Americanized." Intergenerational conflicts often reflect the value struggles of families in adapting to the United States. The third and fourth generations are usually freer to reclaim aspects of their identities that were sacrificed in previous generations because of the need to assimilate.

Families from different ethnic groups may experience diverse kinds of intergenerational struggles. British American families are likely to feel that they have failed if their children *do not* move away from the family and become independent, whereas Italians generally believe they have failed if their children *do* move away. Jewish families often foster a relatively democratic atmosphere in which children are free to challenge parents and discuss their feelings openly. Greek or Chinese families, in contrast, do not generally expect or desire open communication between generations and would disapprove of a therapist getting everyone together to discuss and "resolve" their conflicts. Children are expected to respect parental authority, which is reinforced by the distance parents maintain from their children.

Family life cycle phases vary among different groups. For example, Mexican Americans see early and middle childhood as extending longer than the dominant American pattern (Falicov, 1980). Adolescence is shorter and leads

more quickly into adulthood than in the dominant American structure, courtship is generally longer, and middle age extends into what Americans generally think of as older age.

Any life cycle transition can spark ethnic identity conflicts, because it puts
a person in touch with his or her family traditions. A divorce, marriage, childbirth, illness, job loss, death, or retirement, can exacerbate ethnic identity conflicts, causing people to lose a sense of who they are. A therapist who tries to
help families preserve cultural continuities will assist its members in maintaining and building upon their ethnic identity.

## INTERMARRIAGE

Intimate relationships between people of different ethnic, religious, and racial
backgrounds offer convincing evidence that Americans' tolerance of cultural
differences may be much higher than most people think (Crohn, 1995; Alibhai-
brown & Montague, 1992; McGoldrick & Garcia-Preto, 1984; Petsonk &
Remsen, 1988; Schneider, 1989). Intermarriage is occurring at triple the rate
of the early 1970s. More than 50% of Americans are marrying out of their ethnic groups; 33 million American adults live in households where at least one
other adult has a different religious identity. Intermarriage greatly complicates
those issues that partners from a single ethnic group face. Generally, the greater
the cultural difference between spouses, the more trouble they will have in
adjusting to marriage.

Knowledge about ethnic/cultural differences can be helpful to spouses
who take each other's behavior too personally. Typically, we tolerate differences when we are not under stress; in fact, we may find them appealing. However, when stress occurs, tolerance for differences diminishes. Not to be
understood in ways that confirm with our wishes and expectations frustrates
us. For example, when upset, Anglos tend to move toward stoical isolation to
mobilize their powers of reason. In contrast, Jews seek to analyze their experience together. Italians may seek solace in food or in emotionally and dramatically expressing their feelings. Members of these groups sometimes perceive
each other's reactions as offensive or insensitive, although, within each group's
ethnic norms, such reactions make perfect sense. Much of therapy involves
helping family members recognize each other's behavior as largely a reaction
from a different frame of reference.

Many cultural and religious groups have long had prohibitions against
intermarriage, which is seen as a threat to group survival. Until 1967, when such
laws were declared unconstitutional, 19 states prohibited racial intermarriage.
Until 1970, the Catholic Church did not recognize out-marriages, unless the
non-Catholic partner promised to raise the couple's children in the Catholic
faith. Many Jewish groups have also feared that intermarriage would threaten

the group's survival. In earlier generations the intermarriage rate in Jewish families was very low, but the rates have increased dramatically for the current generation. According to the 1990 National Jewish Population Study, 52% of new marriages were to non-Jews. Extended families may negatively stereotype a new spouse when they feel threatened, to assure themselves of their superiority. In response to this issue, there have been a number of books to guide couples in dealing with issues from a religious and ethnic perspective.

The likelihood of ethnic intermarriage increases with the length of time individuals have lived in this country, as well as with higher educational and occupational status. In a nationwide survey of Catholics, 80% reported their parents were from the same ethnic background, but this was true for only 55% of the respondents.

Couples who choose to "marry out" are usually seeking to rebalance their own ethnic characteristics, moving away from some values as well as toward others. The extended families may stereotype the new spouse negatively, which is often a self-protective maneuver to reassure themselves of their superiority. During courtship, a person may be attracted precisely to the loved one's differentness, but when he or she is in a marital relationship the same qualities can seem grating.

Consider an Anglo-Italian couple in which the Anglo husband takes literally the dramatic expressiveness of the Italian wife, while she finds his emotional distancing intolerable. The husband may label the Italian "hysterical" or "crazy" and in return be labeled "cold" or "catatonic." Knowledge about differences in cultural belief systems can help spouses who take each other's behavior too personally. Couples may experience great relief when they can come to see the spouse's behavior as fitting into a larger ethnic context rather than as a personal attack. Yet cultural traits may also be used as an excuse for not taking responsibility in a relationship: "I'm Italian. I can't help it" (i.e., the yelling, abusive language, impulsiveness); or "I'm a WASP. It is just the way I am" (the lack of emotional response, rationalization, and workaholism); or "I can't help being late. We Puerto Ricans have a different conception of time."

## THERAPY ISSUES

Appreciation of cultural variability leads to a radically new conceptual model of clinical intervention. Helping a person achieve a stronger sense of self may require resolving cultural conflicts within the family, between it and the community, or in the wider context in which the family is embedded. A part of this process involves identifying and consciously selecting ethnic values we wish to retain and carry on. Families may need coaching to distinguish deeply held convictions from values asserted for emotional reasons.

What is adaptive in a given situation? Answering this requires appreciation of the total context in which behavior occurs. For example, Puerto Ricans may see returning to the Island as a solution to their problems. A child who misbehaves may be sent back to live with an extended family member. This solution may be viewed as dysfunctional if the therapist considers only that the child will be isolated from the immediate family, or that the living situation in Puerto Rico may be inadequate to meet the child's needs. However, rather than counter the parents' plan, the therapist might encourage them to strengthen their connectedness with family members in Puerto Rico with whom their child will be staying, for they will be using a culturally sanctioned network for support.

The therapist's role in such situations may be that of a cultural broker, helping family members to recognize their own ethnic values and to resolve the conflicts that evolve out of different perceptions and experiences.

Often it is very difficult to understand the meaning of behavior without knowing something of a client's value orientation. Clients may not talk openly in therapy for many different reasons. Black clients may be uncommunicative, not because they cannot deal with their feelings, but because the context involves a representative of a traditional "White" institution that they never had reason to trust. The Irish client's failure to talk might have to do with embarrassment about admitting feelings to anyone, especially to other family members. Norwegians might be withholding out of respect and politeness, which involves not openly stating negative feelings they have about other family members and may have nothing to do with either the therapy context or guilt about "unacceptable" feelings.

There are many examples of such misunderstood behavior. Puerto Rican women are taught to lower their eyes and avoid eye contact, which American therapists are taught to read as indicating an inability to relate interpersonally. Jewish patients routinely inquire about the therapist's credentials, which many groups would perceive as an affront, but is for them a needed reassurance. Iranian and Greek patients may ask for medication and give every indication of taking it but then go home and not take it as prescribed. Irish families may not praise or show overt affection to their children for fear of giving them a "swelled head," which therapists may misread as lack of caring. Physical punishment, commonly used by many groups, including, until recently, the dominant groups in the United States, may be perceived as idiosyncratic pathological behavior. This is not to justify child beatings, which have been widely accepted among many cultures. Rather, we must consider the cultural context in which a behavior evolves, even as we try to reshape it when it does not reflect humanitarian or equitable values. The point is that therapists, especially those from dominant groups that tend to take their own values as the norm, must be extremely cautious in judging the meaning of behavior they observe.

There are many who believe that "cross-fertilization" between ethnic groups is the best antidote to the "stuckness" families experience when their cultural adaptations fail. Thus, Irish reserve may be a good balance for Italian impulsiveness, whereas Italian expansiveness counters Irish repression.

Jewish families who become stuck in endless verbal analyses may be helped by the "Anglo" ethic that pushes to resolve the matter and move on. Conversely, English constrictions in dealing with emotional distress may be greatly helped by the Jewish value of sorting through the painful experiences and sharing the suffering.

## ETHNICITY TRAINING

In our view, the most important part of ethnicity training involves the therapist coming to understand his or her own ethnic identity. Just as many family therapists emphasize helping families sort out the relationships in their own families of origin, we believe that differentiation requires coming to terms with one's own ethnic identity. This implies, ideally, that therapists would no longer be "triggered" by ethnic characteristics they may have regarded negatively, nor would they be caught in the ethnocentric view that their group's values are more "right" or "true" than others. Ethnically self-aware and sensitive therapists achieve a multiethnic perspective, which is open to understanding values that differ from their own, and no longer need to convert others or give up their own values.

Our experience has taught us repeatedly that theoretical discussions about the importance of ethnicity are practically useless in training clinicians as are "cookbook" formulations (McGoldrick & Green, in press). We come to appreciate the relativity of values best through specifics that connect with our lived experience of group differences (McGoldrick, 1994). Thus, in our training we try to fit any illustration of a cultural trait into the context of historical and cultural experiences in which that value or behavior evolved. We ask trainees to think about how their own group and perhaps that of their spouse or close friends differ in responding to pain, in their attitudes about doctors, in their beliefs about suffering. Do they prefer a formal or informal style in dealing with strangers? Do they tend to feel positively about their bodies? About work? About sexual intimacy? About children expressing their feelings? We try to help them broaden this understanding to other groups through readings, film, and conversation that illustrate other ways of viewing the same phenomena.

When beginning ethnicity training, it is extremely important to set up a safe context, including allowing for some stereotyping, that is, for generalizing about cultural differences. Of course, all generalizations represent only partial truths. We begin by discussing the problem of stereotyping (e.g., becoming stuck in an overgeneralization) and the problem of not generalizing (e.g., that it prevents us from discussing the subject at all).

Presentations about one group are rarely successful because participants tend to focus on the exceptions to the "rule." We find that presenting two groups is also problematic, because it leads to polarizing so-called opposites. Thus, the discussion only really becomes meaningful when three or more groups are discussed together. This is especially important because of our society's tendency to polarize: Black/White, male/female, gay/straight, rich/poor. It is always valuable to create a context in which overlapping and ambiguous differences cannot easily be resolved, since that fits better with the complexities of human experience. Presenting several groups also tends to help students see the pattern, rather than the exception. Thus, while all Irish may not be alike, they may have certain similarities when compared to Haitians, Russians, or Greeks.

Unlike the situation 25 years ago, today there exists a growing body of knowledge and innovative techniques to respond to cultural diversity. Some guidelines we have found useful include the following (Giordano & Giordano, 1995):

- *Assess the importance of ethnicity to patients and families.* To what extent does the patient identify with an ethnic group and/or religion? Is his or her behavior pathological or a cultural norm? Is the patient manifesting "resistance" or is his or her value system different from that of the therapist?
- *Validate and strengthen ethnic identity.* Under great stress an individual's identity can easily become diffuse. It is important that the therapist foster the client's connection to his or her cultural heritage.
- *Be aware of and use the client's support systems.* Often support systems—extended family and friends; fraternal, social, and religious groups—are strained or unavailable. Learn to strengthen the client's connections to family and community resources.
- *Serve as a "culture broker."* Help the family identify and resolve value conflicts. For example, a person may feel pride about some aspects of his or her ethnic background and shame about others, or there may be an immobilizing "tug of war" between personal aspirations and family loyalty.
- *Be aware of "cultural camouflage."* Clients sometimes use ethnic, racial, or religious identity (and stereotypes about it) as a defense against change or pain, or as a justification for half-hearted involvement in therapy. A person who says, "I'm late for our session because I'm on Puerto Rican time" may be trying to avoid a difficult issue.
- *Know that there are advantages and disadvantages in being of the same ethnic group as your client.* There may be a "natural" rapport from belonging to the same "tribe" as your client. Yet, you may also unconsciously overidentify with the client and "collude" with his or her resistance. Unresolved issues about your own ethnicity may be "mirrored" by client families, exacerbating your own value conflicts.

• *Don't feel you have to "know everything" about other ethnic groups.* Ethnically-sensitive practice begins with an awareness of how cultural beliefs influence all our interactions. Knowing your own limitations and ignorance and being openheartedly curious will help set up a context within which you will have a mutual learning with your clients.

• *To avoid polarization, always try to think in categories that allow for at least three possibilities.* Consider, if you are exploring Black and White differences, how a Latina might view it. Consider, if you are thinking of how African Americans are dealing with male–female relationships, how a Black lesbian might view it. Consider, when exploring Italian/Irish differences, how an African American might think about them.

## MOVING BEYOND POLARIZING DISCUSSIONS

Whenever we think we are getting two opposites too clearly in focus, we should probably focus on a third perspective and see how the other two points look from there. For example, to break the "Black–White" polarization, we might explore these issues from a Latino or biracial perspective.

There are two common pitfalls in discussions of diversity:

1. Discussion gets polarized, particularly around the Black experience of White racism, leaving other people of color feeling invisible or excluded. Issues of sexism and homophobia are also pushed into the background in such a polarized context, as people argue over which oppression is the worst or most important. This typically leads to the withdrawal of those who feel their issues cannot be included in such a dialogue.

2. People are so inclusive about diversity that it trivializes racism or leads to it being ignored in the multiplicity of other "isms." This often happens in discussions of cultural diversity, in which proposals for inclusiveness are so extensive that institutionalized racism becomes submerged.

We need to keep a multidimensional perspective, that highlights the overwhelming reality of institutionalized racism, while also including other forms of oppression.

In training groups we often ask participants to (1) describe themselves ethnically, (2) relate who in their family experience influenced their sense of ethnic identity, (3) discuss which groups other than their own they think they understand best, (4) explore which characteristics of their ethnic group they like most and which they like least, and (5) discuss how they think their own family would react to having to go to family therapy and what kind of approach they would prefer.

## NOT ROMANTICIZING CULTURE

Just because a culture espouses certain values or beliefs does not make them sacrosanct. All cultural practices are not ethical. Every intervention we make is value laden. We must not use notions of neutrality or "deconstruction" to shy away from committing ourselves to the values we believe in. We must have the courage of our convictions, even while realizing that we can never be too certain that our perspective is the "correct" one. This means that we must learn to tolerate ambiguities and continue to question our stance in relation to the position and values of our clients. And we must be especially careful about the power differential if we are part of the dominant group, since the voices of those who are marginalized are harder to hear. The disenfranchised need more support to have their position heard than do those who feel they are entitled because theirs are the dominant values.

In addressing racism, we must also deal with the oppression of women of color. This cannot be blamed solely on White society, for patriarchy is deeply embedded in African, Asian, and Latino cultures. We must work for the right of every person to a voice and a sense of safety and belonging. We must challenge those who argue: Let cultural groups "speak for themselves." This ignores the issue of who speaks for their group, which is usually determined largely by patriarchal and class factors.

## CONCLUSION

Ethnicity is a social reality that will require the therapist to be more culturally competent as we enter the 21st century. Race, gender, religion, class, immigration status, age, sexual orientation, and disability are also critical identity issues that we must consider in order to understand our clients. Add to this the rapidly changing nature of family life, and it becomes clear that we need to reexamine our therapy approaches in a larger multicultural context.

## REFERENCES

Alba, R. D. (1990). *Ethnic identity: The transformation of white America.* New Haven: Yale University Press.

Alibhai-Brown, Y., & Montague, A. (1992). *The colour of love: Mixed race relationships.* London: Virago Press.

Almeida, R. (1994). *Expansions of feminist theory through diversity.* New York: Haworth Press.

Angelou, M. (1986). *All God's children need traveling shoes.* New York: Vintage.

Banks, J. A. (1991). *Teaching strategies for ethnic studies* (5th ed.). Boston: Allyn & Bacon.

Bell, D. (1993). *Faces at the bottom of the well: The permanence of racism.* New York: Basic Books.

Bloom, A. (1987) *The closing of the American mind.* New York: Simon & Schuster.

Boyd-Franklin, N. (1989). *Black families in therapy: A multisystems approach.* New York: Guilford Press.

Carter, R. T. (1995). *The influence of race and racial identity in psychotherapy.* New York: Wiley.

Cobbs, P.(1972). Ethnotherapy in groups. In L. Solomon & B. Berzon (Eds.), *New perspectives on encounter groups.* San Francisco: Jossey-Bass.

Comas Diaz, L., & Green, B. (Eds.). (1994). *Women of color: Integrating ethnic and gender identities in psychotherapy.* New York: Guilford Press.

Crohn, J. (1995). *Mixed matches.* New York: Fawcett Columbine.

Erdrich, L., & Dorris, M. (1991). *The crown of Columbus.* New York: Harper.

Falicov, C. J. (1980). The family life cycle of Mexican families. In B. Carter & M. McGoldrick (Eds.), *The family life cycle.* New York: Gardner Press.

Falicov, C. J. (Ed.). (1983). *Cultural perspectives in family therapy.* Rockville, MD: Aspen.

Falicov, C. J. (in press). *Hispanic families in therapy.* New York: Guilford Press.

Friere, P. (1994). *The pedagogy of hope.* New York: Continuum.

Fusco, C. (1995). *English is broken here: Notes on cultural fusion in the Americas.* New York: The New Press.

Giordano, J., & Giordano, M. A . (1995). Ethnic dimensions in family therapy. In R. Mikesell, D. Lusterman, & S. McDaniel (Eds.), *Integrating family therapy.* Washington, DC: American Psychological Association.

Giordano, J., & Riotta-Sirey, A. (1981). *An Italian American identity.* Unpublished paper, Institute on Pluralism and Group Identity, New York.

Gopaul-McNicol, S. (1994). *Working with West Indian families.* New York: Guilford Press.

Greeley, A. (1969). *Why can't they be like us?* New York: American Jewish Committee.

Hacker, A. (1995, November 19). Who they are. *New York Times Magazine,* pp. 70–71.

Ho, M. K. (1987). *Family therapy with ethnic minorities.* Newbury Park, CA: Sage.

Ignatiev, N. (1995). *How the Irish became white.* New York: Routledge.

Jamieson, D., & O'Mara, J. (1991). *Managing workforce 2000.* San Francisco: Jossey-Bass.

Katz, J. H. (1978). *White awareness: Handbook for anti-racism training.* Norman, OK: University of Oklahoma Press.

Klein, J. (1980). *Jewish identity and self esteem: Healing wounds through ethnotherapy.* New York: Institute on Pluralism and Group Identity.

Lee, E. (in press). *Asian American families: A clinical guide to working with families.* New York: Guilford Press.

Lorde, A. (1995). Age, race, class and sex: Women redefining difference. In M. L. Anderson & P. H. Collins (Eds.), *Race, identity, class, and gender: An anthology.* New York: Wadsworth.

McAdoo, H. P. (Ed.) (1993). *Family ethnicity.* Newbury Park, CA: Sage.

McGoldrick, M. (1994, June–July). The ache for home. *The Family Networker.*

McGoldrick, M., & Garcia-Preto, N. (1984). Ethnic intermarriage. *Family Process, 23*(3), 347–362.

McGoldrick, M., & Green, R.-J. (in press). *Re-visioning family therapy from a multicultural perspective.* New York: Guilford Press.

McIntosh, P. (in press). White privilege: Unpacking the invisible knapsack. In M. McGoldrick & R.-J. Green (Eds.), *Re-visioning family therapy from a multicultural perspective.* New York: Guilford Press.

"Melting pot moves to the heartland." (1995, October 31). *Wall Street Journal*, p. A10.

Mirkin, M. P. (1990). *The social and political contexts of family therapy.* Boston: Allyn & Bacon.

Mirkin, M. P. (1994). *Women in context: Toward a feminist reconstruction of psychotherapy.* New York: Guilford Press

"The new face of America—How immigrants are shaping the world's first multicultural society" [Special Issue]. (1993, Fall). *Time.*

Petsonk, J., & Remsen, J. (1988). *The intermarriage handbook: A guide for Jews and Christians.* New York: William Morrow.

Pinderhughes, E. (1989). *Understanding race, ethnicity and power.* New York: The Free Press.

Roberts, S. (1995). *Who we are: A portrait of America based on the latest U.S. Census.* New York: Times Books.

Saba, G. W., Karrer, B. M., & Hardy, K. V. (Eds.). (1989). *Minorities and family therapy.* New York: Haworth Press.

Schleshinger, A. (1995). *The disuniting of America: Reflections on a multicultural society.* New York: Norton.

Schneider, S. W. (1989). *Intermarriage: The challenge of living with differences.* New York: The Free Press.

Schwarz, B. (1995, May). The diversity myth: America's leading export. *The Atlantic Monthly.*

Tataki, R. (1993). *A different mirror: A history of multicultural America.* Boston: Little, Brown.

Thiederman, S. (1991). *Profiting in America's multicultural marketplace: How to do business across cultural lines.* New York: Lexington.

Thomas, R. (1991). *Beyond race and gender.* New York: American Management Association.

Thurow, L. (1995, November 19). Why their world might crumble. *New York Times Magazine.*

"What will the U.S. be like when whites are no longer the majority: America's changing colors. (1990, April 5). *Time*, pp. 28–29.

Uba, L. (1994). *Asian Americans: Personality patterns, identity, and mental health.* New York: Guilford Press.

Zborowski, M. (1969). *People in pain.* San Francisco: Jossey-Bass.

Zola, I. K. (1966). Culture and symptoms: An analysis of patients' presenting complaints. *American Sociological Review, 5*, 615–630.

PART I

# AMERICAN INDIAN FAMILIES

# CHAPTER 2

# American Indian Families: An Overview

## CharlesEtta T. Sutton
## Mary Anne Broken Nose

*There is not in the world a better nation. They love their neighbors as themselves and their discourse is ever sweet and gentle.*
—CHRISTOPHER COLUMBUS (cited in P. Matthiessen, 1984, p. 1)

*Their priests . . . are not other such as our English witches are. . . . They esteem it a virtue to lie, deceive and steal as their master the devil teacheth to them.*
—A. WHITAKER (cited in Berkhoffer, 1978, p. 19)

## NATIVE IMAGES

Since the time of Columbus, the dominant culture's concept of American Indians has been characterized by inaccurate and conflicting images. They were romanticized as innocent savages living in a primitive paradise or reviled as heathens and bloodthirsty fiends. Explorers, settlers, missionaries, and political leaders all exploited these images for their own sake. When viewed through the lens of European beliefs and customs, Indian culture has been seen as inferior. In retrospect, the "humanistic" policies of Indian advocates, such as that of 18th-century reformers to "educate the Indian out of the Indian," have been almost as devastating as the U.S. army's genocidal policies (Berkhoffer, 1978).

Early Spanish explorers first gave one name, "Indios" to all the indigenous peoples living in America, rather than seeing them as individual groups (Berkhoffer, 1978). When the Europeans first sailed to this land, at least "two thousand cultures and more societies practiced a multiplicity of customs and life styles, held an enormous variety of values and beliefs, spoke numerous languages mutually unintelligible to the many speakers, and did not conceive of themselves as a single people—if they knew about each other at all" (Berkhoffer, 1978, p. 3).

Europeans' concern was that the new people they encountered were neither Christian nor civilized. By labeling these aboriginal people as "uncivilized," they were able to interact with them and make decisions concerning them more easily, as well as to justify the atrocities they committed. This blurring of distinctions among tribal groups continues today.

The entertainment industry has offered a distortion of American Indian customs and culture. The images created by the early dime novelists and later, Hollywood movies, had little to do with reality. Tribes were placed in the wrong part of the country. A character who was supposed to be Cherokee might speak Lakota and practice the ceremonies of the Mohawk people. What often was portrayed was not an Arapaho, Cheyenne, or Ute, but a generic "Indian." Unfortunately, most Americans have very little day-to-day contact with American Indians; they obtain their main, largely inaccurate impressions through the media.

This is beginning to change. Indians are using the very institutions that have done so much to malign them to portray a more accurate picture of their history and society. Many school systems are developing curricula featuring Indian history. Documentaries produced by American Indians tell the stories of their individual nations. There are Indian-owned and operated radio stations, TV networks, newspapers, and publishing companies. Old concepts and stereotypes are being slowly replaced with a new respect for Indians' positive influences on the dominant culture.

Environmental groups applaud Indians' respect for nature. Theologians, as well as New Age spiritualists, embrace Indian mysticism. Feminists and sociologists study the first nations' democratic social structure. More and more people are searching their family histories for Indian roots.

## DEMOGRAPHICS

The terms "Native American" and "American Indian" are labels that encompass a diversity of languages, lifestyles, religions kinship systems, and organizations (Polacca, 1995). Many tribes have a unique relationship with the U.S. government in that they are recognized as sovereign nations, both in law and through treaties.

There are many ways of defining "Indian": the genetic definition, having a certain percentage of Indian blood as established by the Federal Register of the United States; community recognition, being recognized as Indian by other Indians is paramount because federal and state governments do not recognize all tribes; enrollment in a recognized tribe; and self-declaration, the method used by the Census Bureau.

According to the 1993 census there are almost two million people, from 500 different tribes and 314 reservations, who claim to be of American Indian descent. Over half live in urban areas, and those on the reservtions may spend time away looking for jobs, education, and other opportunities. Most major cities have a substantial Indian population; for example, approximately 30,000 American Indians from over 60 tribes live in New York City.

There is a wide range of cultural identification among Indians. Some consider themselves American Indian because they have a great-grandparent who was Indian, whereas others are born on reservations and enter school speaking a mixture of their native language and English. Others are raised in the city and have no knowledge of tribal language or customs. A large group, however, moves in and out of both worlds, trying to maintain a precarious balance between their Indian and American identities.

## FAMILY THERAPY AND NATIVE AMERICANS

The Indian Way consists of families working together to solve problems. Fortunately, family therapy, with its systemic approach and emphasis on relationships, is particularly effective in working with Indians, whose life cycle orientation blends well with family therapy's approach. Culturally sensitive, nondirective approaches, which incorporate the use of storytelling, metaphor, and paradoxical interventions, are recommended. Networking and the use of ritual are favored over strategic interventions and brief therapy models.

Studies show that Indians come to treatment hoping that the therapist is an expert who can give them concrete, practical advice about their problems and be sensitive to their cultural beliefs and differences (La Fromboise, Trimble, & Mohatt, 1990; Polacca, 1995; Attneave, 1982; Tafoya, 1989; DuBray, 1993). Historically the relationship between American Indians and helping professionals has been marred by racism. Missionaries, teachers, and social workers have usually tried to "help" Indians by changing their value systems, thus alienating them from the strength and support of their own people and traditions (La Fromboise et al., 1990). This has understandably led many to feel wary of therapists and therapy.

American Indians have been victimized by professionals with impeccable credentials. They sometimes will judge therapists by who, not what, they are. When Indian clients enter a therapist's office, they will more likely look for indications of who the therapist is rather than for a particular diploma on the wall. Personal authenticity, genuine respect, and concern for the client are essential.

One important element for successful therapy with American Indians is to be aware of the impact of genocide. Another is understanding the differences between the dominant culture and that of American Indian clients. Special consideration should be given to individual clients and families' levels of assimilation.

## GENOCIDE

Contact with Europeans was devastating for North America's indigenous peoples. Millions died through disease and genocidal warfare. Entire communities and tribes were destroyed. Survivors were subjected to an insidious plan of coerced assimilation and cultural genocide, with many tribes forced to live on reservations distant from their native lands. Thousands of Indian children were torn from their families and put into boarding schools. White authorities denigrated Indian languages, customs, and religions, forbidding their practice (La Due, 1994). These policies led to a profound cultural trauma because American Indian cultures are rooted in family ties, a unique attachment and respect for their natural surroundings, and a distinct spirituality (La Due, 1994).

Efforts at forced assimilation did not end in the 1800s. In the 1950s and '60s, the federal government developed a termination/relocation plan, taking many Indians from their homes and families and relocating them to urban centers (see N. Tafoya & Del Vecchio, Chapter 3, this volume). Alcoholism rates soared. One scholar concluded: "This was another significant loss heaped upon the already present losses of language, elders, family and culture. Suicide, violence, and homicide all increased to epidemic proportions. School dropout rates, teen pregnancies and high rates of unemployment all became markers of a legacy of trauma experienced throughout this country by Indian people" (La Due, 1994, p. 99).

Although these rates are still high, they need to be seen within this historical perspective. Today, many Indians are reclaiming the life-affirming traditions of their cultures and using them to combat grave social ills caused by 500 years of oppression.

## TRIBAL IDENTITY

Although many may think of Indians as a homogenous group, Indian people identify themselves as belonging to a particular tribe, band, or clan. Each tribe's customs and values are critical to individual identity and affect family dynamics (Red Horse, 1981). This tradition of thinking in terms of "we" instead of "I" is a great strength of Indian culture.

All tribes, even those in the same geographic area, are different. Each tribe has its own worldview. The Hopi, Dine'h (Navaho), and Apache all share the Southwest desert, but are dissimilar in religious practices, customs, and family structures. If a Hopi or Dine'h man marries, he usually moves in with his wife's family; the opposite is true of the Havasupai woman, who live with her husband's relatives. American Indian belief system issues have major implications for therapy. The Dine'h have a legend that seizures result from a brother and sister having incest. Recent studies comparing attitudes of Apaches, Dine'h, and Hopis toward epilepsy reveal that the Dine'h epileptics feel more stigmatized, are more ashamed of their illness, and are less likely to seek treatment (Levy, 1987).

American Indian tribes' diversity sometimes leads to conflict. For example, the Sioux and the Ponca are both Plains Indian Nations who may seem similar to outsiders but are traditional enemies. Each nation has legends about it's own warriors, heroes, medicine men, and women. Each has it's own horror stories about encounters with Whites and tales of military, moral, or spiritual triumph. Through tribal traditions, Indian people are offered a radically different view of themselves than the one created by the dominant culture. The importance of this should never be underestimated.

> Families succeeding best in this migration (into the White culture) have two characteristics. Not surprisingly, one is an openness to learning and to using the social and technical skills of the White culture. A second, more startling characteristic, is the interest these families show in keeping alive the language, folkways, crafts, and values associated with their tribal identities. (Attneave, 1982, p. 82)

Some Indians may struggle to maintain their cultural identity in a foreign environment, while others may try to recapture nearly extinct languages and customs. Since a therapist cannot be familiar with all the nuances of a particular Indian culture, he or she might ask questions when on unfamiliar ground and learn what particular cultural traits the client most values and wishes to maintain. Is it language? Is it spirituality? Is it family ties? The therapist might explore such practical resources as a language class, participation in local ceremonies at pow wow, or involvement with Indian organizations or centers. The therapist would do well to acknowledge a client's depth of loss of his or her culture, even for those who are assimilated, and are grieving for what they never had.

## FAMILY STRUCTURE AND OBLIGATIONS

> Family represents the cornerstone for the social and emotional well-being of individuals and communities. (Red Horse, 1981, p. 1)

The ultimate aim of Dakota life, stripped of accessories, was quite simple: One must obey kinship rules; one must be a good relative. No Dakota who has participated in that life will dispute that. In the last analysis every other consideration was secondary-property, personal ambition, glory, good times, life itself. Without that aim and the constant struggle to attain it, the people would no longer be Dakota in truth. They would no longer even be human. To be a good Dakota then was to be humanized, civilized. And to be civilized was to keep the rules imposed by kinship for achieving civility, good manners and a sense of responsibility toward every individual dealt with. Thus only was it possible to live communally with success, that is to say a minimum of friction and a maximum of good will. (Deloria, 1944, cited in Gunn, 1989, p. 11)

While the extended family is typical of American Indians, its core is quite different from that of the dominant culture. Family therapist Terry Tafoya (1989) explains: "In many Native American languages, cousins are all referred to as brother and sister. The primary relationship is not the Parents, but rather that of Grandparents" (p. 32). This reflects the position of Grandparents as caregiver and provider of training and discipline. "The Grandparent role is not limited to what is called a 'grandparent' in English, but is opened up to include other relations such as a 'grand aunt,' and could be extended to include . . . 'godparent.' Parent roles include not only the biological parents, but those who have a sibling relation to the biological parents. The biological parents of the central siblings would then have specific responsibility over their nieces and nephews . . ." (pp. 32–33).

Many Indian cultures do not have a term for in-law; a daughter-in-law is called a daughter; a sister-in-law, a sister. Clearly what this means is that once one marries into an Indian family, no distinctions are made between natural and inducted family members—a concept foreign to white Anglo-Saxon, Protestant family norms. Thus, families are blended, not joined, through marriage. Medicine people and nonblood relatives are sometimes made part of the family. This is akin to African American and Latino families, in which family role is determined by relationship not by blood.

A therapist working with a Sioux couple obtained an initial family history. When Joseph, the father, was told that one of his grandfathers had died, the therapist pulled out the genogram and found that his name was not listed as a grandfather. For the non-Indian therapist, the deceased was the client's paternal great-uncle. The client explained that all his grandfather's brothers were his grandfathers. "So, you call your great-uncles 'grandfather'?" inquired the therapist. "No," replied Joseph, "I don't call them that; that is what they are, my grandfathers." At this moment, the therapist understood that the client's emotional relationship and sense of respect was to a grandfather, not a great-uncle.

The individual tribe determines roles and family obligations. For example, in Hopi society, the uncle is a family leader who provides guidance, nurturance, and support to other family members. A person unable to meet these role obligations can experience a great deal of anxiety and guilt. A non-Indian therapist may have difficulty recognizing these different roles. Thus, it helps to take a good family history, something with which American Indian clients usually feel comfortable because it is nonthreatening and shows the therapist's concern for the extended family.

Traditionally, when strangers meet, they often identify themselves through their relatives: "I am a Navaho. My name is Tiana Bighorn. My hometown is

Tuba City, Arizona. I belong to the Deer Springs Clan, born for the Rocky Gap Clan" (Benet & Maloney, 1994, p. 9). As therapy proceeds, the professional who is sensitive and willing to listen intently will gradually learn more about the family structure and dynamics. Rapport will not happen in one session but will gradually develop over time. He or she might begin by modeling the process. It is very important to say who you are and where you come from in an accessible, nonthreatening way, and then add something like, "What about you? Would you like to share something about yourself?"

## COMMUNICATIVE STYLE

My grandmother always told me that the white man never listens to anyone, but expects everyone to listen to him. So, we listen! My father always told me that an Eskimo is a listener. We have survived here because we know how to listen. The white people in the lower forty-eight talk. They are like the wind, they sweep over everything. (Coles, 1978, cited in Nabokov, 1991, p. 431)

Native cultures value listening. Long periods of silence by Indian clients can be confusing for the therapist. Silence may connote respect, that the client is forming thoughts, or that the client is waiting for signs that it is the right time to speak. Indian people may be very indirect. In some native cultures, it is considered disrespectful for one relative to directly mention the name of another. A Lakota woman may refer to her father-in-law as "he" rather than speak his name.

The non-Indian therapist may treat silence, embellished metaphors, and indirectness as signs of resistance, when actually they represent forms of communication (Attneave, 1982). The professional needs to monitor his or her feelings about these differences. They must resist the urge to interrupt and be willing to admit to confusion and misunderstanding. Good Tracks (1976) states that Indians may perceive the therapist as "an authority figure representing a coercive institution and an alien dominating and undesirable culture" (p. 57). The therapist can counter this by joining with the client, following his or her directive, and being willing to admit to confusion and misunderstanding. Professionals need to be especially aware of nonverbal communication, particularly when "nothing is taking place." How one enters a room, what is in it, and how one responds to silence are all forms of communication. Having coffee and food can make an office seem safer and more comfortable.

## WHO COMES TO THERAPY AND WHY

American Indians come to therapy for the same reasons as other Americans, including marital problems, chemical dependency issues, and depression. An American Indian family's underlying racial and cultural characteristics may resemble those of an immigrant family that has acculturated for several generations. But the Indian client, one of many American Indians in a metropolitan area, may still be very close to his or her reservation roots (Attneave, 1982).

The stress of intermarriage often brings couples into therapy. Working out the details of everyday life results in the collision of Indian and dissonant cultural values.

Ruben, a Cheyenne, and his wife Angie, a Hungarian, were at an impasse. Living on the East Coast and childless, with financial problems, they came to therapy when Ruben was offered an apprentice job with a large manufacturer, a position arranged by a member of Angie's family. Angie worked as a secretary, while Ruben held a series of temporary jobs. Instead of being happy about the new position, Ruben had become depressed and even was thinking of turning it down. Furious, Angie was threatening to leave him.

———————— ❧ ————————

The therapist and clients explored how problems were resolved in their families of origin. Angie came from a family in which women typically made decisions about work and finances, and thus helped direct the family's mobility. For her, financial stability was critical.

In Ruben's family, asking for guidance and direction through healing rituals was a way to begin to find answers to problems. Before he and Angie married, Ruben had made a commitment to Sundance, a religious purification and peace ceremony for his tribe. This ritual may require a year or more of preparation. The sundancer fasts, prays, and dances in the hot sun under the guidance of a medicine man. Sundance grounds are usually located on reservations. As in most Indian ceremonies the sundancer's family and community participate and provide support. The time and travel involved in keeping this kind of committment often conflict with the demands of employment or education in the non-Indian world.

Ruben wished to Sundance to provide blessings for his family and as a way of promising himself that although he was moving into the dominant culture, he would not lose his traditional ways. He felt that if he did not keep this commitment, something bad might happen to someone he loved or he might lose the marriage he valued so highly. Ruben was caught in a difficult conflict.

Here is a classic counterpoint between the American Indian value of spirituality versus financial security, as well as the Indian way of thinking in terms of "we" instead of "I." Ruben fears that not fulfilling his commitment will hurt someone he loves. If Ruben does not Sundance and his father dies, he may well feel responsible. But if he tells his non-Indian therapist that he feels his father died for this reason, the therapist is likely to think that Ruben is overreacting and will try to diffuse some of his guilt. This will not work, for Ruben has a culturally defined problem that requires a culturally acceptable solution. The therapist's primary task is to allow Ruben to talk about his feelings and explore acceptable ways for him to resolve the situation. The therapist may also encourage Ruben to seek support from family and friends who may want to pray with him. Angie also needs support in learning about the sacredness of the Sundance and its significance for Ruben. Understanding its significance for Ruben may make her feel more comfortable about discussing possible alternatives with her family.

Living in the dominant society can make following culturally prescribed solutions difficult. The therapist can help by supporting such values and rituals and helping the client determine ways of using them to become "unstuck."

## TIME IS ALWAYS WITH US (INDIAN TIME)

Herring (1990) points out that Indians perceive time differently. Indians view time as cyclical rather than linear. Indian time is not limited to a specific minute or hour. It may encompass days, months, even years, and is geared to personal and seasonal rhythms rather than being ordered and organized by external mechanical clocks and calendars. It may mean showing up half an hour after a meeting is scheduled. Non-Indians easily may misunderstand what the "present" means to American Indians. Things take, more or less, as long as they do. A religious observance, for example, may last hours, even days, as opposed to the dominant culture, where church services start and end promptly (Attneave, 1982). Milestones in the individual life cycle, as well, are seen in terms of the rhythmic quality of life. The focus is placed on one's current place, knowing that the succeeding changes will inevitably come.

Technologically-minded White society's encroachment makes it difficult to maintain this highly satisfying approach to time management; this contributes to the culture shock that Indians feel when returning or entering this society after being on the reservation. Conversely, a social worker sent to a Montana reservation to run an alternative school program recalls the following:

"One day I came into work and no one was there. There were no teachers, students, or counselors. At first I thought it was Saturday or some holiday I had forgot about. I checked my calendar and the one the tribe printed to see if it was some special kind of Indian holiday, but it was not. Finally, I went riding around in my car. I saw one of the counselors and asked where everyone was. He said Albert Running Horse had died. I found out later that Albert was one of the oldest men in the tribe and was somehow related to almost everyone at school. When I tried to find out when everyone would be back at work, I couldn't get a definite answer because they weren't sure when some of Albert's relatives would come in from out of state. I was upset because I felt we had been making progress with some particularly difficult cases. I was concerned about the continuity of therapy and the careful schedule we had all worked out. When I expressed my frustration to one of my counselors she just shrugged her shoulders and said we all have to grieve. All I could think of is how am I going to explain this to my superiors."

## THE SPIRITUAL RELATIONSHIP OF MAN AND NATURE

*Mitakuye Oyasin,* Lakota for "To all my relations," is said as a salutation and at the end of prayer. It acknowledges the spiritual bond between the speaker and all people present. It affirms the importance of the relationship of the speaker to his blood relatives, to his forebearers, "his tribe," the family of man, and to mother nature. It bespeaks a life-affirming philosophy that all life forces are valuable and interdependent. Western civilization's orientation is toward control over nature, whereas traditional Indian culture sees harmony with natural forces as a way of life. Only a very few have control over these forces, chiefly through an unusual understanding and alliance with them. Acceptance of overwhelming natural events that cannot be controlled is an integral part of life.

Animals, plants, mountains, and bodies of water may be considered sacred beings, part of the universal family and, as such, involved in a reciprocal system; we care for mother earth and she nurtures us. Just as one strives to be in harmony with one's human relatives, so should a person try to be in harmony with one's spiritual and natural relatives: "My mother told me, every part of this earth is sacred to our people. Every pine needle. Every sandy shore. Every mist in the dark woods. Every meadow and humming insect. The Earth is our mother" (Jeffers, 1991, p. 3).

## COMMUNAL SHARING

"When I was little, I learned very early that what's yours is mine and what's mine is everybody's" (Ivern Takes the Shield, traditional Oglala Lakota, personal communication, June 1989). Traditionally, Indians accord great respect to those who give the most to other individuals and families, and then to the band, tribe, or community. "Giveaways," an ancient custom, where many gifts are presented to others for their help or achievements, are a way of marking such climactic events in the life cycle as birth, naming, marriage, and death, still persist in many tribes. On a day-to-day basis, Indians share material goods. Travelers and visitors are always fed, housed, even clothed and transported (Attneave, 1982 p. 69).

This value of sharing contrasts sharply with the dominant culture's capitalist emphasis on acquisition and can also make it difficult for Indians on reservations to operate businesses. For example, a cafe started by a Dine'h (Navaho) couple should have been very successful, given the lack of competition and the availability of patrons. But the owners felt an obligation to provide food gratis for family members. Since "family" often includes in-laws and the recognition of *their* families, finding paying customers can be difficult. Thus, many successful businesses on reservations are run by people who are part-Indian or nontraditionalists.

Similar issues often occur when the head(s) of an urban Indian family find steady work or a student receives a stipend or fellowship. Whereas White culture focuses on carefully managing cash flow and savings, American Indians are prone to share liquid assets. "Unemployed parents may move in; siblings consume food, wear out clothing, and take up time needed for study. Students realize they can hardly pay tuition nor study in this kind of environment. However, they feel that they cannot be Indian, yet be selfish about helping others whose needs are greater" (Attneave, 1982, p. 69).

## CULTURAL ORIENTATION IN RELATION TO TREATMENT

Until the passage of the Freedom of Religion Act (1977), Indians who practiced their own religion risked, and sometimes suffered, imprisonment. Despite this, Indian religion endured and is thriving today. Some traditional American Indians seek the guidance of medicine people in times of crisis, major decision making, or when seeking spiritual growth. Other Indian people may not even know what a medicine person is, much less have contact with one (Polacca, 1995).

"Indian medicine refers to a traditional and specific cultural approach to health and life for a person, rather than a treatment for a disease or illness" (DuBray, 1985). Generally, a medicine person's approach is holistic, involving healing the body and the troubled soul. Therapists should be alert to any contact that their client may have with medicine people and usually should consider it beneficial.

In 1980, the American Medical Association revised its code of ethics, giving physicians permission to consult, and to take referrals from and make referrals to, nonphysician healers, including American Indian medicine people (Polacca, 1995). Even practicing Christians may have an ongoing relationship with medicine people, which may positively or negatively affect a therapist's work with a family, as the following case reveals:

The Shields, a Navajo family who relocated to a large city, and were practicing Catholics, had three children: Tony 16, Kensil 12, and Shell 9. The children were enrolled in a parochial school system with a large Indian population. They were referred by the school's guidance counselor because Tony clearly had a substance abuse problem. After initially feeling that things were going well, the therapist began to sense that the family had become resistant, particularly after Tony was placed in detention for a drinking episode. The therapist had instructed the family to have Tony remain there so that he could really experience the consequences of his actions. Without notifying the therapist, the family had him released and brought back to the reservation to stay with an aunt and uncle. When the therapist contacted the family about this, they scheduled an appointment, but did not show up. When Tony returned to school, the family resumed therapy, only to have the same pattern repeat itself.

------------ ✦ ------------

The Shields had brought their son home to be with an uncle, a person who traditionally plays an important role in their son's upbringing. They also utilized the services of a medicine man and were involved in the Native American Church. They were reluctant to discuss these involvements with the therapist, feeling that she would not understand their decision and would reject their traditional approach. Rather than having to explain why they had not followed her instructions, the family tried to avoid her. Instead of assuming the family was rejecting treatment, the therapist began to explore why the family had chosen another path. Gradually she began to integrate some of their healing methods into therapy.

Many Indians utilize traditional and Western practices, viewing both as vital to the healing process. Using the clients' own language, the therapist can strongly support such approaches as prayer meetings and herbal medicines, as well as encourage American Indian healing rituals. With regard to the Shields, the therapist might say something like, "The ceremonies you are doing to get rid of these bad spirits, while Tony is in treatment, are helpful. I am glad you're helping him in this way."

Family therapists must examine their own personal values. How do their religious beliefs affect those of their clients? Therapist need to respect and value cultural differences and help clients use their own traditions for personal or familial healing.

Today, Indian people are developing their own approaches and responses to alcohol, drug abuse, and suicide, as well as incorporating recovery techniques used in the broader society. The Native American Church, for example, has been described as "the most important pan-Indian movement in this country. It is political, cultural and spiritual, a source of pride, power, and psychological health" (Hammerschlag, 1988, p. 60). The Native American Church has many members, especially in the West.

## CONCLUSION

Therapists wishing to work effectively with American Indian clients need to discard not only stereotypes perpetuated by the media and by Euro-centric history, but also must be willing to suspend assumptions regarding family roles, relationships, and communication. Each native client's degree of identification with his or her own tribe must be fully understood and respected. Therapists must listen carefully, ask questions, and assume nothing when gathering information about Indian clients, all of which not only will provide them with important information, but also helps foster the trust of American Indian clients, who often are wary of non-Indian therapists. Therapists might also wish to read literature about individual tribes so as to become more effective in determining and understanding the best course of treatment.

American Indian clients deserve the care and understanding of competent professionals, including treatment that respects and supports their culture, customs, traditions, and values.

## ACKNOWLEDGMENTS

Both authors would like to express enormous gratitude to Mona Polacca, Hopi-Havasupai, and Helen Rende, Kahnewke-Mohawk and council members of the Intertribal Indians of New Jersey, for their many patient reviews and suggestions regarding this chapter.

Mary Anne Broken Nose would like to extend special thanks to Mildred Potenza, Coordinator of Community Services at the COPSA Institute for Alheimer's Disease and Related Disorders at the CMHC-UMDNJ in Piscataway, for her support and encouragement of my personal and professional growth.

## REFERENCES

Attneave, C. (1982). American Indians and Alaska Native families: Emigrants in their own homeland. In M. McGoldrick, J. K. Pearce, & J. Giordano (Eds.), *Ethnicity and family therapy* (1st ed., pp. 55–83). New York: Guilford Press.

Benet, N., & Maloney, S. (1994). *Keeper of the culture.* Intertribal America, Collectors Edition.

Berkhoffer, R. (1978). *The White man's Indian: Images of the American Indian from Columbus to the present.* New York: Vintage Press.

DuBray, W. (1985, January). American Indian values: Critical factors in casework. *Social Casework: The Journal of Contemporary Social Work, 66*(1), 30–38.

DuBray, W. (1993). *American Indian values: Mental health interventions with people of color.* St. Paul, MN: West Publishing Company.

Good Tracks, J. (1976). Native American non-interference. *Social Work Journal,* 55–59.

Gunn, P. A. (Ed.). (1989). *Spider Woman's granddaughters: Traditional tales and contemporary writing by Native American women.* New York: Fawcett Columbine.

Hammerschlag, C. (1988). *The dancing healers: A doctor's journey of healing with Native Americans.* New York: HarperCollins.

Herring, R. (1990). Understanding Native America values: Process and content concern for counselors. *Counseling and Values, 34,* 134–136.

Jeffers, S. (1991). *Brother Eagle, Sister Sky: A message from Chief Seattle.* New York: Dial Books.

La Due, R. (1994). Coyote returns: Twenty sweats does not an Indian expert make, bringing ethics alive. *Feminist Ethics in Psychotherapy Practice, 15*(1), 93–111.

La Fromboise, T., Trimble, J., & Mohatt, G. (1990). Counseling intervention and American Indian tradition: An integrative approach. *The Counseling Psychologist, 18*(4), 628–654.

Levy, J. (1987). Psychological and social problems of epileptic children in four Southwestern Indian tribes. *Journal of Community Psychology, 15*(3), 307–315.

Matthiesen, P. (1984). *Indian country.* New York: Viking Press.

Nabokov, P. (Ed.). (1991). *Native American testimony: A chronical of Indian–White relations from prophecy to the present.* New York: Penguin.

Polacca, M. (1995). *Cross cultural variation in mental health treatment of aging Native Americans.* Unpublished manuscript, School of Social Work, Arizona State University.

Red Horse, J. (1981, April). *American Indian families.* Paper presented at the conference on American Indian Family Strengths and Stress, Tempe, AZ.

Tafoya, T. (1989). Coyote's eyes: Native cognition styles. *Journal of American Indian Education—Special Issue,* 29–40.

U.S. Bureau of the Census. (1993, September). *We, the first Americans.* Washington, DC: U.S. Department of Commerce, Economics and Statistics Administration.

# CHAPTER 3

# Back to the Future: An Examination of the Native American Holocaust Experience

Nadine Tafoya
Ann Del Vecchio

## NATIVE AMERICANS TODAY: ROSE P.'S STORY

"What is it like to be an Indian in today's society? I live in shame and feel oppressed. I know that the stress and strain of oppression takes its toll on my psyche, on my sense of self, and on my ability to live a good life.

"When I was thinking about this question, I remembered a time when my son was about 4 years old. He was angry at me. He wasn't ready to come in from playing outside. He was very angry and crying in his rage. I sternly told him to go to his room until he could calm down. As he headed for his room, he narrowed his eyes at me and whispered something under his breath. He stood before his bedroom door and raised his little fist in the air and shook it wildly at me. I will always picture that raised fist clearly in my mind.

"That raised fist is what comes to mind first when I think about being an Indian in America today. I have been scorned and squashed down as an Indian because my culture, my traditions, and my identity are different from mainstream America's. My son raised his fist to me. To whom do I shake my fist in rage at the daily frustration of being humiliated for simply being Indian? My boss? My husband? My teacher? My tribe's governor?

"I learned very young that I was different. In school, I learned not to try to answer the teacher's questions. The teacher only called on the blond children. When she looked at me, I saw disgust, or worse, pity. I felt dirty and stupid. If I had tried once in the past to raise my hand and offer my answers, I learned to stop trying. I hid my pride, my pain, and my tears. I didn't talk to the other Indian kids about it. We all kept quiet.

"As an adult, I don't try much. I don't shake my fist but the pain is still there. I see the teacher's look of disgust on my boss's face. I drink alcohol. I gamble. One of my cousins killed herself. I think about how easy it would be to kill myself too. The pain would be gone then.

"For 500 years, my people have been told in so many ways, 'You're no good. You are a savage. Change your ways. You are not civilized. Your ways are heathen and witchery. Your ways are not Christian!' My grandfather gave up his tribal religion and customs. He adopted Christianity. He, my grandmother, and the other people on the reservation did their best to give up the old ways, become farmers, quit hunting, go to church and be 'good Indians, civilized Indians.' They wept when the federal agents rounded up their children to take them away to boarding school. Some of the children never came home. Some came home to be buried. My grandparents and the people wept again because their children grew up learning alien ways, forgetting their language and customs in schools too far away to visit.

"My parents married soon after they came home from the boarding school. They came from different tribes. They left my father's reservation encouraged by the U.S. government and the boarding school system to find jobs in the 'real world.' He signed up with a job training and education program and moved to San Diego with my mom. My parents were full of hopes and dreams when they started out but like so many boarding school graduates who tried to make a place for themselves in the city, they became urban Indians lost in the city ghettos of poverty, crime, despair, and alcohol and drug abuse.

"The promised jobs never materialized and stuck between two worlds, the big city and the reservation, the Indian world and the White, my father drank and beat my mother. My mother worked at menial jobs to support us. My life was built on this foundation. I was never parented because my parents, raised in government boarding schools, had nothing to give me. They had lost their languages and retained only traces of their cultures. They had never been parented themselves. Boarding school nurturing was having their mouths washed out with soap for talking Indian and receiving beatings for failing to follow directions.

"So this is my legacy and the legacy of many Indians, both reservation and urban. Our loss extends back over many generations to the time of first contact with the Europeans. We have lost our ethnic identities, our cultures and traditions. We have lost our languages, our customs, our lifestyles, and our religions. We have lost our parents and grandparents, our extended family and clans, our sense of community and our knowledge of ourselves as 'people.' We have found systematic oppression and racism. We have found depression and anxiety. We have lost ourselves again in alcohol, drugs, and suicide. We are survivors of multigenerational loss and only through acknowledging our losses will we ever be able to heal."

## DOCUMENTING OUR HISTORICAL LOSS

Memories are all we have. And when the memories are dreadful—when they hold images of the pain we have suffered or, perhaps even worse, inflicted—they are what we try to escape. (Corliss, 1993, p. 110)

Corliss makes the point in a popular press review of the movie *Schindler's List* that the movie is essentially a plea to remember, and that to remember is to speed the healing. This is the case for Native Americans in the United States today. We are at a crossroads, and actively remembering our past and the historic trauma that has occurred to us is one way we can recover a happy, healthy, and productive existence as a separate and distinct ethnic/cultural group in the United States today.

It is important for tribal people to remember that the problems of the present, including loss of our traditional lands and means of economic survival, alcoholism, suicide, depression, anxiety, posttraumatic stress, and many other forms of mental health problems that attack the well-being of minority ethnic/cultural groups in the United States, are both directly and indirectly the result of a devastating and traumatic history. This history includes the destruction of traditional ways of economic survival, destruction of our nuclear and extended family systems, rape, mutilation, and overt and covert genocide. These atrocities form the backbone of our loss and have deprived Native American people of our languages, values, beliefs, and traditions—in short, our cultural and ethnic identities.

It has only been within the last two decades that historians have begun to detail the legacy of oppressive and racist federal policies that were aimed at forcibly and nonnegotiably assimilating and/or annihilating the indigenous peoples of the North American continent. Ethnohistorical methods of inquiry have helped to paint a picture of the historical trauma visited upon Native Americans without further victimizing us. "Ethnohistory enables scholars to move beyond traditional methods in providing a balanced assessment of cultures meeting in the arena of contact" (Axtell, 1981, p. 5). Ethnohistory has allowed a more balanced and complete rendering of the historic trauma to enter mainstream America through video, audio, and other forms of commercial mass media (television and movies), as well as through history and social studies textbooks and popular press.

# LIFE BEFORE CONTACT BETWEEN NATIVE AMERICAN AND EUROPEAN CULTURES

Prior to any contact with Europeans, the tribes of North America existed with intact community self-awareness and purpose that included a complete educational system for raising their children. Each tribal group lived in relative isolation from the other native peoples, and most tribes had a name for themselves in their language that translated loosely meant "the people" or "the true people." Some groups, for example, members of the Tewa speaking San Juan Pueblo, had ritual precautions and purification ceremonies they used when they returned from hunting or foraging expeditions that put them into contact with "other people" (Szasz, 1988). These other native groups were not always recognized as people; rather, they were identified as a source of contamination or sometimes as a source of trade goods, slaves, different foods, and other ways of life. Some tribes were more receptive to the cultural ways and innovations of other people.

Although each tribal group used distinct linguistic and cultural methods to educate their children, all tribes required that certain skills be mastered before a youth was accepted as an adult member of the tribe. These knowledge requirements and skills can be loosely categorized in three areas: (1) knowledge of cultural heritage; (2) spiritual/religious practices; and (3) economic survival skills (Szasz, 1988). This tripartite emphasis provided an effective educational system for childrearing and the transmission of indigenous languages and cultures. The child's special skills, temperament, or proclivities might shape his or her role in the community. However, each child was expected to be knowledgeable and competent in all of the three areas. A child who was an exceptionally good hunter might spend more time hunting and supplying meat to the community, but that child was expected also to know the tribe's ethics, values, and religion, and to practice them accordingly.

These competencies were interwoven. Religious rituals were performed to ensure abundant harvests and hunts. Storytelling during cold winter months entertained adults and youth confined because of the weather, while simultaneously passing on the traditions and beliefs of the tribe. Cultural ideals, mundane lessons, and moral instruction were passed on through a rich oral tradition (Szasz, 1988). Cultural continuity was ensured by the accumulation of stories told each winter as a child grew up. Economic/survival skills were passed on through stories and through direct, hands-on instruction with supervised practice throughout the year. When the European explorers first encountered Native Americans, they were exposed to these traditions, beliefs, and skills, but most viewed indigenous ways of life as primitive, and only a few explorers were able to experience and understand the Native American ways of life as complete, elaborate, practical cultures that were intact and not in need of "civilization."

## LIFE AFTER CONTACT BETWEEN NATIVE AMERICANS AND EUROPEANS

Traditional history books are full of detail about the conquest of the New World by European immigrants. However, the French, Spanish, English, and other European settlers who arrived in the New World were rarely referred to as immigrants in the history books. To the indigenous cultural groups who lived in the New World, they were immigrants to begin with, and later, interlopers and usurpers.

Ethnohistory documents persistent pressure from the European immigrants on the Native Americans to give up their land. Once homelands were usurped by the Europeans, pressure was exerted on Native Americans to conform to the immigrants' European customs. With a loss of traditional lands as the foundation of Native American economic survival, and with associated policies and pressure to assume European ways and means of economic survival, Native Americans were caught in a vise that crushed the traditional tripartite educational systems for the transmission of tribal cultures and ways of life.

By the 1800s, the press of European immigrants had become massive in scale and was reaching the Great Plains west of the Mississippi River. Pushed into the domains of neighboring tribes, which resulted in bloody conflict between tribes, attacked by Old World diseases such as smallpox, exposed to the insidious corruption of alcohol abuse, ravaged by starvation and malnutrition, the Native American population of the New World was decimated; Native Americans numbered some 600,000 in the 1840s, and the population dropped again to about 250,000 by 1850. European "civilization" resulted in more direct Native American deaths than did actual warfare between the immigrants and the North American tribes (New, 1964).

## THE MISSIONARY SYSTEM OF ASSIMILATION

A concomitant of the European immigrants' greed for the tribes' lands was the need to Christianize the heathens. The underlying assumption was that Native Americans would fit better with immigrants' schemes for the New World if they practiced real religion and gave up their savage religious customs. The U.S. government approached the Indian pragmatically by encouraging missions.

Missionaries cost the government little beyond minimal military support to suppress any hostility on the part of the indigenous population, and the missionary system of education bought the government a ready means of annihilating the remainder of the tripartite tribal system of educating children. Through missionary schools, Indian children lost their languages, their tribal customs and beliefs, and came home strangers to their parents, clans, and tribal communities. Szasz (1988) provides an excellent ethnohistorical description of the missionary system of schooling Indians from 1607 to 1783. Beyond 1783, missionary schools continued to educate Native American children and can be found today on reservations throughout the United States. However, the missionary schools proved to be insufficient as a means of assimilation and annihilation of the tenacious Native American cultures.

## THE BOARDING-SCHOOL PHENOMENON

It was 1915, during the harvest season. I was a little girl. I remember it was in October and we had a pile of red chile and we were tying chile into fours. And then my grandfather was putting them onto a longer string. We were doing that when they came to get me. Then right away my grandmother and mother started to cry, 'Her? She's just a little girl! She's just a little girl, you can't take her' . . . I was 5 years old. (Hyer, 1990, pp. 5–6)

The boarding-school method of removing the Indian from the child was implemented toward the end of the 1800s. Tribal leaders were informed that all Indian children were required to be formally educated, and that this would be accomplished through boarding schools. The Carlisle School in Carlisle, Pennsylvania was established in 1879. By 1902, a total of 25 Indian boarding schools were established in 15 states. The schools were located often in old army forts and commonly staffed by ex-military personnel (old army types).

Native American children, parents, and tribes were not given a choice or a voice in the matter of the education of Indian children. The aim of this system was twofold: (1) to remove all traces of Indian from the child, and (2) to immerse the child totally in Western culture, thought, and tradition. In this way the Indian problem would be solved by raising the children in a Western civilized manner and away from their wanton, savage ways. The boarding-school system was one of the most ruthless and inhumane methods of assimilation available to the U.S. government. All-out warfare, with associated atrocities, was a much more humane method of dealing with the Native Americans. McLaughlin (1994) included this description from a 40-year-old Navajo parent who was left at boarding school at 7 years of age. She spoke only Navajo, no English.

It was the first time I've seen a brick building that was not a trading post. The ceilings were so high and the rooms so big an empty. There was no warmth. Not as far as "brrrr, I'm cold," but in a sense of emotional cold. Kind of an emptiness, when you're hanging on to your mom's skirt and trying hard not to cry. Then when you get up to your turn, she thumbprints the paper and she leaves and you watch her go out the big metal doors . . . you see her get into the truck and the truck starts moving and all the home smell goes with it. . . . Then them women takes you by the hand and takes you inside and the first thing they do is take down your bun. The first thing they do is cut off your hair and you been told your whole life that you never cut your hair recklessly because that is your life. . . . And you see that long, black hair drop, and it's like they take out your heart and they give you this cold thing that beats inside. And now you're gonna to be just like them. You're gonna be cold. You're never gonna be happy or have that warm feeling and attitude towards life anymore. That's what it feels like, like taking your heart out and putting in a cold river pebble. When you go into the shower, you leave your squaw skirt and blouse right there at the shower door. When you come out, it's gone. . . . They cut your hair, now they take your squaw skirt. They take from the beginning. When you first walk in there, they take everything that you're about. They jerk it away from you. They don't ask how you feel about it. They never tell you anything. They barely speak to you. They take everything away from you. . . . (pp. 47–48)

The trauma described in this passage was typical of the boarding-school experience. The boarding-school system was inhumane by virtue of the fact that children as young as 5 years of age were separated from their parents and transported far from home. As most Native American families lived on poverty-level incomes, travel to these schools to visit was impossible. A multifaceted process of assimilation commenced as soon as the children reached their destination. The process involved the following features:

- English-language immersion with punishment for speaking tribal languages.
- Destruction of traditional garments and replacement with alien, Western clothing.
- Braids and traditional hairstyles were shaved and replaced with Western-style haircuts.
- Buildings, dormitories, campuses and furnishings of Western design.
- Forced physical labor in the kitchens, stables, gardens, and shops necessary to run the schools.
- Corporal punishment for the infraction of rules or for not following the work and school schedules.
- Immersion in a Western educational curriculum with associated alien goals and philosophy.
- Regimented, time-bound schedules.

This list is not exhaustive. Szasz (1977) described the boarding-school experience as one in which the physical conditions were almost always inadequate. Food was scarce; children were overcrowded, and improper treatment of sick children led to frequent epidemics. Preadolescent children worked long hours to care for the facilities and produce food, because congressional appropriations were woefully inadequate. Staff were usually not prepared with any understanding of the children, their languages, and traditions. Additionally, boarding-school staff and teachers lacked coping strategies and skills for working with confused and sometimes defiant children. At times, staff disciplined children brutally. Emotional, physical, and sexual abuse were common.

As a result of the boarding-school system, several generations of Native Americans were raised without family ties. These generations were not nurtured as they developed. Nurturing, the most essential element of healthy development for young children, was nonexistent and was replaced with forced assimilation, hard physical labor, harsh discipline, and physical, sexual, and emotional abuse. A variety of negative coping strategies have been adopted by Native Americans as a result of the historical trauma and internalized oppression. These survival skills include (but are not limited to) the following:

- Learned helplessness;
- Passive–aggressive behavior;
- Manipulativeness;
- Compulsive gambling;
- Alcohol and drug abuse;
- Suicide;
- Denial; and
- Scapegoating other Indians, especially when they are successful.

The boarding-school generations of Native Americans survived but at the cost of thousands of lives lived in the misery and doubt of damaged self-esteem and linguistic and cultural annihilation. This is the legacy of Native American communities today.

It is the fallout from the historical trauma of the boarding-school system that we as mental health professionals must contend. Our awareness of this trauma and our ability to assist Native American clients to become aware of this trauma must be used as a foundation to *speed the healing.*

## IMPLICATIONS FOR TREATMENT

Middelton-Moz (1986) describes some of the emotional and psychological scarring of forced assimilation. She states that children who were sent to boarding-school institutions became strangers to their parents. The children gave up their traditional cultural values and ways and assumed the values of the majority culture. The children found themselves ill-prepared to cope with either culture and often felt confused and alienated from both the Western and the Indian ways of life. Middelton-Moz found that adults in the therapeutic setting who had been educated through the boarding-school system suffered from a pervasive sense of low self-worth, powerlessness, depression, and alienation from the power and strength of cultural values. Indian adults in therapy were confused about their family roots and traditions and felt abandoned. These young adults who had not been raised by their own parents felt increased confusion when faced with the need to parent their own children.

The boarding-school system has produced a multigenerational problem in Native American communities today. Without positive parental role models to supply children with their culture, and without continuous exposure to nurturing, Native American adults today are forced to invent their own methods and models to negotiate both the Indian and the Anglo worlds. Without positive models, Native American communities and the individuals within have developed a set of survival skills that include numerous self-destructive behaviors, such as alcohol and drug abuse, other addictive behaviors, and suicide. Posttraumatic stress is a concomitant of the boarding-school system. As mental health professionals, we can assist Native American individuals and communities to develop positive methods and models using the following framework.

1. We must be aware of the multigenerational disruption of positive development that is the result of 500 years of historical trauma for Native Americans. Most Native Americans have not been exposed to positive, nurturing, Native American adults who have been able to make their way in both the Indian and the White worlds. In other words, Native American adults have not been taught by their parents and elders how to be happy, healthy parents. They have not been exposed to ongoing, positive role models. We must assist Native American clients to become aware of this history and the impact it may have had on their personal development.

2. We must acknowledge the persistent destructiveness of oppression and racism with which Native American clients have had to deal on a daily basis, and educate clients about the multigenerational impact of the historic trauma and support them through the process of grieving personal and tribal losses of language, tradition, and religion.

3. We must assist Native American clients to grow and move toward health and wellness by (a) providing positive, concrete, well-articulated and well-defined role models as mental health professionals and human beings (practice what you preach); (b) assisting clients to identify elements of personal mental well-being and to design their own model based on healthy traditional values and practices; and (c) assisting clients to discharge anger, shame, and fear associated with oppression and historical trauma.

4. We must work with Native American clients and communities to recognize when denial is used as a strategy to avoid dealing with the consequences of the historical trauma. Especially when addictive behavior is used as a survival skill, it may be difficult for the client or the community to change behavior if denial functions to defend the addictive behavior.

This framework is a simple beginning to use with Native American clients who seek professional mental health care for problems or for growth and wellness. However, on a larger scale, it is important to apply the framework's principles to the larger context of whole communities, reservations, and pueblos. As our tribal governments, social service workers, religious leaders, and other community members have all been through the historical trauma and the fallout from oppressive racist policies to one degree or another, healing must occur at the level of the whole community as well. Remembering and acknowledging the impact of our past is the first step on our road back to the future.

## REFERENCES

Axtell, J. (1981). *The European and the Indian: Essays in the ethnohistory of Colonial America.* New York: Oxford University Press.

Corliss, R. (1993, March 14). Schindler comes home. *Time*, p. 110.

Hyer, S. (1990). *One house, one voice, one heart: Native American education at the Santa Fe Indian school.* Albuquerque: University of New Mexico Press.

McLaughlin, D. (1994, Spring). Critical literacy for Navajo and other American Indian learners. *Journal of American Indian Education, 33*(3), 47–59.

Middelton-Moz, J. (1986). Wisdom of the elders. In R. J. Ackerman (Ed.), *Growing up in the shadow: Children of alcoholics* (pp. 57–70). Deerfield Beach, FL: Health Communications.

New, L. K. (1964). *American Indians: Their past, present, and some predictions about their future.* Unpublished report and lecture transcription, Santa Fe, NM, Institute of American Indian Arts.

Szasz, C. M. (1977). *Education and the American Indian: The road to self-determination since 1928* (2nd ed.) Albuquerque: University of New Mexico Press.

Szasz, C. M. (1988). *Indian education in the American colonies, 1607–1783.* Albuquerque: University of New Mexico Press.

# PART II

# FAMILIES OF AFRICAN ORIGIN

CHAPTER 4

# Families of African Origin:
# An Overview

## Lascelles Black

## HISTORY

The United States is a country comprised mostly of immigrants. People of every race, nation, and culture can be found somewhere within these borders. Most Americans can trace their ancestry to some other nation and culture. Many of them celebrate the blending of the "Old Country" ways and the "American" way. For example, Polish Americans, Italian Americans, and Irish Americans enjoy the richness of both their heritages. They, like many other Europeans who came here, made a choice that spoke of their hope for a better life, a fulfillment of their dreams. In America they hoped to find freedom and an opportunity to improve their lives in ways that were not available to them in their homelands. Their cultures and religious beliefs were accommodated, because these people were valued as productive citizens. Some of these immigrants were more valued than others, some had to struggle against difficult obstacles to attain their goals, but they chose to come to the New World. People of African descent have only recently been able to freely celebrate their connections to their homeland.

Unlike all other immigrants, the ancestors of most people of African descent came to the Americas in fear and terror. Their migration was not a result of choice, but rather of capture. The slave trade that flourished from the 15th to the 19th century brought African captives to the New World of the Caribbean and the Americas and scattered them throughout the hemisphere.

Between the years 1518 and 1870 (when the slave trade ended), approximately 15 million Africans were brought forcibly to the New World. In the 10-year span from 1791 to 1801, the British Caribbean islands imported 1,401,000 African slaves (Parry, Sherlock, & Maingot, 1987). Between the years 1811 and 1870, 550,000 slaves were brought to Cuba, almost the equivalent to the number brought into Spanish America in the preceding 110 years. In Brazil, where the native populations were also enslaved, millions of Africans were also imported. Of the total number of Africans brought to this hemisphere, 38% of them were taken to Brazil (Segal, 1995).

The mortality rate during the passage from Africa to the Americas called the Middle Passage (Black, 1993), ranged from 10% to 20% (Lovejoy, 1989). Those who survived the crossing and were sold by slavers in the New World saw their numbers decrease by 4% or more each year. The mortality rate for children born to slaves was estimated at 200 per 1,000 births (Segal, 1995).

It has been observed that of all the immigrants who came to the Americas before the late 18th century, those who came by the slave trade were the most numerous (Curtin, 1969). Their skill and labor were major contributors to the development and prosperity of the Americas. This prolonged, forced migration transformed the ethnic structure of the populations of the Caribbean and the Americas.

After the U.S. Declaration of Independence in 1776, Delaware and five other states banned the importation of Africans. In 1808, the federal government banned new imports from the slave trade, but permitted the institution of slavery to continue in such states as maintained it, and allowed slavery to spread unrestricted south of the Ohio River. The Declaration of Independence, and its primary principle that all men were created equal and endowed with certain unalienable rights manifestly did not apply to Africans (Segal, 1995).

In 1860, the population of the slave-owning states and the District of Columbia was 12.3 million, of whom 8.1 million were Whites, 4 million were slaves, and 250,000 were "free colored." The numbers of the slave population varied considerably from one state to another. Whereas slaves made up more than 50% of the populations of South Carolina and Mississippi, they were only 1.5% of the people in Delaware. The majority of Southern Whites did not own slaves. Slavery was practiced by just over 25% of Whites, but the majority of the Southern White population defended the institution because, in one way or another, they thought that their prosperity depended on it. Slavery also provided even the poorest of Whites with a sense of superiority over the African population, a superiority based on skin color.

No consideration was given to the Africans' various ethnicities, cultures, and religious beliefs, except to stamp these out. The people brought as slaves were only valued as "cheap labor," never as people with their own unique humanity. However, culture and spirituality are part of the core of any people's identity and survival skills. Africans in the Americas surreptitiously preserved as much of their heritage as they could. They found the strength and solace they needed to survive in the only things that could not be taken from them, the ideas locked in their minds, the customs preserved in their consciousness.

Africans in the Caribbean and the Americas did not endure their enslavement peacefully. The first slave revolt was on the island of Hispaniola, on December 27, 1522 (Segal, 1995). There were many revolts over the years in all countries where slavery was practiced. In Jamaica, the Maroons, groups of escaped slaves who were once owned by the Spanish, fought the British for 76 years, until they were able to get a treaty granting them the right to their lands and hunting rights. They, in turn, agreed to cease increasing their ranks with the escaped slaves of the British and to assist in quelling rebellions. The Maroons had internal self-government of their communities and paid no taxes (Black, 1993).

The existence of these communities must have been a source of hope to the slaves, for revolts were numerous. Slave owners throughout the Americas used brutal torture and executions to punish acts of insubordination and escape out of fear of what might happen if their captives should seize power. But attempts to gain freedom through revolts continued until the end of slavery as an institution in the societies.

## SIMILARITIES AMONG PEOPLE OF AFRICAN DESCENT

In seeking to understand the characteristics that people of African descent have in common, it is important to know what makes them different from all other immigrants to this country. There are several areas of experience that Black people in the New World share that set them apart from all other ethnic groups. These areas include (1) the African legacy, rich in culture, custom, and achievement; (2) the history of slavery, a deliberate attempt to destroy the core and soul of the people, while keeping their bodies in enforced servitude; (3) racism and discrimination, ongoing efforts to continue the psychological and economic subjugation started during slavery; and (4) the victim system, a process by which individuals and communities are denied access to the instruments of development and advancement, and then blamed for low levels of accomplishment and achievement, while their successes are treated as anomalies (Boyd-Franklin, 1989; Pinderhughes, 1982). These are common experiences of the African in the Americas, whether they lived in the Caribbean, Central and South America, or the United States. What sustained them were the portions of the African legacy that they were able to preserve within themselves and their communities.

People of African descent place great importance on the family. In Africa, close-knit families and kinship groups were the foundations of the larger social structure of the tribe and the nation. Although slavery severed families by scattering their members, it could not destroy their desire to reconstitute themselves. In fact, slavery made regeneration of the family a necessity. Living with the constant threat of separation and loss through the sale of a family member by a White master, the family sustained itself by placing high value on each member, no matter how distant the blood relationship may be. When kinship ties have been preserved, African Americans, African Caribbeans, and African Hispanics are often very aware of their extended families and may speak of distant cousins with as much affection as they speak of brothers or sisters.

This incorporation of extended family members includes their children. It is not unusual to find a child of a distant relative living in a home as a part of the family. This process of inclusion provides support in many ways and on various levels, including child rearing, lending money in times of need, and assistance in negotiating through the labyrinth of larger systems that newly arrived family members will encounter, whether they are from another state or another country. It is expected that members of the family will provide assistance to each other in times of crisis.

## Valuing Religion and Spirituality

Spirituality sustained the slaves during their time of servitude, and when their native religions were forbidden, they adopted the religion of their captors and found support in that. In some places, the African gods were cleverly blended with the Christian God and saints, and so preserved aspects of the "Old Country" faith. This blending of the African religion with European Christianity can be seen in Santeria, the Afro Catholic religion of the Spanish-speaking Caribbean, which draws heavily on its Yoruba roots and identifies its entire pantheon with Catholic saints (Shorris, 1992). Similar combinations of the African and European faiths may be observed in Pocomania and Spiritual Baptists, religions found in the English-speaking islands. *Obeah* is a belief in the power of good and bad spirits, and the influence they may have on the lives of people. Although there are practitioners of these rites, it has not been shown to be a specific, organized cult such as voodoo and other secret religions of the Americas (Gopaul-McNicol, 1993). These religious practices and their healing rites sustained the practitioners and believers when the belief systems of their captors failed them, and gave them a sense of their own power to seek vengeance against their oppressors.

People of African descent who are Christians may be found in almost all denominations. More recently, many people of African descent are converting to Islam, a religion that is practiced in many parts of Africa, although it is not necessarily the primary faith in countries which Black people were originally taken.

The Rastafarian religion emerged in Jamaica in the early part of the 20th century, paralleling the Back to Africa movement of Marcus Garvey's Universal Negro Improvement Association in the United States. In 1930, Ras Tafari Makonen was crowned Emperor of Ethiopia, and he named himself Haile Selassie, "the power of the Holy Trinity." He was a Black, Christian monarch with absolute power and many titles, which suggested that he was the chosen of God. Some people saw in him the hope for African redemption. Rastafarians saw him as the Black reincarnation of the Christ. They started to pray to him and the religion was born (Honychurch, 1981).

Rastafarians rejected the notion of a "White God" and substituted the concept of a "Black God," whose chosen people were Africans. Their religious doctrines were not widely accepted on the island at the time, but over the years, their followers have taken the faith to Europe and North America, and their numbers continue to grow. However, their ideas of Black pride, self-reliance, respect, and admiration for the long-denigrated African countries and cultures inspired many people who were not of their faith to question the "White" standards in society and to rail against discrimination and oppression.

## Music, the Arts, and Food

It is quite clear that the rhythms of jazz and the blues, calypso and reggae, salsa and other Latin beats all trace their roots back to Africa. The differences in the music of the various regions may indicate the impact of the European cultures that ruled them and also the contributions of the indigenous people of the area, but the African origins are clear. The same is true of the visual arts. There is a passionate intensity of form and color in the paintings and sculpture of artists of African descent that echoes the styles of their mother continent.

There are distinct differences in the cuisine of the various regions from which people of African descent came to the United States. The influences of Spain, England, France, and other European countries can be seen in the fare. But Africa traded with India, China, and Arabia long before Europe dominated world commerce. The fondness for strongly flavored dishes and hot spices in the cookery that is shared by people of African descent may be traced back to their original diet, hundreds of years ago. Also the many recipes that provide ways of cooking almost every portion of a slaughtered animal are not just a matter of economy, but a particular ancient, cultural reverence for that which sustains life.

## When Similarities Mask Differences: Women and Work

People of African descent are usually more accepting of women working outside the home. The tradition existed in Africa, where it was recognized that women's contributions to the family and the village life went beyond childbearing and child rearing. Women were also providers of food, organizers of community life, and in some societies, leaders and rulers. In the Americas, slavery also required the women to work in the fields and other workplaces along with the men. In modern times in the United States, it has been easier for women of African descent to find work than for the men. Such work is a necessity for the family's economic survival. Men of African descent coming to the United States from other countries sometimes take a while to grasp this not-so-subtle aspect of racism. This economic fact, rooted in racism, demeans both the man and the woman. It also enables the wider culture to identify the woman as less threatening, while labeling the man as less productive and unable to provide for his family.

Highly skilled Jamaican or Barbadian men who are unable to find employment or are underemployed in the United State are likely to blame themselves and question their own abilities instead of realizing the role racism is playing in their problems. That their wives are able to find work may serve to further confirm their self-blame. African Americans who have faced this kind of discrimination all their lives may be more aware to the true cause of their situation. Race and gender interact powerfully in bicultural Black couples.

Ethan, age 33, and Beverly, age 32, came to see me for therapy. He is an African American, born and raised in New York City, and she is a Jamaican who has lived in this country for 10 years. They have been married for 7 years and have two children: Eldridge, who is almost 6, and Elizabeth, who is 3 years old. Beverly's mother, Pamela, has lived with them since her husband died a year ago. Ethan is a teacher at the local high school, and Beverly is a nurse. Pamela is retired and takes care of the children when the parents are at work. She also does most of the cooking and household chores.

Recently the couple has been arguing a lot. Pamela says that her grandchildren do not respect her. She blames Ethan for their disrespectful attitude. Pamela is hurt because the children call her by her first name, and she thinks they are following Ethan's example. She says the children should address her as Grandma, and Ethan should either call her Mom or Miss Pam. He responds that she is not his mother and "Miss Pam" will never pass his lips. Beverly took her mother's side and soon differences that they thought had been worked out long ago were problems once more. Ethan was complaining about the meals that were being prepared, and Beverly was complaining about his watching too much football on television. She wants to go back to college to get a master's degree in administration, and he thinks that is a waste of time and money because the hospital will never place a Black woman in an administrative position. She thinks he sees everything in terms of race and color, and this attitude impedes his career. He responds that she does not understand that, in America, everything is about race and color. These two people seem to have so much in common, share certain aspects of their backgrounds, and appear to face the same problems in society, yet they see things so differently. Why is this so?

People with dark skin who live within a White, racist context often assume themselves, and are assumed by others, to be more similar than different. The stresses of living with racism often require that critical differences be minimized or even ignored. In order to help Ethan and Beverly, we needed first to explore the differences in their cultural backgrounds that they brought to their marriage and promptly forgot.

When Ethan tells Beverly that she will not be able to rise in her profession due to racism, he is reflecting as an African American man. When Beverly, in turn, tells him he pays too much attention to race and racism, she is speaking of her own cultural experience as a Jamaican woman. She grew up in a society where, as a Black person, she was not a racial minority (82% of the total West Indian population is Black), and she saw that most of the elected government officials and the heads of state were people of African descent. She knows racism, but her experience is different from his. Beverly also has a different view of the United States. She came to the United States by choice; she perceives it as the land that will provide her with the educational and economic opportunities she could not have achieved in her country of origin. A discussion of these differences is crucial to working with Ethan and Beverly.

There is a significant number of people of African descent migrating to the United States from the Caribbean. It is estimated that nearly 30% of all Jamaicans now live in the United States. A tremendous emotional toll is exacted when they leave behind family members, sometimes their own children, to try to make a better life for the family. Often these people endure long periods as undocumented workers until they get their green cards and are able to bring their children here to join them. The children they leave behind grow up with a sense of abandonment. They receive the barrels of gifts and the financial support from their parents abroad, but they are deprived of the relationship that having that parent present in their lives would provide. The parents are worried by the uncertainty of how their children are being raised, and they miss experiencing love and the growth of their children (Larmer & Moses, 1996).

## DIFFERENCES

Although the people of African descent who live in the United States share many similarities, they also have distinct differences, which derive from the myriad cultures they have experienced across the generations, coupled with their particular migration patterns. For example, those who came from the former British Caribbean islands will have incorporated aspects of English culture, customs, and beliefs into their own culture. Some African Americans perceive these characteristics as internalized colonialism but, in fact, these traits are important aspects of the national identity of Caribbean people. Their formal manners and reserved behavior may at times be somewhat different from that of their African American brothers and sisters, but such comportment should not be construed as worse than or better than the manners of other people of African descent.

Sometimes this emphasis on good manners can be problematic for clinicians who do not understand the peculiarities of language. For example, a doctor was quite confused when an elderly Jamaican woman told him that her problem was that she "does not go out" as often as she ought. He thought she was referring to her social life, until the nurse informed him that the lady was trying to tell him she is constipated. To this older lady, with her Victorian manners, some things are just not proper to speak about directly.

The differences among peoples of African descent from the many regions of the Americas, who have now settled in the United States, must be recognized and appreciate as cultural characteristics and not perceived as flaws among various Black groups. Often these differences are not mentioned and, indeed, go underground, because there is a fear that mentioning differences may be used as a wedge to divide the people at a time when unity is the desired goal. It is critical to keep in mind that unity of purpose does not require uniformity of viewpoint, beliefs, or actions.

Those Black people from the former Spanish colonies of Central and South America and the Caribbean will exhibit the influence of Spanish culture. There are also people from French and Dutch colonies. Beliefs and cultural styles for a person from Haiti will be as different from those of a person from Brazil as a White French person's are from a White Portuguese person's. In these countries, distinct cultures developed, and they are not just blends or copies of the European cultures. This considerable diversity of values, customs, characteristics, and lifestyles among Black people living in this country is discussed in the work of Hines and Boyd-Franklin (1982), and they warn of the problems that will arise when therapists and policy makers try to design interventions, solutions, and plans based on the notion of a "typical" Black family.

People from the Caribbean are less likely to think of themselves as minorities than African Americans because where they grew up they were the numerical majority. This formative experience of social context can lead to struggles in bicultural couples, such as Ethan and Beverly.

The word "mulatto" was once used to denote people of both African and European parentage. The complex and racist formulae devised to determine the exact ratio of "White and Black blood" in a person have been abandoned in law (Segal, 1995). In the West Indies some of these people were considered "West Indian Whites" (Gopal-McNicol, 1993). Migrating to the United States, they have had more difficulty adjusting to American society where they are categorized by the majority culture as Black and sometimes pressured by the minority culture to so identify. Biracial people were always more accepted in the Black community than in the White community. Historically, in the United States they have learned to identify themselves as Black, or African Americans. However, a portion of the younger generation now refuse to be identified in that manner: They are calling themselves "biracial" or "multiracial." This group reasons that to identify only with one parent's racial group is to deny the other parent's contribution to their development. They are pressing for the inclusion of these terms in the census and other data collection forms. This biracial, or multiracial, position must also be considered and respected when working with racially mixed couples and their children.

## CONCLUSIONS

There is increasing recognition of the importance of understanding the culture and ethnicity of the client/patient. By understanding the customs, cultural concepts, and norms that the client/patient uses to cope with crises in life, the therapist is better able to formulate interventions that will lead to solutions.

It is critical for any therapist working with people of African descent in the American context to be aware of both cultural similarities and differences. Exploring and resolving problems requires the careful capacity to enable our clients to be anthropologists of their own system. As therapists, it is our job to raise questions and draw distinctions so that those difference that truly matter can be discussed, understood, and celebrated.

## REFERENCES

Black, C. V. (1993). *History of Jamaica.* Kingston, Jamaica: Carlong Publisher Caribbean Ltd.

Boyd-Franklin, N. (1989). *Black families in therapy: A multisystems approach.* New York: Guilford Press.

Curtin, P. (1969). *The Atlantic slave trade: A census.* Madison: University of Wisconsin.

Gopaul-McNicol, S. (1993). *Working with West Indian families.* New York: Guilford Press.

Hines, P. M., & Boyd-Franklin, N. (1982). Black families. In M. McGoldrick, J. K. Pearce, & J. Giordano (Eds.), *Ethnicity and family therapy* (1st ed., pp. 84–107). New York: Guilford Press.

Honychurch, L. (1981). *The Caribbean people: Book three.* Walton-on-Thames, Surrey, England: Thomas Nelson.

Larmer, B., & Moses, K. (1996, February 19). The barrel children, *Newsweek*, p. 45.

Lovejoy, P. E. (1989). The impact of the Atlantic slave trade on Africa: A review of the literature. *Journal of African History, 30.*

Parry, H. H., Sherlock, P., & Maingot, A. (1987). *A short history of the West Indies.* London and Basingstoke: Macmillan Education.

Pinderhughes, E. (1982). Afro-American families and the victim system. In M. McGoldrick, J. K. Pearce, & J. Giordano (Eds.), *Ethnicity and family therapy* (1st ed., pp. 108–122). New York: Guilford Press.

Segal, R. (1995). *The black diaspora.* New York: Farrar, Straus & Giroux.

Shorris, E. (1992). *Latinos: A biography of the people.* New York: Norton.

# CHAPTER 5

# African American Families

Paulette Moore Hines
Nancy Boyd-Franklin

For decades, psychological theorists and practitioners have not given significant attention to the implications of race. Some deny that there is an African American culture (Staino, 1980) or ignore many aspects of this heritage. We believe there are distinctive core values and behaviors that are characteristic of African Americans.

Families of African heritage have come to the United States from many different countries over four centuries. The largest group, and our focus here, are those whose ancestors were brought here as slaves. Although all immigrant groups have had acculturation problems, many African Americans question whether the social, economic, and political hardships they encounter as a result of racial discrimination will ever render the American dream attainable for the larger group of African Americans in this country. This group is very diverse in terms of geographic origins, age, acculturation, religious background, skin color, socioeconomic status, and strategies employed to cope with racism and discrimination; these variables interact to generate a host of variations that cannot possibly be fully articulated in a single chapter. Our intention is to provide an overview that will sensitize clinicians to the cultural context in which African Americans live in the United States.

## REVIEW OF THE LITERATURE ON AFRICAN AMERICAN FAMILIES

Many early studies of African American families by mainstream researchers adopted a pejorative, deficit view that characterized African American families as "disorganized, deprived, disadvantaged" (Moynihan, 1965; Frazier, 1966; Deutsch & Brown, 1964). In recent years African American researchers and scholars have challenged this deficit view and adopted a more balanced perspective that includes the strengths inherent in these families (Billingsley, 1968, 1992; Boyd-Franklin, 1989; Gary, Beatty, Berry, & Price, 1983; Hill, 1972; Hines & Boyd-Franklin, 1982; Hines, Garcia-Preto, McGoldrick, Almeida, & Weltman, 1992; Jones, 1980; Lewis & Looney, 1983; McAdoo, 1981; McAdoo & McAdoo, 1981, 1985; Royse & Turner, 1980; Staples, 1971, 1994; White, 1972, 1984).

In the last 20 years, an African psychology movement has developed that views the psychological behavior of African Americans through the lens of African culture, including such concepts as spirituality, "wellness" or collective unity, extended family systems and strong kinship bonds, and pride in one's heritage and ancestry (Nobles, 1985, 1986; Nobles & Goddard, 1984; Mbiti, 1970; Akbar, 1974, 1981, 1985; Baldwin, 1980, 1981; Asante & Vandi, 1980).

## CULTURAL CONTEXT

African Americans comprise about 12% of Americans. Until recent decades, the vast majority lived in the South. Between 1940 and 1970, over 1.5 million African Americans migrated, most frequently to the North and sometimes to the West. Over 84% now live in urban areas (Henderson, 1994).

This migration, in response to greater employment opportunities, has resulted in a substantial number of African Americans moving into the middle class. In 1989, one in seven black families earned $50,000 or more compared to one in 17 in 1967. African Americans also have made major advances in income as well as in education, employment, home ownership, and voter participation (Billingsley, 1992, 1994; Staples, 1994; Tidwell, 1994.) Between 1982 and 1992, the percentage of African Americans living below the poverty level decreased by 10.5% for 18 to 24-year-olds and 6.5% overall.

Still, racism and oppression make it extremely difficult for African Americans to enter and remain in the economic mainstream. In 1992, African Americans averaged just 80% of the income of Whites ($21,609 vs. $27,325). The average income of families in poverty (approximately one-third of all African Americans)—$12,675 for a family of four in 1989—was lower than that of poor Whites (O'Hare, Pollard, Mann, & Kent, 1991). The unemployment rate for African Americans aged 35–44 in 1991 was almost double that of their White counterparts; the rate for those aged 20–24 was almost 2.5 times that of Whites (Tidwell, 1994). Since the Civil Rights era, college and university enrollments have declined and residential segregation has largely persisted. Average life expectancy remains substantially lower than for Whites, and the number of deaths due to homicide exceeds the rate of any other group.

The disillusionment and frustration that evolve from persistent poverty and oppression have caused some African Americans to turn to drugs and alcohol, a dependence that makes for what we view as "psychological slavery." Yet, as Billingsley (1968) noted, African American families generally are noteworthy for their "amazing ability to survive in the face of impossible conditions." They have retained a sense of peoplehood and pride in "Blackness."

Therapists frequently overfocus on deficits and ignore strengths that will help families with "what needs to change." Hill (1972), one of the most important researchers who has focused on adaptive strengths, attributed the group's survival to strong kinship bonds; flexibility of family roles; and the high value placed on religion, education, and work. This perspective provides a framework for the discussion that follows.

## KINSHIP BONDS

Strong African American kinship bonds are traceable to Africa. Although it is problematic to make generalizations about history and culture in such a large continent, various tribes shared "commonalities" in the area of kinship (Akbar, 1985; Nobles, 1980, 1985). In contrast to the European premise "I think, therefore, I am," the prevailing African philosophy is, "We are, therefore, I am." In effect, individuals owed their existence to the tribe (Nobles, 1985).

Torn from their homelands and tribal lives by slavery, men, women, and children had to abandon native languages, names, occupations, mates, religions, foods, and customs. Mortality rates were high (Pinkney, 1975) and life expectancies were low (Ernst & Hugg, 1976). Families were frequently dissolved by the sale of members to slaveholders on near and distant plantations.

Male and female slaves were prohibited from marrying, either through their original tribal ceremonies or through the legally sanctioned rituals of their masters. Frequent changes of partner became the rule. Black men were used as breeders to increase the labor supply, while their owners sexually exploited Black women. Despite these extreme hardships, slaves sought to form new family units to compensate for losses due to death and slavery. Even after emancipation, many former slaves remained on plantations, hoping that lost family members might return.

African Americans thus share a heritage of ongoing trauma and strong kinship bonds. Their kinship network, which is much broader than traditional "bloodlines," remains key in coping with the pressures of an oppressive society (Boyd-Franklin, 1989; Billingsley, 1992; Staples, 1994). White (1972) has noted the number of "uncles, aunts, big mamas, boyfriends, older brothers and sisters, deacons, preachers, and others who operate in and out of the African American home" (p. 45).

# GENDER ROLES

The identity of African American fathers, regardless of income, is linked to their ability to provide for their families. Success in being a provider, however, often is limited by discrimination. Franklin (1993) introduced the concept of the "invisibility syndrome" to explain the marginalization of African American men. This refers to the paradox that White Americans, while keenly aware of Black Americans' skin color, fear them and treat them as if they were "invisible," thus denying African Americans validation and marginalizing them. Frequently therapists assume that Black fathers are absent and uninvolved, particularly if there has been no formal marriage. It also is not uncommon for therapists to overlook males in the extended family system, including the father's kinship network and the mother's male friends, who may be involved in the children's lives.

It is important for therapists to involve fathers and other significant adult males in family treatment, although this may be difficult when fathers hold several jobs or cannot take off from work to participate in therapy sessions. Many African American men also are reluctant to enter therapy, because they associate it with distrusted mainstream organizations. Therapists should explore signs of ambivalence and respond with creativity and flexibility. A father who is regarded as unavailable may come for an evening session or attend a single, problem-focused session (e.g., Hines, Richman, Maxim, & Hays, 1989). Therapists might use phone contacts and letters to keep fathers apprised of developments in their families' treatment. Recognizing fathers' family roles can decrease sabotaging; even limited involvement may lead to individual or family structural changes.

African American women, who often are more actively religious than their mates, tend to be regarded as "all sacrificing" and the "strength of the family." Their identity often is tied to their role as mothers (Hines, 1990). Historically, they have worked outside the home, sometimes as the sole wage earners, particularly in times of high unemployment.

Women's liberation is not new to the average African American woman. Scanzoni (1971) found evidence that African American boys and girls grow up expecting that women as well as men will work in order to survive economically. Thus, African American males do not feel as threatened as men from other cultures by having a working mate, resulting in more egalitarian relationships than among White couples (Willie, 1981; Willie & Greenblatt, 1978). Still, these relationships are affected by the male–female power differential that characterizes our patriarchal society.

African American women are aware that they outnumber African American men, who have a much lower life expectancy than African American women or Whites of either sex. Their availability also is reduced by incarceration, murder, mental and physical disabilities, drug and alcohol abuse, and deaths associated with jobs involving a high degree of danger or health hazards (e.g., military service, blue-collar work in hazardous waste, chemical production, or mining). Thus, many professional African American women have the choice of marrying less educated, lower status men or remaining single. Even if a professional woman is willing to do so, the sex ratio is skewed to an extent that she may not be successful in finding a partner. A growing number of women are choosing to become single parents rather than remain childless.

## COUPLE RELATIONSHIPS

African American couples often seek therapy because of child-focused concerns. Some experience great stress from being unable to translate hard work into economic success (Comer & Hills, 1985; Pinderhughes, 1982). Long periods of separation may occur without either partner moving to dissolve a relationship legally. There also is a strong tradition of remaining together for the sake of the children.

Usually, African American women initiate the therapy process. Therapists may get frustrated with women who express intense dissatisfaction yet resist change in dysfunctional relationships. Their discontent frequently is coupled with an awareness of the torment that generations of racism have caused for both African American men and women, and empathy for their husbands' frustration and sense of powerlessness. Women frequently struggle with the challenge of how to avoid further burdening their partners with their concerns and joining society in "beating their men further down" (McGoldrick, Garcia-Preto, Hines, & Lee, 1989).

## EXTENDED KINSHIP NETWORKS

Therapists working with African Americans must be willing to expand the "definition of family" to a more extended kinship system. Relatives often live in close proximity and expect to rely on one another in times of need. They may interchange functions and frequently share responsibilities for child-rearing, even among the African American middle class (Wilson, 1984; McAdoo, 1981).

It is fairly common for a child to be informally adopted and reared by extended family members who are better off than the child's parents or who reside in a more "wholesome" environment (Billingsley, 1992; Boyd-Franklin, 1989). Young adults frequently rely on the extended-kin network's collective support to achieve higher education and make the transition into adulthood and the work world (e.g., establish independent residences).

Such role flexibility is mobilized in times of crisis, such as separation, illness, hospitalization, or death of a family member. For far too many African Americans, there is a growing gap between the cultural ideology that has maintained patterns of extending help and exchanging resources and their ability to be responsive to family members' needs. African American families, particularly those who are poor or working class and reside in urban areas, are disproportionally affected by high unemployment and health crises (e.g., mothers unable to care for their children because of drug addiction and/or AIDS) that financially and emotionally overtax their networks. Even when family members can provide assistance, health, human services, and school policies sometimes raise bureaucratic or legalistic obstacles to extended family members becoming involved in such crises (Staples, 1985).

A genogram is an effective way to gather information about roles of different family members and their relationships (McGoldrick & Gerson, 1985). However, genogram information generally should be gathered only after the therapist feels that he or she has a bond of trust with the family. The therapist should look for natural openings to obtain information rather than force data gathering, for many African Americans are suspicious about the motivation underlying what they perceive as "prying." Illegitimate births, parents' marital status, incarcerated family members, or deaths due to AIDS, violence, or substance abuse, may be "secrets" unknown to all family members or information that members are hesitant to discuss with an outsider.

Genograms of African Americans seldom conform completely to bloodlines. Because of the extended family orientation and role flexibility that characterizes African American families, relationships are very complex and emotional ties are not predictable solely on the basis of biological relationship. It is essential to ask who is in the family, who lives in the home, and what family members and significant others live elsewhere, or valuable information may be lost. Often the question, "Whom can you depend on for help when needed?" will uncover key individuals in the family's support system.

Family therapists must explore and select carefully which "significant others" to include in family therapy. Often key family members may be unwilling or unable to come regularly. This obstacle may be overcome by scheduling a family session in the home, provided all key members consent.

Too frequently, it is assumed that certain family structures are inherently dysfunctional (e.g., multigenerational, single-parent). Therapists need to recognize that a family system may be functional even if it is not one that they would expect to work satisfactorily; at issue is not the structure but the functioning of a family. Sometimes, however, family boundaries and authority lines become quite blurred. Role confusion is not inevitable but occurs most frequently in the parental child and three-generation family structures described below.

## PARENTAL CHILD SYSTEMS

Sometimes, a child is "parentified," particularly when parents work or there are many children. This may involve a conscious decision on the part of adults to have the child assume or assist with parental responsibilities, or the child may take on this responsibility without the direct encouragement of adults. If there is no explicit delegation of authority, the child may lack power to carry out responsibilities he or she attempts to assume. Alternatively, if parents abdicate their responsibilities, the child may be forced to become the main source of guidance, control, and decision making, even if developmentally unprepared to do so (Minuchin, 1974). Such children often "act out" in school during late adolescence. Their stress may be externalized through delinquency, sexual impulsiveness, or inappropriate handling of younger siblings when the household demands conflict with their own developmental needs.

The parental child structure can work successfully: "The other children are cared for, and the parental child can develop responsibility, competence and autonomy beyond his years" (Minuchin, 1974, p. 97).

When the structure is operating in a problematic fashion, therapy's goals is not to eliminate a child's parental role, which may be essential to a family's survival, but to redistribute the child's burdens by helping the family to better use other resources.

## THE THREE-GENERATION SYSTEM

As the following case reveals, three-generation systems—typically involving a grandmother who plays a central role—often present sensitive boundary issues.

### The Gallop Family

The family consisted of Ms. LaVerne Frazier; her two children, Charlie (age 11) and Mary (age 5); her mother, Mrs. Sarah Gallop; and her aunt, Ms. Pierre. In addition, Charlie had contact with his father, Mr. Frazier, who had major input in decision making concerning him. When Ms. Frazier came to the clinic with Charlie, she reported that he was "out of control" at home and was frequently truant from school. He never listened to her and was involved in many fights.

It became clear that Charlie's grandmother who previously functioned as his mother during his earlier years, could not do so in the last year, because she had been forced to switch from a day shift to an evening shift on her job.

Mrs. Gallop came reluctantly to the session. However, it became clear during the session that she did not believe her daughter was capable of parenting Charlie. It also was obvious that both Ms. Frazier and Charlie responded to her as the real power in the home.

At the second interview, the therapist learned that in Mrs. Gallop's absence, Mr. Frazier (Charlie's father) and Ms. Pierre (Mrs. Gallop's sister) often undermined Ms. Frazier's instructions to Charlie. Mr. Frazier took him on outings even when he knew Charlie was being punished and didn't have his mother's permission to leave the house. Ms. Pierre was a warm, nurturing person who had cared for Charlie for awhile when his grandmother was ill. She would allow Charlie to stay at her home when he became angry with his mother and often supported his refusal to obey his mother.

With Ms. Frazier's and Mrs. Gallop's permission, a session was scheduled with Charlie's father and Ms. Pierre. The therapist was struck by the animosity between Ms. Frazier and Mr. Frazier and by the fact that no family member, including Charlie, responded to Ms. Frazier as an adult.

The adults in the family were asked to discuss Charlie's most serious problem; they eventually agreed on truancy. Mrs. Gallop and Ms. Frazier were then asked to confer on rules for Charlie. With the therapist's help, and after arguing for some time, the two women were able to establish that they would go to the school and discuss the situation with Charlie's teacher and principal. Ms. Frazier also would take Charlie to school for the first week in order to ensure his attendance.

Charlie's father agreed that he would only take Charlie to the movies and bowling—his favorite activities—if he had a positive report from his mother. Ms. Pierre was helped to see how she contributed to Charlie's acting out; she agreed to return Charlie if he ran away to her home.

Mrs. Gallop offered to help her daughter learn how to parent effectively. Ms. Frazier was asked to discuss the plan with Charlie and to gain his agreement to try it, without other adults intervening. Charlie became angry at his mother at one point. When both his grandmother and his aunt attempted to intervene, the therapist blocked their intervention and encouraged Ms. Frazier to complete her discussion and to obtain Charlie's consent.

During treatment, various family members were seen in different subgroups to reinforce the new structure that had been established. For example, Ms. Frazier and Charlie's father were seen together for two sessions to help them stop triangling Charlie in their conflicts. The majority of the sessions involved Mrs. Gallop, Ms. Frazier, and Charlie. Mrs. Gallop became a cotherapist and was able to allow Ms. Frazier to deal directly with her son. A number of sessions also were held between Ms. Frazier and Charlie to help them discuss problems they encountered.

The three-generation issue presented here is not an uncommon problem in African American extended families (Hines et al., 1992). This case illustrates the importance of working with subsystems in African American extended families. A clear parental structure needed to be introduced; later, it was important that other family members, such as Charlie's father and great aunt, support rather than sabotage this structure.

## RELIGION AND SPIRITUALITY

A strong spiritual orientation was a major aspect of life in Africa and during the slavery era. Highly emotional religious services conducted during slavery were of great importance in dealing with oppression. Often signals as to the time and place of an escape were given then. Spirituals contained hidden messages and a language of resistance (e.g., "Wade in the Water" and "Steal Away"). Spirituals (e.g., "Nobody Knows the Trouble I've Seen") and the ecstatic celebration of Christ's gift of salvation provided Black slaves with outlets for expressing feelings of pain, humiliation, and anger.

The church also continues to serve numerous functions for members of the African American community in modern times. African Americans are currently represented in many different religious groups, including Baptists, African Methodists, Jehovah's Witnesses, Church of God in Christ, Seventh Day Adventists, Pentecostal churches, numerous Islamic sects, Presbyterians, Lutherans, Episcopalians, Roman Catholics, and Jews (Billingsley, 1992; Boyd-Franklin, 1989). The impact of these religions on the lives of African American people is a complex subject. Further reading (Nobles, 1980; Mbiti, 1970) is recommended for therapists who wish to expand their knowledge in this area.

However, since a large proportion are Baptist, we will use this denomination as an example of the impact of organized religion in the lives and mental health of many African Americans, whether or not they are active churchgoers. In a Baptist church, as well as in other denominations, an African American family finds a complete support system, including the minister, deacons, deaconesses, and other church members. Many churches also include social activities for the entire family that extend far beyond the Sunday services, such as various choirs and youth, young adult, single parents', men's, women's, Sunday School, and Bible Study groups. Congregates also organize health-promotion classes (e.g., marriage enrichment, exercise, work stress), day-care centers, health fairs, economic development initiatives, tutoring programs, and support groups (e.g., unemployment, alcohol and drug abuse, grief). The smallest church provides a network of people who are available to a family in times of crisis. For example, 12 young men, ages 12 to 14, were suspended from school for fighting and picked up by local police for an immediate court hearing, after which they were transferred back to a lockup facility. Only then were parents alerted to the situation. Several belonged to a church active in the local community. The minister immediately responded to the parents' call for assistance in addressing the youth's pending suspension for the remainder of the school year, as well as anticipated further fighting between the youth.

The local church assisted the parents in grieving the school and court action taken prior to their being contacted. It also made a commitment to support the youth and parents in avoiding the usual institutional responses that exacerbate rather than resolve the difficulties of youth who exercise bad judgment but have been law-abiding. The church created an alternative school on the church premises, and the boys and their families engaged in home-based counseling. In addition, the boys were involved in weekly recreational activities, mentoring and career awareness, entrepreneurship, and conflict-resolution training. Parent education and multifamily sessions were conducted, and the parents were included in periodic outings with the youth, their mentors, and church members.

Mental health professionals are becoming increasingly open to the healthy potentialities of religious involvement and the extent to which a strong spiritual base is central to the resilience demonstrated by individuals when even the therapist is overcome with a sense of hopelessness and/or powerlessness. Bergin (1991) notes that the values endorsed and encouraged by mental health professionals are very consistent with spiritual values; these include sensitivity to others' feelings, responsibility for one's actions, fulfillment and satisfaction, self-discipline, forgiveness, regulated sexual fulfillment, a sense of purpose, and so on. Therapists are all too aware, however, that religion is multidimensional, and there are healthy and unhealthy forms of religiosity. Although the overall effects are generally positive, some interpretations of religious doctrine can have a harmful impact.

Larsen (1976) suggests that therapists work within the confines of a family's belief system rather than attempt to modify their beliefs and that those who are familiar with scriptural passages cite biblical authority to support therapeutic recommendations. He adds that there is a tendency among some clients to "spiritualize" or cope by defining difficulties as God's will, "passively trusting that the problems will somehow be resolved."

Again, even when individuals are not actively involved in organized religion, their core beliefs may be intricately intertwined with religious doctrine. Their religious orientation may be a source of as well as a haven from stress. Therapists also should be aware that when individuals convert from one denomination or religious group to another, they frequently encounter conflicts with family members who have different beliefs and practices, which can become a treatment issue.

Mitchell and Lewter (1986) in their book *Soul Theology* provide an excellent reference with clinical examples for therapists interested in learning more about the extent to which biblical references intertwined with cultural values provide a frame of reference that can serve as a source of affirmation, hope, freedom, and positive behavioral change.

## WORK AND EDUCATION

Many writers (Hill, 1972, Boyd-Franklin, 1989; Billingsley, 1992; Staples, 1994) have addressed the importance that African Americans traditionally place on work and educational achievement as critical to success. Yet many White Americans believe that most African Americans do not work and survive only because of welfare, despite the fact that the overwhelming majority work, often on more than one job. At the same time, they receive less pay for the same work, secure less desirable jobs, are last hired, and are more likely to be underemployed and/or stuck under "glass ceilings" than their White counterparts. Most no longer believe that the American dream is intended to include them. Unlike their mainstream counterparts, most perceive work and educational achievement as essential to psychological and physical survival, a means to an end rather than a source of self-actualization. A small but growing number of teens and young adults, relatively small in contrast to those who operate within the system, are reacting to their perceived exclusion from the world of legitimate work by generating income through underground activity. This type of adaptation is not new in the African American community. However, this subpopulation receives significant media attention, because they represent a threat to the community's safety; their creative approach to survival sometimes involves self- and other-destruction—drug sales and the violence that often accompanies this type of activity.

African American parents generally expect their children to pursue careers offering security and to surpass them in achieving the "comforts of life." Those who succeed to levels formerly denied Blacks are held in high regard. However, because African Americans place great value on character and generally believe in the basic worth of every individual regardless of his or her success, children who earn an honest living and are self-supporting may win as much parental approval as those who are professionals.

Concern about the consequences of poor school adjustment often leads African American families to treatment. In addition to the typical stresses of adolescence, low-income African American youth have fewer ways of acting out their anxieties, anger, and frustration as they face an oppressive society and the expectations of parents who have limited resources to assist them in starting out as young adults (Hines, in press). Middle-class African American youth may encounter conflicts with peers and family members related to differences in socioeconomic status, Black ideology, experiences of and style of coping with racism. Their parents, who often enter the middle class without financial assets and struggle to retain a tenuous hold on their status, are likely to demand high achievement from their children. Concern for their children's futures may reactivate parents' sense of powerlessness and rage about racism, sometimes resulting in self-defeating behavior. It is helpful for therapists to assist parents to distinguish between their own and their children's issues and goals. In coaching parents to assist their children in coping with anger and frustration, therapists can help parents to adopt healthier ways of managing their own stress and anger. This includes helping them to reconnect with strategies that have helped them as well as their forebearers to transcend difficult circumstances and coaching them to share these stories with their children in ways that promote dialogue.

Believing that "to whom much is given, much is expected, "successful African Americans often feel they have a responsibility to "give back," especially to needy family members. This sense of responsibility is linked to the notion that individual well-being is tied to the collective welfare. Accomplishments often are considered the consequence of individual effort and, even more, others' sacrifices. Some individuals may experience difficulty because their efforts to help extended family members leaves them feeling depleted emotionally, physically, and/or financially. In such instances, culturally congruent therapists will support the individuals' capacity to develop or maintain a balance between extending help and taking care of themselves, rather than encouraging emotional cutoffs and attention only to individual needs.

## A MULTISYSTEMS APPROACH TO THE TREATMENT OF AFRICAN AMERICAN FAMILIES

In working with African American families, therapists must be particularly willing to expand the context of therapy to include the impact of the social, political, socioeconomic, and other broader environmental conditions. Aponte (1976, 1994) described this broader treatment approach as "ecostructural," whereas Boyd-Franklin (1989) used the term "multisystems," given that poor inner-city African American families are likely to be involved with numerous external systems. Both ask therapists always to consider a family's environment and community in diagnosis and treatment.

African American, inner-city families often are faced with overwhelming socioeconomic problems, such as eviction or termination of public assistance. When these survival issues take precedence over family conflicts, it is important that clinicians not assume responsibility for these families but act as "guides" to help families learn how to negotiate complex bureaucratic systems. This requires therapists to outreach and involves more time and energy than is usually the case in family therapy. For example, if a child is referred for school problems, therapists may need to arrange meetings with the child, family, and school officials. For a child who is being removed from his or her home by a social welfare agency, the family therapist can help the family work with the agency to find the best possible placement. Sometimes, such placements can be avoided by exploring who in the extended family might care for the child until the situation changes.

Middle-class African Americans, like their lower class peers, contend with circumstances that are shaped by racism; however, it is more subtle. For them, there are likely to be no role models as they enter "uncharted territories" in their workplace or neighborhood. For some, the stress from discerning and responding to subtle and overt racism may result in social and psychological isolation. Others derive from their experience exceptional strength, flexibility, and tolerance for diversity.

## OTHER CONSIDERATIONS FOR FAMILY THERAPISTS

Given these cultural and ecological considerations, it is likely that, for African Americans, reliance on individuals within natural support systems stimulates fewer feelings of guilt, defeat, humiliation, and powerlessness than does use of institutional mental health services.

Many African Americans view therapy as a process for "crazy people." Some assume that clinicians will operate in the same way as other agencies (e.g., welfare system, schools) that have been intrusive in telling families what they "can" or "cannot" own (e.g., telephone or television). Others may view serious emotional difficulties as "the wages of sin"; the person who manifests psychiatric symptoms may be seen as "mean" or "possessed by the devil" (particularly if he or she engages in antisocial behavior) and may be regarded as having the potential to change his or her behavior at will. Some believe that emotional, behavioral, and relationship difficulties result from not believing and practicing biblical and cultural guidelines for living. For some, seeking help from a mental health professional rather than through prayer may signify a lack of trust in God; for others, this is perceived as turning to "the system" that has negatively influenced African American well-being.

African Americans also may fear misdiagnosis, prescription of medication for behavioral and population control, and governmental abuse of clinical files. These concerns arise out of incidents such as the "Tuskegee Study," where for four decades, black men infected with syphilis were monitored, but not treated, in a program that involved the complicity of doctors and governmental officials.

Yet, African Americans have been utilizing mental health services in greater numbers than ever before in history. Their major presenting problems include poor school adjustment, acting-out behavior, depression, "nervous breakdowns" or psychotic behaviors, drug addiction, and alcoholism. Among the low-income and working class, the identified patient is frequently a child who has been referred by a school, welfare department, courts, or the police. Although therapists are generally mindful that families who feel forced to come for therapy are likely to be very ambivalent about therapy, it is necessary to translate this awareness into discussion about families' feelings, expectations, and priorities.

African American families often need to be oriented to mental health services; myths need to be discussed and dispelled. They are likely to be most responsive to time-limited, problem-solving, child-focused therapy approaches with an active, directive therapist. Aponte (1978, 1994) emphasizes the need to help a family experience therapy as a process that can help produce immediate change(s) in their lives.

Requesting total family involvement may heighten a family's feelings of responsibility and guilt, so the therapist should be flexible when families resist. Otherwise, those who are participating in therapy may decide that it is not worth trying to coerce unwilling family members to join them. Therapists need to allow for questioning and to clarify the rationale for requesting family involvement. African American families are quite aware of larger systems influences, and therapists who do not acknowledge this are likely to lose credibility.

Communicating respect is key to successfully engaging families. Therapists should openly acknowledge the family strengths, avoid professional jargon, relate in a directive but supportive manner, and avoid assuming familiarity with adult family members before asking their permission. Using first names prematurely may elicit nonverbalized negative reactions, especially from adults who are sensitive to the disrespect that has been purposefully shown to African Americans during and since slavery by Whites who refused to use their names, renamed them, and referred to them with terms intended to convey low status (e.g., boy).

A non-African American therapist may wish to acknowledge his or her difference in racial/ethnic background and to discuss the family's feelings about it early in therapy. The therapist's gauge of his or her personal discomfort with the family's perceived acceptance of him- or herself is probably the best indicator of whether to move in this direction. The risk of raising the race issue and finding it to be irrelevant is not likely to have a devastating effect if the therapist conveys respect and genuiness and can handle suspiciousness and challenge to authority in a nondefensive manner.

Therapists should first become familiar with the culture and value system different from their own. This may not be easily accomplished. For example, a well-meaning therapist may unwittingly undermine much-needed parental authority out of concern about the harshness of parents' handling of their children. Typically, African American parents believe that there is a very narrow "window for error" allowed African American youth in our society. The principle "Spare the rod, spoil the child" is a common rule of thumb, and physical punishment is an accepted mode of discipline. A well-meaning therapist may unwittingly undermine parental authority out of concern about adults' "harshness" in responding to their children. He or she may be more success-ful in assisting a family by acknowledging a parent's need for a deterrent to misbehavior and conveying sensitivity to their concerns. This does not mean that the therapist has to approve or encourage the use of physical punishment. However, rather than argue for the elimination of physical punishment, the therapist can expand upon parents' understanding that this practice is a residual of slavery, as well as teach and emphasize the benefits of positive, alternative approaches.

We can easily become overwhelmed by a family who differs greatly from our own. In some instances, the issues that a family introduces may represent resistance to change. But a family's concerns about investing time and money in the therapeutic process may stem from negative experiences with "helping" professionals or a desire to avoid an additional demand whose value hasn't been proven. Some families also may not recognize the importance of being punc-tual for an appointment or of calling to cancel or reschedule. Low-income fami-lies, in particular, are likely to approach mental health services with a medi-cal-clinic frame of reference, where they are used to waiting long hours for service. "Resistance" also may well be grounded in the difficulties of balanc-ing parenting, household tasks, and one or more jobs.

Therapists frequently characterize African Americans as nonverbal and incapable of dealing with feelings. Sometimes African Americans who appear mute in the therapy room may talk endlessly on home turf (Jones & Seagull, 1977). Furthermore, a lack of trust or "cultural paranoia" may limit family members' willingness to "open up." Finally, some African American families may communicate differently than persons in the therapist's own ethnic group. A therapist might consider working with subgroups of a family when the larger family group's messages are so vague, complex, or incomplete that the fam-ily, as well as the therapist, become overwhelmed.

Minuchin, Montalvo, Guerney, Rosman, and Schumer (1967) have noted that for many low-income families, "affect is communicated mostly through paraverbal channels in the pitch, tempo, and intensity of the verbal messages and the accompanying kinesthetic modifiers" (p. 206), a description that applies to many African American families. Tracking and joining a family can become a difficult and complex process. A therapist might also consider having family members observe each other behind the one-way mirror or using videotape playback to promote improved communication. Because of African American families' suspiciousness about therapy, therapists should clarify how audiotapes and videotapes will be used.

Individual therapists are more likely than therapy teams to "burn out" when working with families who live under oppressive life circumstances. Use of a team of therapists involves many advantages, including the opportunity to get feedback from behind the mirror during the family session via a bug-in-the-ear device. The therapist also may periodically confer with the consulting team on issues he or she otherwise might overlook. Hines et al. (1989) described a model for family intervention in which a multidisciplinary team of therapists meets together with a family for a planned, all-day session. They found that the use of a team with differing personalities, skills, and sensitivities maximizes the possibility that each family member will connect emotionally with at least one therapist. Team members can process their reactions to the family session, use each other in planning and implementing treatment interventions, and follow-up with other community systems.

## CONCLUSIONS

If we are to expand upon our current knowledge and proficiency in working with African American families, we must begin to establish networks of therapists and researchers in different parts of the county. Research populations must be expanded to include "normal" families to permit greater understanding of the factors that contribute to resilience in the face of racism, classism, poverty, and sexism. This analysis must include an exploration of level of acculturation, racial identity, family functioning, religiosity, availability and use of social support systems, history of low-level but persistent stress, social policies, and style of coping.

## REFERENCES

Akbar, N. (1974). Awareness: The key to Black mental health. *Journal of African American Psychology, 1*, 30–37.

Akbar, N. (1981). Mental disorder among African-Americans. *African American Books Bulletin, 7*(2), 18–25.

Akbar, N. (1985). Nile Valley origins of the science of the mind. In I. Van Sertima (Ed.), *Nile Valley civilizations.* New York: Journal of African Civilization.

Aponte, H. (1978). Diagnosis in family therapy. In C. B. Germain (Ed.), *Social work practice: People and environments.* New York: Columbia University Press.

Aponte, H. (1976). The family–school interview: An ecostructural approach. *Family Process, 15*(3), 303–311.

Aponte, H. (1994). *Bread and spirit: Therapy with the new poor.* New York: Morton Press.

Asante, M., & Vandi, A. (Eds.). (1980). *Contemporary Black thought.* Beverly Hills, CA: Sage.

Baldwin, J. (1980). The psychology of oppression. In M. Asante & A. Vandi (Eds.), *Contemporary Black thought.* Beverly Hills, CA: Sage.

Baldwin, J. (1981). Notes on an Africentric theory of Black personality. *Western Journal of African American Studies, 5*(3), 172–179.

Bergin, A. (1991). Values and religious issues in psychotherapy and mental health. *American Psychologist, 46*(4), 394–403.

Billingsley, A. (1968). *Black families in White America.* Englewood Cliffs, NJ: Prentice-Hall.

Billingsley, A. (1992). *Climbing Jacob's ladder: The enduring legacy of African-American families.* New York: Simon & Schuster.

Boyd-Franklin, N. (1989). *Black families in therapy: A multisystems approach.* New York: Guilford Press.

Comer, J., & Hills, H. (1985). Social policy and the mental health of Black children. *Journal of the American Academy of Child Psychiatry, 24*(2), 175–181.

Deutsch, M., & Brown, B. (1964). Social influences in Negro–white intellectual differences. *Social Issues,* 27–36.

Ernst, R., & Hugg, L. (1976). *Black America: Geographic perspectives.* New York: Anchor Books.

Franklin, A. J. (1993, July/August). The invisibility syndrome. *Family Therapy Networker,* pp. 33–39.

Frazier, E. F. (1966). *The Negro family in the United States.* Chicago: University of Chicago Press.

Gary, L., Beatty, L., Berry, G., & Price, M. (1983, December). *Stable Black families final report.* Manuscript submitted to United Church of Christ Commission for Racial Justice.

Henderson, L. (1994). African Americans in the urban milieu: Conditions, trends, and development needs. In B. Tidwell (Ed.), *The state of Black America* (pp. 11–26). New York: National Urban League.

Hill, R. (1972). *The strengths of African American families.* New York: Emerson-Hall.

Hines, P. (1990). African-American mothers. *Journal of Feminist Family Therapy, 2*(2), 23–32.

Hines, P. (in press) The family life cycle of poor Black families. In B. Carter & M. McGoldrick (Eds.), *The changing family life cycle: A framework for family therapy* (3rd ed.). New York: Gardner Press.

Hines, P. M., & Boyd-Franklin, N. (1982). Black families. In M. McGoldrick, J. K. Pearce, & J. Giordano (Eds.), *Ethnicity and family therapy* (1st ed., pp. 84–107). New York: Guilford Press.

Hines, P., Garcia-Preto, N., McGoldrick, M., Almeida, R. & Weltman, S. (1992). Intergenerational relationships across cultures. *Families in Society, 73*(6), 323–338.

Hines, P., Richman, P., Maxim, K., & Hays, H. (1989). Multi-impact family therapy: An approach to working with multi-problem families. *Journal of Psychotherapy and the Family, 6,* 161–175.

Jones, A., & Seagull, A. (1977). Dimensions of the relationship between the Black client and the White therapist. *American Psychologist, 32*(10), 851.

Jones, R. (Ed.). (1980). *Black psychology* (2nd ed.). New York: Harper & Row.

Larsen, J. (1976, October). *Dysfunction in the evangelical family: Treatment considerations.* Paper presented at the meeting of the American Association of Marriage and Family Counselors, Philadelphia.

Lewis, J., & Looney, J. (1983). *The long struggle: Well-functioning working-class Black families.* New York: Brunner/Mazel.

Mbiti, J. S. (1970). *African religions and philosophies.* Garden City, NY: Anchor Books/Doubleday.

McAdoo, H. P. (Ed.). (1981). *Black families.* Beverly Hills, CA: Sage.

McAdoo, H. P., & McAdoo, J. L. (Eds.). (1985). *Black children: Social, educational and parental environments.* Beverly Hills, CA: Sage.

McGoldrick, M., Garcia-Preto, N., Hines, P., & Lee, E. (1989). Ethnicity and women. In M. McGoldrick, C. Anderson, & F. Walsh (Eds.), *Women in families.* New York: Norton.

McGoldrick, M., & Gerson, R. (1985). *Genograms in family assessment.* New York: Norton.

Minuchin, S., Montalvo, B., Guerney, B. G., Jr., Rosman, B. L., & Schumer, F. (1967). *Families of the slums.* New York: Basic Books.

Minuchin, S. (1974). *Families and family therapy.* Cambridge, MA: Harvard University Press.

Mitchell, H., & Lewter, N. (1986). *Soul theology: The heart of American Black culture.* San Francisco: Harper & Row.

Moynihan, D. P. (1965). *The Negro family: The case for national action.* Washington, DC: U.S. Department of Labor.

Nobles, W. (1980). African philosophy: Foundations for black psychology. In R. Jones (Ed.), *Black psychology* (2nd ed., pp. 18–32). New York: Harper & Row.

Nobles, W. (1985). *Africanicity and the Black family: The development of a theoretical model.* Oakland, CA: Black Family Institute Publishers.

Nobles, W. (1986). *African psychology: Toward its reclamation, reascension and revitalization.* Oakland, CA: Black Family Institute Publishers.

Nobles, W., & Goddard, L. L. (1984). *Understanding the Black family: A guide to scholarship and research.* Oakland, CA: Black Family Institute Publishers.

O'Hare, W., Pollard, K., Mann, T., & Kent, M. (1991, July). African Americans in the 1990's. *Population Bulletin, 46*(1), 8.

Pinderhughes, E. (1982). Afro American families and the victim system. In M. McGoldrick, J. K. Pearce, & J. Giordano (Eds.), *Ethnicity and family therapy* (1st ed., pp. 108–122). New York: Guilford Press.

Pinkney, A. (1975). *Black Americans.* Englewood Cliffs, NJ: Prentice-Hall.

Royse, D., & Turner, G. (1980). Strengths of Black families: An African American community's perspective. *Social Work, 25*(5), 407–409.

Scanzoni, J. H. (1971). *The Black family in modern society: Patterns of stability and security.* Chicago: Univerity of Chicago Press.

Staino, K. (1980) Ethnicity as process: The creation of an Afro-American identity. *Ethnicity, 7,* 27–33.

Staples, R. (1971, February). Toward a sociology of the Black family: A theoretical and methodological assessment. *Journal of Marriage and the Family,* 119–138.

Staples, R. (1985, November). Changes in Black family structure: The conflict between family ideology and structural conditions. *Journal of Marriage and the Family,* 1005–1013.

Staples, R. (1994). *Black family: Essays and studies* (5th ed.). New York: Van Nostrand Reinhold.

Tidwell, B. (Ed.). (1994). *The state of Black America.* New York: National Urban League.

White, J. (1972). Towards a Black psychology. In R. Jones (Ed.), *Black psychology* (pp. 43–50). New York: Harper & Row.

White, J. (1984). *The psychology of blacks: An Afro-American perspective.* Englewood Cliffs, NJ: Prentice-Hall.

Willie, C. (1981). Dominance in the family: The Black and White experience. *Journal of Black Psychology, 7*(2), 91–97.

Willie, C., & Greenblatt, S. (1978). Four "classic" studies of power relationships in Black families: A review and look to the future. *Journal of Marriage and the Family, 40*(4), 691–694.

Wilson, M. (1984). Mothers' and grandmothers' perceptions of parental behavior in three-generational Black families. *Child Development, 55*(4), 1333–1339.

# CHAPTER 6

# Jamaican Families

## Janet Brice-Baker

The focus of this chapter is the Jamaican, West Indian family. It will examine some of the experiences of immigrant Jamaican families that may influence psychotherapeutic intervention.

## BRIEF HISTORY OF JAMAICA

Jamaica is the third largest island in the West Indies in terms of size (146 miles long by 50 miles wide) and population (2.4 million in 1990). It is one of a group of islands that comprise the British West Indies. The other islands are Trinidad and Tobago, the Grenadines, St. Vincent, St. Lucia, St. Kitts, Nevis, Montserrat, Grenada, Dominica, the Cayman Islands, the British Virgin Islands, Barbados, the Bahamas, part of Aruba, part of the Netherland Antilles, Barbuda, Antigua, and Anguilla (Gopaul-McNicol, 1993).

Jamaica was "discovered" by Christopher Columbus, in his role as emissary of the Spanish crown, on his second voyage in 1493. The natives of the island were Arawak Indians. Africans first arrived in Jamaica in 1509 and were alleged to have come from the Ashanti, Yoruba, Ibo, and Fanti tribes. By the middle of the 17th century (1655), the British had conquered the Spanish and taken over the island. The emancipation of the slaves occurred in 1834. In addition to the Arawak Indian natives, the Spanish, the African slaves, and the British, there were communities of Hispanic Jews, French, Germans, Scots, Irish, East Indians, Chinese, and Syrians. With the exception of the Jews, the other groups were brought to the island to work as laborers, particularly after emancipation and the loss of slave labor.

## MIGRATION

The migration of West Indians to the United States dates back to the early 19th century. In the 1850s there were only a few hundred West Indians immigrating to the United States each year. By the end of the century, the number had only risen to approximately 1,000 per year (Ueda, 1980).

Recent statistics indicate that in the years 1981–1991 there were approximately one million immigrants in the United States from the entire Caribbean; the Jamaican immigrants numbered one-fourth of that total. In 1991, the median age for Jamaican immigrants was 28, and the proportion of men to women was fairly even. The immigration was characterized by family separations (often prolonged due to the cost of flying back to Jamaica), feelings of dislocation, and adjustment to urban settings and colder weather. New York and Florida received the largest settlement of new Jamaican immigrants. Therapists working in large metropolitan areas are likely to encounter Jamaicans as clients.

One immigration scenario is for a family member to travel to the United States, sometimes with other relatives, and become established. Other family members are sent for later. Several Jamaican families often share an apartment or house, with each family occupying a bedroom. However, when a family moves out, the remaining families do not necessarily move into the other rooms. In an effort to save money, the extra bedroom might be rented.

Because the island of Jamaica resembles a small town, the probability is very high that if an individual runs into a fellow Jamaican, he or she might know the other person's family back home. Even in instances when the two immigrants do not know one another, they are able to reminisce about certain places, foods, and celebrations particular to their home. This familiarity produces a natural support system that a therapist can utilize to help ease the stress of acculturation.

But even with the available support systems, Jamaicans, like other ethnic groups, have faced and still face the problems of adjusting to a new culture. The weather in the United States changes, and it can be cold and brutal compared to the warm, tropical temperatures of the islands. Furthermore, the weather dictates what people do and when they do it, which may be somewhat disconcerting for a people accustomed to tropical temperatures all year round. Modes of dress and daily diet are also unfamiliar. Although jobs are available, there are many times when a skilled Jamaican immigrant must take work that does not utilize his or her training; the mop and pail of domestic work, for example, are often referred to as "West Indian pen and ink."

One of the most difficult things Jamaicans have had to cope with is the physical and psychological isolation. Visiting extended family members is relatively easy on the island because the country is so small. In the United States, however, traveling to see relatives or going to work becomes a lengthy and complicated endeavor. At home, people know their neighbors and are familiar with local shopkeepers, clergy, and teachers. By comparison, the urban atmosphere seems cold and distant. People who were used to living in their own homes and being outdoors now live in cramped apartments far removed from the countryside.

Aside from the physical separation from their families, Jamaicans' experience of racial discrimination adds to their difficulties. Although racism has always existed in various forms on the Caribbean islands, it is perceived and experienced differently by Jamaicans than by American Blacks. Many Jamaicans find the cruelty and insidiousness of racism in the United States quite shocking. Jamaican Blacks did not experience Jim Crow segregation, lynching, hosing in the streets, and other acts of violence that have occurred here against Black people.

## JAMAICAN AND AMERICAN BLACKS

The relationship between Jamaican and American Blacks is often ambivalent. In large part, this ambivalence is due to the extreme levels and types of racism in the United States that have made it not only useful but also necessary for American Blacks and Jamaican immigrants to present a united front in order to make any gains. In doing so, however, the two groups have polarized around certain issues, one of which is immigrant versus native status. Jamaicans have frequently been placed on pedestals by White society as examples of "the good and industrious Black," whereas American Blacks have been stereotyped as lazy, criminal, and willing to live on public assistance. Another manifestation of polarization has been around the issue of phenotypic and genotypic racial definitions. Jamaicans and American Blacks are very sensitive to racial hue and tend to make at least three broad distinctions regarding skin color: black, colored, and white. These color distinctions represent points on a continuum from African skin color to European skin color. The lighter skinned you are, the closer you are to the European end of the continuum and the higher your status in Caribbean society (Garvey, 1973). Here in the United States, however, such color shadings and the meanings assigned to them are overtly ignored, and people are classified as Black or White.

A light-skinned Jamaican who comes to the United States is in a dilemma. In the islands, he or she probably had a certain amount of status, at least more than a dark-skinned Black person. In the United States, however, Whites might reject the Jamaican as "another Black," whereas Blacks may reject or look down on the light-skinned Jamaican because of what seems to be his or her refusal to identify with other Blacks.

Jamaicans, who are sensitive to potential exploitation from a powerful nation (Dominquez, 1975), share American Blacks' ambivalent feelings about the United States. Unlike American Blacks, who were brought to this country in slave ships and have a long history of negative experience here, Jamaicans have come here voluntarily, looking for educational and occupational advancement. Like American Blacks, they are cut off from their African roots, but unlike American Blacks, they retain an ethnic identity associated with their island or region and view themselves as immigrants (Best, 1975).

The two groups differ considerably in their attitudes toward the possibility of social mobility. Both have a strong desire to advance, but they disagree on the extent to which they can control their own destinies in a country with a White majority. American Blacks believe that no matter how hard Black people work, their color will prevent them from being justly rewarded. For some, the frustration has resulted in "learned helplessness," so they view efforts to break the cycle of poverty as futile. Jamaicans have a sense of empowerment that can be said to have been derived from their successful efforts at casting off the mantle of colonialism. The Maroons are probably one of the most vivid examples of this. They were a tribe of Africans who were discharged from the ships in Jamaica. They did not accept bondage easily and fought ardently to escape their captors. Although many of them died in the process, substantial numbers lived and carved out an existence for themselves in the hills. The Maroons and their leader have come to symbolize ethnic pride and strong survival skills. What is even more important is that they provided a legacy of Jamaicans who were never enslaved. This has to have had a tremendous impact on the self-esteem of Blacks from this island.

Jamaicans, as a result of having lived in a predominantly Black society, have had different experiences than American Blacks. Even if they are not well educated, Jamaicans have come to hope, and sometimes expect, that their children and grandchildren will achieve more. There is evidence for this expectation in the fact that West Indians "have been disproportionately over-represented among black professionals" (Sowell, 1981). And the U.S. value of hard work, which was learned primarily from the British, has meaning for the Jamaican (see McGill & Pearce, Chapter 31, this volume).

It is precisely those Jamaicans who are most acculturated and familiar with European culture who "make it" in the Caribbean or in the United States (Glantz, 1978). As a consequence, so runs the argument, the Jamaican immigrant to the United States is not only more apt to be forceful and enterprising than either the native American Black or the stay-at-home Jamaican, but is also more likely to believe that hard work and self-abnegation can lead eventually to reasonable prominence as a professional, local leader, small property owner, small business man, or landlord (Bryce-LaPorte, 1972).

Jamaican people's attitude about money has also been consistent with their British origins and has helped them to make their way in the United States. Because of their future orientation, they have been very thrifty and sacrifice in the present in order to have something in the future.

Jamaicans have always kept in mind their ethnic identity in their attempts to make a place for themselves in the United States. They frequently speak in terms of a region of Jamaica, of being British, of coming from a particular island, or of being from the West Indies. They assert these identities to distinguish themselves from other Blacks in America and from Whites. There is great value placed on all things English. An Englishman represents dignity, grace under fire, an exceptional education, and a possession of class second to none. For this reason, the Whites and Blacks in America are viewed by Jamaicans as crude and often lacking refinement.

## FAMILY RELATIONSHIPS AND CLASS STRUCTURE

Jamaican family relationships and problems can be understood only if you know about their family and social class structure, which is based on an English/Victorian model. At the beginning of White colonialism in Jamaica, the upper, or elite class, as they were called, was composed of the planters and their attorneys, who saw to the administration of each estate. The absence of "quality white women," who would be the wives of these men, led to sexual liaisons with female slaves (Smith, 1988). However, this was not the only reason. Many White men were simply attracted to Black women. The progeny of these unions created a colored middle class. Seventy years after the emancipation of slaves, this mixed-race population, who had the benefits of education and went into the professions, became the elite of the social structure. Business people comprised the new middle class, and darker skinned Blacks, who worked with their hands and could not trace their family origins to the original mixed-race or mulatto families, filled out the lower classes (Smith, 1988).

Upward mobility in Jamaica could be achieved in one of two ways: through education and/or intermarriage with members of the elite class. Before educational opportunities became more widespread, a key factor in the identification of elites, or members of Creole (any mixture of European and Negro ancestry) society, was their white and near-white complexions. Jamaican Blacks wishing to improve their social status strove to "lighten" the family gene pool. In this vein, intermarriage of Black Jamaicans with White or Asian Jamaicans is not necessarily frowned upon in the Black community. Gopaul-McNicol (1993) writes about another type of intermarriage, namely interisland marriage, or that between spouses from different islands. She points out that whether there are problems in a couple's relationship is really dependent on which other island the spouse comes from. She further points out that marriage between Jamaican Blacks and American Blacks is considered intercultural, with unions between Black American men and West Indian women being more successful than that between Black American women and West Indian men.

Jamaica is a society of gender-role paradoxes. On the surface, sex roles are very traditional and stereotypical and vary little by class, race, or age (Smith, 1988). Girls are taught obedience and discouraged from being assertive. Domestic training is emphasized in the belief that confining a young girl to the house and garden will keep her out of trouble (Schlesinger, 1968; Henry & Wilson, 1975). Girls are expected to be pretty but never sexually alluring, and sex education is usually denied them. They date boys whom their parents know extremely well. If there are not enough opportunities for a girl to meet appropriate young men, she is still not permitted to go out.

Despite the emphasis placed on propriety, there are many unplanned, out-of-wedlock pregnancies and a considerable number of extramarital affairs. Having a mistress is an indication of the level of success a man has achieved. His ability to clothe, feed, and house his mistress and any children they might have together (outside children) is a reflection of his status and wealth. Two other hypotheses have been offered to explain the prevalence of extramarital relationships. One theory suggests that because of the very practical considerations that go into the selection of a spouse, men in the upper classes must resort to affairs to find true love and sexual satisfaction/compatibility. It is interesting to note that a woman's happiness and satisfaction with her mate are not taken into consideration. The other theory has to do with certain attitudes about sexuality that assume that some sexual acts are appropriately performed with one's wife. Mistresses, who usually are drawn from the lower classes, are considered suitable partners with whom to explore the full range of the male's sexual desires (Henriques, 1957). This attitude is not at all surprising when it is taken for granted that a "good" woman does not desire or care for sex.

How upper-class wives feel about their husbands' arrangements is an area of some mystery. Therapists need to tread carefully here, because there are many unanswered questions. Making an issue of an affair during a therapy session could be a mistake if the couple has an agreement that the husband can conduct his affair as long as it is done discreetly. Discretion is usually interpreted to mean that the husband does everything in his power to keep the liaison a secret from his wife, her friends, and anyone in their social circle. If the therapist has any suspicions, he or she may want to discuss them with each spouse separately.

Another glaring paradox is the stated attitude toward fidelity. It is seen as important, and adultery is certainly grounds for dissolving a marriage. However, a double standard exists for men and women. A man's extramarital affair, if discovered, is viewed quite differently from a woman's. The infidelity of women is viewed significantly more negatively than that of men.

The Jamaican woman often enters marriage totally ignorant about sex and is far more concerned about being a good mother than a good sexual partner to her husband (Henry & Wilson, 1975). A primary part of the definition of womanhood and femininity is connected in the minds of Jamaicans with motherhood. Her duties revolve around childrearing, and a married woman without children is viewed as deviant. The job of childrearing includes socialization and discipline. Spankings are the primary form of punishment and are often accompanied by a scolding or "tongue-lashing." These punishments are not viewed by Jamaicans as abusive. In fact, a prevailing sentiment among parents is that spankings are a necessary means of teaching children to distin-

guish right from wrong and to learn respect for their elders and other authority figures (Gopaul-McNicol, 1993).

Gopaul-McNicol (1993) cites Payne's (1989) study on discipline, which
lists the following types of corporal punishment: lashing with a belt, slapping
the hand, spanking with shoes, and hitting the knuckles or palm of the hand
with a ruler. Although the study was done in Barbados and not Jamaica, it does
yield some interesting information. First, the subjects were teachers and child-
care workers, as opposed to parents. "The majority endorsed flogging with a
belt or strap as an approved method, with the buttocks most frequently identified as part of the anatomy to which it should be administered" (Gopaul-
McNicol, 1993, p. 109). This would suggest that parents and teachers on the
island are similarly disposed in their attitudes about childrearing and how to
accomplish it. In the United States, many Jamaican immigrants find themselves
at odds with teachers, child-care workers and health professionals. If abuse is
defined as any and all forms of corporal punishment, it is easy for therapists to
condemn parents for these behaviors without giving them closer scrutiny.
Jamaican parents may find themselves on the wrong side of the law and in the
embarrassing position of having to explain themselves to authorities outside
the sphere of the family.

Children are supposed to show a great deal of respect for their elders. It
is considered impolite for them to talk back to or disagree with an older person, because adults are certain that their life experiences guarantee that they
know what is best for children. Male children are socialized to be responsible.
Achievement is emphasized, and education is valued as a means to an end, not
as a goal in and of itself. Boys are encouraged to seek respectable, stable professions and to choose fields of study that offer opportunities for advancement
and upward mobility. There is a strong bond between mothers and sons, and
a son is doted on regardless of his sibling position. If her husband is absent,
there is a tendency for the mother to lean on her male children. A son's closeness with his mother continues even after he marries, and sons are expected to
take care of their mothers.

Although the mother has chief responsibility for raising the children,
British West Indian children have warm and loving relationships with their
fathers. Unfortunately, this close relationship between fathers and children
is frequently disrupted by lengthy separations. The family's economic situation determines the likelihood of separations; the poorer the family, the
more likely it is that the father will have to search for work away from the
community.

Sometimes it is the children who are separated from their families. "Child
lending" is a fairly common occurrence in the islands. This is a practice whereby
school-aged children are sent to live with extended family members. In some
families, this is done because the mother may be forced to work or has died at

a young age. In other families, a child may be sent to live with a relative to have easier access to education. Sometimes the arrangement may be made for the benefit of the relative. For example, a child may be sent to be a companion to a childless woman or a woman whose children are all grown (Sanford, 1974).

## HELP-SEEKING BEHAVIOR

What the American mental health field labels as "psychological problems" may be viewed as either a medical or a spiritual disturbance by Jamaicans (Gopaul-McNicol, 1993). This dichotomous system of classification makes it important for the therapist to understand the role of religion in the lives of Jamaicans.

In Jamaica, the members of the middle and elite classes are predominantly Protestant—mostly Presbyterian, Baptist, Methodist, and Anglican (Lowenthal, 1972). A minority is Roman Catholic. Members of the lower classes are strongly influenced by folk beliefs of African origins.

According to Lowenthal (1972) the meaning and practice of religion has been one way to differentiate the social classes in Jamaica. He suggests that members of the elite class attend church "less as a religious duty than to affirm their role as social, if no longer national, exemplars" (p. 114). He goes on to say that "middle class Protestants take religion more seriously; theirs is a literal, not a perfunctory creed and, whatever their behavior, a symbol of private as well as public morality" (p. 114). Among the working class, the practice of religion is differentiated by the infusion of African rites and emotionality into the Christian service.

One African rite that survived throughout slavery to the present day is witchcraft, or *Obeah*, as it is called in Jamaica. Practitioners of the craft are referred to as obeahmen, obeahwomen, or witch doctors. The people who consult the witch doctor come from all segments of society: male and female, middle and lower class, young and old. *Obeah* is widespread throughout the island of Jamaica, as well as throughout the Jamaican immigrant population in the United States. An exact index of its prevalence is difficult to obtain. During slavery, it was necessary for practitioners of *Obeah* to hide their activities from the White plantation owners. All the slaves on the plantation had a hand in protecting the identity of these people. A strong inducement against betrayal was the individual slave's fear of retribution by the *Obeah* practitioner (Henriques, 1957). To this day Jamaicans continue to be reluctant to discuss *Obeah*. Middle-class Jamaicans, who wish to maintain their status, distance themselves from what the majority society would consider a "heathen superstition" (Lowenthal, 1972).

*Obeah* practitioners are consulted for a variety of reasons: to cure illness, predict the future, interpret dreams, allay fears, exact revenge, or grant a favor.

Many of these goals are similar to the reasons why individuals seek psychotherapy, namely to instill hope in their lives and increase feelings of self-efficacy (Brice-Baker, 1994).

Neki et al. (1986) outline some of the ways in which *Obeah* can become an issue in therapy. First, it can be used by clients to explain an unfavorable plight over which they feel no control.

*Obeah* can also come up in therapy when individuals want to relinquish responsibility for bad and overwhelming feelings they carry about someone else. These feelings can be said to be coming from the witch doctor, and the individuals can claim innocence of any wrongdoing.

Jamaicans often use witchcraft and spiritual possession to explain aberrant behavior and illnesses for which no organic cause can be found. Mental illness is then seen as a form of possession by evil spirits. And it is not uncommon for Jamaican clients to consult a spiritist at the same time they are in psychotherapy.

For people who endorse the "spiritual unrest" view, the duration of possession can range from one day to several years. The major point is that West Indians believe a spiritist can remove the evil spirit and free the individual from this "evil force" (Gopaul-McNicol, 1993, p. 100).

The Jamaican family finds it difficult to admit that there is a problem it cannot handle. If family members do go to a mental health professional, they often do so for a child's problem that may come up at school, or for a medical complaint, at the suggestion of a physician who was unable to find a physiological basis for the client's symptoms. For many family therapists the genogram is a major assessment tool (Barker, 1986; McGoldrick & Gerson, 1985; Bowen, 1980). When interviewing Jamaicans, it is important that the therapist begin by explaining the genogram construction process. Black people in the United States, regardless of nationality, may have an appropriate "cultural paranoia," given the levels of racism inherent in many institutions (Grier & Cobbs, 1968). It is, therefore, the responsibility of the therapist to make the connection between the type of information asked for and its utility in therapy. The therapist should be aware of the identified patient's use of "family" titles (aunty, uncle, etc.) to denote people who are not actually related by blood. Jamaican children grow up using these titles out of respect for adults. Family titles are also used to obfuscate the paternity of outside children. Young children who grow up in close proximity to their father's outside children may be told those children are cousins. A child's inability to explain certain family relationships should not be taken as a sign of "slowness" but instead as the possibility that a family secret should be explored. In the case of minor children, it is particularly important that an exploration of the "secret" be done with the parents, because Jamaicans do not believe children should be privy to everything that goes on.

One factor that is not reflected in the typical genogram is racial hue. Black family members exist in an array of colors. Skin color can be a potent issue in a Jamaican family. The hopes and aspirations that a parent has for a particular child may be related to that child's skin tone. Perceptions of attractiveness and choice of marriage partners are among the other issues tied to color. The non-Black therapist must be willing to go beyond an introductory query about how the family feels about seeing a White therapist and address the more subtle intrafamilial color concerns.

One significant source of stress is the immigration process. This is not to say that all families in which parents and children have been separated for a period of time are subject to dysfunction. But the therapist needs to consider several factors: the length of the separation, the reason for it, how old the child was at the beginning of the separation, how separation was explained, who was responsible for the child's physical care, whether the parents continued to make major decisions about the child, the nature and frequency of contact during the separation, and whether the child had a sense of when family reunification would take place.

Once the family is referred, the therapist should have little trouble getting members to come in because Jamaicans take seriously the advice of professionals (i.e., teachers and doctors). However, the therapist must choose a time for an appointment that will not require the father or mother to miss work. Jamaicans take the adage "time is money" very seriously.

It is difficult at this time to make any definitive statement about the impact of the therapist's race on the family in treatment, largely because of the paucity of research that examines a therapist's race and therapy outcome. The research that has been done has focused primarily on individual treatment as opposed to family therapy (Davis & Proctor, 1989). Overall, the existing studies seem to indicate that individuals do have a preference for therapists of their own race, but there are a number of methodological problems with these studies. In some cases, "preference" and "expectation" were not operationally defined and were used interchangeably. In other cases, variables such as therapeutic style, age, and attitudinal similarity were not controlled for (Davis & Proctor, 1989). The general consensus has been that racial similarity between client and therapist is an important, but perhaps not the most important, factor. What is potentially more important to the Jamaican client is the cultural and values similarity between therapist and client.

The therapist's gender has also not been studied (Davis & Proctor, 1989). For Jamaican families, males are certainly viewed as future figures of authority. However, the role of therapist is not consistent with the culturally ascribed male role. Since the domain of females is considered to be the emotional well-being of the family, a female therapist could be accepted and have validity (Gopaul-McNicol, 1993).

## CONCLUSIONS

It is important for therapists who treat Jamaicans to be sensitive to their unique heritage, which is varied in its subcultures. Their history of enslavement, colonization by Europeans, migratory labor, and migration to the United States has had profound effects on their family systems and their behavior.

The strength of Jamaican families lies in their being so closeknit, something that can work to a therapist's advantage. Throughout history, extended family members have been an important resource for Jamaican families. What therapists of the dominant culture often refer to as "enmeshment" has been, and still is, adaptive, because it provided individuals with emotional and practical support in their times of stress. Therapists working with these families will find their work rewarding because the individuals are truly motivated to help one another.

## REFERENCES

Barker, P. (1986). *Basic family therapy*. New York: Oxford University Press.

Best, T. (1975). West Indians and Afro-Americans, A partnership. *The Crisis, 82*, 389.

Bowen, M. (1980). Key to the use of the genogram. In E. A. Carter & M. McGoldrick (Eds.), *The family life cycle: A framework for family therapy*. New York: Gardner Press.

Brice-Baker, J. (1994). West Indian women: The Jamaican woman. In L. Comas-Díaz & B. Greene (Eds.), *Women of color: Integrating ethnic and gender identities in psychotherapy* (pp. 139–160). New York: Guilford Press.

Bryce-LaPorte, R. S. (1972). Black immigrants: The experience of invisibility and inequality. *Journal of Black Studies, 3*, 29, 56.

Davis, L. E., & Proctor, E. K. (1989). *Race, gender and class*. Englewood Cliffs, NJ: Prentice-Hall.

Dominquez, V. (1975). *From neighbor to strangers*. New Haven, CT: Yale University, Antilles Research Program.

Garvey, M. (1973). The race question in Jamaica. In D. Lowenthal & L. Comitas (Eds.), *The consequences of class and color*. New York: Anchor Books.

Glantz, O. (1978). Native sons and immigrants: Some beliefs and values of American-born and West Indian Blacks at Brooklyn College. *Ethnicity, 5*, 189–202.

Gopaul-McNicol, S. (1993). *Working with West Indian families*. New York: Guilford Press.

Grier, W., & Cobbs, P. (1968). *Black rage*. New York: Basic Books.

Henriques, F. (1957). *Jamaica: Land of wood and water*. London: MacGibbon & Kee.

Henry, F., & Wilson, P. (1975). Status of women in Caribbean societies: An overview of their social, economic, and sexual roles. *Social and Economic Studies, 24*, 165–198.

Lowenthal, D. (1972). *West Indian societies*. New York: Oxford University Press.

McGoldrick, M., & Gerson, R. (1985). *Genograms in family assessment.* New York: Norton.

Neki, J., Jornet, B., Ndase, N., Kilonzo, G., Haule, J., & Duninage, G. (1986). Witchcraft and psychotherapy. *British Journal of Psychiatry, 149,* 145–155.

Payne, M. (1989). Use and abuse of corporal punishment: A Caribbean view. *Child Abuse and Neglect, 13,* 389–401.

Sanford, M. (1974). A socialization in ambiguity: Child lending in a British West Indian society. *Ethnology, 13*(4), 393–400.

Schlesinger, B. (1968). Family patterns in the English-speaking Caribbean. *Journal of Marriage and the Family, 30,* 149–154.

Smith, R. (1988). *Kinship and class in the West Indies.* New York: Cambridge University Press.

Sowell T. (1981). *Ethnic America.* New York: Basic Books.

Ueda, R. (1980). West Indians. In S. Thernstrom, A. Orlov, & O. Handlin (Eds.), *Harvard encyclopedia of American ethnic groups.* Cambridge, MA: Harvard University Press.

CHAPTER 7

# Haitian Families

Amy Bibb
Georges J. Casimir

*Dèyè mòn'n gen mòn'n.*
*[Beyond the mountains, more mountains.]*
—OLD HAITIAN PROVERB

Although two-thirds of Haiti consists of rugged mountains, this Haitian proverb refers as much to Haiti's history as to its terrain: When one problem is solved, another appears. In 1804, a revolutionary struggle led by slaves against French colonists led to the establishment of the Republic of Haiti as the first independent Black Republic in the world. Other Caribbean islands remained under colonial rule for another century (Laguerre, 1980).

Since that time, Haitian political life has been checkered, characterized by both oppressive conditions and liberation. Indeed, this political condition is metaphoric to the Haitian psyche. They are proud of their revolutionary history, which became a model for other Black Caribbean nations. Despite its innovative history, Haiti remains the poorest nation in the Western Hemisphere and until recently, struggled against decades of dictatorial rule. The impact of such innovation and harsh realities on Haitian identity cannot be underestimated. Pride and shame are ever present. If "when one problem is solved, another appears," truly reflects Haitians' worldview, then many Haitians are willing to take on the struggle.

Although there is an entire generation of United States-born Haitian Americans, most Haitians in the United States were born in Haiti. Most Haitians have strong ties to their culture and community. Although mobility and time weaken their sense of continuity with Haiti, frequent visitation and the influx of new immigrants sustain interaction with the Haitian culture (Soto, 1987).

Much is misunderstood or unknown about Haitian culture, migration patterns, and utilization of services in the United States. This poses an important challenge for clinicians who are increasingly called upon to serve Haitian clients. It is estimated that between 700,000 and 1.5 million Haitians live outside of their homeland. The majority migrated to the eastern seaboard of the United States, although a sizable number of Haitians have migrated to Canada (Institut Haïtien de Statistique et d'Informatique, 1987, cited in Farmer & Kim, 1991).

Haitians most often seek help only during times of crisis and are not very receptive to the notion of therapy. This attitude transcends socioeconomic and educational boundaries. Problems are minimized, intellectualized, rationalized, or relegated to God (Chassagne, 1995). Efforts to have basic needs met take precedence over alleviation of emotional distress. "I can't afford to be sick. Who will take care of me and my children?" is a humorous or pragmatic way of rationalizing this attitude. When they do come for therapy, Haitians are likely to be referred by a third party, such as schools or protective services, and may perceive these referrals as either punitive or irrelevant to their needs. Undocumented or "illegal" immigrants are unlikely to enter therapy of their own accord because much of their energy is directed toward obtaining basics for survival (e.g., housing, medical care, employment, education). Furthermore, they may fear that institutional services will put them at risk of deportation.

## HISTORY

Two significant periods in Haiti's recent history were the U.S. Marine occupation from 1915 to 1934 and the lengthy Duvalier dictatorship. The U.S. Marine occupation was the beginning of U.S. intervention in Haitian political and social life, a presence that is felt to this day. The regime of François (Papa Doc) Duvalier and later, his son Jean-Claude (Baby Doc) Duvalier, reigned from 1957 to 1986. It was characterized by torture of the dissident masses and political persecution of professionals, politicians, and students. Papa Doc was responsible for the creation of the Tonton Macoutes, a secret military police modeled after the Nazis (Hurbon, 1993). In 1991, Father Jean-Bertrand Aristide became Haiti's first democratically elected President. He won 67% of the vote in an election supervised by the United Nations. Several months later, the army staged a violent coup d'état, forcing Aristide into exile. Following 3 years of military rule, Aristide was reinstated as the legitimate President of Haiti on October 15, 1994. Aristide's presidential term ended in February 1996, at which time René Préval became Haiti's newly elected president. The pattern of migration of Haitians to the United States has tended to reflect the political climate in Haiti.

## MIGRATION

Learning the circumstances of a family's migration will reveal much about their resources, social class, and aspirations. Honorat (1985) describes recent Haitian migration to the United States as occuring in three distinct waves. The first wave, *la migration désirée* (desired migration), comprised professionals who obtained visas and U.S. work contracts prior to entering the United States. This wave began in 1957 and was made up of those who fled Francois Duvalier's harsh regime. The second wave, *la migration acceptée* (accepted migration), lasted from the mid-1960s until approximately 1971 and consisted of the discontented and repressed middle class. The third wave, *la migration indésirable* (undesirable migration), consisted largely of members of the working class as well as peasants who were predominantly illiterate, unskilled laborers. It is this group that is most commonly referred to as "boat people."

Although "boat people" have undergone particularly dangerous, traumatic circumstances in order to arrive in the United States, all Haitian migratory experiences include traumatic disruption in social and psychological support systems and impact on their life cycle of patterns. The repercussions of the Haitian government's torture and violence, either experienced or witnessed by Haitians, should not be minimized.

Rivalries were particularly intense within the first, and most privileged wave of Haitian immigrants to the United States (Schiller et al., 1987). These migrants consisted of two upper-class groups whose mutual animosity followed Haiti's independence from France, when each jockeyed for power. One group consisted of rural landowners, speculators, and merchants who controlled internal commerce and were primarily Black. The second group consisted of mulattos (people of mixed African and European ancestry) who had close ties to international trade. Both groups distanced themselves from the masses of Haitians by aligning themselves to French colonial values. They detached themselves from African-based traditions, preferring the French language over Haitian Creole, and practicing Catholicism, while expressing disdain for the African-derived voodoo. They commonly sent their children to Europe for higher education (Schiller et al., 1987).

The remnants of such historical group differences are ever present within Haitian families today. A clinician may naively ask about language or religious practices and not realize that such inquiries, in essence, uncover emotionally laden issues about social class and access to power. Power and class issues are often symbolic of the Haitian migration experience, for many migrate due to lack of power or in hope of obtaining access to better education and material goods. The therapist needs to explore these factors, because they are at the core of Haitian social and psychological life. The dilemma posed is how to ask such questions, rather than whether they should be asked.

## FAMILY

Structured marital (or cohabiting couple units), and structured parent–child relationships characterize most Haitian families. Western patterns of formalized marriage exist primarily in the middle and upper classes. Many Haitians in the lower socioeconomic classes follow the pattern of *plaçage*, known to Westerners as common-law marriage. Another typical conjugal constellation occurs when men maintain strong cohabiting ties with one or two partners and their respective children. Although men are not a constant presence in the households, they are expected to be financial providers and child disciplinarians. Daily childrearing responsibilities are delegated to women, with men acting as problem solvers in unusual circumstances. They remain distant figures, but with a great deal of authority.

While the practice of *plaçage* has been transferred from Haiti to the United States with some ease, economic reality makes it difficult for men to maintain more than one family in the United States. Financial need and acculturation resulted in Haitian women leaving the household to seek outside employment. This requires greater male participation in domestic life, while increasing female financial autonomy. This change in traditional gender roles is a frequent source of conflict in Haitian American family life.

Within Haitian families, parent–child roles tend to be clearly delineated, with limited tolerance for child self-expression. Children learn to absorb and not to question, as conformity and obedience are expected. Loyalty implies being secretive; family business is expected to stay within the family (Chassagne, 1995). This may become a source of intergenerational conflict for Haitian families when younger generations become more assimilated to the United States. As with African Americans and British West Indians, extended and kinship systems are valued by Haitian families. However, the extended family may shrink considerably in size after immigration to the United States and may no longer be available for support.

Elderly parents are members of the typical extended Haitian family. Frequently they provide caretaking of the grandchildren while parents are at work. In return, they expect to be treated with respect and to be taken care of by their children when they can no longer care for themselves. When children cannot care for elders, they are sent back to Haiti. Nursing homes are usually not desirable options, due to economic constraints, limited access to nursing care, and because extended families tend to provide a nurturing environment.

## LANGUAGE AND COMMUNICATION

Therapists may mistakenly assume that all Haitians speak French, when in fact, Haitian Creole is universally spoken (Boyd-Franklin, Aleman, Jean-Gilles, &

Lewis, 1995). Only a minority of 2–5% of the Haitian population also speak French fluently. However, when asked if they speak French, Haitians will invariably respond that they do, increasing the probability of miscommunication if they are assigned a French-speaking clinician (Laguerre, 1981). Haitians of all social classes tend to accept the superiority of colonial-derived behavior and language over African-derived cultural and linguistic forms (Buchanan-Stafford, 1987). Fluency in French is thus associated with social mobility, high social status, and formal knowledge. Fluency solely in Haitian Creole is associated with lower-class origins, ignorance, and illiteracy. Of equal magnitude is a countermovement that associates the French language with falseness and deceit. French is viewed as a symbol of the inherent color–class hierachy, whereas Haitian Creole connotes equality, authentic Haitian identity, and the national and racial unity of Haitian people.

Haitian patterns of communication include loud, animated speech and touching in the form of handshakes and taps on the shoulder to define or reconfirm social and emotional relationships. Loud speech is frequently misinterpreted by non-Haitians as a sign of anger. Nonverbal cues may convey significant information during a therapy session. Haitians are likely to communicate boredom or dissatisfaction in therapy indirectly. Direct verbal expression of discontent with a therapist or the process will not be part of a Haitian client's repertoire. The folding of arms across one's chest with eyes looking at the ceiling, deep sighs, and eye rolling may be strong evidence of an impasse in communication. If this should occur, the therapist should comment about such behavior in a nonchallenging tone.

## RELIGION AND SPIRITUALITY

Religion is a dominant force in the Haitian community. Belief in religion, including voodoo's curative capabilities, shapes views about emotional distress and mental illness and therefore influences help-seeking behavior. Church and voodoo rituals such as prayer, song, and dance provide opportunities for catharsis and create a sense of renewal and control over external forces. Validating these beliefs and practices will increase treatment compliance.

For centuries, Catholicism was the predominant Christian faith in Haiti. However, over the last four decades there has been a growing influence of various Protestant groups, including evangelical and charismatic movements in both Haiti and the United States. Eighty percent of Haitians identify themselves as Catholics and 20% as Protestants. Voodoo rituals integrate elements of Christian theology in an unusual religious syncretism; it is therefore common for many Haitian Catholics and Protestants to practice and believe in voodoo in varying degrees. Voodoo practice is most commonly associated with the lower socioeconomic classes. Although Haitians of every social stratum may believe in voodoo, members of the lower classes embrace its practice most openly. Cognizant of this class-based linkage, middle, upper-middle, and wealthy classes may be reluctant to acknowledge these beliefs and may practice voodoo in secrecy.

Voodoo encompasses both the religious and medical worlds. Haitians see causes of mental illness as emanating from the supernatural external world and voodoo as providing solutions to problems emanating from this world. Haitians may use belief in God or voodoo gods (*loas*) to explain their joys and sufferings, poverty and wealth, health and illness, hopes and fears. "Spiritual reshaping" is an example of a voodoo practice that solves problems of the external world. This technique, practiced by *houngans* and *mambos* (male and female voodoo priests, respectively) is believed to alleviate depressive and anxiety symptoms generated by bad luck (*guignon*) and feelings of vulnerability. A cure is achieved by the priest or priestess bathing the afflicted with specially prepared ointments and magical lotions, and cleansing their environment with special waters, candles, and incense. An amulet is provided to be worn for self-protection and restoration of self-confidence (Charles, 1986).

Such rituals, performed to please or appease supernatural forces, emphasize the importance of external forces, and minimize the ability of Haitians to self-determine their existence. This emphasis places the responsibility of change on the external world rather than on the individual Haitian.

Therapists believing that interactional or interpersonal change is helpful or curative may consequently have difficulty with the voodoo belief system. This belief is certainly dystonic with traditional Western views about psychotherapy that often emphasize internal self-reflection and individualistic change as curative. Discussions about conflicting belief systems should be avoided because they will exacerbate guardedness and distrust. Instead, therapists should acknowledge the importance voodoo beliefs and practices play in Haitians lives and explore how they help them cope on a daily basis. If Haitians initiate discussion or allude to voodoo, it should be explored immediately because it is often at the core of Haitian identity. The authors caution against raising such issues precipitously (early in treatment, when clients haven't raised it) or in a random fashion. Again, this will increase guardedness and may be interpreted as an underhanded way of assessing one's class status or "family secrets." Whenever possible, the therapist should consult with Haitian colleagues who are knowlegeable about these spiritual beliefs. The significance of spirituality may vary among family members. Clinicians should avoid making alliances with any subsystem or individual family member and, rather, help clarify and understand how such differences came about. Eliciting family members' solutions to such differences is an important intial step.

## AIDS

During the 1980s, Haiti received widespread publicity as a probable source from which AIDS was exported to the United States. Numerous Haitian refugees in Florida hospitals met the diagnostic criteria for AIDS, yet most had never had a blood transfusion and denied engaging in high-risk behaviors such as male homosexual relations or intravenous drug use (Farmer & Kim, 1991). As a result of denial of these risk factors by Haitian AIDS sufferers, the Centers for Disease Control (CDC; 1982) erroneously inferred that Haitians were a risk group and included being Haitian as a high-risk category for developing AIDS. The CDC reached this conclusion despite the fact that accurate estimates of the number of Haitians living in the United States were lacking, therefore compromising accurate population-based judgments (Farmer & Kim, 1991).

In some instances, AIDS became known as a "Haitian disease," reinforcing the belief that if Haitians have AIDS, it is simply because they are Haitian (Farmer & Kim, 1991). Although medical opinion has abandoned this idea, the linkage of Haitians to HIV/AIDS persists. Sensationalized media coverage and misinterpreted medical data created stereotypes about Haitians having AIDS, resulting in many U.S. Haitian adults losing their employment and residences, and their children being ostracized in school. Some Haitians began identifying themselves as Guadeloupean, Martiniquan, or Jamaican, either out of shame, or in an attempt to avoid discrimination (Farmer & Kim, 1991).

Initial AIDS cases recorded in Haiti suggested the same modes of transmission as in the United States and Europe, namely, homosexuality or bisexuality and blood transfusion. Preliminary publicized reports of Haitian patients residing in the United States failed to demonstrate the presence of the same risk factors that had been found in American patients. Health officials failed to recognize that most Haitians would not identify themselves as homosexual or bisexual if asked directly. However, Desvarieux and Pape (1991) noted that their careful questioning of a Haitian patient population in Haiti revealed markedly different results. Seventy-two percent admitted high-risk behaviors, the most frequent being closeted homosexuality or bisexuality, and 22% had a history of blood transfusion.

For Haitians, homosexual behavior is often not correlated with a self-definition as gay or bisexual, so certain practices were underdescribed. Haitians may admit to engaging in "economic prostitution" (i.e., engaging in homosexual intercourse with foreign tourists for pay), yet never view themselves as homosexual. Interestingly, during the early 1980s the prevalence rate of men with opportunistic infections in Carrefour (a principal center of male prostitution in Haiti) was significantly higher than in Port-au-Prince (Pape et al., 1983).

Marked changes in HIV transmission in Haiti have been documented since the early 1980s. A huge decrease occurred in cases attributed to homosexuality or bisexuality. Intravenous drug use is not prevalent in Haiti (less than 1% of HIV transmission is attributed to intravenous drug use). Cocaine (especially crack) use is rumored to be commonly used by certain segments of the Haitian population. Cocaine and crack use per se are not associated with increased spread of infection; however, crack users are likely to engage in prostitution and high-risk sexual behavior (Fullilove & Fullilove, 1990, cited in Desvarieux & Pape, 1991). Seropositivity rates in females are rising, and are expected to constitute a larger proportion of the AIDS cases in the 1990s (Desvarieux & Pape, 1991).

Haitians have reacted to the linkage of themselves with AIDS with outrage, anger, and mistrust of U.S. health-care providers. For many, it shattered their pride, self-esteem, and cultural identity. They may experience visceral reactions to any association of themselves with HIV/AIDS. Therapists should inquire about this issue with directness and sensitivity.

Lionel, a 38-year-old Haitian male, and his 30-year-old African American wife, Denise, came to therapy for marital difficulties. Several months earlier, Lionel had been passed over for a well-deserved and previously guaranteed job promotion. Since that time he was increasingly depressed, withdrawing from Denise and their 7-year-old son, Alix. He had drastically changed his eating and sleeping habits and had lost a significant amount of weight. Denise was especially concerned about Lionel's despondence. He had not begun a search for a new job as he had previously agreed with his wife, and most recently was underfunctioning in his current job. This was uncharacteristic of him.

Lionel and his family had migrated to the United States 17 years earlier, following his completion of undergraduate studies in Haiti. As planned, he completed graduate studies in the United States. He and his parents believed that a United States degree would enhance employment prospects in the United States as well as Haiti, should he ever decide to reside there. Lionel came from a middle-class Haitian family who frequently visited relatives in the United States prior to their migration. Over the years, the family had always maintained strong ties to relatives in Haiti. Although initially displeased with Lionel's decision to intermarry, his family eventually accepted Denise. They were especially pleased with her efforts to instill a positive sense of Haitian identity in Alix. They, too, were puzzled by Lionel's recent lack of ambition.

Lionel's symptomatology was compounded by his renewed sense of loss due to the family's migration. The recent professional setback increased his sense of alienation and reminded him that despite many years in the United States and obtaining higher education, he and his family of origin never regained the status and material comforts enjoyed in Haiti. They were acutely aware of stigmatization of Haitians in the aftermath of the AIDS epidemic. Such stigmatization reinforced the feeling that they would never really be at home or welcome in the United States.

Lionel was skeptical about therapy, yet came at Denise's insistence. Although highly recommended, the therapist was an American White. Attempts to work with a Haitian or any other Black therapist had not been successful. Aware of both racial and cultural differences, Lionel was especially concerned that Denise and the therapist's common American identity would result in his being stereotyped or misunderstood. He was eventually able to voice concern about cultural and national differences.

One particularly difficult moment occurred when the therapist began inquiring about his health status. Aware of his sleep and eating difficulties, the therapist specifically referred to Lionel's weight loss. Lionel responded by making a sarcastic joke about Haitians and AIDS. The therapist knew this was an important moment, particularly since Lionel was normally restrained and somewhat distant. The therapist responded by acknowledging that Haitians had been stigmatized regarding AIDS and began inquiring about the impact this had on Lionel.

Issues around racism, cultural identity, and loss became predominant themes in the therapy. For the first time, Lionel acknowledged his devastation that a junior, non-Haitian coworker had been promoted in his stead. This was especially important since Lionel had been socialized never to use ethnocentricism or racism as "an excuse" for lack of achievement. Growing up, he had often been reminded of Haitians who acheived despite obstacles. Lionel eventually realized that pursuing the "American dream" had been preferable to acknowledging and experiencing denied loss. These discussions in therapy helped Lionel articulate his identity as a Haitian raising a family in the United States. While the pain due to migration, racism, acculturation, and it's inherent demands did not change, he became clearer about how he wanted to cope and was able to regain a pride in his heritage. These discussions also helped Denise and Lionel resolve marital differences around their respective cultures. At the end of therapy, Lionel was less isolated and actively seeking employment elsewhere.

---- ❧ ----

## SYSTEMIC CONSIDERATIONS

In working with Haitians, it is especially important to consider the wider context. What distinguishes treatment models with Black families from other systems therapies has always been the explicit attention paid to inclusion of extended family, nonblood kin, and friends, in the treatment (Aponte, 1976; Boyd-Franklin, 1989; Minuchin, 1974; Moore-Hines, 1989), as well as community structures (such as the church, or schools) in the therapy. This model has been termed "ecostructural" (Aponte, 1976) and "multisystems" (Boyd-Franklin, 1989), and has also been applied by Gopaul-McNicol (1993) to work with British West Indian families.

Like British West Indians, Haitians value solving their own difficulties over seeking assistance from professionals (Brice, 1982). When problems cannot be solved, families tend to seek spiritual or community assistance. Pastors, ministers, *houngans*, and *mambos* are typically sought out. At times they are sought to the exclusion of Western helping professionals (i.e., medical doctors, psychiatrists, psychologists, social workers) Frequently, Haitians will utilize the services of "professionals" and traditional healers simultaneously. A multisytems model affirms use of spiritual assistance and is therefore syntonic with Haitian patterns of seeking help and facilitating engagement in the therapeutic process.

## ATTITUDES TOWARD MENTAL HEALTH INSTITUTIONS

Many Haitians, like other West Indians, are surprised when mental health clinics, protective services, and schools seek to become involved with their families, since their view is that such matters are private and should not be scrutinized by outside institutions. Just as problem solving is relegated to the individual, familial, or spiritual domain, so are issues around childrearing, education, and gender roles.

Referrals regarding childrearing practices are often experienced as punitive by Haitian families. For them, corporal punishment has been a time-honored and essential disciplinary tactic of childrearing. Parent–child roles are rigid and structured. Parents are expected to be authoritarian, and children obedient. They may be puzzled and angered by allegations of abuse; indeed, they may view the absence of corporal punishment as spoiling or ruining the child. Furthermore, corporal punishment is sanctioned by educational institutions throughout the French and British West Indies.

It is helpful to explore the family's need to utilize corporal punishment. Haitians, like other Blacks, may be well aware of the repercussions of their children's real or imagined misbehavior. Attempts to discipline their children may be viewed as a preventive measure to obviate the need for White institutions to punish their children. Haitians in the United States may justifiably fear that racism and ethnic predjudice will cause their children to be even more harshly punished by the White-dominated society at large if such behavior is not "nipped in the bud."

Interestingly, a correlation exists between rigid family and societal roles. In Haiti's previously oppressive government, questioning authority and free thought were viewed as a threat to the state and discouraged. As with children, expression was limited, circumscribed, and the consequences for challenging role structures were dire. Emphasizing the similarities between child and adult role expectations can lead to reexamination of structures and rigidity and result in greater flexibility. Within the therapeutic setting, analogies between oppression of Haitian adults and potentially oppressive, abusive practices toward children might be made.

Successful therapy with Haitians requires incorporating knowledge of Haitian culture into the treatment approach. This is especially important because Haitians utilize other supports rather than mental health systems when attempting problem resolution. Without this incorporation, therapists will have no leverage in engaging Haitians, and will continue to function as social controllers (i.e., providing treatment only when mandated by involuntary hospitalizations, protective service referrals, etc.).

## SYMPTOMATOLOGY

Mood symptoms in patients who belong to different cultural groups are often missed by clinicians (Kiesling, 1981). Depression, in particular, is frequently misdiagnosed and should be reviewed carefully. Although there are universal features of depression, such as neurovegetative signs and feelings of hopelessness, as described in the DSM-IV, culturally specific depressive equivalents such as pain syndromes, denial, and stoicism are also common. According to Haitian health jargon, "depression" represents a state of physical depletion characterized by weakness, easy fatigability, which can be due to malnutrition and anemia. Depression is often conveyed through a somatic and supernatural idiom. Pain syndromes such as headaches or feelings of emptiness in the head, and "gas" sensations in different parts of the body are common features. Denial, stoicism, and religiosity are not unusual.

The common presence of suspiciousness, frank paranoid ideation, or delusions of persecution in depressed Haitian patients may lead to diagnosis of more severe disorders such as schizophrenia (Hillel, Turnier, & Desrosiers, 1994). Even well-intentioned clinicians may miss subtle clues necessary for the perception of depressive experience across a cultural gulf (Draguns, 1994). Anger and irritability, and indifference resembling catatonia, although not specific to Haitians, have been frequently reported as nonuniversal depressive symptoms in this population (Hillel et al., 1994).

## SUSPICIOUSNESS VERSUS PARANOID/PERSECUTORY IDEATION

At times Haitian clients may exhibit a paranoid discourse. In addition to psychological implications, this syndrome has historical, political, and religious underpinnings. In the past, slaves were required to report on those who aspired toward freedom. More recently, agents of dictatorial regimes (e.g., Tonton Macoutes) were hired to monitor and harass anyone deemed threatening to the Haitian government. The collective effects of colonialism, torture, and other types of oppression, coupled with magical thinking and belief in voodoo, often explains secretiveness and the lack of personal disclosure to others. Therefore suspiciousness, paranoid or persecutory ideation, in Haitians may not be an indicator of psychopathology unless accompanied by other clinical features.

## IMPLICATIONS FOR TREATMENT

It is important to define and clarify the process of therapy as well as the family's expectations about it. Families may have different understandings of the process and its potential benefits. Clinicians are perceived as strangers, and Haitians are not used to relying on strangers to resolve their problems. Psychoeducation can expedite engagement.

We have found a flexible approach to attendance is most useful with the Haitian population. A combination of individual, family, and subsystem sessions is recommended. Including fathers in family therapy sessions is critical when working with Haitians. The phenomenon of the "absent father," familiar to North American clinicians, is less familiar or acknowledged by Haitian families. The practice of *plaçage* and/or males heading several families does result in a diminished male presence in domestic life yet should not be equated with absence. These fathers often retain an active role in their children's lives.

The family is likely to perceive the exclusion of the father as disrespecting his authority. This creates a dilemma for the therapist, since the father might not attend treatment beyond initial sessions. Exploration of the mother's primary responsibility for child care should occur after attempts at engagement of the father has been established. Tradition-bound Haitian women may be reluctant to challenge or question gender-proscribed roles or patriarchy in the presence (or the absence) of the father. Exploration of how such roles work, as well as how satisfying they are, should occur with both fathers and mothers later in treatment. Watts-Jones (1992) noted the difficulties inherent in challenging patriarchy without also considering the dominant culture's racism and hostility toward West Indian men. She noted that challenge of such roles is riskier when West Indian men do not have the support of their native setting. Furthermore, Haitian womens' vulnerabilities cannot be underestimated when addressing power imbalances. Many lack the social and economic supports of women who are White, middle-class, and legal citizens of the United States. The authors recommend careful, well-timed exploration and intervention around these vital treatment concerns. There is a need for further research and clinical development in these areas, particularly as Haitian women assimilate to North American culture.

Rigid family roles can make encounters between adolescents and parents particularly difficult. Almeida and Bograd (1994) have suggested initially separating the parental and adolescent subsystems when working with immigrant populations with rigid hierarchical family roles. While their work focuses on therapy with Asian families, some of the ideas are also relevant to work with Haitians. They describe the tensions between adolescents who wish to assimilate to North American culture and their parents who want to maintain traditions of their native country. Consequently, parents frequently experience family sessions as a challenge to their prerogative and therefore find the process to be shameful. North American clinicians are cautioned against encouraging parents and children to assimilate rather than developing a lifestyle which balances tradition with healthy adaptation to the host setting.

Assimilation challenges the Haitian adolescent's prescribed role. The adolescent life cycle stage, characterized by rebellion and challenge of parental authority may have been nonexistent or minimized in Haiti. In the United States, it is a rite of passage. The need to assert identity is more complex for the immigrant adolescent. Unlike other adolescents who may demand freedom without responsibility, immigrant adolescents often have more responsibility than they want. Functioning as brokers and translators for less assimilated, less fluent parents can skew the parent–child hierarchy.

Frequently, Haitian adolescents will not express themselves in the parents' presence for fear of being viewed as disobedient. This does not suggest however, that Haitian adolescents are universally compliant with their parents. Adolescents can avoid active participation in family sessions unless they have additional individual time with the therapist. Anger about parental expectations and resistance to assimilation, as well as adolescent individuation concerns is powerful enough for them to want their own time.

It is not unusual for Haitian parents to be suspicious of requests for separate subsystem sessions. Suspicion and resistance can be reduced by presenting separate sessions as part of the intake and therapeutic structure. If the parents agree, alternating parental subsystem sessions with individual or sibling adolescent sessions, in addition to full-family sessions is recommended. The frequency of family sessions with all members present is often determined by the family's ability to schedule and tolerate such sessions.

When the client and the clinician share the same racial and ethnic background, assumptions are frequently made about the therapeutic relationship. A common assumption is that this relationship yields increased understanding and empathy. Non-Haitian therapists (including Black therapists not of Haitian ancestry) may question their ability to engage and treat Haitians. Haitian therapists might have the advantage of developing a rapid rapport with Haitian clients because they can rely on common experiences, cultural understandings, and so on. It is important for non-Haitian therapists to develop confidence in working with Haitians, particularly in the beginning stages of therapy. Knowledge and discussion of Haitian politics often facilitate a positive therapeutic exchange. School-based clinicians note that discussions about Father Jean-Bertrand Aristide during his presidential exile and subsequent return to power helped develop positive therapeutic relationships with Haitian adolescents. For many, Father Aristide's plight symbolized the struggle for freedom and was syntonic with Haitian adolescents' personalized developmental concerns (G. Drew, personal communication, 1995). Some Haitians have been opposed to Father Aristide's political views and actions. Eliciting political viewpoints as well as opinions about successor René Préval is useful. This approach can reveal Haitians' sentiments about the future of their homeland. Such viewpoints will invariably shape current and future aspirations for themselves and family members.

## CONCLUSIONS

Haitians have a unique heritage encompassing a range of subcultures and experiences. Political, social, and cultural realities shape their identity, worldview, and psychological life. They are both proud and stigmatized, marginalized and highly visible. Often they experience themselves as being outsiders in the United States. Among Whites, they may be perceived as "Blacks," among African-Americans and other non-Whites they may be perceived as "West-Indian," and among British West Indians they may be perceived as French Caribbeans. Despite the obstacles, they continue to make a life for themselves in the United States, whether temporarily or permanently. Clinicians can better treat Haitians when they are familiar with this contradictory phenonmenon. They can better appreciate their fortitude, guardedness, and aspirations while in the United States.

## ACKNOWLEDGMENTS

The authors wish to thank Monica McGoldrick, Pierre Jean-Noël, M.D., Yolette Jean-Williams, C.S.W., Carl Cohen, M.D., John Palmer, Ph.D., and Margareth Casimir for their helpful comments on an earlier version of this chapter.

## REFERENCES

Almeida, R., & Bograd, M. (1994). *When East meets West: Exploring the cultural bias of therapy.* Family Therapy Network Symposium.

Aponte, H. (1976). The family–school interview: An ecostructural approach. *Family Process, 15*(3), 303–311.

Boyd-Franklin, N. (1989). *Black families in therapy: A multisystems approach.* New York: Guilford Press.

Boyd-Franklin, N., Aleman, J., Jean-Gilles, M., & Lewis, S. (1995). Cultural sensitivity and competence: African-American, Latino, and Haitian families with HIV/AIDS (pp. 53–77). In N. Boyd-Franklin, G. L. Steiner, & M. G. Boland (Eds.), *Children, families and HIV/AIDS.* New York: Guilford Press.

Brice, J. (1982). West Indian families. In M. McGoldrick, J. K. Pearce, & J. Giordano (Eds.), *Ethnicity and family therapy* (1st ed., pp. 123–133). New York: Guilford Press.

Buchanan-Stafford, S. (1987). Language and identity: Haitians in New York City. In C. Sutton & E. Chaney (Eds.), *Caribbean life in New York City: Sociocultural dimensions* (pp. 203–205). New York: Center for Migration Studies.

Centers for Disease Control. (1982). Opportunistic infections and Kaposi's sarcoma among Haitians in the United States. *Morbidity and Mortality Weekly Report, 31,* 353–354, 360–361.

Charles, C. (1986). Mental health services for Haitians. In H. P. Lefley & P. B. Pederson (Eds.), *Cross-cultural training for mental health professionals* (pp. 183–198). Springfield, IL: Thomas.

Chassagne, R. (1995, May 23). *Cultural consideration in providing mental health services to Haitians.* Paper presented at the annual meeting of the American Psychiatric Association, Miami Beach, Florida.

Desvarieux, M., & Pape, J. W. (1991). HIV and AIDS in Haiti: Recent developments. *AIDS Care, 3*(3), 271–279.

Draguns, J. G. (1994). Pathological and clinical aspects. In L. Adler & U. Gielen (Eds.), *Cross-cultural topics in psychology* (pp. 165–177). Westport, CT: Prager.

Farmer, P., & Kim, J. Y. (1991). Anthropology, accountability, and the prevention of AIDS. *Journal of Sex Research, 28*(2), 203–221.

Gopaul-McNicol, S. (1993). *Working with West Indian families.* New York: Guilford Press.

Hillel, J., Turnier, L., & Desrosiers, P. (1994). La dépression chez l'Haitien: Essai ethnosociopsychiatrique [Depression in the Haitian: Ethnosociopsychiatric essay]. *Le Médécines du Québec, 29*(2), 121–123.

Honorat, J. J. (1985). La Communite Haitienne de New York. *Perspectives: The Haitian Enterprises, 1,* 16–18.

Hurbon, L. (1993). Voodoo search for the spirit. New York: Harry N. Abrams.

Kiesling, R. (1981). Underdiagnosis of manic depressive illness in a hospital unit. *American Journal of Psychiatry, 138,* 672–673.

Laguerre, M. S. (1980). Haitians. In S. Thernstrom (Ed.), *Harvard encyclopedia of American ethnic groups.* Cambridge, MA: Harvard University Press.

Laguerre, M. S. (1981). Haitian Americans. In A. Harwood (Ed.), *Ethnicity and medical care* (pp. 198–199). Cambridge, MA: Harvard University Press.

Minuchin, S. (1974). Families and family therapy. Cambridge, MA: Harvard University Press.

Moore-Hines, P. (1989). The family life cycle of poor Black families. In B. Carter & M. McGoldrick (Eds.), *The changing family life cycle* (pp. 513–544). Needham, MA: Allyn & Bacon.

Pape, J., Liautaud, B., Thomas, F., Mathurin, J., Amand, M., Boncy, M., Pean, V., Pamphile, M., Laroche, A., & Johnson, W. (1983). Characteristics of the acquired immunodeficiency syndrome (AIDS) in Haiti. *New England Journal of Medicine, 309*(16), 945–950.

Schiller, N. G, DeWind, J., Brutus, M. L., Charles, C., Fouron, G., & Thomas, A. (1987). All in the same boat? Unity and diversity in Haitian organizing in New York. In C. R. Sutton & E. M. Chaney (Eds.), *Caribbean life in New York City: Sociocultural dimension* (pp. 184–186). New York: Center for Migration Studies.

Soto, I. M. (1987). West Indian child fostering: Its role in migrant exchanges. In C. R. Sutton & E. M. Chaney (Eds.), *Caribbean life in New York City: Sociocultural dimension* (pp. 131–144). New York: Center for Migration Studies.

Watts-Jones, D. (1992). Cultural and integrative therapy issues in the treatment of a Jamaican woman with panic disorder. *Family Process, 31,* 105–113.

# CHAPTER 8

# African American Muslim Families

## Vanessa Mahmoud

Many African Americans have found themselves influenced by Islam and Islamic values in their search for identity and self-determination. Much of what African Americans are taught about Islam, before conversion, has come through organizations or individuals who have attempted to blend the culture of African Americans with the practice of Islam. This reconciliation of culture and religion is not an unusual occurrence in the Islamic world. Although the tenets of the religion do not change from culture to culture, usually there is a distinct cultural stamp placed on the everyday habits and practices of the religion. The Chinese Islamic community will vary in cultural practices from the Pakistani, the Sudanese will vary in cultural practices from the Egyptian, but all are Muslim, perform the same *salat*, or prayer, and read from the same book, the Holy Qur'an.

Islam first arrived in America with the enslaved Africans Yorro Mahmoud, Ayub Ibn Sulayman Diallo, and Abdul Rahman (Nyang, 1985, cited in Rashad, 1991). There were numerous others, whose practice of Islam was often done in secret and passed down to others surreptitiously in oral history or through family members imitating behaviors, without attribution of source. Often when I have done genogram work with African Americans, a story might surface of a distant relative, who refused to eat pork, always prayed facing east, named the children "funny" names, or refused to allow them to be baptized. This behavior was often remembered because it caused some dissension in the family, which was usually seeking to acculturate and conform to dominant community norms. Other family members had no way of placing such behavior in context, because the practice of traditional African religions, the speaking and writing of Arabic, all were generally suppressed and punished by slaveowners. There is some evidence, however, that a very few slaveowners valued the habits of Muslim slaves except when they sought their freedom (Rashad, 1991).

Some African American families preserved some fragments of Islamic practices. The most famous example of such an occurrence is told in Alex Haley's *Roots*. Haley's ancestor, Kunta Kinte, fought to maintain his identity and his Islamic faith fiercely. He also passed down the practice of maintaining one's lineage in one's memory as did the *griots* of his people, the Muslims of Gambia. It was through this tenacious practice that his descendant was able to journey back to Gambia and be reunited with his relatives.

In addition to the anecdotal and behavioral remnants of Islam that persist within African American family life and culture, there have been a number of attempts to reestablish Islam among African Americans. Although there were Muslims of other nationalities settling in the United States of America (Arabs, Albanians, Indian Muslims, etc.), there was no recorded effort by those communities to establish Islam among African Americans until 1928, when Sheikh Dau'wd was granted a charter by Sheikh Khalid of Jordan and King Saud of Saudi Arabia to establish an Islamic mission in the western hemisphere (Rashad, 1991).

The most powerful combination of cultural necessity and Islamic principles came about in the pairing of black nationalism and Al-Islam. Noble Drew Ali founded the Moorish American Science Temples in 1913. He was influenced heavily by Marcus Garvey's movement, the United Negro Improvement Association. Garvey himself was influenced by Muslims and indeed the Garveyite hymn for the President stated,

> Father of all creation
> Allah Omnipotent
> Supreme O'er every nation
> God bless our president. (Rashad, 1991)

The Honorable Elijah Muhammad was taught by a man named Wallace Fard and built his organization based on the principles of both Garvey and Ali. All three sought to do similar things in their mission with African Americans:

1. Reverse the effects of enslavement by introducing an alternative set of values about self (renaming, alternative explanations of history, self-pride, nationalism and loyalty) to a people long alienated and denied access to full citizenship.
2. Introduce an alternative social milieu in which to practice these values and set goal that expanded the aspirations of the people.
3. Develop a family life and model roles of ideal male and female behavior.
4. Establish bases of economic independence from the dominant culture.
5. Protest and reject the oppression of African American people.
6. Educate children and indoctrinate them with these values, so that they would base their lives on these principles.

7. Establish a land base that could be controlled by African Americans, a homeland, with boundaries that could be protected from oppression.

Indeed, the Honorable Elijah Muhammad promised his followers "money, good homes and friendship in all walks of life," if they adhered to his program and to Islamic principles. Malcolm X, or Al-Hajj Malik al-Shabazz, was the son of a Garveyite who was murdered for his principles. However, his break with Muhammad later in his life was symbolic and significant, for it mirrored the experience of many Muslims who were first attracted to the combination of Black nationalism and Al-Islam. Many later began to study and to practice orthodox Islam. The son of the Honorable Elijah Muhammad, Warith Deen Muhammad, led a massive demonstration of his father's followers into the orthodox practice of Islam in the late 1970s. Minister Louis Farrakhan, a protégé of the Honorable Elijah Muhammad, continued in the tradition of the Honorable Elijah Muhammad and maintained the blend of Black nationalism and Islam among his followers.

The growth of orthodox Islam has been rapid in the last 30 years. In the United States, now, in every major city and large town, there are African American Muslims who identify as *Sunni* or orthodox or those who follow the example of Prophet Muhammad (PBUH). Other schools of thought, such as the Ahmadiyya, the Hanafi, as well as those who are members of esoteric Sufi circles, are flourishing in their studies and in the establishment of communities and *masjid* (places of worship and congregation).

A family therapist who works with an African American who is Muslim needs to know to which community the family belongs and how they feel about their particular religious community. I would put African American Muslims in three very broad categories.

1. *Cultural nationalists:* those who belong to a community that stresses Black nationalism and Islam; stresses separation and independence from the dominant community.
2. *Sunni or orthodox (African American-centered leadership):* those who belong to communities that practice and adhere to the traditional practice of Islam and while stressing self-determination and pride, see themselves as believers whose faith defines them, in parallel with their secular culture. Their communities are usually led by another African American.
3. *Sunni or orthodox (African- or Arab-centered leadership):* those who belong to communities that practice and adhere to the traditional practice of Islam but stress the universality of the religion and are most comfortable in an international, multicultural Islamic community.

During recent years, there has been increasing contact between African Muslims and African American Muslims at all levels. Minister Farrakhan led a large delegation of African American Muslims to Ghana, where Marcus

Garvey and W. E. B. Du Bois are buried. The possibilities of dual citizenship with the country of Ghana have been explored and proposed for African Americans. *Sunni* Muslims sponsor annual trips to complete the Hajj in Saudi Arabia. They are attending African universities in Saudi Arabia, Senegal, Egypt, and so on, and are studying Qur'anic Arabic with teachers from Africa who live in the United States. As a result, conscious adoption of African and Islamic practices, customs, habits, dress, and symbolism is on the increase in many African American Muslim families.

## IMPACT ON FAMILY LIFE

The adoption of the *adab* (conscious Islamic behavior, manners, and customs) by African American families can alter family life subtly or dramatically. In a cultural nationalist family, changes will impact on diet (no pork or pork products, more emphasis on "eating to live" one meal per day, fasting for religious and health reasons), dress (conservative suits, uniforms for men, long dresses, head coverings, uniforms for women), and relationships with non-Muslim family members (sometimes encouraging socialization only with Muslims, nonparticipation in Christian religious holidays that might be celebrated by other family members). Strong commitment to the goals of the group is expected. Chivalry, marriage, and traditional roles are emphasized; classes are held for men and women on these duties and responsibilities. Scholarship is prized if it is paired with a strong knowledge of African/African American history and afrocentric views. Cultural nationalists also stress the development of small businesses, salesmanship, economic independence (do for self), and the appreciation of African American cultural identity.

*Sunni* Muslims base their family life on the five principles of Islam (Al-Qaradawi, 1960):

1. *Shahadah:* The declaration of faith, the affirmation that there is no god but Allah, and Muhammad is the Messenger of God.
2. *Salah:* the five daily prayers.
3. *Zakah:* the giving of charity (about 2% of annual income) to the needy.
4. *Sawm:* fasting during the month of Ramadan (the month in which the Holy Qur'an was revealed).
5. *Hajj:* the performance of the pilgrimage to Mecca once in a person's lifetime.

Conversion to these traditional tenets means that each family, each individual, must somehow reconcile the demands made upon them by everyday life, with the requirements placed upon them as Muslims and as African Americans. Therefore, the ability to synthesize and balance these demands varies with each family and with each individual. The stress this synthesis places upon the individual should not be minimized. Traditional Islam also places dietary restrictions on Muslims (no pork or pork by-products, bloody meat, food that is intended for sacrifice, etc.), ritual cleanliness (for prayer, after sexual contact, sleep, etc.), prohibitions against alcohol and gambling; dress codes, modesty in dress and behavior for both men and women (head covering for women, only face and hands should be seen, modest dress that covers the body and *kufi* (hats) for men; the color red, silk, and gold are prohibited for Muslim men. Islamic manners and greetings are used in conversation, for example, *Al hamdu lillah* (All praise is due to God), *Allah U Akbar* (God is Greatest), *As salaam uAlaikum* (Peace be unto you). Shoes are not worn into a Muslim home, but are left at the door. The decoration of the home should be free of images of people. There are other cultural and religious adaptations possible in the home and in the lives of Muslims based on the *hadith* and *sunna* (sayings, practices, and example) of Prophet Muhammad (PBUH).

The ability to adapt and synthesize these aspects of their faith will vary from family to family, from individual to individual. There is a degree of stress that comes with each additional adaptation. The decision to wear *hijab* (full ritual covering) for women, in a society that sees such covering as oppressive, is quite stressful for some women, and for others it is not. Finding a place to pray, as a Muslim, is difficult when you work in certain settings or are in school all day. Eating school cafeteria food, going out to lunch with peers, being invited out for drinks with colleagues, are all situations in which a Muslim must make conscious decisions to adhere to the prohibitions set upon them, without undue alienation or difficulty.

African American Muslims must endure stereotypes and distorted images projected upon them as Muslims, as well as those they endure as African Americans. It is very stressful when these views are held by other African Americans, in particular, relatives who are not Muslim. However, there is also general respect for the moral standards of Muslims, when sincere in their practices, as well as for their staunch pride in self and for their belief in standing firm against oppression within the African American community.

## Cultural Nationalist Muslim Family

A young couple had come in for their initial visit with me after being referred by a friend. They sought me out because I was African American and Muslim. He was dressed in a suit and wore a bow tie. She was dressed in a blouse that covered her hips and a long skirt. They had been having marital troubles, after having been married only 1 year. He was 23 and she was 21. He had converted to Islam, 3 years ago and she had converted 1 year ago. When asked what had been disturbing them, the husband Samuel stated that his wife Mary did not support his work. He was a vendor and sold jewelry as well as dedicating some time to selling his organization's newspapers. She wanted him to get a job and sell his jewelry part-time. She stated that she wanted to be supportive and she helped him to sell his jewelry from time to time, but she wanted more security. He accused her of not having faith and being materialistic. He also stated that he was the provider and that she had married him, knowing how important his business was to him. She admitted being ashamed sometimes of not living in a better place and of her family giving her a hard time, because she "married one of those Muslims." She had been close to her family before her conversion, but recently she had had an argument with her mother about putting pork in her food to season it without telling her. Her dad often muttered about her going to hell and said ugly things about her husband. She stated that she was so proud of her husband for what he was trying to do for their community, but she did not like the feeling that she had to choose between her husband and family. Her husband felt that she should just leave her family alone, associate more with Muslims and cultivate Muslim friends. She, however, felt that other Muslims could not take the place of her family.

———————— ➷ ————————

In this couple, the stresses of adopting a new set of values were straining their relationship. They had changed their last name to an Islamic one, changed their diet, stopped drinking and smoking, did not go to nightclubs, changed some of the music they listened to, and attended their temple regularly. The hostility of the wife's family of origin to these changes in her life was a great source of pain for her. It was worthwhile, with this couple, to explore the conversion experience and determine if it was a well-thought-out action and decision, an attempt to rebel, or an effort to achieve some boundary or cutoff from the family of origin. We explored the kind of mother Mary had, and the kind of mother Samuel had, and also looked at the influence of their fathers on their relationship.

We were able to talk about their concept of the "ideal Muslim couple" and compare how closely their relationship resembled that ideal. We were able to talk about how difficult it was to live up to that ideal. With her husband Samuel, we were able to talk about his father and the type of provider he was for his family. He was able to contrast this with the type of provider he was striving to be. We also talked about the meaning of their conversion to Islam and the spiritual aspects of their relationship. Mary was able to reveal that her family was afraid that she would be dominated by her husband and made a prisoner in her home. She also thought that they were offended that she would not eat certain foods anymore, for one of her mother's primary ways of expressing affection was by preparing elaborate meals. She was aware that she was still seeking her parents' approval in a lot of ways and still felt in need of her mother's guidance. Samuel was concerned about being a good influence on his family, for he was the oldest of four sons. His mother was a widow and his father had been ill with cancer for a long time before he died. He felt that the model of manhood that he found in his community was one he could emulate and teach to his brothers, who looked to him for leadership. His family was enthusiastic about his involvement and very supportive. He was also able to reveal how much he admired Mary's father, who owned a scrap-metal business. We decided to have Samuel approach Mary's father formally and discuss his plans for providing for her, and ask for his advice in getting started with a stable business. Mary also decided to go back to nursing school to further her own needs for autonomy and economic stability. They agreed that she would stay home with any children they had and postpone having children until Samuel was better established financially.

We talked about the importance of internalizing the ideal roles of Muslim husband and wife, but stressed the fact that they were human beings and therefore fallible and still learning.

Both seemed relieved to have a safe place where they felt understood, accepted, and not judged. They felt that it was helpful to express their beliefs without censure and judgment from another. We met for only four sessions, but the tension was relieved greatly as we strategized how Samuel could assist Mary in bridging the gap with her parents. They decided to continue demonstrating their positive regard for them, inviting them into their home and lifestyle, and reassuring them that she was happy but still needed them.

### African American Sunni Muslim Family

A family was referred for therapy by a local *imam* (religious teacher) and head of a local *masjid* (place of worship and congregation). The husband Na'im, his wife of years Amira, and his new wife Salima came into the first session. All had been Muslims for over 15 years, performed daily *salat*, and attended *masjid* regularly. Both women wore *hijab* (traditional Islamic dress that allows only the uncovering of face and hands), and Na'im wore a *kufi* (small, close-fitting hat, often worn by Muslim men). Salima was a widow who had approached Amira and asked if she would consider her as a cowife. She had two sons and her husband had been friends with Na'im. Amira liked Salima, and after consultation with the *imam*, she agreed to the marriage. Na'im also expressed his attraction for Salima and soon they had a lovely wedding ceremony, which Amira helped to plan.

However, 8 months into the marriage she began to have second thoughts. The women maintained separate households and Na'im strove mightily to provide for both families. He and Amira had four children of their own. Amira felt, however, that since Salima was younger, she began to feel more like her mother than her cowife. Salima was extremely dependent and somewhat lazy with her housework. Over five or six sessions, it became clear that Na'im was getting increasingly irritated with Salima as well. However, when he would argue with her, she would regress and begin to talk in a baby-like voice. At one point, he found her in a closet, curled up in a fetal position. It was clear that she had severe emotional problems that had been exacerbated by the death of her husband. He did not feel it would be right to divorce her at this point, but things were worse and worse between them. Salima had also discovered she was pregnant, and an Islamic divorce would be impossible while she was pregnant anyway. They thought that they should come in for counseling because both households were in turmoil.

———————— ⋘ ————————

In this family, it is clear that another value system and even another legal code is operative. Islamic law recognizes marriages with up to four wives. Although these marriages are not recognized by secular legal institutions, they are recognized by the Islamic community. When people divorce, they seek divorce in the secular court and from the Islamic community as well. Most African American Muslims have only one wife, for the practice of polygamy is viewed with hostility and/or mistrust by many African American Muslim women. However, other African American Muslim women believe that polygamy is justified in their communities because of the shortage of eligible African American Muslim men.

In Islamic countries, the *shariah*, or code of Islamic law, carries more weight, and there is also the force of custom that supports the practice. In therapy, it is important to know how each individual feels about the marriage and also whether the customary limits of fairness to all wives are being observed.

The way this marriage was contracted was proper in the eyes of all parties, and in the eyes of their imam and religious community. Its polygamous nature was therefore not an issue. The main problem was the emotional impairment of the cowife and the additional strain this caused on the extended family finances and family harmony. Because of her dysfunction, her children were often being cared for by Amira. Amira felt overwhelmed, resentful, and guilty about agreeing to a situation with which she could not live. She wanted to help Salima, but she wanted to regain the peace that he and Na'im had developed over the past 13 years, prior to her addition to the family. Na'im felt as if he were trapped, but he felt obligated to live up to his duties. He also began to feel alienated from both women, because he could find little peace with either.

We worked on setting priorities in the family and arranged to have Salima evaluated by a psychiatrist and tested by a psychologist. She was severely depressed and was experiencing dissociative episodes. She disclosed that she had been sexually abused as a child, and her husband had rescued her from a very dysfunctional family. While he was alive, she was able to function well and put her past behind her. After he died, she felt as if she could no longer function. She was still grieving his loss.

She began attending individual therapy throughout her pregnancy and had one hospitalization during this time. Amira arranged for the children to go to a playschool during the day, so that she could have some time for herself. She also started a small business, sewing garments for other Muslim women and children. Salima's mother came to live with her after the baby was born, which gave her the support that she needed, and she began a course of antidepressants. Na'im remained married to both women, but he and Amira were gradually able to realize that they had not lost each other by bringing Salima into their lives. They took some trips together during the time he was allotted to spend with her. They also maintained a boundary between their relationship and Salima by refusing to discuss their relationship with her. Na'im and Salima settled into a nonsexual relationship. He maintained his financial support of her and her children, but both realized that neither wanted the sexual relationship any more. Salima continued to work on her survivor issues in therapy and gradually became more functional as a woman and a mother. She and Amira are cordial but formal with another. They occasionally do things with the children as an extended family during Ramadan, and so forth, but not on a daily basis. At this point, the family is no longer in therapy.

Being a cowife is honorable in Islam, because it allows women not to have to live their lives deprived of the company, support, and sexual contact with men, or to become only girlfriends to whom the men have no social or moral responsibility. Sex outside of marriage is considered *haram*, or forbidden, in Islam.

It is important that therapists not impose their values on these arrangements that are consistent with this belief system, unless they are being used as a cover for abusive behavior. I have seen occasions where this is so and it is, of course, not Islamic for women to suffer oppression at he hands of men who use polygamy as a cover to have more than one woman in their lives.

The *shariah*, or Islamic codes of law, are extensive and based on the Holy Qur'an and *hadith* (collections of observations of the life and sayings of Prophet Muhammad, PBUH) by authors such as Al-Bukhari and Sahih Muslim. It may be helpful for therapists to know the following:

1. Contraception is allowed, and abortion is not allowed after the fetus is fully formed.
2. The best of Believers are those who are good to their wives.
3. Among all lawful things, divorce is most hated by Allah.
4. A representative from the husband's family and wife's family are often appointed to settle marital disputes that the couple cannot solve themselves.
5. Fathers retain custody of their children after divorce, unless otherwise arranged by the couple.
6. Muslims are not allowed to change the birth name of adopted children, for the children should always know their lineage.
7. Anything that intoxicates is forbidden (*haram*): alcohol, other mood altering drugs, and so on.
8. It is considered modest for a man or a woman who are not married to look down and away when speaking directly.

There are many other traditions and customs that come from this belief system, and within many Islamic communities there are scholars who are experts on these customs and traditions. I have mentioned some which might have some relevance to therapeutic interventions. Violation of these traditions is sometimes a source of guilt in Muslims who struggle to be devout.

## PARENT–CHILD ISSUES

Raising children in an Islamic family, but not in an Islamic society, is a difficult task. Some African American Muslims have their children in public or private secular schools and others may do home schooling or educate their children in private Islamic schools. In the latter, classes are separated by sex, and along with their regular curriculum, Arabic and Qur'anic studies are taught. Great emphasis is put on education in Muslim families, and studious, well-behaved children are prized.

As with any religion, parents who are too strict, punitive, or shaming in their parenting raise rebellious children. These children will sometimes find attractive all the things their parents forbid. Children also are subject to all of the pressures that maturation brings and have to struggle to define their identity and the place that Islam has in their lives. Because of the restriction on dress, girls will often have a struggle with wearing *hijab* in their adolescence, unless they are in a community where this is supported. Muslim girls who go to secular high schools sometimes wear *hijab*, but others choose not to, because of the negative stereotypes about covering one's hair. Making *salat* five times a day is difficult as well when children attend a secular school. School lunches that contain pork may cause the child to go hungry, and the schools are not always supportive of special diets due to religious reasons.

Pressures to date, when dating is not allowed in Islam unless there is intent to marry, are also difficult to manage for both sexes. Parents must work very hard to ensure that their children have a large enough peer group with which to relate. Muslim girls are not supposed to marry non-Muslims, but Muslim men can marry non-Muslims if they are believers in the oneness of God (Christians, Jews, etc.). Since the male is supposed to be the spiritual leader of the home, a girl is thought vulnerable to oppression for her beliefs if she marries a non-Muslim.

The importance of siblings taking care of one another is often stressed among African American Muslims, and this is culturally consistent with the extended and augmented family systems of African Americans, anyway. Parental children are common in these families, as large families are often valued.

Parents must be sensitive to the issues, pressures, and emotions of young people who are struggling to synthesize their sense of personal and cultural identity with their religious and spiritual beliefs.

### Identity Issues in Adolescence

A 14-year-old boy was brought in to therapy by his parents. They complained that he had been skipping school and lying to them about it. He had attended an Islamic elementary school and had to transfer to a public high school. He was sullen and angry since this transfer. He began to pay attention in the session, however, when we began talking about all of the changes he was going through and how difficult it must be for him. He slowly began to admit hating his new school. He talked about how rude and profane some of his classmates were. He also gradually talked about how he had been teased because of his dark skin color and because of the way his mother and sister dressed. He also was upset because of the things his teacher had said about Islam and the way they always mispronounced his name, Mustafa ibn Abdul Rahman. He also was shamed by news reports that always portrayed Muslims as evil terrorists, especially when he had to do a report on them for his class. His parents were shocked that his feelings were so intense, because he had always been a relatively happy, obedient son.

––––––––––––––– ◡ –––––––––––––––

His parents resolved to advocate for him at school, with his teachers and with the principal. His mother and sister volunteered to go with him to school when he did his report, so that they could explain the significance of their dress and answer questions about the myths surrounding Muslim men and women. Mustafa was surprised at the support he received, for he had felt that the had to handle the situation and stand up for Islam on his own. He was ashamed to admit that he was scared to do so. His father was able to share with him his experiences at work and how he dealt with prejudice, and he gave him some suggestions. Both parents reassured him that they were a team and that they had to help him stand up for who he was. This, they taught him, was the truest meaning of *jihad* (holy war).

## BIRTH AND DEATH

In *Sunni* Muslim families, the first words that a child hears after birth should be the *shahadah*, or declaration of faith, and often Al-Fatiha, the first *sura* (chapter) in the Holy Qur'an. This is usually done by the father. Other ceremonies follow in 7 days, according to tradition, as well as the official naming of the child. Names are usually Arabic and chosen for their meanings. For example, Abdul means servant of, and when paired with an attribute of Allah (one of the 99) like *Rahman* (the beneficent) you get servant of the most Beneficent. The highest appellation for a Muslim is to be considered a faithful servant of Allah; therefore, there are many Muslims who have taken on the names of the attributes of Allah and declared themselves servants of that attribute.

Muslims bury the dead as quickly as possible, preferably before sundown on the day of death. The corpse should be cleansed by persons of the same sex as the deceased and given a ritual ablution, as if preparing for prayer.

In both of these rituals, the importance of belonging to a greater Islamic community is important, for both are observed communally among other Muslims.

## SOCIAL SEPARATION OF THE SEXES

On most social and religious occasions, the separation of the sexes is observed. At a party, women will be in one section of the home and the men in the other. This seems to reinforce intimacy within the sexes and gives emotional support and security. It must be emphasized that Muslims do not view this as oppressive but rather as natural and modest. In the homes of Muslims who are cultural nationalists, separation is observed publicly but may not be so observed within the home. Gender roles are clear in all groups, and strong, positive identification with one's gender role is encouraged. It is honorable to observe the traditional roles of husband/protector/provider and wife/nurturer. Marriage is considered "half of the religion" and is promoted and supported. For women who work outside the home, this traditional split is maintained as well. The sharing of duties will vary with families. Homosexuality is considered forbidden and abominable, and there is not place in Islamic communities for acknowledged homosexuals. Past homosexual behavior that is renounced and not practiced is considered a matter between the individual and Allah (God).

Again, the laws and ideals are as stated, but real life is another issue. It is difficult then for a person who has homosexual feelings and who is raised a Muslim to reconcile these with Islamic law. Conflict can result from a husband and wife being unable to manage their individual interpretation of what constitutes a balance of gender-role expectations with career aspirations. Within the extended families of African American Muslims as well, there will be expectations according to social class and blood relationship that can conflict with the individual's interpretation of his obligations as a Muslim. Some examples of this include brothers and sisters who are homosexual and who wish to be accepted, or parents who wish for a college-educated daughter to pursue a career rather than stay home and raise a family. There may be cousins who tease Muslim husbands about their fidelity to their wives, an uncle who derides his relative's refusal to accept a position with a company that sells products that are forbidden, or a social club that bars Muslims because of their religion and style of dress, even though family members have always belonged to them in the past. Muslims who have a previous history of addiction and convert to

Islam may have extra guilt because of a relapse. There are many other challenges in reconciling an Islamic belief system with life in a non-Islamic society.

## BARRIERS TO TREATMENT

There is a great deal of suspiciousness of Euro American therapists among the African American Muslim communities, both cultural nationalist and *Sunni*. It is rare for members to go outside of their community for advice or guidance. This suspiciousness I believe has grown out of the acute awareness of oppression brought about by intense study of African American history by many members, the historical reality of how Islam in this country has been closely associated with cultural nationalism, and the individual experiences of the members with racism, which may have contributed to their conversion. There are also a lot of prejudicial articles, media attention, and books that foster fear and dislike of Muslims and do little to educate the public about the religion as it is practiced by different groups.

I would characterize the relationships between African American Muslims and foreign-born or other ethnic Muslims as polite and cordial overall. Tensions between African American Muslims and American Jews are sometimes present because of the identification of African Americans with the Palestinians and the history of some African Americans of feeling exploited by groups that take money out of their communities and really don't care about their development. Some Muslims resent economic dependence in any form and see that dependence as a form of oppression. The Civil Rights struggle was about social accommodation and equal opportunity. There has always been, however, a dual approach to progress in the United States by African Americans, as characterized by its leaders. People such as Frederick Douglass, W. E. B. Du Bois, and Martin Luther King were integrationists. Others, such as Booker T. Washington, Marcus Garvey, and Malcolm X, were separatists and stressed self-determination. Each approach has been useful to the overall cause of freedom for African Americans at various times. The desire for self-determination is often viewed as segregation revisited. The important difference is that segregation was imposed from without for purposes of blocking opportunity, progress, and equality. Self-determination is seen as a desirable state that is positively group-driven. Members engaged in self-determination feel empowered and free to choose their course of thought and action within the society. Any therapist who works with people from these groups needs to understand these differences. Some Euro American therapists may encounter these clients in hospitals, community mental health centers, or in court-mandated situations.

Distrust of the therapist, skepticism about the therapist's attitudes toward Muslims and African Americans and sensitivity to misperception and distortion are common concerns one may encounter within the therapeutic relationship. Knowing even a little about Al-Islam will take the therapist a long way in forming a positive relationship with members of all sectors of this population. I think this is because the choice of a religion is often based on one's most deeply held beliefs. If your client sees that you truly respect those beliefs, you have something on which to build a therapeutic relationship. It is a mistake to fail to explore the belief system of a Muslim client by simply asking questions such as the following:

How did you first hear about Al-Islam?
How long have you been Muslim?
What difference has being Muslim made in your life?
How many members of your family are Muslim?
Do you have mixed feelings about how Muslims are viewed by others?

## CONCLUSIONS

Family therapy with African American Muslims is greatly facilitated by constructing collaborative genograms and gathering extensive family histories. The skills that therapists have developed in working with African Americans are certainly applicable to this group. Particular attention should be paid to the client's subcultural style, use of dialect/Arabic phrases, style of dress, sensitivity to nonverbal cues, double-consciousness, and sensitivity to race and power issues within the therapeutic relationship and setting.

This therapeutic relationship is enhanced by the therapist's appropriate demonstration of some familiarity with the tenets of Al-Islam or African American nationalism. As in any therapeutic relationship, the therapist should be aware of any prejudice or countertransference issues related to the client and in particular to clients whose belief systems are distasteful to the therapist. Most therapists are sincere in their desire to help others, and that sincerity, interest, and openness, combined with culturally effective therapeutic skills, can assist the therapist in constructing appropriate interventions.

This particular group however, suffers from two sets of negative stereotypes that may make bridging the cultural gap more difficult for Euro American therapists. There is the set of stereotypes that the dominant culture holds about African Americans and the set of stereotypes that are held about Muslims, which may interfere with accurate assessment and intervention. Bowen's theory of the societal projection process is certainly operative in the dynamics of the dominant society's perception of both of these groups. Both experience frequent scapegoating by the dominant society, and such scapegoating stabilizes the worldview of some "White" and "Black" Americans, serves as a source of gratification, defines social meaning, absorbs aggression, and facilitiates a sense of virtue as observed by Kovel (1970; cited in Pinderhughes, 1989).

Muslims are often the targets of self-appointed patriots when any negative press is aired regarding Islamic political activity. African Americans are often subjected to police harassment and community suspicion whenever the level of public safety is endangered due to increases in crime. A willingness to listen and affirm the experiences of the client who experiences racism and cultural oppression is essential to a good working relationship.

It is also true that some people use their religion as a way to run away from certain difficulties in their lives, and use religiosity as a defense against personal growth. It is important to explore the extent to which adherence to religious tenets mask other problems.

It is helpful for the therapist to be somewhat familiar with the Holy Qur'an, for the use of Islamic concepts will help to illustrate examples, interventions, metaphors, and so on, and will further mutual understanding. If customs and behaviors are exhibited that the therapist does not understand, a friendly, respectful request for explanation will usually be answered with enthusiasm.

Respect for the patriarchal nature of Islamic family life is important. Most African American Muslim women are familiar with feminist concepts but have consciously chosen their lifestyle as more meaningful for them. Often, they view themselves as far more fortunate than the women who have chosen less traditional lifestyles. Feminist therapists should have respect for the different model of womanhood and femininity chosen by these women. If there is not discomfort on the part of the parties with the way their relationships are constructed, we need to pay attention to what they feel *is* painful to them and reserve judgment for our supervision sessions.

Prayer, fasting, and rituals are important in the lives of Muslims. Suggesting that participants pray, especially for their relationships, is often an appropriate intervention. Prayers are often said communally, with all of the family praying together. Increasing the number of prayers increases family contact.

Female therapists should pay particular attention to their dress during family therapy sessions with Muslims. Low necklines, short skirts, and bare arms will lessen the sense of respect that these clients will have for them. Male therapists should pay particular attention to acknowledging the husband's place in the family by asking him if he has any objection to his addressing questions to his wife or daughters. Please remember that this does not imply male dominance but is a matter of good manners and chivalry. It implies purity of intent to a Muslim man and woman.

In the Holy Qur'an, in Al-Fatiha, the first *sura* has a phrase, "Guide us along the straight path." The idea of the straight path is dear to all Muslims and speaks to their belief in the oneness of God and of unswerving devotion and conviction in the path to His grace and blessings. Encouraging Muslims to continue on that straight path in ways that support healthy family life, communication, truth, personal growth and wisdom is consistent with the goals of family therapists interested in family preservation. The constellation of that family life may be vastly different from the therapist's own but is a valid choice for that family. Facilitating the functioning of these families is interesting and challenging to the therapist willing to be flexible and affirming of the values of these families.

Interest in and conversion to Islam is growing rapidly in our country and it is more likely that therapists in urban areas may have an opportunity to work with this population. Many African Americans identify positively with the values of Muslims and have relatives who are Muslim. The Honorable Elijah Muhammad, speaking of the millions of slaves brought to this country who were Muslim and lost contact with this faith, referred to them as the "lost–found" Nation of Islam, hence the name of the organization, now headed by Louis Farrakhan.

African Americans who practice traditional Islam usually became attracted to the faith as an outgrowth of their study of African/African American history. Many were or are active in Pan-African studies and activities or were former members of the Nation of Islam who progressed to a greater appreciation of the traditions of Islamic cultures and the Holy Qur'an. Islam is attractive to many African Americans because it corrects the damage inflicted upon them by enslavement and oppression by addressing alternative structural solutions for family and community life. It is also attractive as a spiritual path and discipline. It is a complete lifestyle and in some Islamic countries a governmental/legal system as well.

There is a strong emphasis on the community, or *ummat*, among all Muslims. Obligations to the group sometimes supercede family obligations. As a family therapist, it is important to explore how the family relates to the greater *ummat* in order to assess its full functioning.

As we become more adept as family therapists in negotiating cross-cultural relationships with families who have different values systems and beliefs, I believe that we are engaged in extremely important work. This work involves efforts that are designed to increase understanding and healthy functioning in the basic building blocks of our society. It is hoped that this work will contribute to the greater health and well-being of our communities, one family and one microcommunity at a time. We also become ambassadors of cultural knowledge that we transmit to our peers, colleagues, and students. Who can doubt that we need greater understanding of one another? Who can doubt that understanding and corrective actions are the greatest weapon against division and fear, scapegoating and racism?

It is my hope that this chapter will contribute in some small way to such understanding of this growing and interesting group of Americans.

## REFERENCES

Al-Qaradawi, Y. (1960). *The lawful and prohibited in Islam.* Indianapolis, IN: American Trust Publications.

Pinderhughes, E. (1989). *Race, ethnicity and power.* New York: Free Press.

Rashad, A. (1991). *The history of Islam and black nationalism in the Americas.* Beltsville, MD: Writers Inc.

CHAPTER 9

# Nigerian Families

## Emeka Nwadiora

Africa is a vast continent, encompassing a great diversity of cultural values too great to be captured in a short chapter. The continent is nearly 12 million square miles, approximately the size of the United States, China, India, and Europe combined. Several ethnic groups exist, and hundreds of languages are spoken there. Despite the impact of European colonialization over several centuries, most people have maintained their ethnic languages in addition to speaking the languages of their former colonialists, which have primarily been the English, French, and Portuguese. For example, although the official language in Nigeria is English, the country also has three major ethnic languages—Igbo, Yoruba, and Hausa—that are spoken by the three largest ethnic groups within the country. Two religions, Christianity and Islam, dominate the continent through the legacy of colonialization and slave trade. Although many Africans profess to belong to one of these faiths, they may still identify with their own indigenous religions (Mbiti, 1969).

According to the 1990 U.S. Census, there are over 250,000 Black Africans currently residing in the United States legally, mostly in major cities. A sizable number living in the United States have not been accounted for by the Census due either to their illegal or nonimmigrant status (i.e., visitors, students, and the undocumented). There are 91,000 Nigerians in the United States alone (U.S. Census, 1990).

The family is the cornerstone of African cultures. Their definition of family is an extended one, including all persons related by blood over several generations. When a problem arises, there is usually a meeting comprised of male and female elders who democratically deliberate and sometimes invite younger family members to express their views. If the elders agree to invite the younger generations to participate in the problem-solving process, their views may be taken very seriously.

Marriage and procreation are major values among Africans. Children are perceived as carriers of the future and disseminators of cultural values, and as economic insurance for their aged parents. In most countries, there are no social security benefits except the pensions received by government or corporate workers.

In general, Africans have deep respect and honor for their elders, who are perceived as the depositories of wisdom and as persons whose time to join their ancestors is fast approaching. Africans pay homage to ancestors, whom they believe are still spiritually alive and influencing daily affairs. In fact, in times of psychological or physical distress, Africans may consult the ancestors for spiritual guidance and counsel. This is why a proper burial is crucial to Africans. This could be a tool for therapists who might prod their clients to state what they believe their ancestors' views might be on a given problem.

For the purposes of this chapter, I will use Nigeria as a case example. Nigeria is situated on the West Coast of Africa. It is the richest, most populous country in Africa, with a population of over 100 million, according to the recent census. Most of the population resides in rural villages, although there are several modern cities. The gulf between the rich and poor is very wide. A former British colony, Nigeria gained its political independence in 1960. Since then, the country has experienced ethnic problems, a civil war and several military governments, as well as a succession of military coups. The country's political instability may be partially responsible for Nigerians unwillingness to return to their country after completing their education in the United States.

## THE LIFE CYCLE

Among Nigerians, the life cycle revolves around birth, initiation to womanhood or manhood, marriage, and death. These events are marked by unique festivities, rituals, and celebrations, which usually take place strictly within the domain of the extended family and community structure.

Marriage in Nigeria is usually an alliance between two extended families, rather than a contractual agreement between two individuals in love. It is the norm for both men and women. Polygyny, a symbol of high status for men, is the ideal (Uchendu, 1965). Yet most marriages are monogamous, reflecting modernization and the influence of Christianity. Among the Igbos of Nigeria, the process leading to marriage is often long and ceremonious, sometimes lasting for several months or even years. In the first place, the man asks for the woman's consent, which is followed by some negotiations from a middleman and middlewoman. These middlepersons are usually trusted and experienced adults who have knowledge of the histories of the two families and the backgrounds of the woman and man. They are charged to investigate for any profound negative attribute or behaviors from members of these families, for example, history of mental illness, incidence of unexplainable premature deaths, history of convictions, and so forth.

They then seek a soothsayer (diviner) to determine the auspiciousness of the marriage. If both families receive satisfactory news from the inquiries, the courtship ends with a dowry. In fact, no marriage is consummated or approved without a dowry. It is a token of appreciation for the approval of the bridegroom's family to marry the bride. In no way does this ritual indicate that the woman is chattel. In fact, according to Uchendu (1965), the Igbo woman can leave her husband or summon him to a tribunal of elderly women and men if she believes she is physically or psychologically violated by him. This counsel of elders will adjudicate her case and sanction her husband before she returns to the home. Provisions such as these indicate Nigerian respect of the woman's rights and denies allegation of women as chattel. Courtship and marriage among this ethnic group involve the entire families of the man and woman. After the ceremonies, families of both partners are sealed in  permanent relationship exercised through the exchange of gifts, visits, and other ceremonial activities. The man and wife are charged with the importance of maintaining moral virtues and responsibilities to each other, and not to bring shame to their families, which are eternally tied through their marriage. The pervasive sense of community dictates that individuals remain conscious that the eyes of their families and the community, both living and dead, are constantly watching them regardless of where they may reside.

## IMPLICATIONS FOR THERAPY

Many Africans arrive in the United States as single adults, intending to return home to get married in the "proper way." Unfortunately, quite often this idea does not materialize, for they begin courtships and eventually marry in the United States. This phenomenon can create tensions and distress for the African family of origin, which may perceive it as an assault to their dignity in that the proper marriage process was not adhered to, because the roles of the middlepersons and the diviner and the tradition of approval and dowry were not utilized.

Problems can also occur if the bride or bridegroom is not of the same racial, cultural, or ethnic background as his or her mate. In Nigeria, loyalty to one's individual ethnic group is very strong irrespective of their location or level of Western education they have obtained. In assessment of families it is important to include such variables as socioeconomic background of families of origin; the ages of both spouses; place of marriage; and each spouse's ethnicity, language, and skin color. Although skin color may not be an overt issue, too often this can compound other unresolved issues. Due to contact with the European culture, lighter complexioned persons are perceived more favorably than the darker skinned Nigerians. Several families can become estranged from each other over this issue. Having light skin can lead to privileges that may be denied to the darker skinned persons (Boyd-Franklin, 1989).

Diete, a dark-skinned, 32-year-old doctoral student at a prestigious American university, met Nnenna, a light-skinned, 25-year-old woman who was working on her medical degree, while both were attending religious services. They also saw each other frequently at cultural events. After several months of courtship, they became engaged and eventually married in the church and had a baby. This matter angered her parents at home, who disapproved of the union. Nnenna's bouts of depression were related to her parents' disapproval. Her "improper" marriage to a "stranger" in America, although he was Nigerian, constituted shame and guilt to her highly revered parents in Nigeria because he was dark skinned, of lower class, and of another ethnic group of lesser social status. Her family also resented the interruption of her medical education. They ceased responding to her correspondences for over a year.

In my weekly therapy sessions, I explained to the couple that this phenomenon is not uncommon among Nigerians in America, and mentioned several other "American marriages" that have struggled through the crisis. I referred the couple to two such families in the area, who were willing to act as support systems. We discussed the importance of continuous contact with the family at home through letter writing and phone calls. I encouraged them to send gifts as often as possible, and to send some money to Nnenna's parents, explaining that the distance was the reason why they could not perform the marriage in the "proper way." One year later, Nnenna's mother wrote to her daughter for the first time, indicating her parents' preparedness to reconsider acceptance of the marriage with the provision that she would send money so that the elders could perform all the necessary rituals, including the dowry. Eventually, the couple visited Nigeria, and the final marital rituals were completed. Nnenna has since then resumed her medical studies. The psychocultural conflict, the result of a clash between traditionalism and modernity, had been managed effectively.

In Nigerian culture, the elders mediate conflicts, teach the younger generations ethical and moral values through storytelling and use of proverbs, and investigate the backgrounds of potential brides and bridegrooms. (In fact, in Nigerian marriages, particularly among the Igbo people, the elders of both the bride and bridegroom play the most significant role in the ritual process.) In therapy, I usually employ the wisdom of older Nigerians who came in and use stories, jokes, and proverbs called *inu* by the Igbos and *owe* by the Yorubas to encourage analytic thinking and behavioral changes among my clients. For marriage counseling, it is important to understand that the concept of divorce among Nigerian families is an extreme rarity, as it is not limited to the husband and wife, but directly affects the jointed families and the community. The elaborate wedding rituals and ceremonies eternally join the entire families and communities into the marriage. In therapy, couples must be reminded of their responsibilities to their families, communities, and each other in their union, and should be encouraged to recognize their interests in working toward resolutions within their sealed marriages. The use of cultural consultants, such as the elders, is highly suggested.

Because of the relational nature of their culture, Nigerians are more likely to respond to therapists who are more active, personal, sharing of their own life experiences, and who honor the dignity of the traditional family structure. It is not uncommon for the clients to ask therapists about their own family status, age, and number of children. For example, respect for the traditional family structure dictates that in therapeutic interventions, it is necessary to initially align with the husband first since he is assumed to be the head of the family. This could be followed by the wife and finally the children, beginning with the oldest male child (Baptiste, 1993). Therapists can later engage the family in developing a more democratic form but must begin with the traditional, patriarchal family structure. This concept requires adjustment among European American-educated therapists, as they are taught the counselor/therapist should remain indifferent and maintain personal distance from the client(s). Therapists who have older children and may have been married longer than the client family may engage faster and produce better with Nigerian families.

The typical Nigerian family is patriarchal, the man being the provider, whereas the woman is perceived as the nurturer; both roles are equally important to the success of the family. All Nigerian women independently engage in some form of education, business, or employment. It is an anomaly for a woman to stay only at home and raise children. This hierarchy begins with the man, the woman, the son, and daughter with males before females, mostly because males propagate the lineage of the family name and identification. (In families, the oldest male is usually given the honor of being the third parent of the family.) This structure may be a source of major conflict in the United States, where a female spouse may earn a higher income than her male partner. Although the idea of inequality in salaries is unacceptable to Nigerians (they believe in equal pay for equal work), the patriarchal nature of the society allows men to be promoted much faster than women. In fact, major policies and key positions are exclusively male dominated. This gender inequality permeates other social institutions of education and career mobility largely because of patriarchy and the perception that men are the heads and keepers of the family name. Women may struggle with these cultural complexities and stressors which are internal and external to their immediate family. Unlike the mainstream feminist, whose struggle is characteristically independent and may often be adversarial to male participation, the Nigerian woman invites her male to share in these cross-cultural stressors and feelings of alienation in the new culture in which they now live. Everything is usually done within the context of the entire family. Faced with such a case, I have intervened successfully by encouraging a man to seek alternative ways to improve his education and status to at least a comparable worth with his spouse, or in some cases have worked with the family to appreciate the wife's laurels rather than compete or be adversarial. Several successful marriages of Nigerians were cited for the couple to review.

Marriage and parenting are certainly the most important social institutions in Nigeria. Marriage is considered as the fortress for individual well-being, the first level of collective social order, and is the fundamental spiritual union that teaches and improves the couple's ability to withstand the tests and difficulties of life. Those who do not marry or have children may be viewed as having incomplete and unfulfilled lives (Uchendu, 1965). There is enormous pressure exerted on young adults by family member and peers to get married. For a Nigerian to express lack of interest in marriage is a rarity that may be accompanied by community suspicion.

Although homosexuality is a worldwide phenomenon, it is perceived as a moral aberration in Nigeria. The fact that there are no words for it among the Igbos and other Nigerian ethnic groups reflects the degree to which the orientation is a taboo. Nigerians of this orientation understand the taboo and may have a problem with their homosexual identity; in many cases, they resort to marriage or other excuses to hide their identity. It is important for therapists to understand and to explore with clients the complexities, the emotional and cross-cultural stressors that this subgroup may experience because they are immigrants, Black Africans, and homosexual, coming from a culture that abhors their orientation, and are now in a country that discriminates against people of this demographic. The comfort level of the client needs to be respected, and therapists should assist client who express this sexual preference to find support groups within their locale.

Parenthood, particularly motherhood, is probably more valued than career mobility.

Ubani, a medical doctor, and his wife, Ada, a neurologist from the same ethnic group in Nigeria, have lived for 10 years in New Jersey. They agreed that since Ada was infertile, a woman related to her could volunteer to be a second wife. The couple went home to perform the wedding ceremonies, and now Dr. Ada plays the role of "big mother" to the children, who tell me about their "big mother" and their "small mother" (the biological mother). The idea and practice of having two mothers is normal among Nigerians due to polygyny and the extended family system. If infertility is a male problem, there is usually an inconspicuous arrangement for a member of his family to be a sperm donor.

Although Nigerian families have many opportunities for educational and economic advancement in the United States, they experience the loss of extended families and the lack of pervasiveness of Nigerian tradition and ritual, which manifests in isolation and loneliness. One such loss is the role reversal in gender relations, and another is the attitudes of teenagers. They are usually in a state of constant mourning for these losses and will seek opportunities to recreate the traditional structures as a way of managing these losses. For example, the inability of the men to gather traditional support, and the trends toward gender equality in America, may precipitate psychological problems ranging from anger, distrust, depression, suspiciousness, and anxiety for both spouses. Some Nigerians may try to overcompensate for this loss by directing extreme energy into their work. Many less educated Nigerians work two or three jobs in order to make good incomes. Some Nigerians in America may be obligated to send money to their relatives or build home in their native country out of loyalty to their extended families.

Odiambo, an artist, was referred to a mental health clinic due to his constant agitation, restlessness, and distrust over his wife's behavior. He had a serious alcohol problem and had on several occasions assaulted his wife Nneka for coming home late from work. The fact that he had to participate in cleaning, cooking, and caring for their two toddlers angered him, as he was raised in a patriarchal culture where such responsibilities were the domain of women. He perceived such tasks as an assault on his identity as a man and a husband. His depression could be traced back to the loss of his ascribed status and responsibilities as a man. His inability to cope with this loss led to alcoholism resulting in the abuse and emotional estrangement from his wife and children. The major source of family stress was the difficulty he had in taking responsibility for chores that for him were culturally gender specific. Additionally, Nneka and Odiambo had become too emotionally dependent on each other due to isolation from culturally relevant ties.

When necessary, therapists can use other professional helpers to assist in relieving family stress. In therapy, I referred Odiambo to Alcoholics Anonymous but also encouraged him to attend more culture- and gender-specific meetings and organizations. Because the family was Catholic, I encouraged Odiambo and his wife to seek counseling with their priest on a regular basis. I also encouraged them to visit an older Nigerian couple who lived outside of their suburbs for emotional support, offering them ties to the wisdom and inclusion of elders that are traditionally important to them. Nneka was linked to an informal network of other Nigerian females for support that she visited often. I kept contact with the family, the cultural helpers, and the priest for updates on their marriage and his alcoholism. In the end, it was more the culture-specific and gender-specific supports that normalized Nneka and Odiambo's relationship.

———————— ✦ ————————

Nigerian families that reside near other Nigerians or Africans tend to have a better sense of belonging due to the shared values than those who may be isolated. I encourage isolated Nigerians, who may drive for many hours every month, to spend time with their fellow country people. Therapists should recognize and encourage such trips, for they are extremely important to their sense of "belonging" within an alien context. Invisibility and identity crises also beset these families. Too often they are labeled as "Black" with all the negative American stereotypes toward African Americans; in fact, they may be further perceived as uncivilized jungle people. Several Hollywood and other media forms have perpetuated this stereotype for racist and commercial reasons (e.g., Tarzan movies; Herrnstein & Murray's [1994] *The Bell Curve*). But their major reality is that of being African immigrants with a distinct cultural base. This is compounded with the fact that they must live in a Caucasian/European American dominated country. The Nigerian therefore has to struggle and juggle successfully within these three dominant identities—human, African, and Black—in a White, racist culture, and these will constantly and profoundly influence their mental health status. It is the therapist's function to encourage clients to clarify these daily challenges and entanglements.

The therapist's role is also to encourage clients to gradually weed out values and practices that may no longer be useful from the traditions that must be maintained within the context of American culture. Recently there has been much ado in the media about clitorectomy, an ancient practice once common in Africa. This practice is now extremely rare in modern Nigerian society. It is highly unlikely that a Nigerian family in America will practice such a procedure. However, should clients suggest this procedure, therapists should not only discourage the idea, but also encourage them to evaluate the psychological and physical harm to the female. The illegality and penalties accompanying such an activity should be made clear to them also. The fact that this issue has been exaggerated and sensationalized in the media, and even in the helping professions, as opposed to highlighting cultural strengths of Africa, leaves much to be desired and exposes another instance of institutional racism in this society and in our professions.

In most Nigerian families, children are extremely important, because they ensure the longevity and continuity of several generations. Girls are perceived as sources of potential wealth to families because of the anticipated dowry the bridegroom will pay. Boys and girls are groomed to remember their responsibilities to assist their parents in their old age. Among the Igbos, there is a special burden of responsibility given to the oldest male child, called *Okpara*. He is perceived as the heir of the family and must take care of his younger siblings and parents.

Chidi is the oldest son and is married, with three teenagers. He recently returned to America after attending his father's funeral at home, where his elders cautioned him about living in the United States and neglecting his primary responsibilities at home. The village elders urged him to "come back home to fix things up and continue the work your father left behind." Chidi's conflict between his loyalty and desire to respect his family's wishes and traditional values and the need to live independently with his nuclear family in the United States precipitated depression that brought him, and eventually the whole family, to treatment. Chidi became a workaholic, avoiding intimacy with unpredictable bursts of anger. A balance was brought about in the family through an agreement for Chidi to visit home every 2 years in order to "take care of things," and the family's need to remain in the United States but visit their home every 5 years. The family was also exposed to several other Nigerians in the area for cultural support.

———————— ❧ ————————

Nigerian families in the United States often experience crises of identity, devaluation of their personhood, lack of appreciation for their cultural values, and invisibility in a racist country where their skin color automatically labels them as inferior.

African or Nigerian families in the United States possess an intense drive for themselves and their children to succeed. Their upbringing gives them strong family bonds and kinship ties, and a collective approach toward problem solving. Several of them are obligated by family responsibilities at home while at the same time managing their own challenges in the United States. Although physical and cultural distances between the United States and Africa may exacerbate their feelings of loss, many have succeeded in working out these conflicts through consultations, correspondences, and regular visits during which they take the time to approximate and perhaps atone through participating in specific family rituals and crucial events (e.g., funerals) they may have missed due to their stay in the United States. Their elders are usually present to guide them through the process.

Due to the novelty of Western-type therapy to Nigerians, there are no clear-cut ways to manage stress within the American culture or to handle situations of missing rituals or being mentally ill. Each situation will call for a unique approach. The major overriding issue here is the importance of cultural support groups. Therapists should ask clients how much access they have to their distinct or larger cultural support groups. In an environment where there may be no Nigerians, any African people will suffice in serving as cultural buffers.

A major source of stress for Nigerian families in the United States is acculturative stress (Nwadiora, 1995) that results from attempting to live in two worlds. It is the therapist's role to assist in finding a middle ground and some peace with their multiple cultural identities. Families should be allowed and encouraged by therapists to make their own choices in utilizing culturally appropriate support systems (Landau, 1982).

## ACKNOWLEDGMENTS

I wish to express many thanks to Monica McGoldrick and David McGill for their encouragement, Joe Giordano for his insistence in presenting this information, and Nataki MacMurray for emergency clerical work in preparing this chapter.

## REFERENCES

Baptiste, D. (1993). Immigrant families, adolescents, and acculturation: Insights for therapists. In E. Settles, D. Hanks, & M. Sussman (Eds.), *Families on the move—migration, immigration, emigration, and mobility.* New York: Haworth Press.

Boyd-Franklin, N. (1989). *Black families in therapy: A multisystems approach.* New York: Guilford Press.

Herrnstein, R. J., & Murray, C. (1994). *The bell curve: Intelligence and class structure in American life.* New York: Free Press.

Landau, J. (1982). Therapy with families in cultural transition. In M. McGoldrick, J. K. Pearce, & J. Giordano (Eds.), *Ethnicity and family therapy* (1st ed., pp. 552–572). New York: Guilford Press.

Mbiti, J. (1969). *African traditional religion.* Portsmouth, NH: Heineman.

Nwadiora, E. (1995). Alienation and stress among Black immigrants: An exploratory study. *Western Journal of Black Studies, 19*(1), 59–71.

Uchendu, V. C. (1965). *The Igbo of South East Nigeria.* Philadelphia: Holt, Rinehart & Winston.

U.S. Bureau of the Census. (1990). *1990 census of population.* Washington, DC: U.S. Government Printing Office.

# PART III

# LATINO FAMILIES

CHAPTER 10

# Latino Families:
# An Overview

## Nydia Garcia-Preto

During the past decade the Latino population in the United States has grown at an incredible rate. According to the 1990 U.S. Census Bureau, Hispanics, as they are labeled by the government, numbered 22,354,059, in contrast to 16,940,000 in 1985. These numbers, however, do not reflect the undocumented and illegal migrants who come into this country daily and cannot be adequately counted. When this rapid growth in population is combined with the fact that most Hispanics are below the age of 30 (U.S. Census, 1991) we can see why Latinos are the fastest growing ethnic group in America, and why the 1980s had been marked to be the "Decade of the Hispanic." But their numerical increase has not resulted in greater economic or political power. Instead, Latinos, especially those who are here illegally, are experiencing increased social oppression as they face the effects of laws such as Proposition 187—the California initiative denying public educational, medical, and social services to undocumented immigrants, which is now being considered in other states (Griffin, 1995; Falicov & Falicov, 1995)—and the backlash against bilingual education.

Although Mexicans, Puerto Ricans, and Cubans continue to be the three largest Latino groups in this country, there has been an increase in the number of Dominicans, Central Americans, and some South American groups, especially Brazilians in the United States. Considering these changes, we have expanded the section on Latino families in the second edition of *Ethnicity and Family Therapy* to include this overview, as well as chapters on Central America and Brazil. The chapter on Central Americans focuses on the effects that war has had on many families who come to the United States as refugees, and interventions for working with them. The chapter on Brazilians will address the influence of Portugal on their culture and the position they hold here. Although many Brazilians consider themselves Latinos, they are not classified as Hispanics. The chapters on Mexicans, Puerto Ricans, and Cubans have also been

141

revised to reflect changes in society that have affected family organization and functioning. This overview will provide some perspective on the migration, socioeconomic, and political history of Latinos in this country, and on cultural factors that may influence the treatment of families.

## HISPANIC OR LATINO?: SOCIOPOLITICAL PERSPECTIVE

Hispanic or Latino are adjectives used to describe people who come from different countries with different cultures and sociopolitical histories, and who in their countries of origin would never describe themselves in that way. They are Cubans, Chicanos, Mexicans, Puerto Ricans, Argentinians, Colombians, Dominicans, Brazilians, Guatemalans, Costa Ricans, Nicaraguans, Salvadorians, and all the other nationalities that comprise South America, Central America, and the Caribbean. Proclaiming their nationality is very important to Latinos; it provides a sense of pride and identity that is reflected in the stories they tell, their music, and their poetry. Longing for their homeland is more pronounced when they are unable to return to their home either because they are here as political exiles, or as illegal aliens, or because they are unable to afford the cost of travel. In therapy asking the question, "What is your country of origin?" and listening to the client's stories of immigration helps to engage the therapist and gives the therapist an opportunity to learn about the country the client left behind, the culture, and the reasons for leaving.

Although Latinos may hold on to their national heritage with pride, when they arrive in this country, what is most apparent to others are their similarities. They speak Spanish, except for Brazilians who speak Portuguese, most are Roman Catholic, and they have in common values and beliefs rooted in a history of conquest and colonization. To outsiders Latinos look alike, since their physical features, such as skin color, facial structure, and hair texture are often similar due to the mixing of races that has taken place in most of these countries. Once they arrive in the United States, they are officially categorized as "Hispanic": the label used by the U.S. Census to track population growth, as well as trends in education and socioeconomic levels. For Latinos, the label takes away their nationality and symbolizes a loss of identity. Among the different groups there is opposition to this term. Some say that "Hispanic" is an English word, and that it does not have gender, unlike Latino and Latina. Others claim that "Hispanic" is a politically conservative term, while Latino/Latina is seen as a more progressive label (Gonzalez, 1992). Yet, others oppose the use of Latino because it refers to an even older empire, the one that took over Spain. In any case, the use of "Hispanic" by the U.S. Census has become a political statement and a source of conflict among Latinos. However, whatever label is used, it is beneficial for the different Latino groups in this country to have some unity in order to gain political power, especially since as a group they are significantly socially oppressed.

The history of Latinos in the United States, as well as in the Caribbean, Central America, and South America, has followed a cycle of conquest, oppression, defeat, and struggle for liberation. Social oppression has been deeply rooted in Latin American history. Latinos are the descendants of the oppressors and the oppressed, and for generations they have struggled for liberation. The destruction of culture and religion of native inhabitants was rampant as Spaniards and Portuguese took the land, raped the women, and killed the men. In the Caribbean, especially, the Tainos, Arawaks, and Caribes were enslaved, killed, and gone within 50 years after the conquest, and African slaves were brought to do the work. Slaves were also brought to Central and South America, mostly along the coastline, and in large numbers to Brazil (Chasteen & Tulchin, 1994). As in the United States, the power was held by White, European immigrants who owned the land. Wanting control of their own government, the landowners led revolutions against Spain, fighting and winning wars for independence. The liberation movement swept across Latin America, giving the promise of hope and independence to a population of mostly impoverished and uneducated peasants who owned no land and had no power. The power remained in the hands of the wealthy White Europeans, who, in turn, oppressed the indigenous population, the slaves, and the racially mixed people known as "mestizos." Socioeconomic and political oppression still persists in many Latin American countries, and as the poor struggle for survival, many look to the United States as a possible solution.

## U.S. IMMIGRATION AND SOCIAL OPPRESSION

For many Latinos, the United States has represented a place in the sun, a place to be free, yet upon arrival, they are dismayed by the attitude that non-Hispanics have toward them. Their color, language, and culture, essentials to their being, become cause for oppression. A majority see themselves as victims of discrimination and at the bottom of the social ladder, below Blacks. They often view the American people as cold and the American way of life as hostile to what they describe as their tradition of family unity, personal warmth, respect for their elders, and for their own and other people's dignity. For most, especially those with darker complexions and less money and education, feeling respected for who they are outside of their families, out there in the street among the gringos, is a daily struggle. It is not surprising that in an attempt to protect their self-respect, many are unwilling to call themselves American or to let their language, traditions, or way of life disappear.

The history of Latinos in the United States dates back to the 1500s, when the Spaniards settled Santa Fe, conquering and oppressing the indigenous population of what is today New Mexico, Texas, and California. Spain lost the territory to Mexico in the 1800s during the Mexican War for independence, and in the same century the Mexicans lost it to the United States. By the time the Mexicans lost the war to the United States, their possession of land had expanded to include New Mexico, California, Texas, Nevada, Utah, parts of Arizona, Colorado, Kansas, Oklahoma, and Wyoming (Calvert & Calvert, 1993). Although the Treaty of Guadalupe Hidalgo promised citizenship, freedom of religion and language, and maintenance of their lands, the Mexicans who lived in these territories became the subject of discrimination and social injustice soon after the war. They became strangers or immigrants in their own land, losing their rights and private property (Falicov, 1982).

Although there are Spaniards and Mexicans who have lived in the United States since before the *Mayflower* landed (Shorris, 1992), the major waves of Latino immigrants came after World War II. Mexicans, Puerto Ricans, Cubans, Dominicans, Colombians, Brazilians, Argentinians, other South Americans, and more recently, growing numbers from Central America, have made the journey north. The pattern of migration usually follows economic depression or political revolution. Those who come are usually the poor, the wealthy who are able to flee with their money, and the intellectuals who are persecuted for the expression of their ideas. The majority, however, are the very poor.

Once in the United States, poverty is a way of life for the majority of Latinos who live in this society, and their inability to access resources keeps them locked in a cycle that is oppressive and demoralizing. Jobs are scarce, even when they are willing to work for peanuts, housing is substandard and unaffordable, and difficulties with understanding and speaking English often keep them on the periphery. This is especially true for dark-skinned Hispanics who, according to research, are more highly segregated from non-Hispanic Whites than are lighter-skinned Hispanics (Denton & Massey, 1989; Massey & Bitterman, 1985; Massey & Denton, 1992). The darker the skin, the more difficulty Latinos experience finding housing (Hakken, 1979; Yinger, 1991), and the more likely they are to earn low wages (Rodriguez, 1991; Telles & Murguia, 1990).

They come looking for a place in the sun, but are burned by the scalding rays of oppression. Somehow the institutions that provide help are not sheltering; instead, they tend to reinforce the feelings of shame and failure that Latinos feel when their dreams about improving their lives are truncated. Extended family members, when present, are usually caught in the cycle themselves, unable to provide the emotional and financial support that has been traditionally an expectation in Latino cultures. Resentments among family members about lack of support cause cutoffs and exacerbate feelings of isolation in Latinos. Those who are White or educated and have financial resources are in a better position to live out their dreams, especially if they understand

and speak English. Inability to speak English lowers their potential to earn higher wages and to attain higher paying jobs (Bean & Tienda, 1987; Reimers, 1985). Without English, they are relegated to low-skill-level jobs. And, depending on how much emotional support they have at home from their families and friends, they may experience less isolation and a greater connection to the community in which they live.

The base of knowledge on Latino poverty remains inadequate, because most of the studies about Latinos are analyzed using models developed with Blacks in mind. Standard methods and theories for studying Blacks, however, are inappropriate for learning about Latino poverty because there are essential differences between the two groups. For instance, there is a lack of coherence among Latino groups, race has different connotations for Latinos than for Blacks, the level and extent of segregation among them also differs, the effect of immigration is extremely important, and the role of language and culture is very significant (Massey, 1993).

## DIFFERENCES AMONG GROUPS

Although once here Latinos may experience similar injustices, there is often competition among the different groups. The conflict is sometimes related to a history of war between the countries of origin due to struggles about natural resources such as land, access to waterways, or opposing political ideologies. Distinct sociopolitical histories and different historical ties to the United States have affected their entrance and acceptance in this country, leading to resentment and distrust among the groups. Racism and classism influence relationships within and among the groups and contribute to a pecking order marked by prejudice and stereotypes. One group may be afraid that the other will take over jobs, businesses, neighborhoods, receive more help from the government, or attain a higher education. Often the prejudice is subtle and the groups coexist peacefully; however, resentments can quickly surface. Intermarriage among groups is one of those triggers that tends to make prejudice among groups salient.

The prospect of defining unique cultural characteristics that describe different Latino groups is intriguing and painfully controversial. Differences can be subtle and complex, making the process of teasing out specific and categorical statements about each group difficult. It would be an injustice and clinically detrimental to make a chart assigning values, patterns, and attitudes to certain groups without having enough pages to analyze, compare, and define the sociopolitical context in which the cultures have evolved. It would be ludicrous to assume that this type of summary could do justice to such rich heritage. However, I want to offer a brief introduction to the history and pattern of migration of some of the major groups we may encounter in treatment: The next few chapters will offer more specific information about several groups.

## MEXICANS

Mexicans have been in this country since the 1600s and 1700s, when with the Spaniards they established missions and communities that later became important cities in the United States (Falicov, Chapter 12, this volume). However, they first came to this country in large numbers in the early 1900s, attempting to escape the economic depression that Mexico was undergoing and the violence of the Mexican Revolution of 1910 (Falicov, Chapter 12; Shorris, 1992). The wealthy and the poor settled mostly in Texas, California, New Mexico, and Arizona. They are the largest group of Latinos in this country and have been here the longest. According to the latest census bureau report (1991), there are 12,110,000 Hispanics of Mexican birth or ancestry. Mexican Americans, or Chicanos, are mostly mestizos or of mixed Native American (Mayan, Aztec, Hopi) and Caucasian descent (Novas, 1994). The major concentration of Mexican Americans remains in California and the Southwest. The latest official count shows that there are 7.68 million Mexican Americans living in California and 4.33 million in Texas (U.S. Census, 1991). These figures don't include those Latinos who lived in this region before these territories were annexed by the United States after the war with Mexico in 1848. It is difficult to accurately ascertain how many Mexican Americans live in this country, since many of them are here illegally or have become assimilated and do not identify as Latino.

Although some Mexican Americans have been able to move up socioeconomically, the majority of the population remains below the poverty line. After World War II, Mexican Americans made more efforts to gain political power in towns where they were in the majority, and to assert their rights, especially after their men had fought so valiantly in the war. There was a reawakening to the historical cruelty and unfairness by which they had lost their land, language, and culture after the Mexican War. The descendants of those early residents who lost all they had are often among the poorest today. In the 1960s, the Chicano movement emerged, progressive and radical, but it did not become a unifying force for Mexican Americans because many could not identify with its politics (Shorris, 1992). There continues to be a constant movement north, across the Mexican border and into this country, even though the protection at the gates has become stronger and opportunities for finding jobs here have lessened (Massey, 1993).

## PUERTO RICANS

Puerto Ricans, the second largest group, began to arrive in great numbers after the war and the great depression, in the late 1940s and early 1950s. According to the 1990 census, there are about 2,471,000 Puerto Ricans in the United

States. Most are settled in the Northeast, especially in New York City. Puerto Rican communities, however, are also found in other states such as Texas, Florida, and Illinois. Puerto Ricans say, "We are like white rice; you can find us anywhere you go." Many are racially mixed, representing the native Tainos, African slaves, and White Europeans, mostly Spaniards, who settled the island. Unlike other Latinos, they do not need special papers to come into the United States. U.S. citizenship was granted to them in 1917, when the island, a possession of the United States since 1898, gained more participation in its own government and obtained a Bill of Rights. Their pattern of migration has been characterized by a back-and-forth movement, different from other groups who must establish residency in this country before they can move about freely. For Puerto Ricans, going back to the island often represents a solution to the problems they face here, an oasis from the prejudice, discrimination, and isolation that plagues their lives.

Although they have citizenship, they are not acknowledged as citizens. Instead, most are relegated to an existence of marginality and hold the status of being the poorest among the Latino groups (Massey & Eggers, 1990). One-third of all Puerto Ricans living in the mainland live in poverty, and of great concern is that the unemployment rate is 31% for all Puerto Rican males and 59% for all females over the age of 16 (U.S. Census, 1991). Another compounding problem is that of all the Latino men in jail in New York, the majority are Puerto Rican (Novas, 1994). Drug addiction, alcoholism, and AIDS have also plagued the Puerto Rican population at home and on the mainland. It is interesting that those Puerto Ricans who migrate to regions in the United States other than New York seem to fare better economically than other Latinos in those areas. In Texas, for instance, Puerto Ricans graduate from college at a higher rate than Mexicans and have a higher income per capita. In Lorain, Ohio, and in San Francisco, they also have done well economically (Novas, 1994). Perhaps the high rate of unemployment and crime in New York City, as well as the history of discrimination they have experienced there, has led those with some potential to seek advancement elsewhere.

## CUBANS

Cubans are the third largest group of Latinos in the United States. According to the 1990 U.S. Census, there are about 1,000,000 Cubans presently residing in this country, and their population is concentrated in Florida, New York, and New Jersey. They began to arrive in large numbers in the 1960s, after Fidel Castro won the revolution in 1959 and established a revolutionary government. The United States, fearing the threat of communism so close to its shores and having to face its loss of economic control of the island, opened its doors to Cubans fleeing the new government (Bernal & Shapiro, Chapter 11, this volume).

Those who first arrived were mainly white, from the upper socioeconomic classes, with educational resources, business know how and financial backing (Bernal & Shapiro, Chapter 11, this volume). Most settled in Miami, in what became known as "Little Havana," and saw themselves as exiles waiting to return when the revolution was over. In the meantime, they used their skills, knowledge, and desire for enterprise to adjust and prosper. Unlike any other immigrant or exile group in the history of the United States, they also had the benefit of the "Cuban loan" and other government programs that provided direct assistance (Shorris, 1992). In fact, the $2.1 billion in aid for Cubans was greater than the entire budget for the Alliance for Progress, designed to finance what President Kennedy called "a true revolution for progress and freedom" throughout the whole of Latin America (Allman, 1987).

The common belief among Latinos that all Cubans are rich is, however, a fallacy. Despite the fact that Cubans are more affluent and have the highest rate of incorporation into the labor force of any Latino group, their average family income still falls below the national average (Novas, 1994). This is especially true when one considers the second wave of Cuban immigrants who came in 1980, known as "Marielitos," a pejorative label given to them after the name of the port in Cuba from which their boat departed. They differed from the first wave of Cuban immigrants in that the majority came from a lower socioeconomic background and were more racially mixed. Although many of them have done well, this group of Cubans, especially the darker ones, had to contend more directly with the negative effect of racism and prejudice in this country, as well as with a lack of welcome from sectors of the Cuban community who feared that their image would be tarnished by the new immigrants (Perez-Stable, 1981; Bernal & Shapiro, Chapter 11, this volume). They may experience closer identification with other Latino groups who see themselves as minorities in this society, unlike the earlier group who were primarily White and identified themselves with Spain and the elite classes.

## DOMINICANS

The number of Dominicans arriving in the United States has steadily increased in recent years as the economic situation in Santo Domingo worsens. In 1993, an estimated 800,000 lived in New York alone (Novas, 1994). The Dominican Republic occupies two-thirds of the island of Hispaniola, whereas Haiti occupies one-third on the western side. Columbus landed there in 1492, and it became the first colony settled by Spaniards in the New World. However, it soon became neglected after Mexico and Cuba were discovered, which made it easier for the French to settle the western part of the island. They brought massive numbers of slaves to work the land, who eventually rebelled against their owners and proclaimed their independence as Haiti. In 1822, the Haitians took over the eastern part of the island but lost it in 1844, when the Spanish-speaking people rebelled against them and proclaimed their independence as the Dominican Republic.

A source of conflict for many Dominicans has been that even though about 80% of the population is mulatto, a mixture of Black and White races, the government has held an unofficial policy against negritude or descendants of African slaves and an official policy in favor of the island's Spanish roots (Novas, 1994). This may be partly in reaction to the 1822 invasion by Haiti, a nation built by African slaves. Unlike other Caribbean islands, the government also seems to have a pro-Columbus attitude and almost a denial of the cruelty and devastation that the indigenous population and slaves underwent under the Spaniards.

To escape poverty and economic devastation, Dominicans often take the risk of crossing the ocean to Puerto Rico. If not caught by the patrols on the coast or killed in the treacherous waters, travel to the United States is almost guaranteed, since they can easily pass for Puerto Rican. Like Puerto Ricans, they tend to be more racially mixed than Cubans, who have traditionally kept more separation between the races. Also similar to Puerto Ricans, those who migrate tend to be of lower socioeconomic status. Among other Latinos, they are known to be industrious and, like Cubans, are perceived as aggressive. Most Dominicans have settled in New York and New Jersey, and as of 1991, 70% of Latino small businesses in New York City were owned by Dominicans (Novas, 1994).

## CENTRAL AMERICANS

Recently there has also been a large influx of Central Americans migrating to the United States, especially from Nicaragua, Guatemala, and El Salvador, due to the devastation of war in those countries. There are seven countries that comprise Central America: Belize, Costa Rica, El Salvador, Guatemala, Honduras, Nicaragua, and Panama. As of 1991, Central and South Americans represented 15.8% of the total Latino population in the United States (Novas, 1994). Most Central Americans leave their countries illegally and arrive as refugees, settling in cities where they find sanctuary. The aid and welcoming that the government offers to these groups is a far cry from what Cubans received when they first came in the 1960s. The movie *El Norte* portrays with much accuracy and sensitivity the plight that many Central Americans experience as they make the journey north. The character Rosa conveys the hopelessness that many experience as she sadly tells her brother prior to her death, "We couldn't stay in our village because they wanted to kill us, and we couldn't stay in Mexico because of the extreme poverty, and here we can't find a home because they don't accept us. Perhaps the only place where we will be able to find a home is when we die."

Foreign intervention and nationalism fueled the war in Nicaragua, and ideology, class tension, and poverty did the same in El Salvador, where, as in Guatemala, racial wars between the Mayan Indians and the White Ladinos (the Guatemalan term for all non-Indians, including Whites and mestizos) continue steadily to kill the Mayans (Krauss, 1991). Thousands of Nicaraguans have settled in Florida (Shorris, 1992), whereas the largest concentration of Salvadorians is in Los Angeles. Some studies indicate they number almost one million, but their numbers, as with many other Latino groups, cannot be documented, because most Central Americans living in the United States are here illegally (Montes Mozo & Garcia Vasquez, 1988). In California, some of the agencies dealing with Central Americans, such as the Central American Refugee Committee and the Central American Refugee Center, are confronted daily with the traumatic effects of war on many of the refugees (Shorris, 1992). In therapy their experiences with torture and terror are frequently major themes for treatment.

## SOUTH AMERICANS

South Americans represent a complexity of cultures that is markedly affected by geography and climate, as well as by the different races and groups of people who settled in the specific countries. "Differences in land, climate, and resources in pre-Columbian societies, and in degrees of a cultural influence by European colonial administrations led to major political and economic variations in South America." (Hopkins, 1987, p. 39). Colombians, for example, especially those on the Caribbean Coast, seem to have more in common with Costa Ricans than with Argentinians or Uruguayans, probably due in part to their location on the Caribbean and the effect of slavery on their cultures. The foods they eat and some of the linguistic colloquialisms they use are similar. Ecuador, Bolivia, and Peru have large indigenous populations that have significantly influenced the culture of these groups, yet they have also been at war with each other. Argentina, Chile, and Uruguay tend to be more European in nature, and their culture reflects the separation of immigrant groups and races (Calvert, 1993). Brazil is the only country in South America that was colonized by Portugal, and the Portugese influence can still be seen in the music, food, and language. As in the Caribbean, the indigenous population was killed by hard labor and punishment, and African slaves were brought to do the work. The mixture of races is reflected in the population, and there are also very strong indications of indigenous and African culture in the beliefs, values, and religious practices in Brazil. Many South American immigrants in the United States were Jews who had migrated there from Europe around the turn of the century or later. Although this group identifies as Latino, their experiences in those countries often kept them marginalized.

Although these differences are acknowledged among Latinos, once here, the process of being lumped together as one group by the rest of society takes place. Becoming citizens, or legal residents, does not necessarily stop others from perceiving them as "aliens" who are not as good as other citizens. In response to their experience of prejudice and discrimination, many change their names and try passing for White or Black "Americans," depending on their skin color and ability to speak English well. Others react by holding on very tightly to their native language and traditions as protection against the unwelcoming outside world. Regardless of differences, living in a country that is racist and unwelcoming, and that does not acknowledge their history is a common experience.

## CULTURAL IMPLICATIONS FOR TREATMENT

Although it is crucial to differentiate the ethnic identity of Latino families in therapy, there are certain commonalities that can inform therapeutic interventions. Spanish is a common language, except for Brazilians who speak Portuguese, and most belong to the Roman Catholic Church. There is an emphasis on spiritual values and an expressed willingness to sacrifice material satisfactions for spiritual goals. Personalism, a form of individualism that values those inner qualities in people that make them unique and give them a sense of self-worth, is another value that most Latinos seem to hold. In contrast, American individualism values achievement. Dignity of the individual and respect for authority are closely linked to personalism. Most Latinos will also agree that *machismo* and *marianismo* are constructs that tend to organize gender roles in their culture.

Perhaps the most significant value they share is the importance placed on family unity, welfare, and honor. The emphasis is on the group rather than on the individual. There is a deep sense of family commitment, obligation, and responsibility. The family guarantees protection and caretaking for life as long as the person stays in the system. It also offers individuals a measure of control for aggression and violence. The expectation is that when a person is having problems, others will help, especially those in stable positions. The family is usually an extended system that encompasses not only those related by blood and marriage, but also *compadres* (godparents) and *hijos de crianza* (adopted children, whose adoption is not necessarily legal). *Compadrazco* (godparenthood) is a system of ritual kinship with binding, mutual obligations for economic assistance, encouragement, and even personal correction. *Hijos de crianza* refers to the practice of transferring children from one nuclear family to another within the extended system in times of crisis. The others assume responsibility, as if children were their own, and do not view the practice as neglectful.

Often their respect for authority, a value that many of these groups have in common, keeps them from speaking up and asserting their rights. Especially for those who are here illegally, this becomes more problematic, because they live in constant fear of being caught and sent back to situations that were even more dangerous and oppressive, both socially and politically. With the passing of Proposition 187 in California, this fear has escalated, causing increasing stress for families already feeling displaced. For people in these situations coming to therapy, seeking social services, or health care becomes a threat, in addition to the fact that for most Hispanics or Latinos, going outside the family for help is only done as a last resort. People from countries such as Nicaragua, Salvador, Honduras, and Guatemala may be in the minority; however, their numbers seem to be rising, and like Mexicans, many face difficult encounters with immigration.

As with any other group, the most important concern they bring to therapy is a wish to improve their lives. Living in communities that are infested with crime, drugs, rape, and AIDS, most are frightened, especially for their children. Many are experiencing intense feelings of loss, missing the family left behind, or even fearing they may never be able to see them again because of politics or immigration laws. There is also a feeling of loss for the social status and connections in the country of origin, the smells and sounds of their surroundings, their friends and neighbors. Feeling isolated and pressured to change in ways that are not always understood often causes disruption and conflict in their lives. Adjustment to this culture depends on the reasons for coming to the United States, plans for staying or returning, the support received from family and friends, and their ability to assimilate new values without giving up the strengths of the old culture.

In therapy, eliciting, listening, and validating stories about how their lives are affected by living in this country will help families to view themselves and their problems in relation to a larger context, to see themselves beyond their problems, not circumscribed by them (Korin, 1994). Helping them to understand the cultural journey they have embarked upon is essential, since many, even after living here for decades, are still struggling with cultural shock. Some may experience living here as being caught between two worlds, without a secure foundation in either (Garcia-Preto, 1994). This is true of adolescents, especially females, who have spent their childhood here and have learned some of the cultural rules of this society, but at home are expected to behave according to the cultural traditions of the family. Couples also find themselves often struggling with conflicting cultural values. Engaging them in discussions that force them to reflect on cultural contrasts and on what they see as positive and negative about each culture may lead them to ways of relating that take from the old and the new. The idea that to make it in this country both men and women have to struggle together is generally accepted by Latinos and can be used to join the couple in a more egalitarian relationship. After all, they chose to come to this country in order to improve their situation. The metaphor of building bridges to connect the world they come from to the world they live in now helps them to take what is needed from both (Garcia-Preto, 1994). Validating the positives in their culture is essential to help Latinos rid themselves of shame, regain their dignity, make connections, and have a sense of community.

## REFERENCES

Allman, T. D. (1987). *Miami*. New York: Atlantic Monthly Press.

Bean, F. D., & Tienda, M. (1987). *The Hispanic population of the United States*. New York: Russell Sage.

Calvert, S., & Calvert, P. (1993). Latin America in the 20th century. New York: St. Martin's Press.

Chasteen, J. C., & Tulchin, J. S. (1994). *Problems in modern Latin America*. Washington, DC: Scholarly Resources.

Denton, N.A., & Massey, D.S. (1989). Racial identity among Caribbean Hispanics: The effect of double minority status on residential segregation. *American Sociological Review, 54*, 790–808.

Falicov, C. (1982). Mexican families. In M. McGoldrick, J. K. Pearce, & J. Giordano (Eds.), *Ethnicity and family therapy* (1st ed., pp. 134–163). New York: Guilford Press.

Falicov, Y. M., & Falicov, C. (1995). The effects of Prop. 187 on families: What therapists can do. *AFTA Newsletter, 59*, 51–54.

Garcia-Preto, N. (1994). On the bridge. *Family Therapy Networker, 18*(4), 35–37.

Griffin, K. (1995). Proposition 187. *Family Therapy Networker, 19*(2), 12–13.

Gonzalez, D. (1992). What is the problem with Hispanic? Just ask a Latino. *New York Times*.

Hakken, J. (1979). *Discrimination against Chicanos in the Dallas rental housing market: An experimental extension of the housing market practices survey*. Washington, DC: Office of Policy Development and Research, U.S. Department of Housing and Urban Development.

Hopkins, J. W. (1987). *Latin America: Perspectives on a region*. New York: Holmes & Meier.

Korin, E. (1994). Social inequalities and therapeutic relationships: Applying Freire's ideas to clinical practice. *Journal of Feminist Family Therapy, 5*(3/4), 75–98.

Krauss, C. (1991). *Inside Central America*. New York: Summit Books.

Massey, D. S. (1993). Latinos, poverty and the underclass: A new agenda for research. *Hispanic Journal of Behavioral Sciences, 15*(4), 449–475.

Massey, D. S., & Bitterman, B. (1985). Explaining the paradox of Puerto Rican segregation. *Social Forces, 64*, 306–331.

Massey, D. S., & Denton, N. A. (1992). Racial identity and the spatial assimilation of Mexican Americans in the United States. *Social Science Research, 22*, 1–27.

Massey, D. S., & Eggers, M. L. (1990). The ecology of inequality: Minorities and the concentration of poverty, 1970–1980. *American Journal of Sociology, 95*, 1153–1189.

Montes Mozo, S., & Garcia Vasquez, J. (1988). *Salvadoran migration to the U.S.: An exploratory study.* Washington, DC: Center for Immigration Policy and Refugee Assistance.

Novas, H. (1994). *Everything you need to know about Latino history.* New York: Plume/ Penguin Books.

Perez-Stable, E. J. (1981, February). *Cuban immigration: A socio-historical analysis.* Presentation at the Bicultural Association of Spanish Speaking Therapists and Advocates (BASSTA), San Francisco.

Reimers, C. W. (1985). A comparative analysis of the wages of Hispanics, Blacks, and non-Hispanic Whites. In G. J. Borjas & M. Tienda (Eds.), *Hispanics in the U.S. economy* (pp. 27–76). Orlando, FL: Academic Press.

Rodriguez, C. E. (1991). The effect of race on Puerto Rican wages. In E. Melendez, C. Rodriguez, & J. B. Figueroa (Eds.), *Hispanics in the labor force: Issues and policies* (pp. 77–100). New York: Plenum Press.

Shorris, E. (1992). *Latinos.* New York: Norton.

Telles, E. E., & Murguia, E. (1990). Phenotypic discrimination and income differences among Mexican Americans. *Social Science Quarterly, 71,* 682–696.

U.S. Bureau of the Census. (1991). *Statistical abstract of 1991.* Washington, DC: U.S. Government Printing Office.

Yinger, J. (1991). *Housing discrimination study: Incidence of discrimination and variations in discriminatory behavior.* Washington, DC: U.S. Department of Housing and Urban Development, Office of Policy Development and Research.

# CHAPTER 11

# Cuban Families

## Guillermo Bernal
## Ester Shapiro

Thirty-year-old Daisy Fuentes, the MTV veejay and one of the most visible icons of the Cuban American migration, was in Namibia to cohost the 1995 Miss Universe pageant. She was overheard by Cuban music producer Emilio Estefan, shrieking into the phone loud enough to be heard in the hotel hallway: "Mami, mami! It's me! Estoy en Africa. Sí, mami, AF-RI-CA!" (Balsameda, 1995). Ms. Fuentes is a member (as are this chapter's authors) of what Cuban American literary critic Gustavo Pérez-Firmat (1994) calls the "one-and-a-half": children born in Cuba and growing up in the United States among the 1.1 million Cubans who migrated after the 1959 triumph of the Cuban revolution. The story of the Cuban American family experience must be told as an intergenerational narrative of love, loyalty, and longing, within which memory is a highly contested political territory. Socioeconomic, political, cultural, and historical events spanning centuries, but accelerating in the last 35 years, have impacted directly on intimate family relationships and their expression in the developmental pathways of all its members.

Intergenerational tensions within Cuban families have been documented not only within the family therapy field, but also by Cuban American writers, many of whom evocatively describe their struggles to preserve family loyalty while defining their own relationship to both Cuban and American identities. Christina García's *Dreaming in Cuban* (1992) describes the humorous and tragic dialogues between a mother, Lourdes Puente, for whom Castro is the devil incarnate barring return to that Caribbean Gulag, and her daughter, Pilar, whose own developmental search requires an emotional and physical return to the island, with its lost landscapes and severed family relationships. Performance artist Alina Troyano, who created the outrageous theatrical persona Carmelita Tropicana, documents in the autobiographical "Milk of Amnesia/ Leche de Amnesia" (1995) her own problematic attempts at Americanization and the return of the repressed "Cubanidad." Cuban American critic and performance artist Coco Fusco (Fusco, 1994, 1995) displays a photograph of her mother carrying her as an infant as they descend from the plane after leaving Cuba. Like Ester Rebeca Shapiro Rok's photo (Shapiro, 1994a) of her family's last Purim in a Havana synagogue, Fusco's photograph marks a moment of migration frozen in time to which the family returns, again and again, in building and rebuilding the dislocated intergenerational relationships out of which Cuban American family life is made. This chapter draws from literary sources, such as *testimonios* and memoirs, as well as social science and family therapy sources, to describe Cuban American family experience and to suggest effective therapeutic responses that understand our families in socioeconomic, political, cultural, and historical context. Since we believe that an understanding of the broader social context is an inseparable aspect of working with Cuban families, we begin with a brief description of the context.

Cuba is the largest island in the Caribbean, with a total area of 44,218 square miles (about the size of Pennsylvania). Because of its unique geographical position between the Florida and Yucatan peninsulas, some historians have suggested that Cuba's historical significance is out of proportion to its size (Foner, 1962). To the Spanish, Cuba was quite literally the "key" to the Americas, since traffic bound to and from Mexico, Peru, and other points in South America generally stopped in Havana. Indeed, at different moments in history, access to the Americas was possible only through Cuba.

The strategic economic, political, and military significance that Cuba had for Spain was evident to the emerging powerful nation only 90 miles away. Cuba's War of Independence from Spain eventually attracted a major U.S. intervention nearly 100 years ago (1898). The United States invaded Cuba as well as Puerto Rico, the Philippines, and Guam, during the Spanish–American War. Cuba was able to achieve independence, while Puerto Rico, the Philippines, and Guam became U.S. colonies. However, independence came at the price of a military base (Guantanamo Bay) and an amendment to the Cuban Constitution giving the United States the right to intervene in internal Cuban affairs. After three decades of political conflicts and subsequent interventions, the Platt Amendment was repealed in 1933.

Cuba remained bound to U.S. interests until the revolution in 1959. An analysis of the historical developments that preceded the revolution is beyond the scope of this chapter; there are a number of volumes available on this topic (e.g., Castro, 1972, 1975; Pérez-Stable, 1993; Thomas, 1977).

The radical programs promoted by the revolutionary government produced changes in the social, economic, and political structures of society. These changes, together with a U.S. economic blockade, produced dissatisfaction within sectors of Cuban society leading to a unique migration, primarily to the United States. The abruptness of the Cuban migration, its magnitude within relatively brief periods, and its predominantly middle- and upper-class composition (particularly during the early migration waves) amplified its impact and created a special situation in relation to other Latinos and Latinas in the United States.

## CUBAN MIGRATION IN CONTEXT

Cubans have been migrating to the United States since the middle of the 19th century. The two countries share a common history that dates back almost 200 years. The Cuban wars of independence (1868–1878 and 1895–1898) also sent many Cubans to the United States as exiles, where often they were a support community for the proindependence forces. Overall, there were perhaps 30,000 Cubans in the United States by 1958 (West, 1995). The largest Cuban immigration has occurred since the triumph of the Cuban revolution in 1959: Over 1.1 million Cubans have left their homeland. Almost 90% of Cuban Americans live in four states: Florida, New Jersey, New York, and California, with a majority (60%) in Florida. Puerto Rico also has a large Cuban community (Cobas & Duany, 1995).

Although Cubans number less than 5% of the overall Latino and Latina population in the United States, they have been singled out as a success story and viewed as a "model minority." Cuban Americans currently earn about 17% more than other Latino groups, although they still average 12% less than Anglos (Bernal & Enchautegui, 1994; West, 1995). However, the relative success of Cubans in the United States must be understood in terms of the sociohistorical context of the Cuban migration and its political meaning in the context of the Cold War (1945–1990) and U.S. foreign policy. The Cuban migration served a number of U.S. foreign policy interests, such as destabilizing Cuba, pointing to the dangers of communism, and highlighting a contemporary example of the rag-to-riches story of an immigrant group (Bernal, 1982; Bernal & Gutierrez, 1988; West, 1995).

Cuban success in the United States is associated with the nature of the Cuban migration and its historical context (Bernal, 1982; Bernal & Gutierrez, 1988). For example, in sharp contrast to the characteristics of Mexicans and Puerto Ricans (see Chapters 12 and 13), the Cuban migration of the 1960s primarily included White, educated, upper- and middle-class professional groups that were less likely to experience racial barriers. Also, these waves of immigrants had educational and business know-how, shared U.S. cultural values, and received financial support from major federal programs (Bernal, 1982; Bernal & Gutierrez, 1988).

For our purposes, four phases of migration may be identified, the first from 1959 to 1965. During the beginning of this phase, immigrants left Cuba for "political" reasons and families were primarily from the upper and upper-middle classes. Later, after the failure of the Bay of Pigs invasion, a second group constituted the "real refugees" (Amaro & Portes, 1972) since they left with no idea of possible return. This group comprised primarily middle-class professionals who could not adapt to the revolutionary changes.

The second phase began in 1965 and ended in 1973. The Camarioca port was opened to Cubans in the United States who wished to pick up their relatives by boat. Approximately 5,000 people left prior to the negotiations that resulted in the "Freedom Flights" or airlifts from Havana to Miami. Cubans leaving at this time were more likely to be middle and lower-middle class migrants who resembled traditional immigrants who came to the United States in search of better economic opportunities. These early phases of Cuban immigration did not represent the Cuban population as a whole (Bernal, 1982; Fagan, Brody, & O'Leary, 1968), being primarily comprised of Whites, females, and older immigrants.

When the Carter administration negotiated with Cuba to permit family visits for the first time, Cuban families living in the States appeared in Cuba with U.S. dollars and the visible products of a consumer culture. These contacts helped unleash social forces that exploded in April 1980, when a group of Cubans crashed the gates of the Peruvian embassy in Havana, requesting political asylum. When the Peruvian embassy did not immediately return the refugees, Castro again declared that anyone wishing to leave Cuba should seek exit visas at the Peruvian embassy. In a matter of days, 10,000 Cubans poured into the embassy. Negotiations then began with the U.S. government, which opened the way for 135,000 Cubans to immigrate during the next 5 months, mostly through the port of Mariel. This third phase of refugees, disparagingly identified as *Marielitos*, was mostly working class or unemployed and had a larger percentage of Afro-Cubans. Although the United States and Cuba negotiated an orderly immigration policy after the 1980 Mariel incidents, Cuba broke off the agreement in May 1985, when Washington began broadcasting Radio Marti.

A fourth phase of migration began to coalesce beginning in 1990, when the Cuban economy began its *periodo especial* (special period) after the disintegration of the Soviet Union and the end of aid to Cuba. Compounded by the U.S. economic blockade, the years from 1991 to the present have been characterized by extraordinary economic hardship for the Cuban people, and an increased number of them are willing to take great risks to reach the United States. This crisis reached its peak in the summer of 1994, when thousands of Cubans tried to elude their coastal police and attempted to cross the straits of Florida on makeshift rafts. In July and August, when the flow of *balseros* (rafters) was becoming impossible to control, and in the absence of any U.S. interest in opening talks on immigration policy, Havana again declared that anyone wishing to leave Cuba could do so. Over 37,000 *balseros* attempted passage. About 20,000 were intercepted by the U.S. Coast Guard and sent to Guantanamo Bay. Subsequently, Cuba and the United States negotiated a settlement to the crisis that allows the *balseros* at Guantanamo to emigrate to the United States and permits 20,000 Cubans to legally emigrate each year.

The political and economic situation in Cuba remains difficult. Although the recent legalization of the dollar and diversification of the economy has improved the daily life of Cubans, these measures have also polarized society between those who have and those who do not have access to U.S. dollars. The

U.S. government continues its policy of economic blockade, under the misguided notion that continuing to do so will promote change. As the two countries continue their polarized ideological battles, an increasing number of Cubans in both Cuba and the United States are softening political barriers and seeking greater contact between the two communities, which share an intense if embattled kinship.

## CUBAN CULTURAL HERITAGE

The creative integration of many cultural threads, including those found in the new Cuban American context, characterizes the struggle of Cuban families to define new identities in the United States while preserving continuity with and retaining loyalty to the culture of origin. This process of cultural transformation[1] can best be understood in its intergenerational and developmental context (Bernal, 1982; Bernal & Gutierrez, 1988; Shapiro, 1994a, 1994b, 1996), as will be emphasized throughout the remainder of this chapter.

Researchers and clinicians have focused on an appreciation of cultural values in working with Cuban families (Bernal, 1982; Queralt, 1984; Rumbaut & Rumbaut, 1976; Szapocznik, Kurtines, & Hanna, 1979). Cubans share many Latin American and African cultural patterns (Bustamante & Santa Cruz, 1975; Ortiz, 1973), such as the value of the family, language, and social supports. Here, we provide a brief sketch of Cuban cultural traits.

### The Family

The role of the family is central to Cubans. *Familismo* is a cultural attitude and value that places the interests of the family over the interest of the individual and is the basis of the Cuban family structure (Bernal, 1982; Queralt, 1984). The bonds of loyalty and unity, which include nuclear and extended family members, characterize the Cuban family.[2]

Maintaining a traditional family hierarchy with the man as provider depends on social and economic factors. *Respeto* is a means of reinforcing male authority over women and children. Conflicts may arise when the wife works, shifting the economic basis of the marriage. Also, as family members acculturate, conflicts emerge from the clash of values between generations (Bernal, 1982; Bernal & Gutierrez, 1988; Szapocznik & Truss, 1978). As previously noted, the nature of Cuban marriages and family life is related to social class, degree of acculturation and migration stage, and the legacy of Latino family values remains strong. The notions of *machismo* and female purity are apparent in contemporary Cuban relationships. For example, childrearing practices emphasize protection of the girl's innocence. Indeed, the use of chaperones in courtship remains common with many Cuban families (Bernal & Gutierrez, 1988).

## Language and Values

While the preservation of language has been, for the most part, possible among Cuban American families in the "one-and-a-half" generation, language preservation has been much more difficult for children born in the United States to Cuban families. Miami public schools pioneered well-organized programs of bilingual education, but current "English only" movements have made bilingual education a much less supported program. The erosion of language as a rich resource for cultural heritage, especially in the face of hostile monolingualism reflected in the dominant North American culture, is a problem for most Latino and Latina families in the United States, whose ethnic socialization includes language as a key dimension of cultural continuity (Bernal & Knight, 1993). The intergenerational tensions created by the political cutoff between Cuban Americans and their culture and country of origin contributed to families within which the parents protect a status image of the lost country. By holding onto a lost and idealized Cuba, such static images imposed on the younger generation limit the children's access to developmental resources as they become adults in a new context. An understanding of the intergenerational and political dimensions of the loss of culture in overassimilated "de-Cubanization" is critical. Such an understanding may make it possible for therapists to support the recapturing of language and the return to cultural roots, that is, to facilitate a "re-Cubanization" (Bernal, 1982).

Cuban values have been studied by various clinicians and investigators (e.g., Bernal, 1982; Queralt, 1984; Marín et al., 1986; Szapocznik, Kurtines, & Hanna, 1979). Overall, Cubans value and interpersonal orientation over impersonal abstractions and ideas. *Personalismo* represents a preference for personal contacts and social situations. Perhaps the *choteo* is the incarnation of Cuban *personalismo*. *Choteo* is a form of humor directed at ridiculing everything and anyone (Bernal, 1982). Ortiz (1973) considers *choteo* a typical Cuban phenomenon that involves exaggerating things out of proportion. *Choteo* is a means of reducing tension in difficult social encounters and establishing interpersonal closeness. When combined with *tuteo*, the informal use of "you," an even closer interpersonal contact is achieved.

Marín et al. (1986) found more similarities than differences among the main Latino and Latina groups in the United States. However, Cubans scored closer to the Anglo groups on values than to other Latinos and Latinas in the sample. Cubans tend to endorse individualistic responses in problem solving more often than other groups. Also, Cubans tend to prefer hierarchy and linearity in family relations. The values of action in the "here and now" are favored (Bernal, 1982; Szapocznick, Scopetta, Arnalde, & Kurtines, 1978). Clearly, in considering a treatment strategy, therapists that are present oriented, focus on problem-solving, consider the family hierarchy, and involve the family are more likely to achieve effective results.

## Social Supports

Traditional and nontraditional systems of support are firmly established in the Cuban community. Religious, social, health, political, and neighborhood organizations are an important part of community life. One of the first organized systems of support was established by the Federal Government—the Cuban Refugee Center—which provided food, clothing, and shelter. In fact, at the time of this writing, U.S. Government loans and financial assistance to Cuban families total over $2 billion, which is greater than what Washington spent on the entire Alliance for Progress program during the 1960s for all of Latin American. This has enabled Cuban Americans, especially those in the first wave of migrations, to achieve a degree of social mobility that has been rare among foreign-born U.S. populations. The existence of economically successful Cuban American enclaves in Miami, West New York, and New Jersey has created highly visible, politically organized, and powerful communities that have supported the successful preservation of a strong Cuban American presence with a distinct cultural identity (Lamphere, 1992).

Religion is another instrument of support, primarily through the Church. Catholicism is the major religious preference, but the number of practicing Catholics has decreased (Cobas & Duany, 1995; Rogg & Cooney, 1980). The formal structures for spiritual support may be an important resource in therapy, particularly for elderly Cubans.

Less traditional forms of support are found in the folk-healing systems that are part of the Cuban heritage. *Botánicas* are visible in most Latino and Latina communities; these are stores that sell herbs, potions, and candles, and often are operated by *santeros* or *espiritistas*. *Santeros* are priests from the Afro Cuban Santeria religion that integrates Catholic and African Yoruba beliefs, and is described elsewhere (Bernal, 1982; Bernal & Gutierrez, 1988). Clinician should be aware that mobilizing the support systems available through *santeros* and *espiritistas* can serve as an important resource to the family in therapy.

## CLINICAL CONSIDERATIONS

Cuban families have created distinctive intergenerational family relationships under the influence of the cultural, political, and historical forces described earlier as they intersect with the evolving family life cycle (Carter & McGoldrick, 1980; Shapiro, 1994a, 1994b). Because the political circumstances of Cuban migration have caused family cutoffs and profound losses, strong tensions around family ethics and loyalty obligations have characterized the evolving relationships of Cuban families in the United States. In the 1982 edition of this volume, Bernal described cases in which members of the "one-and-a-half" generation voiced, at times directly, at times symptomatically, the burdens of immigration hardship and loss, as well as the wish to join the new culture while honoring a living, evolving image of the Cuba left behind. The danger in these families was an unacknowledged confrontation over the image of Cuba, which on the one hand was idealized and frozen in time, and on the other, represented forbidden political territory.

As Cuban American families establish roots in the United States and face the reality that the myth of return is fading, they present in family therapy in different ways. The birth of a new generation of children and grandchildren, the intermarriage of Cubans with Anglos (as well as with other ethnic groups), and the difficulty maintaining language in the U.S.-born generation all contribute to the evolving family life cycle relationships, which must still incorporate dialogue concerning cultural continuity as well as cultural creativity and change. Partly because of the many losses, partly because of a strong Cuban presence in large enclave communities, Cuban families have tenaciously succeeded in preserving language, family, and culture, which creates dilemmas for a generation growing up exposed to North American values emphasizing individual strivings over family attachments.

Guidelines for the engagement and treatment of Cubans in therapy have been the focus of a number of chapters and volumes (Bernal, 1982; Bernal & Gutierrez, 1988; Szapocznik & Kurtines, 1989). In general, the clinician is required to have family therapy skills, cultural competence, and sensitivity to cultural issues. More specifically, knowledge of the Spanish language is essential, as it is often through language that cultural issues are expressed. It is also important to appreciate the phases of migration and the connectedness to the culture of origin, and to evaluate the impact of the stress of migration, value conflicts, and developmental conflicts. Our focus here is on the interface between sociohistorical issues and cultural processes relevant to the family evaluation and treatment of Cubans in the United States.

Some examples are offered to illustrate issues faced by Cuban families in the States.

## The Ruiz Family

Juan Prado and Marta Ruiz, a Cuban-born couple, both age 32, with a 2-year-old daughter, Susan, entered couple therapy because Juan had an affair. Both were born in Cuba and immigrated to the United States in the early 1960s as children; they had been high school sweethearts in Miami, where their families had known each other in a predominantly Cuban neighborhood. They moved to Boston to attend college and graduate school, with the shared expectation that they would return to the Miami area to raise their family. At the time Susan was conceived, Juan was completing his business studies and Marta was completing a graduate degree in education, so they had been able to persuade their families that they needed a little more time before they returned to Miami to raise their family and for Juan to begin work in the family business.

Juan had initiated an affair with an Anglo classmate at his business school, just prior to graduation and to the negotiated deadline when they would move back to Miami. Although Juan and Marta could acknowledge that completing graduate school and starting a family had taken a great toll on their marriage, they were less aware of how Juan's affair might be a response to the moment when they might feel obligated to return to Miami and an all-encompassing involvement with their families. Once these issues of loyalty obligations were brought into the couple therapy, Juan was able to explore with Marta their own family decision making, as it included their extended families. They decided a return to Miami made sense for them as a couple, but Juan needed some time to establish himself in work outside the family business before making a commitment to Marta's family in that sphere of his life as well.

———— ✄ ————

## The Dominguez Family

Carlos and Nancy Dominguez brought in their 8-year-old son, Bobby, for an assessment because his behavior was out of control at home and at school; they wondered if their child was hyperactive. Carlos, 42, had been born in Cuba and had grown up in Queens, New York. He met Nancy Owens, 32, of Boston Irish Catholic background, when he was completing his surgery residency and she was a student nurse. Although he had told her about his Cuban background, his lack of an accent and physical distance from his family in Queens made their close-knit family habits a distant reality. She saw her own parents, who lived in Boston, once or twice a year, far less often than Carlos had been visiting his parents when they first met. As the family grew, first Bobby and then Lindsay, 3 years later, Carlos began to make less frequent visits to his parents. Upon evaluating Bobby, who was mildly distractible but quite responsive to consistent structure in school and at home, a recommendation was made for family therapy as a way of exploring parental inconsistency and other family issues contributing to Bobby's behavior problems. In collecting a family history, it emerged that Carlos's younger sister, Irma, had stayed close to home, attending Queens College and marrying the son of a Cuban refugee family. When Irma's husband and 12-year-old son were killed in an automobile accident 1 year earlier, Carlos's family's needs and expectations for support increased enormously. Carlos felt terribly caught between his obligations to his sister and grieving parents, and his wife's expectations that their family would come first. He had attended his brother-in-law's and nephew's funeral and wake, but then had permitted work obligations to provide the justification for why he couldn't make regular return visits to his grieving sister and parents. In a poignant family session, Bobby expressed his sense of sadness and confusion at the death of his uncle and especially his cousin, who provided a literally understandable bilingual link to the more foreign world of his old-fashioned Dominguez grandparents, who still spoke Spanish at home and called him Robertico. Bobby's grief, and its reflection and resonance in his father's grief, had gone underground in the family because exposing their shared grief might push Carlos too far over into the gravitational pull of his extended family obligations. When Nancy realized the burden of family grief that Bobby was carrying, she began to accept the importance of strengthening ties to the Dominguez family, as well as opening up communication within their own family about Bobby's connections to his Cuban cultural identity. Carlos, too, needed to explore how he had used Nancy's more distant family style as a means of extricating himself from family connections he did not know how to negotiate in a more modulated way. His work hours had conspired with his parenting responsibilities to make it hard to travel to Queens and easy to lose contact with his parents. The crisis of death and grief in the Dominguez extended family renewed a family conversation concerning the preservation of family connections, and Carlos began to make more frequent weekend visits with both children without Nancy, as well as visits in which she was included.

—————— ❧ ——————

## The Otero Family

Yvette, 24, was referred for treatment due to a major depression. She had migrated with her brother to Florida through a third country in early 1994, and went to live with their father, who had migrated to the United States about 5 years earlier. During a professional visit to the United States, her mother decided not to return to Cuba, shortly after the United States and Cuba immigration agreement of 1994. Although Yvette's parents had been divorced for over 10 years, her mother now lived with her ex-husband and two children in a small studio apartment. During an initial interview, it became clear that Yvette and her brother had been pawns in their parents' marital struggle. During the economic hardships of the *periodo especial*, the father convinced his children to migrate to the United States. The mother felt that life without her children lacked meaning and took the first opportunity to join them. However, the land of plenty was not what she had expected, as her ex-husband had painted a rosier economic picture of the exile reality. He held a professional job, but his means were limited. The mother, a professional in Cuba, now worked as a salesperson at a local flea market. Yvette and her brother, both college graduates and with professional degrees, were unemployed. Acknowledgment of Yvette's multiple losses (work, family, country), a validation of the complex family situation in which the conditions they had in Cuba have been recreated, and the mobilization of resources to deal with the crisis of migration were central in her treatment.

—————— ❧ ——————

## CONCLUSIONS

In this chapter, we have proposed the integration of contextual, developmental, and cultural approaches consistent with the concept of transculturation as a way of describing creative cultural encounter and intergenerational dialogue that creates new cultural forms. While at the international level, the Cold War has been over since 1989, it has remained a reality between the United States and Cuba. In fact, when we began to write this chapter, the Clinton administration had announced the lifting of sanctions allowing visits to Cuba by Cuban Americans, and permitting other cultural and professional exchanges. At the same time, the U.S. Congress was preparing a bill to tighten the economic blockade on Cuba. More recently, an incident over the downing of two planes over Cuba has magnified the Cold War rhetoric. The political, social, and economic context remains an inseparable aspect of work with Cuban families.

Despite the tensions of a continued Cold War rhetoric and the public protection of not negotiating with Castro, privately, the Cuban community in the United States is undergoing an important transformation as it is "re-Cubanized" with the more recent waves of migrants. Individually, Cubans who have opted for an integration of both U.S. and Cuban cultures (Szapocznik & Kurtines, 1989) and who longed to be reunited with their families searching an affirmation of their cultural heritage have continued to do so despite the public anti-Cuba discourse. Pérez Firmat's (1995) *Next Year in Cuba* offers powerful insights into the Cuban cultural experience and it stands out as a testament of cultural affirmation. At one point he writes:

> Although sometimes I have been unwilling to admit this, I can stop being Cuban no more than I can get out of my skin . . . unlike what I once thought, being Cuban does not depend on the pictures on your wall or the women in your bed or the food on your plate or the trees beyond your window. Because Cuba is my past, Cuba is my present and my future. I will never not be Cuban. Whether a burden or a blessing being Cuban in America is for me inescapable. (p. 259)

Recently, in *Bridges to Cuba* (Behar, 1995), and earlier in *Contra Viento y Marea* (Grupo Areito, 1978), autobiographical descriptions of efforts to reconnect with Cuban cultural roots are described. These effort in facing losses, establishing reconnections with the culture of origin, and dialogue between families who migrated and those who chose to stay are encouraging signs of a reintegration among Cuban families. The time may be near when it might be possible to go beyond bridging cultural, political, and generational rifts, and toward a true integration among the different sectors of Cuban families outside as well as inside Cuba. Such integration is only possible if it is based on tolerance, acceptance, and respect for difference. We believe this process has begun.

## NOTES

1. Writers have described the Cuban culture as offering the example of "transculturation," in which cultures meet and transform one another. Anthropologist Fernando Ortiz first offered the term "transculturation" in the 1940s to oppose the

newly coined and still tenacious anthropological term "acculturation," which Oritz (1973) found too unabashed in its colonializing assumptions and inaccurate in describing the Cuban experience. Ortiz, followed by Afro-Cuban poet Nancy Morejon (1993), views Cuban culture as the creative intermingling of indigenous Spanish, African, and Asian cultures, each newly arriving group contributing something to the *ajiaco*, or stew, whose ingredients are enriched by the presence of all the others. The slave trade in Cuba increased its activity relatively late in the declining years of slavery, and Cuba always had a substantial proportion of its Black population who had been permitted to buy their freedom and lived as poor laborers with working-class links to poor Whites. These coalitions of free Blacks, poor Whites, and slaves created the persistent independence movements, and provided the unified political base for the triumph of the Cuban revolution. While Cuba, like other Caribbean and Latin American countries, has retained its share of skin-based racism, social integration was always determined by socioeconomic and political factors as well as race and was not polarized as Black–White racism in the United States.

2. If we follow Ortiz and Morejon to explore the implications of transculturation as an alternative to acculturation in the intergenerational experience of Cuban families, we find that the possibility for cultural creativity is enhanced. Whereas acculturation implies the culture loss of Cubanidad as a primary source for individual and family identity, transculturation emphasizes the continuity, mutual transformation, and culture change. American-style independence grants both men and women greater personal freedom for role inventiveness, as long as it is well balanced by the needs for interdependence and family connections which are an important contribution of Cuban identity. Testimonials of Cuban Americans in the "one-and-a-half" generation describe their journey—as adults whose images of Cuba have frozen in time, and who have experienced politically motivated family cutoffs—to return and bring back living images of Cuba and restored family connections. These bridges to Cuba enrich the family's ongoing development (Fusco, 1994, 1995; Gonzales-Mandri, 1994; Risech, 1994; Shapiro, 1994a, 1996; Torres, 1994; Troyano/Tropicana, 1995).

## REFERENCES

Amaro, N., & Portes, A. (1972). Situación de los grupos Cubanos en Estados Unidos. *Aportes, 23,* 6–14.

Balsameda, L. (1995). The drive of Miss Daisy. *Sí, 1,* 28–32.

Behar, R. (1995). *Bridges to Cuba/Puentes a Cuba.* Ann Arbor: University of Michigan Press.

Bernal, G. (1982). Cuban families. In M. McGoldrick, J. K. Pearce, & J. Giordano (Eds.), *Ethnicity and family therapy* (1st ed., pp. 187–207). New York: Guilford Press.

Bernal, G., & Enchautegui, N. (1994). Latinos and Latinas in community psychology: A review of the literature. *American Journal of Community Psychology, 22,* 531–557.

Bernal, G., & Gutierrez, M. (1988). Cubans. In L. Comas-Díaz & E. E. H. Griffith (Eds.), *Clinical guidelines in cross-cultural mental health* (pp. 233–261). New York: Wiley.

Bernal, M., & Knight, G. (Eds.). (1993). *Ethnic identity: Formation and transmission among Hispanic and other minorities.* Albany, NY: SUNY Press.

Bustamante, J. A., & Santa Cruz, A. (1975). *Psiquiatria transcultural.* Havana: Editorial Cientifico-Técnica.

Carter, E. A., & McGoldrick, M. (Eds.). (1980). *The family life cycle: A framework for family therapy.* New York: Gardner Press.

Castro, F. (1972). *Revolutionary struggle.* Cambridge, MA: MIT Press.

Castro, F. (1975). *Discursos* (Vol. 1). Havana: Editorial de Ciencias Sociales.

Cobas, J., & Duany, J. (1995). *Los cubanos en Puerto Rico: Economia, étnia e identidad cultural.* San Juan: Editorial de la Universidad de Puerto Rico.

Fagan, R. R., Brody, R. A., & O'Leary, T. J. (1968). *Cubans in exile: Disaffection and the revolution.* Palo Alto, CA: Stanford University Press.

Foner, P. S. (1962). *A history of Cuba and its relation to the United States* (Vol. 1). New York: International Publishers.

Fusco, C. (1994). El diario de Miranda/Miranda's diary. In R. Behar & J. Leon (Eds.), Bridges to Cuba/Puentes a Cuba. *Michigan Quarterly Review, 33,* 477–496.

Fusco, C. (1995). *English is broken here.* New York: New Press.

Garcia, C. (1992). *Dreaming in Cuban.* New York: Ballantine.

Gonzales-Mandri, F. (1994). A house on shifting sands. In R. Behar & J. Leon (Eds.), Bridges to Cuba/Puentes a Cuba. *Michigan Quarterly Review, 33,* 553–556.

Grupo Areito. (1978). *Contra viento y Marea.* Havana: Casa de las Américas.

Lamphere, L. (Ed.). (1992). *Structuring diversity: Ethnographic perspectives on the new immigration.* Chicago: Univerity of Chicago Press.

Marín, G., VanOss Marín, B., Sabogal, F., Otero-Sabogal, R., & Pérez-Stable, E. J. (1986). *Subcultural differences in values among Hispanics: The role of acculturation.* San Francisco: University of California Hispanic Smoking Cessation Research Project.

Morejon, N. (1993). Race and nation. In P. Sarduy & J. Stubbs (Eds.), *AfroCuba: An anthology of Cuban writing on race, politics and culture* (pp. 227–237). New York: Ocean Press and Center for Cuban Studies.

Ortiz, F. (1973). *Contrapunteo Cubano de tabaco y el azúcar.* Barcelona: Editorial Ariel. (Also published in English by Duke University Press in 1995)

Pérez Firmat, G. (1994). *Life on the hyphen.* Austin: University of Texas Press.

Pérez Firmat, G. (1995). *Next year in Cuba: A Cubano's coming of age in America.* New York: Anchor Book (p. 256).

Pérez-Stable, M. (1993). *The Cuban revolution: Origins, course, and legacy.* New York: Oxford University Press.

Queralt, M. (1984, March–April). Understanding Cuban immigrants: A cultural perspective. *Social Work,* 115–121.

Risech, F. (1994). Political and cultural cross-dressing: Negotiating a second generation Cuban-American identity. In R. Behar & J. Leon (Eds.), Bridges to Cuba/Puentes a Cuba. *Michigan Quarterly Review, 33,* 526–540.

Rogg, E. M., & Cooney, R. S. (1980). *Adaptation and adjustment of Cubans: West New York, New Jersey.* New York: Hispanic Research Center.

Rumbaut, D. R., & Rumbaut, R. G. (1976). The family in exile: Cuban expatriates in the United States. *American Journal of Psychiatry, 133,* 395–399.

Shapiro, E. (1994a). Finding what had been lost in plain view. In R. Behar & J. Leon (Eds.), Bridges to Cuba/Puentes a Cuba. *Michigan Quarterly Review, 33,* 579–589.

Shapiro, E. (1994b). *Grief as a family process: A developmental approach to clinical practice.* New York: Guilford Press.

Shapiro, E. (1996). Exile and identity: On going back to Cuba. *Cultural Diversity and Mental Health, 2,* 21–33.

Szapocznik, J., & Kurtines, W. (1989). *Breakthroughs in family therapy with drug abusing and problem youth.* New York: Springer.

Szapocznik, J., Kurtines, W., & Hanna, N. (1979). Comparison of Cuban and Anglo-American cultural values in a clinical population. *Journal of Consulting and Clinical Psychology, 47*(3), 623–624.

Szapocznik, J., Scopetta, M. A., Arnalde, M., & Kurtines, W. (1978). Cuban value structure: Treatment implications. *Journal of Consulting and Clinical Psychology, 46*(5), 961–970.

Szapocznik, J., & Truss, C. (1978). Intergenerational source of role conflict in Cuban mothers. In M. Montiel (Ed.), *Hispanic families.* Washington, DC: Consortium of Spanish Speaking Mental Health Organizations.

Thomas, H. (1977). *The Cuban revolution.* New York: Harper & Row.

Torres, M. (1994). Beyond the rupture: Reconciling with our enemies, reconciling with ourselves. In R. Behar & J. Leon (Eds.), Bridges to Cuba/Puentes a Cuba. *Michigan Quarterly Review, 33,* 419–436.

Troyano, A. (a.k.a. Tropicana, C.). (1995). Milk of Amnesia/Leche de Amnesia. *The Dream Review, 39,* 94–111.

West, A. (1995). Cuba and Cuban Americans: History, politics and culture. In F. Menchaca (Ed.), *American journey: The Hispanic American experience.* [CD-ROM]. Woodbridge, CN: Primary Source Media.

# CHAPTER 12

# Mexican Families

## Celia Jaes Falicov

This chapter focuses on four key parameters for understanding Mexican American families: migration/acculturation, ecological context, family organization, and family life cycle. A rationale for the use of these four parameters in culture and family therapy appears in a recent article (Falicov, 1995). My observations derive from extensive clinical work with Mexicans in the Midwestern and Western United States.

## MIGRATION/ACCULTURATION

Descendants of Mexicans have lived in the Southwest for several generations prior to the United States appropriation of those lands. However, the majority of Mexican Americans are either born in Mexico, or are the offspring of Mexican-born parents (Vega, 1990). Spanish is their native tongue, or it was spoken in their homes as children. They are voluntary immigrants who are motivated to improve their economic situation.

Complementarity of economic needs between Mexico and the United States has resulted in a historical roller coaster, with periods when the United States recruits workers, encourages relocation, and legalizes migration, and periods of avoidance, when immigration is discouraged, made illegal and punished with repatriation. Although, starting in the 1960s, Mexicans are no longer granted U.S. legal-alien status, immigration has risen steadily. Economic decline fueled antagonism toward immigrants and led California voters in 1994 to approve Proposition 187, which denies care to nondocumented immigrants and compels employers to report them to government officials. Fear of detection results in negative consequences for their use of mental health services (Falicov & Falicov, 1995; Ziv & Lo, 1995).

## Meaning Systems

Personal stories, views of reality, and adaptive behaviors are anchored in the lived experiences of one's race, ethnicity, or social class. Perhaps the most fundamental dislocation of migration is the uprooting of a structure of cultural meanings, which has been likened to the roots that sustain and nourish a plant. With the disruption of lifelong attachments, internal and external meanings are severely challenged (Marris, 1980). New contexts slowly generate new meanings and accommodations.

The uprooting of established values and exposure to new life constructs create various types of psychological distress, including culture shock (Garza-Guerrero, 1974); marginality, social alienation, and psychological conflict (Grinberg & Grinberg, 1989; Shuval, 1982); psychosomatic symptoms such as palpitations, dizziness, insomnia; and anxiety and depression (Warheit, Vega, Auth, & Meinhardt, 1985). Posttraumatic stress may occur if migration involved trauma: for example, for women who were raped and robbed when attempting to cross the border, often by men who had promised to help them (Zamichow, 1992).

Over time, many symptoms decrease as the immigrant gains language and cultural competence. In fact, "acculturation theory" assumes that maintaining, rather than shedding, one's original culture and language increases the mental health risk of immigrants. Nevertheless, the emphasis on acculturation as the solution to the immigrant's stress has been challenged recently (Griffith, 1983; Portes & Rambaut, 1990). Several studies indicate that Mexican Americans who try to "Americanize," or assimilate, actually have *more* psychological problems and drug use than those who retain their language, cultural ties, and rituals (Ortiz & Arce, 1984; Warheit et al., 1985; Burnam, Hough, Karno, Escobar, & Teller, 1987).

A recent model, "alternation theory," assumes that it is possible to know two languages and two cultures, and to appropriately use this knowledge in different contexts (La Framboise, Coleman, & Gerton, 1993) without giving up one for the other. Among factors that make this model particularly well suited to Mexican Americans are their concentration in border cities between Mexico and the United States, land transportation, and improved connections between the two countries, which create active interchange of people, information, and goods that span "the here and the there." These connections concretize the circular, recursive nature of what has been called the two-home, transcontext lifestyle for Mexicans (Bustamante, 1995; Schiller, Basch, & Blanc- Szanton, 1992; Turner, 1991). Studying Mexicans in Redwood City, California, Rouse (1992) observed a "cultural bifocality," that is, the capacity to see the world through two different value lenses. Immigrant men maintained for many years their language and values within the family, while also learning English and the American work ethic.

## Structural Dilemmas

Migration changes many family interactions, primarily because of recurrent separations and reunions among family members. This may lead to increased closeness among members of the nuclear family that cushions culture shock, but ultimately limits the reincorporation of other family members or curtails individual development.

When prolonged separation between nuclear family members occurs, it is usually the father who migrates first, while the mother may become a one-parent unit supported by relatives in Mexico. When the parents reunite, they undergo a second reorganization, analogous to the incorporation of a step-father. Children may be left behind not only for practical reasons, but perhaps also for less conscious ones, such as loyalty to the family of origin. Reincorporation is often traumatic for all involved, especially children. Recently, more women have begun migrating alone. They often become distant breadwinners who are peripheral to their childrens' lives, compared to their mother or sisters; ironically, they may become more attached to children that they may be hired to take care of.

Other gender and generational dilemmas occur when wives remain isolated in their homes and do not learn English, or when children serve as intermediaries in the United States, situations which may eventually weaken parental authority. The presence of two or three generations, each speaking a different language and holding different cultural values while partaking in some common customs and traditions, creates tensions.

## Clinical Implications

Obtaining a "migration narrative" provides the therapist an entree into the family's cultural and migratory experiences. The clinician might ask how long the family has resided in the United States, who immigrated first, who was left behind, who came later or is yet to be reunited; what stresses and learnings were experienced by various family members over time, and what strengths and resources they discovered.

The therapy should not become bogged down by conflicting testimony, dates, places, or events. The family's vagueness may be an attempt to conceal its undocumented status. More importantly, a migration narrative helps family members find meaning in their uprooting in terms of a unique personal history and continuity of personal outlook that can incorporate gains as well as losses. I previously explored family stressors and various therapeutic approaches for different immigrant generations (Falicov, 1988). Other helpful tools are Ho's cultural transition map (1987), Comaz-Díaz's ethnocultural assessment (1994), and McGill's cultural story (1992).

The alternation model suggests that a therapist who quickly becomes an agent of adaptation may create more rather than less emotional distress. I have illustrated in several clinical examples the importance of maintaining continuity and not overburdening an already unstable situation with more suggestions for "adaptive" change (i.e., the wisdom of "no change"; Falicov, 1993). Promoting acculturation goals may also in effect "impose" values without awareness of cultural biases, for example, when the therapist supports the "Americanized" second generation against "old-fashioned" parents.

## ECOLOGICAL CONTEXT

Migration transports Mexican families to a new social terrain. Bombarded with differences, they attempt to recreate elements of the culture they left. Most Mexican Americans, including those of the second generation, live in urban *ethnic neighborhoods* that serve as buffers against culture shock and a continuity of faces, voices, smells, and food. But the illusion of a safe haven is offset by the fear and loathing of discrimination and persecution. Precisely because of its homogeneity, the ethnic neighborhood is vulnerable to intrusion by the "migra," the Immigration and Naturalization Service, which may suddenly approach, apprehend, and deport individuals—actions that are often witnessed by children (Rouse, 1992).

Relocation disrupts the structures of emotional support, advice, and material aid that *social networks* provide, which are so essential for physical and emotional well-being (Berkman, 1984; Pilisuk & Hillier Parks, 1986). Enduring intimate relationships, whether husband–wife or parent–child, are taxed with many more requests for companionship and understanding than before (Sluzki, 1989). Lacking the watchful eye of nearby relatives, parents compensate with restrictions on adolescents' activities, which may aggravate intergenerational conflicts. Yet, many Mexicans migrate into or quickly recover an expressive supportive network of family and friends, but this network may lack the financial resources to change the stressful situations they are in (Valle & Bensussen, 1985).

Roman Catholicism provides continuity for more than 90% of Mexican Americans. For many, it is a private affair, centered around commitment to marriage and fertility, the sanctity of mothers, the condemnation of premarital sex, abortion, contraception, and homosexuality. Guilt and shame about one's sinful acts or thoughts are common inner experiences.

The church in the *barrio* also provides public support (e.g., sanctuaries for undocumented immigrants, crisis counseling, space for activist groups and community celebrations), and priests that officiate at such life cycle celebrations as communions, baptisms, and weddings. Parochial schools decrease parents and children's school anxiety, perhaps because of their attunement to

Mexicans' religious culture. Having a child go to a Catholic college often is a source of pride and status in the community. It also appears to correlate highly with future professional success.

It has been questioned whether the Catholic church really is attuned to its Mexican American followers. Services often are in English and led by Anglo or Irish priests who may be ambivalent and condescending to Mexicans (Davis, 1990; Shorris, 1992). Younger parishioners, and older men, are leaving the Church, attracted by such other evangelical religions such as Pentecostalism and Jehovah's Witnesses or Fundamentalist Protestantism.

Folk medicine and indigenous spirituality, which coexist with mainstream religion and medical practices, are embodied by "witches," those in charge of creating and diffusing goodness ("white witches") and bad ones ("black witches") who can inflict curses and personal harm.

*Curanderos* (folk healers) are consulted for many maladies and are trusted the most for folk illnesses with psychological components, such as *susto* (fright), *mal de ojo* (evil eye), *empacho* (indigestion), or *envidia* (envy). The latter is recognized as a factor in relationships perhaps more than by other groups (Gonzales, 1976; Teller, 1978; Kiev, 1968; Torrey, 1972; Rumbaut, Chavez, Moser, Pickwell, & Wishile, 1988).

Most Mexican Americans are poor, working hard for little pay and low prestige. They are often exploited and have one of the highest unemployment rates (11.9%). Mexican American women's participation in the labor force has increased very rapidly and is now near that of American women in general. Although some fulfill the immigrant's dream and others send money to their home towns, many experience disappointment and depression at having to lower expectations of a stable and moderate income. Some cling to dreams of starting their own small business, which is the model of progress in Mexico (Rouse, 1992).

Because most Mexicans are dark-skinned, they experience discrimination in housing, education, and jobs, and also are deported more readily than others. Although they comprise only 18% of all undocumented immigrants, they constitute 86% of all Immigration and Naturalization Services (INS) detentions (Bustamante, 1995). *Racismo*, or internalized self-loathing (Shorris, 1992), is commom because of racial discrimination in Mexico itself, which then is massively aggravated by discrimination in the United States. Disempowerment may lead to depression, low school achievement, learned helplessness, or dependence on mental health help (Korin, 1994). For example, the 45% high school dropout rate among Mexican American adolescents is due to a combination of language difficulties, ethnic discrimination, and cultural dissonance.

Many social ills that affect minorities who have been discriminated against, such as drugs, alcohol, teen pregnancy, domestic violence, gangs, and AIDS, are visited upon Mexican Americans; they appear even more frequently in the second and third generations than in the first (Padilla, 1995).

## Clinical Implications

Common problems of Mexican Americans in the social and cultural spheres are isolation, ignorance about community resources, and tensions between home norms and those of the school, peer group, or work situation. To inquire about such ecological issues, the therapist might explore the family's neighborhood (housing, safety, crime, gangs); racial acceptance; employment (income, occupation, job stability); extended family and friendship networks; and school and parent–teacher relationships. It is useful to help the family draw an *ecomap* that depicts family–environment relationships (Hartman & Laird, 1983).

If ecological tensions affect the family's ability to cope, the therapist may need to become a "social intermediary" or "matchmaker" between the family and various communal institutions (Minuchin, 1974; Falicov, 1988). He or she can mobilize the family to use existing networks (Erickson, 1975) or facilitate building new reciprocal ones. If they are sensitive to problems of poverty, priests can offer spiritual support, particularly when dealing with physical illness, old age, and death. In addition, relatives can be advocates for a child and a temporary relief for parents. The therapist often needs to help the family with larger systems and direct them to specialized mental health programs.

## FAMILY ORGANIZATION

Mexican American families can be nuclear, extended, "blended," single-parent, or comprised of never married, divorced, or widowed persons. Nuclear families usually live near, but separate from, extended family members. This preserves their boundaries and identity.

Families usually are large, consisting of the parents and four or more children. Birth rates among Mexican Americans are close to 25% higher than among most other ethnic groups at all socioeconomic levels.

Parent–child lifelong connectedness and respect for parental authority are valued over the husband–wife bond emphasized by the Western nuclear family. Certain dyads, such as mother–eldest son are very strong. Important interactional aspects tied to the emphasis on the parent–child bond can be discussed along several dimensions: (1) connectedness and separateness, (2) gender and generation hierarchies, and (3) communication styles and emotional expressivity. These preferences may remain over several generations, but stir up dilemmas with Anglo American values.

### Connectedness and Separateness

Family collectivism and inclusiveness are central to Mexican Americans (Ramirez & Arce, 1981; Keefe, 1984; Vega, 1990). Family boundaries easily expand to include grandparents, uncles, aunts, or cousins. Children who are orphaned, or whose parents have migrated or divorced, may be incorporated in the family along with adults who have remained single or become widowed or divorced.

Strong sibling ties are stressed from a young age and throughout life. Kinship ties up to third and fourth uncles, and to cousins, often are close. Close friends of one's parents often are called "uncle" or "aunt." Relatives provide a type of individual attention that is hard for parents in large families to provide. Often, a family will bring an unannounced relative to the session. The therapist should invite this person to participate, for the family is unlikely to make a direct request for inclusion.

*Familismo*, or family interdependence, involves sharing by extended family members of nurturing and disciplining of children, financial responsibility, companionship for lonely or isolated members, and problem solving. Concomitantly, there is a low reliance on institutions and outsiders. The idea of a "familial self" (Roland, 1988) is useful in understanding Mexicans' dedication to family unity and family honor. The process of separation/individuation, so highly regarded in American culture, is deemphasized in favor of close family ties, independent of age, gender, or social class.

## Gender and Generational Hierarchies

Affiliation and cooperation are stressed; these values are supported by clear hierarchies. Mexican American men and women, as well as parents and children, try to achieve *simpatia*, or smooth, pleasant relationships that avoid conflict. Both the mother and father are owed *respeto*, a word connoting more emotional dependence and dutifulness (Díaz-Guerrero, 1975) than is conveyed by the English "respect." In general, parents' status is high, whereas that of children, including adult offspring, is low. Most parents neither expect nor wish to be friends with their children, although they enjoy each other's company. Childrearing practices reflect this stress on hierarchies. Punishment, shaming, belittling, deception, promises, and threats sometimes are used in response to children's misbehavior.

Although a patriarchal view of gender roles persists among Mexican Americans, more complex dynamics are evolving. For example, a double standard of gender socialization and sexuality persists (Falicov, 1992), yet decision making often is shared by both parents or involves a process in which the mother commands much authority (Kutsche, 1983; Ybarra, 1982). Increasingly, Mexican American family life is characterized by a wide range of structures and processes, from patriarchal to egalitarian, with many combinations in between (Vega, 1990).

Given the centrality of the parent–child dyad, romantic ties in the marital pair often fade soon after marriage. Women's status rises when they become mothers, for Mexican Americans believe that maternal love is greater and more sacred than spousal love. Often, the father disciplines the children and compels them to obey the mother, while she tends to defend and protect them. This dynamic sometimes generates father–mother–child triangulation that needs to be seen contextually, rather than simply regarded as "pathological" (Falicov & Brudner-White, 1983).

Although Mexican women usually initiate consultation, their husbands generally participate. Stereotypes about Mexican *machismo*, which emphasize a man's resistance to asking for help, may cause a therapist to be hesitant to engage the father. Instead, the therapist should take care to remember that *machismo* also involves a father's dedication to his children and his responsibility for the family's well-being. Thus, *machismo* may be a bridge, not an obstacle, to therapy (Ramirez, 1979).

## Communication and Emotional Expressivity

Indirect, implicit, or covert communication is consonant with Mexicans' emphasis on family harmony, on "getting along" and not making others uncomfortable. Conversely, assertiveness, open differences of opinion, and demands for clarification are seen as rude or insensitive to others' feelings.

The use of third-person ("One could be proud of . . ."), rather than first-person ("I am proud of . . .") pronouns is a common pattern of indirectness, and is viewed as a way of being selfless as opposed to self-serving. Thus, Mexican Americans sometimes are left guessing rather than asking about the other's intentions; they often make use of allusions, proverbs, and parables to convey their viewpoints, which may leave an impression of guardedness, vagueness, obscurity, or excessive embellishment, obsequiousness, and politeness.

Harmony is also obtained by curtailing public displays of anger within and outside of the family ("The one who gets angry loses" a Mexican saying states) by the use of *indirectas*. These take the form of criticism by allusion rather than naming a person ("Some people just never change"), diminutives used in a sarcastic way, and belittlement. Yet positive emotional expressivity is highly valued also. Words of endearment and compliments about a person's appearance, dress, or smile or support for his or her positive qualities, spice up conversations among intimates. These communication modes may be maintained even among acculturated families.

## CLINICAL IMPLICATIONS

It is helpful for the therapist to understand his or her own values, as well as discuss with the family theirs, so that the worldview of each is clear.

The therapist can assume the role of *family intermediary,* serving to clarify expectations, "translate" cultural behavior, justify conflict, encourage compromise and negotiation, or ameliorate imbalances in connectedness or hierarchies that occur as a result of migration. It can further the therapeutic process to interview siblings and parents separately and then bring them together. Siblings can explore the kind of issues they are too inhibited to discuss with parents, such as violence, drug use, or sexual orientation, or rehearse how to present those issues in a respectful way. Parents usually respect siblings' solidarity and opinions.

Language also can be a boundary strategy. If the generational boundary is too rigid, young people can be asked to make the effort to speak in Spanish in the sessions. Alternating Spanish and English highlights intergenerational differences, while also being a metaphor for including bicultural and bilingual needs.

A therapeutic focus on individual over family needs is likely to run counter to cultural preferences. Communications that convey acceptance rather than pressure toward disclosure are desirable. Disclosure is easier when the therapist uses such culturally syntonic conversational modes as metaphors, proverbs, or humor that transmit an existential sense of the absurd, the impossibility of "winning the game," or life's propensity for sudden reversals.

An intense emotive tone is more appealing than an efficient, structured behavioral or contractual approach. When feelings are subtly elicited by the therapist, Mexican Americans respond much more openly than when they are directly asked to describe or explain their feelings and reactions. An experiential approach, with an emphasis on "telling it like it is" or "baring one's soul," and interpretations about nonverbal language, may well inhibit clients.

Manifesting real interest in the client rather than gaining data via referral sheets or obtaining many behavioral details about a problem is essential given the Mexican American emphasis on *personalism*, or building personal relationships. Similarly, a therapist who suggests an explicit contract about number of sessions or treatment goals may be too task- rather than person-oriented.

The therapist might assign "conditional homework," that is, asking the family to think about or to engage in a particular task should the occasion arise. Such a technique is consonant with a culture that values serendipity, chance, and spontaneity in interpersonal relationships. Conversely, Mexicans would not be comfortable with the idea of scheduling certain times to be intimate, express affection, or resolve problems.

Because of their culture's emphasis on cooperation and respect for authority, clients may feel that it is impolite to disagree with the therapist. Encouraging the family to express their reactions, both positive and negative, to the therapist's opinions helps to establish a tone of mutuality.

Externalizing conversations, that is, separating a client from a problem and stimulating personal agency or choice (White, 1989), may be used also, particularly in the form of "inner" rather than "outer" externalization. According to Tomm, Suzuki, and Suzuki (1990), an outer externalization involves talking about a problem as if it eventually could be defeated or escaped, and therefore, conversations about conflict and control prevail. An inner externalization, on the other hand, encourages talking about a problem as if it will be necessary to coexist with it. This latter formulation is more syntonic with the Mexican worldview that encourages accepting or being resigned to problems rather than confronting or struggling against them.

## FAMILY LIFE CYCLE

The values of collectivism and respect for authority, the large family networks, and Roman Catholicism influence the definitions, stages, and rituals of the Mexican American family life cycle.

Examples of life cycle differences with Anglo American norms include a longer state of interdependence between mother and children and a more relaxed attitude about children's achievement of self-reliance skills (often mistaken for overprotection); the absence of an independent living situation for most unmarried young adults; the absence of an "empty nest" syndrome, or a crisis and a refocusing on marital issues in middle age; and a continuous involvement, a respected position and a usefulness of parents and grandparents in the family. With acculturation, these developmental expectations persist alongside the new considerations of individual pursuits and romantic love espoused by the younger generations, sometimes causing intergenerational tensions.

Because leaving home occurs primarily through marriage, boundary or loyalty issues with families of origin are common, particularly because the second generation has begun to stress husband–wife exclusivity. Given the strong mother–son bond, a resolution of the relationship between the mother-in-law and daughter-in-law is crucial to marital success.

Most Mexican families are led by two parents throughout their lifetimes. The number of divorces is considerably smaller than for Anglo populations (Ramirez & Arce, 1981; Becerra, 1988). However, common-law marriages and desertions are common among the urban poor.

Godparents share financial and other duties at life cycle events. The two most important types of godparents are those "of baptism" and "of marriage" from the most important life cycle rituals. The former assume responsibilities throughout the child's lifetime; the latter contribute to the wedding costs and, at least in theory, can function as mediators during marital quarrels.

Some developmental impasses can be linked to the stresses of migration. Leaving home can become more problematic when parents have depended on their older children to be intermediaries with the larger culture. Younger siblings, too, may cling to older siblings who appear to be more understanding than the parents.

Family therapy usually is easily accepted by Mexican Americans. In fact, they tend to attribute their emotional problems largely to family conflicts and financial difficulties, which may be felt more intensely during life cycle transitions (Moll, Rueda, Reza, Herrera, & Vasquez, 1976). Many Mexican Americans believe that emotional problems are rooted in family interactions, particularly between the nuclear and extended family. Even folk illnesses are often attributed to interpersonal problems, such as infidelity or jealousy.

## CLINICAL IMPLICATIONS

To deal with life cycle dilemmas, the therapist can assume the role of *family intermediary*. Acting as a "cultural mediator," he or she might encourage conversation between parents and offspring about developmental expectations and their loyalties to both Anglo American and Mexican culture.

Mexican culture prescribes many life cycle rituals that can be used to deal with developmental impasses. The therapist can encourage the family to perform "initiation rites" or fiestas at such life cycle transitions as engagements, weddings, baptisms, and graduations (from kindergarten on through graduate school). Sometimes the absence of such a ritual suggests uncertainty about whether a certain stage has been reached. For example, because many Mexican girls have a *quinceanera* (cotillion) at age 15 to announce their entrance into womanhood, and there is no equivalent ritual for boys, a family might be encouraged to invent an entrance-to-manhood ritual.

## CONCLUSION

Quick perusal of the four parameters presented here may help therapists navigate the Mexican family's external and internal cultural landscape. This facilitates decisions about what areas should be the focus of treatment.

Exploring the family's migration history and acculturation, and its environmental resources or constraints will help "place" both family and therapist in the family's changed external landscape. Conversations about the cultural values, particularly those related to family organization and life cycle markers delineate the internal cultural landscape.

The therapist might note similarities and contrasts with dominant cultural meanings, and the possible dilemmas and enrichments precipitated by the meeting of the two sets of values. Among these contrasts are collectivism and individualism, hierarchies and egalitarianism, and communicative directness and indirectness. These explorations should set a tone of respect, curiosity, and collaboration in understanding the philosophical and behavioral consequences of a Mexican way of life in the midst of American society.

# REFERENCES

Becerra, R. M. (1988). The Mexican American family. In C. H. Mindel, R.W. Habenstein & R. Wright Jr. (Eds.), *Ethnic families in America: Patterns and variations* (3rd ed., pp. 141–159). New York: Elsevier.

Berkman, L. F. (1984). Assessing the physical health effects of social networks and social support. *Annual Review of Public Health, 5,* 413–421.

Burnam, M. A., Hough, R. L., Karno, M., Escobar, J. I., & Teller, C.H. (1987). Acculturation and lifetime prevalence of psychiatric disorders among Mexican Americans in Los Angeles. *Journal of Health and Social Behavior, 28,* 89–102.

Bustamante, J. (1995). *The socioeconomics of undocumented migration flood.* Presentation at the Center for U.S.–Mexican Studies, University of California, San Diego, Spring Quarter.

Comaz-Díaz, L. (1994). Integrative approach. In L. Comaz-Díaz & B. Greene (Eds.), *Women of color: Integrating ethnic and gender identities in psychotherapy* (pp. 238–261). New York: Guilford Press.

Davis, M. P. (1990). *Mexican voices/American dreams.* New York: Henry Holt.

Díaz-Guerrero, R. (1975). *Psychology of the Mexican: Culture and personality.* Austin: University of Texas Press.

Erickson, G. D. (1975). The concept of personal network in clinical practice. *Family Process, 14*(4), 487–498.

Falicov, C. J., & Brudner-White, L. (1983). The shifting family triangle: The issue of cultural and contextual relativity. In J. C. Hansen & C. J. Falicov, (Eds.), *Cultural perspectives in family therapy* (pp. 51–67). Rockville, MD: Aspen.

Falicov, C. J. (1988). Learning to think culturally. In H. A. Liddle, D. C. Breunlin, & R. C. Schwartz (Eds.), *Handbook of family therapy training and supervision* (pp. 335–357). New York: Guilford Press.

Falicov, C. J. (1992, Summer). Love and gender in the Latino marriage. *American Family Association Newsletter, 48,* 30–36.

Falicov, C. J. (1993). Continuity and change: Lessons from immigrant families. *American Family Therapy Association Newsletter, 50,* 30–34.

Falicov, C. J., & Falicov, Y. M. (1995, Spring). The effects of Proposition 187 on families: What therapists can do. *American Family Therapy Association Newsletter, 59,* 51–54.

Falicov, C. J. (1995). Training to think culturally: A multidimensional comparative framework. *Family Process, 34*(4), 373–388.

Garza-Guerrero, A. C. (1974). Culture shock: It's mourning and the vicissitudes of identity. *Journal of American Psychoanalytic Association, 22,* 408–429.

Gonzales, E. (1976). The role of Chicano folk beliefs and practices in mental health. In C. A. Hernandez, M. J. Haug, & N. N. Wagner (Eds.), *Chicanos: Social and psychological perspectives* (pp. 84–109). St. Louis: C.V. Mosby.

Griffith, J. (1983). Relationship between acculturation and psychological impairment in adult Mexican Americans. *Hispanic Journal of Behavioral Sciences, 5*(4), 431–459.

Grinberg, L., & Grinberg, R. (1989). *Psychoanalytic perspectives on migration and exile.* New Haven, CT: Yale University Press.

Hartman, A., & Laird, J. (1983). *Family-centered social work practice.* New York: Free Press.

Ho, M. K. (1987). *Family therapy with ethnic minorities.* Newbury Park, CA: Sage.

Keefe, S. (1984). Real and ideal extended familism among Mexican Americans and Anglo Americans: On the meaning of "close" family ties. *Human Organization, 43,* 65–70.

Kiev, A. (1968). *Curanderismo: Mexican-American folk psychiatry.* New York: Free Press.

Korin, E. C. (1994). Social inequalities and therapeutic relationships: Applying Freire's ideas to clinical practice. *Journal of Feminist Family Therapy, 5*(3/4), 75–98.

Kutsche, P. (1983). Household and family in hispanic northern New Mexico. *Journal of Comparative Family Studies, 14,* 151–165.

LaFromboise, T., Coleman, H. L. K., & Gerton, J. (1993). Psychological impact of biculturalism: Evidence and theory. *Psychological Bulletin, 114*(3), 395– 412.

Marris, P. (1980). The uprooting of meaning. In G. V. Coelho & P. I. Ahmed (Eds.), *Uprooting and development: Dilemmas of coping with modernization* (pp. 101–116). New York: Plenum Press.

McGill, D. (1992). The cultural story in multicultural family therapy. *Families in Society, 73,* 339–349.

Minuchin, S. (1974). *Families and family therapy.* Cambridge, MA: Harvard University Press.

Moll, L. C., Rueda, R. S., Reza, R., Herrera, J., & Vasquez, L. P. (1976). Mental health services in East Los Angeles: An urban community case study. In M. R. Miranda (Ed.), *Psychotherapy with the Spanish speaking: Issues in research and service delivery* (Monograph No. 3, pp. 52–65). Los Angeles: University of California, Spanish Speaking Mental Health Research Center.

Ortiz, V., & Arce, C. H. (1984). Language orientation and mental health status among persons of Mexican descent. *Hispanic Journal of Behavioral Sciences, 6*(2), 127–143.

Padilla, A. M. (Ed.). (1995). *Hispanic psychology: Critical issues in theory and research.* Thousand Oaks, CA: Sage.

Pilisuk, M., & Hillier Parks, S. (1986). *The healing webb: Social networks and human survival.* Hanover, NH: University of New England Press.

Portes, A., & Rambaut, R. G. (1990). A foreign world: Immigration, mental health, and acculturation. In *Immigrant America: A portrait* (pp. 143–179). Berkeley: University of California Press.

Ramirez, R. (1979). Machismo: A bridge rather than a barrier to family counseling. In P. P. Martin (Ed.), *La Frontera perspective: Providing mental health services to Mexican Americans.* Tucson, AZ: La Frontera Center.

Ramirez, O., & Arce, C. H. (1981). The contemporary Chicano family: An empirically based review. In A. Baron, Jr. (Ed.), *Explorations in Chicano psychology* (pp. 3–28). New York: Praeger.

Roland, A. (1988). *In search of self in India and Japan: Toward a cross- cultural psychology.* Princeton, NJ: Princeton University Press.

Rouse, R. (1992). Making sense of settlement: Class transformation, cultural struggle, and transnationalism among Mexican migrants in the United States. In N. G. Schiller, L. Basch, & C. Blanc-Szanton (Eds.), *Towards a transnational perspective on migration: Race, class, ethnicity, and nationalism reconsidered.* New York: New York Academy of Sciences.

Rumbaut, R. G., Chavez, L. R., Moser, R. J., Pickwell, S. M., & Wishile, S. M. (1988).

The politics of migrant health care: A comparative study of Mexican immigrants and Indochinese refugees. *Research in the Sociology of Health Care, 7,* 143–202.

Schiller, N. G., Basch, L., & Blanc-Szanton, C. (Eds.). (1992). *Towards a transnational perspective on migration: Race, class, ethnicity, and nationalism reconsidered.* New York: New York Academy of Sciences.

Shorris, E. (1992). *Latinos: A biography of the people.* New York: Norton.

Shuval, J. T. (1982). Migration and stress. In L. Goldberger & S. Breznitz (Eds.), *Handbook of stress: Theoretical and clinical aspects* (2nd ed., pp. 641–657). New York: Free Press.

Sluzki, C. E. (1989). Network disruption and network reconstruction in the process of migration/relocation. *The Bulletin: A Journal of the Berkshire Medical Center,* 2(3), 2–4.

Teller, C. H. (1978). Physical health status and health care utilization in the Texas Borderlands. In S. R. Ross (Ed.), *Views across the border: The United States and Mexico.* Albuquerque: University of New Mexico Press.

Tomm, K., Suzuki, K., & Suzuki, K. (1990). The Ka-No-Mushi: An inner externalization that enables compromise? *Australian and New Zealand Journal of Family Therapy, 11*(2), 104–107.

Torrey, E. (1972). *The mind game: Witchdoctors and psychiatry.* New York: Emerson Hall.

Turner, J. E. (1991). Migrants and their therapist: A trans-context approach. *Family Process, 30,* 407–419.

Valle, R., & Bensussen, G. (1985). Hispanic social networks, social supports, and mental health. In W. Vega & M. Miranda (Eds.), *Stress and Hispanic mental health* (pp. 147–173). Rockville, MD: National Institute of Mental Health.

Vega, W. A. (1990). Hispanic families in the 1980s: A decade of research. *Journal of Marriage and the Family, 52,* 1015–1024.

Warheit, G., Vega, W., Auth, J., & Meinhardt, K. (1985). Mexican-American immigration and mental health: A comparative analysis of psychosocial stress and dysfunction. In W. Vega & M. Miranda (Eds.), *Stress and Hispanic mental health* (pp.76–109). Rockville, MD: National Institute of Mental Health.

White, M. (1989). The externalizing of the problem and the re-authoring of lives and relationships. In M. White (Ed.), *Selected papers* (pp. 5–28). Adelaide, Australia: Dulwich Centre Publications.

Ybarra, L. (1982). Marital decision making and the role of machismo in the Chicano family. *De Colores, 6,* 32–47.

Zamichow, N. (1992, February 10). No way to escape the fear. *Los Angeles Times,* pp. B1–B3.

Ziv, T. A., & Lo, B. L. (1995). Denial of care to illegal immigrants: Proposition 187 in California. *New England Journal of Medicine, 332*(16), 1095–1098.

CHAPTER 13

# Puerto Rican Families

## Nydia Garcia-Preto

In times of stress, Puerto Ricans turn to their families for help. Their cultural expectation is that when a family member is in crisis or has a problem, others in the family are obligated to help, especially those who are in stable positions. Because Puerto Ricans rely on the family and their extended network of personal relationships, they will make use of social services only as a last resort (Badillo-Ghali, 1974; Comas-Díaz, 1989). This chapter provides family therapists with a beginning framework for working with Puerto Rican families by presenting some information on sociopolitical history, cultural values, family patterns, and the effects of migration and culture shock on couple relationships, parent–child issues, and three-generational relationships. Clinical examples are used to illustrate certain typical family patterns and therapeutic interventions that are culturally appropriate. The sections on migration and therapeutic intervention focus primarily on low-income Puerto Rican families who usually are referred to social welfare agencies and mental health centers.

Before the Spanish settled Puerto Rico in 1500, the island was populated by Taino Indians (Boas, 1940; Pane, 1973). It is believed that most of the Taino died of hunger, overwork, or suicide shortly after the Spanish invasion (Fernandez-Mendez, 1970). Of those who survived, the men generally worked for the Spaniards and the women became their consorts. Even though the Taino way of life soon faded, a few remnants of their culture are still visible. For instance, the value that Puerto Ricans place on preserving a peaceable demeanor is reminiscent of Taino tranquility, as well as the emphasis the culture places on kinship and dependence on the group. Some Puerto Rican physical characteristics such as skin color, hair texture, and bone structure have also been identified as Indian. The names of certain fruits and vegetables (e.g., *yuca*, *guineo*) are believed to be Indian, as are the names of a number of towns (e.g., Yabucoa and Humacao). In contrast, the Spanish influence is widely evident today. The Spaniards brought their language, literature, and food preferences to Puerto Rico, as well as the Roman Catholic religion and its rituals for birth, marriage, and death. Other Spanish legacies include the family's patriarchal structure and a double standard regarding sexual behavior. Many aspects of Spanish culture, such as the Catholic worship of saints and belief in an after-life and the strong sense of family obligation, blended well with the Indian culture. This may account for some of the difficulty in sorting out Puerto Rican traits that are distinctly Taino.

The Spaniards brought African slaves to the island to work in the pro-duction of sugar cane (Wagenheim & Wagenheim, 1973). The Africans in turn contributed their language, food, musical instruments, religion, and medicine men to the cultural mix of the island. They also carried with them the fatalism of an enslaved race. Although there were fewer slaves in Puerto Rico than on other islands, such as Haiti, Jamaica, or Cuba, Puerto Rican slaves suffered the same horrors as those elsewhere.

In 1898, the United States colonized Puerto Rico, after taking the island as war booty of the Spanish–American War. In 1900, a U.S. governor was appointed to head a civil government made up of island residents. The United States retained the power to veto laws they might pass and the resident com-missioner, who represented Puerto Rico in the U.S. House of Representatives, had no vote. The United States also mandated the use of English as the lan-guage of instruction in the public schools. Considering that few people on the island, not even the teachers, spoke English, this was perhaps the cruelest aberration imposed on the people of Puerto Rico. In 1917, the island's partici-pation in its own government was increased. A Bill of Rights was established and U.S. citizenship was granted, while military service became obligatory for all eligible males. Puerto Rico elected its first governor in 1948, and in 1952 it became a commonwealth. With this latter change, Spanish was reinstituted as the language of instruction in public schools, with English becoming the sec-ond language.

Real political power over Puerto Rico, however, still rests in the U.S. House Committee on Insular Affairs and the Senate Committee on Territorial and Insular Affairs. Puerto Ricans continue to have little power over the fate of their island, because they do not vote in U.S. elections. The political party in power favors statehood for Puerto Rico; however, the results of the 1991 referendum reflected a majority of Puerto Ricans preferring the present structure over state-hood or independence. Thus, the most significant result of the referendum is the conflict among the three major political parties—the Popular Democratic Party (Commonwealth), the New Progressive Party (Statehood), and the Independence Party—about the status question, and Washington's indiffer-ence to the issue. For Puerto Rican activists, however, the question of how to move beyond colonialism remains unanswered (Melendez & Melendez, 1993). Generalizations about Puerto Ricans are dangerous. For example, we may say that they emphasize spiritual and human rather than commercial values. How-ever, the middle and upper classes value possessions as highly symbolic of personal worth. The following section focuses on values that have been characterized as Puerto Rican and that seem to permeate all classes and groups.

## SPIRITUALITY

Puerto Ricans celebrate life. They emphasize values that pertain to the spirit and soul, as distinguished from physical nature, and are willing to sacrifice material satisfaction for spiritual goals. For them, being is more important than doing or having (Papajohn & Spiegel, 1975). They live for the present; the future and past are given little attention. Puerto Ricans, although not resigned, are accepting of fate. Most Puerto Ricans are nominally Roman Catholics, although the Protestant denominations and Pentecostal sects have been growing on the island since about 1900 (Fitzpatrick, 1976). Their methods of worship differ from U.S. Catholicism, which is strongly influenced by Irish customs. Most Puerto Ricans somewhat distrust organized religion, the Church, and the priest, believing that these are dispensable for making contact with God and the supernatural. They tend to personalize their relationship with God through special relationships with saints, who become their personal emissaries to God. Promises and offerings are made, prayers said, and candles lit, all in attempts to show gratitude and faith. They will call on the Church primarily for weddings, christenings, and funerals. Many Puerto Ricans believe in spiritism, an invisible world inhabited by good and evil spirits who influence human behavior (Delgado, 1978). Spirits can either protect or harm, as well as prevent or cause illness. Everyone has spirits of protection, which can be increased by good deeds or decreased by evil ones. Spiritist beliefs also include the use of incense, candles, and powders, which are alleged to have magical properties to cure illnesses and ward off the "evil eye."

## THE DIGNITY OF THE INDIVIDUAL

Puerto Ricans define self-worth in terms of those qualities that give them self-respect and earn them the respect of others. A man can achieve this by being able to protect and provide for his family and by being honorable and respectful in his behavior. Such individualism, often referred to as "personalism" stems from the social situation in most Latin American countries in which the rich and poor are fixed in their socioeconomic status, with little chance for mobility. Focusing on inner qualities allows a person to experience self-worth regardless of worldly success or failure, in clear contrast to American individualism, which values achievement above all else. Respect is vital in the Puerto Rican culture. Respect acknowledges another's social worthiness; it is the social lubricant in the flywheel of interpersonal relationships. Not to show the proper respect to the Puerto Rican man assaults the very core of his manliness and the integrity of his family, and puts in question his self-esteem as a human being (Puerto Rican Congress of New Jersey, 1976). Respect plays a major role in preserving the network of close, personal relationships. Respect for authority is first learned in the home and then expands to the outside society, especially when dealing with superiors. Its rules are complex. For instance, most Puerto Ricans believe that a child who calls an adult by his or her first name without using "Dona," "Don," "Sr.," or "Sra." is disrespectful. To make direct eye contact with strangers, especially women and children, is also unacceptable.

## CONTROL OF AGGRESSION

Puerto Ricans fear losing impulse control and expressing violence. Aggression in Puerto Rico is controlled by pressure from the group, which may be the extended family, the community, or both. Furthermore, the repression of aggression is culturally reinforced by the system of *compadrazgo*, the mutual-aid expectations among family members, and social rules fostering respect. Puerto Ricans' need to preserve an appearance of outward dignity and calm may require suppression and repression of assertiveness and aggressiveness at the expense of inner psychological needs (Rothenberg, 1964). For women, common outlets for aggression are gossip (often about sexual behavior) and psychosomatic complaints (such as headaches, stomach- or body aches, and fatigue). Drinking, verbal threats, and angry political complaints against the government and large corporations are some ways in which men commonly release aggressive feelings.

## FAMILY STRUCTURE

Puerto Ricans value the family's unity, welfare, and honor. Family ties and relationships are intense, and visits are frequent when family members are not living in the same household (Mizio, 1974). Separations cause extreme grief, and reunions cause extreme joy. The group rather than the individual is emphasized. The family guarantees protection and caretaking for life as long as the person stays in the system. Leaving it implies taking a grave risk (Papajohn & Spiegel, 1975).

Family is usually an extended system that encompasses not only those related by blood and marriage, but also *compadres* (godparents) and *hijos de crianza* (informally adopted children). *Compadrazgo* is the institution of *compadres comadres* (coparents), a system of ritual kinship with binding mutual obligations for economic assistance, encouragement, and even personal correction (Mizio, 1974). In Puerto Rico, transferring children from one nuclear family to another within the extended system in times of crisis is common and not necessarily seen as neglectful by the child, the natural parents, or the community. Thus, some children may be adversely affected psychologically or experience rejection and loss, as do the parents. But unless the practice is regarded as a problem by the family, it is better for a therapist not to criticize or attempt to alter such arrangements.

Marriage is still considered much more a union of two families in Puerto Rican culture than in America (Fitzpatrick, 1976). Traditionally, Puerto Rican families have been patriarchal, a structure that gives men authority over women, as well as the power and privilege to make decisions without consulting them. Men have been expected to protect and provide for the family, whereas women's responsibility has been to take care of the home and keep the family together. These gender roles are rooted in Spanish culture and Western European tradition, and have been reinforced by the constructs of *machismo, marianismo*, and *hembrismo*.

In the United States *machismo* has a negative connotation and is used to describe sexist behavior of Latinos and men in general. In the mental health field, the concept has been pathologized, especially by psychodynamic theory. De La Cancela (1991) looks at the construct's negative and positive aspects, and tries to contextualize the definition, claiming that a dialectic view is more conducive to helping Puerto Rican men change when working with them in family therapy. Culturally, *machismo* emphasizes self-respect and responsibility for protecting and providing for the family. Yet, De La Cancela (1991) points out that this value can become negative when it leads to possessive demands and expectation that all decisions be made by the man. *Machismo* dictates that a man must signal that he is always ready for sex (Sluzki, 1982). The paradox is that virginity is very important in traditional Puerto Rican culture and that a man is also responsible for protecting the honor of the women in his family. The double standard about sex usually continues after marriage. Only men are free to engage in extramarital affairs.

The concept of *marianismo*, which stems from the cult of the Virgin Mary, considers women morally and spiritually superior to men and therefore capable of enduring all suffering inflicted by them (Stevens, 1973). Also implicit in the concept is women's repression or sublimation of sexual drives and consideration of sex as an obligation. The cultural message is that if a woman has sex with a man before marriage, she will lose his respect so that he will not marry her, and she will bring dishonor to herself and to her family. Traditionally, the line separating *donas* (a respectful term for Mrs.) from *putas* (whores) has been clear: no sex before marriage and afterward an accepting attitude without much demonstration of pleasure (Garcia-Preto, 1990). *Hembrismo* means femaleness and connotes strength, perseverance, flexibility, and the ability to survive. It can be likened to the concept of superwoman, that is, an attempt to fulfill all female role expectations at home and at work (Comas Díaz, 1989).

Marital respect was eloquently defined by a male client who said to his wife: "Respect between a husband and wife means that as a wife you must be loving, considerate, and never have negative thoughts about me." Women expect men to show respect by remaining loyal to the family's sense of propriety, especially regarding affairs. A woman who discovers that her husband is having an affair may refuse to have sexual intercourse with him, complaining of body aches and nervousness, and therefore rebels against the expected submissiveness to men (Maldonado & Trent, 1960). The extended family is a source of strength for a couple; its absence may cause marital stress and tension. For example, women usually depend on other females in the extended family for help with childrearing and domestic tasks, because husbands are not expected to share these responsibilities. Without extended family assistance, she may experience those tasks as unbearable and begin to demand the husband's help. He may resent this and become argumentative and distant, often turning to drink, gambling, and affairs. The extended family also helps control aggression and violence. Without relatives to intervene in the arguments and advise the spouses to respect each other, couples may have serious difficulties.

## PARENT–CHILD RELATIONSHIPS

Traditionally, Puerto Ricans have married young and have many offspring. Children are seen as the poor man's wealth, the caretakers of the old, and a symbol of fertility. Parents, especially mothers, often make sacrifices for them. During infancy, children are loved and enjoyed by all of the adults in the family. They are expected to be obedient and respectful and, as they mature, are taught to show gratitude by assuming responsibility for younger siblings and older parents. Unlike WASP or Jewish families, Puerto Ricans do not often encourage their children to think for themselves and speak their own minds. Instead, children who talk back are likely to be punished. Parents often speak harshly to them, demanding to know why they did something and then proceeding to answer the question themselves or to complain about the child's refusal to answer before he or she has a chance to speak. They also view spankings as an acceptable form of discipline and often resort to it. Parents may be hesitant to reward good behavior for fear that children will lose their feelings of respect; this may cause familial tension and lead the child to act out feelings outside the home.

Although fathers are supposed to be the real enforcers, mothers have the major responsibility for disciplining children. This yields them a degree of power that is reflected in the alliances they often build with children against authoritarian fathers, who are perceived as lacking understanding of emotional issues. Relationships between sons and mothers are particularly close and mutually dependent. It is fairly common for a son to protect his mother against an abusive husband (Garcia-Preto, 1994). A family therapist working with this type of family may want to help the son to separate from the mother, who may be labeled passive and manipulative. But, the problem is not the mother–son bond, but the lack of power women in these positions experience. Instead, a more useful approach would be to empower women to stop the abuse. It also is important to challenge the dependence that mothers foster in sons, and to address the emotional distance between fathers and children when men are uninvolved or abusive at home. Mothers and daughters have more reciprocal relationships. Mothers teach their daughters how to be good women who deserve the respect of others, especially males, and who will make good wives and mothers. Daughters who take care of their elderly parents often take their widowed mothers into their homes. In turn, older women help out at home, enabling their daughters to attend school or work.

Relationships between Puerto Rican women and their fathers vary greatly. In families in which fathers assume an authoritarian position, there tends to be more distance and conflict. While attempting to be protective, fathers may become unreasonable, unapproachable, and highly critical of their daughters' behavior and friends. But in families in which fathers are more submissive and dependent on mothers to make decisions, they may develop special alliances with their daughters, who may assume a nurturing role toward them. With an increasing number of Puerto Rican families being headed by single women, children often grow up having memories of absent and distant fathers, whose behavior may have been abusive (Garcia-Preto, 1994).

## LIFE CYCLE ISSUES

Birth, marriage, and death are the most important events in the Puerto Rican life cycle. The first two are very happy occasions, celebrated by the family and community. Family members gather when there is a death to comfort each other and to pray for the deceased. Religious rituals such as masses, rosaries, and novenas (prayers to the saints) are said to help the dead and the living. Crying, screaming, and *ataques* (hysterical, convulsive reactions) are common ways of mourning at a funeral. Despite these visible expressions of grief, there is an underlying acceptance of death in the Puerto Rican culture. In the world of Puerto Rican spiritism, a person's potential for power and peacefulness may be perceived as being greater in the afterlife than in this one.

## PATTERNS FOR HANDLING STRESS

Puerto Ricans tend to attribute stressful situations to external factors and to express stress through somatic complaints. When in distress, they turn to their families, who ordinarily recommend visiting a physician. Nonphysical problems usually are categorized as spiritual. Examples of this pattern are guilt, shame, sin, and disrespect for elders or for family values (Padilla, Ruiz, & Alvarez, 1975). In these cases, the family will probably suggest a visit to the clergy. Many Puerto Ricans in distress are treated by a spiritist, who has power over spirits, rather than by a mental health professional (Garrison, 1977, Comas-Díaz, 1989). However, most Puerto Ricans who visit spiritists do so after a doctor tells them there is nothing physically wrong with them (Delgado, 1978). The spiritist, unlike many therapists, takes into account the family situation and cultural milieu when evaluating and treating behavior (Sager, Brayboy, & Waxenberg, 1972). Spiritism helps to alleviate anxiety and focus on change by helping individuals gain control over their lives and by positive reframing of dysfunctional behavior (Delgado, 1978). When working with clients who believe in spiritism, the therapist's goal would be not to change the belief but to help clients gain self-trust and control over their lives.

## THE EFFECT OF MIGRATION ON THE FAMILY

Puerto Rican migration to the United States began in the early 1900s. The granting of U.S. citizenship to Puerto Ricans in 1917 accelerated the process. They primarily moved to Northeastern cities in search of jobs, education, political refuge, and new opportunities. After World War II, the migration rate increased, peaking in 1952, when it surpassed 52,000 (Rodriguez, Sanchez-Korrol, & Alers, 1980). Since then, it has fluctuated depending on economics and employment opportunities both in the United States and on the Island. For example, in 1969, there were more people returning to Puerto Rico than arriving in the United States (Rodriguez et al., 1980). Yet recently, migration to the mainland has been picking up, since attempts to industrialize Puerto Rico by external investors has resulted in less employment, with fewer than one-third of working-age Puerto Ricans on the island actually having jobs (Melendez & Melendez, 1993). There is also an alarming increase in the brain drain of professionals leaving the island, because salaries and the standard of living are much higher on the U.S. mainland (Garcia-Remis, 1993). Some families migrate to solve internal problems. For instance, a relative abroad may need help with childrearing, marital problems, or a sick relative. Other reasons are avoidance of difficult personal situations, such as the aftermath of a marital separation or legal difficulties.

Since no visas are needed for travel, migration from the island to the mainland continues to be marked by a back-and-forth movement that has strongly influenced Puerto Rican family life. This phenomenon reinforces many links to the island, although it also reflects repeated ruptures and renewals of ties, dismantling and reconstructing familial and communal networks in old and new settings (Rodriguez et al., 1980). For Puerto Ricans, going back to the island also may represent a solution to the problems they face here, an oasis from the prejudice, discrimination, and isolation that plague their lives. Their colonial experience has perhaps contributed to a worldview that tends to be fatalistic, rewarding of self-sacrifice and personal struggle, and afraid of the consequences that being aggressive and fighting for their rights may bring.

## EFFECT ON SOCIOECONOMIC STATUS

Although Puerto Ricans have U.S. citizenship, they often are not viewed, acknowledged, or received as citizens. Instead, most are relegated to a marginal existence and are the poorest Latino group (Massey & Eggers, 1990). One-third of the 2.5 million Puerto Ricans in the United States live in poverty. In 1991, the unemployment rate was 31% for all Puerto Rican males and 59% for females over the age of 16 (U.S. Census Bureau, 1991). Another compounding problem is that of all the Latino men in jail in New York, a majority are Puerto Rican (Novas, 1994). Fewer difficulties are experienced by White, middle-class families who come from urban centers in Puerto Rico and have marketable skills. In addition, Puerto Ricans who migrate to other U. S. regions seem to fare better economically than other Latinos in those areas. For example, only 6% of those who recently migrated to New York have college degrees versus 24% of those who migrated to Texas (Novas, 1994). Proportionally, second-generation Puerto Ricans are closer to the national level in education and occupationally seem to be advancing steadily (U.S. Census Bureau, 1991).

## EFFECT OF RACISM

Racism not only affects Puerto Ricans' economic situation, but also presents serious problems for the family. Tomas (1967) describes how color affected his self-image and his relationships with other family members. Comas-Díaz (1994) addresses how racism affects Black Puerto Rican women's interactions with family members and with the outside world. Although racism has always existed in Puerto Rico, racial differences are seen as a continuum between White and Black, with many words describing shades of color and physical characteristics (Rodriguez, 1990). A family's exposure to the racial dichotomy and prejudice in this country may lead to resentment, rejection, and family rifts. Rabkin and Struening (1976) found that non-White Puerto Ricans were more frequently admitted to mental health hospitals than White Puerto Ricans.

## CULTURAL SHOCK

Puerto Ricans on the mainland quickly find that some of their cultural attitudes are undermined by U.S. society. Culturally, Puerto Ricans learn to be dependent on the group and the community, and are rewarded for submissive and respectful behavior. Conflict and anxiety are experienced when they confront a society that frowns on passivity and expects independent, individualistic behavior. The rules of respect that bind relationships in Puerto Rico are not understood in the United States. For instance, the concept of *machismo* has negative connotations that cause conflicts for traditional Puerto Rican men. This culture shock tends to produce significant changes in Puerto Rican family structure.

## EFFECTS ON GENDER ROLES AND MALE–FEMALE RELATIONSHIPS

Conflict in the marital relationship may erupt when traditional sex roles are reversed. Sometimes a wife is able to obtain employment, while the husband stays home to take care of the children. This role reversal does not become problematic if the woman continues to accept the traditional view of family life. Puerto Rican women always have been influential in the home, as well as in the island's political and academic life (Fitzpatrick, 1976). This may be in part because a large percentage of women always have worked to supplement the family income. In 1920, women constituted 25% of the work force in Puerto Rico (Fernandez & Quintero, 1974). However, the wife who becomes the breadwinner will tend to feel more independent and self-confident. Consequently, her husband may feel emasculated, especially if she openly challenges his authority. If he is unable to regain his dominant position through employment, he may experience panic and confusion. His wife, in turn, may develop contempt for her spouse when he no longer fulfills his *macho* role (Mizio, 1974). Some women also experience emotional pain and feelings of helplessness in such a situation. Marital discord and separation are common outcomes. According to the 1990 Census, an increasing number of Puerto Rican households on the mainland are headed by single females, reflecting an increase in divorce and separations.

## EFFECTS ON PARENT–CHILD RELATIONSHIPS

Children have an easier time learning English and often are asked to interpret for their parents. This dependence on their children to express their wishes, concerns, and conflicts often puts Puerto Rican parents in an inferior, powerless position. Asking a child to speak for his or her parents is also contrary to the cultural expectation that children should be quiet in front of strangers. Children caught in conflicts of cultures and loyalties may develop a negative self-image that can inhibit their chances for growth and accomplishment. Parents, not knowing how to respond in the new culture, often feel they have lost control and may give up. They usually react by imposing stricter rules, using corporal punishment, and, if necessary, appealing to the traditionally accepted values of respect and obedience.

When children reach adolescence, parents may become extremely strict and overprotective, especially with daughters who demand independence and freedom to date, due to the conflict in cultural values and the realistic fears of crime, drug addiction, and different sexual mores (Badillo-Ghali, 1974; Garcia-Preto & Boyd-Franklin, 1994). In Puerto Rico, parents relied on other adults in the extended family and the community for help with discipline, which they may be unable to do in the United States. A lack of extended family and friends may also precipitate feelings of anxiety, loss, isolation, and being overwhelmed and resentful. Individuals may feel obligated to fulfill roles and functions that were previously performed by others in the extended system. Consequently, they may experience extreme anxiety. In Puerto Rico, the nuclear family was never expected to take care of all of their needs. Understandably, they may feel overwhelmed and resentful.

Engaging the Puerto Rican family in a warm and personal relationship during the first interview is critical to the outcome of therapy. Puerto Ricans are more likely to respond to a therapist who is active, personal, and respectful of the family's structure and boundaries. They may take directives more readily from a male therapist because of the authority men have in the culture, but may feel more comfortable speaking to a female about emotional problems, because women handle those concerns in the family. If the family was referred by another agency, the therapist might mention the referring person, state that he or she seemed concerned about them, and express the wish to assist them in whatever way possible.

The language factor may be a major therapeutic issue and barrier. When the family is unable to speak English, conducting the interview in Spanish is essential in engaging them. Older Puerto Ricans often are hesitant and afraid to learn English. They may feel humiliated when they try to speak English but are not understood and are asked to repeat themselves. Using children as interpreters is problematic because it shifts the family structure by placing children in a superior position. Even when Puerto Rican families speak English, lack of fluency may lead to distorting information or vagueness (Gonzalez, 1978; Marcos, Alpert, Urcuyo, & Kesselman, 1973). When the therapist is able to speak Spanish but is unfamiliar with the culture, he or she may overestimate or underestimate the degree of family dysfunction. When there are no Spanish-speaking therapists, using interpreters, preferably Hispanic adults, is advisable. However, it has been found that reliance upon translators, even Hispanics, introduces distortions that result in limitations and frustrations for both therapist and client (Abad & Boyce, 1979).

Puerto Ricans may not easily accept an agency's expectation that they keep scheduled appointments due to the informality of their culture and the environmental circumstances. In some cases, home visits may be the only way of initiating or maintaining a relationship (Mizio, 1979; Pittman et al., 1971; Hardy-Fanta MacMahon-Herrera, 1981). Knowing where the family lives and who is helpful in the extended family and in the neighborhood will help the therapist determine what support systems are available to it. The use of a genogram (Guerin, 1976; McGoldrick & Gerson, 1985) can be helpful in determining who comprises the extended family.

Since many family problems are basically social, learning to deal with environmental stresses needs to be part of therapy. The therapist's willingness to meet the family's request for concrete services and to act as its advocate is an important vehicle for establishing a trusting relationship (Aponte, 1976; Mizio, 1979). For instance, in the case of the Martinez family, helping the mother deal with the school alleviated the stress at home.

Mrs. Martinez, a 34-year-old, separated, Puerto Rican female, was referred by the school to a mental health center for therapy. She had left Puerto Rico with her two sons, Mario, age 8, and Hector, age 2, after separating from her husband. Mario, who enrolled in a bilingual class, refused to do schoolwork and disturbed the other children in the classroom. At the time of the referral, Mrs. Martinez had been living in the United States for only 5 months. The therapist facilitated a meeting between Mrs. Martinez and the teacher. The goal was to agree on the classroom behavior they expected from Mario. They were helped to formulate a strategy that improved the child's behavior, which increased Mrs. Martinez's sense of personal power. The therapist also gave Mrs. Martinez tangible advice about setting consistent and clear limits for her son at home. She had been most worried about Mario's physical expression of anger, which she saw as similar to her husband's violent outbursts. Frustrated by her inability to control Mario, Mrs. Martinez often spanked him, which caused her to feel guilty about her own loss of control. The therapist gave Mrs. Martinez advice, which met the expectation that most Puerto Ricans have when they go to a professional for help. The therapist, who wanted to ensure the mother's cooperation with the task, engaged her in the formulation of a plan that seemed feasible.

Women comprise a large percentage of the Puerto Ricans who seek help. They often complain about their husbands' drinking, abusive behavior, and general absence from the home. Although they may have attempted to change the situation at home by threatening to leave their spouses, their lack of resources makes carrying out this threat difficult. Because they are unable to change the situation at home, they experience themselves as failures. Their relatives and the other women in the community often advise them to be strong and accepting. This advice reflects the cultural belief that it is a woman's role to hold the family together. There is a tendency among Puerto Ricans to admire a woman who carries her "cross." Wives usually are ambivalent about accusing their husbands in therapy. On the one hand, they feel disloyal, and on the other, they feel betrayed. They try to clarify that their husbands are basically good human beings, and that they believe their behavior is caused by alcohol, lack of job opportunities, friends, and this country's lifestyle. Mrs. Conde illustrates the bind in which some of these women find themselves.

During the past 5 years Mrs. Conde has come to therapy on different occasions when the situation at home has reached a crisis. In therapy she claims to feel embarrassed about coming with the same problem and not taking steps to change. She wants to do things by herself but feels helpless. She wants the therapist to help her think clearly. She states that she wants to go away from her husband and her family of origin to a place where she can live in peace with her children. She holds back for fear that she will not be able to handle the children, especially her son, alone. She would prefer to stay home and help her husband. She does not want to talk about him behind his back, but he refuses to seek help.

Women like Mrs. Conde often drop out of therapy when the crisis is over and return when another arises.

It is highly unusual for Puerto Ricans to initiate therapy for marital problems. Those who do are more likely to be acculturated into the American society. Most families who seek help present child-focused problems. However, marital conflicts are common in these families. In most cases, the couple will resist therapeutic attempts to explore these conflicts directly, with the husband sometimes stating that he refuses to come again.

In general, Puerto Rican men refrain from asking for help. Abad, Ramos, and Boyce (1974) attributed this avoidance to their sensitivity to any situation that threatens their *machismo* image. Often, wives will ask therapists to convince their husbands to come to therapy. The therapist should assess the situation carefully before interpreting the request as manipulative. Puerto Ricans who ask an outsider to intervene in this fashion usually feel powerless and embarrassed, and view authority figures as influential and this type of request as legitimate. Pushing the woman to do the convincing herself may alienate her and result in her withdrawal from therapy. In some cases, a call from a therapist may prove more effective because of the cultural rules of respect for authority. Every effort should be made to include the husband by appealing to his sense of responsibility and to his traditional role as family head, as the following case illustrates.

Mr. and Mrs. Arce, referred to therapy by a local Puerto Rican community agency, were having difficulties managing their children, especially a 12-year-old son. Therapy focused on helping the parents set clear limits and provide a reward system for the children. The parents appeared distant and angry, and had difficulty working together. The therapist commented that they seemed to be having difficulties, and that she sensed tension between them. They denied any difficulty and quickly agreed on an issue. The next therapy session was attended by Mrs. Arce alone. She stated that her husband had refused to come. He did not believe in therapy and was angry with her for seeking help. It was her fault, he felt, that the children were disobedient and disrespectful. She went on to complain about his lack of interest in her, his absence from the home, and his outbursts of anger. She wanted the therapist to call her husband and ask him to come to therapy. The therapist called Mr. Arce and told him that his absence had shown how much his wife needed his help to discipline the children. The husband's traditional role in the family was supported, and his boundaries regarding intimate matters were respected. An attempt to personalize the relationship was made through a home visit. The therapist supported the wife by involving the husband in the family as a father. Uniting them as parents strengthened generational boundaries and had a positive effect on the children's behavior. In the privacy of their home they were able to perceive the therapist as a friend and as part of their support system. The trust level was heightened, enabling them eventually to share more about their relationship.

Regardless of the therapist's ability to engage Puerto Rican couples in therapy, he or she will find that it is often extremely difficult and embarrassing for them to talk about sexual problems and physical abuse. Issues around lack of respect, jealousy, and problems with in-laws are easier. If the husband refuses to come in, his wife may be coached to mobilize the extended family for support. In cases in which the extended family is unavailable or unsupportive, the therapist may help to break the impasse by mobilizing such external systems as welfare, child-care facilities, and women's self-help groups to support the woman.

Engaging children in therapy will vary depending upon their ages. Since young children may be shy and frightened in front of strangers, play therapy may be more appropriate than conversation. If adolescents are unable to speak in front of their parents, it may be necessary for the therapist to see them alone. Due to respect and fear, they might not be able to speak about sex, drugs, problems at school, or cultural conflicts at home and in the community. Appropriate goals may be to help adolescents express their concerns, to help them share with their parents issues relevant to family problems, and to find ways in which parents and children can compromise. Sometimes, discussing the family's migratory process will clarify conflicts caused by contrasts between cultural values. Redefining roles in terms of privileges and responsibilities may be helpful. The therapist can be helpful by encouraging the parents to discuss their genuine concern for their child, and their fears that the behavior may lead to serious problems. By asking the parents to tell the child about their love, concerns, and fears, the therapist can help them relate to the child in a more positive manner.

Puerto Ricans underutilize mental health services, perhaps because the therapist and family have different expectations from therapy, which are largely determined by their sociocultural contexts. Lack of knowledge about the family's frame of reference may limit the therapist's ability to engage it in a trusting and personal relationship. Health-care providers need to think of forums that are culturally appropriate when providing services to Puerto Ricans. For instance, since Puerto Ricans under stress are likely to go to medical clinics rather than mental health centers, those settings may have to expand their boundaries to provide therapeutic services that respond to the crises presented. Agencies that treat Puerto Ricans may need to operate on a walk-in basis and with considerable flexibility. Due to the complexity and multitude of problems presented by these families, more than one therapist may need to intervene. A team of therapists that is familiar with Puerto Rican culture and fluent in Spanish may increase the effectiveness of treatment.

## REFERENCES

Abad, V., & Boyce, E. (1979). Issues in psychiatric evaluations of Puerto Ricans: Sociocultural perspective. *Journal of Operational Psychiatry, 10*(1), 28–30.

Abad, V., Ramos, J., & Boyce, E. (1974). A model for delivery of mental health services to Spanish speaking minorities. *American Journal of Orthopsychiatry, 44*(4), 584–595.

Aponte, H. (1976). The family–school interview: An eco-structural approach. *Family Process, 13*(3), 303–312.

Badillo-Ghali, S. (1974). Culture sensitivity and the Puerto Rican client. *Social Casework, 55*(1), 100–110.

Boas, F. (1940). *Puerto Rican archeology.* New York: Academy of Sciences.

Boyd-Franklin, N., & Garcia-Preto, N. (1994). Family therapy: A closer look at African American and Hispanic women. In L. Comas-Díaz & B. Greene (Eds.), *Women of color: Integrating ethnic and gender identities in psychotherapy* (pp. 239–264). New York: Guilford Press.

Comas-Díaz, L. (1994). Lati Negra. *Journal of Feminist Family Therapy, 5*(3/4)35–74.

Comas-Díaz, L. (1989). Culturally relevant issues and treatment implications for Hispanics. In D. Koslow & E. P. Salett (Eds.), *Crossing cultures in mental health.* Washington DC: Sietar.

De La Cancela, V. (1991). Working affirmatively with Puerto Rican men: Professional and personal reflections. In M. Bograd (Ed.), *Feminist approaches for men and women in family therapy* (pp. 195–211). New York: Harrington Park Press.

Delgado, M. (1978). Folk medicine in Puerto Rican culture. *International Social Work, 2*(2), 46–54.

Fernandez, C. C., & Quintero, R. M. (1974). Bases de la sociedad sexista en Puerto Rico. *Revista/Review Interamericana, 4*(2).

Fernandez-Mendez, E. (1970). *La identidad y cultura.* San Juan: Instituto de Cultura Puertorriquena.

Fitzpatrick, J. P. (1976). The Puerto Rican family. In R. W. Habenstein & C. H. Mindel

(Eds.), *Ethnic families in America: Patterns and variations* (pp. 192–217). New York: Elsevier.

Garcia-Preto, N. (1990). Hispanic mothers. In Ethnicity and mothers [Special Issue]. *Journal of Feminist Family Therapy, 2*(2), 1–65.

Garcia-Remis, M. (1993). Los cerebros que se van y el corazon que se queda. In *La ciudad que me habita* (pp. 11–19). Rio Piedras, Puerto Rico: Ediciones Huracan.

Garrison, V. (1977). Doctor, *espiritista*, or psychiatrist? Health-seeking behavior in a Puerto Rican neighborhood of New York City. *Medical Anthropology, 1*(2), 65–188.

Gonzalez, J. (1978). Language factors affecting treatment of schizophrenics. *Psychiatric Annals, 8*, 68–70.

Guerin, P. J. (1976). Evaluation of family system and genogram. In P. J. Guerin (Ed.), *Family therapy* (pp. 449–450). New York: Gardner Press.

Hardy-Fanta, C., & MacMahon-Herrera, E. (1981). Adapting family therapy to the Hispanic family. *Social Casework and the Journal of Contemporary Social Work, 62*(3), 138–148.

Maldonado-Sierra, E., & Trent, R. D. (1960). Neuroses and traditional beliefs in Puerto Rico. *International Journal of Social Psychiatry, 6*, 237.

Marcos, L., Alpert, M., Urcuyo, L., & Kesselman, M. (1973). The language barrier in evaluating Spanish speaking patients. *Archives of General Psychiatry, 8*, 655–659.

Massey D. S., & Eggers, M. L. (1990). The ecology of inequality: Minorities and concentration of poverty. *American Journal of Sociology, 95*, 1153–1189.

McGoldrick, M., & Gerson, R. (1985). *Genograms in family assessment.* New York: Norton.

Melendez, E., & Melendez, E. (1993). *Colonial dilemma: Critical perspectives on contemporary Puerto Rico.* Boston: South End Press.

Mizio, E. (1974). Impact of external systems on the Puerto Rican family. *Social Casework, 55*(1), 76–83.

Mizio, E. (1979). *Puerto Rican Task Report—Project on Ethnicity.* New York: Family Service Association.

Novas, H. (1994). *Everything you need to know about Latino history.* New York: Plume/Penguin Books.

Padilla, A. M., Ruiz, R. A., & Alvarez, R. (1975). Community mental health services for the Spanish speaking/surnamed population. *American Psychologist, 30*, 892–905.

Pane, F. R. (1973). Account of the antiquities or customs of the Indians. In K. Wagenheim & O. J. Wagenheim (Eds.), *The Puerto Ricans.* New York: Anchor Books.

Papajohn, J., & Spiegel, J. (1975). *Transactions in families.* San Francisco, CA: Jossey-Bass.

Pittman, F. S., Langsley, D. G., Flomenhaft, K., De Young, C. D., Machtka, P., & Kaplan, D. M. (1971). Therapy techniques of the family therapy unit. In J. Haley (Ed.), *Changing families—A family therapy reader.* New York: Grune & Stratton.

Puerto Rican Congress of New Jersey. (1976). *Folk medicine in a homogeneous Puerto Rican community.* Trenton, NJ: Author.

Rabkin J., & Struening, E. L. (1976). *Ethnicity, social class and mental illness* (Paper Series No. 17). New York: Institute of Pluralism and Group Identity.

Rodriguez, C. E. (1990). Racial classification among Puerto Rican men and women in New York. *Hispanic Journal of Behavioral Sciences, 12*, 266–380.

Rodriguez, E. E., Sanchez-Korrol, V., & Alers, J. O. (1980). *The Puerto Rican struggle: Essays on survival.* New York: Puerto Rican Migration Research Consortiumo.

Rothenberg, A. (1964). Puerto Rico and aggression. *American Journal of Psychiatry, 20*(10), 962–970.

Sager, C., Brayboy, T. L., & Waxenberg, B. R. (1972). Black patient—White therapist. *American Journal of Orthopsychiatry, 8*(3), 128.

Sluzki, C. E. (1982). The Latin loner revisited. In M. McGoldrick, J. K. Pearce, & J. Giordano (Eds.), *Ethnicity and family therapy* (1st ed., pp. 492–498). New York: Guilford Press.

Stevens E. (1972). Machismo and marianismo. *Transaction-Society, 10*(6), 57–63.

Tomas, P. (1967). *Down these mean streets.* New York: Knopf.

U.S. Bureau of the Census. (1991). *Statistical abstract.* Washington, DC: U.S. Government Printing Office.

Wagenheim, K., & Wagenheim, O. J. (Eds.). (1973). *The Puerto Ricans.* New York: Anchor Books.

CHAPTER 14

# Brazilian Families

## Eliana Catão Korin

Over the last decade, an increasing number of Brazilians have migrated to the United States, making this population one of the fastest growing immigrant groups in many U.S. cities. Brazilians have migrated to this country before, but since the mid-1980s, their immigration rate has risen considerably as the economy in Brazil deteriorated, threatening the middle class and making its standard of living difficult to maintain (Margolis, 1994).

There is a paucity of information on Brazilian immigrants to the United States, except for a few publications (Margolis, 1989, 1990, 1994) and some studies (Moretto, 1991; Sacks, 1993). Often confused with Hispanics and Portuguese, it is only recently that Brazilians have started to be noticed as a distinct group in the diverse cultural mosaic of this country (Margolis, 1994; Sacks, 1993). Brazilians, of course, do not speak Spanish, and their culture is quite different from other Portuguese-speaking people. And, in spite of their culture or language affinity with these two groups, Brazilians resent the lack of recognition by U.S. citizens of their unique heritage.

This immigrant group is relatively small—estimated to be between 350,000 and 400,000[1]—but its impact is becoming quite noticeable in some communities because of its concentration and visibility in particular areas, where Brazilian restaurants, small businesses, and news publications have proliferated (Margolis, 1994; Franklin, 1992). Significant numbers of Brazilians are now found in the Boston area; Southeastern Massachusetts; Connecticut; greater New York City; Newark, New Jersey and surrounding communities; Miami and other cities in South Florida; and California, particularly the San Francisco Bay Area and Los Angeles (Margolis, 1994; Sacks, 1993; Fôlha de São Paulo, 1994).

Initially mostly male, this group now includes an increasing number of women and families. Most recent arrivals are from urban, middle-class, relatively educated backgrounds. Most enter legally as tourists and become "visa overstayers." Brazilians migrating to larger cities are mostly from the middle-

or lower-middle class, are racially more mixed, and come mostly from large urban centers. Those from the interior prefer to settle in small towns in the United States, where larger numbers of lower- and working-class Brazilians are concentrated. The majority of Brazilian immigrants have an educational background of at least high school level, and others have had some years of college and have held professional or semiprofessional positions back home. In contrast, as recent immigrants, most often lacking proper documentation and English-language skills, they are confined to menial and dead-end jobs, positions considered undesirable by U.S. workers (Franklin, 1992; Margolis, 1994). They work hard, usually at two or three jobs, so they are able to make enough money to pay debts related to immigration expenses (often around $6,000 dollars), and to help their families in Brazil. They see themselves at least initially as "sojourners" not "settlers" in this country (Margolis, 1994; Moretto, 1991), planning to return when they have saved enough money to buy a home or start a business back home. Many wealthy Brazilians have also emigrated to escape economic uncertainty and a surge of violence (such as recurrent kidnappings for ransom) threatening the stability of their lives. In the last few years, a number of upper-middle-class and professional people have also come with plans to continue their professional careers or to invest in business.

Class, regional, and educational background, conditions of migration, and immigrant status are then determining factors regarding the needs and adaptation of this group to the new culture. The recency of their immigration, fear of the authorities, and linguistic barriers are factors restricting most Brazilians' access to and contact with mental health and human services.

This chapter describes the Brazilian middle-class immigrant population in the United States, presents an overview of the Brazilian culture, and discusses its implication for clinical work.

## BRAZIL: A SOCIOPOLITICAL PERSPECTIVE

Brazil is a large and populous country, almost the size of the United States. Its population of almost 155 million[2] is mostly concentrated in large urban areas close to the Atlantic. Brazil comprises distinct subcultures, sharing the Portuguese language as a common denominator.

Colonized by the Portuguese in the 1500s, Brazilians are descendants of a mixture of people. Portuguese colonizers mixed with the indigenous population and African slaves (mostly of Yoruba and Quimbundu origin), from whom they borrowed many customs and words. Brief Dutch and French colonizations in the Northeast, and the 19th-century waves of German, Italian, Polish, Ukrainian, Lebanese, Japanese, and other immigrants added new elements to this mixture. Brazilian culture is therefore a composite of rich ethnic traditions that have blended differently in various regions. The African influence is most visible in Bahia (a northeastern state), in contrast with the European south. The southeast reflects a confluence of all cultures and races, with a Luzo African predominance.[3]

Though the majority of Brazilians are Catholic, their religious practices are also influenced by spiritualist religions of African origin, such as Candomble and Umbanda. Brazilians do not necessarily follow all Church dogmas, for example, in contraceptive practices and views on sexuality. Also, Catholicism in Brazil has been largely influenced by the ideology of Liberation Theology.[4] Protestant, Jewish, and Espiritism faiths are also present in Brazil, although the Evangelical Christian movement has gained an increasing number of adherents among Brazilians.

Initially an agrarian society, Brazil has evolved since the World War II into a mostly industrialized society, becoming the largest economy of Latin America. Nowadays it is a well developed and modern country with a relatively advanced infrastructure, modern educational institutions, and well-equipped health facilities, where large cosmopolitan urban centers flourish and many Brazilians enjoy a high standard of living. But there is also another Brazil: a country where enormous wealth coexists with rampant and visible poverty; where an internationally competitive industry is shadowed by an escalating inflation and a huge external debt, and where social opportunities are limited for many because of well-defined class and racial hierarchies.

The social fabric of the country is defined by a system of privileges according to class status and racial background. Higher-status Brazilians (most likely White or light-skinned) always expect special treatment, and social inferiors (White, Brown, or Black) easily yield to elites. In Brazil, authority and hierarchy rule, in contrast with the United States, where a pervasive, although idealized, egalitarian ethos prevails (DaMatta, 1991). The legal system is less important than a network of powerful and influential contacts. A system of patronage and favors becomes an acceptable way to get on in life. A Brazilian's social identity originates mostly in class background and family connections.

Compared with other countries, Brazil has been often recognized for its harmonious race relations. The Portuguese colonizers' acceptance of intermarriage, the absence of outright segregation, and the national consensus against public discrimination are factors that have contributed to racial integration in Brazil (Wood & Carvalho, 1988).[5] However, racism (Telles, 1993a) and racial inequality still remain unquestionable facts (Fernandes, 1979). Although this society recognizes and values the African contribution to its culture, especially in food, religion, music, dance, and arts in general, few Blacks are in positions of power and privilege. Brazilians are also confronted with the fact that the average non-White person in Brazil is poorer and less educated than the average White person. Nonetheless, most Brazilians (Whites, Browns, and most Blacks) would deny or disregard the presence of racism in Brazil, which is often obscured by high levels of racial interaction.

Race relations in Brazil are far more subtle and complex than in the United States. Because of miscegenation, the interplay of shades of blackness and the complex perceptions of social standing, race is defined differently in Brazil (Rodriguez, 1995). Brazilians understand race as a continuous color variable rather than as a categorical variable, as in the United States (Telles, 1993b). Also, racial identification is somewhat flexible and may reflect a tendency toward whitening. Persons near boundaries of color are likely to identify with the lighter category. For instance, a middle-class darker Brazilian might be classified as Black—and eventually discriminated against—for the first time in his or her life on coming to the United States, in contrast with his or her experiences in Brazil where he or she might be seen and identify him- or her-self as White or *mulato/a*. Discrimination is not simply racially determined in Brazil; it also requires class considerations. Afro Brazilians are more likely to choose class over racial identity (Telles, 1993b). Brazilians of all shades often say, "He is a Black of good position," meaning that he can be accepted by an elite group in spite of his color. Race and class are two intertwined realities in this country; they both determine racial identity and social status.

Paradoxically, in this highly hierarchical society, money and social power are not absolute values. For instance, music, dance, and play are equally important elements, acting as social regulators of power between different social groups. This is a culture full of contradictions, where opposing values maintain each other, and where special rituals (such as the Carnival) provide outlets that question and reaffirm a hierarchical social order. Social spaces such as the beaches, soccer games, and "the schools of samba" are also places where hierarchies are ignored and people of all colors and classes congregate, becoming part of the same world. As the Brazilian anthropologist, Roberto Da Matta (1991) says, "[Brazilians] unlike the people of the United States, never say 'separate but equal'; instead we say 'different but united,' which is the golden rule of a hierarchical and relational universe such as ours" (p. 4).

## CULTURAL VALUES

The descriptions that follow refer primarily to middle-class Brazilians, mostly from the Southeast region, from which the majority of U.S. Brazilian immigrants come. Ethnic distinctions are not highlighted because in Brazil, differently from in the United States, there is a tendency toward cultural integration and/or biculturality. For instance, German, Jewish, Italian, and Japanese immigrants, in spite of their higher levels of ethnic identity, tend to acculturate upon contact with the mainstream culture. Intermarriage (usually to native Whites) among second-generation immigrants is common.

The importance and value of the family is probably the most central element of Brazilian culture. Indeed, the family constitutes the most important source of support throughout a person's life. Brazilians maintain a close relationship with their families, even when distant geographically. This close-knit unit includes nuclear and extended family members, as well as nonblood kin. Personal needs and issues are dealt with in the context of the family. Social life commonly involves weekly family meals and celebrations of special occasions, when stories are shared, games are played, and problems are addressed and solved. Concepts of loyalty and obligation or accountability toward the family influence personal choices and often compromise individual aspirations. Generational or marital conflicts often involve mediation by other relatives or family friends. Children receive a lot of attention, nurturance, and protection. Traditionally, family life has been based on a patriarchal structure, thereby reinforcing hierarchical relations within the family. Nevertheless, sex roles among Brazilian men and women have been changing. Younger couples tend to adopt a more egalitarian view of marriage, abandoning the idea that a woman should always accede to the husband's demands (Miller, 1979). Although many women hold public positions of power, most Brazilian women agree with prevailing attitudes, commonly accepting the burden of most responsibilities for family caretaking functions.[6] Among middle-class urban groups, marriage tends to be postponed until after education and employment are secured by both women and men (Miller, 1979). Parenthood is highly valued, but the marital relationship also involves mutual fulfillment through a sense of intimacy and sexual love.

Brazilians are extremely gregarious people; they enjoy being together, sharing tasks, and helping others at time of need. Solidarity, empathy, and hospitality are important values in this culture. They are also known for a basically positive outlook toward life. For every problem there is a solution, or a way out (*um jeitinho*)[7] as Brazilians often say. If there is no solution, problems are accepted as an inevitable part of life, and life goes on (*fatalismo*). Conflict avoidance and denial of problems can be a result of this sense of optimism. When sufferings, frustrations, and losses occur, the norm is not to dwell on suffering or negative feelings.

Brazilians differ from Americans regarding notions of privacy. They are not usually very concerned about "having their own space." They prefer physical closeness, touching often when talking, standing close to strangers, and hugging and kissing when greeting friends or expressing affection. Boundaries are also defined differently at an emotional level. People are expected to acknowledge others' problems and needs—"Be considerate"—even when they are not expressed verbally. As with other Latin cultures, social interactions among Brazilians are guided by the concept of *personalismo* (Garcia-Preto, 1982), which means that relationships are more important than accomplishments. Unlike the United States, where identity emerges from what one does, social identities in Brazil are based on what one is. As the American anthropologist Conrad Kottak (1990) says, the contrast is one of "doing" (United

States) versus "being" (Brazil). Good social standing is established by gaining *respeito* (respect) from others, through recognition of personal values such as honor and dignity, and not necessarily through achievement. However, to "be somebody in life" (*ser alguém na vida*), meaning to succeed through work and education, is a value reinforced especially by the middle and lower-middle classes. With industrialization and urbanization, an increasing orientation toward social mobility and achievement is occurring in Brazil (Miller, 1979).

Sexuality is more openly expressed in Brazil: Nudity and graphic scenes in the theater, movies, and TV are usually acceptable (Kottak, 1990), and sexual language is commonly used in lyrics and plays. Both men and women are very expressive with their bodies. Despite the patriarchal nature of the society, women are not necessarily assigned passive roles. Virginity before marriage is expected for young women but adolescents are not as supervised as in other cultures. On the surface, homosexuality is accepted but not legitimized. Within the family, it is dealt with as a secret that everybody knows. In general, Brazilian culture allows for greater fluidity of sexual roles than other cultures, in spite of its patriarchal norms.

## BRAZILIANS IN THE UNITED STATES

Most Brazilians' lives in the United States are shaped by the typical challenges faced by first-generation, middle-class immigrants arriving in this country, such as poor English-language skills, issues related to immigration and occupational status, and economic difficulties. Isolation, fear of deportation, and loss of social status are specific stresses that affect many Brazilians here. Brazilian immigrants often succeed, counting on their disposition for hard work, their sense of determination, and their capacity to improvise when faced with unexpected problems. However, they are often unaware of some of the challenges awaiting them in this country. Coming from a culture where emotional closeness, fun, and reciprocity are important values, loneliness, absence of social life, and lack of nurturance and support by loved ones become major blows to their sense of well-being. A common dilemma constantly and continuously voiced by Brazilians who come searching for the American dream, independent of class, occupational status or, to a certain extent, their success in the new country, is "Is it better to live poor and happy in Brazil or rich and unhappy in the United States?"

Juvenal, a man in his mid-30s, who immigrated to the United States 3 years ago, leaving behind his wife and children, shares his dilemma of "here or there." "Here I am making more money than I was in Brazil. I work hard but I make enough money to send to the kids and survive here. But this is not life! Here is just work, work and money. No respect and consideration for you at work. Nobody cares for anybody."

———————— ᵂ ————————

The opportunities offered in the United States are offset for Brazilians by the loss of a nurturing and stimulating culture, which they have had to leave behind and for which they continue to yearn. The dream of return is always present among most Brazilians, even when they are well adjusted to this society.

The patterned and programmed style of American culture is also difficult for many Brazilians, who are accustomed to a more spontaneous social life. Loneliness is particularly acute for those many individuals who immigrated alone, leaving behind their spouses and/or children (Sacks, 1993). The immigrant's adjustment to a new culture depends a great deal on whether one family member migrated alone or whether a large portion of the family, community, or a nation came together (McGoldrick, 1982).

Juvenal, in his report, was also referring to his frustration with the lack of support among Brazilians here and his experiences of discrimination at work. Unfortunately, lack of solidarity among members of their community here is definitely a source of major stress for Brazilian immigrants (Sacks, 1993). Negative experiences with compatriots, which often involve loss of money or abuses of some sort, are not infrequent among Brazilian immigrants. Lack of support in a highly competitive environment might promote these maladaptive behaviors. Typically, Brazilian communities are not as well organized and supportive as other ethnic communities that were able to develop an economic enclave in the United States (Margolis, 1994). Churches in general are the major source of support to Brazilian immigrants. Increased religiosity, or in the other extreme, alcohol intake, are coping mechanisms used to deal with loneliness and lack of support.

When families come together, both parents often work extensive shifts and children might be neglected or overwhelmed by the responsibility of taking care of siblings. A sense of mutual nurturance and connection is often eroded in this new life situation. Marital distress may result, especially when one member of the couple is not awarded the same opportunity as the other or if there were previous disagreements about the very idea of migration. However, most couples overcome initial stresses, renegotiating relationships to adjust to the new reality. This is especially the case of achieving, goal-oriented families.

Stresses are obviously worse for families for whom the American dream is not accessible. Without a job or income, these families feel trapped, unable to earn enough money to pay for migration debts at home and survive and, on the other hand, unable to return home due to lack of resources.

## CLINICAL IMPLICATIONS[8]

Most Brazilians come to treatment when an acute emotional crisis occurs and support is not available in their immediate network. Nonetheless, psychotherapy or counseling for emotional and family problems is not an alien concept for most middle-class Brazilians, especially the younger generation. When compared with other ethnic groups, Brazilians in the United States seem to be more receptive to the idea of psychotherapy if a personal connection is provided with a particular therapist, someone who can relate to them culturally and linguistically. However, linguistic barriers, time and financial constraints (Sacks, 1993), the lack of information about resources, and the scarcity of culturally sensitive professionals keep Brazilians away from clinical settings.[9]

Brazilians are a proud and self-reliant immigrant group; they avoid being viewed as a problem and do not want to be dependent on social services. Brazilians respond better to a friendly, personal manner rather than a business-like one, expecting the therapist to be personally interested in their problems and to take an active role in their lives. Curiosity about Brazilian culture, reinforced by the therapist's empathic statements regarding the cultural differences between him or her and the family, and also the dominant society, are very instrumental in facilitating the therapeutic relationship. Most Brazilians tend to be initially deferential with authorities but will exhibit a casual and spontaneous style once a relationship is established. People from the interior part of the country are more formal: personable and cordial, but reserved and less verbal. Those from the coastal areas are more expansive and demonstrative. They are likely to be very open and trusting about sharing their vulnerabilities and personal problems. This spontaneous and easy dialogue might be changed in family sessions, however, where fear of conflict and a need of mutual protection might interfere with the communication flow. These mechanisms are intensified in the first years after migration. Together with an acknowledgement of family strengths, indirect techniques such as circular questions are useful to address conflicts without direct confrontations, which do not work well with this group. Reflecting Brazilian immigrant patterns, adults represent the largest number of clients coming for treatment in the United States. Common reasons for seeking therapy include depression, family problems, anxiety, somatization, grief, and issues related to sexual dysfunction and sexual identity. Referrals for family treatment are increasing as families are formed here, and as more families migrate together. Many Brazilians come for treatment for problems related to marital conflicts. However, separations and divorce might happen in many families. Among recent immigrants, marriage might be a buffer for loneliness and other stresses. Couples who migrate together may experience increased closeness in the period just after migration, becoming a major source for support for each other; but as the new culture offers new opportunities, they are challenged into revising previous modes of partnership and renegotiating their relationship. Many Brazilian women marry non-Brazilian men, thus facing additional difficulties related to cultural differences between partners (Sacks, 1994).

School referrals are often generated by a conflicted and depressed adolescent who has difficulties adjusting here and wants to return to Brazil. Antisocial behaviors are not usual among first-generation adolescent immigrants, which most Brazilian adolescents here are. Adolescents might also immigrate alone, joining a parent (usually the father) who has constituted a new family here. These reunions tend to be very distressing for the adolescent, who has to accept a new family and whose idealized dream of coming to the United States contrasts with the reality of the daily lives of families here.

The current wave of immigrants is younger than previous waves (Kantrowitz, 1994); therefore, more young adults are coming for therapy. Depression, usually related to loneliness and separation from their families of origin, is the most common presenting complaint. Coming from a culture with another model of individuation, in which a young adult could live many years with his or her parents, this sudden separation, with many miles in between, can be a disorienting experience for many Brazilians and can cause unanticipated distress.

As with other immigrants, in assessing the emotional problems presented by Brazilian immigrants and their families, it is crucial that the therapist examine the interface of family, life cycle, and cultural transitional issues. Furthermore, situational stresses need to be distinguished from dysfunctional patterns already existent before migration, in order to determine the type and level of intervention.

Life cycle issues are usually amplified by the stress of migration. For instance, an adolescent with problems of school adjustment might be challenging his parents in dealing with their own developmental dilemmas in the context of cultural transition: "Did we make the right choice by immigrating? How can we cope with these feelings of loss and uncertainty?" The therapy has to include a consideration of both the impact of cultural and developmental stresses affecting the individual and of the family at a particular stage.

Fortunately, many crises are situational, requiring only brief counseling. There are cases though, in which the cultural conflict involves complex, unresolved past issues.

In a family whose depressed and suicidal adolescent daughter insisted to her parents that she wanted to return to Brazil, a focus on the parents' adolescence uncovered an important secret (unknown to the daughter): When her mother was about her age, her grandfather had abandoned the family and was never seen again. The mother avoided any family and marital conflict for fear of a new abandonment. Typically, as with other less functional families, these parents blamed the new culture for their child's problems.

———————— ❧ ————————

In these situations, the therapist's initial "acceptance" and validation of the cultural conflicts are crucial for building a therapeutic alliance. An inquiry focused on pre- and postmigratory stresses is most relevant to facilitate an understanding of the migration in the context of the unfolding life script.

Often the very idea of the migration comes about as a way to deal with a particular conflict. Fortunately though, migration might also provide a successful "solution" for individual and family impasses. For example, a gay man who immigrated as an attempt to legitimize his sexual identity, thus escaping constant criticisms by his father, was able to achieve success and change his image in his family of origin after coming to the United States.

Class, gender, and skin-color dynamics, as well as stages of migration and immigration status, are important factors to be considered in formulating problems and designing therapeutic interventions with Brazilians. The following case illustrates how the therapist's attention to these issues elicited crucial information for the understanding of the conflicts faced by this family.

Fernando is a White, 38-year-old man with a technical degree, who arrived in the United States 8 years ago with his wife, a specialized nurse, and two children. Well-adjusted to this country and speaking English fluently, he has been able to provide for his family with a modest but stable income, working as a carpenter for a small contractor. Very depressed and facing escalating marital fights, he came for therapy, referred by his employer. In therapy, Fernando shared his pain of seeing his marriage fail and his disillusionment with his limited financial accomplishments. "I should never have left," he said, an untimely statement for an immigrant who would soon receive a permanent resident status in this country.

At this migration stage, earlier immigrants are reexamining their initial goals and considering new life directions. When dreams are not fulfilled, unresolved family conflicts and the fantasy of return might emerge.

When asked about the fights with his wife, Fernando described her as the instigator, easily upset with his family and sensitive about being excluded from family social events. She was portrayed as prone to emotional outbursts whenever "she does not get her way." He blamed her for alienating his family and others with her angry outbursts. Initially, migration brought them back together, but the fights had escalated during the last 2 years as she started to become more independent.

In eliciting his story, we learned that Fernando met his wife in Sao Paulo after migrating from a small conservative town in the interior of Brazil. He, a serious and quiet man, was attracted (and still seemed to be) to her vivacious and engaging manner. In response to the therapist's questions about her background, he reported that he had chosen a type of woman his "proper" family did not consider to be a good enough match for him: She was an illegitimate child raised by a poor, Black, adoptive, single mother. Her qualifications as a specialized nurse and main provider had been dismissed both by Fernando and his family.

This case shows how Brazilians' concerns with family status and social class affect personal and family dynamics, requiring the therapist's understanding of the peculiarities of gender, class, and skin color dynamics in Brazil. Marly, the wife, considered a *mulata* (born to White and Black parents, often considered a symbol of beauty in Brazil), was discriminated against mostly for her poor and illegitimate background and less for her skin color, which, in the Brazilian context, gave her some social power.

In describing her drama, Marly, a woman of high aspirations, but who has been unable to advance professionally here, revealed that all along what had mattered most to her was to be treated "as a wife should be." Her personal history (illegitimacy) and racial background (dark in a country where to be White is best) made her more vulnerable to being dependent for legitimacy and affirmation on the acceptance of her husband and others of higher social status.

Therapy with this couple involved a process of life review to examine their individual behaviors in relation to their specific family and cultural legacies and to power differences dictated by gender and skin color. A narrative model integrating Paulo Freire's problem-posing method (Korin, 1994) is most valuable in the treatment of Brazilians and other immigrants, as it provides a framework to relate their personal conflicts to a larger sociocultural context. This approach involves therapist and clients in a process of reflection and mutual learning about the client's personal and social realities. The client and family's migration story is validated and reexamined within a historical and sociocultural context to promote empowerment. Therapy with Brazilians will always require a family orientation. Family-of-origin work, with focus on losses related to cultural transition and social status changes, is a necessary approach in doing therapy with this immigrant group.

## CONCLUSION

The formulations outlined in this chapter are presented as an initial map for orienting therapists' work with Brazilian clients and their families. Clients themselves are always the best source of information about their culture (Korin, 1994).

Therapists need to examine and recognize the impact of their own value orientation and that of the dominant society's in assessing their clients' problems; they should avoid ethnic stereotyping and be aware of pathologizing normal processes. The individualist orientation predominant in middle-class U.S. culture is not a universal value; in many cultures, attachment to one's family of origin continues throughout life, in spite of the inevitable changes of relationships that occur over time. Brazilian clients in treatment with U.S. therapists often experience that their attachment to their family of origin is misunderstood and pathologized. Discussing differences in communication style, many Brazilian women have expressed their dissatisfaction with the ways in which their more demonstrative and body-oriented communication style has been often misunderstood by therapists and supervisors. This style has been interpreted as sexualized/seductive behavior contributing to stereotyping and discomfort in therapeutic and professional relationships.

It is my belief that a culture-sensitive practice requires therapists' self-reflection and knowledge about their own cultural values as much as their knowledge about their clients' culture. As a final reminder, it is important always to bear in mind that the therapeutic encounter is an interactive process that always involves the interface of three cultures: the client/family's, the therapist's, and the dominant culture (Sluzki, 1979).

## ACKNOWLEDGMENTS

The author would like to thank the many Brazilians interviewed for this chapter for their generosity with time and insightful contributions. Special thanks to Maxime Margolis, Ph.D., and David Sacks, Psy.D., for their connections with other Brazilian professionals.

## NOTES

1. There are no reliable data regarding the total number of Brazilians living in the United States. In the categories offered by the 1990 Census, Brazilians are not precisely classified; in addition, many Brazilians are undocumented and are therefore not included in official reports.
2. Based on the 1990 census, the 1995 population has been projected at 154,507,291 (Instituto Brasileiro de Estatística e Geografia, Censo Demográfico).
3. Brazilian culture, in general, while predominantly of Portuguese origin, has strong African influences. Whites, along with Brazilians of color, share this Luzo African culture, seeing the African elements as an integral part of the national culture (Telles, 1993b).
4. A liberal movement led by priests working in the Third World, urging the Catholic church to become more responsive to the needs of the poor, questioning therefore its traditional power structures. This movement gave birth to many leading voices in Brazil, such as Bishop Helder Camara and the educator Paulo Freire, who became known around the world for their work with disenfranchised populations.
5. Census racial categories in Brazil (1990) include four categories: White (55.3%), Brown (39.3%), Black (4.9%), and Yellow (0.5%). Afro Brazilians, almost half of the national population, usually refer to Brown and Black categories considered together. The Brown category includes primarily mixed-raced people. Also, Whites are often not purely White, as in the U.S. definition, but relatively White (Telles, 1993a).
6. As the literature on sex roles indicates, balance of power in any marriage is largely dependent on the wife's level of education and employment.
7. This famous expression *dar um jeitinho* may be translated as "find a way out," "clever dodge," or "bypass," and might also imply the use of playful "chicanery" (*malandragem*).

8. Given the limited clinical knowledge available about Brazilians in the United States, what follows are very preliminary formulations, largely based on this author's clinical experience, as well as on interviews conducted with therapists who work with Brazilians, and with Brazilians who have been in therapy in the United States.

9. From 1991–1992, in Cambridge, Massachusetts, in a clinic serving especially the Portuguese-speaking population, 45.4% of the new intakes were Brazilians. (Goldfajn, 1994).

## REFERENCES

A Fôlha de São Paulo. (1994, July 11). *Migração se Intensificou Durante os Anos 80*, pp. 4–9.

Da Matta, R. (1991). *Carnival, rogues and heroes: An interpretation of the Brazilian dilemma.* Notre Dame, IN: University of Notre Dame Press.

Fernandes, F. (1972). *O negro no mundo dos brancos.* São Paulo: Difusão Européia do Livro.

Franklin, J. (1992, February 3). Homeland troubles bring Brazilian influx to region. *Boston Globe*, pp. 1, 14.

Garcia-Preto, N. (1982). Puerto Rican families. In M. McGoldrick, J. K. Pearce, & J. Giordano (Eds.) *Ethnicity and family therapy* (1st ed., pp. 164–186). New York: Guilford Press.

Goldfajn, D. S. (1994). *Brazilian immigrants living in the Boston area: Subsidies in understanding their acculturation process.* Unpublished manuscript, Massachusetts School of Professional Psychology, Boston.

Kantrowitz, F. (1994, July 31). Brazilian beat: New immigrants seek the dream. *Boston Sunday Globe*, p. 1.

Korin, E. C. (1994). Social inequalities and therapeutic relationship: Applying Freire's ideas in clinical practice. In R. Almeida (Ed.), *Expansions of feminist family therapy through diversity* (pp. 75–88). New York: Haworth Press. (Published simultaneously in *Journal of Feminist Family Therapy, 3/4*, 75–88)

Kottak, C. P. (1990). *Prime society: An anthropological analysis of television and culture.* Belmont, CA: Wadsworth.

Margolis, M. (1989). A new ingredient in the melting pot: Brazilians in New York City. *City and Society, 3*(2), 179–187.

Margolis, M. (1990). From mistress to servant: Downward mobility among Brazilians in New York City. *Urban Anthropology, 19*(3), 215–231.

Margolis, M. (1994). *Little Brazil: An ethnography of Brazilian immigrants in New York City.* Princeton, NJ: Princeton University Press.

McGoldrick, M. (1982). Ethnicity and family therapy: An overview. In M. McGoldrick, J. K. Pearce, & J. Giordano (Eds.), *Ethnicity and family therapy* (1st ed., pp. 3–30). New York: Guilford Press.

Miller, C. (1979). The function of middle-class extended family networks in Brazilian urban society. In M. Margolis & W. Carter (Eds.), *Brazil: Anthropological perspectives* (pp. 305–316). New York: Columbia University Press.

Moretto, D. (1991). Descriptive study of the Brazilian immigrants living in the Boston area and identification of their major pre- and post-immigration stress. *Dissertation Abstracts.* Boston: Boston University School of Education.

Rodriguez, C. (1995). *Race in four dimensions.* Unpublished manuscript, Fordham University, New York, NY.

Sacks, D. (1993). *Recent Brazilian immigrants to the United States: Human service needs and help-seeking behaviors.* Psy.D. dissertation, Rutgers University, Piscataway, NJ.

Sluzki, C. E. (1979). Migration and family conflict. *Family Process, 18*(4), 379–390.

Telles, E. E. (1993a). Racial distance and region in Brazil: Intermarriage in Brazilian urban areas. *Latin American Research Review, 28,* 141–162.

Telles, E. E. (1993b). *Afro-Brazilian identity and segregation.* Paper presented at the conference on Racial Politics in Brazil, Austin, TX.

Wood, C., & Carvalho, J. A. M. (1988). *The demography of inequality in Brazil.* Cambridge: Harvard University Press.

CHAPTER 15

# Central American Families

## Miguel Hernandez

This chapter focuses on the unique challenges Central American refugee families experience in adapting and integrating to U.S. society. I will explore here the complex historical events that triggered their migration to the United States, the impact of their exposure to war, the difficulties emanating from their political status in the United States, and the effects of migration on individual and family life. My ideas are based on clinical work with families in New York City. The suggestions made in this chapter are intended to be a general clinical framework with which to approach Central American refugee families living in the United States.

## HISTORICAL BACKGROUND

Central America, the region that links North and South America, includes seven countries: Belize, Guatemala, El Salvador, Honduras, Nicaragua, Costa Rica, and Panama. Belize and Panama, while geographically part of Central America, have a fairly distinct history from that of the other countries in the region. Belize is an English-speaking republic that became independent from Great Britain in 1981 and does not figure significantly in what has been called the "Central American" problem. Panama, although often lumped with the other countries of the region, is not technically Central American; its pre-Columbian indigenous cultures were South American and, until 1903, it was part of Colombia (Booth & Walker, 1993).

Nicaragua, Honduras, El Salvador, and Guatemala were conquered two decades after the first Spanish penetration in 1522. Costa Rica was not settled until the 1560s because, unlike other areas, it offered no easily exploitable gold or Indian slaves. The massive extermination of the country's native inhabitants, as well as its geographical isolation from the rest of the isthmus, lent to a distinctive political, economic, and social history. For instance, in Costa Rica the population became heavily Iberian and therefore a racially distinct and exploited underclass never developed (Booth & Walker, 1993).

Elsewhere in Central America, Spaniards were able to impose their domination without destroying the entire native population. By the end of the conquest, however, fighting, diseases, and enslavement caused a drastic reduction of the Indian population. Only in Guatemala did a large number of Indians survive. Perhaps this was due to the greater difficulty Spaniards had in subjugating completely the relatively more advanced society they encountered in the region (Booth & Walker, 1993). Today, Guatemala continues to have a large native Indian population, which has kept its culture and language alive and has made others feel its presence in the political history of the country.

During the colonial period, Spain ruled Guatemala, Nicaragua, El Salvador, Honduras, and Costa Rica. The region was controlled by a Spanish-born elite, and everyone else belonged to a downtrodden lower class. Biological unions between Spaniards and Indians produced *mestizos* (of Spanish Indian blood), who were never considered equals to Spaniards, but were nonetheless of higher social status than pure Indians. This class configuration changed drastically as new groups were added to the population: African slaves, and later the mulatto offspring of White–Black unions. Today, there are still clear racial divisions where non-White people are socially, politically, and racially discriminated against.

The White elite controlled the human and natural resources. The economy became focused on exportation of products that were not essential for supporting the lower-class population. After the region's independence from Spain in the 1820s, those who had inherited economic power and social standing perpetuated an unregulated, agro-export economy for their own benefit. Out of this pattern, complex social, political, and economic conflicts later developed (Booth & Walker, 1993).

The 19th century was characterized by American and British efforts to expand their political influence in the region. Laissez-faire liberals, who advocated unregulated free enterprise, dominated Central American nations during the late 19th century and part of the 20th, introduced new export products such as coffee and bananas, and advocated modernization, development of governmental institutions, and the infrastructure that could facilitate their economic plan. By the century's end, their coffee business had produced a large class of wealthy landowners who tolerated military and civilian dictatorships and the oppressive sociopolitical system that contributed to important revolutions in the 20th century (Skidmore & Smith, 1992).

In Costa Rica, political reforms began in the late 19th century and culminated in 1948, with the abolition of the army and development of local democratic reforms. The rest of the region, however, made limited progress toward democracy in the 1950s, only to witness a renewal of military rule in the 1960s (Skidmore & Smith, 1992).

During the mid-20th century, changes in the export crops took land away from the rural poor, provoking an exodus to the cities. Landownership and agricultural production became even more concentrated. To varying degrees in each nation, the surge in domestic and foreign investment was concentrated in the production of consumer goods. The number of factory and middle-class jobs grew as the region became more industrialized during the 1970s, but rural and urban unemployment rose because of urban migrations by unemployable peasants (Booth & Walker, 1993).

Nicaragua, Guatemala, and El Salvador entered the 1970s with numerous common problems, including even greater concentration of wealth, increased rural and urban lower-class unemployment, and decreased agricultural self-sufficiency among large segments of the rural poor. The rapid enrichment of the national bourgeoisie in these three countries, rapid growth of the middle classes, and improvement of their living standard increased socioeconomic inequality and stimulated class conflict and widespread protests throughout the region (Booth & Walker, 1993).

Supported by the United States, the countries' governments responded to the massive rebellions with sharply escalating military force and violence. Subjected to repression and to governmental refusal to carry out political and economic reforms, the aggrieved began to organize, mobilize economic resources from poor and wealthy opposition leaders, and engage in armed resistance (Booth & Walker, 1993). The escalating conflicts resulted in two decades (1970–1990) of civil wars within the three countries.

During the wars, many human rights crimes were committed. Physical and psychological torture, intimidation, massive killings, and other persecution of individuals, families, and communities left many with profound psychological and physical wounds (Booth & Walker, 1993; Garcia & Rodriguez, 1989). With the wars, poor socioeconomic conditions and human terror increased, and record numbers of refugees escaped to the United States. From the early 1970s throughout the late 1980s, more than one million Salvadoreans, Nicaraguans, and Guatemalans entered the United States (Arredondo, Orjuela, & Moore, 1989). Still the U.S. government did not recognize them as political refugees, but as illegal aliens who came to the United States for economic gain. Thus, they did not have the benefit of the Refugee Act, which provides political asylum to individuals who flee their homeland because of founded fear of social or political persecution (Drachman, 1995). Consequently, many Central Americans have been forced to remain hidden without proper legal documentation (Conover, 1993).

## TREATMENT CONSIDERATIONS

Assessment and therapy with Central American families in the United States require an understanding of their status as political refugees (Arredondo et al.,

1989). Therapists should be alert to the complex psychosocial stresses that many Central American families have experienced before, during, and after migration, which sets important parameters for their individual and family stories.

Whether or not a family fled illegally, immigrants may have witnessed the terror and violence that recently have dominated the region. Families generally have experienced the loss of members or friends, the horrors of torture and other crimes, and other profound political and socioeconomic repression that leaves deep emotional and relational wounds (Garcia & Rodriguez, 1989). In addition to the trauma from these wars, losses, and disruptions, refugees suffer from survivor's guilt, self-recrimination, unresolved grief, and dissociation.

One commonly sees alliances and coalitions among family members concerning "untold stories" about the family's experience or history with political and socioeconomic repression. Like some Holocaust survivors, many Central American refugee families present an impenetrable silence that can perpetuate the trauma and create a culture of fear and secrecy among family members, who may develop rigid extrafamilial boundaries, social isolation, and a convoluted language of emotional and physical symptoms. These can be startlingly specific metaphors for the unspoken truths (Lang, 1995).

Often families that were victims of direct persecution remain anchored in a state of permanent collective remembrance and mourning, engaged in a constant conversation about the circumstances from which they escaped while others did not. Although the fixation on the trauma can be detrimental, it also can be healing if directed to participation in political and social activism by survivors speaking out and sharing their personal testimony.

A lack of legal status adds another psychosocial stressor to the strain of the postmigration period. Unlike most other refugees, Central American families usually lack access to federally funded medical, educational, and food programs, which has a direct impact on their adaptation and integration into U.S. society (Garcia & Rodriguez, 1989). The Immigration Reform and Control Act of 1986, which penalizes employers who hire illegal immigrants, forces many Central American refugees to work illegally in low-paying jobs in which exploitation and abuse are common. The fear of been captured and deported forces them to hide, live in silence about their past, violate various laws, and tolerate abusive conditions.

José, age 40, a union organizer who has been actively involved in the Nicaraguan revolution, escaped his country after surviving incarceration, torture, and various other forms of persecution. To protect his wife and his two children, José left his family and remained hidden while preparing for his long journey. His goal was to secure a job, housing, and obtain some legal status in order to bring the rest of the family to the United States legally.

Three months after leaving Nicaragua, José arrived in the United States and presented a well-documented case for political asylum, but his petition was denied. Motivated by his fears of being deported, he moved to a different state. In order to find work and housing, and to save money to pay for his family's trip, José obtained a false Social Security card, committed fraud in getting his driver's license, lied to his landlord, and assumed a new identity as a Puerto Rican. His efforts in remaining inconspicuous and remaining silent about his past and his identity had a profound psychological impact. In addition, the pressures to make money, the difficulties in keeping contact with his family, and the long hours at two demanding jobs finally triggered an emotional collapse.

José fell into a severe depression and began to have nightmares, anxiety attacks, and flashbacks about his traumatic experiences in Nicaragua. Overwhelmed by the intensity of his memories, he dealt with his symptoms by drinking heavily every night. One year after immigration, José had become a different person. Later he would tell his therapist that he came to the United States, escaping from death only to die in a more painful way. He was bitter and felt cheated by the U.S. government, which he accused of invalidating his experiences and forcing him to live in a constant lie.

———————— ✎ ————————

## THE MIGRATION EXPERIENCE

The events preceding migration are often just as distressful as the act of migrating. Many Central American refugee families have to depart suddenly, with no time for farewells. Their fears of not ever returning, the uncertain future of those left behind, and the expectation of freedom increases their anxiety and makes the experience of uprootedness and expatriation more difficult.

Because most Central American refugees cannot enter the United States legally, they have to resort to the services of "coyotes," who will take them by risky alternative routes. During the trip, which may last weeks or months, the travelers are frequently mistreated, robbed, and raped by their guides. The final part of the trip, the border crossing, is usually undertaken under inhuman conditions (Garcia & Rodriguez, 1989). Many refugees are captured by officers of the U.S. Immigration and Naturalization Service and either imprisoned or deported to the country from which they came (Conover, 1993).

The mode of migration has a direct impact upon refugees' family structure and development. Often, a few members of the family emigrate first. Those who stay behind are forced to assume new roles and responsibilities for keeping the family functioning. Women often become the sole breadwinners and assume responsibility for the family's financial and emotional support. A parental role may be taken by the oldest child, and dependence on the family's extended networks increases.

If the family eventually is reunited, it will need to negotiate and reorganize structure, roles, and functions in order to include the newly arrived members. It is important to remember that the family almost certainly will go through readjustment conflicts as they are struggling with the new cultural environment (Garcia & Rodriguez, 1989).

The prologue for Julia's migration began the day that José left Nicaragua. After he disappeared, she was interrogated about his whereabouts and lost her job as a factory worker. To protect her two children, Juan, age 10, and Rosa, age 6, she left them with her parents in the countryside. Julia stayed with friends in Managua, where she held different jobs to help support her children and make the necessary arrangements for their escape.

During the following 17 months, Juan and Rosa became very close to their grandparents. The children were told that José had been transferred to the United States by his company and that Julia was preparing everything for their reunion. José's letters promised a big house, new friends, and a happy new life. The children, however, were forbidden to discuss their plans with anybody.

Julia and the children left Nicaragua with a one-way ticket to Mexico City. The departure was sudden and unannounced, and the children did not have the opportunity to say good-bye to their friends and extended family. They spent a week hidden in a stranger's house, where the children were not allowed to go out and play. Frequently, Julia had to leave them alone to make the arrangements for the rest of their journey. Juan was instructed to protect and care for Rosa.

From Mexico City, the family was driven to Tijuana, hidden in the back of a truck. The final part of the trip was the most traumatic for them. Julia had to give her children to a woman she did not know in order to cross the border. While the children crossed by car, Julia had to cross through the fields in dangerous and stressful conditions.

After the long, tiring, and stressful journey, Julia and the children were finally reunited with José. It did not take long for Julia to notice that José was a different person. He was emotionally detached and his drinking problem provoked martial conflicts. The children missed their grandparents and did not find their new home and immediate environment as friendly and beautiful as it had been described by their father. Their discontent would grow when they began school and were forced to keep secret their migration history and use false documents to hide their illegal status.

———————— 🥢 ————————

## SETTLEMENT AND ACCULTURATION

Once the refugee family enters the United States, a complex psychological process begins. Not having time to process the traumatic experiences accumulated during their migration, the family now is confronted with the stresses of survival, adaptation, and integration to a new environment. During this time, many refugees feel "cheated," for the "Land of Liberty" is not as welcoming as they were told (Garcia & Rodriguez, 1989). Central American refugees often end up in marginal positions within the U.S. social structure because they lack legal documentation, support networks, and socioeconomic status.

Perhaps the greatest difficulties result from trying to adapt to the new culture. Acculturation is a complex, multigenerational process in which constant negotiation between the culture of origin and the new culture forces the family to reshape values, behaviors, belief systems, relational patterns, and attitudes (Rogler, 1994). The process usually triggers relational and emotional conflicts as family roles, rules, and values that were culturally congruent and effective in Central America become less functional in the United States.

Although the Central American family's cultural context largely varies with each country, along with the family's social class (pre- and postmigration) and the historical factors surrounding migration, the legacy of Latino cultural values remain strong. There are probably more similarities than differences among Central Americans, Mexicans, and South Americans in language, religion, family values, sex roles, and life philosophy. In this sense, clinicians need to be attuned to central organizing cultural values such as familism; *machismo* and *marianismo*; the importance of extended family and other social networks; the values of respect, dignity, and honor; and the impact of patriarchal and agrarian ideologies on the distribution of power between men and women. These values have been discussed in depth elsewhere (Bernal, 1982; Falicov, 1982; Garcia-Preto, 1982).

An important factor to consider is that as in the Andes and Southern Mexico, there is a strong Indian heritage in Central America. In countries such as Guatemala, the Indian population continues to be sufficiently concentrated to preserve their traditional cultural and social identity. Thus, many of the cultural values discussed in this chapter are not necessarily relevant when the families have a Mayan cultural heritage rather than a Latino one.

Another important difference is the unique political and economic history of Central America and its impact on family values. For instance, during the revolutions in Nicaragua, El Salvador, and Guatemala, the boundaries of acceptable social behavior for women greatly broadened. Many women, who had been confined to the private sphere, joined the guerrillas and became important participants in the region's political transformation. Some became heads of household after their husbands were killed or disappeared during the war. What impact this shift in gender roles will have on Central American society is uncertain. It is clear that with the crushing of the revolutions, women have been redirected toward more traditional roles.

## ACCULTURATION AND FAMILY CONFLICT

Central American refugees are often forced to assume unaccustomed roles in U.S. society. Women are often first to obtain jobs, because they are more open to performing menial tasks, or because the available jobs are seen as more appropriate for females. Through work, they usually develop an outside network that exposes them to more rapid learning of the new culture. Even when they are not part of the workforce, women are more prompt to develop social relationships through traditional duties such as shopping and involvement with the children's school (Garcia & Rodriguez, 1989). This exposure and newly developed strategies to negotiate their traditional gender roles are felt in the family when women begin to demand more participation from children and husbands in the home care.

As expected, new behaviors unbalance the family's and particularly the marital dyad's traditional power structure. For example, traditional husbands, who are used to being considered the main providers and protectors of the family, resent the changes and challenge the newly acquired independence of their wives by reclaiming old role patterns. Women are often accused of abandoning their culture and family. In my experience, out of guilt and confusion, many women try to reassume old roles, isolate from friends, and work extra hard to please their husbands. Their resulting discontent usually is manifested in somatization, depressive symptoms, or relational conflicts.

Traditional Central American masculine gender roles are also challenged by the new cultural environment. Without the public recognition given by the cultural notions of *machismo* and the strong patriarchal ideology to which they are accustomed, many Central American men feel they have lost their power. Their new ethnic-minority status and social invisibility invalidate their domain of the public sphere. Losing power in the public sphere due to racism, ethnic prejudice, and paradoxically, societal change toward gender equity, has a direct impact on the men's family life. Confusion, anxiety and depression, substance abuse, and domestic violence are common manifestations of its effect.

Acculturating Central American families also experience change in their traditional hierarchical structure. Through formal education, children generally become proficient in English before their parents do and often become their culture brokers; parents become dependent on their children to negotiate with the outside world.

As they acculturate, children demand to be heard in the home and begin to challenge their parents' traditional values and cultural beliefs (Garcia & Rodriguez, 1989). Parents frequently feel that they have lost their credibility as authority figures when children move toward a more "American way," becoming increasingly "lost" to the new culture. These conflicts usually generate family tension and disorganization. A breakdown in family cohesion leaves members without support and at risk of developing emotional, psychological, and relational symptoms.

Usually the problem has reached critical proportions before they come to therapy. Because their illegal status makes them hesitate to look for outside help, it is often the mother who breaks their isolation and fears of being known to the authorities and seeks outside help.

Rosa's school truancy was the presenting problem that led the family to seek help. Julia was concerned about her disrespectful behavior and did not approve of her friends or of her rejection of obeying their traditional family values, including speaking Spanish in the house. Rosa was also accused by Julia and Juan of making José suffer.

The initial interview revealed important information relevant to Rosa's problem. There was a clear under/over functioning pattern among the family related to Jose's drinking. He was unemployed and usually spent his days sleeping, drinking heavily every night. He appeared to be very depressed and was cut off from the family. Julia was working at two jobs and spent most of the day out. Juan was responsible for the house chores, supervising Rosa and José. The family was socially isolated and living in a one-bedroom apartment in a crime-ridden neighborhood. There were serious financial problems and, because of their undocumented status, the family did not qualify for public assistance.

While Juan and Julia undermined José's alcoholism, Rosa would openly call him a drunk and hold him responsible for the family's misfortune. She resented Julia's strong alliance with Juan and their tendency to make excuses for José's drinking. Rosa reported that living with her family was unbearable and accused them of being stuck in the past.

Although Rosa's symptomatic behavior occurred 9 years after the family emigrated, it soon became clear that their migration history, cultural transition process, and political refugee status had a direct relationship with the family's problem.

Soon after José was reunited with his family in the United States, Julia found out about José's flashbacks and nightmares. For the first time, she heard about the terrors he experienced while in a Nicaraguan prison and the traumatic experiences he had had during and after his escape. His revelation made Julia become tolerant of his drinking and compensate for his underfunctioning role performance in the family by becoming an overfunctioning parent and spouse. Julia took on all his responsibilities and, when Juan turned 13, told him about José's problem and placed him in a parental role. Since then Juan also became tolerant and protective of his father. During the day, he would try to distract him by engaging him in talks about his daily routine.

Many nights Juan had to pick up his father at the corner *bodega* and bring him home drunk. Rosa was protected from this because she was too young. Although Juan had vague memories of his father's incarceration and his escape, Rosa was unaware of the events that triggered the family's migration. She only remembered that her father had been relocated to the United States by his company and that she was promised a better life and future, which had not happened yet. She felt neglected by her mother, overprotected by her brother, and disappointed in her father.

Paradoxically, her problematic behavior made her feel for the first time that her parents cared for her. During family sessions, Rosa had the opportunity of learning about her family history and finally began to feel like a member of the family. Revealing Jose's and the family's past helped the family to process their trauma, mourn their losses, and move on from being stuck in the past toward a better integration of their present. In many ways, talking out the secrets released Rosa from her acting out, which exposed her family to new challenges they needed to confront in order to become a part of a new sociocultural context.

At treatment's end, this family was able to understand that Rosa's school truancy and rebelliousness toward the family's traditional values were distinctive ways of confronting their isolation and need for help.

────────── ✦ ──────────

## A THERAPEUTIC ALTERNATIVE

This case illustrates some aspects of the Central American refugee experiences that are distinctive to this group. Underlying the symptomatic behaviors was a unique history that defined specific parameters for the family's problems. As political refugees, the individual and family stories were influenced by José's experience of torture, the family's exposure to war and political repression, the traumatic experience of migration, and the vicissitudes of their own personal and family struggles in adapting to a new environment.

To gain access to this aspect of their story, the following specific clinical strategies were adopted based on the Culture and Migration Dialogue technique (Inclan & Hernandez, 1992). The first step was to establish a contract in which, after exploring the presenting problem, the therapist stressed the relevance of the family's history. This was organized by gathering information in the following sequence and noting the feelings accompanying the events described: (1) premigration history (focusing on their exposure to war), (2) migration history (focusing on the emotional impact of the uprooting experience), and (3) arrival in the United States (focusing on the process of cultural transition and the psychosocial impact of their illegal alien status). It was made clear that adaptation, far from being a straightforward process, is characterized by variability and fallbacks.

Reporting and discussing traumatic events served several purposes. It had a cathartic effect of releasing the pressures of secrecy and pain associated with their past. When the family had the opportunity to openly discuss its story, analyze its impact on their lives, and receive support and orientation toward connecting past history with present conflict, they were better able to appreciate strengths that are indispensable for adapting to the new environment. There was a natural depathologizing effect when the family's complex psychological realities were placed within the context of normal adaptive processes. Finally, the family's participation in this therapeutic encounter facilitated the mobilization of intrafamilial resources and the development of supportive relations among its members.

## ACKNOWLEDGMENTS

The following colleagues made important contributions to this chapter and I am gratefully indebted for their unconditional support: Mabel Quiñones, Manuel Muñoz, Jaime Inclan, Monica McGoldrick, and all the Central American families that shared with me their rich and heroic stories.

## REFERENCES

Arredondo, P., Orjuela, E., & Moore, L. (1989). Family therapy with Central American refugee families. *Journal of Strategic and Systemic Therapies, 8*(2), 28–35.

Bernal, G. (1982). Cuban families. In M. McGoldrick, J. K. Pearce, & J. Giordano (Eds.), *Ethnicity and family therapy* (1st ed., pp. 187–206). New York: Guilford Press.

Booth, J., & Walker, T. (1993). *Understanding Central America* (2nd ed.). Boulder, San Francisco, Oxford: Westview Press.

Conover, T. (1993, September 19). The United States of asylum. *New York Times Magazine*, pp. 56–58, 74–78.

Drachman, D. (1995). Immigration statuses and their influence on service provision, access and use. *Social Work, 40*(2), 188–197.

Falicov, C. (1982). Mexican families. In M. McGoldrick, J. K. Pearce, & J. Giordano (Eds.), *Ethnicity and family therapy* (1st ed., pp. 134–161). New York: Guilford Press.

Garcia, M., & Rodriguez, P. (1989). Psychological effects of political repression in Argentina and El Salvador. In D. R. Koslow & E. P. Slett (Ed.), *Crossing culture and mental health* (pp. 64–83). Washington DC: International Society for Education, Training, and Research.

Garcia-Preto, N. (1982). Puerto Rican families. In M. McGoldrick, J. K. Pearce, & J. Giordano (Eds.), *Ethnicity and family therapy* (1st ed. pp. 164–183). New York: Guilford Press.

Inclan, J., & Hernandez, M. (1992). Cross-cultural perspectives and codependence: The case of poor Hispanics. *American Journal of Orthopsychiatry, 16*(2), 245–255.

Lang, M. (1995, September–October). The shadow of evil. *Family Therapy Networker*, pp. 55–65.

Rogler, L. (1994). International migrations: A framework for directing research. *American Psychologist, 49*(8), 701–708.

Skidmore, T., & Smith, P. (1992). *Modern Latin America* (3rd ed.). New York: Oxford University Press.

PART IV

# ASIAN AMERICAN FAMILIES

# CHAPTER 16

# Asian American Families: An Overview

## Evelyn Lee

The term "Asian Pacific Americans" refers to the collective set of Asian American and Pacific Islander American populations. Although many Asian Pacific groups share certain common cultural characteristics, appearance similarities, and migration experiences, use of this term is in no way meant to imply that these populations or communities are homogeneous in nature. In fact, the term "Asian Pacific American," which has been in common use since the 1960s, applies to 43 ethnic groups, including 28 Asian groups and 15 Pacific Islander groups (Asian American Health Forum, 1990). This population has increased from less than 1 million in the United States in 1960 to over 7 million by 1990, and represents the fastest growing ethnic community in the United States today.

This chapter gives a brief overview of Asian Americans, their similar cultural values and experiences, and major differences. The primary focus is on major groups such as Chinese, Japanese, Koreans, Pilipinos, East Indians, and Southeast Asians. Specific assessment and treatment approaches in working with immigrants and refugees are described. More detailed discussion of several major Asian American groups will be covered in other chapters.

## DIFFERENCES AMONG ASIAN AMERICAN GROUPS

Asian American groups differ in terms of migration history, population, language, religion, education level, occupation, income, degree of acculturation, preferred residential location, political involvement, and so forth. Unfortunately, very little attention has been devoted to intraethnic differences among Asian American groups (Uba, 1994). Most of the mental health research, in particular, has focused on Chinese Americans, Japanese Americans, and, more recently, on Southeast Asian refugees. The following discussion is largely drawn from the U.S. Bureau of the Census 1990 statistics, population statistics analysis by the Asian American Health Forum (1990), and limited descriptive data from authors in the fields of sociology and mental health.

## Population

According to the 1990 U.S. Census, the six largest Asian American groups are Chinese (23% of the Asian American population), Pilipino (19%), Japanese (12%), Asian Indian (11%), Korean (11%), and Vietnamese (9%). Groups with less than 2% include Thai and Hmong.

## Residential Preferences

Except for isolated communities of Southeast Asian refugees settled throughout the United States, Asian American communities are scattered among the West and East coasts. About 70% of the total population reside in five states: California (35%), Hawaii (16%), New York (9%), Illinois (5%), and Texas (4%). The cities with high concentrations of Asian Americans are Honolulu, Los Angeles, San Francisco, New York, Chicago, and San Jose. Various groups favor certain cities. For example, Chinese favor San Francisco, Boston, New York, and Washington, D.C. Japanese like Honolulu, Los Angeles, and Seattle. Pilipinos favor San Diego, San Francisco, and San Jose. And, the Vietnamese concentrate in Orange County (California), San Jose, Houston, and Minneapolis.

## Immigration History

Each Asian American group has a complex migration history in the United States. Details are discussed in individual chapters. In summary, Chinese Americans were the first Asians to immigrate to the United States in large numbers and have come in three waves over a 150-year period. The 1965 Immigration Act brought a large number of Chinese, as well as Koreans and Pilipinos. Most Japanese Americans today are the descendants of Japanese who migrated to Hawaii or the U.S. mainland before 1924. With the end of the Vietnam War in 1975, a large number of Southeast Asian refugees arrived. Those who came were mostly educated Vietnamese. Since 1978, a second wave came to the United States to escape persecution, and these included Vietnamese, Chinese Vietnamese, Cambodians, Lao, Hmong, and Mien.

## Foreign-Born Population and Acculturation Rate

In 1960, most Asian Americans were descendants of early Japanese and Chinese immigrants. Now, over half of Asian Americans are foreign born. The 1990 U.S. Census revealed the following foreign-born percentages: Vietnamese

(92%), Cambodian (80%), Korean (71%), Pilipino (64%), Asian Indian (57%), and Chinese (56%).

Varying degrees of acculturation exist among the different groups. Obviously, a fourth-generation Japanese American is much more acculturated than a recently arrived Korean immigrant. The rate of acculturation is also strongly influenced by an immigrant's prior exposure to urbanization and Western culture. For example, a highly educated professional from Hong Kong will become acculturated much faster than a farmer from the mountains of Laos. Those with facility in English before migration will also adjust more rapidly. Very little attention has been devoted to intraethnic differences among Asian American groups. Immigrants who are less acculturated tend to hold on to traditional family values and gender roles.

## Language

Among Asian American groups, there are at least 32 different primary languages spoken. Within each group (such as Chinese and Pilipino), there are sometimes many dialects. Proficiency and the command of English vary greatly among the different groups. While American-born Asians speak English fluently with no accent, the majority of foreign-born Asians struggle with the English language and continue to speak their primary language at home.

## Education Attainment

As compared to the overall American population, several Asian American groups stand out in their college-graduation rates and postgraduate training, for instance, Asian Indians, Chinese, and Japanese. On the other hand, only 27% of Laotians and 38% of Cambodians are high school graduates.

## Family Income

Although data suggest that Asian Americans as a group have the highest average family income in the United States, Southeast Asians are among the poorest. Those living below the poverty level include 66% of the Laotians, 49% of Cambodians, and 34% of Vietnamese.

## Religion

Religious beliefs vary greatly among the different Asian American groups. Among the Chinese Americans, the most popular religions include Buddhism, ancestor worship, and Christianity. Over 70% of Korean Americans are Protestant Christians and attend church regularly. Pilipinos, under past Spanish influence, are heavily Catholic. Japanese Americans follow Shintoism, Buddhism (especially the Zen sect), and Christianity. Vietnamese practice Buddhism, and, from their French colonial past, Catholicism. The religions of both Cambodians and Laotians are strongly influenced by the Brahmanism of the Hindus as well as by Buddhism. The Hmong and the Mien are usually animistic and believe strongly in supernatural causes. It is important to note that in many Asian countries under Communist rule, religion was essentially abolished. Consequently, many immigrants from those countries may not practice any religion at all. Another observation is that many acculturated Asian Americans have adopted mainstream religions such as Christianity, sometimes causing intergenerational conflicts with the older generation.

## Exposure to War Trauma

Many Asian countries suffered from war or political turmoil. As a result, many immigrants were exposed to losses, separation, torture, and other forms of trauma before immigrating to the United States. The degree of exposure to trauma also varies. For instance, an older Chinese immigrant would have experienced the Sino-Japanese War, the Civil War between the Communists and the Nationalists, and the Cultural Revolution. Another example is the case of Cambodian women who lost their husbands during the bloody Pol Pot regime and have become the head of their households in America. Their painful experiences are vastly different than their younger generation family members.

## COMMON TRADITIONAL CHARACTERISTICS OF ASIAN FAMILIES

Asian family values are very different from Western family values. The agricultural background and the teachings of Confucianism and Buddhism have had a profound influence on Eastern philosophical approaches to life and family interactions. Generally speaking, in Western cultures the nuclear family stresses independence and autonomy of the individual members. A family life cycle begins when two individuals meet, fall in love, marry, and have children. They raise their children to become self-sufficient individuals who will ultimately leave home and repeat the process.

However, in traditional Asian families, the family unit—rather than the individual—is highly valued. The individual is seen as the product of all the generations of his or her family. This concept is reinforced by rituals and customs such as ancestor worship, family celebrations, funeral rites, and genealogy records. Because of this continuum, individuals' personal action reflects not only on themselves but also on their extended family and ancestors (Shon & Ja, 1982). Obligations and shame are the mechanisms that traditionally help to reinforce societal expectations and proper behavior. An individual is expected to function in his or her clearly defined roles and positions in the family hierarchy, based on age, gender, and social class. There is an emphasis on harmonious interpersonal relationships, interdependence, and mutual obligations or loyalty for achieving a state of psychological homeostasis or peaceful coexistence with family or other fellow beings (Hsu, 1971).

## Marital Subsystem

In traditional Asian families, marriages are arranged by parents or grandparents to ensure the family prosperity and propagation of the husband's family line. The dominant relationship is more likely to be placed on the parent–child dyad, rather than the husband–wife dyad. The husband assumes the role of leadership and authority, and is the provider and protector of the family. The wife assumes the role of homemaker and childbearer. Physical and verbal expressions of love are uncommon. When things go wrong, the difficulties may be repaired by other adult mediators or confidants. Divorce is not a common practice. The wife is usually dominated by the authority of her husband, her father, her in-laws, and sometimes her son.

## Parent–Child Subsystem

The traditional role of a mother is to provide nutrients and support. The father's role is to discipline. The father and mother's functions tend to be complementary, rather than symmetrical. The strongest emotional attachment for a woman is sometimes not her husband, but her children (especially her sons). Most parents demand filial piety, respect, and obedience from their children. In many extended families, children are not solely raised by their parents, but are cared for by a wide range of adults (grandparents, uncles, aunts, cousins, wet nurses). Parents expect to be cared for in their old age.

## Sibling Subsystem

Because of the large number of children in many Asian families, the parents usually delegate child-care functions to older siblings (especially the eldest daughter). Cooperation and sharing among siblings are expected. The emotional ties among siblings are especially strong for those who survived war and escapes. Due to historical practices of sexism, sons are favored. Sibling rivalry is not uncommon.

## ASIAN AMERICAN FAMILIES IN TRANSITION

During the past 200 years, many Asians families have migrated to the United States. Repeated contacts with American values over a prolonged period of time have changed their outlook on such issues as gender role, child rearing, and family structure. The values, norms, and role behavior learned in the home country are modified when a family adjusts to the new culture. Many Asian American families are in transition from an extended family to a nuclear unit through the inevitable changes induced by migration, urbanization, and modernization. Family members struggle to hold on to the old way while trying to develop new coping skills. Some eventually accomplish this task, whereas others develop symptoms of stress when attempting to force a blend between two contradictory sets of rules (Lee, 1990). Where the stresses are extreme and the support systems are insufficient, the family may become isolated, enmeshed, or disengaged (Landau, 1982).

Generally speaking, Asian American families in transition can be divided into five major types: traditional families, "cultural conflict" families, bicultural families, "Americanized" families, and interracial families.

## Traditional Families

Traditional families usually consist entirely of family members born and raised in Asian countries. They include families from agricultural backgrounds, recent arrivals with limited exposure to Western culture, unacculturated immigrants who are older at time of immigration, and families who live in ethnic Asian communities (e.g., Chinatown, Little Saigon), with limited contact with American mainstream society. Family members hold strong beliefs in traditional values and regularly speak in their native languages and dialects. Family members still practice traditional rituals and customs. Many are members of family associations and social clubs consisting of people from similar heritage.

## "Cultural Conflict" Families

Such families have American-born children or arrived more than a decade ago, when the children were young. The family system usually experiences a great deal of cultural conflict between the acculturated children and the traditional parents or grandparents. Intergenerational conflicts and role confusion are common problems. Other families have conflicts because one spouse is more acculturated than the other. For example, a husband may have lived in the United States for many years, gone home, and brought back a wife who is not familiar with American culture. Conflicts may be caused not only by different degrees of acculturation, but also by religious, philosophical, or political differences.

## Bicultural Families

These families consist of well-acculturated parents who grew up in major Asian cities and were exposed to urbanization, industrialization, and Western influences. Many came as young adults. Some were born in the United States but raised in traditional families. These parents often hold professional jobs, come from a middle- or upper-class family background, and are bilingual and bicultural. In such families, the power structure has moved from a patriarchal to an egalitarian relationship between parents. Decision making is not solely the father's task; "family discussions" are allowed between parents and children. Such families typically do not live in ethnic neighborhoods. The "nuclear" family members usually visit their "extended" family members (such as the grandparents) on weekends and holidays.

## "Americanized" Families

Some Asian families have become largely Americanized. These families usually consist of parents and children born and raised in the United States. As generations pass, the roots of the traditional Asian cultures begin to slowly disappear, and individual members do not express their interest in or make any effort to maintain their ethnic identities. Family members communicate in English and adopt a more individualistic and egalitarian orientation.

## Interracial Families

Interracial Asian American families are increasing rapidly, currently constituting about 10–15% of marriages. Japanese Americans lead in this trend, with more than half marrying outside their group, followed by Pilipino, Chinese, Vietnamese, and Korean Americans (Karnow & Yoshihara, 1992). Some interracial families are able to integrate both cultures with a high degree of success. However, others often experience conflicts in values, religious beliefs, communication style, child-rearing issues, in-law problems, and so forth.

These five types of families are hypothetical constructs for the understanding of the complexity of Asian American families. There are numerous variations within this continuum, and some families may not fit into a particular type.

## PSYCHOPATHOLOGY OF ASIAN AMERICANS

Available research suggests that Asian Americans have a rate of psychopathology equal to or higher than that of European Americans (Uba, 1994). Immigrants can suffer any or all of the psychiatric disorders or emotional problems that affect the general public. However, certain disorders are altered or influenced by the migration process. For example, an individual with a chronic mental disorder may have achieved a certain level of coping in his home country before migration, but can then become dysfunctional in the new country. Certain premigration factors (e.g., war trauma) or postmigration factors (e.g., loss of social network, language difficulties) may precipitate a psychiatric disorder (Westermeyer, 1989).

The common presenting family problems are usually parent–child conflicts, marital discord, in-law problems, and domestic violence. Individual presenting problems include somatization, depression and anxiety, adjustment disorder, schizophrenia, alcoholism, drug addiction, gambling, and suicide. Posttraumatic stress disorder and dissociative disorder are fairly common among refugees traumatized by war. In addition, children and adolescent problems include learning disorders, attention deficit disorder, conduct disorder, and gang affiliation.

A survey of Asian American therapists (Matsushima & Tashima, 1982) revealed that depression, low self-concept, and relationship conflicts affect at least 50% of their Asian American clients. Between 40% and 50% of the clients were affected by problems with parent–child relationship, acculturation, somatic complaints, and isolation. There were interethnic differences among different Asian American groups. Japanese and Pilipino Americans presented more intrapsychic problems, such as identity conflict. Southeast Asians encountered more employment difficulties. Hawaiian, Pilipino, Japanese, and Samoan Americans suffered from more alcohol and substance-abuse problems.

Research has revealed six predictors of mental health problems among Asian Americans: (1) employment/financial status, (2) gender—Asian women seem to be more vulnerable, (3) old age, (4) social isolation, (5) relatively recent immigration, and (6) refugee premigration experiences and postmigration adjustment (Uba, 1994).

There are also interracial differences on manifestations of psychopathology. Chinese and Japanese Americans have reported more somatic complaints than European Americans in the MMPI (Sue & Sue, 1974). Asian Americans who use mental health services are more severely disturbed than non-Asian counterparts (Sue & McKinney, 1975). The proportion of Asian Americans diagnosed as psychotic was larger than the proportion among European Americans; Asian Americans were also diagnosed as having major affective disorders at a proportionately higher rate than African Americans or Latino Americans (Flaskerud & Hu, 1992).

## ASSESSMENT AND DATA COLLECTION[1]

The proposed approaches are drawn from two major conceptual frameworks: *social systems theory* and its application to family therapy, and *Eastern holistic concepts* of health and illness.

The family is a complex institution that can be investigated and understood from various dimensions. The clinician needs to assess (1) the internal family system, which will include the understanding of individual members and family subsystems; and (2) the external factors, which will include the impact of community and other environmental stressors. Since many Asian families undergo rapid social change and cultural transition, relevant data on migration history, impact of war, cultural shock, racism, employment, and housing are extremely helpful.

Although Western psychological and biological understanding of emotional difficulties is important, we need to incorporate the Eastern holistic way of thinking into clinical practice. A model that takes into account the psychological, social, biological, cultural, political, and spiritual influences on the lives of families is recommended. In addition to the traditional psychosocial assessment or mental health status examination, a holistic model in data collection and assessment as discussed here should be adapted:

*Demographic data on each individual family member*—age, years in the United States, country of origin, immigration status, marital status, birth order in family, educational level, occupation, residence, and so forth.

*Data on the family system*—membership (nuclear or extended family), ethnocultural heritage (both maternal and paternal lines), socioeconomic background (before and after migration), immigration status and history of each member (who came first, who was left behind, and why), basis of marriage (matched or romantic love), acculturation level of each family member, leadership and decision making, sex-role differentiation, child-rearing practices, forms of discipline, role expectation, family communication pattern, and relationships with legal sponsors.

*Data on community system*—neighborhood of family residency, housing conditions, economic climate and job availability, educational systems for children and adults, human service network and support systems, problems of crime, violence, drugs, racism, prejudice, and discrimination.

This data collection to gather relevant personal, familial, and community information applies to many ethnic groups. However, in working with immigrant and refugee Asian families, the clinician should take time to conduct in-depth assessment in the areas discussed below (Lee, 1989).

## Migration Stress and Degree of War Trauma

Most Asian countries have suffered years of war and political turmoil, the stress of which compounds the migration strain that all immigrants experience. Many immigrants and refugees experienced unwilling separations and exposure to trauma, both in the home country and in the search for sanctuary. A systematic and longitudinal understanding of the migration experience is crucial. When taking a thorough migration history, the clinician can apply a chronological approach focusing on two major aspects of the family migration history: premigration history and immigration history. The use of genograms (McGoldrick, 1985), oral history, and family photographs can be helpful.

*Premigration history*—city/village of origin, family composition, major political changes, socioeconomic status, employment status, support system, and so forth.

*Immigration history*—reasons for leaving, means of escape, hardships endured during the trip, type of losses, trauma experience, and so forth.

## Postmigration Experience and Cultural Shock

In assessing the family's postmigration experiences, it is essential to assess the degree of cultural shock and its impact on the family. Many new immigrants are placed in a strange and unpredictable environment. In addition to language barriers and homesickness, they have to adjust to physical, economic, religious, educational, and value orientations of the United States; political changes; and social relationship changes. For many families, there is a sudden lack of extended family and community support at a time when it is most needed. When the stresses are extreme and the support system and the old way of coping are not sufficient, the family in cultural transition frequently cannot adapt to the necessary changes. A family member's failure to handle a particular problem may lead to dysfunction within the total family system.

## Impact of Migration on Individual and Family Life Cycle

The adjustment to a new culture is a prolonged developmental process that will affect many family members differently, depending on the individual and family life cycle phase they are in at the time of transition (McGoldrick, 1982). For example, when families migrate in the launching phase, it is very difficult for the parents to break into new jobs, find new friends, and deal with the "empty nest" syndrome at the same time.

## Differences in Rates of Acculturation of Family Members

Individual family members within one household may differ greatly in their rate of acculturation. In general, the degree of acculturation depends on years in the United States, age at time of migration, exposure to Western culture and people, professional affiliation, work environment, and English-speaking ability.

## Family Stress Caused by Role Reversal

In many Asian American families, role reversals created by their migration cause serious strain. When monolingual adults depend on their English-speaking children as cultural brokers and interpreters, the situation can cause anger and resentment. Role reversals may also occur between husband and wife.

Husbands, who are accustomed to male-dominated Asian cultures, find it difficult to accept wives who may find work more easily and become more independent and assertive.

Many immigrants and refugees have been raised by someone other than their biological parents because of the extended family system and separation from family members. Family reunion in the United States after years of separation may trigger unresolved family conflicts and resentment.

## Work and Financial Stresses

Asian American families value hard work, and studies have found that clinical depression was significantly associated with unemployment (Yamamoto, Lam, Fung, Tan, & Iga, 1977). For Asian Americans, there exist two common types of stress related to employment. Among immigrants, many experience unemployment and underemployment. "Downward mobility" leads to low self-esteem, insecurity, and role reversal in families. For acculturated and professional Asian Americans, a "glass ceiling" (a term that refers to a barrier to promotions and success because of one's ethnicity or gender) and subtle discrimination at work sites often lead to frustrations and job dissatisfaction.

The parents' type of work and work hours often influence the family dynamics. At one extreme, a typical Asian American small-business owner (i.e., laundry, grocery store) requires the whole family to spend long hours together, sometimes resulting in relationships that are intense and "too close." At the other extreme, parents may work extremely long hours (i.e., restaurant or engineering/research office). Family members seldom have sufficient time together to communicate. One recent phenomenon is the so-called "astronaut" family, where the family resides in the United States and one parent still maintains his business in the home country. Such families maintain their relationships by telephone, fax, and "frequent flyer" trips.

## Neighborhood and Community Support

Whether the family lives in an ethnic neighborhood will influence the impact of the family cultural heritage on their lives (McGoldrick, 1982). For those Asians who live in their ethnic communities, the community support systems provide a cushion against the stresses of migration. Unfortunately, due to housing shortages, many recent immigrants and refugees have to live in poor neighborhoods, where they feel isolated from their ethnic communities and encounter problems of crimes, violence, drugs, and inadequate housing. Those who live in areas with relatively small Asian populations, such as small towns and rural areas, generally have more trouble adjusting and are pressured to assimilate more rapidly. The clinician should also explore the effect of racism, prejudice, and discrimination encountered by family members.

## Family's Religious and Spiritual Beliefs

Asian Americans come from a variety of religious backgrounds, such as Christian, Buddhist, Shinto, or Muslim. Family behavior is influenced by religious beliefs. In many Asian countries, religious organizations are highly respected. The priest, minister, or Buddhist monk is a key figure in the process of understanding and solving family problems. The clinician should assess whether the family is a member of a particular church or temple and the availability of emotional support or counseling from the particular organization. In many Asian American households, values that are shared by the grandparents or parents may be challenged by the younger generation, which is typically exposed to Western religions. The clinician should encourage the family members to share their spiritual beliefs in relationship to the presenting problem and problem-solving strategies.

## Family's Physical Health and Medication History

It is crucial to explore the physical health of Asian clients, because they tend to express their emotional problems in somatic terms and usually come to treatment with many physical complaints. Many Asians, especially refugees, are in need of medical attention because of physical injuries, malnutrition, and lack of adequate medical treatment during times of conflict. Often they are not familiar with Western medicine and may become confused by drug names, dosages, and effects. Furthermore, for many Asian Americans, concurrent use of Western and traditional medicine is quite common. A clinician's concern over these health and medication matters is often appreciated.

## Culturally Specific Responses to Mental Health Problems

Many traditional Asians do not accept Western biopsychological explanations of mental illness. A mental health problem may be conceptualized as a manifestation of organic disorders, hereditary weakness, an imbalance between *yin* and *yang*, a disturbance of *chi* energy, supernatural intervention, or emotional exhaustion caused by external environmental factors (Lee, 1982). In the assessment process, it is essential for the clinician to encourage the client and family members to discuss openly their cultural and religious viewpoints on the cause of the problem, their past coping style, their health-seeking behavior, and their treatment expectation. Questions to ask might include the following (Lee, 1990):

- What are the symptoms and problems as perceived by family members?
- What would be the diagnostic label given in the client's home country?
- What are the family's cultural explanations of the causes of the problem?

- What kind of treatment would the family get if they were back in their home country?
- Where did the family go for help before they came to see the clinician?
- What is the family's experience with herbal medicine, indigenous healers, and Asian exercises (such as *tai chi, chi gong*)?
- What were the family's previous experiences with health and mental health care systems?
- What is the family's exposure to mental health professionals?
- What are the family's treatment expectations?

## Cultural Strengths

In addition to the assessment of family stress and pathologies, an assessment is necessary with respect to individual and family strengths in adaptation, coping, and problem solving. The Asian family arrives in the United States with many problems. But, they also bring along very highly developed cultures, religions, and philosophies. Asian cultures place great importance on hard work, education, family, friends, and the ethnic community. During a crisis, Asian families can usually count on support from extended family members, friends, and ethnic community networks and organizations. Such support systems should be explored and recognized.

## CULTURALLY RELEVANT TREATMENT STRATEGIES

Traditional Western psychotherapeutic approaches based on the assumptions of individuation, independence, self-disclosure, verbal expression of feelings, and long-term insight therapy may go counter to Asian American values of interdependence, self-control, repression of emotions, and short-term result-oriented solutions. Many authors offer helpful suggestions in working with Asian American families. Kim (1985) recommended an integrated family therapy orientation drawn from Haley's strategic and Minuchin's structural therapies. Ho (1987) recommended Bowen's intergenerational perspective and Satir's cognitive approach to "teach" family members to recognize the family's rules. Paniagua (1994) suggested several effective treatment strategies, such as exhibiting expertise and authority; maintaining formality and conversational distance; providing concrete and tangible advice; and giving assurance that stress will be reduced as quickly as possible. Sue and Zane (1987) believe two therapeutic processes to be critical: credibility and gift giving (i.e., seeing that the client receives a benefit early in the treatment process).

Effective clinical strategies need to incorporate unique Asian cultural values and family characteristics. The following suggestions are divided into three distinct stages: beginning phase, problem-solving phase, and termination phase (Ho, 1987).

## Beginning Phase

Asian American clients are usually unfamiliar with family therapy. The clinician needs to pay special attention to the first contact phase of therapy in order to avoid premature termination. The following suggestions may be helpful in the establishment of rapport and motivation for the family to continue treatment. Three areas are particularly important in this phase, including engaging the family, assessing family readiness, and deciding on family members involved in therapy.

## Engaging the Family

1. In view of the traditional family power structure, the initial appointment should be made with the "decision maker" of the family, mostly the father. Requesting the English-speaking children to inform the parents of an appointment may reinforce the role reversal in the family. If necessary, ask the interpreter to make the arrangement. Be sure to set an appointment time that is convenient to the working parents because they value work more than therapy. Detailed explanations of the reasons for such an appointment and the location of your agency may be necessary.

2. Many immigrants do not understand the role of the mental health professional and may confuse him or her with a physician. A brief explanation of your role and training background may be helpful.

3. During the first session, the clinician should address the family in a polite and formal manner. In addition, he or she needs to pay attention to "interpersonal grace" and show warm expressions of acceptance, both verbally and nonverbally. Greeting the family with a smile, hanging up his or her coat, offering a cup of tea, and providing comfortable chairs to the older family members are examples of pragmatic expressions for conveying genuine concern and can add greatly to the beginning of a positive relationship (Ho, 1987).

4. Many Asians are used to receiving help from their friends or village elders for advice. They may ask the clinician many personal questions, such as his or her country of origin, marital status, number of children, and so on. The clinician needs to feel comfortable in answering such questions. Appropriate self-disclosure may facilitate positive cultural alliance and a level of trust and confidence.

5. Forming a social and cultural connection with the family during the first session is very important. For the clinician who has lived in the same Asian country or has extensive experiences in working with Asians, it will be beneficial to disclose your familiarity with that culture to make the "cultural connection." For the clinician who is not very familiar with the client's culture, it is important to show his or her interest and appreciation of the client's cul-

tural background. Pictures of Asian countries and culture on the office wall can also convey the clinician's interest.

6. Since many Asian family members are not used to verbal communications in therapy, asking nonthreatening personal questions can put the family at ease. Engaging the clients in small talk may help. Before the establishment of rapport, it is important to avoid direct confrontation, a demand of greater emotional disclosure, or a discussion of culturally taboo subjects such as sex or death.

7. For many Asians, public admission of mental health problems can bring intense shame and humiliation. The clinician may counter those emotions by empathizing with them and encouraging them to verbalize this feeling. It is important to assure family members about confidentiality and anonymity. One helpful technique is to reframe their courage in seeking help as love and concern over family members. If appropriate, the mobilization of the family's sense of obligation to receive help to achieve family harmony or for the sake of the children can be very effective.

8. Many Asian clients come to their first session believing that the clinician is an authority who can tell them what is wrong and how to solve their problems. It is helpful for the clinician to establish credibility right away, to assure that the client will return. Confidence, empathic understanding, maturity, and professionalism are all important ingredients. Other ways to establish credibility and authority include (a) using professional titles when making introductions; (b) displaying diplomas, awards, and licenses in the office; (c) obtaining sufficient information about the client and family before seeing them for the first time; (d) offering some possible explanation for the cause of the problem; (e) showing familiarity with the family's cultural background; (f) providing a set of cues that help the family to judge the clinician's expertise (i.e., "According to my experience working with Asian families during the past 20 years . . ."); and (g) utilizing the crisis intervention approach to offer some immediate solutions to the problems. It is important for the family to feel that they are in good hands, and that there is a sense of hope before they leave the first session.

9. Many Asian Americans do not comprehend the significance and the sometimes lengthy procedures of evaluation. They are either not used to detailed history taking, or they do not understand the relationship between the questions and the presenting problems. Some may even suspect such information will be put to political use, thus jeopardizing their immigration status. The clinician needs to help the client understand the reasons behind such questions.

10. Most of the families come to the first interview during a family crisis. The clinician should plan to allow more time than an usual 1-hour session, especially when an interpreter is used.

## Assessing Family Readiness for Therapy

Even though family therapy can be highly effective with Asian Americans, they are generally quite reluctant to seek treatment and are mostly unfamiliar with the concept of therapy or the role of the clinician. They usually do not see individual problems as family related. They rarely agree to the suggestion that the problem is the group's instead of the identified client's. Because of the traditional hierarchical and vertical structure of Asian American families prohibiting free verbal expression of emotions, especially true thoughts and negative feelings, family members may not be equipped with the communication skills to discuss problems and to express themselves openly in a family group setting. For example, for parents to discuss their "adult" problems or to express their sadness in front of the children is considered to be very culturally inappropriate and is viewed as losing control.

Because of long years of separation among family members of immigrant and refugees families, there are many family secrets and much unresolved grief that members are not ready to share openly with each other. "Conspiracy of silence" is a common way to cope with unpleasant events. Family therapy, which may bring out the "ghosts" in the past, can be very overwhelming and at times damaging to the family relationships. Traditional Asian husbands or fathers are quite resistant to attend family sessions or allow the therapist to enter into the family system. The admission of emotional problems and receiving help from outside the family network may be interpreted as a sign of weakness and "losing face" in the mind of many traditional Asian men. In the event that their children are in trouble and the parents are forced to receive treatment, they usually send their wives to be the "family representative" to deal with service agencies. It is very difficult to conduct family therapy without the cooperation and participation of the male adult figure.

For some, family therapy may be neither feasible nor desirable. However, if the clinician believes that family therapy will be the most effective treatment strategy, family members (especially the decision makers) should be told why it could be helpful.

## Involving Family Members in Therapy

The definition of "family" in traditional Asian cultures may include a wide network of kinship. For example, a Vietnamese teenager who left his homeland with his aunt when he was an infant may have more emotional ties with his aunt and her family than with his own biological parents. In many Filipino families, trusted friends and allies serve as godparents to children and play an important role in their growth and development. The clinician, if appropriate, can ask the identified client to define his or her own concept of family members and discuss who should be included in therapy. In many cases, it is advisable to encourage all family members to come to the first session so that the family dynamics among members can be observed. However, in many instances, family members are either emotionally not ready or physically unavailable to participate in treatment.

Therapy for Asian families does not always require all-encompassing family involvement. A *flexible subfamily system* approach in the establishment of therapeutic relationships with family members at the beginning phase can be very helpful. For example, an effective method is for a clinician to interview the parents first, then the identified client, and then the siblings. The parents can discuss their adult concerns or express their emotions freely in absence of the children. The children, usually more acculturated and fluent in English, can negotiate issues they might not bring up with their parents present. When all parties feel "safe" and have more control over what would be discussed in the family group, they may be more willing and ready to accept family therapy. This "staging" process requires skills in establishing trust and credibility with each family member at the initial phase of treatment.

## Mutual Goal Setting

Many Asian Americans find it difficult to admit having family problems or psychological difficulties. They usually present themselves as victims of some unfortunate environmental events or "impersonal" physical discomfort. The clinician should take their presenting problems seriously and respond immediately to the "concrete" needs of the clients. A *problem-focused, goal-oriented, and symptom-relieving* approach is highly recommended in the beginning phases of treatment. Goals may be best stated in terms of external resolution or symptom reduction. Many clients find loosely targeted and emotionally oriented goals incomprehensible, unreachable, and impractical (Ho, 1987). Long-term goals may best be broken down into a series of easy-to-understand, achievable, measurable, short-term goals. Once the family is engaged in the therapeutic relationship and gain a sense of success, the clinician can gradually introduce other more insight-oriented goals and renegotiate with the family members.

## Problem-Solving Phase

Asian American families often come to counseling with a set of physical or behavioral problems and expect the clinician to "fix it" with immediate results. Therefore, the problem-solving approach seems to be more appropriate. The following eight techniques have been found to be useful (Lee, in press).

## Focusing on the Problems as Presented by the Family

In order to engage the family in therapy, it is important for the clinician to (1) acknowledge the family's feeling that the identified patient has problems, (2) verbalize the family pain caused by the difficulties, (3) assist the family to shift from person-focused to problem-focused in order to minimize scapegoating, (4) focus on the effect of the problem on each family member, and (5) reinforce the sense of family obligation and the importance of solving the problem together. At times, it may be helpful to encourage family members to elaborate previous attempts in dealing with the problem. The realization of their coping failure, and the unpleasant consequences if the problem is uncorrected, may motivate the family to continue in treatment. In some instances, the clinician may capture the family's sense of guilt to participate in treatment for the sake of the family name (Lee, 1990).

## Applying a Psychoeducational Approach

Education is highly valued in Asian cultures. Many Asians consider the clinician as "doctor" or "teacher." The psychoeducational approach based on social learning principles is compatible with Asian values and beliefs. Such intervention focuses on four major areas: (1) education about the illness (or problem), (2) communication training, (3) problem-solving training, (4) behavioral management strategies (McGill & Lee, 1986), and (5) conflict resolution techniques. In addition to providing education on individual and family levels, psychoeducational programs dedicated to multiple families in the Asian community can be very effective.

## Assuming Multiple Helping Roles

Flexibility and willingness to assume multiple helping roles enhance the therapeutic relationship, especially in working with multiproblem families. In addition to being the counselor, the clinician should be comfortable to play the roles of teacher, advocate, intermediary, and interpreter. Show caring by "doing" and "being there" when the family needs help.

## Indirectness in Problem Solving

Most Asians view confrontation as disrespectful and lacking in moderation. Many take criticisms as a personal attack or rejection. The clinician is advised to use an "indirect" means, for example, "Do you ever care about your children?" could be changed to "We all have different ways to care about our children—I wish to learn from you about your ways of caring about your children" (Ho, 1987).

## Employing Reframing Technique

Haley's and Minuchin's reframing technique can be very helpful. Using this technique, the clinician capitalizes on the pragmatics of Asian American cultures by emphasizing the positive aspects of behavior, redefining negative behavior as positive (Ho, 1987).

## Capitalizing on Family Strength and Community Support

In many circumstances, especially when family members are coping with death, losses, and unpredictable changes, one of the functions of therapy is to mobilize the family's cultural strength. Strengths include support from the extended family, the strong sense of obligation and family loyalty, parental sacrifice for the children's future, filial piety, strong focus on educational achievement, the work ethic, and support from their religious and ethnic communities. Strengthening the family's sense of cultural pride can also be very therapeutic.

## Utilizing Intermediary/Go-Between Functions

In some situations, when a large gap exists between certain family members, the clinician may be able to bridge the gap by using an intermediary who can serve the function of linking the two uncommunicative members (Kim, 1985). Such intermediaries can include a trusted uncle, a good family friend, or a leader from the family association.

## Understanding the Family's Communication Style

There is a lack of "common" language spoken in many Asian American households, especially families with "Westernized" adolescents who do not speak their parents' and grandparents' native dialects. It is quite difficult to conduct therapy in two or three different dialects and different communication styles. English-speaking clinicians should avoid the use of bilingual children as interpreters, particularly when the presenting problem involves parent–child issues. The bilingualism of a child can reinforce the problem of role reversal and the monolingual parents' sense of helplessness. Also, clinicians should avoid the use of relatives and friends as interpreters. If interpreters are used, clinicians should try to use interpreters who match the Asian dialects and cultural background.

In addition to determining the preferred language and dialect used in therapy, the clinician must understand a family's communication style. Asian Americans traditionally have been taught to employ indirect styles of communication and to avoid direct confrontations. The clinician is expected to read between the lines in order to grasp the major issue. On the other hand, the family may perceive the clinician to be too blunt, pushy, and insensitive. If emotional difficulties are discussed, Asian clients will often speak in an oblique, understated way, with little obvious emotion, implying that the problem is more mild than it really is (Hong, 1989). Negative emotions such as anger, grief, and depression may be expressed in an indirect way. A culturally naive clinician may mistake this style for denial, lack of affect, lack of awareness of his or her own feelings, deceptiveness, or resistance on the part of the client (Sue, 1990). Even positive feelings, such as expression of love, are frequently not expressed in an open manner. Asian parents may be misunderstood as unloving and uncaring.

### Termination Phase

In this final phase, it is unrealistic for the clinician to expect an Asian client to verbalize anger or separation anxiety. Also, a client may not be able to comment on the progress in public. In showing appreciation, he or she may invite the clinician for dinner or present him with a gift. If clinically appropriate, the clinician should accept such gestures with genuine appreciation. Many Asian Americans went through many losses due to war and migration. A good relationship with the clinician is a permanent one that is to be treasured. A client may want the clinician to continue as a friend after termination, and may include him or her in family celebrations. Such culturally appropriate behavior should not be interpreted as "pathological."

### CONCLUSION

Asian Americans are a heterogeneous group reflecting a diversity of educational, political, socioeconomic, and religious backgrounds, as well as different migration histories. This chapter presents a practical assessment guide and treatment strategies that take into account the physical, psychological, social, spiritual, and cultural background of Asian American families. Many Asian immigrants and refugees are survivors of war, political upheavals, and cultural transitions. They deserve our compassion and respect, and the best we can offer as mental health professionals.

### NOTE

1. This section and the section "Culturally Relevant Treatment Strategies" are adapted from Lee (in press).

# REFERENCES

Asian American Health Forum. (1990). *Asian and Pacific Islander American population statistics* (Monograph Series 1). San Francisco: Author.

Flaskerud, J., & Hu, L. T. (1992). Relationship of ethnicity to psychiatric diagnosis. *Journal of Nervous and Mental Disease, 180*(5), 296–303.

Ho, M. K. (1987). *Family therapy with ethnic minorities.* Newbury Park, CA: Sage.

Hong, G. (1989). Application of cultural and environmental issues in family therapy with immigrant Chinese Americans. *Journal of Strategic and Systemic Therapies, 8,* 14–21.

Hsu, F. L. K. (1971). *Under the ancestor's shadow: Kinship, personality, and social mobility in China.* Stanford, CA: Stanford University Press.

Karnow, S., & Yoshihara, N. (1992). *Asian Americans in transition.* New York: The Asia Society.

Kim, S. (1985). Family therapy for Asian Americans: A strategic–structural framework. *Psychotherapy, 22*(2), 342–348.

Landau, J. (1982). Therapy with families in cultural transition. In M. McGoldrick, J. K. Pearce, & J. Giordano (Eds.), *Ethnicity and family therapy* (1st ed., pp. 552–572). New York: Guilford Press.

Lee, E. (1982). A social systems approach to assessment and treatment for Chinese American families. In M. McGoldrick, J. K. Pearce, & J. Giordano (Eds.), *Ethnicity and family therapy* (1st ed., pp. 527–551). New York: Guilford Press.

Lee, E. (1989). Assessment and treatment of Chinese-American immigrant families. *Journal of Psychotherapy and the Family, 6* (1/2), 99–122.

Lee, E. (1990). Family therapy with Southeast Asian refugees. In M. P. Mirkin (Ed.), *The social and political contexts of family therapy* (pp. 331–354). Needham Heights, MA: Allyn & Bacon.

Lee, E. (in press). *Asian American mental health: A clinical handbook.* New York: Guilford Press.

Matsushima, N. M., & Tashima, N. (1982). *Mental health treatment modalities of Pacific/Asian-American practitioners.* San Francisco: Pacific Asian Mental Health Research Project.

McGill, C., & Lee, E. (1986). Family psychoeducation intervention in the treatment of schizophrenia. *Bulletin of the Menninger Clinic, 50*(3), 269–286.

McGoldrick, M. (1982). Ethnicity and family therapy: An overview. In M. McGoldrick, J. K. Pearce, & J. Giordano (Eds.), *Ethnicity and family therapy* (1st ed., pp. 3–30). New York: Guilford Press.

McGoldrick, M. (1985). *Genograms in family assessment.* New York: Norton.

Paniagua, F. A. (1994). *Assessing and treating culturally diverse clients.* Thousand Oaks, CA: Sage.

Shon, S., & Ja, D. (1982). Asian families. In M. McGoldrick, J. K. Pearce, & J. Giordano (Eds.), *Ethnicity and family therapy* (1st ed., pp. 208–228). New York: Guilford Press.

Sue, D. W. (1990). Culture-specific strategies in counseling: A conceptual framework. *Professional Psychology: Research and Practice, 21*(6), 424–433.

Sue, S., & McKinney, H. (1975). Asian Americans in the community health care system. *American Journal of Orthopsychiatry, 45,* 111–118.

Sue, S., & Sue, D. W. (1974). MMPI comparisons between Asian Americans and non-Asian students utilizing a student health psychiatric clinic. *Journal of Counseling Psychology, 21*, 423–427.

Sue, S., & Zane, N. (1987). The role of culture and cultural techniques in psychotherapy: A critique and reformulation. *American Psychologist, 42*, 37–45.

Uba, L. (1994). *Asian Americans: Personality patterns, identity, and mental health*. New York: Guilford Press.

Westermeyer, J. (1989). *Psychiatric care of migrants: A clinical guide*. Washington, DC: American Psychiatric Press.

Yamamoto, J., Lam, J., Fung, D., Tan, F., & Iga, M. (1977). Chinese-speaking Vietnamese refugees in Los Angeles: A preliminary investigation. In E. F. Foulks, R. M. Wintrob, J. Westermeyer, & A. R. Favazza (Eds.), *Current perspectives in cultural psychiatry* (pp. 113–118). New York: Spectrum.

# CHAPTER 17

# Chinese Families

## Evelyn Lee

In Chinese culture, the family, rather than the individual, is the major unit of society. The sense of the family's importance and its contribution to the individual's core identity have been molded by cultural norms and values over 4,000 years of Chinese history. For many Chinese Americans, particularly for immigrants and refugees, the family often provides the sole means of support, validation, and stabilization. In order to provide a culturally relevant clinical intervention for Chinese Americans, it is essential to understand the cultural aspects of Chinese family systems, functions, and their unique life experiences.

The purposes of this chapter are to (1) give a brief overall description of Chinese Americans—demography, language, migration history, and family structure; (2) discuss clinical considerations; and (3) present a culturally relevant assessment and treatment model.

## CHINESE AMERICANS: A DIVERSE POPULATION

According to the 1990 U. S. Census figures, Chinese Americans, at more than 1.6 million, were found to be the largest Asian Pacific American group, making up 22.6% of the Asian Pacific American population. Between 1980 and 1990, the Chinese American population doubled due to the new influx of immigrants and emerged as one of the most diverse Asian American groups. Their diversity can be examined in terms of country of origin, generations, language, economic background, residential preferences, and religion.

Currently, more than 63% of Chinese Americans are foreign-born, 23% do not speak English well, and 53% live in the Western United States. There are 542,121 Chinese Americans who reside in California; 147,250 in New York; and 55,916 in Hawaii. It is estimated that 13.3% of Chinese Americans live below the poverty level, 69.4% are high school graduates, and 72.5% speak a language other than English at home (Asian American Health Forum, 1990).

## LANGUAGE

There is no single "Chinese language." The major dialects are Cantonese (most commonly used in Chinatowns), Mandarin (spoken by most Chinese from China and Taiwan), Toishanese, Chiuchow, Shanghainese, Taiwanese, Fukien, and Hakka.

The written Chinese characters are less complicated than the variety of Chinese dialects. Generally speaking, there are two major styles: the "traditional" style, practiced by the majority of Chinese from Hong Kong, Taiwan, and Southeast Asian countries, and the "simplified" style of writing, developed by the People's Republic of China.

## MIGRATION HISTORY

The Chinese migration history to the United States tells a complex yet fascinating story of change, adaptation, and survival. Their experience also reveals how the Chinese family system is affected by the immense power of political, legal, social, and economic forces. The Chinese have been residing in the United States in significant numbers for over 150 years. Major national immigration policies and economic upheavals in the United States and in Asian countries have resulted in different waves of immigration and different types of family systems.

### The First Wave: The Pioneer Family (1850–1919)

Although there were Chinese residing in the United States as early as 1785, the impetus for large-scale immigration to this country did not take place until the discovery of gold in California in 1848 and the need for manual labor for the construction of railroads. Many Chinese migrants, mostly peasant farmers, left their village in China to pursue their dreams in *Gam Saan*, the "Gold Mountain."

The Chinese Exclusion Act of 1882 barred Chinese laborers and their relatives (including their wives) from entering the United States. The early Chinese pioneers lived in a virtually womanless world without family life. In 1900, of the 89,863 Chinese on the U.S. mainland, only 5% were female (Wong, 1988). The married men were husbands or fathers of "mutilated" families (Sung, 1967) or "split household" families (Glenn, 1983). This type of "sojourner" family pattern had profound consequences on the personal and social development of family life of the early Chinese in the United States.

## The Second Wave: The Small Business Family (1920–1942)

The discriminatory Immigration Act of 1924 made it impossible for American citizens of Chinese ancestry to send for their wives and families. This law was later changed in 1930 to allow wives of Chinese merchants and Chinese wives who were married to American citizens before 1924 to immigrate to the United States (Chinn, Lai, & Choy, 1969). As a result, sizable family units with second-generation American-born Chinese population were emerging in Chinatowns. At the same time, many first-wave laborers began to leave the mines and railroads, and used their savings to start their own small businesses, such as laundry shops or fishing, either alone or with partners. The small-producer families emerged during this period. This family type consisted of the immigrant and first-generation American-born family functioning as a productive unit (Wong, 1988).

## The Third Wave: The Reunited Family (1943–1964)

During the period from 1943 to the repeal of the quota law in 1965, Chinese immigrants were largely female. After years or sometimes decades of separation from their husbands, many wives were reunited with their husbands for the first time. By the time they arrived in the United States, these women and their children had already established very powerful bonds that were far more intense than the marital tie. Reform in immigration policies also encouraged Chinese men to return to Hong Kong to find wives. These trans-Pacific marriages, with wives who were 10–20 years younger than their husbands, were usually arranged by matchmakers or relatives.

## The Fourth Wave: The Chinatown and Dual Worker Family (1965–1977)

Unlike the pre-1965 immigrants who came over as individuals, most of the Chinese immigrants who arrived under the Immigration Act of 1965 came as families. Many of them initially settled in or near Chinatowns in the major metropolitan areas. Approximately half of them were classified as working class, being employed as service workers or laborers. Most of husbands and wives sought employment in the labor-intensive, low-capital services such as garment sweatshops and restaurants. Unlike the small-business families, there tended to be a complete segregation of work and family life, and family members had very little time to spend together. Economic survival was the primary goal for many families, especially the new immigrant families.

## The Fifth Wave: The New Immigrant, Refugee, and Astronaut Family (1978–Present)

In the past two decades, there has been a tremendous influx of Chinese immigrants from China, Hong Kong, Taiwan, and Vietnam. The reestablishment of diplomatic relations between the United States and the People's Republic of China in 1978 also provided an opportunity for students and professionals from China to study in this country, and many elected to stay. Another group of immigrants, who came from Hong Kong, worried about the 1997 transfer of British sovereignty to China. The recent political climate in Taiwan and the desire to seek higher education for their children also created an impetus for many Chinese to come to this country.

Many of the refugees from Vietnam, Laos, and Cambodia were ethnic Chinese. They constituted the second "wave" of Southeast Asian refugees. A significant number of them were survivors of hunger, rape, incarceration, forced migration, and torture. There are also "overseas Chinese" from countries such as Japan, Korea, Philippines, Singapore, Malaysia, Thailand, Mexico, Canada, and many other countries in South America and Europe.

Another recent phenomenon is the so-called "astronaut families." These are the "frequent fliers" who set up two households, one for the children in the United States and one for the adults who work back in their home country after they have received their "green cards." The increased number of such families is due to the economic boom of the Pacific Rim and the difficulty of finding suitable employment in the United States. In recent years, this phenomenon has not only applied to new immigrants, but also to many Chinese American families who have lived in the United States for many years.

In summary, the influx of immigrants and refugees from many different parts of Asia and from many different socioeconomic and political backgrounds has contributed to the complexity of existing Chinese American communities.

## THE TRADITIONAL CHINESE FAMILY

There were many unique characteristics in the traditional family in China. These were heavily influenced by Confucianism, with its emphasis on harmonious interpersonal relationships and interdependence. Family interactions were governed by prescribed roles defined by family hierarchy, obligation, and duties. Independent behavior or expressions of emotions that might disrupt familial harmony were discouraged. The family was patriarchal. Males, particularly the father and eldest son, had dominant roles. Marriages were commonly arranged, and it was socially acceptable for influential men to have concubines. Husbands dealt with the outside world, and provided for the family. The spousal relationship was secondary to the parent–child relationship.

Filial piety was highly cherished, and respect and shame were used by parents as means of control. The father usually played the role of a stern disciplinarian, whereas the mother was affectionate and caring. The eldest son was expected to carry on the family name and enjoyed special privileges, while the eldest daughter was taught to assist the mother with household chores and attend to younger siblings. The most elevated family dyad was the father–son dyad.

Throughout history, Chinese mothers have been portrayed as self-sacrificing, suffering, guilt-inducing, and overinvolved with their children. Traditionally, in accordance with the custom of "thrice obeying," women were expected to comply with their fathers or elder brothers in youth, their husbands in marriage, and their sons after their husbands' death. As wives, their value was judged by their ability to produce male heirs and to serve their in-laws. In many middle- and upper-class families, children were raised by "wet nurses" who breast-fed the babies and took over the mothering roles. Grandparents and other extended family members also played a significant influence on family life. Due to the strong bond and the intense sense of obligation, many sons never left their parents in their adult lives. Parents expected to be taken care of in their old age, and never experienced the so-called "empty nest" period in their family life cycle.

## CONTEMPORARY CHINESE AMERICAN FAMILIES

The patterns of family systems tend to be molded by economic, political, and sociocultural factors outside the family system, rather than determined merely by emotional and psychological factors within the family (Tseng & Hsu, 1991). In the past generation, the traditional Chinese family has undergone tremendous transformation due to economic and political forces in the United States and Asia. As indicated previously, the structure and composition of Chinese American families are heavily influenced by U.S. immigration policy changes.

With the large number of Chinese immigrants from China, Hong Kong, and Taiwan, the clinician should recognize that economic and political changes in those countries have a dramatic impact on Chinese family system and values. Since the Communist takeover of China in 1949, Confucian thought and religions were largely banned. A one-child family system has replaced the traditional extended family system. During the 10 years of the Cultural Revolution period, many families suffered forced separation. Red Guard youths openly challenged their parents and teachers; filial piety and respect for the elderly no longer dominate life in China. In recent years, the economic boom in China has brought another wave of Western influences and urbanization.

After World War II, both Hong Kong and Taiwan underwent rapid growth in light industries and exports. The forces of industrialization, Westernization, urbanization, and economic affluence brought a change in Chinese social and family structure. Although the older- and middle-generation Chinese still embody some traditional beliefs, the younger generation has shown some evidence of their rejection of conservatism and traditionalism. Political history has also influenced traditional Chinese family values. In the case of Hong Kong, a British colonial past has produced profound effects on the education, legal, and social systems. In Taiwan, a long period of Japanese occupation, until the end of World War II, has had a large impact on the society, especially among the older generation.

In summary, there are several distinct shifts in the contemporary Chinese American family: (1) The traditional Chinese extended family has gradually yielded to a more *nuclear family*, in which functional relations apply instead of actual household structure; (2) the traditional patriarchal family has transformed in many cases to a *biarchal system*, in which a mother shares decision making with the father; (3) the parent–child dyad has diminished in importance, whereas the *husband–wife dyad* has increased; (4) favoritism of sons has slowly decreased, because daughters now attain comparable education and careers, and can be counted on to take care of aged parents; (5) the family life cycle has changed from arranged marriages and no "empty nest period" to one where romantic love occurs before marriage and adult children leave the home; (6) successful child rearing is now measured mostly by the children's academic and career achievements; and (7) earning power is no longer solely the father's, but is shared with other adult family members.

These observations are general ones. There is no one "typical" Chinese American family. There are many individual differences, and they represent a wide range of cultural values from very traditional to very "Americanized."

## COMMON PRESENTING MENTAL HEALTH PROBLEMS

Given the fact that no large-scale prevalence studies have been conducted on Chinese Americans, it is difficult to specify what the rates of mental disorders are within this population, or to compare them with other ethnic minority groups. However, findings from the available research on prevalence and needs strongly imply that major mental health problems do exist among Chinese Americans, which is contrary to the widespread belief that Chinese Americans are a well-adjusted "model minority."

### Somatization and Depression

Several research findings have reported the prevalence of somatization symptoms among the Chinese (Kleinman, 1982; Tseng, 1975; Marsella, Kinzie, & Gordon, 1973). Many Chinese Americans who are treated for mental health problems complain of headache, backache, and chest pains. Chinese American students seemed to have a rather definite pattern of depression associated with somatic functioning (Marsella et al., 1973). Chang (1985) also found ethnic differences in the patterns of depressive symptomatology, and the Chinese were the most likely to exhibit somatic complaints.

There are many hypotheses on why Chinese tend to express their emotional problems in somatic symptoms. It may be a reflection of Chinese cultural values that emphasize avoiding shame and protecting the family's name from the negative stigma of mental problems. Somatization may be a socially acceptable means of suppressing direct depressive affect while allowing the individual to receive secondary gain. Many Chinese women, for example, may use the sick role to seek attention and emotional support from family members who otherwise may not be available. In addition to the psychological and sociological explanations of somatization, one needs to understand the Chinese holistic view of health and illness based on traditional Chinese medicine. There is a strong belief in unity between the mind and the body, an organ-oriented conception of pathology that emphasizes close correspondences between human emotions and body organs. Somatic problems frequently are explained by traditional Chinese as being due to weak kidneys, hot intestines, or *chi* (energy) imbalances.

Depression has been widely found among Chinese Americans, especially among the immigrants and refugees. This may be, in part, a result of social isolation, lowered status, grief (Lin, 1986), acculturation stress, war trauma, financial problems, and other social stressors. Many experience symptoms of exhaustion, weakness, dizziness, diffuse bodily complaints, difficulty with sleep and appetite, and a sense of hopelessness. They may meet the official diagnostic criteria for a major depressive disorder. However, from the traditional Chinese patients' perspective, their chief problem is not depression but "neurasthenia," an official diagnosis in China and a diagnosis widely given by traditional herbalists in Chinatown.

## Suicide

In an earlier study in San Francisco's Chinatown, Bourne (1973) reported a high suicide rate among the Chinese. From 1952 to 1968, the suicide rate among Chinese was 27.9 per 100,000 population per annum, which was three times higher than the reported rate for the national average. Yap (1958) borrowed Lindemann's concept of hypereridism to explain the high frequency of interpersonal stresses as a precipitating factor for female suicide.

In a more recent study of percentage of all deaths attributed to suicide of 15- to 24-year-olds, Chinese Americans have a higher rate in comparison with the European Americans in that age range. The percentage for female Chinese is 20.8% versus 8.8% for European American females. Foreign-born Chinese

Americans have higher suicide rates than American-born Chinese Americans (Yu, Chang, Liu, & Fernandez, 1989).

## Schizophrenia

There is an absence of epidemiological data in the United States on schizophrenia prevalence for Chinese Americans. The prevalence data indicate a band of prevalence rate ranging from roughly 2–10 cases per 1,000 population across a range of populations (Sartorius & Jablensky, 1976). The prevalence of schizophrenia in China ranged from 0.77% to 4.80% (Lin & Kleinman, 1981). In Chinese culture, mental illness is highly stigmatized, and a mentally ill member usually brings shame upon the entire family.

## Other Psychological Problems

Other common manifestations of psychological problems among Chinese Americans include anxiety disorder, dissociative disorder, posttraumatic stress disorder, paranoia, hypersensitivity, identity confusion, low self-esteem, conduct disorder, drug addiction, alcoholism, gambling (a serious problem in the Chinese community that has not been properly studied), family problems (intergenerational conflicts, marital disharmony, in-law problems, domestic violence, child abuse, and neglect), difficulties encountered at work, school, dating, and impaired interpersonal skills. Culture-bound syndromes also have been reported. Two of the most common categories are genital retraction disorder (*suk-yeoung*) and *amok* (Gaw, 1993).

## CLINICAL CONSIDERATIONS IN TREATING CHINESE AMERICAN FAMILIES[1]

In providing culturally competent services to Chinese American families, the clinician needs to understand the cultural meanings of their concept of mental health problems, their help-seeking pattern, the process of healing, ways to deal with psychological problems, and their treatment expectations.

## Conceptualization of Mental Illness and Emotional Difficulties

Western-trained clinicians have paid great attention to either the intrapsychic influences or the biological explanation of the cause of mental illness. For many traditional Chinese, their views are still highly influenced by their religious and spiritual beliefs and, most important of all, the concepts of health and disease in traditional Chinese medicine. Generally speaking, there are several common popular explanations of factors that may contribute to the development of mental illness and emotional problems:

1. *Imbalance of yin and yang and the disharmony in the flow of chi.* In traditional Chinese medicine, humankind is viewed as a microcosm within a macrocosm. The energy in each human being interrelates with the energy of the universe. *Chi* (energy) and *jing* (sexual energy) are both considered vital life energies that are kept in balance by the dual polarities of *yin* and *yang.* If there is an imbalance of the *yin* and *yang,* then the immunity of the body is disturbed, and the body is susceptible to illness.

2. *Supernatural intervention.* Mental illness is seen as some form of spiritual unrest meted out to the individual through the agency of a "ghost" or vengeful spirit. It is a sign of punishment caused by the transgression of family rituals in ancestor worship (Lin & Lin, 1981).

3. *Religious beliefs.* Mental illness is viewed as *karma* caused by deeds from past lives or punishment from God.

4. *Genetic vulnerability or hereditary defects.*

5. *Physical and emotional strain and exhaustion* caused by external stresses such as failing in a business, ending a love affair, death of a family member, and so on.

6. *Organic disorders.* Mental illness is conceptualized as a manifestation of physical disease, especially brain disorders, diseases of the liver, hormonal imbalance, and so on.

7. *Character weakness.* Mental health is achieved through self-discipline, exercise of will power, and the avoidance of morbid thoughts. Persons who are born with weak character will not be able to practice these and are more vulnerable to emotional problems.

## Indigenous Healing Practices in the Chinese Community

Despite the existence of an advanced, highly institutionalized U.S. medical system and the availability of mental health professionals, it is evident that many types of traditional healing methods are still being utilized by Chinese clients for physical health or emotional problems. There are various indigenous healing practices available in major Chinatowns and refugee communities. The most popular ones are herbal medicine, acupuncture, and therapeutic massage. Religious faith healing is also perceived to be helpful. Other practices such as geomancy and fortune-telling are also being used to prevent or to remove "bad spirit."

Nutrition is another popular means to restore health. According to Chinese traditional medicine, foods are categorized in five groups: "hot," "cold," "allergic," "moderate," and "nutrient." Chinese are usually very conscious of good nutrition. Therapeutic cuisine which gives "good *chi*" is very popular in treating health and emotional problems. In addition, many Chinese practice health exercises such as *tai chi chuan* and *chi gong* to bring harmony to their body and mind.

## Dealing with Psychological Problems

Most Chinese Americans try to deal with their psychological problems without seeking professional mental health counseling. Traditional families usually seek help from family members first, because it is considered the collective responsibility of the family to take care of the disturbed member as long as possible. Such problems are kept from outsiders for fear of the shame, guilt, and stigma that this knowledge might bring upon the family. The family will often try to deal with the problem by denying the seriousness of the illness, or by extorting or reasoning with the patient to "correct" his or her behaviors (Lin & Lin, 1981). Each family member may contribute his or her own proposal for treatment. When the family and the troubled person are not able to resolve the problem, they often turn to certain trusted outsiders and helpers within the ethnic community, such as community elders, spiritual leaders, indigenous healers, and physicians (Sue & Morishima, 1982). When these efforts fail, assistance from other agencies and providers, including psychiatrists and other mental health professionals, would be sought while the troubled family member was still kept at home. Family members usually resist hospitalization until all other efforts have failed. The introduction of the label of mental illness seemed to hasten the transition from intrafamilial coping to hospitalization of the troubled member, who ultimately would be rejected, scapegoated, and blamed for things that went wrong within the family (Lin & Lin, 1981; Gaw, 1993).

## Treatment Expectations

For many clinicians, the "success" of a case is measured by the "emotional" growth of the client or the "psychological" understanding of the problem. While some of the acculturated Chinese may expect "insight" therapy, the majority of Chinese immigrants and refugees expect more "concrete" help and the immediate alleviation of symptoms.

## Process of Healing

Many Chinese Americans seek help from mental health professionals only as the last resort after they have exhausted all other resources, and usually come in for help in a state of crisis, with expectation of an immediate "cure." They are used to traditional Chinese healing practice, which usually includes a brief physical observation, diagnosis, and prescription writing—all in one session. They expect a rapid diagnosis and do not understand the purpose of lengthy evaluation and the apparent lack of treatment in the initial process. They may also get upset with initial interviews that probe into their family and personal backgrounds, which they perceive have nothing to do with the presenting problem. To reveal family secrets to an outsider also evokes a sense of guilt. Consequently, many Chinese clients drop out of treatment (Lee, 1982).

## Perception of the Mental Health Professional Role

Many mental health disciplines are not widely recognized in many Asian countries. Most Chinese do not have the sophistication to understand the roles of the clinicians or their special professional orientations. Since the role of a physician is more clearly understood and respected, Chinese patients may expect clinicians to conduct themselves in the traditional role of physicians who prescribe medication. Therefore, especially in the initial stage of the therapeutic relationship, it is very important for clinicians to explore their clients' exposure to mental health professionals in the past and their experiences.

## FAMILY ASSESSMENT OF IMMIGRANT CHINESE FAMILIES

Effective assessment must take into consideration the Chinese holistic view of health and illness and their culturally specific ways of coping with emotional difficulties. The assessment must include information beyond traditional intake data. Relevant personal, familial, community information, and cultural mapping are extremely helpful in the assessment of Chinese families who have undergone rapid social change and cultural transition (Ho, 1987). As in any assessment, it is vital for clinicians to base their evaluation on the physical (constitutional or somatic organization), the psychological (the ego or self-concept as an organizing force), and the sociocultural (the organizing response to the rules and expectations of society and culture) (Lee, 1982).

The assessment guidelines discussed here for Chinese American families follow those presented in Chapter 16 on Asian families (Lee, 1982, 1989, 1990).

## Migration and Relocation History

As a result of the major political changes in China in the past several decades, many Chinese have experienced different wars, such as the Sino-Japanese war and the Civil War between the Nationalists and the Communists. Many families also endured hardships during the Cultural Revolution. It is helpful to understand how much energy clients have spent in coping with their losses and separations, and how much energy they have left to cope with new demands.

Questions to ask include the following: How many times did the family move in the past? From where to where? Who left, and with whom? What were the reasons? Who made the decision? Which family members are still left behind? What was the order of migration? Were these voluntary or involuntary migrations? To what political and economic systems was the family exposed? When did family members come to the United States? Who is the sponsor? What kind of relationship does the family have with the sponsor?

In view of the long history of losses and separation in many Chinese families, it is common for the pain and unresolved conflict of one generation to be suppressed or denied and then passed on and expressed in the next generation. It is very important for clinicians to view the pain an individual brings to the session as pain experienced by the total family, including parents and grandparents.

## Adjustment Problems and Cultural Shock

Many new immigrants arrived in the United States with losses, separations, and unresolved grief. At the same time, they are placed in a strange and unpredictable new environment. As minority members, they have to learn and get used to the behavioral and value orientation of American culture. Problems encountered, such as language, transportation, employment, housing, child care, and racism, can be overwhelming.

## Impact of Migration on Individual and Family Life Cycle

In addition to the overall impact of relocation, migration disrupts both the individual and the family life cycle. For example, how does a Vietnamese Chinese child growing up in a refugee camp with no provision for substitute mothering establish a basic sense of trust? How does an adolescent from mainland China integrate old values with the new ones learned from the media, school, and peer groups? How does a Chinese housewife deal with new values in regard to sexual orientation, independence, achievement, and work? How does a newly arrived, elderly Chinese man who expects to be supported by his children and grandchildren deal with his loneliness in a housing project for the elderly or in a nursing home?

From the family life cycle perspective, families that migrate with young children are perhaps strengthened by having each other, but they are vulnerable to the parental reversal of hierarchies. Families migrating when their children are adolescents may have more difficulties because they will have less time together as a unit before the children move out on their own. Thus, the family must struggle simultaneously with multiple transitions and generational conflicts (McGoldrick, 1982).

## Differences in Rate of Acculturation

There is great diversity among the Chinese in the United States. Given the diversity of languages, norms, and immigration status, clinicians are advised to assess a client's acculturation in the United States very carefully. A non-Chinese-speaking, third-generation Chinese American may be very "Westernized" and have a different value orientation from a non-English-speaking, newly arrived immigrant. However, years in the United States is not an absolute yardstick to measure the degree of acculturation. Many older Chinese, who came to the United States before the Cultural Revolution, still try to preserve their heritage by "freezing traditions," and may be more "Chinese" than newly arrived immigrants from Hong Kong or Taiwan.

The country of origin will also influence the rate of acculturation. A professional from Singapore may absorb American culture much more easily than an adult from China, because Singaporeans have rapidly adopted many Western practices, whereas mainland Chinese are only beginning to do so.

Professional affiliation is also a factor in acculturation. An English-speaking Chinese doctor from Hong Kong who works in an American hospital is exposed to many more American practices than a Chinese cook who works in the kitchen of a Chinese restaurant with other non-English-speaking Chinese.

Age at time of immigration is another factor. A 10-year-old child who immediately enters the public school system is more easily assimilated than an 80-year-old man who lives in Chinatown.

## Family Stress Caused by Role Reversal

Many monolingual Chinese parents and grandparents depend on their English-speaking children as cultural brokers and interpreters. Such dependency can cause resentment and anger (Lee, 1988). Role reversal may also occur between spouses when one is more acculturated than the other. Many Chinese women, for the first time, earn more than their husbands, and demand more rights than before.

## Work and Financial Stress

For the Chinese, the work environment and work roles contribute greatly to a person's self-definition and self-esteem. Work can be a facilitator or a barrier to life adjustment. Hope of improving the family's financial status is one of the major reasons Chinese immigrate to the United States. However, language barriers and other factors have trapped many Chinese in restaurant and garment factory work with no other alternatives. "Status inconsistency," created by underemployment, is one of the major stresses for Chinese in this country. In addition, demands from work have brought about drastic changes in the Chinese family system. Because of long working hours, many Chinese men find it difficult to maintain their traditional family role as husband and father. Women, especially those who did not work before they came to the United States, find it very stressful to be working mothers with little support from their husbands. Becoming the breadwinner is devastating for one who has not faced that responsibility before. For Chinese American professionals, recent economic downturns and "glass ceiling" barriers also cause stress.

## Neighborhood and Community Support

Enclaves of Chinese living in Chinatowns across the United States represent not only a physical sense of community, but also a psychological one. To many Chinese Americans, especially recent immigrants, the community provides the psychological significance of an extended family. Similar to the support formerly available in their "village," the community provides the family with an informal support network for socialization into the behaviors needed for survival and adaptation. Chinese depend on other Chinese to learn about their "new world." Community groups such as family associations and social/cultural clubs provide much needed support. The community may have a much more important psychological meaning for Chinese families than it does for many Western families.

Beause Chinese communities tend to be cohesive, with strong informal communication networks, the clinician must assess the constraints any particular Chinese community places on a particular family or person. Therapeutic problems may arise because of the sense of losing face due to the community stigma of emotional problems, cross-ethnic relationship conflicts involving racism, conflicts within the Chinese community, lack of service alternatives, and the poor reputation of the treatment system in handling Chinese family issues and confidentiality.

Many Chinese live in urban neighborhoods with crime and violence. Special attention should be placed on the effect on family systems from such environmental stressors.

## Religious and Spiritual Beliefs

Among Chinese Americans, Christianity, Buddhism, Taoism, and ancestor worship are the most prevalent religions. The clinician should respect the spiritual perspective of the family. For example, the concepts of *karma*, reincarnation, and compassion are effective in working with Buddhist clients.

## Family Physical Health and Medication History

Because of the holistic view of health and illness, it is important to pay attention not only to the emotional state of the client, but also the physical health.

Gathering information on physical health, nutrition, and medication history is vital. Many Chinese patients take herbal medicines and receive treatment from indigenous healers. Such practice needs to be respected and considered.

## Culturally Specific Responses to Mental Health Problems

The clinician should encourage family members to share openly the cultural beliefs on the causes of the problems, their past coping style, their help-seeking behavior, and their treatment expectations. (See Chapter 16 for a list of questions that may be helpful.)

## Cultural Strengths

The Confucian teaching of "the middle way," the Buddhist teaching of *karma*, and the Taoist teaching of "the way" are some examples of how religious and philosophical teachings can be helpful in coping with life stresses. In addition, the support from extended family members and the strong focus on harmony and interpersonal relationships in Chinese families should be utilized.

## TREATMENT STRATEGIES

Treatment strategies discussed in Chapter 16 can also be applied in working with Chinese American families. In particular, the following strategies have been found to be effective (Lee, 1982):

1. The clinician should convey expertise and use caution in establishing an initial egalitarian therapeutic relationship. Because Chinese families view family relationships in terms of a vertical hierarchy, extreme caution is advised against adopting a democratic attitude in the therapeutic relationship. The clinician will need to take a much more authoritative attitude than may be customary, since Chinese family members view the clinician as the "problem solver" and expect him or her to behave in an authoritative or parental manner. They will feel very uncomfortable if put on a peer level with the clinician.

2. Clinicians need to convey an air of confidence. When asked, they should not hesitate to show off their educational background and work experience. Clients need to know that the clinician is more "powerful" than their illness and will "cure" them with competence and know-how.

3. Receiving information on the personal credentials, qualities, and background of the clinician provides the client with common ground for establishing rapport. Chinese clients usually do not view their clinician as merely a professional involved in this kind of human service or as just an agency staff member providing valuable services. They expect the clinician to care about

them as people. It is not uncommon for clients to ask the clinician many personal questions about his or her family background, marital status, number of children, and so on. The clinician will need to feel comfortable about answering personal questions in order to gain the client's trust and to establish rapport.

4. Nonjudgmental listening and neutrality in the clinician's responses may be viewed as lack of interest. Such a passive manner may be interpreted by Chinese clients as noncaring or lacking confidence. Since verbal expression of feelings is not encouraged in Chinese culture, the client's dissatisfaction may not be made known to the clinician.

5. Flexibility and willingness to assume multiple helping roles enhance the therapeutic relationship. Because of the lack of understanding of the role of mental health professionals, especially among disorganized, multiproblem families, clients expect the clinician not only to be a "talking" doctor, but also to play the role of teacher, advocate, family adviser, consultant to friends and relatives, and so on. Actions such as telephoning the client's physician, making a home visit, or getting the client a job can be very therapeutic. However, the clinician should be aware of which roles are therapeutic to the client. The use of paraprofessionals in a team can be effective in allowing for a diversity of therapeutic roles, although it is important to have one primary therapist.

6. Clients often need demonstrations of caring and empathy. Among Chinese patients with a long history of separation from their loved ones, there is a yearning for an actively empathic parental figure. Clinicians who exhibit warmth are more able to gain the trust of their clients. This requires not only careful listening to the clients, but also trying to do something that will be helpful in relieving symptoms. Due to the strong sense of obligation in Chinese culture, clients may view keeping appointments or taking medication as doing something for the clinician in return for the clinician's concern.

7. Chinese clients may expect to have a dependent role at the outset of the therapeutic relationship. The clinician should encourage "healthy dependency" and set up a therapy plan that will foster future independence when the client is ready. Of course, long-term dependency should be discouraged.

8. It is very important for the clinician to identify the decision makers in the family and gain their support for the treatment plan. Their active participation in the implementation of the plan can be very effective. In the early stages of therapy, individual sessions (some Chinese families refer to these as "secret meetings") can foster unnecessary guilt and isolation within the family and increase the family's resistance to involvement in therapy. It is preferable to establish relationships with multiple family members. In view of the strong Chinese family influence on the individual's behavior, family therapy is generally the treatment of choice. This requires establishing relationships with the client, the parents, the siblings, the grandparents, and with significant others. Each set of relationships may require different intervention skills.

9. Flexibility and informality around case entry and exit are essential. Many Chinese clients come to an agency for help not by formal referral but by word of mouth. They may drop by the office without an appointment because they have heard about the worker from friends with whom they work in the community. They are not used to a formal appointment system. Formal evaluation sessions may scare them away. Termination is another area requiring special attention. The Chinese concept of time and space in relationships is quite different. They invest a great deal of energy in trusting their clinician and in allowing him or her to be part of the family, and they like to maintain contact even after the successful achievement of treatment goals.

10. Appreciating the inherent ambivalence in the relationship with the clinician facilitates the therapeutic relationship. Sharing feelings and family secrets with an outsider can provoke feelings of guilt and uneasiness. On the other hand, many Chinese clients are yearning for a close relationship with someone who is understanding and supportive.

11. Creative use of the client's cultural strength is encouraged. Strengths such as support from extended family members and siblings, the strong sense of obligation, the strong focus on educational achievement, the work ethic, the high tolerance for loneliness and separation, and the loyalties of friends or between employer and employee should be respected and used creatively in the therapeutic process.

12. Special caution is advised for clinicians who share similar cultural backgrounds with their Chinese clients. Those with the same cultural background may have particular difficulties and blind spots. For example, a young Chinese clinician who is still struggling with his or her own cultural identity and dependency toward parents may overidentify with the teenagers in the family. Transference and countertransference issues should be explored and handled appropriately.

## CONCLUSIONS

This chapter provides a historical migration background of Chinese American families. Cultural issues and clinical considerations are presented. Practical guidelines are offered for family assessment and treatment. From the pioneer family to the "astronaut" family, Chinese American families have undergone numerous changes and are continuing to evolve. With the present political and economic trends in the United States and Asia, Chinese American families may undergo more changes in their composition, size, and family dynamics. As clinicians, we need to stay in tune with these rapid changes and be flexible in designing treatment strategies.

Effective cross-cultural family therapy requires not only the knowledge of cultural differences, but also professional skills to bring about positive changes and effective treatment outcome. The establishment of therapeutic relationship is not only based on mutual trust, but also on the clinician's ability to empathize with compassion. A culturally competent clinician should also have a clear understanding of his or her cultural identity, cross-cultural communication style, and countertransference issues while working with Chinese American families. The most challenging task is, however, to take advantage of the long and rich cultural strengths (such as philosophy, religion, and holistic health) of the Chinese and *integrate* them with the best that modern Western medicine and psychology can offer. The author believes that such an integrated model will not only benefit the treatment of Chinese Americans, but can also enhance mainstream American society in its current multicultural setting.

## NOTE

1. This section and the sections "Family Assessment of Immigrant Chinese Families" and "Treatment Strategies" are adapted from Lee (in press).

## REFERENCES

Asian American Health Forum. (1990). *Asian and Pacific Islander American population statistics* (Monograph Series 1). San Francisco: Author.

Bourne, P. (1973). Suicide among Chinese in San Francisco. *American Journal of Public Health, 63*(8), 744–750.

Chang, W. (1985). A cross-cultural study of depressive symptomatology. *Culture, Medicine, and Psychiatry, 9,* 295–317.

Chinn, T. H., Lai, M., & Choy, P. (1969). *A history of the Chinese in California: A syllabus.* San Francisco: Chinese Historical Society of America.

Gaw, A. (1993). Psychiatric care of Chinese Americans. In A. Gaw (Ed.), *Culture, ethnicity, and mental illness* (pp. 245–280). Washington, DC: American Psychiatric Press.

Glenn, E. N. (1983). Split household, small producer and dual wage earner: An analysis of Chinese-American family strategies. *Journal of Marriage and Family, 45*(1), 35–46.

Ho, M. K. (1987). *Family therapy with ethnic minorities.* Newbury Park, CA: Sage.

Kleinman, A. M. (1982). Neurasthenia and depression: A study of somatization and culture in China. *Culture, Medicine, and Psychiatry, 6,* 117–189.

Lee, E. (1982). A social system approach to assessment and treatment for Chinese American families. In M. McGoldrick, J. K. Pearce, & J. Giordano (Eds.), *Ethnicity and family therapy* (1st ed., pp. 527–551). New York: Guilford Press.

Lee, E. (1988). Cultural factors in working with Southeast Asian refugee adolescents. *Journal of Adolescence, 11,* 167–179.

Lee, E. (1989). Assessment and treatment of Chinese-American immigrant families. *Journal of Psychotherapy and the Family, 6*(1/2), 99–122.

Lee, E. (1990). Family therapy with Southeast Asian refugees. In M. P. Mirkin (Ed.), *The social and political contexts of family therapy* (pp. 331–354). Needham Heights, MA: Allyn & Bacon.

Lee, E. (in press). *Asian American mental health: A clinical handbook.* New York: Guilford Press.

Lin, K. M. (1986). Psychopathology and social disruption in refugees. In C. William & J. Westermeyer (Eds.), *Refugee mental health in resettlement countries* (pp. 61–73). Washington, DC: Hemisphere.

Lin K. M., & Kleinman, A. (1981). Recent development of psychiatric epidemiology in China. *Culture, Medicine, and Psychiatry, 5,* 135–143.

Lin, T., & Lin, M. (1981). Love, denial and rejection: Responses of Chinese families to mental illness. In A. Kleinman & T. Lin (Eds.), *Normal and abnormal behavior in Chinese culture* (pp. 387–401). Dordrecht, The Netherlands: D. Reidel.

Marsella, A., Kinzie, D., & Gordon, P. (1973). Ethnic variations in the expression of depression. *Journal of Cross-Cultural Psychology, 4,* 435–458.

McGoldrick, M. (1982). Ethnicity and family therapy: An overview. In M. McGoldrick, J. K. Pearce, & J. Giordano (Eds.), *Ethnicity and family therapy* (1st ed., pp. 3–30). New York: Guilford Press.

Sartorius, N., & Jablensky, A. (1976). Transcultural studies of schizophrenia. *World Health Organization Chronicle, 30,* 481–485.

Sue, S., & Morishima, J. (1982). *The mental health of Asian Americans.* San Francisco: Jossey-Bass.

Sung, B. L. (1967). *Mountains of gold.* New York: Macmillan.

Tseng, W. S. (1975). The nature of somatic complaints among psychiatric patients: The Chinese case. *Comparative Psychiatry, 16,* 237–245.

Tseng, W. S., & Hsu, J. (1991). *Culture and family: Problems and therapy.* Binghamton, NY: Haworth Press.

Wong, M. G. (1988). The Chinese American family. In C. H. Mandel, R. W. Habenstein, & R. Wright (Eds.), *Ethnic families in America* (3rd ed.). New York: Elsevier.

Yap, P. M. (1958). Hypereridism and attempted suicide in Chinese. *Journal of Nervous and Mental Disease, 127,* 34–41.

Yu, E., Chang, C. F., Liu, W., & Fernandez, M. (1989). Suicide among Asian American youth. In M. Feinleib (Ed.), *Report of the Secretary's task force on youth suicide* (pp. 157–176). Washington, DC: U.S. Department of Health and Human Services.

# CHAPTER 18

# Japanese Families

## Wesley Tak Matsui

*Issei seek your fortune.*
*Dual souled nisei reflect the silence.*
*Both sent to the bleakness of camp.*
*Sansei reclaim your identity.*
*Yonsei scatter in the multicultural stream.*

The 1990 U.S. Census reported 845,000 people of Japanese ancestry, with more than three-fourths American born. Since the 1980s, the Japanese comprise less than 2% of the total new Asian immigrant population, which numbers for two or three thousand each year (Kitano, 1995). The experiences of this admittedly small percentage of the U.S. population are awash in each successive decade's mainstream characterizations of Japan. My own ethnic identity reflected the portrayal of the Japanese in the dominant culture. For example, growing up in the 1950s, "Made in Japan" meant something cheaply constructed and I felt ashamed. When Japan constructed quality cars and its industry management methods were emulated, and its education system was a model of excellence, a corresponding pride emerged. An emotional downturn occurred with the return of "Japan bashing." This chapter will explicate the Japanese American story in its historical context, identify preferred family patterns, and describe the therapeutic implications for family therapists.

## HISTORICAL CONTEXT

The immigration experience of Japanese Americans can be understood by the context of conditions in Japan during the *Meiji* Era, the Immigration Period, the Prewar Period, the Wartime Evacuation, and the Postwar Period. The reception of these Japanese immigrants on the Pacific coast was a case study in institutional racism in that numerous legislative actions were taken to exclude or take away rights. Each period will be described briefly to illustrate the immigrant experience.

## *Meiji* Era (1868–1912)

The restoration of the *Meiji* emperor to the throne in 1868 by the coup d'état of the Tokugawa shogunate initiated a major upheaval (Niiya, 1993). The *Meiji* Era marked the change of Japan from an isolated feudal country to a major world power. Japan's modernization was in response to the threat of colonization by Western powers. The transformation set into motion the following: the industrialization of the nation, Western political institutions, a Western legal system, and universal education (Hane, 1972). Farmers took the burden for financing the overhaul of the country. This became a factor in that immigrants sought higher wages in the United States and Hawaii to pay for the taxes on their farms in Japan.

Despite this drastic modernization, the traditional patterns were embedded in the societal fabric. The traditions brought by the *issei*, the first generation of immigrants, are best understood in the historical context of the *Meiji*, not today's Japan. In a conversation about a *nisei*'s (the second generation and the first generation, born in the United States) visit to Japan, there was a sense of disappointment in the search for Japanese food of his childhood. He was told, "Nobody eats that food here; that's peasant food." Reflexively, a Japanese scholar quipped that a good place to study 19th-century France was in sections of Canada, and the best place to study the *Meiji* Era was in sections of California (Kitano, 1969).

The themes of the premodern Japanese family have been summarized by Kitano (1969, p. 61):

1. Filial piety, respect for age and seniority, and preference for male children.
2. Clear-cut patterns of deference, including special words for addressing elders.
3. Cohesion and harmony valued above individual achievement.
4. Recognition of the relationship between generations insisted upon.

These themes will be developed in the sections on family patterns.

## Immigration Period (1890–1924)

For over two centuries before this period, it was illegal for the Japanese to travel outside their country. Takaki (1989, citing a poem by Ichiyo) characterized this first wave of Asian immigration as "overblown with hope."

> Let me take my leave, my mother.
> Earn money and come home, my child,
> As I stay home and pray to the gods.
> To this Hawaii from the far away Okinawa
> We have come all the way for the sake of money.
> Thinking it'd only be a few years we came,
> But we have now grown our roots deep
> and with green leaves.
> (*My Mother Dear*, an Okinawan song, cited in Niiya, 1993, p. 5)

Migrants' initial purpose was *dekasegi* (sojourning) in hopes of making a fortune and returning to Japan to rectify the previously mentioned tax burden. From 1885 to 1894 the flow of migrants went to Hawaii, where contract labor arrangements were made for much needed plantation laborers. The attraction to the United States for the migrants to the U.S. mainland was the lure of higher wages. On the mainland of the United States, a laborer could earn in 1 year the same income as a governor in Japan (Takaki, 1989). To reduce problems associated with a transient bachelor population, the Japanese government encouraged women to immigrate. This ushered in *shashin kekkon* (photo-marriage) based on the system of arranged marriages (Nakano, 1990).

The anti-Japanese movement began in 1905 with the formation of the Asiatic Exclusion League (set up almost completely by organized labor). It should be noted that the reception of the Japanese in Hawaii was quite different, given the desirability of plantation laborers. Organized labor protested the *issei* workers on the grounds of "unfair competition," their low standard of living, and they were "unassimilable." The following letter was written by a farmer urging the legislature to pass anti-Japanese legislation. The letter describes the racial sentiment of this movement:

> Near my home is an eighty-acre tract of as fine land as there is in California. On that tract lives a Japanese. With that Japanese lives a white woman. In that woman's arms is a baby. What is that baby? It isn't Japanese. It isn't white. I'll tell you what that baby is. It is a germ of the mightiest problem that ever faced this state: a problem that will make the black problem of the South look white. All about us the Asiatics are gaining a foothold. (Takaki, 1989, p. 204)

The legalization of this anti-Japanese sentiment took the form of the San Francisco School Board Segregation Order of 1906 (which segregated students of Japanese descent); the Gentleman's Agreement of 1907 (Japan agreed to stop issuing passports to workers headed for the United States); and the California Alien Land Law (which prohibited Japanese immigrants from purchasing agricultural land because these immigrants were not eligible for citizenship). The last law figured strongly in *Snow Falling on Cedars* (Guterson, 1994). This fictional account of a murder trial in a small fishing community in the Pacific

Northwest vividly portrays post-World War II racial tensions. Takaki (1989) described the Japanese American solidarity response to these conditions. Using the language of sociology, Kitano (1969) described the formation of insular communities as the Japanese subculture.

## Prewar Period (1924–1941)

This period began with the Immigration Act of 1924. The effect of this legislation was to halt further Japanese immigration to the United States. The prior window of immigration opportunity for the Japanese accounted for the idiosyncratic counting of generations of families, which will be explicated in the section on generation. The close of the Prewar Period was punctuated by the bombing of Pearl Harbor.

## Wartime Evacuation (1941–1945)

Roosevelt's signing of Executive Order 9066 in February of 1942 allowed the military authority to exclude any person from any location without a trial or hearing. Although this order did not specifically mention the Japanese, the order set the stage for evacuation. In March of 1942, Executive Order 9102 established the War Relocation Authority. Between April and September of 1942, over 120,000 Japanese Americans were sent to what were euphemistically called relocation camps. The names of the 10 American concentration camps were Topaz (central Utah), Poston (Colorado River) and Gila River (Rivers) in Arizona, Granada (Amache) in Colorado, Heart Mountain in Wyoming, Jerome (Denson) and Rohwer in Arkansas, Manzanar and Tule Lake (Newell) in California, and Minidoka (Hunt) in Idaho (Niiya, 1993).

Early in 1943, the War Department realized that many of the Japanese Americans were loyal to the United States. A questionnaire was devised to screen those in "camp" for eventual release and make those previously declared legally ineligible for military service eligible. Two questions that provoked considerable reactions were known as the "loyalty questions." The first asked about willingness to serve in the military. The second inquired about "unqualified allegiance to the United States" and "forswearing any form of allegiance or obedience to the Japanese Emperor." Negative responses to these questions ensured further detainment. The following is a personal example of the legacy of these loyalty questions. During the Vietnam War, I voiced my opposition to the war, including consideration of conscientious objector status. This provoked an intense reaction on the part of my mother, who shouted, "You won't be a 'No-no!'" Only much later did I discover the meaning of "No-no." My objections revisited the reverberations of having to prove one's loyalty and patriotism ruptured the usual silence. John Okada's *No-No Boy* is considered a classic in Asian American literature. Interestingly, the book published in 1957 was initially rejected by the Japanese American community.

## Postwar Period (1945–the Present)

Daniels (1993) distinguished the Japanese American immigrant experience as different from other groups in that the Japanese Americans had to immigrate twice.

In 1970 a movement within the Japanese American Citizens League sought apology and compensation for those detained in the concentration camps. This redress movement served to break the silence and culminated in the signing of the redress bill in 1988. When constructing my genogram during my psychology internship, I met enormous resistance in gathering information about the "camp" from my parents. Even appeals that this was for my education were not initially effective. Following the Congressional redress hearings (where my father offered testimony), access to some of this information was more forthcoming.

## FAMILY PATTERNS

### Generation

Japanese Americans have a particular numbering system of succeeding generations that is sometimes confusing. The *issei* were the first generation of immigrants. Ichioka (1988) provides a highly regarded historical account of the *issei*. The laws restricting immigration created a window of opportunity to come to the United States between 1905 and 1924. The *nisei* (see Hosakawa, 1969) were the second generation and the first generation born in the United States. Most *nisei* were born between 1915 and 1935. The *kibei* are a subset of the *nisei. Kibei* were born in the United States, sent to Japan for education, and returned to the United States. This practice was a form of parental hedging of chances for the children's success. This practice was popular between 1920 and 1940, which was a period of intense nationalism and patriotism in Japan (Kitano, 1969). Upon their return, the *kibei's* exposure to culture and loyalty to Japan put them in conflict with *nisei* and *issei*. In addition, the *kibei* were suspect to the dominant culture. *Sansei* are the third generation. Most *sansei* were born between 1945 and 1965. *Sansei* also connotes reference to the generation born after "camp" (relocation camp). I was startled to read *Turning Japanese: Memoirs of a Sansei* by David Mura (1991). I never expected to see aspects of my ethnic experience in the mainstream press. *Yonsei* refers to the fourth generation. It will be interesting to see whether this counting of generations will continue with acculturation. *Gosei* refers to the fifth generation.

### Gender

When attempting to recapture the history or experience of a people, the lens has typically been through the perspective of men. One source that explicated the notions of gender embedded in language is *Womansword: What Japanese*

*Words Say about Women* (Cherry, 1987). Nakano (1990) expanded this perspective by chronicling the experience of three generations of Japanese American women. Nevertheless, the tradition of male preference by the *issei* was captured in the following poem:

> As if he wished they were boys, for an instant
> Sadness shades his face:
> Our daughters bending in the fields
> In their faded overalls
> (Takaya, 1934, cited in Nakano, 1990, p. 33)

The division of labor was also demarcated along gender lines. *Issei* women complained about their husbands as "*Meiji* men," meaning that they did not even glance at housework or child care (Takaki, 1989).

Women were considered the transmitter of tradition: "All women irrespective of education, preserved and passed on everyday aspects of Japanese culture such as food, medicine, peasant lore, and customs, in their families and in the larger community" (Glenn, 1986, p. 38). New Year celebration was clearly my maternal grandmother's production. She would cook for weeks in preparation for the feast. Her need to have everything done her way precluded anyone from participating. My grandfather, who was a chef at a major hotel in Chicago, was not allowed in the kitchen, nor was my mother. Consequently, when my grandmother died, much of the tradition died with her. Several years later, my mother, brothers, and I decided to revive the New Year tradition. All of us learned to prepare some of the Japanese cuisine. My mother, who is an artist, had complaints about the visual presentation of the food. So we modified grandmother's rule. Everyone cooks, but only one cook in the kitchen at a time. A source for Japanese American traditions is *Matsuri Festival: Japanese American Celebrations and Activities* (Araki & Horii, 1993). Another was the result of a writing project for children, *Kids Explore America's Japanese American Heritage* (Westridge Young Writers Workshop, 1994).

## Hierarchy

The concept of hierarchy is a mainstay in the organizational understanding of the family (Haley, 1977). Given the recent importance of balancing power imbalances, hierarchy has become a controversial lens through which to view the family. Nonetheless, hierarchy remains an important dimension in the Japanese American family. The executive functioning of the family is located in the father–oldest son relationship. Reischauer (1988) attributes the emphasis on hierarchy to the long history of hereditary power and aristocratic rule in Japan. Hierarchy is embedded in the fabric of Japanese society and language. Ranking occurs within the family (based on gender and age) or within groups such as business corporations, and between groups.

## Marriage

Hirayama and Hirayama (1986) examined marriage and sexuality in four generations. They reported that *issei* and, to a lesser extent, *nisei* families maintain traditional, patriarchal, and hierarchical family structures; are restrained and less physically demonstrative in their expressions of affection, love, and intimacy; and rigidly control the sexual expression and behavior of their offspring. *Sansei* and *yonsei* were more physically demonstrative, egalitarian in their marriages, and included more American cultural norms. They still may retain some traditional Japanese attitudes and values.

The history of arranged marriages for the *issei* has structural implication. This marriage pattern places less emphasis on the marital relation for relational satisfaction. Instead, emphasis is placed on cross-generational relationships (e.g., the mother–child relationship [see Parenting section] or the father–son relationship [see Hierarchy section]).

According to Kitano (1995), one-third of all Japanese Americans marry non-Japanese, whereas in Hawaii, where the Japanese make up a larger percentage of the total population, one-half of all Japanese Americans marry non-Japanese. Tinker (1982) found that the *sansei* rate of intermarriage is even greater. Tinker views this pattern of interracial marriage as evidence of thorough assimilation of the Japanese Americans into the dominant culture.

## Communication Patterns

*Enryo* (restraint or holding back) describes a frequently observed communication style. An example of *enryo* is one's hesitancy to ask questions or speak out in a group setting. The adaptive origin of this behavior was located in Confucian ethics conveying thoughtful consideration toward one's superiors. Interestingly, Doi (1981) states that the Japanese dislike *enryo* in themselves but prefer it in others. Reischauer (1988) documents a preference for indirect modes of communication, for example, *haragei* (the art of the belly) is a meeting of the minds, or at least the viscera, without clear verbal interaction (p. 136). Reischauer hypothesized that this indirect mode was developed in a homogeneous society, whereas the development of verbal skills in a diverse society is more valued. *Nisei* remember being told *da-mot-to-le* (keep quiet). This highlights the role of socialization. While grocery shopping at Yaohan (a large Japanese shopping center frequented by many Japanese nationals), a Japanese produce man observed my daughter in intense conversation with my wife. He looked at me and gruffly admonished me, "She talks too much!" The implications about my role as a socialized parent were clear. According to Kitano (1969), "The most distinctive characteristic of Japanese family interaction was, and still remains, the absence of prolonged verbal exchanges" (p. 72). This has implications for family problem solving and points to a preference for indirect patterns of communication over direct patterns.

# Parenting

The difference in emphasis on the dimension of differentiation of self between the West and the Japanese is apparent in divergent parenting styles. Reischauer (1988) describes this difference as follows:

> Japanese infants and small children are treated quite permissively, are in almost constant contact with their mothers, and are practically never left alone. This contrasts sharply with the American tendency to put children on strict sleeping and eating regimes, to have them sleep alone from the start, to separate them in their own rooms, to hand them over on occasion to the care of unknown babysitters, and to have more verbal interplay with them than body contact. Japanese children are nursed for a relatively long period, are fed more at will, are constantly fondled by their mothers, are still often carried around on the back when mothers go out—once an almost universal practice—and often sleep with their parents until quite large. Even after that, Japanese tend to sleep in groups rather than singly in individual rooms. Instruction is not by generalized verbal rules reinforced by punishment so much as by intimate contact and patient example. (p. 144)

The result of increased dependency in relation to the Japanese mother is an attitude called *amae*. *Amae* (the cognate is "sweet") means "to look to others for affection." This seeking of approval generalizes from the mother to the group. The counterpart of ostracism from the mother and later the group is feared. Doi (1986) explicates these dimensions of self in relation to the group in *The Anatomy of Self* and *The Anatomy of Dependence* (1981). *Amae* is related to the previously mentioned *enryo* in that outspoken behavior could adversely affect *amae*. Implicit in the intense mother–child relationship as the psychological precursor to *amae* is the importance of the mother–child relationship. The therapeutic implications of *amae* will be developed later.

White (1993) compares the coming-of-age comparison of adolescence in Japan and America. Although this comparison is more applicable to Japanese nationals, the following select distinctions are instructive in the contrasting values of the two cultures:

> [1.] Americans believe that coming of age means acquiring legally encoded rights and yet we fear the consequences of those licenses to drink, drive, and spend. Japanese believe that young people will meet the moral obligations contained in the responsibilities that are the signal of maturity.

[2.] American folk psychology is based on institutionalized ideologies, such as the principle of individualism, and yet we are confused by the diversity that ensues; Japanese folk psychology is based on pragmatic idealism, such as the ideal of the triumph of effort over obstacles, and Japanese generally get high performances.

[3.] Americans believe that adolescence is the most problematic stage of life and that getting youth through this stage safely is the adult's job; Japanese believe that youth are society's future and that providing motivation to achieve will serve both the child and society, whose fates are inextricably tied.

[4.] Americans believe that a child must both love and leave his or her parents in order to grow up; Japanese feel that the family is the source of ongoing support and that breaking away or leaving home is not a necessary step in maturation. (White, 1993, p. 23)

## TREATMENT CONSIDERATIONS

### Prevalence of Psychological Disorders

In a study that questions the model minority hypothesis, Kuo (1984) reported that the incidence of depression in Asian Americans was at least as high as the White population. This study supports the idea that Asian Americans underutilize mental health services instead of needing fewer services.

The following study has implications for cultural differences in the expression of depression. Tanaka-Matsumi (1979) compared Japanese and Western American's word association to *yuutsu* (depression). The Japanese made referents to concrete external or environmental or somatic words, such as rain, dark, worries, cloud, headache, or fatigue. Western Americans associated depression with such internally negatively connoted mood states such as loneliness, down, or sad. Tanaka-Matsumi (1979) and Mock (1995) contend that the Japanese are more likely to express depression through somatic and/or metaphoric language than their Western counterparts.

The transgenerational effects of internment were examined. Nagata (1990) compared *sansei* whose parents were interned with *sansei* whose parents were not interned. She found little communication between generations about the internment experience. Those *sansei* whose parents were interned described feeling less secure about their rights in the United States, preferred affiliating with other Japanese Americans, and were more in favor of monetary redress than the *sansei* whose parents were not interned.

### Family Therapy Models and Their Applicability to Japanese American Families

Structural family therapy has been offered as a treatment of choice for Chinese families (Jung, 1984) and Vietnamese Chinese families (Ko, 1986). Given the previous descriptions of the Japanese American family as patriarchal, and the importance of hierarchy and generational differences, there would appear to be a fit with structural family therapy.

A discussion about joining is warranted given the high rate of premature terminations of Asian Americans (Sue & McKinney, 1975). The assumption by Japanese American families of hierarchy applies to their perception of family therapists. Credentials based on the gender and seniority of the therapists utilize this preference for the expertness of the therapist. "Giving," based on the tradition of gift giving in Japanese culture, is also advocated by Sue and Zane (1987) to decrease dropouts. Sue and Zane encourage therapists to offer the family a concrete example of therapeutic problem solving during the first session as a "gift" to the family.

The previous discussion on the attitude of *amae* and the negative connotation of dependency is reminiscent of the feminist critique of mainstream family therapy devaluing relationships and the recovery movement's notions on codependency. Tamura and Lau (1992) correct the cultural value valence by translating *amae* to mean connectiveness. Consequently, in order to make the goals of family therapy consonant with the values of the Japanese American family, the direction is toward integration rather than separateness (Tamura & Lau, 1992).

*Ki* is another concept that illustrates the value of connectedness. *Ki* is loosely defined from the Chinese as life force. In the relational sphere, *ki* can be understood "as mental or spiritual energy that floats around one's physical existence and fills the gap between individual in relationships" (Tamura & Lau, 1992 p. 325). To make good use of *ki* is to behave in a way that considers the other's feelings and circumstances without making each party's feelings explicit. This is remarkably similar to the notion of empathy in connection (Jordan, 1991), sans the active listening component. *Ki* also underscores the preference for indirect communication and intuition.

The structural assumptions on boundary making and cross-generational relationships require modification. Pare's (1995) observations on family therapy's paradigm shift from a cybernetic paradigm to a narrative anthropological paradigm is helpful in this alteration. Pare redefines boundaries in terms of valuing those unique structures of the culture. In Japanese American families, this would mean positively connoting those cross-generational relationships such as the mother–child relationship.

## Distal Nature of Ethnicity Factors

Except for the therapist and family sharing the same ethnic background and/ or language, the effect of knowledge of ethnicity factors on the therapeutic outcome is meager (Sue, 1988). Yu (1995) explored the conceptual framework that Asian American family therapists utilized when treating Asian families.

One way of reducing the distal nature of ethnicity factors is to place the behavior in its historic–ethnic adaptive context. Another suggestion is to devise circular questions about family patterns that are important to the family's sense of integration and maintaining their Japanese American identity.

## CONCLUSION

The reception of the Japanese Americans was rife with racial discrimination at the local and national legislative levels. This figured prominently in shaping their immigrant experience. The applicability of family therapy models to the described family patterns of the Japanese Americans was developed. The importance of connection over separateness was emphasized. I hope this chapter has encouraged an appreciation for the historical adaptive nature of family pattern. The family may have a range of adherence to the pattern from rigidity, longing for the old pattern, to an eschewing of old traditions for Western patterns.

## DEDICATION

This chapter is dedicated to my parents, Takanobu and Tsuyako Matsui.

## REFERENCES

Araki, N. K., & Horii, J. M. (1993). *Matsuri: Festival Japanese American celebrations and activities.* Torrance, CA: Heian International.

Cherry, K. (1987). *Womansword: What Japanese words say about women.* Tokyo: Kodansha Press.

Daniels, R. (1993, September 13). *The issei experience.* Paper presented at the Japanese American National Museum, Los Angeles, CA.

Doi, T. (1986). *The anatomy of self: The individual versus society.* Tokyo: Kodansha International.

Doi, T. (1981). *The anatomy of dependence* (rev. ed.). Tokyo: Kodansha International.

Glenn, E. N. (1986). *Issei, nisei, war bride.* Philadelphia: Temple University Press.

Guterson, D. (1994). *Snow falling on cedars.* New York: Harcourt Brace.

Haley, J. (1977). *Problem-solving therapy: New strategies for effective family therapy.* San Francisco: Jossey-Bass.

Hane, M. (1972). *Japan: A historical survey.* New York: Scribner's.

Hirayama, H., & Hirayama, K. K. (1986). The sexuality of Japanese Americans. Special Issue: Human sexuality, ethnoculture, and social work. *Journal of Social Work and Human Sexuality, 4,* 81–98.

Hosakawa, B. (1969). *Nisei.* New York: William Morrow.

Ichioka, Y. (1988). *The Issei: The world of the first generation Japanese immigrants, 1885–1924.* New York: Free Press.

Jordan, J. (1991). Empathy and self boundaries. In J. Jordan, A. Kaplan, J. Miller, I. Stiver, & J. Surrey, *Women's growth in connection: Writings from the Stone Center* (pp. 67–80). New York: Guilford Press.

Jung, M. (1984). Structural family therapy: Its application to Chinese families. *Family Process, 23,* 365–374.

Kitano, H. L. (1969). *Japanese Americans: The evolution of a subculture.* Englewood Cliffs, NJ: Prentice-Hall.

Kitano, H. L. (1995). *Japanese Americans: The immigrant experience.* New York: Chelsea House.

Ko, H. Y. (1986). Minuchin's structural family therapy for Vietnamese Chinese families: A systems perspective. *Contemporary Family Therapy: An International Journal, 8,* 20–32.

Kuo, W. H. (1984). Prevalence of depression among Asian Americans. *Journal of Nervous and Mental Disease, 172,* 449–457.

Mock, M. (1995). Multicultural expressions of clinical depression. *Family Therapy News, 26*(5), 21–22.

Mura, D. (1991). *Turning Japanese: Memoirs of a sansei.* New York: Atlantic Monthly Press.

Nagata, D. K. (1990). The Japanese American internment: Exploring the trangenerational consequences of traumatic stress. *Journal of Traumatic Stress, 3,* 47–69.

Nakano, M. (1990). *Japanese American women: Three generations 1890–1990.* Berkeley, CA: Mina Press; San Francisco: National Japanese American Historical Society.

Niiya, B. (Ed.). (1993). *Japanese American history: An A to Z reference from 1868 to the present.* New York: Facts on File.

Okada, J. (1976). *No-no boy.* Seattle: University of Washington Press.

Pare, D.A. (1995). Of families and other cultures: The shifting paradigm of family therapy. *Family Process, 34,* 1–19.

Reischauer, E. (1988). *The Japanese today: Change and conformity.* Cambridge, MA: Belknap.

Sue, S. (1988). Psychotherapeutic services for ethnic minorities: Two decades of research findings. *American Psychologist, 43,* 301–308.

Sue, S., & McKinney, H. (1975). Asian Americans in the community mental health care system. *American Journal of Orthopsychiatry, 45,* 111–118.

Sue, S., & Zane, N. (1987). The role of culture and cultural techniques in psychotherapy: A critique and reformulation. *American Psychologist, 42,* 37–45.

Takaki, R. (1989). *Strangers from a different shore: A history of Asian Americans.* Boston: Little, Brown.

Tamura, T., & Lau, A. (1992). Connectedness versus separateness: Applicability of family therapy to Japanese families. *Family Process, 31,* 319–340.

Tanaka, M. J. (1979). *Taijun kyfusho: Diagnostic and cultural issues in Japanese psychiatry.* Washington, DC: American Psychiatric Association.

Tinker, J. N. (1982). Intermarriage and assimilation in a plural society: Japanese-Americans in the United States. *Marriage and Family Review, 5*(1), 1–74.

Westridge Young Writers Workshop. (1994). *Kids explore America's Japanese American heritage.* Santa Fe, NM: John Muir.

White, M. (1993). *The material child: Coming of age in Japan and America.* Berkeley, CA: University of California Press.

Yu, A. (1995). *The experience of Asian therapists counseling Asian families.* Unpublished doctoral dissertation, University of Utah, Salt Lake City.

# CHAPTER 19

# Korean Families

## Bok-Lim C. Kim

For centuries, pragmatism, perseverance, and a hierarchical family structure with rules and prescribed role relationships have all served to sustain Koreans through famine, political and social upheaval, foreign domination, and war (Choy, 1971). Although pragmatism and perseverance have persisted, the tumultuous events of the 20th century have drastically altered traditional family organization. In the early 20th century, the Japanese colonized Korea, exploiting its natural and human resources, additionally attempting to eradicate the Korean language and culture (Nahm, 1973). These experiences have made Koreans mistrustful of foreigners and cynical as well as rebellious toward government and authorities in general. The division of Korea along the 38th parallel in 1945 and the Korean War in 1950 both created cataclysmic sociopolitical upheaval. Mass destruction of its people and land challenged the strength and stamina of Korean individuals and families. Loyalty with its tradition of mutual help and obligation were weakened, as no family escaped losing members to death or lifelong separation. Allegiance to different political ideologies and governments divided families, spawning tragedies of sons turning against fathers, as well as brothers against brothers.

During this time, the founding of women's high schools and universities increased the accessibility of education for women (Y.-C. Kim, 1976). These educated women became a major force in abolishing gender-based discriminatory laws and modernizing the education of the Korean masses, for women as well as men. Urbanization and industrialization of the past three decades so greatly increased the demand for skilled labor that unmarried women for the first time broke with tradition, left home, and became a part of the labor force (A.-S. Kim, 1990).[1]

These changes in women's education as well as participation in the workforce brought an increased status and respect for women. However, gender discrimination and class stratification have remained in different forms. Money and academic credentials have replaced inherited class as markers of status, and although women are not barred from higher education, professions, or business, their success is still measured by marriage, not by professional success. No matter what a woman has accomplished, she is measured by her husband's status and the achievements of her children (Mintz, 1990).

## KOREAN IMMIGRATION

Korean immigration to the United States occurred in three distinct waves. The first consisted of only 7,000 desperately poor farmers who came to Hawaii between 1903 and 1905 as contract laborers (Yang, 1982), followed later by their "picture" brides (Chai, 1987). The second wave began around 1950, when a significant number of Korean war orphans and Amerasian children arrived as transracially adopted children of American parents (D. S. Kim, 1978). About this time, Korean women married to U.S. servicemen began to immigrate in large numbers (B.-L. C. Kim, 1981).

The third wave of Korean immigration began with the passage of the 1965 Amendment to the Immigration and Naturalization Service Act of 1955 (Public Law No. 89-236, 79 Stat. 911), which ushered a new era of racial and ethnic equality in American immigration policy (C. Kim & B.-L. C. Kim, 1977). The Amendment opened the floodgates for Koreans and other Asian groups severely restricted by previous quotas. In the past two decades, over 30,000 Koreans have immigrated annually, accounting for the tenfold increase of the Korean American population between 1970 and 1990. This rapid increase has made Korean Americans visible to the American public as a distinct group, different from the Chinese or Japanese. This has been an important change for most Korean Americans, due to their long-standing unfriendly relationship with these two countries. Koreans tend to view it as an insult to be misidentified as Chinese or Japanese, a fact that is rarely appreciated by most Americans.

The third wave of Korean immigrants differed from the earlier ones in a number of ways. Although they are better educated than the first wave of immigrants, they come from a wider range of socioeconomic and educational levels. Most Koreans are emigrating as nuclear families rather than single adults. Close to three-fourths of them have relatives or close friends already living in the United States, who assist with their initial adjustment. Most cities in the United States now have Korean resident associations, ethnic churches, and businesses that offer practical help and ongoing support for ethnic identification. They are coming to a society that has become less prejudiced and more tolerant of minority groups. Emigrating from a country that is modern, industrialized, and relatively affluent, they no longer see the United States as superior. Koreans simply see America as a place that offers better business and career opportunities as well as superior education for their children. The third wave population will be the major focus of this chapter.

## KOREAN AMERICANS IN THE UNITED STATES

Family patterns and cultural values of these third-wave Koreans in the United States and those in Korea are remarkably similar. The immigrants' recent history in the United States, daily contact with Korea through newspapers, radio, television, telephone, and frequent trans-Pacific travel account for the congruence of values. In this chapter, for these reasons, no distinction will be made except when there are marked differences.

Korean Americans are an adventurous, upwardly mobile people who are willing to move wherever education, employment, and business opportunities beckon them. They are widely dispersed throughout the United States, almost exclusively in urban centers. The 1990 U.S. Census reported that 72% of Koreans were foreign born and 84% were married and living as nuclear families (U.S. Bureau of the Census, 1990). Thus, the majority of Korean Americans live in families consisting of immigrant parents and American-born or raised children where two cultures, two languages collide and individual members are undergoing different rates of acculturation and maturation.

Korean Americans are a well-educated people. Over one-third have bachelor's and graduate degrees, and half of them have high-school diplomas with some college education. Fewer women, one-fourth, have bachelor's and graduate degrees, two-thirds having high school diplomas with some college education (U.S. Bureau of the Census, 1990). Such high educational achievement, however, does not translate into high status and high-paying occupations.

Since Koreans are relatively recent immigrants, their English proficiency level is low, while their unfamiliarity and functional discomfort with American social structure is high (B.-L. C. Kim, 1978; Hurh & K. C. Kim, 1984). Most college graduates, educated in Korea, find that differences in job market requirements make the transfer of their education and work experience to the American situation difficult and uncertain.

Koreans have been willing to take skilled and semiskilled jobs that do not reflect their education and experience. Thus, their participation in the labor force has been high. Over four-fifths of men and three-fourths of women work outside the home on a full-time basis (B.-L. C. Kim, 1978). The shrinking job market has turned these people toward labor-intensive, long-hour, small businesses such as convenience stores, groceries, and laundries.

## FAMILY PATTERNS AND VALUES

Hierarchy by gender, generation, age, and class have been a "given" in Korean society. Although it has largely changed on the surface, it remains a powerful force determining thinking and behavior. Strict segregation between the sexes has largely disappeared with traditionally prescribed role differentiation and work division based on gender. Throughout life, the generational boundary between parents and children has continued to remain firm. Parents are to support and guide, while children of all ages are to obey and respect, although their opinions are now being considered.

The legacy of hierarchical relationships can be seen in age stratification in business and social intercourse. The reaction of Mrs. Soonja Du, the Korean grocer in Los Angeles who in 1991 shot the African American teenager who slapped and knocked her down during an argument, can be seen as an extreme reaction to a mind-boggling situation for which nothing in life had prepared her (*People v. Soonja Du*, 1992). Concerning even informal social situations, Koreans determine who is *sun-bae*, older, and *hoo-bae*, younger. Korean language, with more than three classes of nouns and verbs signifying ranking orders of relationships, reinforces this way of thinking (B.-L. C. Kim, 1988). The absence of this kind of differentiation in English creates much discomfort in social interactions with Americans and has special implications for the parent–child relationship. Tension and ill feelings are generated between Korean parents and their American-raised children, who lack the appreciation and fluency of Korean to properly observe the hierarchical protocol.

Korean families have a clear boundary as to who is "in" and who is "out." The term *jip-an* means literally "within the house" and identifies both family membership, values, and traditions practiced within a particular family. *Ka-moon* means "the family gate" and refers to the family standing and reputation within the community. This boundary also determines what information needs to be kept *jip-an* and what can be shared. Whereas many societies conceal family problems and boast about successes, Koreans attach shame to such a wide range of problems that they are highly selective about what is revealed. This boundary tends to be rigid among the upper classes, less so among poor and rural people. Although Korean American family boundaries remain rigid in terms of the larger society, within the immigrant community boundaries are porous and permeable due to the absence of an extended kinship network. Nevertheless, harmony and connection between geographically dispersed extended family members is maintained by frequent telephone calls as well as trans-Pacific travel. Korean immigrants make extraordinary sacrifices of time and money to participate in events such as *han-kap*, the special celebration of the 60th birthday, and *chae-sa* (Janelli & Janelli, 1982) the ancestor-worship ceremony honoring deceased parents and grandparents for six generations past.

## MARRIAGE

Marriage is still considered the joining of two families rather than two individuals. Each family's status in the community, as well as the couple's academic credentials and health are checked discreetly but thoroughly before a decision is reached. Either romantic love or formal matchmaking can lead to marriage, but mutual investigation by the two families and the consent of both sets of parents are "musts."

## WIFE–HUSBAND AND IN-LAW RELATIONSHIPS

Most Korean American couples expect faithfulness, mutual respect, and joint decision making. Money management is usually the wife's responsibility. The gender-ordered rule for the three obediences of women—obedience to her father before marriage, to the husband after she is married, and to her son in old age—is no longer practiced. The power relationship and work division for the couple depends on how close in age they are, their educational level, and their commitment to traditional values. Among older couples and more traditional families, the unequal division of responsibilities and rights remain. It is not uncommon for an unemployed husband to expect his wife to prepare family meals after returning from her job.

There are many forces that impinge on the marital relationship. The Korean Family Legal Center estimates 70–80% of marital problems involve the in-laws of the wife (T. Y. Lee, personal communication, July 1992). Geographic distances protect most Korean Americans from the intricate network of daily obligations for the in-laws. However, even when families live far apart, the influence and interference of the in-laws are ever present. They are involved in all major and many minor decisions from type of car, housing, to the number of children the couple should have. Their influence decreases somewhat as the couple's economic independence increases, and especially with the birth of children.

Problems between mother-in-law and daughter-in-law are most common and can be quite intense. The mother-in-law is generally possessive of her son and critical of the daughter-in-law. The daughter-in-law frequently perceives her mother-in-law's "helpfulness" as controlling. Changing expectations in the relationship between these two further exacerbates their differences. Because the issue of in-laws is so central, it is important for the therapist to inquire about the couple's in-law relationships with every Korean American family regardless of the presenting problems.

In contrast, the husband's relationship with his in-laws is less conflictual because less is expected from him. As long as he is a good provider for the family and a faithful husband, the obligation to his in-laws is fulfilled.

Korean couples are inexperienced in conflict management and resolution. They tend to see the problem to be a matter of right or wrong, to be resolved by proving the other wrong. Men also tend to invoke male superiority to win their point, and frustration is often handled with alcohol. Even though this is culturally condoned, the immigrant wife feels she does not have to tolerate this, and the conflict can easily escalate to violence, which is condoned by all social classes. There is an old Korean saying: "Dried fish and women get softer with beating."

There are a number of acculturation problems that provide fertile ground for stress and conflict. All studies of Korean immigrant families have listed limited English proficiency as the number one stressor (B.-L. C. Kim, 1978, 1980, 1988; Hurh & K.-C. Kim, 1984). For "face" or appearance-conscious Korean adults, the inability to express and be understood is a major blow to self-esteem. The limited English proficiency of many immigrant adults, particularly men, causes them to feel exposed and humiliated in the English-speaking world. One man related his despair by saying, "Overnight I became deaf and mute when I came to America."

Underemployment and long working hours in unsafe neighborhoods are also highly stressful and constitute a major source of marital conflict.

One important avenue for dissipating stress is the ethnic church, where this struggle is tacitly understood and supported. Church membership among Korean Americans is between 70% to 80% (B.-L. C. Kim, 1978; Hurh & K.-C. Kim, 1984) as compared to 47% in Korea (Korean Overseas Information Service, 1990). It is clear that the Korean ethnic church not only administers to spiritual needs but more importantly, it also provides support and a sense of belonging (Hurh & K.-C. Kim, 1984). As Hurh and K.-C. Kim pointed out, the church is both an acculturation agent and a resource for preserving culture and ethnic identity.

## PARENT–CHILD RELATIONSHIPS

Male children have been very important to Korean families in order to carry on the name and ensure continuity of the generations. Female children were viewed as a burden because of the exorbitant expenses incurred in marrying them off and their subsequent joining with their husband's family. Such discriminatory attitudes are slowly disappearing as increasing numbers of married daughters maintain close contact with parents and even care for them in their old age.

The traditional Korean primacy of the father–son dyad from one generation to the next has recently been replaced with the development of the husband–wife dyad, which lasts only until the first child enters first grade. It is then superseded by the mother–child dyad as the key relationship. Koreans place such a high value on *hak-bul*, academic credentials, that the parents' self-esteem is intimately tied to the academic success or failure of their children. The fiercely competitive nature of the Korean educational system has made successful education of children an all-consuming enterprise for most families, requiring much time, energy, and money, with the mother assigned to this task full-time.

This system is not needed in the United States, and working mothers are not available to enforce it. Nonetheless, immigrant parents deprived of traditional sources of self-esteem and feeling undervalued by American culture, insist even more strongly that their children excel in school, as well as gain admittance to prestigious universities.

The hierarchical relationship is extremely stressful for Korean American children who wish to have their feelings heard and opinions respected, but the parents who feel they are losing their children to the "selfish" American culture cannot appreciate their children's wishes. Parents and children are further handicapped because each is using a translated language for communication. Just as the parents' English lacks an American cultural context and mind-set, the children's Korean lacks Korean cultural contexts and social norms. An American-born, English-speaking 13-year-old boy said to his father, "You are crazy!" during their humorous exchange of funny stories, whereupon the immigrant father was offended and got angry.

Immigrant parents' limited appreciation of the wide difference between American and Korean cultures and their ambivalence about their children's acculturation causes them to make incongruent demands on their children (B.-L. C. Kim,1980). They want them to be successful in school but to be obedient, respectful, and humble at home, not realizing that the attributes needed to succeed in American schools are assertiveness, initiative, and independent thinking. They want their children to be proficient in English and to retain fluency in Korean. They restrict afterschool activities with English-speaking peers but expect them to be socially popular. They profess no prejudice toward other racial and ethnic groups, yet resist interracial dating and marriage and explain this in terms of the importance of compatibility between the two families.

On the positive side, we found that parents had nondiscriminatory career goals for male and female children, and there was remarkable agreement between the generations about the children's future goals. The children also recognized their parents' hard work and sacrifice for them and shared their parents' dream of success in America (B.-L. C. Kim, 1980).

## AFFECT MANAGEMENT

Foreigners are often surprised when Koreans, who are usually very reserved and reticent, express themselves more spontaneously. Koreans are most spontaneous among their peers and social equals, and they are reserved and deferential in the presence of superiors and during official occasions. Educated and cultured persons tend to be more controlled and selective in expressing feelings and usually express negative feelings only to their immediate family. Teaching children about appropriate affect management is too important to be left to chance, and children learn from parents and teachers by both lecture and example.

Koreans are variously described as hot-tempered, easily offended, generous, gregarious, and humorous. It is safe to say that Koreans are an emotional people whose overriding concern in all human interaction is the issue of respect. The non-Korean therapist needs to know about several key Korean qualities that orchestrate the expression of respect in all social relationships.

First there is *jeong*, a unique Korean concept that has no English equivalent (L. Kim, 1990). It expresses a combination of empathy, sympathy, compassion, emotional attachment, and tenderness in varying degrees according to the social context. *Jeong* enriches and humanizes social relationships and makes life meaningful. It is expressed by attention to the small but important details that show concern for the person's comfort and well-being. The Korean equivalent of "How are you?" is "Are you at ease?" Without it, a person loses his or her humanity. Korean clients will observe whether the therapist has *jeong*, and if they do not perceive it, treatment is doomed. *Jeong* is easy to miss in cross-cultural encounters, and the therapist needs to be especially careful to demonstrate human qualities, despite the professional nature of the contact. This can be done with "small talk," such as asking if the client had any difficulty finding the office or locating a parking space.

*Hahn* is a pervasive sentiment referring to an unexpressed, ongoing grievance and resulting heartache of an oppressed or abused person who has no recourse to rectify the wrong. Koreans experienced a lot of *hahn* during the Japanese rule and the Korean War. Korean women, who for many centuries had been subordinated by the family system, have accumulated much *hahn*. The resulting condition is now listed in DSM-IV (American Psychiatric Association, 1994) as *hwa-byung* under "Culture-Bound Syndromes." *Hwa-byung* is predominantly seen among middle-aged Korean women. In contrast with Korean men, who can relieve their *hahn* by drinking, these women have no culturally sanctioned outlets other than physical symptoms. In working with this group, it is important not to see *hahn* in a pejorative sense as learned helplessness or somatization, but rather to appreciate its cultural roots. The therapist can label the client's immigrant status as an opportunity to leave behind old practices and learn new ways of active mastery that are more appropriate for this country.

*Noon-chi* and *boon-soo* are closely related concepts born out of the necessity of surviving as a subordinate in a hierarchically ordered family and society. *Noon-chi* literally means measuring with the eyes, learning to pick up external cues in order to choose a course of action that is both nonoffensive and appropriate. Once in America, the Korean immigrant has found that his *noon-chi* skills cannot be practiced in such a different society with a whole different set of cues and meanings. Until they become highly acculturated, Koreans will be extremely uncomfortable and anxious in social interactions with Americans. The therapist must communicate concern for the client's discomfort and anxiety about the therapeutic situation by showing the client that the need for help in no way diminishes the therapist's respect for the client as a human being. Clients will feel less need to rely on their *noon-chi* when the therapist makes the context and purpose of the treatment as explicit as possible.

*Boon-soo* refers to knowing and accepting one's status regardless of the advantage or disadvantage accorded to that status, in short, knowing one's place. The highly stratified social class of the past relied on each person to observe their *boon-soo* to preserve the status quo. When expectations or demands are excessive, that person is said not to know his or her *boon-soo*. The therapist needs to appreciate that the Korean client, trying to act within his or her *boon-soo*, might express such low expectations that in an American context it would suggest serious problems with low self-esteem.

*Chae-myun* is face saving, a concept familiar to many Asians. Making a good impression is very important to Koreans in all relationships other than the immediate family. Maintaining *chae-myun* protects the dignity, honor, and self-respect of the individual and the family. The therapist needs to anticipate that clients will be reluctant to reveal vital information if this will cause loss of *chae-myun*. Respect for the therapist's *chae-myun* will stop them from correcting or disagreeing with the therapist. This needs to be differentiated from passive–aggressive or subservient behavior. Protecting the client's *chae-myun*, especially that of the male clients, is important. The therapist must be very careful about any comments or gestures that could be construed as criticism, put-downs, or indifference. There is no room for error, because just as with *jeong*, loss of *chae-myun* is absolute. The client who loses *chae-myun* will not return.

## TREATMENT CONSIDERATIONS

Traditionally, Koreans have resolved conflict with the help of a mediator chosen for his or her fairness and wisdom. This worked well as long as there was respect for authority. For other Koreans, the help of shamans (*moo-dang*) and fortune-tellers, superb listeners and astute observers of people, have been helpful. Shamans exorcise evil spirits with elaborate and often costly ceremonies (Covell, 1983), whereas fortune-tellers console and prescribe a course of action that may include inaction as well. Faith healing by the Christian clergy has also entered the field of healing.

Deprived of most of these resources in the United States, Korean immigrants are turning to relatives, close friends, clergy, and lawyers for help with emotional, psychological, and relational problems (B.-L. C. Kim & Condon, 1975). They seldom seek professional help because they define both the problems and remedies so differently from Americans (Sue, & McKinney, 1975; Sue, 1977). They consider the emotional pain and worry caused by relational or environmental problems as *pal-ja*, immutable destiny, which needs to be endured without complaint. University students suffering from depression comprise the only group that seeks help voluntarily.

Korean Americans are often ignorant of available mental health services and even when they are willing to consider them, most do not meet the language and cultural requisites of this population (B.-L. C. Kim, 1978). As a result, involvement with mental health services usually comes by way of mandatory counseling when school, court, or child protective agencies require it.

Involuntary clients are difficult to engage and treat even when race, language, and culture are the same. Korean Americans, already very anxious, defensive, and deeply shamed by their encounter with the system, do not expect understanding or help with their problems and assume that the therapist will be critical, punitive, and authoritative.

Therapists who can acknowledge ignorance about the Korean American experience and who take the time to read or talk with people will gain familiarity and appreciation for the client's mind-set. On a more practical level, the therapist needs to find out about the client's level of English proficiency and acculturation before the first appointment. Having a well-trained interpreter available on an on-call basis is ideal. If the clients bring their own interpreter, the therapist must be prepared to screen for bias and English competency to minimize the risk of editing, censorship, or mistakes. Use of family members has the advantage of convenience but is fraught with problems related to family hierarchy or injuring *chae-myun*.

As in all clinical situations, assessment is an ongoing process and particularly essential when working with Korean American clients who begin by presenting their problems in a highly disorganized and inconsistent manner. They are vague about dates, specifics of problems, and they become more evasive about their reactions and feelings. It is difficult to determine whether they are deliberately making themselves unintelligible or are just confused and upset. It is usually better to postpone obtaining factual information and to concentrate on the client's immediate concern. The therapist needs to appreciate the client's high anxiety and fear of being accused or misunderstood. Explanation about how legal, social service, and mental health systems function and how the therapist can make the system work for the client establishes what Sue refers to as therapist credibility (Sue & Zane, 1987). Once clients clearly perceive the therapist's role and sincere desire to help, they can commit to therapy (S. C. Kim, 1985).

Problem-solving and psychoeducational approaches are most effective because Korean Americans are not particularly introspective. Framing problems as acculturation issues common to other immigrant groups may also remove their sense of "blame" and decrease their shame (Szapocznik, Santisban, Kurtines, Perez-Vidal, & Hervis, 1984). Parent–child conflicts and problems can be reframed as cultural conflicts requiring mutual Korean–American "acculturation." New or alternate perspectives and methods of problem solving can be offered as "doing things differently in a new country," like the proverb "When in Rome, do as the Roman's do." The therapist can take the dual position of being a teacher of American ways and a student in Korean ways, thus empowering the client and bridging the distance between therapist and client.

A 14-year-old Korean American boy, youngest of three, the only child born in the United States, was brought by his college-educated, Korean immigrant parents because he had "gone berserk." Primarily well-behaved and high achieving, he had been suspended from school, his grades had fallen, and he was insolent to his parents, who were anguished and deeply ashamed by his behavior. Although the son was infuriated and could not understand why his parents were so upset, his continuing need for their approval had resulted in loss of self-esteem and other depressive symptoms. Inquiry revealed that he was the class clown, had not been doing his homework, and had been found with a cigarette on school grounds. His grades had dropped from A's to C's. The parents complained that he would either ignore them or talk back and sometimes slam the door in anger. Their previous success with the patient's two other siblings, both raised in Korea till puberty, further fueled their outrage and certainty that something was seriously wrong with their son. The therapist was able to help them appreciate how different this child was from his siblings because he had grown up in such a different world. Once they understood this, and some of the pressure he was experiencing as an American teenager, they could work with the therapist to adapt their parenting techniques and become successful as they had been with their other children. At the same time, the therapist worked with the boy to appreciate his parent's need for respect. Furthermore, he was helped to share with his parents his adolescent lifestyle and the importance of peer relationships. She reminded him how important it was to reassure his parents that he was not losing sight of his long-term career goals. As the parents recognized how much their son had incorporated their values, they could overlook some of his disrespectful manners and maintain their commitment to him. This case illustrates mutual ignorance about the extent of cultural commitment that each party has and how it can lead to misunderstanding and miscommunication.

Once the therapist gains the clients' trust, Korean Americans are remarkably open with their feelings and opinions and will expect something of the same from the therapist. They will want to know about the therapist's marital status, age, number of children, and academic credentials. Most American therapists consider such personal questions to be intrusive, but questioning motives will only embarrass and offend. It is best to answer factually without getting too personal. Gift giving is a normal expression of appreciation after the therapist is helpful, and an invitation for dinner, a family birthday, or holiday celebration is not uncommon. As with personal information, the rule is to accept gifts gracefully if they are not expensive and decline meal invitations.

## CONCLUSION

Korean Americans as recent immigrants are experiencing a variety of adjustment and acculturation difficulties they could never have anticipated. Although they are used to major changes, they have no precedent for learning to live in a foreign culture that in itself is undergoing rapid change. Neither these new immigrants nor the American public in general begins to appreciate the magnitude of trying to become grounded in a society where extreme change has become the norm. Under these circumstances, we can expect exaggerated expressions of individual and family dysfunction complicated by cultural stress. The task of the therapist is to discriminate between inner conflict or weakness in family structure and that which is primarily situational and culture generated (Falicov, 1988). The therapist needs to recognize that therapy alone is not the answer. The therapeutic mission must include working with specialized ethnic resources as well as sensitizing mainstream institutions to be responsive to the needs of new immigrants.

## NOTE

1. This issue contains excellent articles regarding Korean women's status of the past and present. For copies write to Subscription Service, *Koreana*, P.O. Box 312, Hartsdale, New York 10530.

## REFERENCES

American Psychiatric Association. (1994). *Diagnostic and statistical manual of mental disorders* (4th ed.). Washington, DC: Author.

Chai, A. (1987). *Feminist analysis of life history of early immigrant women from Japan, Okinawa, and Korea.* Unpublished manuscript, University of Hawaii, Women's Studies Program, Honolulu.

Choy, B.-Y. (1971). *Korea: A history.* Rutland, VT: Charles E. Tuttle.

Covell, A. C. (1983). *Ecstasy: Shamanism in Korea.* Elizabeth, NJ: Hollym International Corp.

Falicov, C. J. (1988). Learning to think culturally. In H. Liddle, D. C. Breunlin, & R. C. Schwartz (Eds.), *Handbook of family therapy training and supervision* (pp. 335–357). New York: Guilford Press.

Hurh, W.-M., & Kim, K. C. (1984). *Korean immigrants in America: A structural analysis of ethnic confinement and adhesive adaption.* London & Toronto: Fairleigh Dickinson University Press.

Janelli, R. L., & Janelli, D. Y. (1982). *Ancestor worship in Korean society.* Stanford, CA: Stanford University Press.

Kim, A.-S. (1990). Economic status and labor conditions. *Koreana, 4*(2), 24–33.

Kim, B.-L. C. (1978). The Korean sample. In *The Asian Americans: Changing patterns, changing needs* (pp. 177–211). Montclair, NJ: The Association of Korean Christian Scholars in North America.

Kim, B.-L. C. (1980). *The Korean-American child at school and at home* (Project Report [09-30-78–06-30-80], Administration on Child, Youth, and Families, U.S. DHEW, Grant No. 90-C-1335 [01]). Washington, DC: U.S. Department of Health, Education and Welfare.

Kim, B.-L. C. (1981). *Women in shadows: A handbook for service providers working with Asian wives of U.S. military personnel.* La Jolla, CA: National Committee Concerned with Asian Wives of U.S. Servicemen.

Kim, B.-L. C. (1988).The language situation of Korean Americans. In S. L. McKay & S.-L. Wong (Eds.), *Language diversity: Problems or resource?* (pp. 252–275). New York: Newbury House.

Kim, B.-L. C., & Condon, M. E. (1975). *A study of Asian Americans in Chicago: Their socio-economic characteristics, problems and service needs* (Final Research Report, NIMH, U.S. DHEW, Grant No. 1, R01 MH 23993–01). Washington, DC: National Institute of Mental Health.

Kim, C., & Kim, B.-L. C. (1977). Asian immigrants in American law: A look at the past and the challenge which remains. *American University Law Review, 26*(2), 373–407.

Kim, D.-S. (1978, Spring). From women to women with painful love: A study of maternal motivation in intercountry adoption processes. In H. H. Sunoo & D.-S. Kim (Eds.), *Korean women in a struggle for humanization* (pp. 117–169). Montclair, NJ: The Association of Korean Christian Scholars in North America.

Kim, L. (1990, December). *The concept of jeong and other Korean ethos.* Paper presented at the meeting of the American Academy of Psychoanalysis, San Antonio, TX.

Kim, S. C. (1985) Family therapy for Asian Americans: A strategic–structural framework. *Psychotherapy, 22*(2s), 342–348.

Kim, Y.-C. (1976). Modern education. In Y.-C. Kim (Ed.), *Women of Korea: A history from ancient time to 1945* (pp. 213–242). Seoul, Korea: Ewha Women's University Press.

Korean Overseas Information Service. (1990). *A handbook of Korea.* Seoul, Korea: Author.

Mintz, B. R. (1990). Changing—for better or worse? *Koreana, 4*(2), 69–73.

Nahm, A. C. (Ed.). (1973). *Korea under Japanese colonial rule—Study of the policies and techniques of Japanese colonization.* Grand Rapids, MI: The Center for Korean Studies, Institute of International and Area Studies, Western Michigan University.

*People v. Soonja Du,* 7 Cal. Rptr. 2d 177, 1992.

Sue, S. (1977). Community mental health services to minority groups: Some optimism, some pessimism. *American Psychologist, 42*(1), 37–45.

Sue, S., & McKinney, H. (1975). Asian Americans on the community mental health care system. *American Journal of Orthopsychiatry, 45,* 111–118.

Sue, S., & Zane, N. (1987). The role of culture and cultural techniques in psychotherapy: A critique and reformulation. *American Psychologist, 42*(1), 37–45.

Szapocznik, J., Santisban, D., Kurtines, W., Perez-Vidal, A., & Hervis, O. (1984). Bicultural effectiveness training: A treatment intervention for enhancing intercultural adjustment in Cuban American families. *Hispanic Journal of Behavioral Science, 6*(4), 317–344.

U.S. Bureau of the Census. (1990). *1990 census of population: Asians and Pacific Islanders in the United States.* Washington, DC: U.S. Department of Commerce, Economics and Statistics Administration.

Yang, E. S. (1982). Koreans in America, 1903–1945. In E. Y. Yu, E. H. Phillips, & E. S. Yang (Eds.), *Koreans in Los Angeles: Prospects and promises.* Los Angeles, CA: Koryo Research Institutes, Center for Korean-American and Korean Studies.

CHAPTER 20

# Vietnamese Families

Paul K. Leung
James Boehnlein

Twenty years ago we witnessed the beginning of the forced exodus of the people of Vietnam from a homeland that was lost to a repressive regime. In 1990 the Census Bureau reported more than 600,000 Vietnamese in the United States, the majority foreign born (Kinzie & Leung, 1993) and admitted as refugees. Toward the second half of the previous two decades, Vietnamese also had come as legal immigrants, because of the sponsorship of financially secure family members, who had arrived earlier and had successfully assimilated into the United States. In the meantime, a whole new generation of Vietnamese Americans born in the United States has come to adulthood with only a minimal emotional tie with the "old country" way of life that their parents so dearly cherish.

Since 1975, many authors have focused on the health and mental health issues facing individual Vietnamese refugees (Strand & Jones, 1983; Kinzie et al., 1988; Kinzie & Manson, 1983; Vignes & Hall, 1979). Several of the studies have discussed the practice of folk medicine among the population and its impact on contemporary medical treatment (Golden & Duster, 1977; Kinzie & Leung, 1993; Muecke, 1983). It has repeatedly been pointed out that, although the prevalence rates of various mental health problems are higher among the Vietnamese than among the general U.S. population (Gong-Guy, 1987), they have underutilized mainstream mental health resources (Nguyen, 1985). Rarely has the family been the focal point of mental health surveys or research studies; however, many authors have pointed out the importance of involving the family in the treatment process (Kinzie & Fleck, 1987; Lee, 1988). In fact, one study has noted the phenomenon of unrelated individual refugees forming a "pseudofamily" for the purpose of mutual emotional support and survival (Lin, Tazuma, & Masuda, 1979).

In this chapter we will examine the traditional Vietnamese family and its values and the changes that have evolved in America. Unique considerations in the treatment setting will also be illustrated with case histories.

## THE TRADITIONAL FAMILY

Vietnamese society has gone through tremendous changes since the turn of the century, and especially since World War II. These changes are due to French colonial rule, Japanese occupation during World War II, and the period of struggle of the Vietnamese people for freedom and reunification. Through this turmoil, the family as an institution has adapted itself and endured in the midst of changes.

### Traditional Vietnamese Culture

Vietnamese culture and history have long been influenced by China (Frieze, 1986). In the middle of the 10th century, Vietnam gained independent sovereignty from China, but it continues to maintain close ties with its bigger and richer northern neighbor. People from all walks of life have traveled between the two countries, assuring a steady stream of mutual influence on their societies. Trades flourished for centuries, and it was an honor for a family to send its favorite son to be schooled in China. Vietnam has adopted Chinese Confucianism with open arms, and this code of conduct has governed its society for centuries. Confucius, a philosopher who 3,500 years ago was regarded as the greatest teacher in the history of China, set forth a code of conduct that still influences Chinese society. In a larger sense, Confucianism demands that an individual revere heaven, earth, the emperor, parents, and one's teachers, in that order. It defines the relationships an individual has with people and obligations to them. Loyalty and forgiveness are always emphasized in any interpersonal relationship. The "self" is to be minimized for the goodness of the family and the society. One is to seek a harmonious existence with the environment and with other people.

The worshiping of ancestors is important in the Vietnamese culture, as it is for the Chinese. The practice is pervasive and commonly found even among the converts to religions rooted in the Judeo-Christian tradition. On important anniversaries, dates, festivals, or significant individual or family events, offerings presented to ancestors are often the first act of the celebration. This is usually conducted by the elderly figures in the family, with active participation expected of the younger members. Children are raised with the constant reminder of never bringing shame to the ancestors.

### Roles of the Old and Young

Traditional Vietnamese society follows other Asian cultures, especially those influenced by Confucianism, regarding attitudes toward elders, who are to be respected and not openly disagreed with. Elders are often called in to resolve conflicts and crises among members of the family. Young people are frequently reminded to remain quiet when in the midst of elders. Age may not be the only factor determining one's status as an elder. One's generation in the family tree, as well as birth order, are other factors.

Little Tuan N. was born in America. He was accompanying his parents to a wedding. At the banquet his parents began to instruct Tuan to greet people around the table. The elderly lady sitting across should be addressed as "Grandma," the young lady next to her would be "Aunt Ngoc," and the young man next to her was "Brother Thanh." The formality had repeated itself for the rest of the evening. Finally after greeting the 20th "relative," Tuan commented to his parents that he had met so many uncles, aunts, and cousins, he wondered where they had been prior to the occasion. His parents replied that these people were not really his relatives and that he was not to ask any more "embarrassing" question in front of the guests.

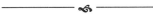

The issue of "eye contact" also needs to be addressed as part of the communication process between different generations, aside from its role in reflecting social status. As a rule, a person of a lower position in the hierarchy does not maintain direct eye contact with elders or those in a higher social position. Otherwise, it would be interpreted as a sign of disrespect. Hand shaking is also handled differently than the Western practice; one shakes the hands of elders with both hands to indicate respect.

## Roles of Husband and Wife

In a traditional family, spouses are governed by a set of rules of etiquette. The spouses may have married as a result of a prearrangement by the respective parents rather than by their own initiative. Before agreeing to the union, the parents usually want to be reassured that the two families are compatible by social status, cultural background, and religious beliefs.

Once married, the bond is regarded as permanent and only breakable if adultery is committed by the woman but not the man. Prior to the World War II, divorce was exceedingly rare in Vietnamese society. However, it was quite acceptable for a man to take on a second or even a third wife, also with a mistress on the side. This situation changed after the 1950s with the institution of laws forbidding polygamy, but the practice of a man "entertaining" or "enjoying" in the "leisure-oriented environment" is still looked upon as somewhat acceptable. The wife usually would overlook the issue as long as her position in the extended family was secure and the provisions for her children had been satisfied.

Mr. Quang D., a man in his late 60s, was from a very affluent family when Vietnam was under the colonial government of France. He had taken a wife before he was sent to Paris for his higher education in the late 1940s. After 7 years he had earned his engineering degree. Throughout those years as a student in the university he was known more for his reputation as a drinker and a womanizer. In the middle of the 1950s, due to changes in the Vietnamese political situation, Mr. D.'s family had followed the refugee tide south and resettled in the city of Saigon. At this time, Mr. D. had also returned to Vietnam and reunited with his family. However, it was not long afterward that he had begun staying overnight frequently in a woman's house. He had often commented to friends that this woman was attractive to him because she was more "Westernized, capable of new thinking." He remained faithful in providing for his wife and children. Later on in his life he had taken on another wife, while remaining married to the first one. In 1975, he came to America as a refugee along with his two wives and seven children. Not long after, both of his wives demanded that each would have her own place, and that he would go to stay with the other one, because neither had time for him. At this time neither of the wives and children is living with him.

───────── ◆ ─────────

As for financial matters, the husband is expected to be the main provider of the family, but he does not discourage his wife from having a small business on the side; sometimes this business can indeed bring in a handsome supplement for the family. Before the fall of Saigon in 1975, it was common to see men holding jobs in the offices and women running shops and businesses in the local markets.

## Roles of Sons and Daughters

Even to the current time, children are regarded as property of the parents, although this belief has been loosened gradually as the culture has become more Westernized since World War II. Parents have the responsibility to provide for their children and be accountable for their actions. Children are expected to follow the parent's advice in all aspects of life, including matters relating to marriage and career selection. From a very young age, children are taught the concepts of obligation and shame. Children learn that they have the obligation to provide for their elderly parents. They will be reminded throughout life that they have an obligation to fulfill the dreams of their parents, often presented in the name of the "family." Failing to carry out the obligations would only bring shame to one's life and might even cause the individual to become an outcast within the extended family and the community.

The firstborn of a family holds a special position; this is especially true for a son. In the absence of the father, the eldest child can assume the leadership among the siblings and is regarded as the head of the household. The eldest child, especially the son, is expected to provide good modeling for the rest of the children and take the blame for the wrongdoings of his siblings. Parents most likely favor the oldest son, but also expect to be cared for by him. The oldest son is expected to carry on the name of the family.

Trinh L., while a sophomore majoring in business administration, had his heart set on going for an MBA degree after his undergraduate years. Trinh's father, a hardworking man who had to struggle in order to provide for the family after their resettlement in America, came to the son one day and said, "We need a doctor in the family. You are my eldest son, and it is my wish for you to pursue this career in order to bring honor to the family." Trinh took his father's words seriously and changed his career goal. This decision did not come without great struggle for Trinh. He had discussed the matter at length with his counselors at the college and church and finally accepted the challenge. Eventually Trinh graduated from medical school and is now a successful practitioner in his community. Very often in his own private moments, Trinh wonders when he will have an opportunity to return to school for the degree that he had to cast aside for the sake of the family honor as well as the fulfillment of the wish of his father.

———————— ✺ ————————

## THE FAMILY IN TRANSITION

### Historical Facts

In order to appreciate the changes that the traditional Vietnamese family has endured, we have to first understand the forces behind these changes. As we begin to examine the disruption of the traditional family system in Vietnam, we find that the root of the problems really started prior to the Indochinese conflict. As early as the turn of the 20th century, the struggle to gain independence from the French colonial government had already pitched members of families against each other because of differences in political ideology. In 1954, at the signing of the agreement in Geneva, two Vietnams were created (*The New Columbia Encyclopedia*, 1975). This separation brought about an exodus from the north of people seeking to flee communist rule. As a result, many families were broken up, with their members not able to see each other for the following 20 years, and some never again. Throughout the Indochinese conflict, the breakup of the Vietnamese family continued to take place due to the very destructive and disruptive nature of the war. Although they had to endure this turmoil, Vietnamese families were still able to maintain their integrity because they could draw upon the support of their innate cultural environment. However, for the group of Vietnamese who left the country after the collapse of the Saigon government in 1975, the devastation of the family system was nearly complete. This group consisted of millions who had gone to foreign lands under much stress. For them, a way of life that treasured harmonic living among people related by blood and marriage largely disappeared.

## Changes in the Family Structure

For the Vietnamese who live in America, one of the biggest changes facing them is the loss of the extended family structure. In Vietnam, they would expect to live among a network of family and relatives, which sometimes would encompass many layers of relationships. As they sought refuge in foreign lands, some were fortunate to have their nuclear family with them, but others remained separated. For those who came at the beginning of the influx of Indochinese refugees into America, assimilation was complicated by the stresses associated with upward mobility. Many Vietnamese parents were shocked to see their children moving away for better job opportunities after finishing their education. The loss of this extended family structure meant the loss of a natural and familiar supportive system and an associated identity that one could only attain while living among a network of related people.

## The Confusion of Role Identities

In the traditional society, the role identities were always clear. The husband was the head of the family, he was the chief provider for the family, and the rest of the family would look to him for guidance. The wife would be the caregiver and comforter of the family, who was not required to deal with the outside world unless she chose to do so. Children were always under the protective wings of the parents and in the presence of the parents, they were not expected to provide leadership for the family. Often, once the family was transplanted outside of its natural environment, the role identities of its members were altered.

Most Vietnamese have discovered in America, as well as in most Western countries, that it is a matter of survival for all able family members to participate in the workforce. As women have increased their contribution to the family's financial well-being, they also have become increasingly forceful in demanding that their status in the family and in the society be elevated. Sometimes the wife becomes the primary wage earner for the family because of age or because of employment options available in the community favoring low-paid female workers. The husband may lose his leadership role if his ability to contribute to the family's finances is the only gauge of measurement. Children are also encouraged to be financially independent as soon as they can, further eroding the leadership base of the parents. In addition, children who grow up in America become more proficient in English and often act as the bridges to the outside world for the non-English-speaking parents. This has further contributed to role confusion for many members of the family.

Mr. Phuoc V., a 57-year-old former South Vietnam Army intelligence officer who was released from the reeducational camp after an incarceration of 12 years, had come to America 2 years ago to be reunited with his wife and three children; they had come to the United States in the late 1970s. The wife has been working as a housekeeper in a motel and was able to get by with her English. The three children had completed their formal education and each had been working in a high-technology industry. Mr. Phuoc was referred to the mental health clinic for treatment of depression and previous trauma-related symptoms. In the course of therapy it was discovered that Mr. Phuoc had developed severe low self-image since his arrival here. In his own words, Mr. Phuoc had said, "I have felt so useless now because I have to rely on my wife to support me. My children have changed; they are too Westernized, they do not listen to me, they do not honor me anymore. I am just a dumb old man who cannot even speak or understand the language here." We have engaged Mr. Phuoc in therapy with our program. At the beginning he was receptive only to medication therapy, but resisted attempts by the counselor to engage in talk therapy. The psychiatrist and the counselor continued to meet with him together for medication management and gradually enticed him to talk about his family problems. Eventually, Mr. Phuoc has become increasingly comfortable in this way of meeting, beyond just talking about medications. The frequency of meeting with the psychiatrist were gradually reduced while increasing the time and frequency with the counselor alone. Through a process of active education, explanation, and refocusing, he began to understand the need to reshape the structure of his values system. He has accepted that his wife is an equal partner in providing for the family, that it is equally fair for him to stay home to attend to the chores. As for his children, he has accepted that it is different in America, and the children have their lives to live, and he could not expect them to behave as if they were in Vietnam. Mr. Phuoc's famous quote was, "The world has to change too."

───────── ◈ ─────────

## TREATMENT CONSIDERATIONS

### Resistance to Seeking Help

Studies repeatedly have shown that Asians underutilize mental health treatment facilities (Brown, Stein, Huang, & Harris, 1973; Sue & Sue, 1974). Some authors have attributed this to the inability of mainstream providers to meet the needs of Asian patients (Chien & Yamamoto, 1982; Sue & Morishima, 1985), but others have identified different factors (Kleinman, Eisenberg, & Good, 1978). When working with Vietnamese families, it is important to remember that they reserve outside intervention as the last resource to be utilized only when all internal family options have failed. Like other Asians, Vietnamese prefer to resolve problems among family members by dealing with them within the family circle. Sometimes a respected relative or an elderly friend of the family is invited to play the role of referee to help with settling differences. The concept of going to a total stranger for advice and discussion about family or personal problems is an alien concept to most Vietnamese. It is important for the family therapist to recognize that the step taken by a Vietnamese family to seek help is itself a significant and stressful event and needs to be handled with patience, respect, and gentleness.

## The Therapeutic Alliance

It is important for the therapist to gain the trust of the Vietnamese family. With the exception of some urban areas, most of the communities where Vietnamese families have congregated are relatively small. One issue that concerns Vietnamese clients is confidentiality. There must be reassurance that the matters brought to the therapist will not be spread among the community. Often it takes more than a few visits before the client can feel reassured and comfortable with the therapist. It is necessary to repeatedly educate the client about the professional obligation of upholding confidentiality.

Once trust has been established, the therapist may need to take an active role in the therapeutic process rather than taking the traditional passive and facilitory position, as favored by most Western-trained therapists. Vietnamese clients are likely to see the therapist in the role of teacher, adviser, and someone who is there to give guidance in a time of trouble.

Huyen H. was 23 years old when she was referred to the mental health clinic by the caseworker in the community, who had taken note of Huyen's extremely withdrawn behavior and her sad affect. During the evaluation it was obvious that the young lady was severely depressed with vegetative signs and symptoms. However, the patient was quiet, passive, and denied having any problems. In subsequent months she was asked to return to the clinic for follow-up care. Although Huyen came back faithfully, she persistently refused to take part in any group therapy or activity. It was determined that the therapist would see her for treatment. Huyen remained passive, quiet, and took her medicines as instructed. The therapist met with the patient regularly, engaged her actively in conversation, and educated her about the new country. Five months into the process, one day Huyen asked for permission to tell the therapist about the ordeal she went through when she had escaped from Vietnam. The therapist had subsequently learned that Huyen was raped by Thai pirates seven times on three separate occasions and twice by the guards when she was jailed on an island somewhere in Malay. Huyen remained in treatment 8 years after her initial evaluation. In the beginning, Huyen was seen by the psychiatrist and the Vietnamese counselor for medication, and engaging in talk therapy when the opportunity presented itself. As time passed Huyen began to meet with the counselor for therapy, with more space in between visits with the psychiatrist. For the last 5 years she has been coming to a group that is focused on depression and posttraumatic stress disorder issues. She has also joined a work group as part of the job training program of vocational rehabilitation.

———————— ✦ ————————

## The Communication Process

For Indochinese parents in general, regardless of the length of stay in America or the stage of assimilation into American culture, one of the biggest problems is when the therapist puts all family members on the same level in open and "equal" discussion of family problems. Therapists often encourage children "to speak their minds" with the parents listening in. This is no doubt useful when all parties involved know the rules of the game. But unless Indochinese parents have been thoroughly prepared, this style of therapy may undermine their sense of parental authority and immediately discredit the counselor.

Another major therapeutic issue is the use of interpreters. Although many have written about the need of using trained interpreters to reach non-English-speaking clients (Kinzie, 1981; Lee, 1982), it is still very common to see those well-tested principles being violated. Many service providers make the fundamental mistake of equating an interpreter simply with someone who can speak the language of the client and some English. In many situations a family member with some English capability, who could be the child of the client, is drafted into the role of interpreter. Sometimes a friend, or even a bystander who happens to be present, is asked to be the interpreter. There is little regard for the training and professionalism of the person who does the interpretation. In reality, no effort should be spared to have a person who has professional training in medical and mental health interpretation, and preferably with credentials recognized by the public, to assist the therapist or counselor to bridge the gaps of language and culture in the treatment process. It is better if ethnic professional therapists or counselors can be recruited to provide services in their respective communities. The Indochinese Psychiatric Program in Oregon over the last 18 years has successfully trained a group of highly experienced ethnic mental health professionals who can provide services to clients of all Southeast Asian ethnic groups.

## High Prevalence of Severe Mental Illnesses

Over the past decade an accumulated body of data has revealed that there are high levels of distress and mental illness among refugees, especially those from Southeast Asia (Gong-Guy, 1987; Kinzie et al., 1990; Lin et al., 1979). Depression and posttraumatic stress disorder (PTSD) are the most prevalent problems, although other major psychiatric illnesses are common among this population (Kinzie & Manson, 1983; Mollica, Wyshak, & Lavelle, 1987). Studies involving nonpatient Southeast Asian high school students have also shown high rates of both depression and PTSD (Kinzie & Sack, 1991). Furthermore, other studies have shown that parents with chronic mental illnesses can adversely affect the development of interpersonal skills of their children, as well as fostering a sense of distrust of the outside world (Anthony & Cohler, 1987; Freyberg, 1980; Westermeyer, 1991). It is therefore important to keep in mind the dual effects of mental illness and the distress of being a refugee on the integrity of the family.

## CONCLUSION

Providing mental health care for Southeast Asian families, including the Vietnamese, will continue to pose a tremendous challenge to professionals for a number of reasons. These include language barriers, different expectations of treatment resulting from different cultural perspectives, and a severe shortage of adequately trained professionals in the field. The development of human resources in the areas of health, mental health, and other human services is an urgent issue that needs to be addressed in order for care to be effective. Working with families of a different ethnicity, like the Vietnamese, also should receive more attention from family researchers and from health-care providers.

## REFERENCES

Anthony, E. J., & Cohler, B. J. (Eds.). (1987). *The invulnerable child.* New York: Guilford Press.

Brown, T., Stein, K., Huang, K., & Harris, D. (1973). Mental illness and the role of mental health facilities in Chinatown. In S. Sue & N. Wagner (Eds.), *Asian Americans: Psychological perspectives* (pp. 213–231). Palo Alto, CA: Science & Behavior Books.

Chien, C. P., & Yamatoto, J. (1982). Asian-American and Pacific-Islander patients. In F. X. Acosta, J. Yamamoto, & L. A. Evans (Eds.), *Effective psychotherapy for low-income and minority patients* (pp.117–145). New York: Plenum Press.

Freyberg, J. (1980). Difficulties in separation–individuation as experienced by offspring of Nazi Holocaust survivors. *American Journal of Orthopsychiatry, 50,* 87–95.

Frieze, R. (1986). The Indochinese refugee crisis. In J. Krupinsk & G. Burrows (Eds.), *The price of freedom.* New York: Pergamon Press.

Golden, J. M., & Duster, M. C. (1977). Hazards of misdiagnosis due to Vietnamese folk medicine. *Clinical Pediatrics, 16,* 949–950.

Gong-Guy, E. (1987). *The California Southeast Asian's mental health needs assessment* (California State Department Mental Health Contract #85-7628-2A-2). Oakland, CA: Asian Community Mental Health Services.

Kinzie, J. D. (1981). The evaluation and psychotherapy of Indochinese refugee patients. *American Journal of Psychotherapy, 35,* 251–261.

Kinzie, J. D., Boehnlein, J. K., Leung, P. K., Moore, L., Riley, C., & Smith, D. (1990). The high prevalence rate of PTSD and its clinical significance among Southeast Asian refugees. *American Journal of Psychiatry, 147,* 813–917.

Kinzie, J. D., & Fleck, J. (1987). Psychotherapy with severely traumatized refugees. *American Journal of Psychotherapy, 41,* 82–94.

Kinzie, J. D., & Leung, P. L. (1993). Psychiatric care of Indochinese Americans. In A. C. Gaw (Ed.), *Culture, ethnicity, and mental illness* (pp. 281–306). Washington, DC: American Psychiatric Press.

Kinzie, J. D., Leung, P. K., Bui, A., Rath, B., Keopraseuth, K., Riley, C., Fleck, J., & Marie, A. (1988). Group therapy with Southeast Asian refugees. *Community Mental Health Journal, 24,* 157–166.

Kinzie, J. D., & Manson, S. (1983). Five years experience with Indochinese refugee psychiatric patients. *Journal of Operational Psychiatry, 14,* 105–111.

Kinzie, J. D., & Sack, W. (1991). Severely traumatized Cambodian children: Research findings and clinical implications. In F. L. Ahern, Jr. (Ed.), *Refugee children traumatized by war.* Baltimore, MD: Johns Hopkins University Press.

Kleinman, A. M., Eisenberg, L., & Good, B. (1978). Culture, illness and care: Clinical lessons from anthropological and cross-cultural research. *Annals of Internal Medicine, 88,* 251–258.

Lee, E. (1982). A social systems approach to assessment and treatment of Chinese American families. In M. McGoldrick, J. K. Pearce, & J. Giordano (Eds.), *Ethnicity and family therapy* (1st ed., pp. 527–551). New York: Guilford Press.

Lee, E. (1988). Cultural factors in working with Southeast Asian refugee adolescents. *Journal of Adolescence, 11,* 167–169.

Lin, K. M., Tazuma, L., & Masuda, M. (1979). Adaptational problems of Vietnamese. *Archives of General Psychiatry, 26,* 955–961.

Mollica, R. F., Wyshak, G., & Lavelle, J. (1987). The psychosocial impact on war trauma and torture on Southeast Asian refugees. *American Journal of Psychiatry, 144,* 1507–1572.

Muecke, M. A. (1983). In search of healers—Southeast Asian refugees in the American health care system. *Western Journal of Medicine* [Special Issue], *139*(6), 835–840.

*The new Columbia encyclopedia.* (1975). New York: Columbia University Press.

Nguyen, S. D. (1985). Mental health services for refugees and immigrants in Canada. In T. C. Owan (Ed.), *Southeast Asian mental health: Treatment, prevention, services, training, and research.* Washington, DC: U.S. Department of Health and Human Services.

Strand, P. J., & Jones, W., Jr. (1983). Health service utilization by Indochinese refugees. *Care, 21,* 1089–1096.

Sue, S., & Morishima, J. (1985). *The mental health of Asian Americans.* San Francisco: Jossey-Bass.

Sue, S., & Sue, D. (1974). MMPI comparisons between Asian-American and non-Asian

American students utilizing a student health psychiatric clinic. *Journal of Counseling Psychology, 21,* 423–427.

Vignes, A. J., & Hall, R. C. W. (1979). Adjustment of a group of Vietnamese people in the United States. *American Journal of Psychiatry, 136,* 442–444.

Westermeyer, J. (1991). Psychiatry services for refugees' children: An overview. In F. L. Ahearn, Jr., & J. L. Athey (Eds.), *Refugee children: Theory, research, and services.* Baltimore, MD: Johns Hopkins University Press.

# CHAPTER 21

# Cambodian Families

## Lorna McKenzie-Pollock

This chapter is intended as an introductory guide for clinicians beginning to work with Cambodian families. The bilingual, bicultural treatment model described here can be adapted for use with other refugee and immigrant families. Clinicians are going to be increasingly called on to treat highly traumatized non-English-speaking groups, as refugees from Bosnia, Rwanda, Haiti, and Somalia arrive and need services, and clinicians are not yet available from the newly arrived groups.

## BACKGROUND

Cambodia is a Southeast Asian country situated between Thailand, Laos, and Vietnam. The Cambodian people, known as the Khmer, are a racial mix of indigenous tribal people and invaders from India and Indonesia. Unlike some of the neighboring countries, they are a very homogeneous group, 97% of which are Theravada Buddhists (there is a very small Moslem minority). Prior to 1970, the country was largely agrarian. Over 85% of the population were small rice farmers. Although the country had been colonized by the French, and the upper classes and many of the people in the capital city Phom Penh spoke French, most of the population had been exposed to little Western influence prior to 1970.

Khmer social structure was based on the extended family. The social order was highly stratified. Social relations were clearly defined, so that people knew what to expect from each other. This hierarchical, stratified nature of the society is even revealed in the language. For example, a different word for eating is used depending on the rank of the person being referred to.

Relationships within the family are also highly stratified. The husband as head of the household expects to be deferred to on all matters. The eldest son has a special position in the family. Siblings refer to each other as older or younger brother or sister. This familial ranking carries over to social relationships in all spheres. For example, a Khmer counselor will address a client as older sister, *bong*, or younger sister, *pu'on*, depending on her relative age and social standing. A woman client who is actually chronologically younger than the counselor may be referred to as older sister if she came from a prominent family in Cambodia.

Central values in Khmer society are harmony and balance. Conflict is to be avoided at all costs (Ebihara, 1968). In a clinical setting this means that if clients are angry or upset with something a therapist said, they will not indicate this directly. Instead they will tell the therapist very politely and pleasantly that it is simply not possible to come in for another session because their hours at work are about to change or transportation is too difficult. Or they will simply not show up for the next session. Cambodian clients expect this same indirectness from an American therapist and experience confrontation or direct questioning by a therapist as very rude. For example, a Cambodian widow came to see me recently with two of her children for support in dealing with recurrent depression. She told me about an experience she had with a psychiatrist 2 years earlier, whom she described as conducting an interrogation, which she said felt like a torture session. Curious, I sent for her records and found that the psychiatrist in question, a female resident, had simply been conducting a mental status exam as part of a medication evaluation. There was no indication in the record that she was aware that the client was upset.

On the other hand, it should be noted that Cambodians are very willing to overlook what they consider rude or incorrect behavior by an American therapist if they understand that the therapist is well meaning. For example, early on, in an attempt to be culturally sensitive, I began greeting clients at the beginning of a session in the Khmer language. I did this for a year before someone finally told me that I was using a very impolite, slangy form of greeting. When I asked the bilingual counselor what people had thought of that, she told me that clients knew I meant well and had not been offended.

The importance of harmony and politeness is further illustrated by the following: I once asked a Cambodian teacher for advice about the most effective way to intervene in a case where teachers were referring a child who had talked about domestic violence. She said she would handle this situation by visiting the couple with a gift of food. She would sit with them and chat about family life and values without mentioning the reports of violence. Therefore, the couple would not be shamed by having the problem named, but they would get the message that there was a problem with their or his behavior.

## HISTORY

In 1970 Cambodia was thrown into turmoil by saturation bombing in the eastern part of the country by the United States military, with the aim of stopping the flow of supplies and personnel from North to South Vietnam along the Ho Chi Minh trail, part of which ran through eastern Cambodia. There were many casualties, many people were left homeless, and considerable political destabilization ensued, with the overthrow of the longtime Cambodian political leader, Prince Sihanouk, and the installation of a short-lived pro-Western government led by Lon Nol. In April 1975, just 2 months after the fall of Saigon, the government of Cambodia fell under the control of the Khmer Rouge, a Maoist-inspired government led by Pol Pot. They declared the Year Zero and embarked on a program to rid Cambodia of all Western influences. What followed was another of the holocausts that have marred the 20th century.

The Khmer Rouge ordered the cities evacuated. People were sent to rural labor camps. All wealthy, educated, and professional people were sought out and executed. Teachers, doctors, and soldiers were killed or had to disguise their identity in order to survive. A systematic program of thought control by the Khmer Rouge followed. Children were separated from their parents, put into children's camps, and made to inform on their parents. People were put in forced labor camps and made to work long hours. With the dismantling of the old social order, the once relatively prosperous country went into collapse, and famine and disease became endemic. Conditions in the labor camps became even more nightmarish. The Khmer Rouge maintained control by mass public torture, execution, and disembowelment of all dissidents or suspected dissidents. Family members, neighbors, and coworkers were forced to watch without showing emotion; any outpouring of emotion was punished by similar brutality. It is estimated that over two million Cambodians died during the Pol Pot regime.

In 1978 the Vietnamese army invaded Cambodia. At this point people became able to move around and discovered the full extent of their losses. Amid the mass confusion, people began pouring over the border on foot into neighboring Thailand—a long, dangerous journey through a mine-studded border region where many died or lost limbs. A series of refugee camps were set up along the border region of Thailand.

Cambodian refugee families spent anywhere from 1 to 12 years in these camps, in austere, overcrowded, and often unsafe conditions, awaiting resettlement in a third country. Most Cambodian families currently in the United States came here between 1980 and 1989 from one of these refugee camps.

On arrival in the United States, refugee families are generally resettled in poor urban areas, where, as the new group on the block, they are often preyed upon by other minority and immigrant groups. Many Cambodians become symptomatic and are referred for therapy after a violent incident in the neighborhood revives memories of events back home.

## THE TREATMENT MODEL

Because Cambodians are such a newly arrived group, and because of the tremendous upheaval in their country, few mental health or social service people who speak the Khmer language are available. Various interim treatment models have therefore had to be devised to meet the need for services in this community.

The model presented here involves a bilingual cotherapy team consisting of a bilingual Cambodian paraprofessional working together with an American clinician. A trio consisting of the bilingual worker, the American clinician, and the family or individual client are in the room at all times. This triadic cotherapy model can be confusing and difficult to get used to. It can present two traps for the unwary. The first is the danger of a struggle for control between the bilingual and the English-speaking clinicians. This can take the form of the English-speaking clinician trying to take control by insisting that the bilingual person be nothing more than a mouthpiece by doing direct translation. This results in discomfort and loss of face for the bilingual worker, who feels disempowered and can be asked to make culturally inappropriate interventions. It also robs the English-speaking clinician of the insights and expertise of the bilingual person and does not make effective use of the empathic connection between bilingual worker and client. A frequent outcome of this model is that the bilingual worker resorts to what has been called the "10 to 1 phenomenon" in which bilingual worker and client engage in lengthy animated exchanges and when the English-speaking clinician asks for clarification, the bilingual worker responds with a short or uninformative response (e.g., "They said yes"). Another trap is that of the disengaged American clinician, in which the American clinician remains detached from the details of the case by busying him- or herself with notetaking, prescription writing, or going in and out of the room to supervise other cases. This results in the bilingual worker feeling unsupported and overwhelmed by having to pick up all the details of follow-up for what are often complex and demanding cases. It can be difficult for bilingual staff to negotiate the maze of the American social service system alone without the "clout" provided by professional licensure credentials. This latter model protects the American clinician from having to sit with the feelings engendered by hearing overwhelming stories of sadness and loss, and leaves the bilingual worker, frequently a trauma survivor him- or herself, to sit with the stories alone.

The model I use (McKenzie-Pollock, 1988) is adapted from the Milan systemic model (Palazzoli, Boscolo, Cecchin, & Prata, 1981). The Cambodian staff person and I meet before each session to clarify our goals and make sure we are headed in the same direction. We attempt to resolve differences in how we see the issues before meeting with the family. Since the family and I do not speak the same language, it feels comfortable to sit back slightly and mentally assume the position of the coach behind the one-way mirror (formed in this case by the language barrier). In this way, I have removed myself from the temptation to vie for control and can make use of my particular vantage point to be an effective coach or advisor.

Throughout the session I observe the family interactions very closely. I maintain close contact with the bilingual worker, who frequently stops (at his or her discretion) and tells me in English what is being said. I also periodically share my observations with him or her. Since our communications are in English, we are usually not understood by the family. I will therefore frequently ask the bilingual person to fill the family in on what we have discussed. Sometimes, if the situation is particularly sensitive or complex, or if a split is developing in the team, the bilingual staff person and I will leave the room and confer.

At the end of the session, the team confers and gives the family our impressions and frequently a task to work on. This kind of directive approach tends to be acceptable and reassuring to Cambodian families. I find it helpful for both team members to keep a model of triadic communication in mind. The effectiveness of the therapy breaks down if avenues of communication are not constantly kept open between the three points of the triangle, namely, the American clinician, bilingual clinician, and the family.

I have found it useful to conceptualize the two therapists' positions as "emic" and "etic"—terms popularized by anthropologist Marvin Harris. "Emic" refers to a cultural insider's view, the position taken by the bilingual worker, whereas "etic," the position I take, involves being on the outside looking in. The idea is that both are valid and potentially useful. For families in cultural transition this can be a particularly powerful model. An additional benefit of having an American clinician present, taking an engaged, empathic role, is that many newcomer refugee families have relatively few warm and friendly relationships with Americans. I have been told repeatedly by Southeast Asian clients that their only other interactions outside the refugee community were with welfare workers, policemen, and other authority figures who were often impatient with their hesitant attempts to negotiate the new culture. Westermeyer and Williams (1986) state that in order to "regain a stable sense of self" refugees need both to "reestablish a foothold in their culture" and "to develop a new foothold in the receiving culture" (p. 242). This model is a means of facilitating this process.

Treatment issues of Cambodian families are often complex and multilayered. In trying to understand a family's presentation, I often find myself dealing with two or three levels of reality or "explanatory models" (Kleinman, 1980) simultaneously.

For example, a 35-year-old married Cambodian woman was referred because of depression and marital conflict. She was extremely withdrawn, avoided interacting with the neighbors, and had angry outbursts. Her husband told her, her children, and neighbors that she was crazy. He spent much time out of the house and had several affairs. The family's explanation of the problem was that a spell had been put on the wife. She dated the onset of the spell to 5 years earlier in a refugee camp in Thailand when she was hospitalized as a result of complications following childbirth. She was given an intravenous drip and believed this was how the spell had entered her body. The psychiatric–biomedical explanation appeared to be a major affective disorder, probably originating in a postpartum depression. The systems explanation would be that her symptoms were a response to her husband's behavior. A treatment plan should address all of these levels to be effective. In this case the plan included attempts to find a *kru Khmer*, or shaman, who would remove the spell, couple therapy to explore their difficulties, and a trial of an antidepressant medication.

————— ❧ —————

It should be emphasized that the treatment model outlined here is an interim model, and is in the process of being replaced by a new generation of Cambodian mental health professionals. It is also important to note that it is possible to work very effectively within this model. It is my experience that working with non-English-speaking families provides excellent training. When you are deprived of comprehension of words, you develop hyperacuity to other areas such as affect, body language, and your own response to what is going on. This in turn enriches your repertoire of skills in working with English-speaking families.

## TREATMENT ISSUES

### Trauma and Loss

Trauma and loss are, understandably, the most common treatment issues in Cambodian families. Clinicians therefore need to be familiar with the symptoms and treatment of posttraumatic stress disorder (Mollica, Wyshak, & Lavelle, 1987; Mollica, 1989; Kinzie, 1985). Saly Pin Riebe, a Cambodian social worker, movingly described the Cambodian experience: "Most trauma survivors run into situations from time to time that trigger memories of their trauma, but for Cambodians the reminders are everywhere. Every time they move, something reminds of a lost husband and father. When they look at a child, they remember their lost children So they are constantly in a state of distress, fright, and sorrow " (Interview, in Doepel, 1989).

Savuth was referred to Svang Tor and me for an evaluation by a physician because he was not complying with medication he had been prescribed for suspected tuberculosis. When we met with him and asked him about his family, he told us he was married and had three daughters ages 3, 4, and 6. When he informed us that his 6-year-old had not yet started attending school, even though it was a month into the school year, we brought in the whole family. On meeting his wife, Saroeun, I immediately became concerned. She was a thin, attractive woman in her mid-30s, whose face wore a blank frozen stare. The three daughters, well dressed and healthy looking, ran around my office, and she barely appeared to notice them. The older daughter looked out for the younger ones and the father would set limits periodically. Saroeun hardly spoke.

Svang, my Cambodian cotherapist, suggested we set up a meeting with just Saroen, Svang, and me. We first asked her about her physical symptoms, a way we had found helpful in connecting with Cambodians about their distress. She told us she could only sleep for a half-hour at a time before being woken up by terrifying nightmares. She would then spend hours shaking violently and sweating, with her heart pounding. In the nightmares she would hear the cries of her three young children who had died. As she began to tell her story, she became intensely distressed and sobbed uncontrollably.

When the Khmer Rouge came to Saroeun's village, they lined people up and began shooting. Eighteen people died. They put her in prison and starved and tortured her for 6 months because they suspected her brother had been a soldier. She said she did not tell on him, but they executed him anyway. During her imprisonment, her three young children were repeatedly brought to her, then taken away. She watched them deteriorate and eventually two of them died of starvation. The third died of typhoid in a Thai refugee camp. We had a series of individual meetings with both Sarouen and Savuth in which they each recounted their trauma stories, hers with intense outpourings of emotion, his with quiet sadness. We then began meeting with them as a couple, and they began to talk about these events that they had never discussed together. Sometimes these meetings were emotional and sorrowful; at other times they were able to use humor in talking about their situation. In one session they jokingly portrayed a typical night in their household with their alternating episodes of nightmares and flashbacks, humorously pantomiming how each would awake shaking and terrified. We then began talking about the children and had several meetings with them. By this time, Saroeun was much more actively involved with the children.

At one point Saroeun announced that she did not want to come in more than once a month because the nightmares had gone and only came back the night before she came to meet with us. We scheduled the meetings in accordance with her wishes. About 6 months later, Saroeun came in with a gift for me, a tapestry in startlingly bright fluorescent colors. She said she was feeling better and this was to thank me. By this time I was familiar enough with the culture to know that this meant she would not be coming in any more.

———————— ❧ ————————

## Difficulty Negotiating Life Cycle Transitions

Danieli (1985) and Krugman (1987) have both described the intergenerational effects of traumatization continuing into the third generation. In Cambodian families this can take the form of difficulties when the younger generation tries to separate in some way or go off to form their own nuclear family. Members of the older generation, deprived of the companionship of spouse, extended kin, or peers that they would have enjoyed in Cambodia, sometimes experience these attempts to leave as total abandonment. Because of the tradition of close extended family relationships (enmeshment is not a relevant concept in a discussion of Cambodian families), the distress of the older generation can cause the younger people enormous pain. Because families have endured so much together, there is a tremendous loyalty that can sometimes result in families accepting extremely difficult and even out-of-control situations.

For example, an elderly Cambodian widow was brought in by her two sons, ages 32 and 28, who were very concerned about her multiple somatic complaints. The oldest son told us, "When she hurts, I feel pain too." When this son went on a vacation to another city, with the intention of looking into moving there, the mother developed such terrible aches and pains that the son had to be summoned back immediately to perform coin rubbing (a traditional healing practice). She began attending regular biweekly sessions with us, sometimes with the sons and sometimes alone, and this became a place for her to talk about her aches and pains, complain about her daughter-in-law, and talk about her loneliness. In time her aches lessened and the emergency calls to her son decreased. Trips to the emergency room stopped. She became very active in a local Buddhist temple, at times spending all day there meditating and chatting with other women. It was at this point that her symptoms improved dramatically. The oldest son also reported that his life was going much more smoothly. He was no longer torn between his wife and mother.

———————— ❧ ————————

## ACKNOWLEDGMENTS

Some of the clinical material presented in this chapter is based on work done at the Indochinese Psychiatry Clinic, Saint Elizabeth's Hospital, Brighton, Massachusetts. I am indebted to Richard Mollica and James Lavelle, whose Herculean efforts to found and maintain the clinic allowed this work to be done. I would also like to express my gratitude to my Cambodian cotherapists Svang Tor, Franlinette Khuon, and Diane Kay—my windows into Cambodian culture. Working with them provided some of the most wonderful and enriching moments of my career as a therapist. I would also like to thank Saly Pin-Riebe, who reviewed the chapter for accuracy.

## REFERENCES

Danieli, Y. (1985). The treatment and prevention of long-term effects and inter-generational transmission of victimization: A lesson from Holocaust survivors and their children. In C. Figley (Ed.), *Trauma and its wake.* New York: Brunner/ Mazel.

Doepel, D. (Series Producer). (1989). *Understanding psychological trauma* [video]. Boston: Echo Bridge Productions.

Ebihara, M. (1968). *A Khmer village in Cambodia* (Doctoral dissertation). Ann Arbor, MI: UMI.

Harris, M. (1968). *The rise of anthropological theory.* New York: Thomas Crowell.

Kinzie, D. (1985). Overview of clinical issues in the treatment of Southeast Asian refugees. In T. C. Owen (Ed.), *Southeast Asian mental health.* Washington, DC: National Institute of Mental Health.

Kleinman, A. (1980). *Patients and healers in the context of culture.* Berkeley & Los Angeles: University of California Press.

Krugman, S. (1987). Trauma in the family: Perspectives on the intergenerational transmission of violence. In B. van der Kolk (Ed.), *Psychological trauma.* Washington, DC: American Psychiatric Press.

McKenzie-Pollock, L. (1988). A model for cross-cultural family therapy. In *The Newsletter.* Newton, MA: Society for Family Therapy and Research.

Mollica, R. (1989). Developing effective mental health policies and services for traumatized refugee patients. In D. Koslow & E. P. Salett (Eds.), *Crossing cultures in mental health.* Washington, DC: Sietar.

Mollica, R., Wyshak, G., & Lavelle, J. (1987, December 12). The psychosocial impact of war, trauma and torture on Southeast Asian refugees. *American Journal of Psychiatry, 144.*

Palazzoli, M. S., Boscolo, L., Cecchin, G., & Prata, G. (1981). The treatment of children through brief therapy of their parents. In R. J. Green & J. Framo (Eds.), *Family therapy: Major contributions.* New York: International Universities Press.

Westermeyer, J., & Williams, C. L. (1986). Planning mental health services for refugees. In C. Williams & J. Westermeyer (Eds.), *Refugee mental health in resettlement countries.* Washington, DC: Hemisphere.

# CHAPTER 22

# Indonesian Families

Fred Piercy
Adriana Soekandar
Catherine D. M. Limansubroto

In the 1994 film *Body Snatchers,* a frantic doctor points a pistol at a general and his military followers, all aliens who have taken over human bodies.

BODY-SNATCHED GENERAL: We traveled light-years throughout the universe, always surviving because we've learned that it's the race that's important, not the individual.

DOCTOR: The individual is always important.

ANOTHER ALIEN: Accept it.

ANOTHER ALIEN: It's a better way.

DOCTOR: (*pointing the gun*) Stand back!

GENERAL: It's a matter of survival.

DOCTOR: Stay back, stay back. I'm warning you, stay back!

GENERAL: Doc, put the gun down.

DOCTOR: You are never going to get my soul! (*The doctor then points the gun at his own head and pulls the trigger.*)

To understand Indonesian culture, it helps to see it in contrast to our own. *Body Snatchers* is a thoroughly American allegory about the primacy of individual freedom. The point, of course, is that the individual is more important than the community. Like other Asians, many Indonesians would disagree, particularly when it comes to the importance of family solidarity. Higher Indonesian values include family loyalty, obligation, and respect. Children must obey their parents. All must preserve the family's honor. Collective obligation is also reflected in the traditional practice of parents approving whom their children will marry. (A film that more positively reflects this collective influence of the family is *Age of Innocence*.)

Still, it is as dangerous to pigeonhole Indonesians as it is to generalize about Americans. This is because of the vastness and diversity of Indonesia.

## INDONESIA: A LAND OF DIVERSITY

Indonesia, formerly known as the Dutch East Indies, is a developing country in Southeast Asia that stretches over 3,200 miles of tropical ocean and spans 17,508 islands (6,000 of them inhabited). It is the land of Spice Islands; Boogeymen (pirates); Bali; Komodo dragons; and a rich history of artistic, religious, and cultural diversity. With over 190 million people, Indonesia is the fourth most populous country in the world.

Indonesia is also the world's largest Muslim nation, with almost 90% of the population registered as Muslims. However, the Muslim faith practiced in Indonesia is less doctrinal than that found in many other countries (Guest, 1992). Indeed, one can see the influences of animism (e.g., spirits within objects) and Hinduism (e.g., reincarnation) in the beliefs of many Indonesians.

Diversity among Indonesians also comes from differences in language, customs, class values, and cultural identities. There are over 100 distinct ethnic groups in Indonesia, each with its own cultural identity. Together they speak a total of more than 300 distinct languages.

One Indonesian "tall tale" highlights through humor and exaggeration the cultural variations in Indonesia. If, on a crowded bus, you were to accidentally step on an Indonesian's foot, the way the Indonesian would respond can depend on where in Indonesia he or she is from. If from East Java, the tale goes, the Indonesian might speak to you in a convoluted, respectful way about the bus being crowded, in hopes that you would realize that you are standing on his or her foot. If from Central Java, the Indonesian whose foot you're stepping on might simply smile at you and say, "I'm sorry." If from Bali, the person might silently pray for your enlightenment. If from North Sumatra, the person might shout and push you away.

Although each description stretches the truth (like saying that all New Yorkers would shoot you), the real truth in this tale is that all Indonesians are not alike. With such wide cultural differences, it is important that American family therapists learn as much as they can about their Indonesian client families. What part of Indonesia is the family from? What is the *adat*, or custom, of their ethnic group or community? How does their economic class and religion influence their values and beliefs? What is their level of acculturation or acceptance of Western values? How do they feel about coming to therapy, and what do their parents or other relatives think about their problems? In short, what is their view of the world and their place in it?

In this chapter, we will give a broad-brushed view of several Indonesian social, cultural, political, and class issues that may relate to presenting problems of Indonesian families and how best to address them. However, because of the differences among Indonesians, the reader should think of them as issues worth exploring rather than rigid formulas for intervention.

## ISSUES TO CONSIDER

### Family Closeness

Indonesians value family closeness. Until they marry, most young Indonesian adults live with their parents and extended families. Their families expect young people to stay at home, and Indonesians don't understand why so many Americans are in such a hurry to move out of their parents' house after high school. Indeed, after a young Indonesian couple I (F. P.) know gave birth to their daughter, they buried the placenta in their backyard and said a prayer in the hope that their daughter would always stay close to home (Piercy, 1991). Of course, Western values of independence will influence Indonesian youth growing up in America. When these Western values clash with more traditional Indonesian values of family togetherness, sparks can fly.

### Hierarchy

Hierarchy in Indonesian families is very important. The wife should respect and obey her husband, and the children should respect and obey their parents; all should defer to elder grandparents, aunts, and uncles. Again, problems can occur when the more egalitarian or feminist values of American culture clash with the more traditional hierarchical and patriarchal values held by some family members.

Since hierarchy is important, and since Indonesian adults may be uncomfortable—even ashamed—to be in therapy, it is important for the therapist to show all family members a good deal of respect. It will be important, for example, for the therapist to speak first to the extended family members, and not to call adults by their first names until asked to do so.

It is also important not to begin by talking with the children. In fact, in certain subcultures in Indonesia, such as traditional Javanese or Indonesian Chinese, children are not allowed to talk about their parents to outsiders, at least in front of their parents, since it might result in the parents losing face. It may be better in such families for the therapist to meet separately with the children.

## Difficulty in Being Direct

In many areas of Indonesia, it is more polite to "talk around" sensitive issues rather than to discuss them directly. To be too direct is impolite. It is important for the therapist to take time for small talk and to follow the lead of the Indonesian client in what may be a rather circuitous discussion. The therapist should also realize that "maybe," "sometime," and "yes, but" from an Indonesian may all mean "no" or "never." For some Indonesians, it is better to not say what one means than to say something that might cause the therapist or family member to lose face.

## Shame

Scheper-Hughes (1992) states that "without our cultures, we *simply would not know how to feel*" (p. 431). Indeed, culture both defines and shapes emotions. For example, the concept of shame takes different shapes across cultures. Americans often feel shame about getting older, looking older, or experiencing the infirmities of age. These are not reasons for shame among Indonesians.

However, shyness (*sungkan*) and shame (*rasa malu*) are important in understanding Indonesian behavior. Many Indonesians feel shyness in the presence of higher-status people. Similarly, anything that calls undue attention to an Indonesian—a loud laugh, a misbehaving child, or a comment that could be seen as bragging—all may illicit extreme shame (*malu*).

*Malu* can play a role in the problems that bring an Indonesian into therapy. Collins and Bahar (1995) report a case in which an Indonesian woman was brought to a psychiatric facility because her husband found her compulsively rocking back and forth in her home. In later discussions with a doctor, the woman stated that she had lost 25 pounds over the last few months. She also revealed that she lived in a small, three bedroom house with 14 other family members, did most of the laundry and cooking, and was worried about expenses. The doctor privately told the husband that he believed that the wife's strange behavior came from the exhaustion, depression, and irritation related to these living conditions. The husband was surprised, for his wife had never complained to him. Even though she did admit to the doctor (in private) that he was indeed right, she still could not express her feelings to her husband, since it would not be proper (*kurang pantas*) for her to complain. She also wanted to protect her husband from feeling *malu*. The only way she could express herself was in her symptoms. Fortunately, the husband listened to the doctors and asked several of his brothers to move from the house.

Indonesian men who are made to feel *malu* may become aggressive. An extreme example of this is seen in the syndrome known as *amok*, which is specific to the culture of the Malay world (Simons & Hughes, 1985). In *amok*, the person dissociates in reaction to extreme frustration, anger, or an affront to his honor and literally "runs amok," committing random acts of homicidal violence. However, this is rare among Indonesians today.

For many Indonesians, the problems that bring them into therapy, as well as therapy itself, may cause *malu*. Divorce, for example, is a great source of family shame. And since admitting marital problems to strangers is also a source of *malu*, Indonesians are more likely to seek therapy for child-related problems.

## Gender Roles and Homosexuality

Indonesian men are expected to marry and be the providers and leaders of their families. Muslim men in Indonesia may have up to four wives, but few do, since the husband must secure the previous wives' permission and treat each one equally (which may mean providing a separate house for each).

Indonesian women are expected to defer to their husbands and are responsible for tasks related to home and family life—cooking, housekeeping, and child care. This is true even in West Sumatra, one of the few matrilineal societies in the world, where women are the landowners and seek the man's hand (and his family's blessings) in marriage. Ideally, the Indonesian family is strong, and each member takes pride in his or her prescribed gender roles.

But what about Indonesians who are gay or lesbian? Since a heterosexual marriage is expected, some gay men marry but seek sex with men outside marriage (Stevenson, 1995). Other gay men and lesbians remain single but keep their sexual orientation hidden. The many cultural sanctions against homosexuality (i.e., religious orthodoxy; traditional beliefs about marriage, family, children, and gender; and the lack of support from friends and family) make it difficult for many gay or lesbian Indonesians to "come out," much less develop a gay or lesbian identity (Tremble, Schneider, & Appathurai, 1989; Troiden, 1991; Stevenson, 1995).

Generally, Asians have less trouble than Westerners in keeping their public and private selves separate. In order to avoid shame, their public identity must conform to gender and familial roles that are consistent with social and cultural norms. They may reveal their private selves to very few people, if anyone (Chan, 1994; Jackson, in press; Stevenson, 1995).

It is clearly easier to establish a gay or lesbian identity in America. Indonesians living in the United States, thus, are faced with the choice of keeping their same-sex sexual relationships secret, sharing their sexual orientation with a select few, or developing a more open gay or lesbian identity. We believe that any of these choices is legitimate, given the cultural context of Indonesian Americans. However, each will provide challenges that will require the therapist's support and understanding.

## Social Class

Being wealthy, middle class, or poor bring their own cultural legacies and challenges for an Indonesian. For the wealthy Indonesian who has emigrated to America for a better life, the challenges may relate to the different levels of acculturation of family members. For example, family members may have very different ideas about working hard in school, courtship, and parental respect. On the other hand, those Indonesians in the U.S. on scholarships to study for a few years will face a different set of problems. Indonesian graduate students are often separated from close family and friends. They may face returning to Indonesia with their Ph.D. to make less money and work longer hours than they did on their university assistantships.

## Political Influences

The many years of Dutch domination and the strong nationalism that exists today in Indonesia may have produced the current sensitivity of Indonesians to forms of foreign domination. In terms of therapy, Indonesians may distrust American experts who do not try to understand or appreciate their way of doing things. Clearly, Indonesians will be sensitive to being "colonized" in the therapy room. For this reason, the therapist would do well to look for ways to appreciate and empower Indonesian family members, and to provide options rather than directives. Instead of assigning homework, I (A. S.) usually suggest some tasks that my Indonesian clients "might like to try" at home. Rather than direct a client who is older than I am to do something, I always let him or her decide whether to do a particular task.

## Length of Therapy

Indonesians generally seek short-term advice when they seek therapy. At the psychology clinic at Udayana University, in Bali, the average number of therapy sessions is two. The American therapist may need to discuss the concept, purpose, and process of therapy in order to broaden the Indonesian client's conception of what can or should take place in the therapy session.

## WHAT FORM OF FAMILY THERAPY FITS INDONESIANS?

Family therapy will need to be modified to fit Indonesian families (Limansubroto, 1993; Soekandar, 1993). For example, since extended family members are so central to the lives of Indonesians, therapists should consider involving them in therapy. At the same time, many Indonesian clients do not want others, even those close to them, to know about their problems. They would rather solve them privately and may feel shame at not being able to do so.

The family therapist, therefore, will need to present therapy as something that capable, caring people engage in, foster respect for the clients, and, when appropriate, invite extended family members into the therapeutic process (but perhaps not in the same session as the primary client).

A therapy appropriate to Indonesians will also be one that is consistent with, and makes use of, their religious faith, their commitment to family, and their rich culture and customs. The family therapist needs to be a good listener and collaborative partner in the change process. For example, it would be more helpful to ask a devoutly Muslim family, "How has your religion helped you through other difficult times?" or "How can Islam help you face this issue?" rather than to either assume or ignore the personal meaning of religion in their lives.

We have found certain family therapy techniques to be particularly helpful with Indonesians. We like to use genograms, for example, to help client families see their problems in a wider context. Since some Indonesian families are enmeshed in ways that disadvantage certain family members, Murray Bowen's ideas about differentiation and taking "I positions" can be useful. Feminist discussions about differential power, exploitation, and personal agency can be helpful also, although some Indonesians might resist them if the therapist labels them as "feminist."

We also see the caring, direct communication style of Virginia Satir as a useful way to help Indonesians communicate more straightforwardly with each other. In addition, the respectful nature of many current social-constructionist family therapies seem to fit Indonesian cultural values. Reflecting teams, for example, are a great way to share different viewpoints without the Indonesian client feeling forced to conform to a particular one. Similarly, narrative and solution-focused therapies respectfully recognize and amplify an Indonesian's strengths. Home-based family therapy may also be appropriate because it allows the therapist to involve all family members, especially fathers and extended family, on nonthreatening turf.

Finally, it is important for the family therapist working with Indonesians to see the transcendent qualities that link us together. We are all more alike than we are different. Thus, the very best therapy for Indonesians—and anyone else, for that matter—is one that is both sensitive to our differences and recognizes, embraces, and nurtures our shared humanity.

## ACKNOWLEDGMENTS

We wish to thank Hadar Gumay and Tia Ali-Nafis for their feedback on a previous draft of this chapter.

## REFERENCES

Chan, C. S. (1994). Asian-American adolescents: Issues in the expression of sexuality. In J. M. Irvine (Ed.), *Sexual cultures and the construction of adolescent identities* (pp. 88–99). Philadelphia: Temple University Press.

Collins, E. F. & Bahar, E. (1995). *Malu: Shame, gender, hierarchy, and sexuality.* Unpublished manuscript, Ohio University, Athens, OH.

Guest, P. (1992). Marital dissolution and development in Indonesia. *Journal of Comparative Family Studies, 23,* 94–112.

Jackson, P. A. (in press). Kathoey × gay × man: The historical emergence of gay male identity in Thailand. In L. Manderson & M. Jolly (Eds.), *Sites of desire/economics of pleasure: Sexualities in Asia and the Pacific.* Chicago: University of Chicago Press.

Limansubroto, C. (1993). *A compilation and organization of a family therapy teaching curriculum for Indonesian university students.* Master's thesis, Purdue University, West Lafayette, IN.

Piercy, F. (1991, November/December). Of progress and palm trees: Indonesian families feel the strains of modernization. *Family Therapy Networker,* pp. 57–62.

Scheper-Hughes, N. (1992). *Death without weeping: The violence of everyday life in Brazil.* Berkeley: University of California Press.

Simons, R., & Hughes, C. (Eds.). (1985). *The culture-bound syndromes: Folk illnesses of psychiatric and anthropological interest.* Dordrecht, The Netherlands: D. Reidel.

Soekandar, A. (1993). *Selected family therapy interventions and their application in Indonesia.* Master's thesis, Purdue University, West Lafayette, IN.

Stevenson, M. (1995). *Searching for a gay identity in Indonesia.* Unpublished manuscript, Ball State University, Muncie, IN.

Tremble, B., Schneider, M., & Appathurai, C. (1989). Growing up gay or lesbian in a multicultural context. *Journal of Homosexuality, 17*(3/4), 253–267.

Troiden, R. R. (1991). The formation of homosexual identities. In J. C. Gonsiorek & J. D. Weinrich (Eds.), *Homosexuality: Research implications for public policy* (pp. 191–217). Newbury Park, CA: Sage.

CHAPTER 23

# Pilipino Families

## Emilio Santa Rita

The Philippines is a tropical archipelago of some 7,000 islands located at the crossroads of the trade routes of Asia. The islands have attracted a variety of settlers and colonizers, which is reflected in more than 80 identified dialects and in the diverse racial and ethnic characteristics of the population.

Between 700 A.D. and 1400 A.D., colonizers came in separate waves from China, Indonesia, Malaysia, Indochina, India, Borneo, and Java. Colonizers from Spain occupied the islands between 1521 and 1898. American colonizers, from 1898 to 1946, further contributed to the racial diversity and genetic pooling referred to as the "Pilipino" blend (Agoncillo & Guerrero, 1987).

The Spanish Christian missionaries instilled in the people fear of retribution, submission to authority, and resignation to divine will. American colonizers shaped the Philippine economy toward meeting America's need for a steady market and a source of cheap labor and raw materials.

There were profound psychological and cultural consequences of this form of colonialism. The Pilipino self-concept as powerless and inferior was further ingrained, and the perceived dependence on the benevolence of envied Western masters detracted from the development of a strong national identity and solidarity. Pilipinos accepted their subservient, dependent, and mendicant role, perpetuating a culture of dependency and passive resistance (Fallows, 1987). For the immigrant Pilipino community in the United States, this colonial mentality detracted from its ability to organize and assert itself, resulting in political and economic stagnation (Lott, 1976).

## PILIPINO IMMIGRATION TO THE UNITED STATES

There have been three waves of immigration from the Philippine Islands to the United States. The first wave was composed of farmworkers in the 1920s and 1930s, known as "old-timers," who found themselves the objects of racial discrimination, social segregation, economic exploitation, and even violence.

The second wave were World War II veterans and their families. This group has had difficulty adjusting to the American way of life, a problem that often leads to social isolation and alienation. They frequently found themselves assigned to menial jobs far below their training and experience. The third wave were professionals who, even now, have difficulty keeping up with the image assigned to them as members of the "model minority" (Lott, 1976).

Class separation still exists among Pilipinos in the United States. The conflict among different generations of Pilipino Americans is characterized by the clashes between traditional and Westernized cultural beliefs, values, and behaviors, and differences in communication styles. This clash of values and behavior styles also threatens many interracial marriages (Atkeson, 1970). Some traditional Pilipino values and psychodynamics conflict with the egalitarian ideals and individualism of the American society. This "cultural baggage" includes the following:

1. The primacy of family and small-group affiliation over the individual (Agpalo, 1976), a value strongly held by Pilipinos, inhibits free expression of dissent and tends to detract from the creativity and autonomy that are highly prized by Americans.

2. The strict adherence to gender-role stereotypes and patriarchal family structure goes against the egalitarian norms in the American family.

3. The primacy of smooth interpersonal relationships (SIR) conflicts with the American ideal of openness and frankness.

4. The attitude of "optimistic fatalism" (Marsella, Escudero, & Gordon, 1971), or *bahala na*, is opposed to the American beliefs in future orientation, careful planning, and the drive for excellence and economic development through determined effort.

5. The sensitivity to slights and criticism, which springs from an exaggerated need for self-importance, *amor propio*, often leads to withdrawal and/or vengeance, in direct opposition to the American style of directness and sportsmanship.

6. The dread of *hiya* (devastating shame; Bulatao, 1964) often inhibits competitiveness. This concern over face-saving is fostered by the use of ridicule and ostracism in child training.

7. Conceding to the wishes of the group (*pakikisama*) to maintain interpersonal relationships does not afford the intellectually stimulating and broadening benefits of dissent.

8. The practice of *delicadeza*, or nonconfrontational communication, most evident among females, is ineffectual in U.S. society, where directness is appreciated and competitiveness is encouraged.

9. *Utang nang loob*, or reciprocity of favors, that derives from the sentiments of gratitude and belongingness is incongruous in a society that gives primacy to individualism and the "bottom line."

10. The strict adherence to Catholic beliefs on abortion, contraception, and homosexuality contributes to a self-righteous, judgmental stance that is out of place in a pluralistic society with alternative lifestyles.

## EXPRESSIONS OF MENTAL ILLNESS

Tompar-Tiu and Sustento-Seneriches (1995) identified the most common manifestations of mental illness among Pilipinos. Among Pilipino Americans with schizophrenic disorders, paranoid symptoms predominate. As with other ethnic groups with strong supernatural orientations, influence by malevolent spirits, witches, and demons dominate the Pilipino patient's delusions. The prevalence of major depressive disorder among Pilipinos is very grossly underestimated. This is because Pilipino culture places a special premium on endurance and silent suffering (Bulatao, 1964).

Organic mental disorders are the more readily recognized and accepted mental disorders among Pilipinos. Perhaps this is because virtually every Pilipino family has had an elderly, often senescent member living at home. Medical care is, therefore, more likely to be sought relatively early in the evolution of an organically based disorder, without too much apprehension about stigma to the family.

The incidence of suicide among Pilipinos is not known. The notion of suicide as a mortal sin is very deeply engraved in the Pilipino conscience through a Catholic upbringing.

Although the use of alcohol is popular at Pilipino gatherings, alcohol abuse and alcoholism are reported to be relatively low by Western standards. Among women, alcohol use is very rare and is still generally considered to be socially unacceptable. It is equated with promiscuity and low moral standards in most circles. Although alcohol and drug use (marijuana, heroin, and cocaine) have not become a significant mental health issue, the incidence of casual use among the young is reported to be increasing. Child abuse and incest are rarely reported because children are afraid their parents will be deported or prosecuted (Tompar-Tiu & Sostento-Seneriches, 1995).

Adjustment disorders due to the process of immigration and acculturation are manifested in family and marital conflict, extramarital affairs, embarrassment and inadequacies in work situations (including perceived discrimination), estrangement from the Pilipino family, and family problems related to school and adolescent behaviors. Unemployment or underemployment weighs heavily on the the Pilipino male's sense of his own masculinity, and he frequently takes his frustration out on his spouse and children. Pilipino women internalize their frustration against male dominance by developing symptoms of depression (Araneta, 1993).

## ATTITUDE TOWARD MENTAL ILLNESS

Among Pilipino Americans, the intensity of stigma regarding mental illness is reflected by the vehemence and indignation with which the occurrence of such illness is denied, and by the lengths to which families go to hide the presence of any disorder among their members (Flaskerud & Soldevilla, 1986; Tompar-Tiu & Sustento-Seneriches, 1995).

The cultural roots of this stigma are deep and pervasive. First, Pilipinos believe that only people who are dangerously insane and socially disruptive require psychiatric care. Therefore, apprehension and disdain toward anyone believed to be mentally ill persists. Second, the notion that mental illness is indicative of "bad blood" (*na sa dugo*) or a familial disorder is very strong in the Philippines. Third, having debilitating symptoms without demonstrable physical origins is seen as reflecting weakness of will, lack of moral courage, or frailty of character (Araneta, 1993).

## RESPONSE TO THERAPY

A response consistently noted among Pilipino families reacting to a relative's mental illness is an initial refusal to accept the possibility of the illness's existence. Following the initial denial phase, the next family response consists of concerted efforts to convince the patient and themselves of the susceptibility to change of naturalistic factors that may have led to the illness. "Prescriptions" include rest cure; avoidance of mental stress; building physical and moral strength by going to church, praying, making spiritual offerings, gratifying physiological needs; indulging the patient's wishes; and encouraging thoughts of contentment and peace (Lapuz, 1978). If still no improvement occurs, a period of tolerant accommodation follows. The paramount concern is to prevent the patient from causing embarrassment to the family. Progressively stricter disciplinary measures, including isolation or seclusion in his or her room, are imposed on the patient in order to avert publicly embarrassing situations. At this point, the family begins to consider the need for external sources of help. The families that are more traditionally oriented are more likely to seek a priest, a spiritual counselor, or healer. If the ministrations of these healers do not achieve the desired results, then the patient is taken by a family elder to a family doctor. It is through the family doctor that the patient and his or her family eventually become involved with mental health workers.

## FAMILY THERAPY WITH PILIPINO AMERICANS

Family therapy, utilizing a natural group, is the treatment of choice for Pilipino families. Mental illness is perceived as social in nature, and Pilipinos seek a cure in "sociotherapy," that is, the restoration of harmonious relationship and smooth functioning in the family.

From the initial interview on, the therapist can designate the wife/mother as the "elder," a kind of cotherapist empowered in relation to the therapist. This intervention signals to the family the shift from a patriarchal, male-dominated family structure to the egalitarian pattern modeled in therapy sessions. As an "elder," she and her family can work toward getting rid of the "cultural baggage" of the Pilipino's colonial mentality. In family therapy, the themes opposed to this "cultural baggage" may be "enacted" utilizing alternative Pilipino cultural norms and practices. Enactment is a technique by which the therapist stages scenarios that suggest alternative ways of family transacting (Minuchin & Fishman, 1981). Enactments are similar to role plays and rituals familiar to Pilipinos because of their affinity for *zarzuelas* (plays) and religious ceremonies.

1. The *bayanihan* (mutual sharing) of chores, child care, and decision making may be redrawn without regard to sex-role stereotypes. The signing of this contract may be enacted in the therapist's presence, duly witnessed by him or her, and monitored in subsequent sessions as the family puts into practice the new rules in family transactions.

2. The *kapulungan ng pamfamilia* (family council) can be run such that mother and father are experienced as equally "strong" in decision-making power. The therapist stages an enactment so that mother and father rehearse until they "get it right" in presenting a "united front." Thus, children will not be able to play one parent against the other.

3. *Lakas ng loob* (assertiveness) may be enacted during the sessions in scenarios contrasting *mahinhin* (self-effacing) and long-suffering, passive behaviors of Pilipino women with assertive behavior. Assertiveness is an alternative to playing the martyr, which exacts such a high psychological price in the form of depression and other medical symptoms.

4. The therapist can encourage Pilipino families to invite teachers, counselors, nuns, and priests to come attend *fiestas* (home parties). These social contacts not only expand the family's support system but also may serve as deterrents to possible concealment of abuse or incest in the family.

5. Pilipino children's "doing their thing on their own" usually incurs parental punishment in the form of shunning, banishing, or declaring the child as "unofficially dead." The therapist may enact *despedidas* ("going-away" parties) by asking the family to bring food, going-away presents, and music to play during the therapy session. The *despedidas* legitimize the transition to independence necessary if children are to compete, succeed, and bring "honor" to the family.

6. *Pakikibaka* (to struggle) can be enacted through the popular Pilipino game of "tug-of-war," in which winning is based on strength and on outwitting the opponent. This friendly game of competition suggests that merit is an

alternative to the Pilipinos' reliance on displays of gratitude (*utang na loob*) and "personal connections" as the sole basis for recognition, achievement, and job promotion. Such a reliance is often thwarted, and Pilipino men may then take out their anger on family members.

7. *Tinikling* (a bird in a bamboo trap) is the traditional Pilipino dance simulating how the bird skips and jumps its way through clashing bamboo poles. This dance can be enacted during the session to remind the family that, like the bird (symbolizing the Philippines), it is resilient, resourceful, and can escape traps (of the Colonial masters) of any kind. This resourceful dancing-bird image suggests an alternative to maintaining *amor propio* (need for self-importance) and *hiya* (shame) at all cost. These traits are so exaggerated in both men and women that failures and disappointments lead to depression and adjustment disorders.

8. "God helps those who help themselves" is a study theme that can be enacted in a "family Bible session" as "*actively* working with God" through labor and accomplishments that "glorify" Him. This view suggests an alternative to *Bahala Na* (fatalism) that results in lack of initiative and impedes economic and social mobility.

9. *Kanya-kanya* (self-interest) can be enacted in role plays of "agreeing to disagree" and holding firm to one's position on an issue. These role plays suggest an alternative to the Pilipino's need to be overly agreeable (*pakikisama*). *Pakikisama* usually causes the use of drugs and alcohol among Pilipino adolescents who cannot resist peer pressure.

10. "In my father's house, there are many mansions" is a study theme that can be enacted in a "family Bible session" as an exercise in "hospitality"—welcoming fellow human beings. This "Christian welcome" would help Pilipinos become more accepting of other people's beliefs and lifestyles.

## CONCLUSION

Major obstacles to the mental health of Pilipino Americans stem from their sense of vulnerability over their perceived and acutely subordinate status in this society, reminiscent of their colonial history. In this situation, "enacting" opposite but functional ways for implementation will not only neutralize the family's low image of self but will also provide the family an opportunity to discover its inner strengths and resources. This discovery should help the Pilipino family gain self-respect.

## REFERENCES

Agoncillo, R. A., & Guerrero, M. C. (1987) *History of the Pilipino people* (7th ed.). Quezon City, Philippines: Garcia.

Agpalo, R. (1976). The politics of Philippine modernization. In L. Lapuz (Ed.), *Psychopathology* (pp. 17–41). Quezon City, Philippines: New Day Publishers.

Araneta, E. G. (1993). Psychiatric care of Pilipino Americans. In A. Gaw (Ed.), *Culture, ethnicity, and mental illness* (pp. 377–411). Washington DC: American Psychiatric Association.

Atkeson, P. (1970). Building communication in interracial marriage. *Psychiatry, 33,* 396–408.

Bulatao, J. (1964). Hiya. *Philippine Studies, 12,* 424–438.

Fallows, J. (1987, November). A damaged culture. *Atlantic Monthly,* pp. 49–58.

Flaskerud, J., & Soldevilla, E. (1986). Pilipino and Vietnamese clients: Utilizing an Asian mental health center." *Journal of Psychosocial Nursing and Mental Health Services, 24*(8), 32–36.

Lapuz, L. (1978). *A study of psychopathology.* Quezon City, Philippines: New Day.

Lott, J. (1976). Migration of a mentality: The Pilipino community. *Social Case Work, 57,* 165–173.

Marsella, A., Escudero, M., & Gordon, P. (1971). Stress, resources, and symptom patterns in urban Pilipino men. In W. Lehre (Ed.), *Transcultural research in mental health* (pp. 148–171). Honolulu: University of Hawaii Press.

Minuchin, S., & Fishman, C. (1981). *Family therapy techniques.* Cambridge, MA: Harvard University Press.

Tompar-Tiu, A., & Sustento-Seneriches, J. (1995). *Depression and other mental health issues: The Pilipino American experience.* San Francisco: Jossey-Bass.

# PART V

# MIDDLE EASTERN FAMILIES

.

CHAPTER 24

# Arab Families

## Nuha Abudabbeh

There is a distinct difference between Western and non-Western cultures in their perceptions and attitudes toward the concepts of psychology and the treatment of mental illness. Years of practice and research within the Arab and Arab American communities have shown that culture, religion, and even history can significantly impact a person or a society's receptiveness toward seeking assistance for psychological problems and in determining the most effective approach to treatment.

To provide a broad overview and best illustrate the fundamental differences between the Western and Arab cultures, this chapter covers their history, religion, language, the family (marriage and children), Arab Americans, and how community outreach programs are affecting treatment.

The most basic question to ask is: *Who is an Arab?*

If asked to define "the Arab Nation," most Arabs would say it includes all peoples who speak the Arabic language and claim a link with the nomadic tribes of Arabia, whether by descent, affiliation, or by appropriating the traditional ideals of human excellence and standards of beauty. This definition includes reference to a historical process that began with the preaching by Mohammed of a religion called Islam, a process in which all Arabs play a leading part and by virtue of which they can claim a unique role in the history of mankind (Hourani, 1970).

The cultural traits of modern Arabs have been impacted by several significant historical events. Although there are limitations in generalizing about a whole population, it is important to note that a new cultural entity was forged by Arab immigrants whose experience of acculturation was varied. Despite these environmental, historical, and sociological changes, Arab Americans have emerged as a cultural group with its own unique values and norms.

Today, Arab Americans and Arabs can be described as a heterogenous group that is a "multicultural, multiracial, and multiethnic mosaic population"

(Abudabbeh & Nydell, 1993). Because the term "Arab" is based on the person's language and culture and is not an ethnic origin, there is a great deal of diversity among Arabs.

# A HISTORICAL PERSPECTIVE

The period between the 7th and 10th centuries A.D. witnessed the emergence of one of the most profound and influential historical changes in the Arab World: the growth and spread of the religion of Islam. In the early 7th century, the Prophet Mohammed called upon the people of the Arabian peninsula to submit to the will of God as expressed in a book called the Qur'an. Uniting the tribes in the name of Islam, Mohammed guided them to the conquest of the surrounding countries. By the end of the century, this new empire, called the Caliphate, extended from central Asia in the east and to Spain in the west. This era saw the spread of both Islam and the Arabic language, and the building of an urban civilization.

The Arab world was dominated by the Ottoman Empire for the next four centuries (15th–19th). Upon conclusion of World War I, it was divided up among the European victors. In this latter period, Muslim states were forced to adopt new systems of government and law to face the new developing realities as first Egypt and Tunis fell under European control and were eventually followed by Morocco and Libya.

Islam's legal practices were preserved, but new thought emerged to rationalize the strength of Europe and to proselytize the merit of adopting European ideas without being untrue to Islamic beliefs and culture. A new class of Arab "intelligentsia" was created, one that was convinced of the need to adopt European ideas to improve living conditions in Arab countries. Their ideas provided the foundation for the crystallization of 19th-century Arab nationalism.

The partition of Palestine in 1948 and the creation of the state of Israel ignited a political reaction that led to the fall of most of the old regimes in Arab countries. The new regimes were committed to nationalism that aspired to the close union of all Arab countries, independence from the superpowers, and social reform in the direction of greater equality. These ideas were embodied throughout the 1960s in the personality of Egyptian President Gamal Abdel Nasser. The defeat of Syria, Egypt, and Jordan in the 1967 Arab–Israeli war halted the advance of these goals and led to a period of disunity and increasing dependence by Arab countries on one or the other of the two superpowers.

In the 1980s the Arab world witnessed the reemergence and strong expression of Islamic feelings and loyalties. This filled an identity vacuum for the uprooted urban population, providing a solid base for their lives and filling a need for their own traditions and customs as opposed to adopting those of the Western world. The 1991 Gulf War, which provoked conflict among the Arabs, was the most recent of historical events to impact Arabs and Arab Americans vis-à-vis the world and Arab nationalism.

## ARAB AMERICAN POPULATION

The Arab American population in the United States is currently estimated to be nearly three million people, who are deemed to have arrived in the United States in two distinct waves. The first wave, which came between 1890 and 1940, consisted mostly of merchants and farmers who emigrated for economic reasons from regions that were then part of the Ottoman empire. Ninety percent of this first-wave immigrant population was Christian and originated from the regions known today as Syria and Lebanon. They seem to have assimilated in their new country with a good deal of ease.

The second wave of Arab immigrants began after World War II and continues today. Unlike their predecessors, this group consists mostly of people with college degrees or those seeking to earn them. It also differs in that it came from all over the Arab world, from regions of post-European colonization, and from sovereign Arab nations. This wave, dominated by Palestinians, Egyptians, Syrians, and Iraqis, arrived with an "Arab identity" that was absent in the first wave of immigrants. With the crystallization of an Arab identity came also the practice of traditions and customs that affected either a hyphenated identity as "Arab Americans" or sometimes alienation from the majority of society. By the 1970s, the trend of easy assimilation began to change into a cultural separateness, built on political ideology centered on the Arab–Israeli conflict and based on rejecting Western norms and customs.

## RELIGION

### Islam

The essence of Islam, as preached by the Prophet Mohammed, was transmitted through the Qur'an, which is believed to be the literal word of God. In addition to the Qur'an, the laws of society were elaborated upon by adding the Prophet's own traditional sayings (*hadith*) and his practices (*sunna*). A fourth dimension was also added, taking into account certain pre-Islamic traditions and also integrating other existing societal norms and customs.

Except by implication, the Qur'an does not contain explicit doctrines or instructions; basically, it provides guidance. The *hadith* and *sunna*, however, contain some specific commands on issues such as marriage and the division of property. They also address such daily habits as how often the believer should worship God and how all people should treat each other.

Based on the general guidance of the Qur'an, five basic obligations of Muslims emerged in the form of the "Pillars of Islam." These consist of (1) oral testimony that there is only one God and that Mohammed is His prophet, (2) ritual prayer practiced five times a day with certain words and certain postures of the body, (3) the giving of alms, (4) keeping a strict fast of no liquid or food from sunrise to sundown during the month of Ramadan, and (5) holy pilgrimage to Mecca (*hajj*) once in a lifetime at a specific time of the year. A general injunction was added, *jihad*, which carries the universal meaning that every Muslim must exercise strenuous intellectual, physical, and spiritual efforts for the good of all.

## Christianity

Approximately 14 million Arabs follow the Christian faith. Lebanon contains the largest Christian population, where they comprise almost 50% of the population. Christians remain a minority in all other Arab countries, with the highest percentage in Sudan, followed by Syria, Egypt, Jordan, and Palestine. The largest Christian congregation in the Middle East is the Coptic Orthodox Church, numbering nearly six million believers, most of them in Egypt. Other Christian denominations include the Assyrian Church of the East, the Syrian Orthodox Church, the Eastern Greek Orthodox Church, the Eastern Rite Catholic Churchs, that is, the Maronite Church (predominantly in Lebanon).

Although Christians comprise only 10% of the overall Arab population, Arab Christians are described as having played a disproportionate part in the political activities of post-World War II Arab countries. This is especially true in the nationalist movement in the Middle East and in the Palestinian movement (Carmichael, 1977).

Often Christians would impress outsiders as more "Arab" than Muslim Arabs in their Arab nationalist position. Among Arab Americans it is not uncommon to find Arab Christians holding traditional and conventional attitudes toward a variety of issues synonymous to those held by Muslim Arab Americans. After World War II, most Arab nationalist movements were led by Christian Arabs. Christian Arabs in the United States are very active in fighting to oppose the negative image of Arabs in the United States and the West. Some of the most prominent spokespersons for Arabs are Christians (e.g., Professor Edward Said, Dr. Hanan Ashrawi, etc.). Christian Arabs often become quite irate about any hint of not being seen as part of the Arab community.

When the first major split in Christianity occurred (fifth century), Western church leaders affirmed the dual nature of Christ (Christ was both spirit and body) in contrast to Middle Eastern Christians, who adhered to a Monophysite definition of Christ—that he was of a single nature, divine and spiritual. The Arab Christians belonged to the Monophysites.

The Assyrians are unique in that they use neither paintings nor sculpture in worship, using a plain cross above the altar. Prayer and worship are conducted in Aramaic, the language of Christ, and are led by laymen.

The Coptic Orthodox, located primarily in Egypt but also in Ethiopia, believe that their church originated from St. Mark the Evangelist. Today the Coptic Cathedral is located in Cairo, Egypt, and the head of the Church has the title of Pope and is revered as the successor to St. Mark.

The Syrian Orthodox Church, also known as the West Syrian Church to distinguish them from the East Syrian Church, is also referred to as the Jacobites, after bishop Jacob Baradaeus. Numbering about 160,000, the Syrian Orthodox Church consider the Patriarch of Antioch in Damascus as their spiritual leader. Worship is conducted in Syriac (a dialect of Aramaic) and the sign of the cross is made with one finger, signifying their Monophysite belief.

Eastern Rite Catholics are Arab Christians who maintained their ancient languages of worship and continue their tradition and rites but have split from the rest of the Arab Christians by accepting papal supremacy and by returning to the Catholic Church. Unlike the Eastern Rite Catholics, the Maronites claim never to have been outside the Catholic Church. The Maronite church became the first Eastern church to accept papal supremacy in 1180. The Maronites have preserved their ancient Syriac liturgy, although most of their worship is conducted in Arabic (Shabbas & Al-Qazzaz, 1989).

## LANGUAGE

Albert Hourani (1970), in describing the relationship between Arabs and their language, termed them "more conscious of their language than any people in the world, seeing it not only as the greatest of their arts but also as their common good."

Arabic today is spoken by 130 million people. It was named the sixth official language of the United Nations and is ranked as the fourth most widely spoken language in the world (tied with Bengali). Although spoken Arabic is as varied as the different parts of the Arab world, classical Arabic and written Arabic are the same in all the Arab countries and are used for formal speech, broadcasting, and writing.

The Arabic language is extremely difficult and grammatically complex, its structure lending itself to rhyme and rhythm. While many other people feel an affection for their native language, Arab feeling for their language is much more intense. The Arabic language is one of the greatest Arab cultural treasures and achievements (Nydell, 1987). Because it is difficult to achieve, a good command of the Arabic language is highly admired.

## THE FAMILY

If the Qur'an is the soul of Islam, then the family can be described as the body. Although pre-Islamic Arabs found their strength in tribes, Islam emphasized the extension beyond the tribe, focusing on the *umma* and considering all Muslims as brothers and sisters belonging to the same *umma*. Within the *umma*, families are given importance as units. Men are given specific duties toward their wives and children, wives are given instructions as to how to treat their husbands, and children are advised to honor their mothers. The empowerment of the family unit reassures women of economic and emotional support within their social position in the world. Both men and women are expected to contribute to the support and maintenance of the family unit according to traditional codes of family and honor and are responsible for the rearing of children. In crisis, both also are expected to view the good of the family above the fulfillment of individual wishes.

There are today many signs of strain on the system due to factors such as industrialization, urbanization, war and conflict, and Westernization. Despite these pressures, however, the family remains the main system of support throughout the Arab world and for Arabs living elsewhere. For the majority of Arabs, as for virtually all other cultural groups, no institution has replaced the family as a support system (Fernea, 1985).

The Arab family can be described as patriarchal, pyramidically hierarchal with regard to age and sex, and extended. Despite moves toward a more Westernized nuclear family, the extended family remains important. Although families may have established their own households, they nevertheless maintain the concept of extension by considering their own kin as being worthy of the most attention, of being confided in and of being worthy of allegiance.

Bedouins are the part of Arab society that mostly came from the Arabian Peninsula and migrated to other parts of the Arab world with the spread of Islam. As opposed to city people, Bedouins are a migrant, tribal society. The family in Bedouin, rural, and urban areas constitutes the dominant social institution through which persons inherit their religion, social class, and identity. Whatever befalls one member of the family can bring either honor or shame to the whole family. Family dynamics involve a great deal of self-sacrifice and also provide satisfaction based on the happiness of others or by vicarious living through others.

Another feature of the Arab family is its style of communication, which is described by both Sharabi (1975) and Barakat (1985) as hierarchal, creating vertical as opposed to horizontal communication between those in authority and those subservient to that authority. This relationship, according to Barakat (1985), leads to styles of communication between parents and children in which parents use anger and punishment and the children respond by crying, self-censorship, covering up, or deception.

# MARRIAGE

The author's focus on Islamic regulations governing marriage derives from the fact that the majority of Arabs are Muslim, which establishes an undeniable Islamic influence on the entire society. Islam considers marriage an important duty of every Muslim and a safeguard for chastity. Marriage (*nikah*) is recognized as a highly religious, sacred ceremony, and is regarded as central to the growth and stability of the basic units of society (having moved away from the pre-Islamic tribalistic emphasis on kinship and blood relation). In Islamic law it is a contract legalizing intercourse and the procreation of children. Under Hanafi law, a Muslim man is allowed to marry a non-Muslim woman as long as she belongs to the "people of the Book," meaning either Jewish or Christian. Women, however, are not allowed to marry non-Muslims (Esposito, 1982).

Marriage is seen as a family affair, in which partners are chosen by one's family and not based on the Western concept of romantic love. However, despite some changes in this regard, this method of marriage remains the rule and romantic marriage an exception. Although the girl's opinion is supposed to be respected in accepting or rejecting a certain suitor, this is seldom practiced. In Islam, when the marriage contract is drawn, some *Sunni* sects allow the inclusion of clauses that would give women the power to terminate the marriage. Despite changes in family laws in some Arab countries, women continue to be shortchanged due to the long-standing traditional pre-Islamic and persisting post-Islamic attitudes toward women's role in society.

Practices such as endogamy continue to occur in many Arab countries where marriage within the same lineage (cousins) still is a norm. This is another indication of the fact that the family and the tribe, rather than the individual, are the basis of a community. The reasoning behind this type of marriage remains rooted in tribal tradition, which is pre-Islamic. Marriage to close kin assures the kind of economic and blood kinship needed to ensure and enhance the position of the tribe. However, studies conducted in several communities indicate that endogamy constitutes only 3–8% of all marriages and is higher among the more traditional and conventional Arab groups (Barakat, 1985).

Muslim law allows women to be contracted for marriage by their guardian (in most countries, this is their father). This is the case at all age levels, unless they have been married before. Several Arab countries, however, have enacted laws more favorable to women in this respect, allowing adult women to draw their own marriage contract. The minimum age for marriage for a Muslim girl is 15 in most Arab countries and 18 for boys (Barakat, 1985). The more education a woman has, the more likely she is to marry at an older age (Barakat, 1985).

Traditional Islamic law allows men four wives. Although the Qur'an qualifies the multiplicity of wives by stating that a man should not marry more than one unless he is able to treat them equally, the choice is left to him to determine whether to marry more than one.

In recent years, some Arab countries have forbidden the practice of polygamy (Tunisia), whereas others have required that a husband obtain a court's permission prior to taking a second wife (Iraq). In others (Lebanon and Morocco), a wife can insist on a clause in the premarital contract, giving her the option of divorcing her husband in the event he decides to take a second wife (Beck & Keddie, 1978). In practice, polygamy is rare in modern Arab societies.

Most Arab Christians belong to denominations that do not allow divorce. Among Muslims, it is permitted with certain legal stipulations. Mohammed is reported to have said, "Of all permitted things, divorce is the most abominable to God." Many verses in the Qur'an were intended to limit the frequency and facility of divorce, which existed in pre-Islamic Arabia (Esposito, 1982).

Barakat (1985) describes the divorce rate as having risen in Arab countries, attributing it to the pressures of modern life. When analyzing the divorce trend, however, it was noted that most divorces occurred in the "engagement" period or during the first 2 years of marriage. This probably is related to the nature of these marriages (i.e., arranged marriages). It may be that what Western couples are able to discover in each other before marriage is only possible for Arab couples to discover after "engagement" (which in Islam is usually a binding contract) or during the early period of marriage.

## CHILDREN

Children are raised to perpetuate the customs and traditions of the family. Methods of discipline vacillate between mild punishment for unacceptable behavior and putting fear in the child with warnings of what happens to those who do bad things. This is often accompanied by a great deal of unconditional love, especially toward the sons.

Differential treatment of boys is not uncommon, and the instilling of traditional expectations in girls is common practice. Although these trends are changing, Arab children are encouraged to maintain close ties with their families and are not encouraged, as Westerners are, to be individualistic and separate from their parents.

In the event of divorce, a woman retains custody of her children for only a limited period of time, and then places them usually with the father or the closest male relative as guardian. The age at which the mother relinquishes custody of her children varies according to the Muslim sect to which she belongs.

As the Arab family is more likely to use an authoritarian style in interaction with their children, it is not uncommon to observe that parents are more likely to lecture children than to invite them to discussion and dialogue. It is also more common for the children to respect the father's authority, and therefore they are encouraged to obey orders as opposed to exploring ideas or thoughts with him. It is more likely that the children will spend more time with their mother and are more likely to be open with her, at times using her as a messenger or go-between with their father. Therefore, there is a greater likelihood of acting out on the part of the children and also of triangulation, as opposed to open communication among all members of the family.

## ARAB AMERICANS AND MENTAL HEALTH PROBLEMS

The emphasis on family as the source of support and also the concept of the *umma* in Islam discourage Arabs from seeking professional help for their emotional problems. The likelihood of an Arab family seeking psychotherapy is even less probable. In addition to the threat of revealing much treasured family values and traditions, the therapeutic intervention may also be seen as interference with the father's authority and with religious teachings.

Since the Gulf War and a concentrated effort to educate Arabs via the medium of radio, there has been a change in their attitude about seeking professional assistance (Abudabbeh, 1994).

At the Naim Foundations, a nonprofit Arab educational, social, and health organization in Washington, D.C., a hotline for callers is available and assistance in the different dialects of the Arabic language is given. It appears Arabs are more likely to telephone for help than to come in for treatment, for problems ranging from loneliness and depression to physical abuse by spouses. Men are as likely, if not more likely, to seek treatment as women. Two other institutions, ACCESS (Arab Community Center for Economic and Social Services) and the Arab American Chaldean Community Center, both located in Detroit, Michigan (where the largest number of Arab Americans live), also have information available on Arab Americans who seek assistance.

Treatment can be enhanced if the therapist relinquishes traditional approaches, such as adherence to the most formalized aspects of conducting psychotherapy. In that vein, a therapist is more likely to be able to work with a family if he or she is willing to go to their home or is willing to talk the resisting party into coming by calling them and convincing them to come. These methods fit in with the Arab response of kinship and respect for those who make an effort, in contrast to a negative reaction to formalized relationships with caretakers.

As the Arab community in the United States continues to be pulled between Western values and its conflicting Arab customs and traditions, some of the problems its members bring to the therapist include generational conflict, in which parents have difficulty instilling Arab cultural norms and children have difficulty accepting their parents' norms; male–female issues, in which women (either as daughters or wives) insist on changes in how they are dealt with, as they see women being treated more equally in the surrounding culture; choosing a partner, in which a struggle exists between a partner that the family wants and choosing Western-style, someone a person falls in love with (a dilemma that occurs among both men and women); cross-cultural marriages, which usually present cross-cultural problems and often experience conflict over child rearing and other culturally divergent expectations.

As the community, however, becomes aware of the impact of the loss of the major support systems that were available to them in their country of origin, its members begin to see the merits of seeking help where it is available. Because of the secrecy that envelops the whole area of emotional problems, no information is available for those Arab Americans who seek help outside Arab cultural centers. For the most part, those who use American health professionals are English-speaking, more educated, and more Westernized. Arabic-speaking families turn instead, where available, to Arab-oriented services and Arabic-speaking therapists.

## ARAB AMERICANS IN THERAPY

In seeking professional help, the Arab American is usually referred by an outsider. A major deterrent to seeking help is the fear of exposing oneself to the outsider. The revelation of family secrets and the risk of exposing family shortcomings to outsiders, where any "shameful" behavior is a reflection on the whole family, makes therapy a challenge. Most Arabs approach therapy as a visit to the doctor who knows more than they do and who, in turn, will teach them how best to change the situation at home. This applies to the less-educated class, in contrast to what occurs among the educated.

In circumstances in which the family is not dealing with a clear diagnosis, such as an eating disorder or a psychotic breakdown, the family is likely to present obstacles by engaging in denial. If forced to accompany his spouse to treatment (in most cases, men are more resistant) he, unlike the uneducated parent, will challenge the authority of the therapist and compete for control of the family. Outside highly Westernized families, it is difficult to conduct family therapy with Arab families. The highly structured relationship of authority that exists between parents and children make this a difficult modality for treatment. However, to enhance treatment the therapist should use didactic and structured therapies, rather than in-depth or insight therapy, which is contraindicated. In the event a spouse or a father is unwilling to come for therapy, calling the unwilling spouse and asking him might bring the hesitant party in.

A 15-year-old Lebanese Arab American male was brought to treatment by his mother, who was an American married to an Arab. Although the children in this family were not raised as Arab Americans, during intake it became clear that the father's background had played a significant role in determining the family's methods of punishment. His role in the family contrasted to that of the mother and presented factors that further complicated the family dynamics. With a possible inherited susceptibility to depression (on the mother's side), exacerbated by the father's rejection of a Western understanding of mental illness, issues of treatment became a power struggle between the husband and wife. Despite the fact that every facility that became involved in treating either of the siblings was consistent in recommending family therapy, this never materialized. Innovative approaches were used by the therapist, such as using different dyads to deal with different issues and supplementing this with meetings of all family members whenever a crucial stage in treatment was reached. The ideal alternative of ongoing family therapy was therefore relinquished in favor of a hands-on solution of seeing the family as the situation allowed.

———————— ❧ ————————

The hierarchal and patriarchal nature of the family dynamics should be kept in mind while helping the parents to accept some new norms for the family. In dealing with Arab families, the definition of family must be expanded to encompass parents who may come to therapy with their mature, adult children.

A 38-year-old Egyptian Arab male was referred by his treating psychiatrist for psychotherapy to help him resolve his intricate family situation. Sayed had met his non-Arab wife while she was visiting his country. They fell in love and became intimate. She became pregnant and wished to have the baby, as this was possibly her last chance to have a child. She did not pressure Sayed to marry, as she was already married but separated. Sayed, however, wanted to marry her because he loved her, but also because of the pressures of obligation and blood ties to the then unborn infant. An amicable divorce occurred, following the interest of Sayed to marry the mother of his child-to-be. Certain agreements were made regarding the future right of Sayed with respect to the child. The years subsequent to the marriage and the birth of the child were years that crystallized all the differences between the couple, leading to a marriage that both parties described as pure "hell." Sayed's Arabic notion of marriage (a permanent commitment to wife and child) rendered the seemingly obvious solution of separation unfathomable.

Unconventional methods of treatment in this case included discussing the Western versus Arabic concept of marriage. Therapy sessions included such significant others as the wife, Sayed's mother, and the ex-husband, who were all part of the problem and possibly the future solution. Short of all the principles that comprise family therapy, telephone conferences and other means were used to help Sayed work through his conflicting feelings with regard to a healthy resolution of a family crisis. Sayed did not come for therapy as defined by Western norms; he came for guidance from an outsider to assist him in "fixing" his home situation. Because his English was extremely limited, the work had to be done by a counselor who spoke Arabic and was also perceived by Sayed as being an ally of his since there was a shared background and the counselor could help without trying to offer him insight into his situation.

———————— ᴈ ————————

## COUPLE THERAPY

The experience at the Naim Foundations is that, unlike other ethnic groups, Arabs are more likely to seek help for couple problems than for individual or family problems. Although families have had to be "lured" into treatment, couples have represented a steady stream of patients. This is likely due to the motivation to keep a marriage going, since divorce is frowned upon and keeping the family intact is paramount.

Problems presented by couples cover many different areas. There are those who seek help following physical or emotional abuse by the spouse, most often the husband. Other problems include couples who are unable to consummate their marriage for a variety of reasons, women whose husbands are seeking a second wife but are unwilling to give them up, and men or women who married to please their families but found they were not compatible.

Samir, a highly-educated Palestinian, was a self-referral who had spent a considerable amount of time in the West. When it was time for him to marry, he chose to please his family by marrying a woman that they decided upon. In opting to marry someone of his family's choice, Samir had given up another woman whom he had loved. The problems in the marriage began as Samir discovered that his wife was physically unattractive to him. In reality, the wife was quite attractive. As he began rejecting her and her ways, she also became critical of him but was unwilling to terminate the marriage without trying. At that point, methods for mending the marriage also caused further disagreement between the two. By the time the couple arrived for therapy, the issues between them had already polarized to a great extent, and Samir had already informed his wife about his first love. The wife was willing to come into therapy but continued to call her family to complain. The family subsequently pressured Samir to work harder at the marriage. These family pressures included attacks on seeing an outsider—the therapist. Major issues, in addition to Samir's obvious ambivalence if not rejection of the marriage, were issues such as the role of religion in the marriage, friendships, and the extent to which their families would be allowed to interfere.

Initial sessions with the couple were devoted to exploring their backgrounds and the points of difference between them, with the idea of helping them to develop better communication skills and conflict resolution. These attempts to help the couple were ineffectual, however, because both sides of the family became increasingly anxious about the failure of the marriage. With the heightened anxiety, several traditional solutions that contradicted the therapeutic process were suggested to the couple. This culminated with the wife refusing to continue therapy. The husband, however, continued his sessions to help him terminate the marriage despite family threats and pressures.

Fadwa, a Jordanian, called complaining about physical abuse. She had two children from her marriage and lived in an isolated area where she did not know any other Arabs. She did not call the police because she did not want to break up her family. In addition to physical abuse, her husband was psychologically abusive, preventing her from learning to drive or take English classes.

Initial counseling via telephone assisted Fadwa to finally approach her husband, insisting that he seek professional help with her, as a couple, threatening that she would leave him if he did not. She had been assisted to make proper arrangements with a third party with whom the therapist had also spoken. Following the threat, Fadwa came with the husband for several sessions. Home visits were made to enhance trust between the therapist and the couple. Gifts from Fadwa were accepted and an invitation to the birthday of the daughter also was accepted. These acts of hospitality and the exchange of gifts facilitated treatment for the couple, whose main problems were related to isolation. The husband had become abusive in his desperate effort to keep his family together. Initial sessions made it clear that this was a viable marriage. This was apparently an accurate assessment since the marriage has remained intact. The wife is presently driving and the husband has cooperated and made appropriate changes to make his wife feel better and consequently have a better life.

## CONCLUSION

Similar to other minorities or culturally diverse groups, Arabs are newcomers to the benefits of psychotherapy. Seeking psychotherapy is not an instinctual behavior; it is a learned behavior. The benefit of psychotherapy or psychological intervention as we see it today is the outcome of at least half a century of ongoing research and education in this country. Our sensitivities to incorporating other cultural norms into understanding the delivery of services is even more recent. Ensuring the delivery of optimal services to non-Western people calls for educating both the service providers and those who receive the services.

To provide the appropriate services, the emphasis should be put on education. The experience to date supports the impression that when Arab families, like others, become aware of the benefits of psychotherapy as an essential tool in achieving a better or less stressful life, they are good candidates for psychotherapy. As with other non-Western populations, Arabs also could benefit from changes in the approach used in the delivery of service, changes that would incorporate some of the expectations Arabs may seek from a therapist.

## REFERENCES

Abudabbeh, N. (1994). Treatment of post-traumatic stress disorder in the Arab American community. In M. B. Williams & J. F. Sommer, Jr. (Eds.), *Handbook of post-traumatic therapy* (pp. 252–263). Westport, CT: Greenwood Press.

Abudabbeh, N., & Nydell, M. (1993). Transcultural counseling and Arab Americans. In J. McFadden (Ed.), *Transcultural counseling: Bilateral and international perspectives* (pp. 261–284). Alexandria, VA: American Counseling Association.

Barakat, H. (1985). Arab families. In E. Fernea (Ed.), *Women and the family in the Middle East: New voices of change* (pp. 27–48). Austin: University of Texas Press.

Beck, L., & Keddie, N. (Eds.). (1978). *Women in the Muslim world.* Cambridge, MA: Harvard University Press.

Carmichael, J. (1977). *Arabs today.* New York: Anchor Books.

Esposito, J. L. (1982). *Women in Muslim family law.* Syracuse, NY: Syracuse University Press.

Fernea, E. (Ed.). (1985). *Women and the family in the Middle East.* Austin: University of Texas Press.

Hourani, A. (1970). *Arabic thought in the liberal age: 1798–1939.* London: Oxford University Press.

Nydell, M. K. (1987). *Understanding Arabs: A guide for Westerners.* Yarmouth, ME: Intercultural Press.

Shabbas, A., & Al-Qazzaz, A. (Eds.). (1989). *Arab world notebook.* Berkeley: Najda.

Sharabi, H. (1988). *Neopatriarchy.* New York: Oxford University Press.

# CHAPTER 25

# Iranian Families

## Behnaz Jalali

Iranian immigrants comprise a small but steadily growing ethnic group in the United States. Because many are under stress, their families may come to the attention of mental health professionals. Most Iranian families in the United States are first-generation immigrants and, thus, have many of the same characteristics as families in their homeland. They mainly come from several specific socioeconomic groups; because social class is a central factor in Iranian society, it greatly influences the nature of migration to the United States.

Social class in Iran is more clearly defined than in the United States, comprising distinct, identifiable elements (Bill, 1972). Therapists should be sensitive to these important distinctions to an Iranian family and should not assume that all Iranians identify with each other's experience. For example, the therapist should not assume that financial circumstances alone signify Iranian families' class distinctions, and they should inquire about the family background, belief in traditional values, and exposure to Western lifestyles.

Most Iranians who have migrated to the United States are generally from the elite, Westernized, educated, and business classes. They reflect, in fact, a relatively small portion of the Iranian population, which is primarily rural and agrarian. I will focus here on basic Iranian cultural characteristics that influence each person, irrespective of social class.

## WAVES OF IRANIAN MIGRATION

There have been three waves of Iranian immigrants to the United States. The first (1950–1970) was mostly from large Iranian cities. The migrants generally had an understanding of Western culture, were highly educated, affluent, and belonged primarily to the elite and professional middle-class groups. Most were engineers, doctors, dentists, teachers or scientists, and their skills allowed them to adapt well to the new culture (Adams, 1968; Baldwin, 1963).

The second wave (1970–1978) was both affluent and city oriented and came from various social classes which, during these years of economic boom and rapid growth, had become wealthy. Like the first wave, most were professionals in a good position for gaining employment and thus were usually able to remain in the social class they had enjoyed in Iran. Of 14,500 Iranian immigrants who came from 1970 to 1975, 30% held advanced degrees, including 10% who were physicians (Askari, Cummings, & Izbudak, 1977). Some were from less Westernized families more rooted in the traditional culture, and thus not as prepared to manage cultural change (Bill, 1973).

Although economics was still a major factor in this group's immigration, they also came for professional possibilities and to provide opportunities for their children (National Science Foundation, 1973) or for political reasons, such as opposition to the ruling political regime. Second-wave immigrants are scattered all over the United States, with the highest concentration in the Northern, Eastern, and West Coast urban centers.

The third wave (1978–1984) came immediately before and after the Iranian revolution, largely for personal, economic, or political security. This is a more heterogeneous group in terms of education and age, although again, most were affluent. Some have had exposure to Western culture, others have not. Unlike the first two waves, many were forced to flee Iran. Like those from any culture who are forced to do so for political or economic reasons, they experienced extreme cultural shock, alienation, frustration, and depression in adjusting to life in the United States. Some had to break ties with their families, at least temporarily. Their future remained uncertain; many had lost their social positions and power and could not practice their professions; their strong ties to their homeland made them reluctant to settle and acculturate. This group probably had the highest incidence of symptomatology. Since 1984, an even more heterogeneous group of immigrants than the third wave have continued to come.

Within a few years, many Iranians were able to acquire the necessary education, licenses, or other qualification to either continue in their professions or begin new ones. Many businesses were set up with entrepreneurs hiring other Iranian employees or seeking Iranian partners. Iranian newspapers, TV and radio stations, and yellow-pages have been created. In Southern California alone, there exist three 24-hour radio stations and multiple TV programs, which are an excellent source providing news, networking, and entertainment, especially for older immigrants. Most of these immigrants settled where they had family members or friends who could help them with the transition and provide financial and psychological support.

## NATIONAL AND PERSONAL CHARACTERISTICS

Cultural characteristics are interwoven into Iranians' everyday lives and inter-actions with family members, friends, fellow workers, and authority figures (e.g., the therapist). Given the regional and ethnic diversity among them (there are several regions in Iran that have their own ethnic characteristics, includ-ing their own dialect of the language), any collective profile has only limited applicability (Banuazizi, 1977).

Iranians have assumed several cultural characteristics to ensure their self-preservation and to cope with political instability and turmoil over centuries. They tend to be individualistic, fatalistic, and nostalgically tied to the past (Haas, 1946). Iranians are proud people who believe deeply in their uniqueness, which is rooted in Iran's history. They survived several foreign invasions and repeated internal turmoil. Repeatedly Iran has managed to absorb cultural influences without losing its own identity and continuity. Thus when the Arabs invaded, Islam was assimilated into their culture; in fact, most of the religion's rules became the governing laws of Iran. However, Iranians opted for a new branch of it, called Shiism. This differentiates them from most of the Moslem world, who are Sunnis. (Currently, 98% of Iran's population is Moslem, and 93% of these are Shiites.) Shiism, a highly emotional, mystical form of Islam, focuses on a series of martyrs: the twelve divinely designated, martyred descendants of the prophet, or the Imams.

Iran's spoken language is Persian (*Farsi*), which has Indo-European roots. Although the Arabic alphabet has been integrated into Persian writing, the language is distinctive from the Arabic spoken by Lebanese, Jordanians, and Iraquis.

Individuality and nonconformity are especially evident in the diversity of Iranians' opinions and behavior (Arasteh, 1964). Iranians' sense of individu-ality has always been so powerful that authoritarian controls were needed to ensure their allegiance and support. Rulers are authoritarian in order to guar-antee the submission and respect of their subjects. Iranians simultaneously accept authority and indirectly resist it, or they may passively accept authori-tarian treatment from their superiors and act in the same manner toward their inferiors. Iranians also express their individuality through creativity in their art, poetry, literature, and philosophy.

Iranians' cultural, historical, and individual pride may account for their boastfulness, impatience with learning, and difficulty in admitting mistakes (Zonis, 1976).

Basic to the culture is the belief that this world and its material belong-ings are not worthwhile, a worldview evident in the Sufi philosophy common in Iran that started to grow in the beginning of the ninth century. Its doctrine has some links with Islam, but it was influenced by such other philosophies and religions as Zoroastrianism, Buddhism, Christianity, and Neoplatonism, which it views as shadows of the central truth that it seeks. Sufism essentially seeks to give the individual a spiritual union with God, devoid of the rituals and intermediaries of a religious hierarchy. Through self-renunciation, spiritual realization, and concentration, the individual may reach a stage of unity with God (Arasteh, 1964). Iranian epicurean poets, such as Omar Khayyam, also express the worldview that, since life is short, we should enjoy the present; this has become part of the Iranian philosophy of life.

Iranians share the Western preoccupation with time, since their view of life is oriented to the present. Iranians greatest concern is to extract the most from the present. Plans are not necessary, since the future is either uncertain or preordained (Gable, 1959). Iranians may work 5 to 6 days a week only to spend all of their earnings on the 7th by having fun. From rapidly changing political circumstances, they have learned to live with uncertainty, distrust, and cynicism (Zonis, 1976). They also manifest mistrust in interpersonal relationships. Individuals must always be on guard to protect themselves; they fear that others will take advantage of them. Trusting relationships exist mainly with family members and lifelong friends.

Iranians usually believe deeply in fate, or *Taghdir*, they are expected to accept with grace the outcome of their lives. Their respect for strength and submission to superior forces is part of this concept (Vreeland, 1957). However, this fatalism has decreased visibly among educated Iranians over the past 30 years, as their experience has led them to believe instead that it is up to the individual to change his or her own life.

Iranians are very hospitable; guests are treated with unusual courtesy and generosity. They also tolerate verbal exaggeration (Gastil, 1958). Since Iranians try to avoid publicly criticizing or embarrassing one another, truthfulness is avoided if it hurts another (Arasteh, 1964). Rather, they express disagreement through socially acceptable humor and wit.

Friendships, which often begin in school and are close, intimate, and of long duration, are very important in Iranian culture. Friends remain loyal and are likely to meet regularly, make mutual demands, exchange favors, and have high expectations of each other. There is also a large circle of less intimate friends and acquaintances, who are an important part of Iranians' social and professional life. Iranians of both sexes are emotionally expressive people. Both men and women show their pain, anger, and affection easily. Kissing and hugging as a way of greeting are common both between men and women, but are less socially acceptable between a man and a woman. Iranians' social code prescribes correct behavioral patterns toward those in each position in the hierarchy. People of a lower rank respond to those of higher rank with deference, politeness, and respect, even though they may feel resentment and hostility toward them. Since pride and identification with one's occupation is more important than materialistic rewards, Iranians will not perform a job that they consider beneath them. For example, they usually do not perform well on assembly lines.

Iranians have a predictable pattern to resolve conflicts in families and among friends; fighting ensues and overt communication stops for days, weeks, or months. Eventually, mediators (a family member of authority, a powerful and persuasive friend, a wise elder) may be used to reconcile the parties. These mediators are extremely important, because they facilitate compromise, while allowing each party to save face by not "giving in." They arrange separate negotiations with each party and try to reach compromises. Afterward the two parties will meet and make up.

As far as cultural prejudices are concerned, Iran has historically always been in interaction with many different cultures and races and has tended to show a tolerance of different races and cultures.

## FAMILY STRUCTURE AND RELATIONSHIPS

My view here is based largely on personal, cultural, and treatment experience with Iranian families, since little formal research is available on them. In Iran the individual's total life is dominated by the family and family relationships (Gable, 1959). People rely on family connections for position, security, influence, and power. The importance of the family as a social unit for Iranians dates back to Zoroastrian times (the pre-Islam period), when rearing children and duties of children toward their parents were considered sacred.

The extended family has traditionally been the basic social unit, as befits the society's predominantly agrarian nature. In villages and tribes this pattern is crucial for survival in hard times. However, in urban areas, geographical dispersion of the extended family and differences in status and material holdings diminish the extended family's significance. Still, it has preserved its significance as an important psychological and bonding entity. Iranian society's hierarchical organization is apparent in the ascending order from family, to village, to tribe, and finally, to country (Wilber, 1963).

## The Traditional Family Structure

The traditional Iranian family unit is patriarchal: The father is the undisputed family head. Sons and their wives may live in his household or compound. An extended family consisting of a couple, their unmarried children, plus their married sons with their wives and children, is common. Old Iranian houses were built to accommodate families. A wall surrounded the home to ensure privacy, and each nuclear family had its own sleeping quarters. Many extended families continue to maintain close ties, which frequent marriages between cousins serve to strengthen.

The father has authority over his wife, children, and grandchildren; no one dares to question his decisions openly. In the extended family authority is almost always invested in the oldest man—a father who is head of his household. He may discipline his younger brothers and sisters, as well as his nieces and nephews. The patriarch's responsibility is to unify the group and to resolve internal conflicts. Religious laws define a wife's relationship to her husband as one of submission. He expects her to take care of the home and children, and her actions at home and in public should enhance his and the family's status. The father expects respect and obedience from others in the family and he, in turn, supports them materially and socially. He is expected to be a strict disciplinarian, but is also a provider of affection and love. As the only legal guardian of his children, he allows more freedom to his sons than to his daughters. At times he may make decisions for his children, even when they are adults. When the father dies, the eldest son inherits the authority and accepts responsibility for his mother and any unmarried brothers and sisters.

The mother's authority and power are more subtle and indirect and depend in part on the relationship she has built over time with her husband, sons, brothers, and the other women in the family. In public, women address men in a more reserved fashion than in private; they may add words to their names such as *agha* or *khan*, to indicate respect and formality.

The mother never openly disagrees with the father, but may use other relatives, such as her children or mother-in-law, to intervene on her behalf as she expresses her opinions or requests. Iranian women are particularly close to their children and devote much time to them. When conflict arises between father and children, the mother tries to intervene and mediate. She attempts to soften the father's attitude, while encouraging her children to respect his authority (Nyrop, 1978).

Mothers are also very affectionate toward their children, especially their sons. They attempt to persuade rather than order sons, but often dominate their daughters. Sons may show great love and devotion toward their mothers and, when married, encourage their wives to be friendly with them. If the relationship between mothers-in-law and daughters-in-law becomes conflictual, as frequently happens, the son/husband serves as mediator, a role fraught with difficulty since he is pressured to take sides and must behave wisely and diplomatically.

Relationships between brothers and sisters are complex, stemming both from their bonding and their mutual responsibility. A brother assumes the role of supporting his sister, but if she behaves inappropriately, his disapproval is as powerful as a husband's. Should a sister lose her husband, her brother automatically becomes her protector.

The most difficult relationship may be that between fathers and sons. The father continuously dominates his son but also encourages him to assume more responsibility. A son's identification with the father is strongly encouraged, because it is assumed that he will someday not only take on his father's role, but also become the head of his own nuclear family and possibly the patriarch of an extended family. This pattern stimulates conflict, since both submission and competition are expected.

## Marriage

Women are often 10–15 years younger than their spouses. In traditional families they marry at about age 16–18, although among urban modern families the age may be 22–25 or older, particularly among the most Westernized families, in which men try to develop economic independence before marriage. Financial demands are made on the man by the woman's family prior to marriage, which depend upon the family's wealth and social status. When marriage occurs, the two families become united; they join their wealth and increase their power and influence.

Generally the woman goes to live among her husband's relatives; however, she maintains close ties with her family. Conflicts among in-laws are a common source of stress. To marry, women must obtain their fathers' agreement, whereas men do not have this legal prerequisite, although it may be a moral one. Depending upon the family's social class and tradition, premarital sex for women may be viewed with disdain and contempt. If a man has premarital sex with several other women, it is tolerated, but a woman who has premarital relations becomes stigmatized as a "loose" woman.

In traditional rural and urban families, parents choose the ideal young woman for their son, arranging meetings and undertaking negotiations with her family. If these go well, a time is set for the wedding, at which time a sum of money, of *Mehr*, is guaranteed to the wife if her husband dies or divorces her. Very few meetings occur between the man and the woman until they officially marry. Their meetings are usually in the presence of the family. Arranged marriages and betrothals at birth are declining but are still common, as are marriages between cousins.

A woman gains status when she gets married, which increases further when she has a child, especially a boy (Arasteh, 1964). Sons are regarded as economic assets; Iranians desire large families with as many sons as possible. Conflicts among in-laws are a common source of stress. Men may be allowed to have as many as four wives, although with some restrictions. Polygamous marriages, although very infrequent, invariably lead to rivalries and jealousies among wives, as each competes for her husband's attention and favor. However, the first and oldest wife maintains a senior position. A Moslem man may marry a non-Moslem woman, but a Moslem woman cannot marry a non-Moslem man unless he converts. Also, men can divorce their wives, but the reverse is not true unless there is an exceptional situation. The father is the legal custodian of the children, and he retains this custody after a divorce. Once divorced, a woman has less chance of remarrying than does a divorced man, and particularly of marrying one who has not been married before.

Depending upon its wealth, the traditional family usually has a number of servants who stay with the family for years. Wealthier families may also have nannies, who take a very active role in rearing their children, and with whom a child may have a very special relationship, at times even closer than that with the mother (Arasteh, 1964).

The mother receives guidance and advice in rearing children from her mother, mother-in-law, and other relatives. Because of Iran's relatively high infant mortality rate, she may fear losing her children, as expressed in the old belief in the evil eye, which is still believed by some in the middle and upper classes. The evil eye, which explains misfortunes and focuses fear on the envy or hostility of outsiders, has both supernatural and personalized aspects. Consequently, people refrain from commenting on a child's health, beauty, or even intelligence, for fear that it may make them vulnerable to the evil eye (Arasteh, 1964).

## Child Rearing

Children, especially young boys, are the focus of attention and affection from both the nuclear and extended families and may be spoiled by aunts, uncles, and grandparents. As they grow older, they are expected to be polite and respectful toward adults. The Iranian child is typically well-mannered and can sit quietly for hours in an adult's presence.

Boys learn to respect their fathers' authority and dominance, yet are also encouraged to be assertive and independent. They tend to bully their sisters and sometimes tyrannize their mothers, but their misbehavior and aggressiveness are often affectionately praised even while they are scolded. Both parents are more permissive toward their sons than their daughters. A girl is expected to be submissive and to give in to her brother. Boys grow up believing themselves superior to girls, but, by adolescence, are strongly protective of them.

Fathers maintain discipline, which may consist of scolding or slapping. There is no specific pattern to the punishment; depending upon the father's mood, a child may be punished for a trivial misbehavior, while at other times, he or she may be laughed off or overlooked for a more serious act. For example, a child may be slapped if he or she misbehaves in public or in front of a family guest, yet in private the same misbehavior might only merit a scolding.

Since the parents' authority, especially the father's, is visible and respected, his mere expression of disapproval and scolding is quite effective, even without any spelling out of the consequences of bad behavior. Western methods of disciplining, such as withholding favorite foods or sending children to their rooms, are rarely used.

Child training involves many prohibitions that parents express repeatedly. For example, children are told to be obedient, to behave like adults, and to be quiet. However, most of the social learning occurs through experience with either a peer group or the extended family unit. Finally, it should be noted that parents consider even adult married children to be children.

## LIFE CYCLE AND TRADITION

Parents gain more respect and power as they get older. In old age, they may retain their own residence and be cared for by the children or live with one of them. In Iran there are no nursing homes. When death occurs, mourning ceremonies are an important function for the family and the neighborhood where the person has lived. Mourning is expressed quite openly, especially by women, who sometimes faint from extreme grief. The neighborhood and community are very much involved in supporting the bereaved, soothing them, bringing food, visiting, and talking with them about the deceased person.

No formal funeral homes exist, and the dead body may remain in the home for 1 to 2 days—in a secluded area of the house in the presence of a clergyman reciting prayers. Then the body is taken to the cemetery. The mourning lasts for 3 days; the family holds a memorial for the dead on the 7th and 40th days, and the first-year anniversary. When the extended family, friends, and community visit the mourners, they remember the deceased. It is generally believed that a person is judged after death and, depending upon his or her behavior in life, is sent to hell or heaven (Nyrop, 1978).

Inheritances pass from husband to wife and children, but the shares are unequal: Sons receive a full share, daughters a half-share, and the wife even less, although they can own property in their own name.

The traditional family's structure is relatively immune to conflict and tension. While to an outside observer this structure may appear as a source of conflict, the values and roles are internalized and accepted as norms, and conflicts are at a minimum. Women generally accept their husbands' dominance, at least on the surface, and complain little about it outwardly. Family loyalties and a sense of obligation go a long way. Foreigners are repeatedly astonished that Iranian women accept when their husbands bring their mothers, sisters, and other relatives to share their home.

# MODERN IRANIAN FAMILIES

Upper and middle-class families in urban areas of Iran are caught between the pull of traditional religion and culture and an acceptance of more Western family relationships. The mass media and modern schools have changed urban children's attitudes toward traditional values. However, these developments have not penetrated all levels of society, and traditional forces remain strong. In fact, they have grown since the mid-1970s.

Industrialization and urbanization have weakened parental authority and increased young adults' choice of marriage partners. Young people in particular often experience conflict between their desires for independence and their strong sense of duty toward their fathers.

Among the upper and middle classes, married men tend to establish households separate from their families of origin, perhaps even in a different neighborhood. But ties remain strong and visits frequent. The attitudes toward women remain conservative, and premarital sex is uncommon. A spouse is usually chosen from the same social group, although often with parental interference.

Western education and travel abroad have profoundly changed women's roles and have resulted in demands for change in family relationships. More women have sought higher education and many have begun working outside of the home. Modern Iranian women marry later than their traditional counterparts; with no servants, child caretakers, and housekeepers, they also have fewer children. However, although some women have entered the workforce, traditional culture retains a strong grip, and sex roles have been enormously difficult to change.

Western influences have caused families to become more oriented toward the nuclear family, which has led to a partial breakdown of the extended family. Consequently, family members have become conflicted about their obligations and sense of responsibility toward elders.

Immigrant families' stability is threatened by the many stresses they encounter and they may abandon cultural standards of behavior in favor of Western norms of more freedom of expression. There is a striving and competition to achieve more status and wealth. A father may resent his children not respecting his authority as much as he respected his parents. He may also have ambivalent feelings toward his professional wife.

Like other immigrants who have emigrated from patriarchal societies, Iranian women have gained more familial power and equality after living in the United States for several years. Iranian men, on the other hand, have not enjoyed the powerful role that they held in the family prior to immigration. The extended family network usually is no longer available to either intervene when conflicts arise or to provide a context for diluting relationship conflicts.

All of these factors have contributed to an increase in the separation and divorce rate among Iranian immigrant couples compared to the homeland. The generation gap among parents who grew up in Iran and their children who grew up in the United States has widened. Families express a great deal of conflict and ambivalence regarding adolescents and young adults, especially daughters' dating. Hardest hit with adaptive difficulties are older Iranian immigrants who lack English fluency.

The combination of loss of their social-network status, position, friends, plus cultural alienation between them and their children and grandchildren, has added to states of isolation and loneliness. There is a better chance of cultural adjustment for the children if the family has a strong and positive sense of their cultural identity and heritage as well as openness and flexibility to add on new values.

## ADAPTATION TO IMMIGRATION

Iranian families' adaptation to American culture vacillates between acculturation and holding onto the old culture (Jalali & Boyce, 1980). At times Iranians preserve aspects of their culture no matter how Westernized they are in appearance, mode of thinking, and behavior. Since Iranian immigration is so recent, it is unclear how these patterns will develop over several generations. The most common modes of adaptation are:

1. *Denigrating the old culture.* Some families sever the old ties, avoid other Iranians, and denounce the old traditions and beliefs. This amounts to an effort to deny their cultural origin by adopting the external features of American culture, including especially materialistic habits and values.

2. *Denying the new culture.* The new becomes so frightening that the old cannot be abandoned. Families turn inward, associating only with Iranians and attempting to reproduce a microculture similar to that in Iran. They eat the same foods, follow the same traditions, and criticize Western values and beliefs. However, their children become acculturated through schools and friends, and frequently develop conflicts with their parents.

3. *Biculturation.* The family attempts to integrate the two cultures and tolerates the conflict and anxiety of crossing cultural boundaries. Important attachments to the old culture are maintained, along with a productive assimilation of the new culture. Therefore, they can integrate without disrupting their basic sense of identity.

Often some family members adhere to one mode, whereas others follow another, which leaves the family prone to internal intergenerational conflicts. In the United States, family relationships remain important, although they have undergone significant transformation, with family ties less close, mainly because the extended family is not available. The father retains some of his authority; the mother, while having more social freedom, maintains many traditional patterns.

Decision making lies with the nuclear family. The extended family is informed after decisions are made, although at times they may be consulted for their special expertise. The sense of obligation to the family exists but is ambivalent.

The first wave of Iranian immigrants, due to their prior exposure to the West through education, the media, and travel abroad, adjusted easily to the new culture. They also had marketable skills and were affluent, which allowed them to survive the insecurities of a new environment. Many married Americans, which also facilitated acculturation. However, because of cultural differences, the American spouse often became a source of conflict, especially when not accepted by the Iranian spouse's extended family. Conflicts would erupt, especially when the extended family arrived for long visits. The extended family felt resentful and resented; the Western spouse found it difficult to grasp the intricate system of the Iranian extended family.

Immigrant Iranians who married Iranian spouses did better, particularly if well educated. Less-educated and more traditional Iranian spouses were less employable and did not speak English as well. They often retreated from the new experiences, while their partners were employed and fully exposed to the new environment. American-born children usually grew up with very little command of Persian language, even if both parents were first-generation Iranian Americans. (This was even more likely if one parent was American.) Children strongly influence the behavior of their parents through school and peer relationships. Children become a vehicle to acculturate their parents into the details of the new culture. Initially many second-wave families were enthusiastic and excited about immigration. But later they began to miss their extended families, neighborhoods, and communities, and felt isolated and alienated in the new culture. The second wave is particularly prone to intergenerational conflicts. Their children may attempt to dissociate themselves from the old culture, ridicule their parents, and reject ethnic food. Fathers, in particular, are threatened by these changes in their children; they may blame the new culture and criticize its values. These families are also prone to developing marital conflicts as wives welcome more social freedom, which further threatens their husbands.

The third wave of Iranian immigrant families is very prone to develop psychosocial stresses and psychological symptoms. The family's integrity and unity has been disrupted by political, ideological, and physical separation. Some fled their homeland but hope to return to it. This subgroup's traumatic entry to American culture has often been marked by disappointments, failures, and a sense of hopelessness.

When such immigrants cannot use their skills or professions, they also have financial worries, worry about their extended families back home, and have difficulty merging with their subgroup. These factors may contribute to a resistance to becoming acculturated, which makes them feel alienated from their surroundings.

Children's ability to cope with their new environment depends considerably on their parents' ability to adapt with their conflicting loyalties and anxiety. They may feel unaccepted and shy, avoid peer relationships, or may develop school problems, or delay learning the new language, which makes adaptation even more difficult. Most of these families suffer cultural, physical, and emotional isolation with concomitant anxiety and depression.

## TREATMENT ISSUES

The American therapist's lack of familiarity with Iranians' cultural expression of psychological stress and mistrustful view of outside helpers often leads to misunderstandings. This may result in problems in the therapist–patient relationship. The following segments highlight some of these issues.

Among Iranians, sadness and melancholy are seen as indicating inner depth (Good, 1985); however, depression, *Narahati*, is experienced as distress. It may be experienced in various verbal forms as well as physical ones (Pliskin, 1987) and includes such symptoms as worry, anxiety, sadness, and distress.

Problems are frequently expressed through somatization and projection. Heart symptoms such as aching, pounding, fluttering, rapid beating, pains, or discomfort, almost always reflect anxiety that can be traced to interpersonal problems, work, or worry (Good, 1976). Heart-related symptoms that reflect depressed moods are reflected in comments such as "My heart is closed in" and requests for the therapist or doctor to "open it up," which in essence means a request for sympathy and listening. The brain is the center of the mind, but the heart is the center of emotions (Good, 1976).

Weak nerves, tired nerves, shaking hands, lack of sensations, and numbness may indicate neurological problems but can be psychosomatic equivalents of depression and anxiety. General body pain, especially pain in the limbs, exhaustion, and lack of strength are also somatic symptoms, as are complaints of upper gastrointestinal pains, a weak stomach or liver, digestive problems, and vitamin deficiency.

Physical symptoms are more acceptable and less stigmatized than psychological ones. Symptomatic individuals can make demands of the family for special privileges, caretaking, or other changes in family behavior. It is thus difficult to convince them that they may have psychological problems, and therefore, it may be important not to confront them directly about the meaning of the symptoms but to accept the presenting complaint and use more subtle interventions.

Problems are also explained using outside events, people, or forces, such as grief, school failure, or heartbreak. Usually the precipitating stress is seen by the family as the sole cause of problems; they may not talk about larger cultural factors unless questioned in detail about their situation. Iranians with problems usually turn to same-sex friends or relatives for advice and support. Younger people turn to parents or older relatives; and friends gossip about problems to other relatives or friends. Only as a last resort do they turn to an outside "helper" or "doctor." By this time a whole network of people is aware of the problem, even though the confidants are all sworn to secrecy.

## THERAPIST–PATIENT RELATIONSHIPS

To understand the complex nature of the doctor–patient relationship we must appreciate its roots. Iranians are ambivalent, even mistrustful of a "helper's" expertise, although in specific instances people may have a trusting relationship with one physician, assigning him or her special healing powers. Iranians are also "doctor shoppers," going from one specialist to another, requesting medication and demanding quick results, particularly if the illness is serious or difficult to diagnose. If a cure is not imminent, the patient will visit another doctor, hoping that he or she will express a different opinion, which only increases mistrust toward the previous physician.

Ensuring family support is essential, because families take an active part in decisions about which specialist to consult, or which course to follow (Good, 1976). If satisfaction is not achieved, the family will consider sending their ill member elsewhere, even abroad, although it may disagree also with the foreign physician's diagnosis. Nonmedical health-care professionals may be treated with particular mistrust, for in Iran nonphysician professionals are not involved in direct patient care; even the nurse's role is based on a purely medical model. Noncompliance with physicians' orders is common and does not necessarily indicate rejection of a particular physician. Iranian doctors often view their patients as exaggerating symptoms and holding unscientific beliefs; thus, they frequently prescribe vitamins, minor tranquilizers, and intramuscular medications to partially satisfy patients. Iranians may have more trust in American physicians but still seek prescriptions for vitamins and for laboratory tests. Special diets that avoid certain foods, herbs, or spices have been a basic therapeutic element in traditional Iranian medicine, and patients often expect their doctors to prescribe such regimens. Indeed, when he or she does not do so, the patient may feel an incorrect diagnosis has been made. In addition, Iranians may be embarrassed to provide personal information (e.g., about sexual problems) and may screen the information they give.

## FAMILY THERAPY WITH IRANIAN FAMILIES

Reluctant about psychotherapy, Iranian families are almost always referred by an internist or family physician but do respond positively to a call for a family interview, because it deemphasizes the identified patient. The family expects the therapist to address the father first, as family head, and he or she should proceed with respect and caution in challenging patriarchal power hierarchies or role patterns to avoid alienating the family.

Every attempt should be made to involve the extended family in therapy if they are available. Most often, such invitations are accepted readily. Extended family members may act as experts on family matters during sessions; it requires therapeutic skill to ally with them and, when possible, use them as cotherapists.

Compared to Westerners, Iranians are neither conforming nor obedient patients. Although seeming to follow a therapist's suggestions and orders, they will often modify suggestions to suit their own evaluation of a situation. Iranian men, in particular, have difficulty following a female therapist's directions and recommendations, and sometimes avoid discussing painful feelings, personal concerns, weaknesses, vulnerabilities, and sexual matters with her. Women patients will use the same avoidances with a male therapist. Therefore, the therapist should address marital issues with utmost tact and scrutiny, preferably with a man and woman cotherapy team, if at all possible.

One difficult bicultural situation involves therapy with an Iranian husband and an American wife. Conflictual situations include the Iranian husband's closeness to his friends and extended family, while the American wife is comfortable with greater distance and wishes to be more independent of them. They may also clash about male–female roles and child-rearing practices. Therapists should recognize that for a successful bicultural marriage, they should help the couple to communicate across their differences so that cultural identity does not become threatened (Bateson, 1994).

A 42-year-old, first-generation Iranian physician who immigrated 12 years earlier from a middle-class family was referred with his 38-year-old American spouse because of chronic marital conflicts. They had a son, age 8, and a daughter, age 5.

The couple's relationship had been fraught with difficulty because the husband was chronically ambivalent about making a commitment to stay in the United States. He occasionally entertained serious thoughts of leaving his job and home here and returning to Iran. The husband's extended family still lived in Iran, and four or five of them at a time periodically visited the couple for months at a time, which was always a source of stress for the couple. The wife never felt accepted by her husband's relatives and resented the intrusion into their lives.

The couple also disagreed about child rearing, male–female roles, socializing, and other cultural issues. Each ridiculed aspects of the other's culture to assert his or her own values. Their son was repeatedly triangulated as each tried to bring him up their own way. The husband insisted on frequent entertaining and would spend several evenings a week with his Iranian friends. The wife wanted more time together as a family and couple. Even though the husband was quite open and Western in his thinking, he repeatedly accused his wife of being aggressive and demanded more traditional and submissive behavior from her. She demanded that he share in domestic tasks and decisions. Actually, he had adjusted and changed in response to some of these demands. When his extended family visited, he reverted to old ways, refusing to share any domestic tasks and attempting to dominate his wife.

The therapist attempted to focus the couple on their marital problems, highlighting their similarities and encouraging them to accept the differences. The husband was encouraged to teach his wife Farsi, so that she could communicate better with him and his extended family. She was urged to resolve conflicts with her in-laws on a one-to-one basis, instead of pressuring her husband. Surprisingly, his sister responded quite positively to her sister-in-law's request for privacy and control of household affairs. The wife was encouraged to ask her in-laws about recipes for ethnic food and supplies of ethnic herbs and spices, to which the extended family's response was overwhelmingly positive. She was encouraged to talk to her mother-in-law about her husband's childhood.

The husband was instructed to support his wife when she needed it but generally to let her work out her own relationship with his family. The extended family then began to accept her more and actually began to brag about her new talents. No attempts were made to decrease the number and length of the extended family's visits, but arrangements were made for relatives to visit other members of the extended family during their stays. As the two families got along better, the husband's focus on the integrity of his nuclear family became evident.

─────── ◄§ ───────

Cultural family patterns such as a mother's closeness to her children, especially to boys, and her permissive attitude toward them, should not be confronted directly. Instead, the therapist should try to strengthen the child's sibling, peer and father–child relationships, rather than weaken mother–child bonds. Similarly, the mother may be encouraged to present a united front with the father when disciplining the child. The therapist might be a mediator and use his or her power and authority to resolve conflict and unify the family group.

The most effective family therapy technique with Iranian families is either the structural or the strategic problem-oriented approach, possibly because the power–hierarchical orientation matches the culture. The Iranian family usually responds positively to directives and may actually request them.

Finally, therapists will help by encouraging their Iranian patients to ventilate their feelings, listening to them with empathy and compassion, developing an appreciation of their cultural isolation, and treating real symptoms as they emerge.

# REFERENCES

Adams, W. (1968). *The brain drain.* New York: Macmillan.

Arasteh, A. R. (1964). *Man and society in Iran.* Leiden, The Netherlands: E. J. Brill.

Askari, H., Cummings, J. T., & Izbudak, M. (1977). Iran's migration of skilled labor to the United States. *Iranian Studies, 10,* 3–35.

Baldwin, G. B. (1963). The foreign-educated Iranian: A profile. *Middle East Journal, 17,* 264–270.

Banuazizi, A. (1977). Iranian "national character": A critique of some western perspectives. In L. C. Brown & N. Itkowitz (Eds.), *Psychological dimensions of Near Eastern studies.* Princeton, NJ: Darwin Press.

Bateson, M. C. (1994). *Peripheral visions: Learning along the way.* New York: HarperCollins.

Bill, J. A. (1972). *The politics of Iran: Groups, classes and modernization.* Columbus, OH: Charles E. Marrill.

Bill, J. A. (1973). The plasticity of informal politics: The case of Iran. *Middle East Journal, 27,* 131–151.

Gable, R. W. (1959). Culture and administration in Iran. *Middle East Journal, 13,* 407–421.

Gastil, R. D. (1958). Middle class impediments to Iranian modernization. *Public Opinion Quarterly, 22*(3), 325–329.

Good, B. J. (1976). Medical change and the doctor–patient relationship in an Iranian provincial town. In K. Farmanfarmaian (Ed.), *The social sciences and problems of development.* Princeton, NJ: Princeton University Press.

Good, B. J., Good, M.-J. D., & Moradi, R. (1985). The interpretation of Iranian depressive illness and dysphoric affect. In A. Kleinman & B. Good (Eds.), *Culture and depression: Studies in the anthropology and cross-cultural psychiatry of affect and disorder.* Berkeley: University of California Press.

Haas, W. S. (1946). *Iran.* New York: Columbia University Press.

Jalali, B., & Boyce, E. (1980). Multicultural families in treatment. *International Journal of Family Psychiatry, 1*(4), 475–484.

National Science Foundation. (1973). *Immigrant scientists and engineers in the United States.* Washington, DC: Author.

Nyrop, R. F. (1978). *Iran: A country study.* Washington, DC: American University Press.

Pliskin, K. L. (1987). *Silent boundaries: Cultural constraints on sickness and diagnosis of Iranians in Israel.* New Haven, CT: Yale University Press.

Vreeland, M. M. (1957). *Iran.* New Haven, CT: Human Relations, Area Files.

Wilber, D. N. (1963). *Contemporary Iran.* New York: Praeger.

Zonis, M. (1976). *The political elite of Iran.* Princeton, NJ: Princeton University Press.

# CHAPTER 26

# Lebanese Families

## James P. Simon

*I am Lebanese and I'm proud of that . . .*
*No matter how many days I stay away*
*I shall remain an Easterner—Eastern in my manners,*
*Syrian in my desires, Lebanese in my feelings—*
*No matter how much I admire Western progress.*
—KAHLIL GIBRAN, LEBANESE AMERICAN POET
(GIBRAN & GIBRAN, 1981, p. 290)

Apart from being familiar with the political tensions of Lebanon or with this country's foods, the average American is probably largely unfamiliar with Lebanese culture. I hope that being the son of a second-generation Lebanese American family that arrived as immigrants and passed through Ellis Island in 1910 qualifies me to offer these thoughts on Lebanese families.

Prior to ancient Greek and Roman cultures, the Lebanese were known as Phoenicians and reached the height of their early civilization between 1200 and 700 B.C. One of their greatest contributions to Western culture was to teach their alphabet to people of the Mediterranean region. Lebanon in the past has been referred to as Syria when both Lebanon and Syria were part of the Ottoman Empire, but since Biblical times, Lebanon has always enjoyed a separate identity as a region, despite being under the authority of other nations and powers at various times in its history.

Lebanese citizens immigrated to the United States in two major waves: The first occurred between 1880 and 1914; the second between 1975 and 1994, when thousands fled Lebanon during the civil war. Although Lebanese Americans represent a small percentage of the overall population of the United States, they are well represented in leadership, sports, and entertainment. Among well-known Lebanese Americans are Donna Shalala, U.S. Secretary of Health and Human Services; Michael DeBakey, pioneer heart surgeon; Ralph Nader, consumer advocate; Senator George Mitchell; James Abourezk, former Senator and now head of the American Arab Anti-Discrimination Committee; Doug Flutie, 1984 Heisman Trophy winner; Casey Kasem, radio personality;

F. Murray Abraham, actor; Paula Abdul, pop singer; Danny Thomas, entertainer; Kahlil Gibran, poet/artist; and Elias Corey, 1990 Nobel Prize winner for Chemistry.

My experience has been shaped by being a Lebanese Christian, of Maronite Catholic heritage. Also, in the course of this chapter I will occasionally use the words "Lebanese" and "Arab" interchangeably when the cultural habits are similar. It should be noted, however, that "Arab" is a much more general term than "Lebanese" and may imply differences, that is, religious sects.

## FAMILY

*The mother is everything—she is our consolation in sorrow, our hope in misery, and our strength in weakness. She is the source of love, mercy, sympathy, and forgiveness. He who loses his mother loses a pure soul who blesses and guards him constantly.*

—KHALIL GIBRAN (1957, p. 92)

Identity for the Lebanese does not exist apart from the family. In fact, the proper introduction of a Middle Easterner does not end with the announcement of his name—his family group must also be established. Thus, the individual in isolation is nothing and only complete when related to his family (Kayal & Kayal, 1975). The extended family is viewed by the Lebanese as a source of both identity and strength.

The typical Lebanese views the family as an extension of him- or herself (Kayal & Kayal, 1975). Lebanese families are traditionally patrilineal, endogamous, and extended, with wide and complex kin relationships that help to sustain traditional functions of the culture. Relations between kin were, and still are, institutionalized, with obligations and rights clearly delineated. The family would assume the role of a welfare unit regarding the care of elderly relatives and orphaned or disabled kin (Hassan, Healy, & McKenna, 1975).

Kinship ties are extremely strong in all cultures of traditional Arab society. The extended family remains influential even after members have moved away to faraway cities or even overseas. Illustrative of the strength of these ties is the well-known fact that Lebanese emigrants regularly send financial contributions to their relatives back home, including both immediate and extended family members. In Patai's *The Arab Mind* (1983), the author cites the case of an Arab friend who happened to have read a news item in *The New York Times* to the effect that a first cousin of President Nixon was receiving social-welfare benefits. The Arab friend remarked to the author with utter incomprehension that such a thing would be unimaginable in his country: To support a cousin or any other relative is as much a moral duty as supporting one's own children.

An example of how family ties remain effective even after emigration overseas is clearly reflected by the Lebanese economy. In 1961, when the total merchandise exports of the country resulted in an income of 231 million Lebanese pounds, the income from emigrants' remittances was 92 million pounds, or almost 40% of the export income for the country (Patai, 1983). One Lebanese American recalls that when growing up in a working-class family, his parents sent yearly gifts of cash to relatives in the old country, despite the fact that the parents had never been to Lebanon and, in fact, had never met the relatives who were recipients of the gift.

Even in thoroughly Westernized upper-class, urban Arab families, the bond of kinship is still much stronger than anything known in the West. Arab culture can still be considered "kinship culture," and is still typified by "familism," as it has been in the past (Patai, 1983).

Members of many second-generation and third-generation Lebanese American families can remember feeling more Lebanese than American while growing up. In fact, to describe someone as behaving in an *Umircan* (Arabic word for American) fashion would tend to be derogatory. An example would be that someone (including a fellow Lebanese) might be described as acting *Umircan* for serving small portions of food at dinner, whereas a traditional Lebanese meal would be large portions. Since the civil war in Lebanon began in 1975 and brought a tremendous influx of emigrants from Lebanon to the United States, second- and third-generation Lebanese Americans have, in my opinion, come to realize that they are more acculturated into the American mind-set than originally thought and are at least as American in outlook as they are Lebanese.

For a Lebanese family or individual to move to a higher social status is very common, because they form, in large part, a mercantile class of people, and because advanced education is stressed. It is also common for a person from one social stratum to socialize with other Lebanese families or persons of a lower stratum, with friendships based in large part only upon a shared Lebanese heritage.

When Lebanese Americans need a commodity, medical care, or other services, they look first either to relatives or persons already known to them. Rather than being concerned with a doctor's credentials and training, they are more likely to seek a physician known to the family. Support is commonly derived from the extended family in times of crises. When my father had a heart attack on his 82nd birthday, in addition to the immediate family coming to the hospital, 19 other relatives took planes or drove to see him. The doctor seemed amazed by this and stated at one point that it was impossible to tell where this family ended.

An important factor for therapists to be aware of is that couple relationships in Lebanese families often focus more on children than on the partners. Mothers, even in present generations of Lebanese families, tend to be very solicitous of their children, often placing even adult children before their husbands in terms of time and attention.

The Lebanese family support system, with its large network of relatives, provides the means to borrow money to start a business or get help with staffing or expanding a business. Similarly, the network provides support in child rearing. The family in Lebanese culture provides a tremendous support system in the event of illness, disability, or financial problems. There seems to be a tremendous willingness to participate in the support or alleviation of these problems. When death strikes, the widow or widower has many visitors and will be encouraged to visit in exchange: Eating alone or spending a lot of time alone runs counter to typical Lebanese culture. As both married and widowed persons traditionally spend a great deal of time with extended family members, the experience of isolation is rare.

## FOOD, MEALS, AND DRINK

Lebanese Americans have a great affinity for the foods of their homeland, and Lebanese families in the United States place great importance on family meals and hospitality when entertaining friends and others. In fact, social events attended by Lebanese persons might well be judged solely by the variety and amount of food served at the event rather than by the more usual factors such as the size of the gathering or the backgrounds of the participants and their number.

Great expectations are placed on Lebanese mothers to cook elaborate meals for their nuclear and extended families. However, this requirement has diminished noticeably in assimilated, career-minded second-generation families. Even so, second- and third-generation Lebanese Americans who have only minimal knowledge of Lebanese culture or language frequently continue to cook and eat the foods of Lebanon. One Lebanese American relates the story of how his family judges personality traits of other Lebanese people by their cooking (e.g., the individual is "cheap" because he or she put too much bulgur wheat, the least expensive ingredient, into a *tabouli* salad, or "lazy" because he or she does not cut the stems from parsley in the *tabouli*).

The expectation of serving food was so ingrained for a *situ* (grandmother) of a Lebanese performing artist that when his grandmother traveled on a bus to New York City to meet her family for a weekend, she sent spinach pies, via Federal Express, ahead of her. Knowing that her children and grandchildren were taking her out to a restaurant for dinner, she wanted to provide something for them that was home cooked as a means of expressing love for her family.

Lebanese Americans still exhibit a traditional custom: When offered food, it is impolite to accept upon the first offer. The host is expected to offer food or drink several times before it is considered proper to accept. At the same time, if a host is not aggressive in offering food or drink to a Lebanese guest, the host is considered inhospitable. A two-part play is expected whereby the Lebanese guest denies that he or she wants anything and that the host should just sit down and chat. At the same time, the guest takes offense if not pressured to take food or drink. I remember as a child visiting a friend whose mother asked if I wanted a soda. I replied, "No thank you," and waited for her to repeat the offer. When she responded "okay" and walked away, I was offended by what I perceived to be her rudeness and lack of hospitality.

Given this ritual of expecting a host to repeatedly offer food, it is difficult to ascertain if a Lebanese guest really does or does not want anything to drink or eat. The host may believe the refusal is only politeness on the part of the guest, and that as a host, he or she must continue to press the guest aggressively to accept the offer. The Lebanese would be very critical of a person who did not display strong hospitality.

Socializing typically takes place in the home, and bars are regarded as a place for lonely, isolated people. Alcohol consumption tends to be moderate and confined to the home (Kayal & Kayal, 1975).

## LANGUAGE

For the therapist treating a Lebanese patient, several points regarding language may be worth considering. Inasmuch as the structure of the Arabic language is conducive to graceful and adorned reporting of experiences and emotions, the language also encourages exaggeration in expression, which is not conducive to scientific precision. It is important for the therapist to realize that it is the grace of the words and fluency of the expression rather than the logic of the argument and veracity of the statement that count (Khalid, 1970).

Along these same lines, anthropologist Judith Williams, in a study of youth in a Lebanese village, noted that Arabic does not easily lend itself to distinguishing between two different past time periods. Hence, for the Arab, it is of little distinction whether two past actions, events, or situations recalled were simultaneous, or if one of them preceded the other. Past events were almost one huge undifferentiated entity (Patai, 1983).

## ANGER/CONFLICT

Volatile behavior on the part of men is easily accepted in Lebanese families. Patai (1983) addresses the Arab's susceptibility to anger in discussing that demonstrating feelings under heavy affliction is not considered unmanly. The Arab "flares up easily and does not refrain from outbursts; and once aroused, his wrath has no limits" (p. 161). Patai's chapter "Control and Temper" discusses the quick change from quiet self-control to uncontrollable outbursts of temper. Sania Hamady observes that "the Arab communicates by shouting accompanied by signs of anger" (cited in Patai, 1983, p. 160). But the Lebanese quickly forget these outbursts and within short periods of time respond as if nothing has happened. Lebanese men have a particular reputation in the Middle East for cursing when upset. When aroused, they may "let loose a verbal barrage of obscene sexual abuse. . . . The slightest quarrel or disagreement can easily provoke angrily hissed references to '*qus ummak*' (your mother's vulva), followed by an exchange of even more explicit and therefore more damaging and more infuriating obscenities" (Patai, 1983, p. 135). Ayoub, in a study in a Lebanese Druze village, found that generally the important issue in a conflict is not which party is right, but rather an obligation to support your relative in the conflict, irrespective of who might be right or wrong (Patai, 1983). This goes back to the primary importance of the family, for whom justice is viewed differently. Although it would be acceptable to criticize a relative privately, a Lebanese would feel obligated to support a relative in a public conflict.

Regarding conflicts within the family, there is an expectation that one will "side" with one party in the conflict. It is generally not possible to be neutral in Lebanese family arguments. The therapist, being trained to be impartial, might need to clarify the therapist's position of neutrality, since a neutral position will generally be interpreted either as a lack of concern, opposition, or even as betrayal.

Resolution of problems between family members would generally not involve long discussions but would favor a "letting-go" period after problems are presented. Working through problems in Lebanese families is not necessarily verbal, and solutions would favor "quick-fix" types of resolution.

Issues that threaten family cohesiveness probably create the strongest reactions in terms of family conflict.

One Lebanese American patient, John A., described his family life as loving and supportive. He remembered being hit by his parents only one time at age 18 when he decided to attend a university away from home rather than a local college. They saw his decision as selfish and counter to the unity of the family.

———————— ✦ ————————

## INDEPENDENCE

*Nothing humiliates a man like being subject to someone else's authority.*
— Syro-Lebanese Proverb

*Work on Sunday and holidays, and be not in need of your fortunate brother.*
— Arabic Proverb

In Kayal and Kayal's *The Syrian–Lebanese in America* (1975), the authors discuss the Arab distrust for organization and preference for letting fate dictate the outcome of events. Syrians–Lebanese tend not to organize their communities for collective security or ethnic survival. The needs of the family and the church take precedence. Kayal and Kayal discuss the example of a Lebanese Democrat who ran for office in Bay Ridge, Brooklyn, and failed to win the election, even though the area in which he was a candidate had the largest density of Arabic-speaking people in the United States. The predominantly Republican voters in the area did not change party lines even to put one of "their own" in office.

There would appear to be a polarity, in my experience, between being independent in employment (Lebanese have frequently gone into business for themselves and constitute a mercantile class) and being independent in private life. The American ideal of "independence" in personal life is an anomaly to Lebanese culture. For the Lebanese, time outside of work is an occasion for gregariousness, hours to be spent with family members gathering in a common area of the home (i.e., the kitchen with its central table).

One factor that may inhibit strides toward independence is the enormous pressure an individual feels from both the nuclear and extended family when making independent choices that are contrary to what the family believes to be best. The extended family often does not consider it inappropriate to pressure a family member to conform to family wishes (although stated more briefly and with less authority than the immediate family). This type of behavior seems to contrast with that of many non-Arabic families, who would consider it impolite to pressure family members on major life decisions, although they may have strong opinions on the issues. Pressure and criticism from the traditional Lebanese family on an independent member can be severe.

The American ideal of expecting some "personal space" is also not valued in Lebanese culture. Consequently, privacy becomes another issue. Family members who are living together are not expected to have or need personal space. Since gregariousness as a reinforcement for family cohesion is so highly valued, wanting private time within the home (e.g., to read a book) would be considered an oddity. Watching television together or talking around the family table are the natural—and preferred—activities.

Also related to the issue of privacy is the Lebanese custom of not withholding information from each other. One second-generation Lebanese American woman described how she had to teach her children that it is acceptable not to tell everything to everyone. Along these same lines, Kayal and Kayal (1975) referred to the Lebanese and Syrians as not saying "Mind your own business," since the problems of one are the common concern of all.

An American custom that is not part of Lebanese culture would be the typically observed custom of calling on the telephone before visiting. Also related to issues of privacy would be the decision by adult sons or daughters to move into their own apartments prior to marriage. This is often met with resistance and suspicion by parents. It is not uncommon for unmarried adult children to live at home well beyond the point at which their American counterparts have set up their own households. One son relates the story of how, when setting up his first apartment, both parents told everyone they met that they were not "throwing their son out" and wanted him to stay at home. He was 25 years old at the time. Although education is highly valued, as described earlier, going away to college for the added experience of living independently might also be met with discouragement or resistance. Second-generation Lebanese Americans might feel a tremendous sense of isolation when they do leave home for college or jobs, having been acculturated to want American-style independence and success but still being tied to their traditional Lebanese society.

## RELIGION

Lebanese Christians have a strong affiliation with the church and have looked to religion as a source of their identity. According to Kayal and Kayal (1975), in both Syria and Lebanon, religion is the practical equivalent of nationality, with various religious sects being recognized within the structure of the governments.

As Lebanon has been a focus of much religious warfare for centuries, its citizens have been taught to fight for religious ideals and make a direct correlation between personal strength and religious fidelity. Along with a fierce allegiance to their religion, deeply ingrained prejudices exist regarding other religious sects, even within their own religious tradition. Much of the language of the everyday conversation of Lebanese Christians is cast in religious terms (i.e., on leaving a friend, good-bye is replaced with *Allah ma'ek* (God go with you).

## HONOR AND SHAME

The concepts of honor and shame are important in Lebanese culture. Honor (*sharaf*) is the collective property of the entire family (Kayal & Kayal, 1975). In Patai's *The Arab Mind* (1983), if any single member of a family incites dishonor, the entire family is disgraced (cited in Kayal & Kayal, 1975). Honor in the Arabic world is a generic idea that entails many different forms. For example, there is the type of honor a man receives from his virility, as shown in having numerous sons; or honor that is displayed by being employed in certain types of work and refraining from others (Patai, 1983). Honor is also closely monitored by participation in the family. If a person acts dishonorably, he or she "blackens the family name." Examples of dishonoring the family would include pregnancy outside of marriage, not supporting a relative in a public conflict, or betraying a family member in business. To act without discretion, particularly regarding matters of sexuality or sobriety, reflects upon the entire family (Kayal & Kayal, 1975). Sania Hamady observed that the barometer by which an Arab performs an action or refrains from it is judged by whether the person would be ashamed if people knew about it. "What would people say" becomes the gauge in making a choice (cited in Patai, 1983). Shame is imparted to young persons by shaming techniques, for example, comparing one child to another who is more talented and berating the child who is less talented, a technique that Hamady believes is widely used in Lebanon and Egypt (Patai, 1983). One important difference between the Arab and Western cultures concerns guilt. What pressures an Arab to "save face" is not guilt but shame, or more precisely, the psychological drive to escape or prevent negative criticism of others (Patai, 1983).

## SEX ROLES

The role of women in Lebanese culture is subordinate to that of men except in the domestic domain, where women have considerable influence and status, particularly as mothers (Hassan et al., 1985). The male has special privilege from babyhood in areas of educational, financial, and social matters (Sweet, 1974, cited in Hassan et al., 1985, p. 186). One anecdote relates the story of a Lebanese husband who bought a new house that his wife had never seen. After moving into the home, his wife maintained control over major domestic decisions such as the schedule of the family and the discipline of the children.

## MARRIAGE/DIVORCE

In Khalaf's (1976) and McKay's (1980) studies of Lebanese families in Australia, the Maronite community of Lebanese Catholics showed a high rate of endogamy: 70% in the second generation and 49% in the third generation (cited in Hassan et al., 1985). The Orthodox Christian sect also had a high rate: 55% in the first generation and 40% in the second generation. The Melkites (similar to Syrian Orthodox liturgy but under the Catholic Church), showed a much lower rate of 28% in the first generation and 16% in second generation (Hassan et al., 1985).

Divorce among the Lebanese in Australia was rare for all religious sects. The Muslim respondents did not even want to discuss it. The Druze respondents were willing to discuss it, implying that divorce was a last resort, and the Christian respondents implied that the marriage state was permanent in spite of impediments that were put in the way of it becoming pleasant or peaceful. Adultery was not seen by any group as reasonable grounds for divorce, and it was agreed that it was better to repair a marriage than to arrange a divorce. The reason given was that divorce maligned the family name and honor

(Hassan et al., 1985). The stigma attached to adultery among Lebanese Christians varies by gender. Although for women it is taboo, men are criticized for adultery but not shunned.

## AFFECTION

Open display of affection is important to Lebanese families and tactility is very common. A lack of physical tactility is often associated with emotional coldness. Displays of affection between men and between women are acceptable, and Lebanese Americans are also demonstrative in language toward family members using terms of endearment from the Lebanese language even though the person may not speak Lebanese (i.e., *yahabooboo*, or darling). Grandparents typically have entire litanies of terms of endearment that they use with their children and grandchildren.

## SEXUAL EXPRESSION

Lebanese culture is primarily male-dominated, and sex is considered primarily in terms of male privilege. The sexual expression of women is limited and defined in terms of their relation to their husbands. Although premarital sex is approved of for sons, it is frowned upon for daughters. This view of sexual expression as the domain of aggressive males is reflected in the Arab view that masturbation is far more shameful than visiting prostitutes. The reasoning is that the active sex act is at least being performed with a prostitute, whereas masturbation does not reveal an ability to perform sexually (Patai, 1983). Although Arabs might typically be shy in discussing sex publicly, they may be no different from Westerners in average onset of activity or frequency. Patai discusses how perplexing it may be for a Western person to observe the bipolarities of the Arab mind in this and so many other areas. Homosexuality is not an open issue in Lebanese society, and there are no gay or lesbian communities. The Lebanese would be reserved in regard to discussion of homosexuality. Not much is known about homosexuality among the Lebanese in general, but I suspect that a good number of gay or lesbian Lebanese Americans marry opposite-sex partners due to family pressures and expectations to have spouses and children.

## DEATH

Lebanese families are generally very expressive in their response to death, even after several generations of living in the United States. Extreme displays of emotion are common, and it is not unusual for older family members to ask the deceased to get up and perform a favored deed one last time (i.e., to *dubkee*, a Lebanese dance, or cook a favored meal). After the deceased is unable to respond to the request, the grief of the family is amplified and followed by wailing and crying. For immigrant Lebanese several decades ago, it was not uncommon to jump into the grave at the cemetery if a child had preceded a parent in death. In recent times Lebanese American reactions to death are less dramatic but still highly emotional and demonstrative. Calmness at wakes is perceived as a lack of love for the deceased, and emotional outbursts are perceived as respect for the deceased. Because of the strong bonds and emotional attachments of Lebanese families, wakes and funerals are highly charged experiences. Immediately following the death of family members, it is also common to remain with the body of the deceased until a funeral director has taken over. One Lebanese woman recounts how her aunt died on a holiday weekend and it was difficult to find a coroner. Eight members of the family felt unable to leave the hospital until a coroner arrived many hours later.

Yousef, a 38-year-old male from Lebanon, had emigrated to the United States at age 28. He came from an upper-middle-class family in Tripoli and emigrated to the United States along with his sister and brother-in-law for better job opportunities. Yousef stated that his family pressured him to marry and had "picked" a wife for him. He returned to Lebanon and met the woman; they married and returned together to the United States. One year later, the couple had a baby, followed shortly by Yousef becoming disabled in a construction accident. After he received 6 months' rehabilitation, his wife returned to Lebanon for 1 year, leaving the child in the care of Yousef, his sister, and his cousin. Yousef reported feeling pressured by his family to divorce his wife, who the family felt was not supportive of him with his disability. He entered therapy at this time on the advice of his physician, stating that he felt depressed. He also had difficulty accepting his limitations from the disability and handling his feelings about not working. In addition, he felt resentful that his family began treating him like a child since the time of the accident. His wife returned after 1 year and their relationship immediately began to deteriorate, with frequent arguments. He reported some anxiety over this and also reported feeling ashamed because he accepted financial help from his family in order to live. Yousef returned to Lebanon for a visit at this time. His in-laws requested a meeting with Yousef and his parents. It was discussed at the meeting that in light of the presenting problems with Yousef's marriage, his wife should be "obedient" to Yousef and that he should have more control over his temper and abusive language toward her. The therapist worked with Yousef to help him get more self-control. This resulted in the verbal abuse diminishing but not stopping. Family relations continued to be tense. At the therapist's recommendation, a family therapy session was arranged with Yousef, his wife, and his sister, at which some of the interpersonal strains were discussed, in addition to his sister affirming continued support for him in the future.

———————— ✦ ————————

In working with a Lebanese patient, the therapist should know that "individualism" or "leading one's own life" is not of value to a Lebanese. Family obligations, which are often extremely demanding, may take precedence over individual needs or marital expectations. The role of a wife would be to display submissiveness in public, although women typically have much influence within the Lebanese family in the privacy of the home. Among first-generation Lebanese, critical life decisions may be made by the family rather than by the individual. Among second- and third-generation Lebanese, the individual may be more strongly influenced by the family of origin than typically observed among persons of Western heritage. In addition, the Lebanese family typically provides a rich support system, assisting the individual in many areas including child rearing, care of sick or elderly members, and finances.

## ACKNOWLEDGMENTS

My thanks to Mary Saba, Nancy Pointek, Peter Skinner, Christine Archambault, Scott Nagel, Karen Haboush, Psy.D., and Catherine Kano Kikoski, Ed.D., for their suggestions and feedback.

## REFERENCES

Gibran, J., & Gibran, K. (1981). *Kahlil Gibran, his life and world.* New York: Interlink Books.

Gibran, K. (1957). *The broken wings.* New York: Citadel Press.

Hassan, R., Healy, J., & McKenna, R. B. (1985). Lebanese families. In D. Stoner (Ed.), *Ethnic family values in Australia* (pp. 173–198). Sydney: Prentice Hall.

Kayal, P., & Kayal, J. (1975). *The Syrian–Lebanese in America.* Boston: Twayne.

Khalid, M. (1976). The sociocultural determinants of Arab diplomacy. In G. N. Atiyeh (Ed.), *The conference on Arab and American cultures, Washington, D.C.* (p. 130). Washington, DC: American Enterprise Institute for Public Policy Research.

Patai, R. (1983). *The Arab mind.* New York: Scribner's.

CHAPTER 27

# Armenian Families

## Steve Dagirmanjian

Many times when meeting people, I will be asked the origin of my name. After I identify myself as Armenian, the person asking the question very often responds by telling me a story of a favorite neighbor, a close friend from college, or a helpful coworker he or she has known who was Armenian. Commonly this will be followed by a fond recounting of the various Armenian culinary delicacies that they have sampled by way of the friend. Sometimes the truly initiated will even recite an Armenian phrase or two, almost as if delivering the secret handshake of some esoteric fraternal organization. In a certain regard, that is exactly what they have done.

Living at the crossroads of competing civilizations, Armenians were perpetually overrun by powerful outside groups. For centuries a dominating theme in Armenian culture has been to maintain its unique identity while living side by side with people Armenians considered outsiders at best and, more often, enemies.

In environments such as this, there are certain adaptive benefits in assessing quickly a new acquaintance's hostile, friendly, or neutral posture. For many Armenians such "sizing up" of outsiders is almost reflexive—as basic as looking both ways before crossing the street. It is something therapists attempting to work with Armenian families would be wise to recognize. Given this ancient cultural narrative of survival and the acutely refined wariness of outsiders, and the attention to group affiliations embedded within it, it is not without some irony when someone asks an Armenian the origin of his or her name.

The counterpoint to the hypervigilance Armenians may exhibit before getting to know someone is the warmth and affection they typically shower on people whom they accept as friends. Friends visiting an Armenian family's home for the first time are often surprised by the red-carpet treatment and the "one-of-the-family" kind of acceptance they instantly receive. Sam, an Armenian college student, described how touched his best friend was by the hugs he received the first time he met Sam's parents, when the two students were home for a holiday break. The friend was received more like a member of the extended family than a guest.

The paradox of wariness versus emotional warmth and openness suggested by these brief examples is one of several that appears to characterize Armenian Americans and the often contradictory images they present. These contrasting currents of identity will be explored throughout this chapter, along with their historical antecedents and proposed clinical responses.

## HISTORY

Historically, the lands of Greater Armenia are located northeast of the Euphrates River on the high Eastern Anatolian Plateau of Asia Minor. Mount Ararat (17,000 feet), located at the eastern edge of modern-day Turkey, is considered by many Armenians to be the spiritual, as well as geographical, center of the homeland. It is here that the Bible says Noah's Ark landed.

Located in the midst of major caravan routes linking the West with the East and Middle East, Armenia was a battleground throughout most of its history, as powerful neighbors (Greeks, Romans, and Byzantines on the west, and Persians, Arabs, and Turks on the east) vied for control of its strategic lands. Regardless of who were the political rulers of the regions of Armenia in the centuries following the birth of Christ, local control essentially was dominated by a feudal system. Whether paying tribute to Roman or Persian rulers, the local Armenian feudal lords (*nakharans*) remained fiercely independent. Local rivalries abounded and the *nakharans* were constantly fighting with each other. Such was their localized focus that it was not uncommon for these Armenian feudal lords to ally with Arab or Greek forces if it might gain them an advantage over a nearby Armenian rival. As a result, Armenians never presented a unified front to outside aggressors (Der Nersessian, 1945).

This separatism was further exaggerated by Armenia's inaccessible geography and the "excessive individuality" (Der Nersessian, 1945) of its inhabitants. The skillful exploitation of these rivalries by both Arab and Greek interlopers added to the divisiveness of an already fractious people.

The "excessive individuality" is amusingly reflected in an apocryphal comment my grandfather used to make. He would say that Armenians were fierce fighters but lousy soldiers, because every private in the army thought that he knew more than the generals. So it would seem that this narrowly focused, hyperprotectionism has not always served Armenians well.

By the 15th century, Armenians were subjects of the Ottoman Empire. In an attempt to find a governmental mechanism for the Muslim Turkish rulers to coexist with their Christian Armenian minority, the Ottomans created the *millet*. Essentially, the Armenian *millet* was a separate religious, political, economic, and administrative entity that functioned independently within the

Ottoman Empire, while still under the ultimate authority of the sultans. Although this structure allowed Armenians cultural and religious autonomy, it also added to the political inequality and social distance between Armenians and the Turkish majority. The oppression and prejudice this system nurtured eventually led to Genocide early in the 20th century (Bakalian, 1993).

Another early historical event in which Armenians take great pride is the establishment of Christianity as its state religion. King Tiridates was converted by St. Gregory in 301 A.D., making Armenia the first country to adopt Christianity as its official religion (Der Nersessian, 1945). However, even with this, Armenians carved their own independent path. Rather than ally themselves with the larger Greek Orthodox Church, they maintained their own church doctrine and hierarchy. This further accentuated their separateness (for better or worse) from neighboring peoples and cultures.

A final critical element in the maintenance and development of Armenian culture as a distinct entity was the invention of the Armenian alphabet in the fifth century by the monk Menob Mashtots. His translation of the Bible paved the way for a burst of intellectual expansion that established Armenians "as part of the civilized world and consolidated their Christian identity" (Bakalian, 1993). The language and the church can be said to have provided the intertwining backbone of Armenian identity throughout centuries of living under outside domination. Many Armenians hold the language in the same kind of reverence as they do the church.

Following World War I, an independent Republic of Armenia existed for a short time (1918–1920) before becoming partitioned by its powerful neighbors, Turkey and the Soviet Union. For many years, the only "Armenia" was the Soviet Socialist Republic of Armenia. In 1991, with the dissolution of the Soviet Union, Soviet Armenia declared its independence and joined the world community as an independent nation.

## GENOCIDE

The single most defining element of 20th-century Armenian identity is the Genocide of the Armenian people, perpetrated by the Turkish government during the early part of this century. Large-scale massacres, which were begun in the 1890s at the direction of the Ottoman Sultan Abdul-Hamid, culminated in the Genocide of 1915, in which the new government of the Young Turks orchestrated the slaughter of 1.5 million Armenians. The impact of such a horror on a group who presently number approximately six million, worldwide, is incalculable. It is a rare Armenian family who has not been touched by these events (e.g., each of my four grandparents was the sole surviving sibling in his or her family). However, what keeps the Genocide alive in the hearts and minds of most Armenians today is the unyielding denial of its occurrence, maintained by the present Turkish Government.

When the Young Turk government came to power in 1908, few Armenians could have imagined the implications of the new rulers' xenophobic vision of a pan-Turkic empire, which excluded non-Turkic minorities such as Christian Armenians. Early in 1915, using the pressures of World War I to justify suppressing "subversive" Armenian activities, the Young Turk government set into motion a simple yet startlingly effective plan of mass murder. Men of fighting age were arrested, removed from their villages, and killed by the military away from populated areas. The remainder of the defenseless population of women, children, and elderly men were collected and deported out of their homelands. These "deportations" were nothing more than death marches into the desert, where the Armenians were stripped of their possessions, even their clothing, denied food and water, and subjected to attacks by marauding bandits (Miller & Miller, 1993).

The Genocide resulted in the death of approximately 1.5 million Armenians, one-quarter of the total Armenian population, worldwide. It cut through all strata of Armenian society, rending the fabric of Armenian life in unimaginable ways and imprinting its abominable spin on subsequent generations of Armenian family life cycles, which in some ways remain little diminished after 80 years.

## RESPONSES TO THE GENOCIDE

Responses to the Genocide are varied and complex. Miller and Miller (1993), in their collection of oral histories from 100 survivors of the Genocide have categorized their responses into six types: (1) avoidance and repression, (2) outrage and anger, (3) revenge and restitution, (4) reconciliation and forgiveness, (5) resignation and despair, (6) explanation and rationalization. The range of response reflects, perhaps, the difficulty inherent in attempting to move beyond an event of such enormous proportions. Herein lies another Armenian paradox. The Genocide, more than any other single aspect of being Armenian, can muster feelings of solidarity and unity among broadly disparate subgroups of Armenians. Yet, it creates intolerable dissonance for a self-reliant, industrious, and vibrant people to be identified primarily by a generations-old tragedy.

Although survivors' responses may vary according to the degree to which they were directly exposed to atrocities and are not limited to simply one category, a dominant response among many has been avoidance and repression. Apparently, many surviving children raised in Turkish families or in orphanages were discouraged from speaking about what they had seen (Miller &

Miller, 1993). Survivors I have known never mentioned the Genocide unless questioned directly about it, and then only to state in rather matter-of-fact, dismissive terms, "My father and brothers were killed by the Turks"—end of story. My maternal grandmother simply would not discuss how she came to have the tattooed cross on her wrist. Apparently Hitler's Germany was inspired by the Turks in more than one way.

Miller and Miller (1993) also say that survivors were more likely to say positive things about the Turkish people than subsequent generations of Armenian Americans. For some survivors, Turks had been instrumental in their survival, some even reporting acts of courage by Turkish citizens to resist the official policies of the government. However, in general, reconciliation and forgiveness seem to be least common among the responses, particularly among second- and third-generation Armenian Americans, primarily because of the continuing denial of the Genocide by the Turkish Government.

Non-Armenian therapists might be surprised by how deeply resistant contemporary Armenians may be to feelings of forgiveness for the Genocide. For example, many years ago, I saw a Harvard-educated hippie client in a drug program whose speech was full of love and peace and brotherhood. But when I happened to mention the assassination of a Turkish government official by a militant group of Armenians, he said he was glad, adding, "It's paying the Karmic debt, man."

The stigmatizing story of victimization and its subtle ripple through the generations is not unlike that reported by adult survivors of sexual abuse. Life has moved on, and the survivors can be functionally quite successful, but an irrational undertow of guilt and shame seems to blight their self-esteem like an oil slick untouched by the tides of time.

Boyajian and Grigorian (1986) describe a "survivor syndrome" in which survivors feel apologetic for being alive while the "good" family members died. However, I believe a subtler form of shame may be lingering with subsequent generations of Armenians. This shame, again, is more like that of the incest survivor's and may be described as the unassimilated debris of the abject humiliation of the Genocide. It is the survivor's enduring, if irrational, feeling that there is something irreparably wrong with him or her for having experienced such heinous crimes. As a result of the perpetrators' denial of responsibility and the unwillingness of the community at large to recognize the crimes, the victim's narrative of shame may burrow further from the light of discourse to remain hidden and unaltered.

Bruno Bettelheim (1979) described a similar avoidance among Jewish survivors of the Holocaust. The memories of endured atrocities do not fade, and the survivors seem to fear that if they were to talk about the past, they would once again become crushed and consumed by these horrors constantly lurking in the shadows of their present lives. Yet talking is the "cure" Bettelheim prescribes. This may be true of descendants of survivors, as well, as the story of Katchi will illustrate.

Katchi was a 44-year-old, third-generation Armenian, whose second marriage was foundering at the time she sought therapy. She felt overwhelmed by the demands of her two children and burnt out by the routine of nearly 20 years of teaching. On the face of it, her problem appeared to be a familiar one. Overresponsible, caretaking wife is unable to satisfy or engage with her emotionally aloof and exacting husband. Therapeutic efforts involving the husband yielded some early positive changes, which eased the crisis in the marriage. However, Katchi remained depressed and listless. A new therapeutic avenue presented itself when it was noticed that her depression seemed to coincide with her mother's hospitalization for emphysema. In this new conversation, Katchi, who had openly expressed pride in her Armenian heritage at the outset of therapy, now revealed more contradictory feelings. Her mother's illness had stirred memories of her grandmother, who lived with her when she was a child. Her grandmother, a survivor of the Genocide, was beset with multiple health problems—many quite real, some seemingly imagined. Katchi recalled how she felt embarrassed and smothered by the infirmed old woman's neediness and fears, by how she was different from the "American" grandmothers of her friends. Katchi was ashamed of her grandmother's broken body and spirit and hated herself for feeling so. It was not until she allowed herself to talk about how oppressed she felt by her grandmother's painful existence that she recognized the genocidal origins of her own despair. As she considered the grotesque ways in which the Genocide had twisted her grandmother's life, Katchi became less ashamed and more accepting of her grandmother and herself. Concurrently, her depression dissipated and eventually disappeared.

---

## CHURCH AND POLITICS

As mentioned earlier, Armenia was the first country to adopt Christianity as its state religion. As in many ancient cultures, church and state were not separate. The church served as the hub of cultural and political activities almost as much as it served as a religious center.

In the early 19th century, a small proportion of the Armenian population left the "mother church" to become Protestants and Catholics, due to the proselytizing efforts of Roman Catholic and New England Protestant missionaries (Bakalian, 1993). These three different denominations, Apostolic, Catholic, and Protestant, remain active today in the United States; the Apostolics being by far the largest group, and Catholics the smallest.

These denominational categories are further divided by political affiliations. Through much of the 20th century, Armenian politics have largely been defined by the conflict between militant proponents of Armenian nationalism (the Tashnag Party) and advocates of accommodation with the Soviet Union (the Ramgavar and Hunchag Parties). Each side believed that their philosophy was best suited to preserving the integrity of Armenian culture in a hostile world. The factionalism was further accentuated by periodic outbreaks of violence, the most infamous being the assassination of the Armenian Archbishop of New York in 1933 by members of the Tashnag Party. This resulted in the development of a separate Tashnag wing of the Armenian Apostolic Church.

The divisiveness continues to have practical consequences for generations of Armenians far removed from the politics of their homeland. Typically, Armenian families will attend American churches of various denominations before attending a nearby Armenian church of the wrong political persuasion. Once, while attending the funeral of an old family friend, I was reminded of the immediacy of these old political squabbles, which are largely irrelevant to most latter-generation Armenians. As an old friend of the deceased was delivering a heartfelt eulogy, I began to hear a strange noise coming from the gathered mourners. Several old women were literally hissing their disapproval as the speaker had made reference to the deceased's past political activities.

Another significant aspect of the Apostolic Church is its flexibility with regard to doctrinal beliefs. Again, individuality is encouraged. The church does not strictly enforce rules of observance. This religious tolerance seems to be balanced by moral values among the families of the church community that are quite conservative (Bakalian, 1993). Behavior that dishonors the family is likely to be more strongly censured than the religious implications of a misdeed. A paradox emerges again—Armenians are religiously liberal while being morally conservative.

In some circles the Armenian Church has come under criticism. Critics claim its chief function has become the promotion of Armenian nationalism, whereas its theology has not evolved since the Genocide. It has been said that the Church functions more like a social club and less as a place for spiritual guidance (Guroian, 1987). Many Armenians, who will attend church picnics and enjoy the Armenian food and music, attend non-Armenian churches because the theology seems more relevant to their current spiritual needs.

## IMMIGRATION

Although there are records of Malcolm the Armenian in the Jamestown Colony in 1618, the first significant influx of Armenian immigrants to the United States did not occur until the 1890s when the first wave of massacres in the Ottoman Empire began. From that time until 1924, when an immigration quota system was instituted, tens of thousands of Armenians immigrated to the United States (Bakalian, 1993). The great majority of these immigrants were survivors, directly or indirectly, of the Genocide and the deportations.

In addition to the personal tragedies the newcomers brought with them, they were ill prepared for the demands of a complex, industrialized society, coming as they did from a largely agrarian culture. Their integration into their new home was further hindered by the particularly hostile intolerance for differences prevailing at the time. Yet most Armenian immigrants felt enormous gratitude for their host country and attempted to demonstrate their appreciation by working hard and becoming good citizens.

The second significant wave of Armenian immigrants came following World War II. Another spurt came in 1965, when the quota law was liberalized. Unlike the first immigrants, these Armenians were not survivors of the Genocide and were not coming from the ancestral homeland. They were coming from a variety of the Armenian diasporan communities that had been established following the Genocide in Syria, Lebanon, Greece, France, and elsewhere. These immigrants were generally better prepared to face the exigencies of life in their new home than earlier Armenian immigrants (Bakalian, 1993).

The hardships of settling in a new country and culture are obvious. Nevertheless, Armenians were quick to establish their own connections with each other apart from the majority American culture. Accustomed as they were to preserving their ethnic identity while coexisting with alien cultures, Armenians quickly established fraternal organizations, built churches, and created schools to teach the Armenian language and history in a formalized way to their children. The strong Armenian community became and remains testimony to Armenian cultural pride, as well as being a resource for sustaining it.

The most recent groups of Armenians to come to the United States came following the earthquakes in Soviet Armenia in 1988 and also following the conflict between Soviet Armenia and Soviet Azerbajian over the Nagarno-Karabagh region. This conflict resulted in a modern massacre of Armenians in Baku in January 1990 at the hands of the Muslim majority (Bakalian, 1993). These refugees tended to be middle- to upper-middle-class business people and professionals.

All too predictably, the new arrivals have not been entirely well received by the established Armenian American community. The older community disapproves of what it sees as the arrogant and pushy behavior of the newcomers. The newcomers are often disdainful of the established community's degree of Americanization. Although the Armenian Church has attempted to foster integration between the groups, relations remain strained among them (Sungarian & Guglielmo, personal communication, September 15, 1994).

The earlier immigrants settled primarily in the urban industrial centers of the Northeast and the Midwest—where the jobs were. A small percentage settled in California. Now 600,000–800,000 Armenians are more widely distributed throughout the United States. However, Los Angeles currently is clearly the favorite location of newcomers.

The early immigrants tended to be better educated than immigrants from other countries arriving at the time. Many were skilled artisans or experienced businessmen. Armenians have been referred to as "middlemen minorities" (Bakalian, 1993) because their economic pursuits have been in activities that are liquid and transportable, typical of a merchant class.

Armenians quickly were recognized in their new country for their intelligence and industriousness. For this they escaped the standard ethnic slurs of the time of ignorance and laziness. Instead, a pejorative stereotype of the wily, self-serving, overambitious Armenian was created to account for the group's relative economic successes (Bakalian, 1993). Ironically, these are some of the same criticisms that Armenian Americans have directed at more recent Armenian immigrants from the Middle East and the former Soviet Union (Sungarian & Guglielmo, personal communication, September 15, 1994).

Being hardworking and self-sufficient are clearly cornerstone values for most Armenians. A story common to many Armenian families is how they managed to get through the Great Depression without relying on public assistance.

## THE FAMILY

The traditional, pre-Genocide family structure usually consisted of several generations living together within one household (often within a one-room household). The family was strongly patriarchal, with the elder males dominating the affairs of the family. Marriages were arranged, and new brides were expected to live with the husband's family, where they were clearly subservient to the eldest female in the household (Miller & Miller, 1993). With the division of labor along gender lines, the eldest woman could often be a formidable figure within the family, because of her accrued authority over household matters within the overarching patriarchal structure.

After the Genocide, widows sometimes filled the void as the family elder, because so many of the men had been killed. Clearly, the family remained patriarchal, and the eldest males' authority was not challenged, although there were more instances of family situations in which female voices held sway. Stories abound among latter-generation Armenians about the centrality of beloved grandmothers in their childhood households (Bakalian, 1993).

One second-generation Armenian woman recognized the roots of her own precocious feminism, while warmly recalling days spent with her grandmother as a child. Her grandmother's household was among the poorest in a neighborhood of poor families. The meagerness of what she had to give to her children and grandchildren was further limited by her autocratic husband's self-ishness. His allowance to his wife for food and clothing for the family was given only after he had reserved sufficient money for cigars and gambling (cards and backgammon) at the local Armenian club. This grandmother, who had nothing of her own, was always sharing whatever she did have with neighbors, even temporarily taking in people who had become homeless. The woman recalled wanting to spend all her time with her grandmother. She also recognized as she told her story that kindness such as her grandmother's, in that male-dominated culture, reflected an entire life given over to sacrifice. Her grand-mother had no life of her own by today's standards, and yet she left an indelible mark on many of those who knew her. The storyteller realized that her own quiet resistance to the traditional role expectations of her as an Armenian woman owed much to what her grandmother "gave" her. She had, for example, been earning her own income for more than 40 years.

The close-knit nature of contemporary Armenian families has not diminished much from the days of their ancestors, when the nightly activity consisted of sitting around the circular fireplace (*tonir*) eating and talking (Miller & Miller, 1993). The needs of the family always took precedence over individual needs, and the importance of maintaining a strong sense of family honor was continually reinforced. Armenian children were taught not to bring shame (*amot*) to the family name. The precedence of family over individual needs seems to be maintained among present-day Armenians as well. This was a sentiment to which 80% of Armenian respondents agreed in a recent survey (Bakalian, 1993). Clinicians most often see these values reflected when young adult children have difficulty separating from their parents, as in the example of David, which follows.

Living among hostile majority cultures for many, many years, Armenians developed strong prohibitions against marrying non-Armenians. Obviously, this was a significant aspect of preserving their distinctive culture against the forces of assimilation. This value has not been preserved among subsequent generations of Armenian Americans, for whom marrying outside the group is quite common. In Soviet Armenia, where there was little church influence, marrying non-Christian ethnics, unheard of in the past, has become rather common.

As Armenians have become more assimilated in mainstream American culture, formerly self-defining aspects of ethnicity, such as language spoken or church attended, are no longer universally common to all Armenian Americans. One survey of Armenian Americans revealed that the higher their income or educational level, the less likely they were to speak Armenian (Bakalian, 1993). External expressions of ethnicity, such as language or religion, are no longer automatically predetermined but now are much more a matter of choice. Bakalian (1993) refers to this phenomenon as "symbolic ethnicity." She further explains that it is the middle and upper-middle classes of Armenian Americans who are the chief arbiters of these chosen expressions of ethnicity, whether it be through black-tie fundraisers, the food served at church bazaars, or the scholarships and grants awarded to Armenian American scholars.

Historically, Armenian attitudes regarding sexual mores have been quite conservative and consistent with the familiar male–female double standard. Part of maintaining the family honor involved ensuring the "purity" of the women in the family. Women who had "been around" were not considered good marriage material. In general, however, both men and women tend to be "shy" when interacting with the opposite sex (Bakalian, 1993).

Views about homosexuality among Armenian Americans would be expected to vary according to generation, with older generations being less accepting than younger generations. In this way, Armenian attitudes are unlikely to be very different from popular American cultural values. However, in those families in which negative biases against homosexuality exist, it is likely that the family would encourage secrecy in its gay family member. Preserving the family honor would likely be a greater concern than any personal biases for or against homosexuality itself. A gay family member willing to maintain secrecy about his or her homosexuality could still be regarded as a loved, although misguided, part of the family by family members having negative biases. In all probability, an Armenian choosing to be open about his or her homosexuality would encounter much more conflict within the family than his or her secretive counterpart.

Armenians have shown the greatest affinity toward those ethnic groups with whom they have the widest exposure and the most in common. Social-distance indicators show that Armenian Americans are closest by friendship or marriage to White Americans of European ancestry. They have been particularly close with Italians and Jews, whose travails as immigrants most resembled their own. Despite Armenians' own experiences with bigotry, they are no less racist as a group than other Whites (Bakalian, 1993).

As one might expect within a culture in which great respect was afforded elders, families tended to be adult-centered, with children conforming to needs of the parents. Nevertheless, children have always been highly valued members of the family and especially so following the Genocide. Children came to be seen as "special" in the sense that they carried the hopes and dreams of a ravaged generation into the future. In this light, life is seen by these children as "serious business," and comes with an implicit sadness (Boyajian & Grigorian, 1986).

*Housom,* the Armenian word for a deep feeling of sorrow and sadness, seems to be an unarticulated legacy many of these "special children" unconsciously embrace. As one of my boyhood Armenian friends put it when asked why he, who was usually so boisterous and joyous, seemed so sad, "The sadness is as much a part of being Armenian as is breathing."

Bettelheim (1979) noted a similar vein of emotional intensity among Holocaust survivors. The intensity seems to potentiate the ebb and flow of expectable feelings associated with ordinary life events. The resulting forcefulness of emotions can sometimes become unmanageable. This is evident in Armenian families in which the usual kinds of ambivalent feelings about family members, or struggles between generations or among siblings, are experienced in enormously powerful ways, and small differences are often played out as if major stakes were in the balance.

## THERAPY WITH ARMENIAN FAMILIES

The recent postmodern trend toward a narrative style of family therapy seems to lend itself well to incorporating elements of ethnicity into the therapeutic dialogue. Narrative approaches assume that personal meaning emerges from the intersubjective crucible of one's social environment. The therapeutic conversation, therefore, is oriented toward recognizing the contextual points of meaning within which a client's self-narrative takes form. As the client's own attributions of meaning are encouraged, themes with ethnic origins have the opportunity to be noticed and developed.

In our group at the Catskill Family Institute in Kingston, New York, we emphasize client narratives that are consistent with what we call the client's preferred view of self. People are, of course, more at ease when their preferred view (or ideal sense of self) is consistent with how they think others see them. It is when their preferred views and others' views are contradictory that problems tend to develop (Eron & Lund, 1993). This is obviously a major issue with Armenians, as described earlier, when they sense that others do not acknowledge their history. When therapists acknowledge clients' preferred views, problems seem to diminish; when their comments conflict with clients' preferred views, problems intensify. We find this a helpful guide in conducting therapeutic conversations that are sensitive to our clients' sense of their ethnic identity. I hope that this will be demonstrated through the following case examples.

Not surprisingly, Armenians are unlikely to see psychotherapy as a way of dealing with their problems. The idea of paying someone else for "advice" runs counter to centuries of self-reliant individualism and may even be considered shameful or dishonorable. When Armenians come into therapy, it is probably because they are in extreme distress or there is some external pressure. They will probably present themselves as in better shape than they actually are. An assumption of a viable therapeutic contract should not be made simply because an appointment has been made, as the case with Arikel will show.

Arikel was a maintenance man for the county's administrative offices and the only son of Genocide survivors. He was approaching retirement after 28 years of valued service to the county, when he suddenly began to demonstrate erratic behavior. He was missing work frequently, his work was sloppy and incomplete, and his attitude toward coworkers and the public had become increasingly belligerent. When he had a screaming match with one of his bosses, he had gone too far. This always irascible but beloved employee was given the ultimatum of going to an Employee Assistance Program counselor or losing his job. After stomping out of the counselor's office, his boss gave him one last chance, and he reluctantly agreed to try a second therapist.

The second therapist's questioning did not start out with the assumption that Arikel ("Call me Ace") had a "problem." Instead he expressed curiosity about the circumstances that brought him to the office. This elicited a diatribe, recounting 28 years of county governmental incompetence and how his division head was a phony son of a _____. The therapist took pains to acknowledge Ace's references to how hard a worker he had always been, even when most of his coworkers didn't do half of what he did. Only after the therapist asked how someone as obviously savvy as Ace was about how the civil service game was played did Ace say that he hadn't been himself at work for months. On inquiry, the therapist learned that Ace had never been married but had always lived with his mother, who had died about a year earlier.

Ace could not tolerate being considered needy or incompetent. It was only after the therapist joined with his preferred view of himself as a savvy, hard working person that he could acknowledge the incongruities of the picture he was presenting. Only then could a meaningful treatment contract around his unresolved grief be established and a constructive course of therapy be started. Like many Armenians, Arikel was not about to allow just anyone to be a witness to his grieving for his mother, whom he regarded as an almost saintly figure. Further exploration indicated Arikel and his mother had been the only survivors of their village in Armenia, and his pride in himself as a worker, as a son, and as an Armenian were all part of the same intense life experience.

Armenian preferred views were threaded throughout the course of therapy also in the following case about a son's difficulty leaving home.

Mary made a panicked phone call for help after her 19-year-old son, David, had revealed to her that he had been having suicidal thoughts. David had recently dropped out of college and returned home, where he was working part-time at a local sporting goods store, feeling defeated and depressed. In the first session, the therapist faced a sullen David, a worried Mary (a legal secretary), and her testy husband, Mike, a manager for IBM. Clearly, the men, who were used to getting their own way, did not want to be there, but in a matter of such gravity, Mary would not take "no" for an answer and insisted they come.

David had been an excellent student and athlete in high school. He had been Mike and Mary's pride and joy. Initially he seemed happy at the prestigious college he attended, although a bit bothered by the more modest nature of his achievements. However, over time his dissatisfaction grew and with it the intensity of his parents' advice to him, until he abruptly dropped out of school to everyone's great dismay.

To these second-generation Armenian parents, this turn of events represented a failure of their entire family. All three of them felt out of place as they sat stiffly in my office—confused, hurt, and angry. Recognizing that pride in family and closeness of the family were highly regarded virtues in this Armenian family, I chose a conversational path that accentuated the strengths of this close-knit unit, rather than assuming, as some therapists might, that David's problem stemmed from the family being too enmeshed.

While in college, David had perceived his parents' worry about how he was doing as disappointment. As he came to believe he was failing them, he withdrew further into himself and did worse. His parents perceived his withdrawal as lack of caring about them and what they had taught him. In separate meetings with the parents and with David, I developed a narrative of a young man who had lost confidence, rather than someone who had stopped caring for his family. I described to the parents how much David respected their achievements and feared he could not do nearly as well. With David, I commented on the ambitious plans he had loosely formulated to move away and try another school as evidence that the family ethos of achievement had not left him, rather than dwelling on his frustration with his low-paying job.

Fortified with the understanding that they were the best people to be giving David confidence boosts when he doubted himself, the parents were able to calmly encourage him to finish the semester at his new school when he again wavered in his belief in himself. This supportive nudge from his parents was enough for David to overcome his crisis in confidence and move forward in his life.

By respecting the family's high regard for closeness and utilizing it rather than trying to circumvent it, I was able to help the family help themselves. This allowed them to address David's problem in a manner that remained consistent with their ethnically preferred value of self-reliance.

A final example is of a young, fourth-generation Armenian American woman and her Italian American husband. Again, recognizing preferred ethnic qualities suggested a productive avenue for the therapeutic dialogue.

Ani came into therapy with her husband, Anthony, because she feared her marriage of 3 years was in jeopardy. Although both she and Anthony readily professed their continued love for each other, their arguments had become more frequent and increasingly vile. Ani was mortified at how quickly she would say things that she knew would hurt Anthony. Anthony, a strong, silent type, indicated his refusal to capitulate to his wife's tactics by stubbornly withdrawing into silence. Ani had come to fear that Anthony did not care about her, whereas Anthony believed Ani had to have things her way.

In reviewing how they had become a couple, I learned that the quality to which each of them was most attracted in the other was their willingness to state frankly what was on their minds. Ani, like her ancestors before her, put great stock in her own counsel and did not want to be a deferring wife like her mother was with her father. Anthony knew he was strong-willed and believed he would be unhappy if he had a wife he could dominate as his father had dominated his mother. They quickly got their fighting under control when I observed that they had not made mistakes about each other as they had feared, but that sparks were the inevitable consequences of choosing strong-minded partners. Ani and Anthony then acknowledged that their goals usually were the same, but their approaches differed. Accepting their differences as a good thing, they began discussing how they could express their differences without hostility.

---- ⋟ ----

Identifying ethnically preferred views of self pointed the way to a common ground (Dagirmanjian, Eron, & Lund, 1993) around which the remainder of the couple's therapy was organized. Consistent with her Armenian heritage, Ani highly valued thinking for herself but did not wish to be an Armenian wife like her mother, always deferring to her husband. Anthony had approached their marriage with very similar values. When they recognized their bickering was the by product of what they preferred in each other and not the result of a flaw in either one of them, they were able to address their expectable differences with each other more collaboratively and less adversarially. As these preferred elements of their ethnic identities (i.e., pro-independent thinking and anti-inequality) were respectfully identified, accentuated, and threaded through a mutually acceptable narrative of the marriage, solutions began to emerge.

## CONCLUSION

Probably the single most difficult obstacle to achieving a successful therapeutic experience with Armenian families is getting beyond their heightened wariness of outsiders, coupled with their reflexive self-reliance. Establishing meaningful reasons to meet is essential. Even if a therapist should be able to demonstrate his or her trustworthiness, it may be hard for an Armenian family to believe that a therapist could tell them something they do not already know about themselves. The therapist who successfully engages Armenians in therapy, more often than not, has been "reminding" them of what they already know but may have overlooked in the midst of life's exigencies. In essence, that is what was done in each of the case examples. Arikel would not reveal the pain of his loss to a therapist until his knowledge and competence had been acknowledged. David and his parents interacted more constructively around his leaving-home difficulties only after their closeness as a family was emphasized as a strength and a resource upon which to draw. Katchi was unable to move forward in her life before she realized that her feelings of shameful ambivalence about her Armenianness were an unwanted and unnecessary legacy of the Genocide. By noticing aspects of the clients that were consistent with their preferred ethnic values, the therapists were able to foster feelings of agency that allowed the clients to try alternative solutions to their problems.

As obstreperous as Armenians often may be, there are no people warmer and more devoted to those whom they have accepted into their lives. As Ace was leaving my office at the end of his final session, and after he had emotionally expressed his gratitude for my help, he turned and gave me an expression of genuine puzzlement and stated with total sincerity, "You know, you're a lot smarter than you look."

## REFERENCES

Bakalian, A. (1993). *Armenian-Americans: From being to feeling Armenian.* New Brunswick, NJ: Transaction Publishers.

Bettelheim, B. (1979). Afterword. In C. Vegh, *I didn't say goodbye* (pp. 161–178). New York: E. P. Dutton. (Translated by R. Schwartz, 1984)

Boyajian, L., & Grigorian, H. (1986). Psychological sequelae of the Armenian Genocide. In R. Hovannisian (Ed.), *The Armenian Genocide in perspective* (pp. 177–185). New Brunswick, NJ: Transaction Publishers.

Dagirmanjian, S., Eron, J., & Lund, T. (1993, August). *Mapping the path to narrative common ground with couples.* Paper presented at 101st Annual Convention of the American Psychological Association, Toronto, Canada.

Der Nersessian, S. (1945). *Armenia and the Byzantine Empire.* Cambridge, MA: Harvard University Press.

Eron, J., & and Lund, T. (1993). How problems evolve and dissolve: Integrating narrative and strategic concepts. *Family Process, 32,* 291–309.

Guroian, V. (1987). Incarnate love: *Essays in orthodox ethics.* Notre Dame, IN: University of Notre Dame Press.

Miller, D., & and Miller, L. T. (1993). *Survivors: An oral history of the Armenian Genocide.* Berkeley: University of California Press.

# PART VI

# ASIAN INDIAN FAMILIES

# CHAPTER 28

# Hindu, Christian, and Muslim Families

## Rhea Almeida

The culture of Asian Indians is one that is most "other" to Western cultures. It is a culture that exists within a context of contradictions. Although women are devalued in everyday life, they are also revered in the scriptures. The goddess Durga/Kali is most sought after as well as feared by men, who feel powerless before her. It is often said that cows have a more prominent place than women in daily life. However, the Indian Constitution, unlike the American Constitution or subsequent legislation, provides for equality between the sexes. Yet another contradiction is the fact that Indians have already had a woman Chief of State, Prime Minister Indira Gandhi.

With a population of 800 million people, India is the largest democracy in the world. Tolerance and diversity are central to the Asian Indian culture, as significantly embodied in Hindu beliefs (Almeida, 1990). Some of the most important of these have been embraced in the teachings of Mahatma Gandhi: "Not to hurt any living thing is no doubt a part of Ahimsa. But it is its least expression. The principle of Ahimsa is hurt by every evil thought, by undue haste, by lying, by hatred, by wishing ill to anybody. It is also violated by our holding on to what the world needs" (Gandhi, 1983, p. 4).

Ahimsa is the philosophy of nonviolence toward all living things—the avoidance of killing any living being for food or other purposes. It also embodies the notion of strength in diversity. Ahimsa was particularly important in the struggle for Independence from Britain, as well as the partition of Pakistan from India. Gandhi mobilized the support of women in the struggle for power through nonviolence. Indians believe in the connectedness of all living things and in an immortality to which we are connected by reincarnation. They believe that when we die, the soul is born again into another human being or animal.

Thus patience and a positive relationship to other human beings and to the universe are essential human qualities. These values are embodied in the concepts of *karma* (destiny), *caste* (a hierarchical organization of human beings), and *dharma* (living life in accordance with the principle that orders the universe), which are all essential concepts to understanding the worldview of Asian Indian families, whether they are Hindu, Christian, Muslim, or Parsi. This chapter will present a general overview of the Asian Indian culture and discuss some differences between Hindus and Indians of Christian and Muslim backgrounds. Historically Indians have been tolerant toward cultural and religious diversity—the much publicized strife between Hindus and Muslims being of recent vintage. Deeply entrenched beliefs unite Asian Indians of different religions, although they also have distinct patterns in family development. Although the largest religious groups after Hindus are Muslims (75 million in India) and Christians (16 million), other faiths include Parsis or Zoroastrians (a Persian sect), Buddhists, Jews, and Bahais.

India's location as an entry way to the Orient made it much desired by colonial powers for its spice, tea, and silk. Its history is characterized by numerous invasions, first by Persians and Muslims, later by the European imperialists. When Vasco da Gama first met the Indian traders in the early 16th century, he was unprepared for the sophistication of their production and commerce. When the Indians refused to trade their cotton, silk, jewelry, and spices for the coarse clothes and hardware, the Portuguese took by force what they could not gain by fair trade. They occupied the western coastal areas, while England supplanted France in the interior.

Although not acknowledging the complexity and magnitude of Asian scientific culture, Europeans described India's indifference to the Western concept of time as reflecting an inability to focus on detail or maintain scientific rigor. They self-righteously defended their right to dominate because of their discipline, a routinized work ethic, precision, and organization.

The ranking of non-Western people began with European Colonial expansion. Although color and physical characteristics have played a role in this racial discrimination, their writings (which do not include themselves in the rankings!) described Indian and Chinese cultures as considerably more sophisticated than African cultures in political systems, marriage customs, handicraft technology, and conceptions of the supernatural with regard to time and space. They also revealed massive ignorance of non-Western systems of science and knowledge. This ranking of non-Western peoples together with India's ranking of its people (caste system) creates particular dilemmas around racism in this culture. European colonization lasted from the early 1600s until Indian independence in 1947 (Visram, 1986). India and Pakistan were one country until Pakistan was partitioned off in a religious compromise between Muslims and Hindus in the Independence struggle. Many believe that this religious conflict was intensified by the British presence. There is considerable overlap between the cultures of India and Pakistan in spite of distinct differences between Islam and Hinduism.

## MIGRATION HISTORY AND DEMOGRAPHICS IN THE UNITED STATES

Asian Indian immigration to the United States has recently experienced phenomenal growth. In 1990 the Census revealed that there were approximately 800,000 people of Asian Indian descent in the United States. Three years later, the Census indicated that the number had grown to one million people. This has resulted in part from a change in U.S. immigration policy, embodied in the Family Reunification Act of 1990, which grants preference to relatives of earlier immigrants. This policy is based on the idea that a successful transition cements the economic and social integration of immigrants for the next generation (Papademetrius, 1993; U.S. Department of Commerce, 1993).

The first Indian immigrants to the United States were farmers in the mid-1800s, who settled on the West Coast. They left little trace, because some intermarried Mexicans and others returned to India in the face of the intense discrimination they encountered. The Immigration and Naturalization Act of 1965, which ameliorated previous racial preferences for Europeans, ushered in a second wave of Indian migrants.

Most Indian immigrants to the United States speak English as a consequence of British colonization, which has eased their transition into Western cultural life. Newer rural immigrants are, however, less fluent in English and may require assistance in functioning effectively within the dominant culture. This is certainly evident in the achievements of younger Asian Indian children. Although they historically fit the stereotype of the "model minority," many do not complete high school, work in low-paying and unskilled jobs, are obligated to support extended families, and experience forms of prejudice similar to other immigrants of color (Chandrasekhar, 1982). Our increasing clinical sample reflects this profile. In addition, those immigrating as a result of the Family Reunification Act are not as highly educated or technically trained as their predecessors.

## RELIGIOUS VALUES

The legacy of Hinduism is much more of a cultural tradition than a religious doctrine. To some degree, many of the values I present here ripple through family life for all Asian Indians. The caste system influences much of family life in India. This system may be defined as

> a system of ranked, culturally distinct, interdependent endogamous groups. An individual belongs to the caste of his or her parents and cannot move from one caste to another. Castes are usually associated with traditional occupations, and there are definite social boundaries between castes involving, for example, pro-

hibitions on intermarriage, interdining, and other spatial and social contacts. In India, caste is related to the Hindu ideas of spiritual purity and pollution, and the castes are ranked on the basis of these criteria. While the Indian constitution specifically outlaws the demeaning and oppressive aspects of the caste system, particularly those that limit the full participation of the lowest castes and untouchables (now called scheduled castes), caste consciousness, and hierarchical relations between persons and groups based on caste distinctions, has by no means disappeared from the modern political and social scene. (Nanda, 1990, p. 144)

Purity relates to the ability to lead a totally spiritual life and abstain from bodily "pleasures." Sex, drugs, and alcohol, for example, are viewed as "bodily pleasures" and thus are part of an "impure" or polluted existence. Indians believe that caste is part of your "fate," or *karma*. By leading lives of sacrifice, which often means being a sanitation worker, a farmer, a butcher, or construction worker, and living in abject poverty, they can hope to ascend to a higher caste in the next life. Although the higher caste Hindus do not eat meat, for instance, the lower castes are the butchers for those in the community who do consume meat. The highest caste is the Brahmins, or priestly caste of Indian society; the lowest caste is the scheduled caste (untouchables), or *Harijans*—children of God—as Gandhi named them (McGoldrick et al., 1991; Malayala, Kamaraju, & Ramana, 1984). Asian Indians have greater affiliation across religious than caste lines. Hindu beliefs of caste and *karma* are so deeply pronounced that they influence family life of most religious groups.

These beliefs about purity and pollution create enormous stress at every stage of the life cycle. For instance, good or "pure" births involve preferably boys with no birth defects; proper mate selections must occur within the caste; and adults or children who die young are considered to bring bad luck or "pollution" to their family. Thus, the Hindu *yogi*, whose position in society is even higher than that of the priest, fasts for long periods, eschews sex and sustenance from human relationships, and directs all energy toward spiritual enlightenment in preparation for *nirvana*—the ideal that one strives for.

Gandhi—who said that India had two types of slavery, that of women and that of the *Harijans* (untouchables)—did much to alter the oppression of darker-skinned Indians. He was central to the cause of Indian independence from the British and of liberating women and the "untouchables" (Lynch, 1969). He did this through legislation that offered entry to universities for women and *Harijans*, increased professional opportunities, outlawed dowries, and sanctioned divorces. He was also instrumental in inspiring Indians in South Africa to participate in the struggle against apartheid. In the movie *Mississippi Masala*, the relationship between Meena's father and Okello depicts their closeness in Uganda's post-British rule—a closeness that was destroyed in the face of African nationalism.

The power of these ideas, especially in relation to attitudes toward daughters, cannot be overemphasized. No matter how well educated or apparently acculturated families are, the belief that a daughter's fate is tied up in her sexual purity and her marriage goes extremely deep for families (Almeida, 1990; Hinnels & Sharpe, 1972).

A mother of a 16-year-old girl may constrain her daughter from dating by saying, "It will be difficult for us to find a man for you to marry if the community knows we let you go out with boys."

Although Sikhs (a sect of Hinduism), Muslims, Christians, Jews, Buddhists, and Parsis or Zoroastrians (a Persian sect) constitute 20% of India's population, the overarching Hindu beliefs of caste and *karma* structure Indian society. Caste also has a skin-color component, with Brahmins tending to be light-skinned due to Persian and Aryan ancestry, and *Harijans* (untouchables) largely dark-skinned. In the movie *Mississippi Masala*, when Meena is getting dressed to meet her prospective suitor, Dr. Harry Patel, she comments on the futility of their hopes for a good husband: "Face it, Ma, I'm your darkie daughter." In the context of this history, religious writings about the forces of lightness and darkness in the universe are interpreted literally to mean skin color: Dark skin denotes evil, and light skin denotes rebirth and fairness. Mitter (1991) describes a typical matrimonial advertisement in the *Hindustan Times*: "The girl will in addition be fair-skinned, slim, and tall. . . . A complexion termed 'wheatish' is an admission that the maiden is dark" (p. 19). Asian Indians view all darker-skinned people through this prism.

This concept has particular salience in a Western context with respect to socializing children, intermarriage, and work relationships (Hines, Garcia-Preto, McGoldrick, Almeida, & Weltman, 1992; McGoldrick et al., 1991; Almeida, 1990), as can be seen in the following vignette:

An Indian mother refused to allow her daughter to play with certain classmates, including a Caribbean child and a darker-skinned Asian child. When questioned by the teacher, the parents expressed their concern that any interaction with individuals deemed by the community as "improper" could ruin the daughter's chances for marriage. The child's individual social development is secondary to the preservation of the family's cultural identity.

Many Asian Indians are scholars of racism and devote their efforts toward changing the role of marginal cultures amid Western domination. Others have used a "European" physical appearance to "blend into" the dominant culture. Minority group status is controversial within the first-generation Asian Indian community. The Indian League of America, for example, has not wanted Indians to be given "minority" or non-Caucasian status (Leonard & Tibrewal,

1993) out of concern that it will place them at a disadvantage. The high degree of education and professional skill of many Asian Indians has enabled them to assume a privileged status in the United States. This "quiet privilege" may change, however, with the recent influx of a large number of less-educated, less-skilled Asian Indian immigrants. Britain is a good example of how Asian Indians have been marginalized, in spite of their efforts to blend in. Many neighborhoods in Britain are not unlike the ghettos created by privileged Americans for Blacks and Hispanics.

Because Hinduism does not require regular worship at a temple, practice of the religion occurs mostly at home. In India the society enforces Hindu beliefs. Indian families in the United States are left with no societal support for their values. They themselves bear sole responsibility of enforcing religious and cultural beliefs, which often puts them in a defensive and conservative stance and limits their flexibility to foster acculturation and change in their children (Sodowsky & Carey, 1988). For example, the holiday *Diwali* (the festival of lights), which is celebrated elaborately in India (usually in the early part of November), is honored only modestly in the United States.

## PROCESS OF ACCULTURATION

Acculturation is the process of maintaining an identity with one's culture of origin, while adapting to the host culture. For Asian Indian families in the United States acculturation varies depending on education, class, caste, family size, economic support, connections to their traditional culture, degree of religiosity, past migration history, and how they have dealt with the loss of their country of origin. Families who migrate for better economic and political conditions may also be insufficiently prepared for American competitiveness, lack of social support, and overemphasis on individualism. Families who have lived and received an education outside of India tend to adapt more readily to this culture than those who have not. This process of adaptation to a new culture imposes different levels of stress on families, based upon factors of social class, pattern of immigration (i.e., forced or voluntary, level of community support), exposure to other Western cultures prior to immigration, and level of intergenerational conflict prior to migration (Krishna & Berry, 1992). Asian Indians are considered to have adapted smoothly to American life.

Women as immigrants in general tend to acculturate later than their male counterparts, as they are usually in the home and have less opportunity to interact with the dominant culture (Gune, 1994). Men, on the other hand, are more able to live in both worlds: the work world, where they have a measure of competence and acceptance by the host culture, and in the home, where traditions are maintained by their wives, mothers, and daughters. Similarly, adolescent boys are given more freedom in their social lives than are girls. Thus boys acculturate at an earlier age than do girls. Although female adolescents seem to acculturate at a slower rate than their male counterparts, adult women who work out of the home seem to have more opportunity for role flexibility. In California, for instance, women were found to have highly visible roles as grocery store and motel managers, clerks, restaurant managers, and other professional positions (Leonard & Tibrewal, 1993). Such visibility outside of purely professional roles is nonexistent for women in India. Within the immigrant community, women contribute to family earnings with greater decision making about spending than their mothers-in-law had in either India or the United States. This has encouraged elderly parents to visit and live with both their sons and daughters, rather than the traditional arrangement of living only with sons.

A study of first-generation Hindu immigrants to Canada found that the more religious immigrants believed in male domination, female subordination, and rigid sex roles in the family. The higher the social class and the longer the time since immigration, the weaker was the allegiance to traditional gender roles and the greater the preference for individualistic rather than collective norms (Dhruvarajan, 1993). Exposure to the Western feminist movement and consequent awareness of women's rights threatens traditional Indian male-centered families. Not surprisingly, such ideas are stressful to Indian families even though there are similar movements in India (Ramu, 1988). Good barometers of changing societal patterns are frequent stories in Indian magazines of women launching their careers before marriage and successfully leaving husbands who abuse them.

Young couples, single adults, and families with young children tend to adapt more rapidly because of their contact with U.S. society through schools and the workplace. However, some families who have been in the United States a long time are beginning to have second thoughts about their rapid assimilation. Now that they feel secure enough to share their experience of bicultural adaptation, they speak openly of having suffered discriminatory practices and of the price they have paid for their choice to succeed quietly for fear of being noticed and rejected. These misgivings have often resulted in adults seeking later to rediscover their Indian heritage, a process that can become conflictual if they try to impose these values upon their children. A 26-year-old woman says, "I always viewed my parents as liberal, unlike other Indian parents who forced their children to do things the Indian way. More recently, however, I have become increasingly angry and confused over their return to the Swami and insistence that I marry someone of their choice!"

Many Indians who have immigrated to the United States went first to other countries, where they often confronted very hostile situations. Asian Indians who have been in Uganda for three generations were forced to leave their homes in 1972, and the commercial success of Indians in other African countries has been resented by nationalistic regimes. Naturally, the experiences Indian families have had in these earlier migrations will influence their values and adjustment in the United States. Therapists need to learn about this history if they want to understand the family's adaptive strategies in this country. This complexity was brilliantly illustrated in the movie *Mississippi Masala*, in which the Indian–African American relationships were deeply influenced by the family's earlier, but buried history in Uganda. (I will refer to segments in the movie to emphasize different aspects of family life.)

## THE LIFE CYCLE

Indians are expected to follow a life course referred to as *dharma*, which presents separate patterns for men and women. Traditionally, men had four life stages: studentship, householder, forest-dweller, and homeless wanderer. Within the stages of householder and forest-dweller, men were expected to marry and fulfill family responsibilities. During the studentship and wanderer stages, they were required to live as single individuals, free of any worldly desires. Although few Hindu men achieve all of these stages, the implication of this *dharma* is that men are to be supported in their quest for study, marriage, children, and spiritual self-fulfillment.

Hindu women have a simpler *dharma* to follow. As "good Hindus," they are expected to marry early and produce children, especially sons. When families promote education for their daughters, it is usually with the goal of making them more marketable as brides, and not out of any commitment to their personal development (Hines et al., 1992; Roland, 1988). In the movie *Mississippi Masala*, the encouragement by Meena's parents for her to get an education is solely for this reason.

Asian Indian families have an elaborate network of relationships, determined through male lineage (Ayakar, 1994). When women married, they typically left their family of origin and moved into the home of the husband's family of origin. A new bride's tolerance was measured by her ability to adjust to all of the women in her husband's family with whom she spent the most time. During the early years of marriage, she would see her husband only briefly, at night. In some regions new brides might make long visits to their own parents' home. These practices would continue until the wife's children, preferably sons, gave her status in her in-laws' home. This conjoint home physically and economically supported the sons, their families, unmarried sisters, and paternal aunts (single or widowed), as well as the parents. There, the newly married woman deferred to her mother-in-law and older sisters-in-law, who prepared her for living in her husband's home and for childbirth (Hines et al., 1992). Men, not women, were expected to care for this entire family system financially. It is relevant for families to ask about these intergenerational and regional practices of marriage.

When a man dies, his wife is not expected to remarry and is cared for by brothers-in-law. Although remarriage and divorce may be part of modern-day life in India as in the United States, the consequences are very severe for offending Indian women, as this example from a community of recent immigrants in New Jersey illustrates:

Following the birth of a daughter, a 32-year-old, educated Hindu woman filed for divorce from her physician husband, due to his repeated violence. When she moved into her parents' home, her entire community of friends shunned her and her family as well. In contrast, a widow of 16 years, at 42, said, "It would have been nice to have a father for my children, but remarriage would have created problems between my children and in-laws. Now they respect me."

---------------- ⚮ ----------------

Although the scriptures may revere women, in everyday life their value is not equal to that of men (Almeida, 1990; Bumiller, 1990; Gross & Bingham, 1980). They are not socialized to be independent in any facet of their lives. In dual-career households, money earned by the wife is considered, with few exceptions, to be the property of the husband and his family. A woman's identity comes from marriage, childbearing, and her status as a mother-in-law, wherein she wields tremendous power over her daughter-in-law. Motherhood of sons affords women special status (Almeida, 1990; Bumiller, 1990). The birth of sons is celebrated more than that of daughters (Bumiller, 1990). Daughters are groomed to be married; their dowries are a burden that every father and brother must carry. When a family has only daughters, especially if they are economically disadvantaged, both mother and daughters are vulnerable to abuse by the husband's family and are likely to develop psychological symptoms. *The Times of India* (December 1, 1985) reported the following:

The Rajasthan high court on Friday awarded capital punishment to one Jagdish, . . . for setting his wife, Chand, aflame on September 10, 1981. According to the dying declaration of Chand, she had been having a tussle with her husband and mother-in-law. Her daughter had been ill for a few days. She used to take the child to a doctor. Her husband and mother-in-law had objected to the expenditure on the treatment of a female child. (cited in Mitter, 1991, p. 117)

Boys are highly valued, and having many sons is a way for women to gain power economically and spiritually. Even well-educated families seem to accept this prejudice:

A young college-educated mother of two daughters made a pilgrimage trip to India from her home in the United States to bathe in the water of the Ganges and visit a special temple in order to have the gods assist her in having a son. She indicated that she and her husband, a physician, were both familiar with genetics, but she had confidence that spiritual power would ultimately help her to have a son.

———————— ✎ ————————

Another contradiction in the Asian Indian life cycle is the status of mothers-in-law. Although women in general have low status, mothers-in-law, as evident in the death of Chand, have a tremendous amount of power over their daughters-in-law, increasing their desire to have sons. A mother-in-law may run interference in many aspects of a couple's relationship, even their intimate sex life, asking the son frequently if he is being pleasured in the way a good wife ought to pleasure him. She may offer her opinion about the number of children the couple should have, the preferred sex of these children, the type of child care that is desirable, and make numerous suggestions regarding second-shift responsibilities, money, work, and social activities. A range of abusive behaviors, from emotional intimidation and harassment to murders (including dousing women in gasoline and lighting their saris with fire), arise from dissatisfaction with dowries and the sex of the grandchildren.

Child-rearing practices in the Asian Indian culture are quite similar to those in other Asian cultures. Children are desired and seen as a necessary part of the family life cycle. It would be unheard of for a couple to plan not to have a child. However, families embrace daughters only if they also have one or more sons. Female infanticide and abandoning girl babies to missionary adoption homes is especially common among poor, uneducated families.

In general, children are pampered by everyone, including older siblings and extended family. A 4- or 5-year-old child is often less independent than children of European background. Girls, however, are expected to be more responsible than boys from age 13 onward. Regardless of their studies, girls are expected to help with household chores and care for younger siblings. Boys, on the other hand, are expected to do their studies first and then help with younger siblings, but not necessarily with household chores.

Mr. Amin, a Hindu father, brought his 14-year-old daughter, Sunita, for therapy on account of failing grades and a suspected relationship with a boy. The family, consisting of Mr. and Mrs. Amin, Sunita, and her sister, Shamita, were in treatment for about 6 months to confront transitional issues of adolescence. There were a number of issues that surfaced, including severe mother-in-law conflicts. These conflicts were resolved by Mr. Amin asking his other siblings to share the responsibility of caring for their mother. As the oldest son, this solution would never have been entertained in India or with very traditional families. Acculturated influences made this possible. During the course of this work, Mrs. Amin's sister-in-law and two sons came from India to visit for the summer. Sunita and Shamita complained about the glaring difference in participation in family chores between their cousins and themselves. While she and her younger sister helped out with household chores, her cousins expected to be waited on by the females in the family. Sunita confronted her father for permitting this, insisting that he take a stand against the girls waiting on the boys in their home. Her father tried to explain that the cousins wanted to help out, giving examples of how they helped him do the "manly" work outside the house. He urged his daughter to be patient and understand the context the boys had come from. She did not necessarily need to wait on her male cousins but could explain to them how things might be done differently here.

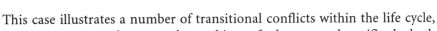

This case illustrates a number of transitional conflicts within the life cycle, but more importantly, we see the teachings of tolerance and sacrifice by both parents. Mr. Amin wants Sunita to be patient as he is patient with her and the extended family members that visit for extended periods of time. Although he is the parent, and the most powerful in this system as compared to his daughter, who has the least power, he empowers her to challenge the male cousins while maintaining the illusion of the male hierarchy: a cultural paradox. Mrs. Amin also shows the tolerance and sacrifice she endured through all the years she has been hospitable toward his mother and other in-laws in their home. Because girls are prepared for marriage at such a young age, mothers may treat their adolescent daughters like adults. They often do not understand the complexities of adolescence in the United States. They tend to personalize the typical rebellious struggles of their daughters, emphasizing the respect and sense of obligation that they always had toward their parents. It may be useful to remind a mother that her daughter is still young and immature, which can help the mother be more compassionate. When families present with adolescent struggles for freedom, it is important not take a position for the independence of the child, but rather to seek a solution within the family's framework of autonomy and interconnectedness. For example, if a family insists that their 16-year-old daughter include some Indian friends in any social activities, the therapist should help the adolescent respect this as a compromise between the generations. Parents need help in understanding that the process of acculturation brings the tasks of adolescence and leaving home into the life cycle.

Children are frequently punished by being held close and spanked or being talked to. Philosophical "talks" are favored over immediate behavioral consequences. Time-out procedures are viewed as too distancing and controlling of individual outcomes. With the continuum of violence and stress that families frequently find themselves in, I would encourage methods of discipline that do not run the risk of physical abuse. Although this is difficult for first-generation parents to carry out, many second-generation families will be more able to adapt time-out procedures with positive reinforcement as a form of setting boundaries, while achieving a balance between independence and respect toward the family. Parents who take their children to Al-Anon or Al-Ateen, for instance, feel this philosophy is too centered on the self and not sufficiently on family obligations.

Indian families in the United States often feel a need to maintain rigid cultural boundaries as a bulwark to protect family patterns and cultural legacies against assimilation and racism. For example, children are encouraged to play and celebrate birthdays with relatives and family friends' children rather than with classmates. Socializing with classmates is discouraged, also, as it is likely to occur across caste lines. This is particularly confusing for Christian children as they share the Easter and Christmas holidays with their Christian classmates.

Sibling roles vary by the region they come from in India (Nuckolls, 1993). In India, siblings are expected to assume certain roles and responsibilities for each other. Brothers are expected to live and cooperate with one another. In many regions, for instance, sisters must leave at marriage to join their husbands' family of origin. In other regions, however, they are expected to return to their own home after the marriage, and in some instances, even until the children are of school age. Brothers are responsible for the general welfare of sisters, including their marriages. After marriage they are expected to turn the responsibility for their sisters over to their husbands, which frequently involves a relationship cutoff with their sisters. Anthropological studies have shown a positive relationship between inheritance rights that favor the brothers in a family, large dowries paid for a sister, and lifelong connections between brothers and their sisters (Kolenda, 1993). Brothers, on the other hand, seem to cultivate stronger bonds toward one another in the interest of preserving the family legacy. Like many other family patterns, immigration, economics, and acculturation do alter this legacy. It is not uncommon for older siblings to assume parental responsibilities over their younger siblings at the early age of 9 or 10, using punitive forms of authority. Paradoxically, strong nurturing bonds may develop between an older brother and younger sister, or an older sister and younger sisters in a family with no brothers. The common term "cousin brother" is representative of the expected ideal of loyalty between brothers, without the acknowledgment of the brother–sister or sister–sister dyad. In Northern India there is a particular celebration of the brother–sister dyad called *raki*. This celebration consists of a ritual whereby sisters give bracelets and cook a meal for their brothers. Brothers, in turn, bring gifts and money for their sisters, whether they are single or married.

Family life cycle transitions can be particularly difficult when they collide with values of passivity, obedience, and sacrifice. The belief that one should be accepting of life difficulties in order to be rewarded in the next life is at odds with the basic belief in the United States that one should pull oneself up by one's bootstraps. For example, a grandmother who lost her adult son to cancer had a difficult time enjoying her new grandchild, as she believes that her past actions caused the death of her son (*karma*) and she must sacrifice her life now for a better future life for all of her family. She was helped to see how a connection with her grandson would facilitate a spiritual connection with her son in the afterlife.

Indians do not generally speak of feelings or personal experiences. The language of personal emotions is viewed as too self-focused, without any concern for respect and obligation toward the family. Communication patterns tend to follow the hierarchical structure of the family. It may be perceived as disrespectful for a therapist to make direct eye contact with older members, and they will feel ashamed of expressing their anger. Difficulties are usually presented through stories, metaphors, and narratives, rather than in the language of personal emotions. This can often result in a set of undifferentiated assumptions between parents and children, as can be seen in the following vignette:

A father of a college student, frustrated over his son's failing grades and interracial relationship with a young White woman, related elaborate stories of attempts by others to tempt him into "bad" behavior in his youth. He told of his stoic struggle over such temptations in order to comply with his role as a dutiful son and remain responsible to his parents. Through this indirect means, he was raising the question of how his son could live a life he considered to be so disrespectful of his parents.

The father's seeking help for his son's academic difficulties is not anomalous in Indian families, where mothers typically handle domestic issues (private), and fathers handle social, school-related, and other (public) matters.

Adolescent sexuality, like other issues of the Indian family, are defined within the value structure of purity and pollution. Free expression of sexuality is viewed as incongruent with spirituality. Boys are not permitted to masturbate but rather are encouraged to meditate in preparation for studentship.

Girls are seen as needing greater protection after they begin menstruating. Frequently this involves restricted interaction with the opposite sex. Although this custom is honored at some level by most Hindus and Muslims, it is more strictly enforced by observant Muslims through *purdah*, or "veiling" of all girls after menarche. The wearing of modest clothes is encouraged for all girls (Papenek, 1973).

The life stages of adolescence and launching young adults do not exist in the Indian culture. A culture that prescribes marriage, childbearing, and economic responsibility for extended family leaves no room for exploration of how to leave home: experimentation within couple relationships in dating; or exploration of one's sexual orientation, career, and work choices. Asian Indian adolescents living in the United States often feel caught between two worlds:

their family and culture, on one hand, and the prevalent values in the United States on the other. This becomes especially difficult because of the absence of cultural permission to discuss emotions, as the following case vignette illustrates:

A 14-year-old Hindu girl and her family were referred for treatment after the girl's suicide attempt as a result of her depression around her feelings that her parents did not allow her to speak to boys and her fears of an arranged marriage. Assisted by the therapist, the girl's parents were able to achieve a compromise between the Hindu tradition of segregation and American norms of total mixing of sexes. The daughter could go on social outings with Indian boys and girls, as long as an older sibling or parent came alone, but she could not engage in relationships with non-Indian boys. The parents assured the girl that she would be given a choice of potential mates and would not be forced to marry anyone not to her liking. They acceded to her request that she not marry until she completed her education, with the caveat that she could expect the field of eligible young men to narrow if she postponed marriage for too long.

—————— ∽ ——————

Interestingly, after the rules were clarified, the parents were able to tell the daughter how much she meant to them and that they wished for her to tell them of any future distress. Such a conversation does not take place in most Asian Indian families, nor had it occurred in this family before, but parents are often willing to adjust their cultural strictures to ease a child's unhappiness. In general, both in India and the United States, new trends are emerging with regard to arranged marriages. Teenage marriages are on the decline, with new brides being from around 23 to even 30 years old. A graduate education and employment for women are also being valued more highly. Intermarriages, dating, and divorce continue to be more acceptable for men than women, although an increasingly larger number of women are confronting these barriers.

Death is a particularly potent symbolic event among Hindus, given their beliefs about *karma* and destiny (McGoldrick et al., 1991). As with weddings, traditional rituals associated with death and mourning are likely to be modified when Indians live in the United States. Mourning cycles vary, but rituals for Christians and Muslims diverge less significantly from American practices than those of Hindus and Parsis, whose customs include a 10- to 12-day mourning ritual that violates American health and funeral home regulations, in addition to requiring extensive absence from work. In keeping with Indian sex-role traditions, widows are expected to perform many rituals of sacrifice glorifying the family, whereas widowers and other family members are not required to observe such rites (McGoldrick et al., 1991). *Sati* is a practice of widow burning on her husband's funeral pyre. This practice was outlawed during the British Raj, but has been practiced as recently as 1987 in the state of Rajasthan. The underlying belief is that, by this glorified sacrifice, a widow brings good luck to her husband and his entire family, as well as herself. The historical reports of *sati* described it as an act of social political protest by women whose husbands were killed in war. Following their defeat, the invading soldiers would come into the villages to rape and steal the women and children. Through time this practice became imbued with patriarchal notions of how widows should behave in the event of their husbands' death, the lack of appropriate status for widows, and economic difficulties. Enforced suicide with new religious meaning became attached to this practice. Death is both an event for mourning and celebration. It is seen as the end of one's life cycle and beginning of another. This is contrary to Western notions that view death with finality.

## HOMOSEXUALITY

I will discuss homosexuality within the larger Hindu context and then more specifically speak to the differences with Muslims and Christians. Identity confusion may also develop around the coming-out process for young gay and lesbian adults. While the notion of a third gender, or *hijra*, is written about in the scriptures, as with many of the other paradoxes in Indian culture, homosexuality is not culturally sanctioned. *Hijras* worship the Mother goddess, saying, "It is the Mata who gives us life, we live only in her power" (Nanda, 1990, p. 26). They have historically held powerful roles in the community around performing for weddings and births, bringing good *karma* to the event and supported in communal living. Gays and lesbians in the United States struggle between the pressures to marry and retain the support of their communities against racism, or to leave the community and choose an alternate lifestyle. There is, however, a steadily growing activist Indian movement, Shakti, for gays and lesbians in India, Pakistan, and the United States. *Shakti* is the potency of female strength represented through the creation of life. Shakti as an organization is critical to the transitional process necessary to solidify the sexual orientation of gays and lesbians in the Asian Indian community.

Contrary to Western norms, the culture of India and Pakistan encourages close emotional bonding and physical affection between male friends. Although this connection among men is embraced, and relationships among women is commonplace, Muslims tend to view gay and lesbian relationships through the prisms of procreation and community good. Therefore, any relationship that does not lead to procreation is not in the best interests of the community. According to Dynes and Donaldson (1992, p. 27), "Islamic law and tradition tend to relate sexuality to the maintenance of the social order rather than taking the Judeo-Christian approach of treating it as a matter of individual morality." The Koran explicitly condemns homosexual behavior "Whenever a male mounts another male, the throne of God trembles" (p. 27).

Islamic's concern is with gender roles and public reputation versus private behavior. An *imam* (priest) recently withdrew his participation at a conference addressing theology and homosexuality, saying, "I cannot sit at the same table with sinners." Homosexuality is considered dishonorable for men, as it places them in the passive or "feminine" sexual role. Lesbianism (*mushqaq*) is considered by Islamic law to be sex outside of marriage and therefore constitutes adultery, but since lesbian sex does not require penetration, it is less punishable than heterosexual adultery (Schmitt & Sofer, 1992). Lesbianism is rarely acknowledged in Muslim society, although it may be assumed to exist, given the gender segregation of females common in India and Pakistan (Dynes & Donaldson, 1992).

Because Muslims prize family life so highly, it is not uncommon for homosexuals to live a gay or lesbian lifestyle until marriage, then marry and have children, while continuing to have a separate homosexual partner. They find that having a family within the boundaries of tradition and also maintaining a gay lifestyle is preferable to risking alienation by pursuing an exclusively homosexual lifestyle (Khan, 1992).

A young male graduate student of Asian Muslim descent presented with fears of not meeting the standards of success defined by his family. He initially defined these standards as the ability to find a high paying job upon graduation as an engineer and support his two younger sisters and parents. In exploring this further, it became evident that he most feared the family's impending plans for his marriage. He was gay and had spent the last 4 years of his life taking various girls home but maintaining a closeted gay lifestyle. As the oldest son in an Asian Muslim family he believed strongly that it was his primary responsibility to marry and raise a family. He seemed unable to entertain the choice of cutting off from his family temporarily in order to experience a full gay lifestyle. While he was aware of a few other Asian gay men, he felt that his community was largely centered around marriage and heterosexual family life. These boundaries offered individuals like himself a barrier against racism and the other struggles of immigrant life. At the end of therapy he was less anxious and fearful believing that he would continue his deep friendships with men but not live a gay lifestyle. This is the dilemma of first-generation Asian men and women. Being Muslim and gay adds another level of isolation.

Values of tolerance and passivity help families to withstand the harsh practices of racism in their lives at work, and toward their children at school. This same strength can prove to be dysfunctional, however, when the pattern of internalizing negative emotions, together with enforcing rules of obedience and respect within the hierarchical family system, leads to the rigidifying of traditional family boundaries as an insulation against assimilation and racism (Hines et al., 1992). The distinction between acculturation and assimilation is not always clear to families. It serves therapists well to delineate these differences for them (Hutnik, 1986; Jiobu, 1988). Acculturation is the selection of dominant norms helpful to the integration process while maintaining one's cultural heritage. Assimilation is the complete adoption of dominant norms to the exclusion of one's own cultural identity.

## ASIAN INDIAN CHRISTIANS

Christianity was brought to India by missionaries in the wake of Portuguese, French, Dutch, and English colonization. This colonial diversity gave rise to Catholicism and different sects of Protestantism. As is common in the colonial experience, converts to Christianity in India integrated their new religion with their original indigenous beliefs, which arose primarily out of Hinduism.

Asian Christians tend to be more flexible than Hindus toward their adolescent children, allowing both boys and girls to attend church and other social activities, including dating. In addition, they place no dietary or dress restrictions on them, as Hindus and Muslims do. Although they might acculturate more rapidly, they experience difficulties similar to other Asian Indian immigrants: family transitions and cultural adjustment.

A Christian Asian Indian family was referred for therapy by the school for the daughter's failing grades and weight loss. Her complaints revolved around intense feelings of isolation due to her parents forbidding her to socialize with anyone out of the extended family. She was also prohibited from youth activities at her church. The father, an engineer, stated that he refused to be controlled by her and did not care if she killed herself. The mother was more willing to consider other options for the daughter. In the father's absence, she confided that she herself felt totally trapped in the family situation, by her need to care for their 10-year-old son, who was autistic. She wished her daughter would help her more. The mother was helped to see that the daughter felt ignored, even though she understood that her brother's needs were greater than her own. The mother expressed her great sadness because of her loss of status within the in-law system and the community over bearing a male child who would not be a productive member of the family.

As mother and daughter discussed their situation more openly, the mother agreed to extending a few privileges to her daughter so that she could expand her social life.

What is clear here is the influence of Hindu beliefs, even with an acculturated Christian family. Girls are taught from an early age that their sexuality is tied to family honor, so any violation of sexual purity before marriage brings disgrace to the family. These ideas, similar to those in Latin cultures, are reinforced through beliefs in Catholicism. Boys are also constrained by taboos around premarital sex but are simultaneously expected to be "Don Juans" when they marry. Although these taboos exist, mixed youth parties, dances, and music are central to the culture of Christian families.

Homosexuality is considered a sin within Christianity, which emphasizes marriage and sex for procreation. Since Indian Christians have greater access to non-Indian Christians who may be homosexual, they may have more of a buffering system than their Hindu or Muslim counterparts, as they experiment with their sexuality. Since priests and nuns are revered by the Indian Christian community, it is not uncommon for gay and lesbian children to join the church or to stay at home and care for elderly parents. Frequently their identities remain a hidden although frequently better option than marriage.

Christians are accepting of a female Asian therapist but prefer to use a priest because of their religious beliefs (Misumi, 1993).

## MUSLIM FAMILIES FROM INDIA AND PAKISTAN[1]

Pakistan, India, and Bangladesh were all one country prior to British colonization over 500 years ago. When India gained independence from British rule (Raj) in 1947, these countries were divided upon religious lines. This partition was based on irreparable sociopolitical differences between Muslims and Hindus, which had heightened during independence from British rule. Prior to this, Muslims and Indians had lived harmoniously together since about the eighth century (Nanda, 1990), with many Hindus converting to Islam. Over the past 1,200 years, some integration has taken place between Hindus and Islam, although in terms of theology the religions are quite different (Nanda, 1990). Unlike Hinduism, Islam does not recognize caste. A major tenet of Islam is that all participants are equal in social, political, and legal status, and the major distinctions occur between believers and nonbelievers of the faith. It is this aspect of Islam that has attracted the *hijras* (all the genders that do not define themselves as simply men or women), as well as Black Americans to the religion.

Pakistan and Bangladesh (formerly East and West Pakistan) are predominantly Muslim nations. India has a very significant Muslim presence—11% of its population. In North America, South Asians are considered one of the three major groups of Muslims, along with Arabs and African Americans. There are no official statistics reflecting the percentage of Muslims among U.S. citizens of Indian or Pakistani heritage.

Islamic law (also known as *Shari'a*, or personal law) is considered inherently incompatible with a secular democracy because it determines religious, social, and political standards that Muslims must follow. Today, Pakistan has both secular laws, which do not infringe on the *Shari'a*, and religious law. Marriage, divorce, family relationships and inheritance remain areas of religious law and are respected even by U.S. courts, as illustrated by the following vignette.

A Pakistani Muslim lawyer sought to divorce his wife of 8 years. At the premarriage ceremony, the woman had been given a sum of $300 in Pakistan as a *tullich* (a gift designed to provide for women so that men can divorce more freely). Upon filing for divorce, the husband documented the *tullich*, which he equated with a prenuptial agreement. The judge accepted the husband's position—a divorce settlement of $300—without considering the proportion of such inequity. Furthermore, there were two children from the marriage, and the wife had not as yet received her "green card" or immigrant visa. This made her ineligible to file suit under U.S. matrimonial law (Saijwani, 1989).

---------------- ❧ ----------------

Muslims in India practice their religion freely, although there have been recent religious conflicts that have resulted in violence. As mentioned, Hindu beliefs in *karma*, caste, self-sacrifice, and purity have influenced Muslim families as well as other religious groups. In addition, many Muslim families in India and Pakistan offer a dowry to the groom and his family when their daughter marries, even though dowry is not a tradition of Islam and is practiced in few other Islamic countries.

Muslim Indians and Pakistanis follow the traditions and beliefs as stated by Allah (God) through Mohammed and recorded in the Qu'ran (holy bible), which embodies Muslim law (*fiqh*). The Qu'ran is a book of revelations that describes five major tenets by which Muslims (men and women) should conduct themselves: (1) a declaration that there is but one God and Mohammed is His Prophet; (2) a prayer performed five times daily, facing Mecca; (3) almsgiving to help the poor and as an act of piety; (4) fasting during the daylight hours of the month of Ramadan, which is usually around Easter and Passover; (5) a pilgrimage to Mecca, at least once in one's lifetime. The Qu'ran also contains certain moral and legal ordinance, forbidding such activities as drinking, gambling, eating pork, and so on. It defines penalties for crimes and sets out rules for marriage, divorce, and inheritance (Cooper, 1993). These practices receive varying degrees of societal recognition in different countries. How observant Muslims are depends on their education, economics, societal influences, immigration patterns, and acculturation influences.

Veiling, a form of *purdah*, or gender segregation, originated as a Byzantine practice and was later incorporated into Muslim tradition. It ranges from totally covering a woman's face, head, and body, to a partial covering. The *salwar kameese*—pajama pants and a tunic with a thin chiffon shawl thrown around the shoulders or head—is used by many Indian and Pakistani women. This covering is viewed by Westerners, feminists in particular, as oppressive. Muslim feminists, in contrast, defend veiling (*hijab*) by explaining its internal meaning in the culture as a symbol of protection against individualism, which is viewed as a Western ideal and a source of trouble. A recent television interview between a Muslim and Western feminists placed the discourse about "veiling" in the same context as "makeup," body image, and all of the other forms of external markers that define and legitimize women as objects of male possession in the Western world.

Veiling maintains boundaries that separate women and organize family and community life in Muslim societies. It also ensures the control by men over women's sexual lives (Mernissi, 1982). Whatever disadvantages such segregation creates, it has, paradoxically, allowed women to excel through female education systems (Mernissi, 1992). Segregated Muslim women have also pointed out that they feel safer from rape and attack than women who live in integrated societies. Muslims generally consider the segregation of women to be a much less serious problem than the segregation between the rich and the poor, which has more implications for children of both genders, who receive little education and have few societal rewards (Mernissi, 1992). This class schism is profoundly impacted by the way other cultures, including especially the United States, relate to Muslim societies, exploiting the poor, and promoting an elite through which their interest, but not necessarily Muslim interests, are served. Oil resources from the Middle East are a good example of this. Thus unequal access to knowledge divides the Muslim world, creating not only animosity between classes but also a polarization between traditional religious practices and modern Western ideas.

In poor Muslim families, women's lives are traditionally confined to marriage, children, and domestic responsibilities. Men are encouraged to receive an education, because they carry the burden of providing for the nuclear and extended family's financial needs. With middle- and upper-class families there is generally more flexibility with regard to women's segregation.

Asian Indian Muslims and Christians, like other Asian Indians, consider marriage the most important life cycle transition (Rege, 1996; Ahmad, 1976). Parents often plan for this event from the time children are very young. It is viewed as bringing together two families rather than two individuals. Intermarriage is discouraged as threatening the integrity of the family, culture, and faith, although Jewish or Christian intermarriage is slightly more acceptable than marriage to a Hindu, atheist, polytheist, or idol worshiper.

According to Islamic religious texts, Muslim men and women have the same religious rights and duties, and it is only the patriarchal interpretation of Islam that defends sexual and economic inequalities in the name of Islam (Al-Hibri, 1992; Baffoun, 1992; Mernissi, 1982). Recent conservative pressure for women to stick to their role in the home as "culture bearer" at the price of any participation in public life is seen as political, not cultural, and, of course, is not in keeping with the idea of women globally to work toward societies that will include both cultural preservation and gender empowerment.

Between 1937 and 1986, Muslim women gained legal rights regarding their consent to marriage, inheritance, polygamy, and divorce. These rights have, however, seldom, if ever, been enforced for women of any religion in India (Lateef, 1990). Rights for Muslim women depend on the particular group. Sunni or Shiite Muslims, for example, are more conservative and traditional, and Halbali Muslims tend to be quite punitive if families deviate from the expected norms of their group. In a recent case of domestic violence, the father from the Halbali sect threatened to kill his 15-year-old daughter and her boyfriend if she engaged in premarital sex.

Even in families where women are not veiled (*purdah*), women are still restricted in many ways, including their involvement in public activities, creating a kind of "*purdah* mentality" (Lateef, 1990). Adherence to Muslim practices creates a number of conflicts within Indian and Pakistani families. It is an especially challenging task for Muslim families to acculturate within a societal context that views them from such an uninformed and prejudiced perspective, portraying them as terrorists or uncivilized barbarians (Mernissi, 1992; Vicente, 1992). A Pakistani may, for example, choose to identify herself as Indian to escape anti-Muslim hostility. Family therapists working with Muslim families must counter the popular notions of Islam as a monolithic, anti-Western, violence-prone group.

An additional challenge for therapists is the tendency for Americans to view Muslim women as representing the epitome of disempowerment and patriarchal control, envisioning their intolerably inferior status, citing polygamy, divorce by repudiation, the wearing of the veil, segregation, imprisonment in household tasks, strict dependence on their husbands, and their lack of legal rights (Arkoun, 1994).

Muslims have had a long-standing belief in the fusing of church and state (Khalidi, 1991). The incongruities between the Muslim belief that the state should support religious tenets, such as gender segregation, and the American position of a strict separation of church and state may give rise to great difficulties for Muslims living in the United States, for whom it is impossible to follow the tenets of the Qu'ran mandating segregation of men and women. For example, attempts to negotiate with men for more independence for their wives to socialize or work outside the home, or for their adolescent daughters to participate in social activities, directly challenge the traditional beliefs of Islam. The reaction to these societal conflicts often parallels the *purdah* mentality of staying in the home/compound. This is more so the case with less educated families, as they have fewer options within our society.

A Muslim couple presented with concerns over their 14-year-old daughter. She was cutting classes and not taking the school bus home. The school seemed concerned as well. All the money the parents earned from their restaurant and hospital jobs that was not needed for strict necessities went to fund the daughter's dowry. When asked why they were so concerned with a dowry, the father reframed it as a sum of money he hoped to give his daughter and son-in-law to buy a home, just like American parents would give their children.

The family was entirely focused on every detail of the daughter's marriage. They would not accept an orthodox (or fundamentalist) Moslem. Nor would a Black American Muslim do, as recent converts would not understand the intergenerational legacies regarding Islam. The parents were also wary that a Black Muslim would be tainted with the American "cult of individualism."

They were determined that marriage had to occur at age 18, and then their daughter could continue her education as she desired, provision for which would be arranged as part of the marriage settlement. They had no difficulty being treated by a non-Muslim Asian Indian female, but they were intransigent on the subject of their daughter's marriage before completing college.

---

❧

---

The ability to adapt is a survival strength of Asian Indian Muslim immigrants, and particularly of women, whose socialization emphasizes their capacity to adapt to different environments with minimal resistance. For example, a professional Muslim woman who conforms to career demands in all respects, including wearing Western dress, may return home to function as an obedient wife and daughter-in-law. Supporting the woman's connection to friends and family members (including extended family) who are sympathetic to her desired role may help her to redefine herself, bridging Eastern and Western concepts.

Although women may greatly desire release from certain roles and relationships, fear of isolation and ostracism may make them ambivalent, anxious, or depressed about the risk entailed. Therapists must help women develop supportive relationships within and outside their community with women who support their changing roles.

As with Hindus, Muslim families are likely to live in a hierarchical, joint family system of three or four generations, which demands respect and obedience toward elders, while encouraging interdependence and conformity (Rizvi, 1989; Williams, 1991). This may limit both a woman's and an adolescent's ability to challenge the hierarchy and thus work through conflicts within the family.

Arranged marriages are often the source of such conflicts. Although arranged marriages are much less common in recent times, young adults and their parents often act as if the old tradition were still the rule. Conflicts arising out of arranged marriages may precipitate a referral for therapy (Vaidyanathan & Naidoo, 1991). Couples have a difficult time adjusting to intimate life with a "stranger" after being raised in this country and experiencing friendship differently. Men in these marriages frequently resort to violence in order to gain the subordination expected in traditional marriages. Women, on the other hand, keep the code of silence for fear of shaming their families within the community.

Although many Asian women and men may present a high level of intellect, there may be a great lag between their intellectual and emotional development. They are often quite naive about sexual and emotional issues. However, the seeming rigidity of Muslim Indian families often gives way to intergenerational negotiation of cultural beliefs, which shows, in fact, remarkable flexibility. Young men and women can be coached to avoid confronting their parents directly with their changing values, to convey a respect and acknowledgment of the parents before gradually beginning a conversation to bring the parents around to tolerating their changing ways of thinking. Young adults most often tell their parents either too much or too little. They are not adept at sifting through what types of information should be offered to their parents; they typically offer too much or too little. A common error among Western therapists is to overidentify with the experience of the younger generation as it most closely resembles their own struggles with adolescence and reflects usually the dominant American values—"doing your own thing." The parents seek what they are most comfortable with—as much control over the lives of their children as possible!

Cultures in transition, such as India, are inevitably stressed by the challenges to traditional women's role as sex object and caretaker of others. Young men in India and Pakistan, as in patriarchal societies universally, are expected to have many brief sexual encounters before marriage, yet marry a virgin (Mernissi, cited in Al-Hibri, 1982).

## TREATMENT ISSUES FOR ASIAN INDIAN FAMILIES

The focus of treatment for Asian Indians and Pakistanis should be on family issues, even when individuals present alone. The family is central to individual development. This group in general expects concrete and time-limited advice in treatment. The concrete therapeutic suggestions should fit the complex familial and cultural issues and not be limited to cognitive approaches. They prefer to attend an extended session of several hours rather than to have weekly sessions for an unspecified time period. Therapy in general as well as its time concept are based on Western notions of individualism and success or happiness. Indians see therapy as a very small juncture in the overall scheme of their lives. Therefore, therapeutic solutions must attend to their definitions of success and happiness: past legacies (*karma*) and future life cycle impact (*nirvana*). With Muslim families, attention to the proper codes of behavior as defined by the Qu'ran is critical.

Asian Indians and Pakistanis vary in their perceptions of professional roles. The less educated see all professionals as "doctors" and authority figures, and accept advice accordingly. More educated men may, however, have difficulty with their power in the family being challenged, although, paradoxically, they like to be seen as tolerant and worldly. This is the leverage for change. Women are more accessible, although it is critical to engage men as well. Most prefer Asian therapists who have greater knowledge of their culture and whom they view as less likely to try to get their children to assimilate to Western culture. There tends to be a general understanding among Asians within a Western context.

The most common mental health problems presented by Asian Indian and Pakistani families are:

- Somatic complaints, such as frequent headaches and stomach pains.
- School-related difficulties with children, adolescents in particular.
- Academic difficulties, depression, malnutrition, and suicidal thoughts among girls and women.
- Boys' exhibiting arrogant behavior toward their parents and teachers (viewed as particularly problematic in light of cultural norms of obedience and tolerance), and, more recently, substance-abuse problems.
- Couples having difficulty with intimacy and with the husband's family of origin. The influence of the extended family is powerful irrespective of whether they live with the couple. Sons often form strong bonds of loyalty with their mothers, leaving the wife in an outside position.
- Domestic violence and child abuse, which are being more widely reported.
- Unresolved loss issues.
- Mother-in-law issues.

Mental illness and emotional difficulties are exacerbated by the intersecting influences of (1) stresses of immigration and acculturation, (2) adaptation to a racist culture, and (3) the hierarchy of the male-centered family system. These factors need to be considered in relation to the help-seeking behavior of all Asian Indian and Pakistani families.

The father of a 22-year-old female was distressed about the emotional well-being of his daughter who was having an "affair" with a "White" man. Their daughter, Mira, attended the first several sessions without her older brother, Viju, who was "too busy with his studies" and viewed this as his sister's "disaster." The parents stressed that their anger and disappointment were not because their daughter's boyfriend was White, but because of his lack of character.

The store manager had informed the father that this boy was a high school dropout, a bad influence, and owed a lot of money. Mira felt that the manager was motivated by racism in telling this to her parents, and that they had little concern for her or her family. She claimed that her parents' disapproval was also race-based. They did not care that her boyfriend was trustworthy and kind to her, but only that he was not an Indian.

Through different combinations of group and individual sessions with both siblings and parents, it became apparent that the father was quite abusive to his wife and children. The mother acknowledged that she had experienced years of depression, psychiatric treatment, and medication, and that the son, Viju, had attempted suicide shortly after their arrival in the United States 5 years previously, all because of the father's insidious control. The father spoke of his anger at being given a small dowry and being told that his wife was a journalist when, in fact, she did not even have a college degree. The parents came to see that what seemed at first glance to be Mira's rebellion, was in fact her reaction to a long history of violence and control by the father.

This case illustrates the importance of never literally accepting a problem definition with a culture where relationships are connected through complex patterns, even when families appear to be "Westernized" in their presentation. Questions about the dimensions of power and control by the father toward the mother and children are critical too. Unlike western cultures it is not unusual for men to call and elicit suggestions about fixing their families.

## CONCLUSION

Muslim and Christian families, similar to Hindu families, may come to the attention of therapists for many reasons: difficulties in school or with peers; conflicts with parents regarding dating, socializing, and sexuality; domestic violence; and, increasingly for young college women, date rape. This population is less likely to present with problems of caring for the elderly and the range of difficulties seen in Western couples who present for therapy. It is more typical that a woman or adolescent child, and sometimes a man, will present with psychological symptoms of depression. Depression is a common mask for mother-in-law issues, couple difficulties, adolescence or troubles dealing with "launching" children, or work problems.

It is crucial that the therapist validate, encourage, and respect the experience of the parents, and respect the family system, because any threat to family integrity is viewed as a failure on the part of the parents as well as the community. An exploration of the family structure and roles of authority in the family is necessary whether working with a couple, a subset of a family, or a larger extended family. As with Hindu families, extended family members who have not immigrated may still exert a strong influence on family members in the United States, as does the religious community here. Therapists can help families work through intergenerational conflicts by helping them to see themselves as a family/culture in transition and identify what is positive in the acculturation cycle and balance this with the preservation of religious, cultural, and family values.

When treating Asian Indian families, as with families of all ethnic, cultural, and racial groups, therapists should respect the existence of diversity and not assume that they are homogenous in their backgrounds or preference for treatment. The following suggestions may be helpful in locating families' experience when they enter treatment:

1. Ask specific questions to clarify their understanding about the family's cultural beliefs and traditions.
2. Find out about their experience with Western colonization.
3. Explore the migration history of the family. This exploration will help to engage the family as well as empower them.
4. Offer direct suggestions with respect to differences in the family rule structure in comparison to dominant nuclear families (i.e., importance of mothers-in-law to the marital dyad might involve the couple's negotiation of money while alluding to the mother-in-law's voice in this negotiation; coach the husband to be generous to his wife while maintaining loyalty to his mother; acknowledge the husband's/father's importance, while offering suggestions of empowerment to the wife/mother.
5. Shift the rule structure carefully to empower alliances between fathers and sons and to strengthen the marital dyad, both economically and socially.
6. Pay special attention to the life stage of the family's culture vis-à-vis mainstream culture, so that the anxiety around loss of cultural identity is lessened, while assisting members in their life choices around adolescence, leaving home or launching, young adulthood, and anticipation of arranged marriages.

## NOTE

1. This section is coauthored with Maya Rege-Colt.

## REFERENCES

Ahmad, I. (1976). *Family, kinship and marriage among Muslims in India*. New Delhi: South Asia Books.

Al-Hibri, A. (1982). *Women and Islam*. Elmsford, NY: Pergamon Press.

Almeida, R. (1990). Asian Indian mothers. *Journal of Feminist Family Therapy*, 33–40.

Arkoun, M. (1994). *Rethinking Islam*. Boulder, CO: Westview Press.

Ayakar, K. (1994). Women of the Indian subcontinent. In L. Comas-Díaz & B. Greene

(Eds.), *Women of color: Integrating ethnic and gender identities in psychotherapy* (pp. 161–181). New York: Guilford Press.

Baffoun, A. (1982). Women and social change in the Muslim Arab world. In A. Al-Hibri (Ed.), *Women and Islam* (pp. 227–241). Elmsford, NY: Pergamon Press.

Bumiller, E. (1990). *May you be the mother of a hundred sons: A journey among the women of India.* New York: Random House.

Chandrasekhar, S. (1982). *From India to America: A brief history of immigration: Problems of discrimination—Admission and assimilation.* La Jolla, CA: Population Review Publications.

Cooper, M. H. (1993, April 30). Muslims in America. *CQ Researcher, 3*(16), 373–380.

Dhruvarajan, V. (1993). Ethnic cultural retention and transmission among first generation Hindu Asian Indians in a Canadian prairie city. *Journal of Comparative Family Studies, 24*(1), 63–79.

Dynes, W., & Donaldson, S. (1992). *Asian homosexuality.* New York: Garland.

Gandhi, M. K. (1983). *Autobiography.* New York: Dover.

Gross, S. H., & Bingham, M. W. (1980). *Women in India.* Minneapolis, MN: Glenhurst Publications.

Gune, R. (1994, October 28). Problems of South Asian women. *India Abroad,* p. 51.

Hines, P. M., Garcia-Preto, N., McGoldrick, M., Almeida, R., & Weltman, S. (1992). Intergenerational relationships across cultures. *Families in Society, 73*(6), 323–338.

Hinnels, J. R., & Sharpe, J. (1972). *Hinduism.* Newcastle upon Tyne, UK: Oriel Press.

Hutnik, N. (1986). Patterns of ethnic minority identification and modes of social adaptation. *Ethnic and Racial Studies, 9*(2), 150–167.

Jiobu, R. M. (1988). *Ethnicity and assimilation.* Albany, NY: State University of New York Press.

Khalidi, U. (1991). Minority role in the U.S.: A model for Muslim Indians. In O. Khalidi (Ed.), *Indian Muslims in North America* (pp. 60–63). Watertown, MA: South Asia Press.

Khan B. (1992). Not-so-gay life in Karachi: A view of a Pakistani living in Toronto. In A. Schmitt & J. Sofer (Eds.), *Sexuality and eroticism among males in Moslem societies.* New York: Harrington Park Press.

Kolenda, P. (1993). Sibling relations and marriage practices: A comparison of North, Central, and South India. In C. W. Nuckolls (Ed.), *Siblings in South Asia: Brothers and sisters in cultural context* (pp. 103–142). New York: Guilford Press.

Krishna, A., & Berry, J. W. (1992). Acculturative stress and acculturation attitudes among Indian immigrants to the United States. *Psychology and Developing Societies, 4*(2), 187–212.

Lateef, S. (1990). *Muslim women in India: Political and private realities.* London & Atlantic Highlands, NJ: Zed Books.

Leonard, K. B., & Tibrewal, C. S. (1993). Asian Indians in Southern California: Occupations and ethnicity. In I. L. Light & P. Bhachu (Eds.), *Immigration and entrepreneurship—Culture, capital, and ethinic networks* (pp. 96–98). New Brunswick, NJ: Transaction Publishers.

Lynch, O. (1969). *The politics of untouchability: Social mobility and social change in a city in India.* New York: Columbia University Press.

Malayala, S., Kamaraju, S., & Ramana, K. V. (1984). Untouchability—need for a new approach. *Indian Journal of Social Work, 45,* 361–369.

McGoldrick, M., Almeida, R., Hines, P. M., Rosen, E., Garcia-Preto, N., & Lee, E. (1991). Mourning in different cultures. In F. Walsh & M. McGoldrick (Eds.), *Living beyond loss: Death in the family* (pp. 86–89). New York: Norton.

Mernissi, F. (1982). Virginity and patriarchy. In A. Al-Hibri (Ed.), *Women and Islam* (pp.183–191). Elmsford, NY: Pergamon Press.

Mernissi, F. (1992). *Islam and democracy* (M. J. Lakeland, Trans.). Reading, MA: Addison-Wesley.

Misumi, D. M. (1993). Asian-American Christian attitudes towards counseling. *Journal of Psychology and Christianity, 12*(3), 214–224.

Mitter, S.S. (1991). *Dharma's daughters—Contemporary Indian women and Hindu culture.* New Brunswick, NJ: Rutgers University Press.

Nanda, S. (1990). *Neither man nor woman: The hijras of India.* Belmont, CA: Wadsworth.

Nuckolls, C. W. (Ed.). (1993). *Siblings in South Asia: Brothers and sisters in cultural context.* New York: Guilford Press.

Papademetrius, D.G. (1993). Critical issues in the U.S. legal immigration reform debate. In I. Light & P. Bhachu (Eds.), *Immigration and entrepreneurship, Culture, capital and ethnic networks.* NJ: Transaction Publishers.

Papenek, H. (1973). Purdah: Separate worlds and symbolic shelter. *Comparative Studies in Society and History, 15*(3), 289–293.

Ramu, G. N. (1988). Marital roles and power: Perceptions and reality in the urban setting. *Journal of Comparative Family Studies, 12,* 207–227.

Rege, M. (1996). Breaking new ground: First generation Indian-American women. In S. Mazumdar & J. Vaid (Eds.), *Women, communities and cultures: South Asians in America.* Manuscript submitted for publication.

Rizvi, S. A. A. (1989). *Muslim tradition in psychotherapy and modern trends.* Lahore, Pakistan: Institute of Islamic Culture.

Roland, A. (1988). *In search of self in India and Japan.* Princeton, NJ: Princeton University Press.

Saijwani, V. (1989). *The law reporter* (Vol. 5). New Brunswick, NJ: Rutgers University Press.

Schmitt, A., & Sofer, J. (Eds.). (1992). *Sexuality and eroticism among males in Moslem societies.* Binghamton, NY: Harrington Park Press.

Sodowsky, G. R., & Carey, J. C. (1988). Relationships between acculturation-related demographics and cultural attitudes of an Asian-Indian immigrant group. *Journal of Multicultural Counseling and Development, 16*(3), 117–136.

U.S. Department of Commerce. (1993). *We the American Asians.* Washington, DC: Economics and Statistics Administration, Bureau of the Census.

Vaidyanathan, P., & Naidoo, J. (1991). Asian Indians in Western countries: Cultural identity and the arranged marriage. In N. Bleichrodt & P. J. Drenth (Eds.), *Comtemporary issues in cross-cultural psychology* (pp. 34–79). Ontario, Canada: Wilfrid Laurier University Press.

Vicente, M. (1992). *Psychosocial dynamics of the Persian Gulf War as reflected in the media*. Unpublished master's thesis, Smith College School for Social Work, Northampton, MA.

Visram, R. (1986). *Ayahs, lascars and princes: Indians in Britain 1700–1947*. London: Pluto Press.

Williams, R. (1991). Asian-Indian Muslims in the United States. In O. Khalidi (Ed.), *Indian Muslims in North America* (pp. 17–25). Watertown, MA: South Asia Press.

# PART VII

# FAMILIES OF EUROPEAN ORIGIN

# CHAPTER 29

# European Families: An Overview

## Joe Giordano
## Monica McGoldrick

While we were working on this book, a colleague commented that, surely, we had nothing to say about Italians or Irish families because, "Come on, White ethnics today don't have ethnic issues; they're totally American." His comment is surprising, especially since he is Jewish and has an Anglo American wife, yet he was expressing many therapists' perceptions that ethnicity pertains only to people of color.

We use "White ethnic" interchangeably with "European American" to refer to all non-Hispanic White families of European heritage. This term, first used to describe primarily Southern and Eastern European immigrants rather than Americans of British or German ancestry, is somewhat ambiguous.

According to the 1990 U.S. Census, Whites make up 80% of the U.S. population of 250 million. There are 53 categories of European Americans, of which the largest are German Americans (58 million), those of English ancestry (British, English, Welsh, and Scottish; 41 million), and Irish Americans (39 million); the smallest are Cypriot Americans (5,000). Yet these groups are barely mentioned in most discussions of "cultural diversity." (Roberts, 1995)

Most families from European American groups have been in the United States for three generations or more, so that the immigration generations' struggles against discrimination and for a satisfactory education, occupation, and residence have largely faded. An increasing number of White ethnics also marry outside of their own group, think of themselves simply as "Americans," and often are unaware of and uninterested in their mixed European heritage.

Also, individuals with common national, racial, and religious origins, or even those who speak the same language, may ignore or reject an ethnic identification if given that choice by society, and it is White ethnics generally who are given that choice. Since "ethnics" are thought to be groups other than "regular" Americans, all European groups can, to some extent, "pass" for "regular" and therefore may choose not to identify themselves ethnically, because this might seem to lower their status. In our definition, however, all people are ethnic, whether they choose to identify with their background or not—it is like not acknowledging your grandparents not to acknowledge your ethnic background. It is just a fact of our identities, one over which we have no choice.

However, there is no guarantee that a shared ethnic heritage produces homogeneity of thought, emotions, or group loyalty. Individuals may embrace, change, or reject aspects of their ethnicity, as well as aspects of their American identity. These actualities have led some social scientists to conclude that ethnicity among European Americans barely exists and has more of a symbolic meaning than a real significance for most Americans (Alba, 1990).

What many people, including researchers and social scientists, have failed to notice is that in periods of stress or personal crisis, individuals often return to familiar sources of comfort and help: their nuclear or extended family, their religion, the ethnic enclaves or community resources they grew up in, cultural rituals and behaviors, or the value and belief systems in which they were raised. In these situations, they call upon behaviors and attitudes that have evolved out of their ethnic background, which may differ from those of their peers or the norms of the dominant society.

Certain deeply embedded features of ethnic and religious identity may persist even after experience indicates they are dysfunctional (e.g., hyper-individualism or family enmeshment). And aspects of ethnicity that were shed or changed (e.g., names, belief systems, language, food rituals, family customs) may reappear later in life or in the next generation. Examples of this are the increasing number of third-generation Jewish Americans who have become Orthodox, the rise of Protestant fundamentalism, and the increased expression of ethnicity on college campuses and in the arts. The conscious and unconscious aspects of ethnicity are what make this subject so complex, yet elusive in research studies.

The clinical importance of understanding and addressing the ethnic differences even among European groups cannot be overestimated. Although therapists have generally ignored these differences, except as they pertain to "minority" groups, even physically similar groups differ on many dimensions, compounded, of course, by class and gender differences, leading to many misunderstandings. For example, Anglo and Irish Americans, although quite similar in appearance, differ profoundly in many character traits. Anglos prefer restraint, decorum, logic, and stoicism in all situations; the Irish are more interested in humor, dream, fantasy and intuition, and less interested in logic. Take the couple Katherine Hepburn and Spencer Tracy. While their differences probably reflect many issues, including class and family variables, their ethnic differences also seem striking. Dorothy Parker once said of Hepburn, a product of a stoic Protestant family of Scottish and English ancestry: "She runs the gamut of emotion all the way from A to B!" (cited in Kanin, 1988, p. 17). Tracy, on the other hand, would go from violent drunken rages to merry times to sullen withdrawal in roller-coaster fashion. Whereas Hepburn was careful, thorough, methodical, and analytical, he was an instinctive, intuitive player, who thought he went stale by overrehearsing and preferred to trust his intuition. With him there was a lot less clarity (Kanin, 1988). "With Spencer it was virtually impossible to know when he was pretending and when he was on the level" (p. 12). Hepburn's values of propriety, cleanliness, frugality, hard work, and rugged individualism are legendary. She took seven or eight showers a day! As a close friend described her: "When you enter her world you are expected to observe its strictness and you do without question. . . . You arrive on time and leave as early as possible . . . you agree with every one of her many opinions . . . you do not get drunk no matter how much you drink; you do not complain (you may, however, rail); you say nothing that may not be repeated; you refrain from lies, dissemblance and exaggerations; you omit discussion of your physical state, symptoms, ailments" (pp. 12–13). Tracy, on the other hand, saw fun in everything, except his religion. A full-scale hell raiser from his youth, full of highs and lows, he announced to his astonished family that he wanted to become a priest, but soon changed his mind and went into the military instead. Tracy was a loner who flitted in and out of relationships from his youth, could shift from charming merriment to week-long alcoholic binges, becoming cantankerous, unshaven, not changing his smelly clothes for weeks, holing up in the dark in a heavy overcoat he wore even in summer. Always a fighter and a rebel, he felt most comfortable in working-class contexts, dropping out of many schools even before he dropped out of college. In our view, acknowledging and helping couples sort through their differences may be essential to good therapy.

## A NATION OF IMMIGRANTS

From the beginnings of colonization, this country has been ethnically diverse, although we have tended to view Americans as European in ancestry (Tataki, 1993). As historian Ronald Tataki has put it, "In the creation of our national identity, 'American' has been defined as 'white'" (p. 2). Indeed, the immigration law of 1790 declared that only European American immigrants could become U.S. citizens. Although the English made up 61% of the 13 colonies' three million White inhabitants, there were many non-English immigrants and settlements. But the colonial English shaped basic American social and political institutions, so that Anglo culture became the ideal by which all subsequent ethnic groups were judged. Acculturation meant acquiring Anglo–Protestant lifestyles, values, and language (Banks, 1991).

Some European American groups adjusted easily to the new culture. Although the Germans did not speak English and were greeted with suspicion and hostility by Anglo Americans when they first arrived in the early 1700s, they adapted with little difficulty. In contrast, Irish adjustment was turbulent, although most Irish spoke English and fit well temperamentally with many aspects of Anglo American culture. But the "English" were threatened by their perceived clannishness, orientation to political power, and fierce loyalty to the Catholic Church (Brookheiser, 1991; Perlmutter, 1992; Tataki, 1993).

From 1880 to 1921 (when the first immigrants quotas for Europeans were adopted), millions of individuals from southern, central, and eastern Europe streamed to these shores. They tended to settle in ethnic communities: Little Italys, Polonias, Greektowns, and Jewish "ghettos." They also transformed America from an overwhelmingly Protestant country to one with millions of Catholic, Jewish, and Eastern Orthodox citizens (Handlin, 1951). The immigrants helped build America, its roads, railroads, bridges, and mines. Many of their children organized and helped build labor unions to fight the oppressive conditions they and their parents had endured.

Like the Irish, the Italians intense loyalty to each other violated the dominant culture's norms. They responded to the hostile dominant culture as they had coped with outsiders for centuries: by relying only on family and friends. Unlike the Irish, the Italians did not organize politically and therefore were not perceived as a threat to Anglo Americans except in terms of crime.

Many European Americans held one particularly deep, persistent prejudice that lingers to this day: anti-Semitism (Singer, 1994; Chanes, 1995). Yet in America, Jews have organized against anti-Semitism and generally have worked to influence the political process, as they never had in Europe. Because of constitutional protections against religious discrimination in America, there is significant discontinuity between the American Jewish and the European Jewish experiences. Despite this, some American Jews still felt a powerful wish to escape their heritage and "pass" for Anglo Americans (Klein, 1980; Gilman, 1986). As film director Steven Spielberg (1994) described his growing up in a non-Jewish town:

> I just wanted to assimilate. I wanted to be like everyone else . . . Being Jewish really made me stand out. I remember taping my nose so it would turn up. My grandfather would call me by my Hebrew name, Schmuel . . . and I wouldn't answer . . . because I was embarrassed. [When] I encountered anti-Semitism . . . I . . . realized there was a world out there in which people didn't like me. I didn't fight back. And that is one of the things I am most ashamed of. I hid it from my parents as long as I could. It has stuck with me for years. It still hurts. I began to question my Judaism. I felt a sense of shame.

After living in the United States for two or more generations, the immigrants from Eastern and Southern Europe called themselves "Americans." But the "native" Anglo Americans viewed them as unassimilable and judged them intellectually and culturally inferior (Banks, 1991; Perlmutter, 1992; Thernstrom, Orlov, & Handlin, 1980). Objects of ridicule, prejudice, and discrimination, they were blamed for a vast array of contemporary urban problems, economic recession, and political corruption, not unlike the current attitudes toward Haitian, Hispanic, and Asian immigrants (Brimelow, 1995).

Such sentiments helped create the extreme nationalism and ethnocentrism that characterized the 1920s "nativist," movements, which restricted immigration and protected the interests of the native-born (Banks, 1991; Thernstrom et al., 1980). The permanent adoption of immigration quotas in 1924 and the Depression (1929–1939) contributed to a sharp drop in immigration during the 1930s and 1940s. During World War II and the Holocaust, hundreds of thousands of Jews and other victims of Nazism were unable to obtain immigration visas because quotas favored Western and Northern Europeans (Tataki, 1993).

Strong religious and family traditions among newer European immigrant groups tended to make them conservative on many social issues, but their own memories of poverty enabled them to empathize with the struggles of other poor Americans and impelled them to vote for candidates favoring progressive economic legislation.

A major change in national policy took place with the Immigration Act of 1965, which repealed national-origins quotas and shifted the flow of immigration from Europe to other parts of the world, particularly Third World nations. Technical skills and kinship, rather than country of origin, became the major criteria for obtaining visas.

By the second and third generation, most European American immigrant families have done well. Their overall history has been marked by upward mobility, with some striking success stories, although a significant minority remain in low-status jobs in the middle-middle, lower-middle, or near-poor classes.

Today, only 20% of new immigrants come from Europe. However, in contrast to the often poor, uneducated Eastern and Southern Europeans who came from 1880 to 1924, most post-1945 European Americans are well educated, skilled professionals: They also have not experienced the discrimination that troubled earlier immigrants. Consequently, earlier immigrants' descendents, and the new arrivals from Europe, are quite different, even when they are from the same country of origin.

## FROM THE MELTING POT TO THE NEW PLURALISM

For some European Americans, the struggles of people of color for equal rights opened up hidden scars and repressed anger about discrimination they had suffered and their alienation from mainstream America. The economic recessions and the social and political changes resulted in millions of working-class, second- and third-generation European Americans becoming bitter and discontented with the direction of American society (Levine & Herman, 1972; Whiting, 1972).

During the 1970s, White ethnic intellectuals began to express pride in their roots, as well as anger for the generations of denial and repression of their ethnic identities. White ethnic writers began to write about the price of "Americanization" (e.g., Richard Gambino [Italian], Paul Cowan and Irving Howe [Jewish], the Rev. Andrew Greeley and Jimmy Breslin [Irish], and Michael Arlen [Armenian]). One of the most articulate was Slovak American Michael Novak (1971):

> My grandparents, I am sure, never guessed what it would cost them and their children to become "Americanized." In their eyes, no doubt, almost everything was gain. From the oppression experienced by Slovaks at the hands of the Austro-Hungarian empire, the gain was liberty; from relative poverty, opportunity; from an old world, new hope. They were injured, to be sure, by nativist American prejudices against foreigners, by white Anglo-Saxon Protestant culture, and even by an Irish church. (Any Catholic church not otherwise specified by nationality they experienced and described as "the Irish church.") (p. xxi)

Novak (1971) articulated the estrangement of European ethnic groups in *The Rise of the Unmeltable Ethnics.*

> I am born of . . . those Poles, Italians, Greeks and Slavs, non-English speaking immigrants, numbered so heavily among the workingmen of this nation. Not particularly liberal, or radical, born into a history not white Anglo-Saxon and not Jewish—born outside what in America is considered the intellectual mainstream. And thus privy to neither power nor status, nor intellectual voice. (p. 53)

Novak and such individuals as Irving Levine, Barbara Mikulski (now a U.S. Senator), the Rev. Andrew Greeley, and the late Rev. Gino Baroni became the intellectual and organizing core of the "New Ethnicity." They helped mobilize a coalition of European American groups that joined with minority groups to advance knowledge about ethnic and racial identity's role in shaping Americans' values, behavior, family patterns and lifestyles. They believed that America could equally promote diversity and foster a common culture. Today, their work is carried on by countless young writers, artists, and filmmakers who no longer feel shackled by a dominant culture sitting in judgment. Rather, they feel free to search out and express their familial and ancestral stories. During the 1980s, as many European Americans felt less alienated from mainstream society, the White ethnic movement faded.

During the 1990s, the United States experienced an ongoing influx of new immigrants and a backlash against them; the rise of new religious groups and a greater political influence of right-wing religious groups; increased ethnic and racial tensions, including Black–Jewish and Black–Korean conflicts (Berman,

1994); the expansion of the African American middle class and an increase in its rage; and a backlash against bilingualism, affirmative action, social welfare, and multiculturalism (Bernstein, 1994; Markowitz, 1994). Thus our country has become highly politicized and polarized along racial and ethnic lines ("Race and Racism: America's Dilemmas Revisited," 1994). The Kerner Commission's 1968 description of our being "Two Societies: One Black and One White" still pertains today.

## THE ISSUE OF RACE

Race and racism have long played a hidden role in European history. For centuries Europe's colonization of Africa, Asia, and the Americas meant that the continent was supported by the labor of people of color. Racism, anti-Semitism, and other prejudices have deeply characterized European countries.

Yet, Europeans fleeing religious persecution also envisioned a New World where all individuals would be legally guaranteed freedom and liberty. Millions of immigrants and refugees from around the world have come to the United States seeking such a society. Yet despite much progress over the past two centuries, racism still exists, although often in subtler forms than previously. It is one of our country's many paradoxes. Even the Irish, who in their own country were treated as an inferior race, though they initially sided with libertarian ideas in the United States, soon took advantage of their superior racial status in this country and participated in promoting the racial divide between Whites and people of color in the 19th century (Ignatiev, 1995). In his classic work *An American Dilemma*, Gunnar Myrdal (1944) had described racism as a "problem in the heart of the American." Sniderman and Piazza (1993) point out that a generation ago, antiracism formed the moral highground of American politics. Today, however, the authors conclude, bigotry has become more implicit than explicit and the politics of race have become more complex, divisive, and morally problematic. The authors ask: "What do whites think about blacks and how do these opinions influence their behavior and support for social programs? How much are Americans prejudiced? Is there a new racism, more subtle and covert than the old? Is racism reinforced by traditional American values such as self-reliance, hard work, and individual initiative" (p. 2).

The national mood on race remains bleak: 75% of Whites and 86% of Blacks view race relations as only fair to poor, and the level of segregation between European Americans and people of color, especially African Americans, remains extremely high (Sheler, 1994), yet most Americans agree that they want full integration (Mayer & Kosmin, 1994). In another study, 71% of adolescents said they would go out with someone of a different race (Pera, 1995). However, racial hostility and interracial alienation persist, while our ability to discuss these issues has declined. In a social climate of isolation and little dialogue, racial and ethnic stereotypes fester.

Blacks and Whites of all social and economic classes sometimes interpret the same event very differently (Terkel, 1992; Whitaker, 1995). The Clarence Thomas nomination hearing, the Rodney King beating, the 1993 Los Angeles riot, the O. J. Simpson trial and verdict, and the Million Man March in 1995 are among the events that indicate the vast chasm in understanding between Blacks and Whites.

In his editorial piece on the aftermath of the O. J. Simpson trial, journalist Eric Zorn (1995) underlines the lack of awareness of many Whites about African Americans' situation and sensibilities today, and the danger of an unbridgeable gap between races:

> Are things still that bad?, I asked myself. Does racism remain so endemic and corrosive that it becomes an occasion for delirious celebration within the African American community when the justice system exonerates one of their own, even one whom many Blacks acknowledge probably committed the double murder?
>
> Many, many African-Americans see us living in separate and unequal worlds and have the experience to prove it. . . . Was I really so naive as to have thought otherwise? . . . The answer is . . . Yes. I see and hear very little overt racism in my daily life, though I know this has a lot to do with both my choice of friends and a certain obliviousness that is a luxury of being white.
>
> I've interviewed haters and read much about discrimination in employment and housing. Even still, I'd allowed myself to pretend comfortably . . . that full equality and general harmony were but a generation or so of enlightened thinking away . . . Those images of blacks celebrating O. J. Simpson's acquittal shattered that for me and, I suspect for a lot of others who considered themselves fair and optimistic, and who thought they had seen significant progress in the last 30 years. In that disillusionment is discouragement and anger at how we've fooled ourselves, at how destructive and dangerous this alienation is to our country, at how far we are from our national goals. (p. 24)

What Zorn describes as a "luxury"—the many advantages and privileges of being White, is something that most European Americans are neither aware of nor prepared to acknowledge (McIntosh, 1988; Katz, 1978). Although interracial marriages have tripled in the last three decades, the actual numbers are relatively small. Likewise, surveys indicate that White Americans are more tolerant today than they were 20 years ago. Yet there is an increasing number of racial incidents and bias-related crimes, and almost complete residential separation of Whites and Blacks. This remains a profound societal problem and one that most Whites tend to be complacent about.

What are the implications of this chasm for therapists? In the clinical literature, racial issues are underrepresented. Many therapists deny or are unaware of this problem until they face a racial issue in either their professional or private lives (Carter,1995; Pinderhughes, 1989).

A. J. Franklin (1993) poignantly describes in his clinical work with professional middle-class Black men the pain of daily indignities and their feelings of being once again reminded to "stay in their place." When they come into therapy and share with a White therapist the accumulation of these indignities, the White therapist often minimizes them or explains them away. "When Black men feel as 'invisible' in therapy as they do in daily life, they don't want to bother" (p. 35).

White therapists and those of color are both also prone to ignore the ethnic differences among White clients, judging them by how well they fit into the dominant group's stereotype.

Family therapists too often treat race and ethnicity as a "special issue," rather than as basic to personal and social identity. Like patriarchal and class hierarchies, and heterosexist ideologies, so racism has been an invisible contributor to the cultural values of America's ethnic groups, as well as to the interactions between therapists and the families they treat.

## RELIGION

The United States is a very religious country. In a 1994 poll, 93% of Americans said they believe in a benevolent God who hears prayers and intercedes in their daily lives (Sheler, 1994).

Most Europeans share the dominant American Judeo-Christian belief in one God, and in the separation of church and state. Today, however, with the flood of new immigrants coming to the United States, other religions are making an impact on established religious institutions. Islam, the third great monotheistic faith, which is expanding through immigration and African Americans' conversions, will soon supplant Judaism as this country's third largest faith.

The Catholic Church, which has absorbed floods of immigrants, is particularly feeling the impact of the new immigration. Today mass is heard in 30 languages in New York City. Millions of Latinos with a fervent Latin approach to worship are challenging the church hierarchy. Latinos are also increasingly being attracted to the Pentecostal and Baptist faiths, creating new competition for the Catholic Church. Likewise Koreans, with their evangelical zeal and religious traditionalism, are causing a stir within Protestant churches.

Ethnicity often has a religious character, while religious life may be largely influenced by ethnic customs and rituals (Thernstrom et al., 1980). In America, such groups as Irish Catholics, German Jews, French Canadians, Armenian and Greek Orthodox, Finnish Lutherans, and Scottish Presbyterians are only a few of the European groups in which ethnicity and religion are inextricably linked (Gordon, 1964; Greeley, 1969,1974; Thernstrom et al.,1980). Yet within each faith community, there is also great ethnic diversity. For example, Danes, Finns, Germans, Norwegians, and Swedes coexist within Lutheranism. It is difficult to talk about religion without also talking about ethnicity.

Religion intersects with ethnicity in striking ways. For example Polish, Irish, and Italian Catholicism are quite varied. For the Irish, the Church is primary; other values, such as family, are secondary. For Italians, the family always comes first and everything else, including the Church, is secondary. For them, the Church serves as the opportunity for a fiesta or festival of family celebration, the reason family members come together. For Poles there is no separation between church and family, but Polish religiosity is tangible and physical, not intellectual or ascetic, as it may be for the Irish.

People use religion as a means of coping with stress or powerlessness, as well as for spiritual fulfillment and emotional support. Institutionalized religion and the church also meet social needs. Unfortunately, practitioners often fail to utilize appropriate religious tenets and support systems that give comfort and meaning to the family (Friedman, 1985; Pinderhughes, 1989).

Given Americans' strong spiritual beliefs and their religious institutions' social service networks, it is surprising that many family therapists treat faith as a private affair that has little or no impact on treatment.

## CLASS

It has been estimated that the "richest 20% of American households now own more than 80% of its wealth" (Vermuelen, 1995, p. 13). With this trend continuing into the next century, poor as well as middle-class families will find themselves in more vulnerable and precarious situations. These class differences will have a serious impact on family relations.

But although class is a major aspect of family life, not all differences can be ascribed to this factor alone. For example, most Italians, Greeks, Poles, and Irish who came to the United States had similar rural peasant backgrounds, yet there remain important ethnic differences among them, even when they move up in class. Individuals may feel compelled to make a choice between moving ahead and group loyalty, which can produce severe identity conflict.

Ethnic distinctions, although a hidden factor across class lines, apparently play a less powerful role among the most educated and upwardly mobile population segments. The royal families of Europe, for example, have been joined repeatedly as cousins marry across ethnic boundaries, making princes and queens in England mostly German or Greek and vice versa.

Groups also differ in terms of how they value education or "getting ahead," which may cause intergenerational, intergroup conflict. A person's country of origin clearly influences his or her class values. For example, the British class system is deeply entrenched, although British individualistic values mitigate against it.

Certain groups, such as Poles and Italians, have reservations about moving up in class, whereas Jews value such change, believing that parents should work hard so that the children will be more successful than they are. The Irish seem to be in the middle, hoping their children will rise in class, yet also having deep skepticism about their children "getting a swelled head."

## THE PERSISTENCE OF ETHNICITY

Even after generations of acculturation and intermarriage, ethnicity still influences in small and large ways how European Americans behave in their daily lives. In his autobiography, former President George Bush (1988) describes his Anglo American mother's advice after she heard one of his campaign speeches: "You're talking about yourself too much, George," she said. When he explained that he was expected to tell voters something about his qualifications, she persisted: "Well, I understand that, but try to restrain yourself." In contrast, when Lee Iacocca had presidential aspirations, he received a spirited response from his immigrant mother, Antonette. In a 1979 film about his career, she is seen serving her son a lavish meal, while he animatedly shares personal feelings and beliefs about his leadership abilities. As the camera focuses in on Antonette, she relates stories about her famous son, ending with the following: "Lee was really a very nice boy right from the beginning. What he got today, he got from God. He was really a good boy to his family. He calls me all the time on the phone for no reason . . . just to say 'Hello, ma. How you doin?'" (Iacocca, 1979).

A 1987 study of 220 mental health professionals clearly indicated the influence of ethnicity on their lives (McGoldrick & Rohrbaugh, 1987). Therapists differed significantly in characterizing their values and practices.

*Anglo Americans* indicated they were raised in families in which men and women were expected to be independent, strong, and able to make it alone. Exploration of the world was encouraged, self-control was highly valued, suffering was to be borne in silence, and conflicts were covered over, especially in public. They were significantly less likely to endorse the idea that you should still give time, money, and other assistance to any family member who needs it, no matter how busy you are.

*Jewish Americans* reported that in their families, children were encouraged to discuss and express opinions on family problems. They learned that talking about problems is the best way to solve them, success is more highly valued than anything else, and suffering is more easily borne when expressed and shared. In addition, you really get attention when you are sick, and you are not supposed to marry outside the group. In their experience, guilt was considered one of the best ways to shape a child's behavior. They were significantly less likely than others to endorse the statement that children should be seen and not heard.

*Italian Americans* learned that nothing was more important than the family, and that eating was a symbol of nurturing and family connectedness and a wonderful source of enjoyment. In their homes, roles were separate and defined; men, who were always dominant, protected and women nurtured. Babies were indulged, cuddled, and allowed to sleep with their parents. Families always liked to have a good time, and family members believed personal connections were the way to get things done. They were significantly less likely than the others to endorse these statements: Men and women should be strong and capable of making it on their own; self-control is very important.

In *Irish American families*, therapists learned that Church rules were paramount; suffering, which was to be handled alone, was their punishment for sins; drinking was an important part of social engagements; and complaining about problems was "bad form." In their homes, children were expected to be seen and not heard, and they were not praised too much so they would not get "swelled heads." Being self-controlled, strong, and psychologically tough was highly valued. Sex was not to be discussed and, in the final analysis, women were expected to take care of things. Irish American therapists were significantly less likely than others to endorse these statements: Eating is a wonderful source of enjoyment; suffering is easier to bear when it is expressed and shared.

In *Greek American families*, babies were indulged, constantly picked up, cuddled, and allowed to sleep with their parents. Sex was not discussed. Males were always dominant, and women were expected to know in their place. Parents warned children about the dangers in the outside world and wanted nothing more than for them to be successful. Older family members were respected for their wisdom.

## INTERMARRIAGE

Intimate relationships between people of different ethnic, religious, and racial backgrounds offer convincing evidence that America's tolerance of cultural differences may be higher than most people think. Thus, intermarriage is occuring at triple the rate of the early 1970s. More than 50% of Americans are marrying out of their ethnic groups: 33 million American adults live in households where at least one other adult has a different religious identity (Mayer & Kosmin, 1994). Lawrence Wright (1995) in his article "One Drop of Blood," points out that marriages between Blacks and Whites have tripled in the last 30 years. Also the number of children living in families in which one parent is White and the other is Black, Asian, or Native American has tripled from less than 400,000 in 1970 to 1.5 million in 1990. The figures do not include single or divorced families. With this trend increasing, therapists will be presented with new challenges in dealing with issues of identity, parenting, and family dynamics.

Some observers argue that the growing prevalence of intermarriage implies that ethnicity is evaporating from the American scene, that the "melting pot" (blending and fusing of European American identities) is finally becoming a reality. Our clinical work indicates the opposite.

We believe that dealing with these cultural differences is often the key to opening the family system. Also, although different cultural values may be deeply held and at the core of serious conflicts between spouses and or among family members, they may also provide a convenient way of rationalizing and displacing anger arising from other family problems. Therapists should be alert to such "cultural subterfuge." For example, a person who claims, "I don't think you understand me because of your different ethnic racial or religious background" may be trying to deflect attention from dealing with a difficult issue (Giordano & Carini-Giordano, 1995).

## CONCLUSION

Ethnicity persists in the consciousness of European Americans, in their perceptions, preferences, and behavior, even while mass production and mass communication homogenizes their outward appearances. Psychologically, European Americans are often ambivalent about their identities, and are constantly trying to balance the pull of their family histories and experiences with their individual desires to be accepted and successful in the larger society. The persistence of ethnicity, although weaker for some groups than for others, challenges therapists to broaden their concept of ethnicity and race and become more knowledgeable and sensitive to all who walk into their offices.

## REFERENCES

Alba, R. (1990). *Ethnic identity: The transformation of white America*. New Haven, CT: Yale University Press.

Banks, J. (1991). *Teaching strategies for ethnic studies* (5th ed.). Boston: Allyn & Bacon.

Berman, P. (Ed.). (1994). *Blacks and Jews: Alliances and arguments*. New York: Delacorte Press.

Bernstein, R. (1994). *Dictatorship of virtue*. New York: Knopf.

Brimelow, P. (1995). *Alien nation—common sense about America's immigrant disaster*. New York: Random House.

Brookheiser, R. (1991). *The way of the WASP*. New York: Free Press.

Bush, G. (1988). *Looking forward*. New York: Bantam Books.

Carter, R. T. (1995). *The influence of race and racial identity in psychotherapy.* New York: Wiley.

Chanes, J. (1995). *Anti-Semitism in America today: Outspoken experts explore the myths.* New York: Birchland-Carol Publications.

Franklin, A. J. (1993, July/August). The invisibility syndrome. *Family Therapy Networker,* pp. 32–39.

Friedman, E. (1985). *Generation to generation: Family process in church and synagogue.* New York: Guilford Press.

Gilman, S. (1986). *Jewish self-hatred.* Baltimore: John Hopkins University Press.

Giordano, J., & Carini-Giordano, M. (1995). Ethnicity and family therapy. In R. Mikesell, D. Lusterman, & S. McDaniel (Eds.), *Family psychology and systems therapy: A handbook.* Washington, DC: American Psychological Association.

Gordon, M. (1964). *Assimilation in American life.* New York: Oxford University Press.

Greeley, A. (1969). *Why can't they be like us?* New York: American Jewish Committee.

Greeley, A. (1974). *Ethnicity in the United Utates: A preliminary reconnaissance.* New York: Wiley.

Handlin, O. (1951). *The uprooted: The epic story of the great migration that made the American people.* New York: Grosset & Dunlap.

Iacocca, L. (1979). *Biography.* New York: Lifeline Productions.

Ignatiev, N. (1995). *How the Irish became white.* New York: Routledge.

Kanin, G. (1988). *Tracy and Hepburn: An intimate memoir.* New York: Donald I. Fine.

Katz, J. H. (1978). *White awareness: Handbook for anti-racism training.* Norman: University of Oklahoma Press.

Klein, J. (1980). *Jewish identity and self-esteem.* New York: Institute for American Pluralism, American Jewish Committee.

Levine, I., & Herman, J. (1972). The life of white ethnics: Toward effective working-class strategies. *Dissent, 19*(1).

Markowitz, L. (1994, July/August). The cross-currents of multiculturalism. *Family Therapy Networker,* pp. 18–69.

Mayer, E., & Kosmin, B. (1994). *National survey of religious identification.* New York City University of New York.

McGoldrick, M., & Rohrbaugh, M. (1987). Researching ethnic family stereotypes. *Family Process, 26,* 89–98.

McIntosh, P. (1988). *White privilege and male privilege: A personal account of coming to understand correspondences through work in women's studies* (Work in Progress, No. 189). Wellesley, MA: Stone Center, Wellesley College.

Myrdal, G. (1944). *An American dilemma.* New York: Harper & Row.

Novak, M. (1971). *The rise of the unmeltable ethnics.* New York: Macmillan.

Pera, G. (1995, August 18–20). "Teens and race: Special report." *USA Weekend.*

Perlmutter, P. (1992). *Divided we fall.* Ames: Iowa State University Press.

Pinderhughes, E. (1989). *Understanding race, ethnicity and power: The key to efficacy in clinical practice.* New York: Free Press.

"Race and racism: America's dilemmas revisited." (1994). *Salmagundi,* pp. 3–136.

Roberts, S. (1995). *Who we are: A portrait of America based on the latest U.S. Census.* New York: Times Books.

Sheler, J. (1994, April 4). Spiritual America. *U.S. News & World Report,* pp. 48–59.

Singer, D. (Ed.). (1994). *American Jewish year book.* New York: American Jewish Committee.

Sniderman, P., & Piazza, T. (1993). *The scar of race.* Cambridge, MA: Harvard University Press.

Spielberg, S. (1994, March 14). In B. Getty (Producer), *Barbara Walters special.* Los Angeles: ABC Television.

Tataki, R. (1993). *A different mirror: A history of multicultural America.* Boston: Little, Brown.

Terkel, S. (1992). *Race: How Blacks and whites think and feel about the American obsession.* New York: New Press.

Thernstrom, S., Orlov, A., & Handlin, O. (Eds.). (1980). *Harvard encyclopedia of American ethnic groups.* Cambridge, MA: Harvard University Press.

Vermuelen, M. (1995, June 18). What people earn. *Parade Magazine,* pp. 4–6.

Whitaker, M. (1995, November 15). Whites and Blacks. *Newsweek,* pp. 50–61.

Whiting, B. (1972). *Race and ethnicity task force report.* New York: Ford Foundation.

Wright, L. (1995, November 6). One drop of blood. *The New Yorker.*

Zorn, E. (1995, October 8). O.J. aftermath shows how divided a people we still are. *Chicago Tribune,* p. 24.

# CHAPTER 30

# Amish Families

## Eric Emery

The Old Order Amish are both an ethnic group with distinct cultural origins and a Christian sect whose commitment to living their faith is reflected in every aspect of daily life.

The Amish believe in a strict interpretation of the Bible, specifically the following passages, which explain why they choose to live as they do: "Love not the world, neither the things that are in the world. If any man love the world, the love of the father is not in him" (I John 2:15). "Wherefore come out from among them, and be ye separate, saith the Lord, and touch not the unclean thing, and I will receive you" (II Cor. 6:17). The Amish choose to live separate from the dominant culture because they believe the outer world to be a place of temptation and sin. Although their religion permeates their culture, it does not totally explain who they are ethnically and psychologically.

Amish immigration to America occurred during two periods, 1727–1790 and again from 1815–1860. They came initially to Pennsylvania from Switzerland because of William Penn's guarantees of religious freedom. Several communities were established in southeastern Pennsylvania, and those in rural Lancaster County, approximately 70 miles northwest of Philadelphia, have been among the most enduring (Hostetler, 1989). As the flow of Amish immigration from Europe continued, they established large communities in Pennsylvania, Ohio, Indiana, and Illinois. Small communities were also eventually established in many Northern and Midwestern states and the Canadian province of Ontario. There are today approximately 900 congregations with an excess of 130,000 members (Kraybill, 1993).

This chapter is intended as a framework for understanding the Amish and those families who have left the culture. In order to fully comprehend the unique complexity of this society, it is important to understand the strict code of conduct Amish families follow. These rules directly emanate from religious doctrine noted earlier and set forth in the 1600s and early 1700s. Although these rules are incredibly specific and would seem to outsiders to be restrictive of individual liberties, they are rarely viewed that way from within the culture. However, refusal to follow any part of these rules by any member of the community is a serious problem.

A young Amish man sought counseling because he recently purchased rubber tires for his tractor and realized that when this was discovered by the bishop, he would be excommunicated. He had been secretly thinking of leaving the church and by purchasing the tires, he had created a dilemma that would force a decision that he had been consciously afraid to make. The therapist helped him examine both what he would gain and lose by leaving the community. In encouraging the young man to consciously accept responsibility for his choices, and ultimately those of whatever decision he made, he empowered the client. The client decided that the benefits of belonging to the community far outweighed whatever restriction of freedom he was experiencing. He removed the rubber tires from his tractor.

There is a tendency among those who break away to want to dissociate themselves from the rigid boundaries and restrictions of the culture. Yet with the increasing distance between mainstream America and the Amish way of being, it is becoming increasingly difficult for those who choose to leave the Amish faith and community to make a successful transition into the dominant culture.

I have witnessed families two and three generations removed who are still struggling to fit. Among those who leave Amish communities, it is the young who make the quickest transitions, sometimes appearing to become Americanized overnight eschewing any trace of their origins. This process is often disempowering to parents who lose their ability to control their children's behavior and what they are exposed to.

My father's family roots were in Old Order Amish tradition. I watched him navigate two worlds during his lifetime. At home he was a strict disciplinarian who stressed the value of hard work. Like an Amish father, he did not communicate much with his family. At work he was a teacher and a school principal who could be charming and socially engaging. As a child I remember being puzzled by this split. However, I have watched this same pattern emerge in me as an adult. I call it the dichotomy between my Amish and mainstream self. I have witnessed this same split between a preference for simplicity and the demands of participating in today's highly complex and technology-driven world with those who have left the Amish faith and community.

The other problem that coincides with this is deciding what is appropriate, having left a culture that always made the decisions. There is a high level of comfort and security for those who stay in this closed society that is lost by those who choose to leave. The price paid by choosing to stay is loss of personal choice and individual identity. The cultural lens never focuses on the individual, only on family and community, so individual rights are nonexistent. This often leads to a struggle for those who leave, as they attempt to figure out how to make individual decisions.

Beyond this internal split between the old and new worlds, I have identified a series of characteristic conflicts that appear common to many who leave the Amish community. Chief among these is knowing what is appropriate and expected in spousal roles. This is often less a problem if both partners had roots in Amish tradition. When only one partner has Amish roots, problems emerge in what the Amish refer to as "willfulness versus submission." In Amish culture, it is a woman's role to be submissive to her husband and follow his lead in all things. Furthermore, communication is often a problem, because men in Amish culture do not discuss their feelings. Any Amish man who leaves the culture and marries an outsider will be ill-equipped for dialogue with his spouse, especially concerning her emotional issues.

A couple married 7 years presented for treatment. They had left the Amish culture 4 years earlier because of their dissatisfaction with the rigidity concerning religious expression. They were both church members and had been shunned by the community but not entirely by their families.

This couple was caught in a kind of limbo between the Amish world and the dominant culture. Their cutoff from the loving community and their families of origin was very painful for them. Both were grieving the loss of friends and family. Their limited contact with their families allowed some relief; however, both sets of parents were extremely judgmental and unaccepting of their new life and how they were raising their children. This couple and their children were caught between worlds. They knew they could not return to the rigid dictates of Amish life, yet they constantly felt they did not fit into the dominant culture.

Therapy consisted of acknowledging their pain, grief, and loss and witnessing their odyssey in search of themselves and of belonging in the world. The couple left therapy after several months because the husband accepted a new job outside the area. They both said talking about their pain and loss helped them move on. However, it is my belief that they remained caught between two worlds, seeking both what they lost in the community and the freedom they endeavored to find in the dominant culture.

---- ⚭ ----

## FAMILY AND COMMUNITY STRUCTURE

Each Amish community is independent of all others, with no formal hierarchy. The community is composed of several families that make up their district. A Bishop is named through the church community of families and is the leader inside the community and in all official interactions with the outside world. Their language is often referred to by outsiders as "Pennsylvania Dutch." It is primarily an oral language that is spoken in the home and the community. The origins of this language are from an Alemannic dialect, which was common to a geographic region of Switzerland, France, and Germany. Learning English is seen as important in order to conduct business in the world outside of the community but is not encouraged within it (Hostetler, 1989).

The Amish are a traditional culture that sees men's and women's roles as dictated by scripture and not open to interpretation or redefinition because of changing times. The father is the head of the household; women must be obedient and submissive to their husbands. In church matters, "women have an equal vote but not an equal voice" (Hostetler, 1980, p. 152). Their influence is essentially limited to the process of raising the children. There is no divorce. Relationships are monogamous. The only end to a marital relationship comes through death.

The Amish do not believe in birth control. Families are large, often numbering seven or more children, who are seen as a gift from God and are received and cared for as such. Large families have been a necessity due to the physically demanding nature of farmwork, conducted without the aid of modern machinery. This may be changing, as it is estimated that only about 50% of today's Amish are actually engaged in farmwork as a primary occupation.

Men do not assist with the duties of the house. The preferable work for men is farming or vocational trades closely associated with the sustenance of the community, including harness and carriage making, carpentry, cabinet and furniture making, and blacksmithing. When no other options are available for work, the Amish will seek employment in trades outside the community, but this is not preferred because of the possible negative impact of regular exposure to the outside world. Amish are now working in factories, building mobile homes and recreational vehicles, and are valued by employers because they are hard workers who do not take coffee breaks, sick days, or cause problems.

The Amish may not join unions, and they have negotiated compromises in closed-union locations that dues collected for Amish workers will be donated to charity. Each work location or factory must be approved by the Bishop for the community. Amish are never allowed to have government jobs, or any job that involves making military hardware (Wittmer, personal communication, November 1994).

Women not only do all of the household tasks, they also assist in farm chores and maintenance. Amish children pattern their lives after their parents in dress and behavior. Responsibility, according to their gender roles, is allotted with each year of age. Amish boys are apprenticed either to the farm or the trade of their fathers. Amish girls follow the path of their mothers in tending to the care of children and maintenance of the household. Some young Amish women are now also working in factory locations, which has been of great concern to the Amish, who are afraid the women will be led astray by exposure to worldly things and ideas (Wittmer, personal communication, November 1994).

Everyone works, except very young children, the ill, and the aged. Each child, beginning at about age 4, is given tasks and chores appropriate to his or her age and capabilities.

The role of women in Amish society greatly restricts their choices. Daughters know they will not be inheriting the farm. It is considered preferable for women to marry. If they do not marry, which is not uncommon, they continue to live with their parents, even after the main house has been turned over to one of the brothers and his family. At this point unmarried women see their options become very limited (Hostetler, personal communication, October 1994).

I have no knowledge of Amish men choosing not to marry. The Amish do not acknowledge homosexuality. It is viewed as abnormal, and those who feel differently about their sexual orientation must see the Bishop. If an Amish man or woman were openly homosexual, he or she would be excommunicated from the church and shunned by the community. Amish men and women are expected to marry and have children, even if they have homosexual feelings.

Amish parenting styles are traditional, and parental authority is unquestioned, with the father seen as the ultimate authority. However, tradition dictates that parents work together in raising the children. In a culture that believes in adult baptism, parents know they are ultimately responsible for their children's souls. Although this system may seem autocratic and dictatorial to outsiders, it is not viewed this way from within the culture. Parents do not disagree in front of the children. They are a united team that the children cannot split (Hostetler, 1980). Parents want children to follow in their footsteps because the children are being prepared to live their lives exactly as previous generations. New ideas on parenting are not available. Ideas of upward mobility or of getting ahead are nonexistent. Competition is frowned upon, and pride in any form is a sin.

## LIFE CYCLE TRANSITIONS

Births are viewed as gifts from God, are joyfully acknowledged by the family and community, and enhance the standing of the family within the community. For the first 2 years of life, children are treated with total loving care and permissiveness. Beyond age 2, the child is exposed to the parental system of strict discipline that continues until adolescence (Hostetler, 1989). Children must learn to conduct themselves in accordance with the Amish way of life, both inside the community and in the outside world.

The transition to school life is probably less traumatic for Amish children than for "English" children because of community size and regular interactions of members. The Amish in most established communities have their own schools. Teachers are not college-educated instructors because the Amish feel it is more important to have someone from inside their culture teaching their children. While in school, the child is taught to speak and write in English (which is not spoken in the home and seldom in community). The family plays an important role in helping children learn basic educational skills and in developing humility, forgiveness, and appreciation. The Amish see eighth grade as the end point in the child's formal school life.

Following eighth grade, Amish young people do expand their horizons, often by working for other families, even beyond their own communities. As with all adolescents, their peer group becomes much more important as a socializing agent than either family or community. Young people spend a great deal of time together when they are not attending to work responsibilities. It is cause for concern when a young person chooses a non-Amish peer group because the choice increases the likelihood that he or she will eventually decide to leave the community.

In the adolescent peer group, a certain amount of acting out is tolerated. Stories of buggy races, slipping traditional garb for "worldly clothing" and going into town to the movies, having a car stashed somewhere, and other "worldly" pursuits are not uncommon, all done without parental and adult knowledge. However, exploring sexuality, use of alcoholic beverages and tobacco, and gambling are not allowed and, if discovered, can result in a strong rebuke from the community.

The life decisions facing Amish adolescents are those that concern joining the church and marriage. The decision to join the church is a sober one that means a young person has decided to become baptized and live by and be accountable to the rules of the community. It also means leaving behind the worldly pursuits of adolescent experimentation. This decision is viewed as one of the symbolic rites of the transition to adulthood (Hostetler, 1980).

Marriage is seen as the other symbolic rite in the passage to adulthood. Amish young people usually choose to wait until early in their 20s to marry. Marital relationships are not viewed from a romantic perspective. Relationships are practical and based on respect. The Amish do not believe in open or public displays of affection. Adults do not hug, kiss, or show other physical signs of affection toward each other in front of their children or anyone else. They form a union of cooperation with each other, working together and making decisions as one.

The single most important issue in all relationships is intimacy. The emphasis on practicality and not romantic love leads most Amish couples to a marital structure that I call "parallel lives." The married couple lives their life on a parallel course, but interpersonally they are distant. My parents' marriage reflected this pattern of parallel lives, and their relationship worked best when they had a distance that I symbolically refer to as "3 feet apart." I remember hearing my oldest sister say at my father's funeral that she had never seen my parents hug or kiss in their 30 years of marriage. I was shocked because even though I had never seen it in my lifetime, being the youngest, I had somehow assumed it must have been there before I was born.

A 34-year-old woman requested treatment for issues concerning her grief following the death of her mother. She had been married for 10 years to a man who left the Amish church. She reported that her husband was unable to respond to her need for emotional support and tenderness and said he was generally noncommunicative and had difficulty expressing his thoughts and feelings. She was angry and frustrated because of what she perceived as his unwillingness to participate in a dialogue of loving intention and support. The therapist, whose attempts to get the husband in for conjoint marital sessions were unsuccessful, explained the cultural origins of his behavior, providing the wife a new way to understand their marital disconnectedness. In follow-up sessions, the wife reported that the cultural interpretation by the therapist allowed her to see their marriage and his behavior in a new light, which enabled her to stop questioning her adequacy as a woman.

Elders in the community are viewed with great respect and are treated accordingly. They may work or not, as they prefer. Many older people pursue hobbies such as making crafts. When aging parents turn over the farm to one of their sons, they move into separate quarters that have been built for them, often attached to the main house. There is no problem with care of the elderly among the Amish because there is no question about where they will live or who will care for them. The Amish do not see the care of their parents and in-laws as a burden but rather as a gift.

Death is a sober occasion (Hostetler, 1980), yet it is seen in context as a natural part of the rhythm of life. It is greeted as the passage to a better life with God. There is no doubt about the hereafter and therefore no anxiety.

## MENTAL ILLNESS

Mental illness is viewed as a tragedy because it affects one's ability to function as a contributing member of family and society. Since the communities are usually small and interdependent, any case of mental illness is widely known. The Amish are unique, as they have no alcoholism, drug abuse, or sociopathy, since these behaviors are culturally forbidden (Egeland & Hostetter, 1983).

Outside counseling and intervention will be sought if the severity of the problem is such that it cannot be tolerated in the community, or if there is a risk to the person's life. The secrecy that surrounds the Amish culture often makes it more difficult for family members to seek outside help. Yet talking to others inside the culture is not an option; if the problem involves some rule transgression or questioning of the way of life, it will be brought to the attention of the Bishop, resulting in some disciplinary response. This is why many suffer in silence.

The issue of extended inpatient psychiatric care is another dilemma. Egeland and Hostetter (1983) conducted a 6-year study on affective disorders among the Amish. In their research, they found the highest percentage of those deemed mentally ill fell into three categories: bipolar (34%), unipolar (37%), and minor depression (8%). They found extremely low rates of schizophrenia (4%), atypical psychosis (2%), paranoid disorder (2%), and schizoaffective disorder (6%).

It is important to note that the Amish have an extremely high tolerance for "peculiar" behavior. This is based on a cultural belief in acceptance and is supported by faith that God made everyone in His image. It is not uncommon for the families of afflicted members to continue to care for them at home, even though the severity of the disorder taxes the families' ability to manage. Steering family members through psychotic episodes or extreme manic states is aided by family willingness to avail themselves of community-based, outpatient psychiatric systems of care and psychiatric medications.

## PROFESSIONAL GUIDELINES FOR OUTSIDERS

As a mental health provider offering services both to those who have left the culture and those who remain isolated in their communities, I offer the following therapeutic guidelines.

- Helping individuals evolve their sense of self and encouraging individual achievement and personal pride will place the Amish in conflict with their culture, and is not advised. Therefore, it is important for therapists to acknowledge their own cultural and personal biases. Beyond this, help clients articulate their dilemmas, allowing them freedom to explore alternatives within and outside the bounds of the culture, if they decide this is appropriate. Yet the guiding therapeutic principle should be not to inject your opinions and beliefs unless there is either a threat to life or a legal mandate to report a problem, as in child physical or sexual abuse.
- Respect Amish requests for separateness both from non-Amish and from things deemed worldly to them. For example, do not attempt to videotape therapy sessions.
- It would be considered incredibly disrespectful for a therapist to curse, use harsh language, or use God's name in vain while interacting with the Amish. If this should happen, the Amish client will never return.

• Be careful when exploring subjects concerning family or community problems, as there may not be permission to discuss these with outsiders. Learn the difference between privacy dictates of the culture, which should be respected, and secrets (e.g., incest) that need to be exposed for healing to occur.

• Be sure the family understands the nature and limits of confidentiality.

• Be sensitive to issues of gender roles and possible conflicts between your personal values and those of the culture.

• Be cautious of counseling instincts that lead you to encourage someone to leave the community.

• Be open to learning about their world. Inform them that you follow a process that is useful to you in interviewing, but you are not an expert on their culture. Ask for their help in navigating the intricacies of their culture. They value medical and professional expertise and will respond to your honesty and personal integrity.

The Amish represent a unique paradox: Their continued existence depends on their ability to hold the ever-encroaching technological world at bay, while clinging to a fragile bond with the past and nature. Their unfailing belief in God and ongoing commitment to living in disciplined communities leaves them with few questions about their way of life. Yet, as the mainstream American society demands greater technological complexity and escalates its rejection of agrarian ideals, it seems there is little room for a culture that emphasizes simplicity and a desire for separateness. This leads me to wonder if this new reformation will result in either a breakdown of Amish society or a new exodus for the Amish in search of a simpler world in concert with nature and God.

## ACKNOWLEDGMENTS

I wish to thank the following people for their invaluable assistance: Betsy Langner, Jeanne Emery, Robert Weaver, La Vern Yutzy, John Hostetler, and Joe Wittmer.

## REFERENCES

Egeland, J. A., & Hostetter, A. M. (1983). Amish study I: Affective disorders among the Amish 1976–1980. *American Journal of Psychiatry, 140*(1), 56–61.

Hostetler, J. A. (1980). *Amish society* (rev. ed.). Baltimore & London: Johns Hopkins University Press.

Hostetler, J. A. (1989). *Amish roots: A treasury of history, wisdom and lore.* Baltimore & London: Johns Hopkins University Press.

Kraybill, D. B. (1993). *The Amish and the state.* Baltimore & London: Johns Hopkins University Press.

# CHAPTER 31

# American Families with English Ancestors from the Colonial Era: Anglo Americans

David W. McGill
John K. Pearce

Approximately one-fourth of all Americans (70 million) have ancestors descended from the English colonists who were recorded in the first U.S. Census in 1790. Scholars call them Anglo Americans—the term used by therapists and the general press to distinguish the descendants of colonial English from other Americans (Gleason, 1980; McGill, 1992; Thernstrom, Orlov, & Handlin, 1980). One-half to two-thirds of these colonial-era immigrants and their descendants have intermarried with other ethnic groups, bringing another one-fourth of Americans into direct family contact with Anglo American values (Allen, 1989). Anglo American core values persist in these families.

Freedom of the individual and the emphasis on psychological individualism are the values that most distinguish Anglo American families from other American families. As exemplified throughout this book, American families across the cultural spectrum value political, economic, and cultural self-determination, but in Anglo Americans self-determination becomes exaggerated into hyperindividualism.

Later in this chapter we focus on the four distinctly different regional groups of Anglo American colonists and their descendants—Puritans New Englanders, Mid-Atlantic Quakers, Southern Tidewater Anglicans, and Border Country Appalachians—and their variations on the theme of hyperindividualism.

## THERAPY AND THE THERAPEUTIC PROCESS

In therapy, Anglo Americans are likely to identify as problems those situations that disrupt autonomous functioning. Usually they will attempt to avoid dependency and direct expressions of anxiety. They may, even when suffering, prefer emotional isolation and withdrawal. Lack of contact, separation from others, difficulty communicating, and blandness are not likely to be regarded as problems.

Family therapist Murray Bowen and his followers have rightly observed that even apparently isolated and detached people may be covertly fused to their families by invisible loyalties and covert dependencies. His recommendation is to encourage even more individuation so they can be separate while together. Anglo Americans are wary of affiliation and attachment. They prefer distance. Individuals in therapy need to be tactfully encouraged to balance dependence and independence to achieve more genuine autonomy.

Starting treatment is difficult and embarrassing for Anglo Americans. Individuals usually come for help only when it is impossible to deny their problems, or when their efforts to solve them alone have failed. Failing to solve their own problems make Anglo Americans feel inadequate. Therapists should see initial awkwardness as a difficulty in seeking help and not as a true reflection of the severity of the presenting problem. Unfortunately, successful treatment may not reduce Anglo American discomfort with therapy. Furthermore, open encouragement may be embarrassing.

Once Anglo American families are talking comfortably, they are likely to get right to the truth of the matter—as they know it. Anglo Americans value insight and reason, including meaningful discussion. The key is "meaningful." They tend to be literal, parsimonious, and careful with words, treating them seriously, as if the words were part of a contract ("My word is my bond"). This characteristic may be underestimated by therapists from cultures that traditionally use words differently.

Anglo Americans will want to clearly define a problem that can be worked on. Once this is done, the family can proceed with confidence, believing that hard work in therapy will be sufficient for success. Hard work is a core value in therapy, as in other aspects of life.

Anglo Americans will be most comfortable making the therapeutic relationship a contractual one, viewing the therapist as the family's consultant. Anglo American families will expect to pay a fair fee, clearly negotiated, promptly and without hassle, and they will expect to get their money's worth in terms of successful treatment.

The therapist should show respect for Anglo American individualism by making contracts with each member of the family, including children. Often, the therapist will be wise to use an objective method (e.g., reason, discussion, education, task assignment, training) as an initial access to more subjective matters. Objective methods lead to core emotional issues and the reduction of emotional isolation.

Although starting treatment is uncomfortable for Anglo Americans, they may terminate quite easily and view the end of therapy as completion of a job well done. They may just stop. Abrupt departures should not necessarily be attributed to resistance, failure to complete work, or separation anxiety—it is simply Anglo American style. They may (like some Irish families) leave therapy quite satisfied, without a word of acknowledgment or validation, only to tell an astonished therapist some years later how the therapy turned their lives around.

## THERAPY AND SHARED VALUES

Anglo Americans have been taught that the meaningful issues and genuine struggles of life all lie within the self, and that few external constraints cannot be overcome by individual effort. All persons can, and therefore should, be individually successful. Failure is almost always ascribed to personal weakness (Pearce & Friedman, 1980).

The value of self-reliance may be illustrated by the case of an upper-class New England couple's marriage that was threatened by the wife's irritability and anger as she attempted to cope with her full-time profession, a 6-month-old daughter, and multiple sclerosis. It was a revelation to her when the therapist suggested she might be doing too much. The couple was better able to understand the origins of her expectations of herself by exploring her family history. Her ancestors, including the women, had been fiercely independent and had striven to make social contributions through professions or social services. Reviewing this history helped to make sense of her difficulty in accepting any disability or asking for help from her husband. She was successful in therapy in revising her expectations to a more realistic level.

——————— ✷ ———————

Anglo Americans would rather not complain.

The father of a Anglo American man developed a melanoma on his back. Eventually it bled so much that he had to change his shirt many times a day, yet he never sought medical attention. Finally, a tumor developed under his arm that was so painful and disabling that he was "forced to get to a doctor." He soon died.

Listening to this description, the son's Jewish therapist suggested that it was too bad that the father had not gotten some help and relief earlier. The Anglo American patient, who was doing grief work for his father as part of the therapy, replied, "No, my father made his choice and died his own way."

——————— ✷ ———————

The Anglo American response to pain may be contrasted with the Irish style. Zborowski (1969) points out that the Irish tend to repress and deny pain—often they cannot accurately identify its location. Anglo Americans can identify pain. They report it fully and accurately to the physician—when they think something can be done about it. They want to assist the physician's work. But where a remedy seems unlikely, they usually prefer to not discuss it. They value bearing pain silently—if they can. This silence contrasts with Jewish and Italian traditions of valuing vivid expression of pain and suffering. The contrast, of course, applies not only to physical pain but to emotional pain.

Anglo American's prefer to "not waste words." The silence is emotional self-containment. Although a caricature, the image of the silent cowboy or rugged frontiersman who says nothing after returning from arduous months on the trail (because "There is nothing to say") exemplifies Anglo American sparse use of speech. Anglo Americans do not use words for drama as do Italians, nor to elaborate reality as do Irish, nor to articulate and share feelings and thoughts about suffering as do Jews. Anglo Americans may feel that if they say too much about themselves, they will burden others.

On Kluckhohn's value-orientation scale of basic cultural choices, Anglo Americans have a strong future orientation, prize individual achievement, and see themselves as dominant in their relationship to the natural world (Papajohn & Spiegel, 1975). Thus, they do not see the point of dwelling on past problems; their attention belongs elsewhere, especially on the future and "getting on with it." This future orientation, once expressed in the ruthless exploitation of the resources of the continent, is now expressed in the passionate cause of preservation of the natural environment "for the future."

Above all, Anglo Americans value work. They may seem to focus more on the external signs of success, probably because they believe success is evidence of virtue. Calvinists believed that success (which was actually achieved by hard work) was evidence of predestined salvation. An Anglo American's identity, relationships, self-esteem, and sense of adequacy and well-being may all be tied to work. Indeed, Anglo Americans have a tendency to transform many aspects of life into work. Men and women "work" at making a living, and "work" at raising the children. Anglo Americans may talk of "working" on relationships, love, sex, fulfillment, and identity. They may even treat their recreation, hobbies, collections, and sports very seriously, with standards of achievement and success in each. They want therapy to be work—so they can do it.

## ANGLO AMERICAN CHILDREN

Anglo Americans raise their children to be self-contained, principled, responsible, independent, self-reliant, self-determining, and, perhaps, from the vantage point of other cultures, self-centered individuals. The more children begin to demonstrate that they can take care of themselves, the more successful Anglo American parents feel.

The following example illustrates how fathers may relate to their children primarily by criticizing their performance. This unintentionally produces feelings of inadequacy.

A man who came into therapy with work problems reported that his relationship with his father had consisted primarily in joining him in doing tasks around the house. The father's role was to show his son how to do things right so the son could take care of himself some day. The man recalled often feeling ashamed and inadequate because, although he had persevered, he could never do things "quite right," and his father would often complete the task himself. The father's self-absorbed task orientation made the child feel that the work was more important than the relationship. In addition, the work required an attention span and mastery of detail beyond a child's reach. Sometimes Anglo American training for individual adequacy can turn out to be training in feelings of inadequacy.

Anglo American children often complain that their parents relate to them in a detached manner. Hovering, worried parental involvement is considered neurotic. Developmental stages are typically passed through without ceremony. Going off to school, reaching puberty, menstruating, leaving home, getting married—each of these milestones may be greeted with understated appreciation. The muted Anglo American approach may be puzzling to the non-Anglo American therapist.

Middle-class Anglo American children typically negotiate school rather well, especially through the latency period. The tasks of school and of latency are a match with Anglo American values. Children are encouraged to go off to school alone, take initiative, and achieve. They are expected to develop a strong sense of their individual capacity and gain self-esteem from individual achievement. Poor Anglo Americans, however, may not appreciate their school years as much; they may consider school a distraction from the real tasks of life—working and coping.

Clubs, sports, and hobbies help socialize Anglo American children in the twin social modes of competition and conformity. They learn to "play by the rules of the game." These friendships remain a model for adult life.

Anglo American children have trouble when they are unable to meet their parents' expectations for achievement and autonomy. Anglo American parents will be distressed if the child is unable to become self-sufficient. Physical or emotional handicaps are upsetting. The child's "bad" neediness makes the parents feel inadequate, which makes the child feel worse, in a vicious circle of mutual failure. Anglo American families are fine when things go well. Things are "supposed" to go well. This expectation, this optimism, contrasts with other cultural groups in which trouble is considered inevitable.

In the real world, because failure and inadequacy of one kind or another are bound to occur, when trying again is not an adequate remedy, Anglo American families may respond quite harshly with scapegoating. Those who do not measure up may be cast aside. They may become marginal, isolated, and eccentric. Even worse, they may stay at home, accept the "defective" role, and increase the family's pain.

## ANGLO AMERICAN ADOLESCENTS

Anglo American culture historically encouraged early separation of adolescents and the development of an individualistic, self-defined, adult identity. In 1750 and even 1850, a 20-year-old couple could be well established in the community—adequately skilled, financially independent with farm and house, and with children on the way. In the 2000s, extended apprenticeship (of one form or another) in our complex vocational and financial world will make buying a house and feeling established in job or career difficult even by age 30 or 40. If contemporary parents, following the frontier model, try to promote independence by withdrawing physical, financial, or emotional support too soon, the Anglo American adolescent will probably feel abandoned. The result may be a kind of false adulthood with premature identity foreclosure.

Anglo American families do not struggle to keep children at home or closely involved in family life as do, for example, Jewish or Italian families, for whom adolescence may be a period of open family conflict. In today's world, however, adolescents are not always ready to move on when they or their families want them to, especially when jobs are scarce and rents high. In the past, Americans have enjoyed a continuously expanding economy based on new, cheap land. There have been financial busts, but the trend of increasing prosperity lasted from the 1600s to the booming post-World War II economy—a very long time. It seems unlikely that the future holds comparable economic opportunity. Without good jobs, it is hard to go off on one's own, to one's own work and one's own new family, whenever one feels it is time.

When Anglo American adolescents have difficulties, they are likely to be considered their individual's business, not the family's. Anglo American parents may be hesitant to intervene. In therapy they need to be encouraged to stay involved, to continue to provide support and clear limits. In other words, a little more family struggle may well be good for Anglo American adolescents, who would otherwise be left alone to struggle. The idea is to invite the adolescent back into the family, to help young people express and validate their pain, and to share their load with the rest of the family.

## ANGLO AMERICAN ADULTS AND COUPLES

In the recent past, traditional Anglo American nuclear family roles denied women the opportunities for the success that their culture so keenly valued, forced them into relatively isolated dependency, and relegated them to lower status. However, asking isolated, dependent women to raise independent children has been a continuing cultural contradiction for Anglo Americans. The depression and "inadequacy" of Anglo American women, which has constituted the most common psychiatric patient profile from the 1950s to the present, is in part a product of their devalued, contradictory position. This has changed substantially in the 1990s, when economic decline has forced most families to depend on two incomes. Women now work outside the home for unequal pay and continue to do most of the housework and child care—the "second shift." They are now suffering from the same stress diseases (e.g., coronary heart disease) as are working men. Anglo American men still expect to be supported in their work-adventures. Things are not getting better or more equal for Anglo American women.

Successful therapy will help Anglo American women make sense of their anger and modify their cultural tendency to take responsibility and blame for all troubles, and to ascribe the troubles to their inadequacy as individuals.

Anglo American men have their problems too. They are still expected to fulfill traditional roles. The man has his job and is, in some ways, encouraged to be a workaholic—he is supposed to be a success and earn more money. In this role he may feel inadequate and irrelevant in child rearing and in maintaining social relationships. The fact is, workaholics may do better at their jobs—while doing worse at home. There are no simple solutions to these dilemmas.

Anglo Americans tend to experience marriage as a contractual relationship between individuals to meet individual needs. The emphasis is not on fulfilling a religious sacrament or joining extended families. Sex, money, and even the delivery of happiness are seen as contractual obligations. If a spouse fails to perform adequately sexually, earn enough money, or provide enough security, he or she has not kept the bargain. Divorce is relatively acceptable for Anglo Americans; however, the individual Anglo American may experience divorce as a painful personal failure.

Anglo American adults and couples often come to treatment with a controlled style that may make the source and nature of their pain and conflict inaccessible to the therapist. Their aggression is often sublimated into competition at work or recreation rather than acted out in family relationships. Alcohol is commonly used to anesthetize aggressive or other painful feelings. Martinis for lunch and cocktails before dinner on a daily basis are more typical middle- and upper-class Anglo American drinking patterns than episodic or binge drinking. An Anglo American may drink a great deal without noticing that it is a problem: Cocktails before dinner, wine with dinner, and an after dinner aperitif may be regarded as gracious living, a matter of pride, not embarrassment.

Anglo American sexual problems often stem from excessive control, avoidance, and distance in intimate relationships. Anglo Americans suffer more from lack of intensity in their sexual and emotional expression than from repressive inhibition or violent acting out. Worry about adequacy is often a prime component in Anglo American sexual problems. High standards of production combined with high expectation of control may cause performance anxiety and failure. Anglo American couples often respond to conflict by distancing and avoidance rather than by active confrontation, as in the following example:

An Anglo American couple at the point of separation came to treatment. They were ambitious and perfectionistic, and they tried always to be cheerful and tolerant. It was apparent to the therapist that they had drifted apart and needed help in ending their marriage so that neither would feel irresponsible. They had no norms for conflict expression or resolution and, indeed, had never had any fights, even small fights, along the way. The therapist observed that their cheerfulness, denial, and sense of righteousness had allowed them to carry problems, without directly addressing them, until they were so far apart emotionally that there was nothing left with which to work.

———————— ◆ ————————

Therapists can teach Anglo Americans an antidote to this cultural pattern. Couples can learn to have small, immediate, frequent, and personal fights instead of letting it all build up. When an Anglo American couple is able to seek help, a variety of techniques can be used: contracting, task assignments, and negotiated (even signed) agreements. Therapists should not be put off by or overinterpret the cool, reasonable, and correct tone of many Anglo American couples in marital conflict. They are maintaining self-esteem by conducting themselves correctly. Conversely, they may feel humiliated at losing their cool in a fight.

The most important factor in a marital conflict may not be readily apparent. For example, money may well be the dominant factor, but it is never brought up. Anglo Americans would rather not talk about money, but money issues are usually crucial whether the family is poor, working class, middle class, or rich.

Anglo American couples may not view their families of origin as resources in either childbirth or child rearing. Their cultural style leads to isolation from support, sharing, and the guidance of an extended family. Any change or intervention that works toward reducing Anglo American family isolation is likely to be helpful. The following is an example:

A successful corporate executive in his 50s had been in therapy for 2 years. His work had been his life. He had little experience with intimacy, and he was separated from his own feelings. Part of his therapy consisted of encouraging him to reconnect with those feelings. As the therapy progressed, the man began to express a wish for more of a relationship with his three brothers and sisters, all of whom lived nearby. As the man put it, "We only get together for Christmas when Mother calls. We enjoy each other, but we all just seem to disappear, except at Christmas."

---

## ELDERLY ANGLO AMERICANS

The fear of aging, with eventual sickness, incapacity, and dependence, can become a matter of almost obsessive concern to Anglo Americans of all ages. The youthfulness and future orientation of the wider American culture make the elderly particularly vulnerable to loss of self-esteem. At best, an older person in reasonable health is able to sustain feelings of adequacy by continuing self-sufficient, independent living, and not becoming a "burden to the family."

When Anglo Americans face extended disability or terminal illness, a stressful situation for any family, their self-contained individualism can be particularly maladaptive. They try to keep their painful feelings to themselves. They may have difficulty asking for help and sharing the stages of loss and grief with others.

## FAMILY THERAPY THEORY AND ANGLO AMERICAN VALUES

Murray Bowen's systems therapy (Bowen grew up in a small town in Tennessee) fits well the values and style of his origins—the Appalachian Anglo American family. Bowen uses individual coaching to promote emotionally neutral, responsible relationships between individuals within the family. Tracing historical, multigenerational family emotional patterns further helps to differentiate the individual. The individuated person can then confront emotionally tempestuous family secrets and arbitrary social rules calmly and with a well-defined sense of self. Bowen's advocacy of a person-to-person relationship with each member of the family counteracts isolation.

Psychodynamic family therapy is also relatively compatible with Anglo American values. Anglo Americans want to face the truth and gain insight into inner truths. They believe in science and readily accept the mechanistic (hydraulic) psychodynamic model. They are usually not that keen on expressing feelings, but if that is what it takes to make progress, they are willing. Appeals to the role of the psychodynamic unconscious are usually viewed with some distaste.

Minuchin's structural family therapy can fit the needs of Anglo American families for connection by clarifying boundaries and alliances.

Strategic/Milan family therapy probably will not work as well with Anglo Americans who expect direct, honest, and aboveboard negotiation. Asking Anglo Americans to maintain secrets and make secret, strategic moves in alliance with the therapist will seem sneaky and dishonest. It may serve to heighten Anglo American emotional isolation by promoting the opposite of direct person-to-person communication. To ask Anglo Americans to continue doing what they are doing conflicts with their desire to work directly on their difficulties.

Narrative family therapy is appropriate. It helps with the problem of isolation by encouraging each family member to have his or her say and be heard. Similarly, Virginia Satir's emphasis on "filling the pot" and Carl Rogers's focus on empathy address Anglo American longing for individual validation. Some therapists may underestimate the power of Rogerian empathic listening to bring relief to emotionally isolated Anglo Americans.

Behavioral approaches, transactional analysis, psychoeducation, and the various self-help and self-training modes of therapy are compatible with Anglo American positivism. Therapies that emphasize the teaching and practice of interpersonal communications skills are also often of great and immediate benefit to Anglo American families.

Overall, when they are able to ask for help, Anglo Americans are willing to try most anything and can benefit from many different kinds of therapy. They are the omnivores of psychotherapy.

## ANGLO AMERICAN FAMILIES AND NON-ANGLO AMERICAN THERAPISTS

Non-Anglo American family therapists may be wary of the ways in which Anglo Americans relate to therapists from other ethnic groups. It should not be a problem. Anglo Americans prefer to see people as having individual worth, especially when encountered in personal relationships. Hence, in therapy, Anglo American families are likely to relate comfortably and individually to therapists of any background.

Anglo Americans do not perceive themselves as "ethnics." They are usually uncomfortable with therapists' encouragement that they talk about their ethnicity. They have been evolving this individualistic culture and calling themselves "American" for a long time—indeed, they fought the English 200 years ago to be American, not English. Their descendants consider themselves "plain, regular Americans."

## INTERMARRIAGE

More than half of Anglo American families are intermarried. Anglo Americans are likely to take cultural differences personally—as if they were individual not cultural differences. They are inclined to regard talking about cultural differences as a lame excuse for not recognizing personal inadequacies.

## SOCIAL CLASS

Because of the visibility of Anglo American wealth, one might suppose that most Anglo American families are especially prosperous. In fact, the census records reveal that the average family income for people who claim English ancestry is very close to the average family income of other White European ethnic groups such as French, German, Irish, Italian, and Polish (Sowell, 1981; U.S. Bureau of the Census, 1993). The Anglo American poor are likely to live in rural areas throughout the 50 states; they are almost invisible.

The English colonists came from a society that had assumed the justice of fixed class differences. But the New World settlers (except those in the Tideland South) softened class and economic differences. The United States was 95% agricultural until the 19th century: Wealth was land, and land was abundant. Upward class mobility, within limits, was possible for all hardworking, thrifty, right-thinking (conforming) citizens.

The Northern colonists, and later their pioneer offspring, shared the belief that individuals could make it, become wealthy, find opportunity, and change class and economic status at will. This was partly true, but many English colonists were poor, their descendants were poor, and they remain poor today.

The belief in boundless opportunity has a far-reaching impact on poor, middle-class, and rich Anglo American families today. Believing that they have all started on a more-or-less level playing field, Anglo Americans have ambivalent feelings about class. They identify with the worldwide struggles for political freedom, but not economic policies that compensate for past injustice. Economic opportunity is assumed to be available to everyone in the United States, and therefore poverty is suspect (Rubin, 1976). As a result, poor Anglo Americans carry a double burden; they feel oppressed not only by poverty but also by feelings of self-blame and inadequacy, overattributing their poverty to inferiority. Middle-class Anglo Americans think they should have done better. Upper-class Anglo Americans are afraid that, because of their personal inadequacy, they are at risk of slipping. Fears of inadequacy are found in all classes.

Some Southerners are different. They continue the Tidewater tradition of class stratification linked to identification with local roots. Southern Anglo

Americans see themselves as living in a highly interdependent world of class and race. They have long lived with contradictions between public and private life, between maintaining themselves and others in their places, and with the contradictions inherent in keeping problems secret.

## THERAPY, ANGLO AMERICAN DOMINANCE, AND RACE

Anglo American dominance means different things to different classes. Upper-class Anglo Americans who are privileged—because of their families wealth, early arrival in North America, expensive educations, connections, and the absence of myriad barriers that others must climb over—may deny that such things matter much. They attribute their privileged status to individual achievement. Poor and middle-class Anglo Americans do not consider themselves privileged or dominant and may fear that other groups are "taking over."

Historically, the four colonial Anglo American regions of the United States practiced systematic racism. Each region tried to eliminate Native Americans, and the South embraced slavery. Race was and is an American dilemma. Anglo Americans live with the awareness of their contradictions; they value individual liberty, yet they have denied it to others. They feel remorse about others' suffering—if they are reminded of it—but believe everyone should look to the future and forget the woes of the past. This is an attitude that can produce conflict with other American ethnic groups.

Although the four colonial Anglo American regional cultures had, in the 16th and 17th centuries, little contact with one another, they had continuous contact with Native American and African cultures. Both the North and the South fought and cooperated with Native Americans and were influenced by them. The Northern tiers of pioneers were particularly involved with Native Americans. Southern cultures were particularly influenced by both Africans and Native Americans. We can expect to see our understanding of these mutual cultural influences grow as many scholars study them (Axtell, 1985; Namias, 1993).

## REGIONAL ORIGINS: FOUR ENGLISH FOLK CULTURES

Since the first edition of this book (1982), new historical studies (especially *Albion's Seed: Four British Folk Ways in America* by David Hackett Fischer, 1989) have enlarged our understanding. Anglo American folk ways were derived from four distinct regional English folk cultures, developed in four geographical regions in England. These folk ways came in four discrete, great migrations to America and evolved into four distinct Anglo American regional cultures. While these cultures shared the political idea of individual freedom,

Anglo American society as a whole continues to be the story of the interaction of these four distinct regional cultures. These four groups and the dates of their migrations are the Puritan New Englanders (1629–1641), Anglicans of the South (1645–1676), Quakers of the Mid-Atlantic States (1685–1715), and Appalachians of the Highland South (1717–1775). These groups have maintained distinctive folk ways and substantially preserved their values. The four Anglo American regional cultures have competing and even contradictory ideas about freedom and individual liberty. Persisting regional differences are shown, for example, by differences in attitudes toward gender equality, as shown by voting patterns for the equal rights amendment; rates of military service; violence, as shown in homicide rates; views about the right to bear arms, as shown in gun ownership and the formation of militias; and large differences in the amount of money spent for local government services and education.

## New England

The Puritan New England idea of freedom was based on the belief in an ordered existence—order in communities, families, and the lives of individuals. The following is the case of a man who took individual responsibility to an extreme:

A 40-year-old high school history teacher came for treatment following hospitalization for major depression (he had a previous hospitalization in his 20s), for feeling inadequate in his work, and for an unhappy marriage. The couple came together (other members of his family were included at various points in the therapy). The man's wife was a social worker from a family with a history of depressive illness. He wanted children; she did not. He did not express sadness or anger about not having children or disappointment in his wife for not appreciating his work. He was critical of himself for failing in the marriage. He directly expressed his exaggeration of New England values in saying, "I believe in the principle of taking responsibility for what goes wrong." He felt completely responsible for the tension in the marriage. He took sole responsibility and did not ask for help. He did not fight with and thereby engage his wife to share problems—a stance that further created distance between them. Treatment encouraged him to shift from his exaggerated sense of responsibility, self-absorption, and isolation toward shared responsibility and an engaged, connected self.

Treatment of Northeastern Anglo Americans may usefully include moderating the impact of family traditions, sometimes by getting the family more directly involved in exploring that history in order to sort the myths from the realities and to reclaim realistic expectations. Pride and involvement in family history tend to be associated with making money. Family myths will be more potent among the rich, or once rich. The most potent family myths are stories of glorious achievement, linked to standard ethnic values, such as independent judgment or service to the community. The poor take pride in the history of making enough money to live and in not asking for handouts.

## Southern

The Cavaliers who developed the southern Tidewater plantations saw freedom as the right to rule one's own lands and servants, in other words, as freedom to maintain a class hierarchy. Frank Pittman (personal communication, 1981), an Atlanta, Georgia, family therapist, observes that a typical Southern family's motivation for seeking help is the experience that something (the socially correct status quo) is out of control, that the family needs help doing the "right thing." Southerners may at times come for help in order not to change.

In Pittman's hands, therapy is a careful, very delicate social transaction. Concerned about social class from a local (neighborhood or county) perspective, Southerners will be concerned about the social standing of the therapist. These families need to feel that they are in control, that they can proceed at a moderate pace, and that they will be able to solve a problem. Coming to therapy does not mean all family business will be discussed. Indeed, trust is likely to be extended only when the therapist agrees, at least implicitly, that the rules of avoiding certain topics (the family secrets) will continue to be honored. Therapists working with Southern families are expected to understand that "their peculiarities are different from their problems." They do not come to therapy, as do some Northerners, to become better people.

## Mid-Atlantic/Midwestern

Quakers, oppressed in their quiet practice of religion, asked only that their rights and the rights of other persons be mutually respected. The value is that you must allow other people freedom in order to be free. Other immigrant groups populated the Midwest more than did the Quakers, but the Quakers were an important formative influence. The following is the case of a man who's privacy was treated with such extreme respect that his alcoholism was ignored.

A law firm partner was drifting gradually into alcoholism, while the other lawyers tactfully looked the other way. His alcoholism progressed to the point that he was failing to meet his professional responsibilities. The partners then confronted him with specific omissions, but could not bring themselves to take on the key issue, alcoholism. They saw his alcoholism as a flaw and his personal business. The managing partner finally, unhappily, consulted the therapist. The treatment amounted to a cultural transplantation, where the ideology of Alcoholics Anonymous and the characterization of alcoholism as a medical disease was advocated. Thus reframed, the alcoholism issue was confronted and the previous privacy-respecting was labeled as "enabling behavior." The disease theory of alcoholism allowed effective problem solving without challenging the core value of respect for individual privacy.

For Mid-Atlantic/Midwest Anglo Americans, having troubles means failure on two counts: the failure to successfully carry on, and the failure of being needy. Effective therapy does not challenge the positive values of work and independence; it adds the value of getting appropriate help when needed. Therapy is a way to reasonably and responsibly "work" on problems. The goal is restoration of adequate emotional self-sufficiency and appropriate interdependence. Of course, even when life is conducted in an exemplary and reasonable way, tragedy will strike. The lack of adaptive fatalism in Anglo American culture can leave them dismayed when bad things happen to good people.

## Appalachian/Southwestern

The Appalachian/Southwestern culture is found in the Appalachians and the rural desert Southwest and Northwest. This is the culture we know from "country and Western music." This culture has it's roots in the chronic wars between Scotland and Northern England. Violence persists. The rate of murder in Texas is four times that of New England. These people are patriotic; they disproportionally serve in the military and participate in private armies—militias. Education is not as highly valued as in other parts of the country. The Southwest has a high school graduation rate of 65%, in contrast to 90% in New England.

Appalachian/Southwestern families are usually seen by family therapists only after preferred modes of problem solving within the extended family have broken down. The successful family therapist will ally with the extended family network, and consider using some form of restorative network family therapy.

## CONCLUSION

Anglo American clients bring to therapy a hyperindividualism that helps in trying new things and hinders in getting help with problems. They do well in treatment that recognizes both the costs and benefits of emotionally self-contained hyperindividualism. The goal of successful family therapy is to increase the Anglo American's ability to reach out of personal isolation, reclaim important emotional experiences, and engage the challenges of life with a spirit of adventure.

## REFERENCES

Allen, J. (1989). *We the people: An atlas of America's ethnic diversity*. New York: Macmillan.

Axtell, J. (1985). *The invasion within: The contest of cultures in Colonial North America*. New York: Oxford University Press.

Fischer, D. H. (1989). *Albion's seed: Four British folkways in America*. New York: Oxford University Press.

Gleason, P. (1980). American identity and Americanization. In S. Thernstrom, A. Orlov, & O. Handlin (Eds.) *Harvard encyclopedia of American ethnic groups* (pp. 31–58). Cambridge, MA: Harvard University Press.

McGill, D. (1992). The cultural story in multicultural family therapy. *Families in Society, 73*(6), 339–349).

Namias, J. (1993). *White captives: Gender and ethnicity on the American frontier*. Chapel Hill: University of North Carolina Press.

Papajohn, J., & Spiegel, J. (1975). *Transactions in families*. New York: Jossey-Bass.

Pearce, J. K., & Friedman, L. (Eds.). (1980). *Family therapy: Combining psychodynamic and family systems approaches*. New York: Grune & Stratton.

Rubin, L. (1976). *Worlds of pain: Life in the working class family*. New York: Basic Books.

Sowell, T. (1981). *Ethnic America: A history*. New York: Basic Books.

Thernstrom, S., Orlov, A., & Handlin, O. (1980). Anglo-Americans. In S. Thernstrom, A. Orlov, & O. Handlin (Eds.), *Harvard encyclopedia of American ethnic groups* (p. 125). Cambridge, MA: Harvard University Press.

U.S. Bureau of the Census. (1993). *U.S. Census of population, 1990: General social and economic characteristics*. Washington, DC: U.S. Government Printing Office.

Zborowski, M. (1969). *People in pain*. San Francisco: Jossey-Bass.

# CHAPTER 32

# Dutch Families

## Conrad De Master
## Mary Ann Dros-Giordano

The Dutch have been characterized as ambitious, hardworking, and frugal, yet quiet and peace-loving. Throughout their history, they have exemplified a people searching for a place of their own, a land where they can keep to themselves and freely practice their religion. They are an intensively active, internally principled, uncompromisingly private people and, at the same time, are often open-minded, receptive, and tolerant of others. If you ask Dutch people how they identify themselves ethnically, many would simply say they are Americans. Despite a high degree of acculturation, however, Dutch Americans continue to display Old World Dutch traits.

In both the Old and New Worlds, core Dutch characteristics and values have been strongly influenced by Calvinism, the theological system developed by John Calvin and his followers. Calvin's teachings contributed significantly to the Protestant Reformation movement, when people sought to practice their Christian beliefs personally rather than under the dictates of the established Roman Catholic Church. Those who were eventually instrumental in establishing the Netherlands as a nation were followers of Calvin.

Calvinism emerged as a distinct interpretation of the Christian faith at the same time as Dutch Protestants attempted to free themselves from outside religious, political, or economic interference. It subsequently contributed toward shaping personal and family behavior, as well as public and political institutions and policies: It certainly inspired many Dutch to focus on establishing a place of their own. The interplay between the religious and the political nurtured a strong sense of self-reliance and individualism, characteristics that gave impetus to creating the Netherlands as a distinct entity, which eventually impelled many to emigrate to America and shaped their settlement patterns.

The Dutch also were strongly influenced by the topography of the Netherlands. Sixty percent of the Dutch population lives below sea level, and because the country is small and densely populated, all space is precious. Not only has Holland always been in danger of being engulfed by the sea, but Dutch lives, of necessity, are impacted by the sea's whims. To survive, the Dutch have learned to live communally and have always worked together, especially during natural disasters.

Fear became reality in 1953 when waters from the North Sea broke through the dikes, taking more than 1,800 lives, and again in 1995, when flood waters rose to force 100,000 from their homes. The Dutch pride themselves on their distinct sense of community and their strong work ethic, values that have made it possible for them to protect their land from the seas.

The Dutch are a complex and sometimes paradoxical people. Because so little has been written about them as an ethnic group, we will draw upon historical sources, our personal experience growing up in Dutch communities, and our professional experience working with Dutch American families.

## HISTORICAL SETTING

The Dutch are descended from three Germanic tribes: Frisians, Saxons, and Franks. The practice of religious tolerance and the separation of church and state were established early in Holland. The move toward separation of church and state and the strong insistence on having freedom of religion resulted in Holland becoming a haven for Europeans suffering persecution elsewhere, often serving as a "foster-parent" country. Eventually Holland served as a conduit for many other Europeans who had suffered persecution elsewhere and were on their way to America. This special ability to incorporate people of diverse backgrounds and religious beliefs enabled Holland to grow and survive and is active evidence of what has come to be known as "Dutch tolerance."

The seeds of tolerance began to germinate during the Middle Ages, when the cities of what was about to become the Netherlands assumed importance in Europe. The Low Countries, as they had come to be known, were developing in many ways, including commercially. Most significantly, they had become the world's greatest shipbuilders. As Olsen (1989) points out, the Dutch and their neighbors resented the oppression of the Catholic Church and bridled at the role of the powerful Hapsburgs of Spain, foreigners who drained banks and businesses dry in order to finance costly wars abroad. Although of differing ethnic, economic, and religious backgrounds, the people of the Low Countries united in their efforts to gain autonomy and freedom. Eventually they developed their own nation.

Originally ruled by the Hapsburgs of Spain, later, in the early 1800s, overrun and ruled by Napoleon of France, and subsequently caught in the cross fire of World Wars I and II, the Dutch, from the beginning of their existence in Europe, have seemed a restless dissatisfied people. They had been in constant struggles politically, economically, and religiously with their more powerful neighbors. They persistently fought to preserve their identity and their freedom from domination, rising up each time they were attacked and even when overtaken. But after many attacks from the outside and a variety of adjustments, the Dutch borders have remained unchanged since the 1830s.

Many Dutch, particularly the poor, chose to leave, hoping to gain a better life elsewhere. Consistent with what occurred at other times in their history, the dilemma for the Dutch, coming from a small country, is revealed in more recent times in the deep impact sustained by the two World Wars.

During World War I, the Dutch were caught in the cross fire between Germany and its enemies: Britain and France. During World War II, Hitler invaded the Netherlands. The German occupation lasted 5 long years, during which time the Dutch endured bombings and severe shortages of food and fuel. Such inconveniences pale in the face of the mass slaughter of nearly 80% of the total Jewish population in Holland, a larger percentage of the Jewish population than was killed in any other European country. According to Oliner and Oliner (1988):

> Despite the notable history of acceptance of Jews in the Netherlands and the concomitant weakness of anti-Semitism there, 115,000 Jewish citizens and 25,000 Jewish refugees suffered a proportionally greater loss of lives "between 75 and 80%" than the Jews in any other occupied country in Western Europe. The primary responsibility for this frightful toll lives with the Germans, who ruled the Netherlands with an iron fist as a protectorate. The near annihilation of the Jews in Holland constituted a radical reversal of the country's long national heritage of religious tolerance and civic equality. (p. 31)

Despite this tragedy, many Dutch people risked their lives to save Jews. An example of Dutch heroism is documented in the poignant diary written by a young Jewish girl named Anne Frank (Frank & Pressler, 1995).

## DUTCH IN AMERICA

It is difficult to determine how many Dutch there are in America today. According to a recent U.S. Census, 6.3 million Americans consider themselves to be of Dutch origin, but this figure is thought low, and estimates run closer to 8 million. It is equally difficult to determine how many people in the United States speak Dutch, but the number is usually set at somewhere between 200,000 and 400,000.

It is worth noting that there was never a mass migration of Dutch to the New World. Of those who immigrated, 9 out of 10 were prompted by economic considerations. Rising birthrates and living costs, periodic food shortages, plant and livestock diseases, unequal and heavy taxation, and a general gloomy outlook in the Netherlands made American land and wage opportunities seem increasingly attractive, particularly during the early migration of the 17th century and also later, during the early 1800s and 1900s. These immigrants were lower-middle-class rural folk: farmers, laborers, and artisans who brought to America an ethic of industrious work, practical farming methods, and a strong desire for agricultural land. Especially during the 17th and early 18th centuries, immigrants were often exploited by the profit-seeking trade companies that had encouraged migration, and by wealthy landlords known as *patroons*, who regulated their lives and deprived them of the freedoms they sought. The Netherlands was not a powerful country that could, nor was inclined to, support its holdings or its people in the new country. Consequently, many settlers became so disillusioned they remigrated back to their old country.

The Dutch have been in America since 1609, when they explored the Northeastern Coast on the *Halve Maen*, under the command of Henry Hudson. In 1626, the Dutch settlers purchased Manhattan Island from the Indians for 60 guilders in trade goods and constructed Fort Amsterdam on the southern tip of the island. Downtown Manhattan still has several streets that bear the original Dutch names, the most famous of which is Wall Street (*Walstratt*).

The 1680s saw some immigration of religious groups to Dutch communities and by about 1700, there were well over 10,000 Dutch people living in America in New York, New Jersey, Delaware, and Pennsylvania. As in Europe, when the Dutch were overtaken politically, which restricted their freedoms, and/or when outside investors attempted to regulate business and trade, the poorer people often left. The same result occurred when New Amsterdam, the main Dutch settlement, was overrun by the British in the late 1600s and the trade companies and *patroons* attempted to regulate workers' commercial endeavors and even their personal lives, many of the Dutch pushed westward.

The land available west of the coastal colonies beckoned as a place where the Dutch could live freely and be left alone. Swierenga (1979) concludes that for the Dutch: "Family, faith and farming were their watchwords, not liberty, fraternity, and equality." Once again, as in Europe, the Dutch strove to have their own land on which to live and prosper, to be free to practice their own faith, and to raise their families as they saw fit.

In their efforts to carve out a place they could claim as their own, the Dutch had a noticeable impact on others. By pushing for and attempting to ensure their own rights and freedoms as a minority group, they paved the way for others. In seeking tolerance for themselves, the Dutch engendered and ensured tolerance for others. Up until recent years, they tended to marry within their own ethnic group and favored doing business with their own folk; the Dutch often were against labor unions, suspicious of any political party and, in general, reluctant to join any organization other than the local church.

Given their history in Europe and their experiences in America, it is easy to understand why the Dutch often display a fierce independence. They tend to be suspicious of authority or of those who aspire to be dominant. They are skeptical about "outsiders" and, as Swierenga (1979) describes, "are notorious for their clannishness, even among the fifth and sixth generations" (p. 6).

## RELIGION

No attempt at promoting an understanding of the Dutch can be adequate without providing at least some insight into their faith and religious life. For a Calvinist, Christ is not a hope, a promise, a set of beliefs, a moral code, or a prescription for life. Christ is seen primarily as an actual historical event; the birth of Jesus Christ, the divine, interrupted and converged with human history, transforming all that occurred subsequently by offering new hope and promise to those who follow His teachings. In a similar, analogous way "acceptance of Christ" refers to an occurrence in human experience in which the divine converges with the human and thereby transforms all subsequent experience through offering new hope and promise for that individual.

Divine action, however, is not limited to the life and death of Jesus. Calvinists believe Christ's intersection in human history remains an ever-present, ongoing process that occurs as the divine, through the action of the Holy Spirit, informs the conscience of those who remain open to His call and direction. To be Christian, therefore, means to live as one perceives, according to the innermost recesses of one's conscience, the way Christ would have lived (Calvin, 1960).

This teaching helps us understand a Dutch pastor's reply when asked how Dutch people try to manage family difficulties or troubling psychological or emotional events. He said:

> "Well, they probably would view the problem as an indication that something was askew in their relationship with God. The event probably would serve as the impetus for fervent prayer. If prayer didn't suffice, then the pastor himself would be consulted in hopes that he would help to determine God's will in solving the problem and thus help the individual or the family develop a closer relationship with God."

What this means for the therapist (particularly since many Dutch have rebelled against and actively reject what they perceive as their religious background) is that Dutch people often feel at a loss when they do not have a sense of what is right or called for in a particular situation, that is, when the message from the conscience remains unclear or confused. Not much stock is placed in expressing oneself or even in uncovering deep emotions; in fact, doing so may often be viewed as presumptive or arrogant.

The strength of conscience characteristic of Dutch folk is illustrated by a Dutch mother of two young children:

She remained steadfastly loyal to her husband despite his continued drinking, drug abuse, and unfaithfulness. Her religious beliefs not only reinforced the sanctity of their marriage but also seemed to foster a sense that merit derives from self-denial and persistent endurance in the face of hardship. This woman expected little for herself, yet remained conflicted about the impact her husband's behavior and the resulting family disruption would have on her children. For many months, she felt unable to do anything constructive, often becoming moody and depressed. She expressed little concern for herself and didn't know what to do, but clearly hoped to do "what is right."

As therapy progressed she appreciated that her anger and frustration with her husband's substance abuse was not the result of "uptightness," puritanical or moralistic judgments. After all, she drank too. How could she judge him? When it came to matters affecting her children, however, she readily set aside her "partying"; she felt it very important to follow through on what was promised to the children, to be emotionally alert and "not in a fog" when her children wished to talk or were struggling with some difficulty. She recognized that it takes energy to discipline and set limits; she realized that raising children often requires 24-hour readiness and doesn't leave room for substance abuse if their well-being is taken seriously. She, in addition, experienced a happy surprise in discovering that her children liked going to church. She shifted from reviewing church attendance as a pietistic practice, which her husband had no interest in, to something that might actually be nurturing the emotional and spiritual yearnings of her children. This experience helped her to reconnect with the positive value and meaning church attendance had for her as a child. This reassessment opened the way for her to feel more accepting of her past and more aligned with the family she grew up in.

After carefully considering which parts of her family heritage and spiritual life she wished to pass on to her children, she came to believe that continued involvement with her husband would interfere with rather than promote what she envisioned for her children. Religious understanding of forgiveness and grace, thought of in regard to both herself and her husband, helped to free her to feel more energized. Her depressed mood lifted, and although she still felt very conflicted, she was able to begin moving toward getting a separation and eventually a divorce. She felt more at peace with herself and left open the possibility she might appear right or righteous in God's view.

——————— ◆ ———————

When the therapist can appreciate the painful dilemma of not knowing, can empathize with the genuine desire to do what is right, and can be sympathetic about the confusing complexities of life, deep emotions often well up and are expressed, albeit in a quiet, reserved manner. Likewise, if the therapist can view silence on the part of an individual or family not as an indication of resistance or uptightness but as evidence of the patient being somewhere on the continuum between being completely overwhelmed and prayerfully searching for enlightenment, the overall emotional process of the session will remain much more alive.

For the Dutch, separation of church and state takes on a far deeper meaning than simply regulating a form of political practice. The Dutch simply do not talk about religion with casual or business acquaintances. Even within families, especially within the extended family, differences in religious beliefs or commitment may be tolerated for the sake of the family. But, if it comes down to a choice, the bonds may be severed if it seems that religious beliefs or values are being compromised.

Also, all of Calvin's teachings persistently admonish followers not to expect any reward from their efforts, because one's true reward comes from "grace" alone, irrespective of any "good works." When issues arise from external "political" events, the Dutch readily become very tolerant, rational, and utilitarian, tending to favor the solution that is most efficient and least conflictual. Individual Dutch people, therefore, live with this internal paradox—an extreme strictness on the one hand, and a live-and-let-live openness and tolerance on the other. In relation to others, the Dutch may often seem aloof, standoffish, or certainly emotionally distant. Individual experience, however, often becomes clouded by persistent soul searching and internal debate, resulting in behavior characterized by the emphasis that all people ought to have the freedom to do as they determine is the best for them.

The dictates of conscience become a powerful influence on decision making as to how and where to live and what one must do to have the freedom to practice one's beliefs—even if it means leaving all one has known to move to another country.

The influential role of spiritual thinking was illustrated by the words of a 30-year-old Dutch woman describing her relationship with a man she adored. She stated:

> "We could fall very easily into a pattern of almost living together. We're fighting it. We each believe the other to be a present from God. We treasure that gift and hope to show God how much we value and appreciate it. Therefore, we want to do what is moral and right. Others, who do not take our religious beliefs as seriously, might see this as being rigid."

## THE FAMILY

There is a strong sense of family responsibility among the Dutch, perhaps originating in another time and place, "born of the dikes and the knowledge that every man and his spade is the keeper and protector of every other man" (Bailey, 1970, p. 35). There is even a Dutch term, *familie-ziekte,* literally "family sickness," that describes a person who is overly conscious of the kinship system and its obligations. The nuclear family (*gezin*) maintains close ties with the family at large (*familie*). Clear boundaries are usually maintained in the family consistent with their individualism and respect for privacy and personal freedom (Bailey, 1970).

Within the nuclear family, role definition and responsibility tended to be very clear. The man is expected to give overall direction to the family, provide for it economically, and set an example of uprightness in the community. The woman is counted on to provide a rich home life for her husband, to nurture the children, and to attend to and promote social and cultural input for the family.

The relationship between husband and wife is considered sacred; a strong emotional commitment, buttressed by religious belief, often exists between them. What adds to the strength of the marital bond is that in several pivotal areas, the spouse's thoughts and feelings are usually held in high esteem. Although the husband, for example, bears major responsibility for implementation, his wife's input regarding business, career, and/or family financial matters often proves to be of determining influence. In like manner, although the wife often holds major responsibility for the care and nurturing of the children, she often seeks her husband's input.

Dutch parents feel keenly responsible not only for the physical nurturing and safety of their children, but also perhaps even more so, for their children's spiritual nurturing and well-being, so family guidelines and admonitions tend to be very stringent. The adolescent struggle toward adulthood seldom occurs smoothly, usually taking on the form of some sort of rebellion. When Dutch people meet and begin to recognize a common background, conversation tends to move easily toward describing the nature of their rebellion against their heritage or family. In most cases, however, there is a return "to the fold."

This process was illustrated by a 32-year-old divorced Dutch woman with two children.

She had experienced a tempestuous adolescence, married a non-Dutch man "outside the faith," and is now solidly entrenched back in the Dutch church and community. Since she had experienced so many crises, she was asked her view of how the Dutch handle family crisis. She said, "If something happens outside of the normal mainstream, the Dutch don't know how to handle it. They may suppress or ignore the happening, but it really disturbs them and it takes them a long time to readjust. If whatever occurs goes against their grain, they don't know how to deal with it."

This woman had often felt alienated and isolated, yet even at her darkest moments, close family and friends tolerated her waywardness and continued to demonstrate an openness. Of her background, she now says, "If I hadn't had some sort of solid background, I wouldn't have been able to keep moving through the difficult times." For those who have rebelled and then wish to return to the "Dutch" way of life, warm acceptance usually remains available. The New Testament parable of the prodigal son gets lived out in Dutch families, particularly for those who repent of their wrong doing.

Part of this tolerance, this willingness to accept the wayward back, also may come out of the long Dutch tradition in which religious or political authority and rule were not well received. The Dutch are a nation of seceders, so it is not surprising that the authority of the Dutch parent often is somewhat circumspect. In subtle ways, it often becomes evident that Dutch parents expect, or may even quietly enjoy, their children's rebellious nature. Parents are often concerned about providing strong spiritual and moral guidance, but they also respect autonomy and cherish the sense of independence. Once children leave the home, parents tend not to intrude. In addition, because of the difference in expectations and concerns regarding one's own as compared with others, there often develops a clear distinction among Dutch folk between "one of us" and an "outsider." Also, subtle gradations often develop as to the degree to which someone exists as "one of us" or an "outsider."

This negotiation of boundaries was played out in a very interesting manner by a family in which three generations were living in the same household.

A 44-year-old divorced mother and her 16-year-old son were living with her parents. The son often insisted on smoking in his room in clear violation of his grandparents' rule that prohibited smoking in the house.

Over time the grandfather, who demonstrated much love and concern for his grandson, became increasingly distressed by the repeated violation of the no-smoking rule. Finally, with the strong support of the grandmother, and stressing health and safety concerns, the grandfather said his grandson could no longer remain living in the house because of his noncompliance.

Initially this strong stand seriously disturbed the daughter, especially since her married sister had smoked in the house while visiting, yet nothing was said to her. When confronted with this partiality and after some initial quandary, the grandfather stated that it was really a matter of respect. His grandson did not show the kind of respect that his visiting daughter did.

Although we might initially view the grandfather's stance as a reaction to the challenge to his authority and family position, subsequent family discussion, linked with the nature of the grandfather's relationship with the grandson, did not substantiate this line of reasoning, although it certainly contributed to the family dynamic. What proved more productive for the family was recognizing that although she was a family member, the married daughter came to the house as a guest. She was therefore treated with the respect and tolerance due guests and, moreover, she responded with the respect one would expect of a guest. Two influential factors came together here: (1) the paradox of Dutch life (i.e., extreme strictness regarding oneself and immediate family living in the house while showing much greater tolerance for all others) and (2) once having left the house, generational boundaries tend to be much clearer and respected.

Many other factors also were operating within the family. The son had previously proven himself errant on many occasions, and at this point the mother considered disowning her son and having him declared an emancipated minor. However, her loyalty to her son eventually won out. She came to understand and accept her father's position. In just a few weeks, she found an apartment for herself and her son and moved out of her parents' home. As soon as this decision was made, the grandfather–grandson relationship improved significantly, becoming better than it had been for a long time.

## CONCLUSION

For the therapist working with the Dutch, it may be beneficial to keep in mind (1) the long history of struggle by the Dutch with forces outside their community, which were perceived as threatening, controlling, and or exploitive; (2) their strong emphasis on self-initiation and self-reliance; and (3) the major part religion, with its emphasis on personal inspiration, served in their development as a people and as a nation.

These influences combine to foster a caution about outsiders and a negative reaction to those who do not share their strong sense of personal responsibility or do not appreciate the depth of their religious conviction. Once involved in treatment, however, Dutch folk tend to be determined and thorough, and will diligently work until they have reached an internal sense of "right."

## REFERENCES

Bailey, A. (1970). *The light in Holland*. New York: Knopf.
Calvin, J. (1960). *Institutes of the Christian religion* (Vol. I) (J. T. McNeil, Ed.). Philadelphia: Westminster Press.
Frank, O., & Pressler, M. (Eds.). (1995). *Anne Frank: The diary of a young girl*. New York: Doubleday.
Oliner, S., & Oliner, P. (1988). *The altruistic personality*. New York: Knopf.
Olsen, V. (1989). *The Dutch Americans: The peoples of North America*. New York & Philadelphia: Chelsea House.
Swierenga, R. (1979). The Dutch in America: An overview. In L. P. Doezema (Ed.), *Dutch Americans*. Detroit: Gale Research.

# CHAPTER 33

# French Canadian Families

## Régis Langelier

Franco Americans[1] have settled throughout the United States, but their largest concentration is in New England. One out of every seven persons in New England is of French Canadian descent, constituting the largest non-English-speaking ethnic group in that area. Yet, while some cities and towns boast voter lists with a majority of French surnames, Franco Americans go almost unnoticed. They have traditionally been quiet and unassuming as a group and have led private lives, characterized by persistence in preserving their language and culture.

Except in the first edition of this book (Langelier, 1982) little has been published on psychotherapy with Franco Americans. The therapist's task is made difficult by the lack of research on counseling members of this ethnic group and by the variations within the group itself: urban and rural; educated and noneducated; first, second, or third generation in the United States. In spite of these differences, there is a common family profile to consider for effective treatment of the Franco American. Certainly, as McGoldrick, Garcia-Preto, Moore-Hines, and Lee (1991) warn us, the reader is "urged to consider the characterizations made here not as statements of absolute fact that apply to all men and women in a given culture, but as suggestions of patterns to increase our cultural awareness" (p. 170). This ethnic group has been shaped by influential Catholicism, by language, by dedication to duty, and a conservatism arising from rural descendants. Two sections of this chapter, "Family Patterns" and "Family Therapy," make use of material collected in a survey of professionals who educate and counsel the individuals and families from New England. Case examples and anecdotal commentary were gathered from 20 years of the author's clinical practice and friendships with this group.

## HISTORICAL AND CULTURAL INTRODUCTION[2]

Franco Americans, sometimes called French Canadians, are descendants of farmers who left Quebec in massive numbers between 1860 and the 1920s. The flow slowed considerably when growing industrialization and urbanization in Canada created jobs, thus reducing the necessity to immigrate to the United States[3] and when U.S. immigration law changed in 1960, making it more difficult for Canadians to emigrate to the United States. Currently they share very little of Quebec's new identity and nationalist orientation.

Although the Franco Americans were immigrants in New England, they had been North Americans for generations. French Canadians descend from the 17th-century settlers of the New World. Their ancestors explored the continent, fought and won wars, often with the Indians as allies. But they also fought and lost. Indeed they lost the last battle and, abandoned by France, became subjects of the British monarch in the 18th century.

Although defeated by the English, most French Canadians were not subjected to overt persecution. The Acadians, French colonists of what are today Nova Scotia and New Brunswick, however, suffered severely. They were brutally deported, starting in 1755. Many ended up in Louisiana, where they are known as Cajuns. Some Acadians escaped deportation by hiding out in the woods. Louisiana claims close to one million people with French ancestry, both Cajun and Creole.

French Canadians "hid out" from the English in a psychological sense. They lived apart and turned in upon themselves. In isolated rural settings, dominated culturally as well as religiously by the Catholic Church, they led simple lives. Education was minimal. Early marriage and the begetting and raising of children were given the highest priority by the Church hierarchy, which saw large families as the only hope for the future of the race. Few French had come originally. There were only 60,000 French Canadians and fewer than 15,000 Acadians in the French colonies at the time of the conquest, when the population of the 13 American colonies was 1,610,000. Further French immigration was totally cut off by the English victory.

When French Canadians left Canada for New England, they usually came to cities where relatives or friends had preceded them. They had a place to go and a family to receive them; often, they even had jobs waiting.

Family and religion are central to the lives of Franco Americans, just as they had been for their French Canadian rural forebears. The family handed down its essentially conservative, traditional values through the generations, aided by the powerful impact of the Catholic Church's code of behavior. It is a rigid code, particularly about sexual matters. Until quite recent times, the Church's teaching on moral matters was dominated by priests and nuns trained in the seminaries and novitiates of Quebec, where the doctrine of original sin was emphasized and human nature was viewed with profound pessimism. In *Visions of Gerard* (1963), Jack Kerouac, himself a Franco American, summed up the view of self that resulted from this teaching: "But you bumbling fool you're a mass of sin, a veritable barrel of it, you swish and swash in it like molasses. You ooze mistakes thru your frail crevasses" (p. 41).

Life was seen as full of temptations, offering opportunities to sin rather than to strike out constructively and to choose wisely. Franco Americans had defeatism in their blood. They set limited goals. They settled for less and had to be content because the best reward of all, paradise, could be attained if they had been faithful in the fullest sense of the word to Mother Church and to Mother-tongue language being perceived as the guardian of their faith.

As a result of being constantly subordinated to strong authority at home, within the Church, and at work (where Franco Americans rarely occupied positions of authority), anger and resentment were (and still are) often intense. Franco Americans felt helpless in the face of powerful outside forces. They could count only on themselves as individuals, or, as was more often the case, as individuals surrounded by a caring family.

As the speakers of one of the privileged languages of the world, French,[4] Franco Americans could have regarded their language as a badge of honor. Such an ability could have enhanced their status within any community. But educated Americans admired only Parisian French. The French spoken with a rural accent in New England was disdained. It lacked the polish, sophistication, elegance, and style that are associated with the French from France. Thus, the French language, to which Franco Americans were profoundly loyal, also became a badge of inferiority.

Due to their distrust of others, they felt that no one, not even members of other ethnic groups who, like Franco Americans, had been the butt of prejudice, could truly understand their special position. They saw themselves, because of their religion and their language, as better than they were judged to be, but they were well aware that they were looked down upon. Survival as a separate entity, against all odds, became a mystique.

In spite of this mystique of *survivance* (survival) as an ethnic group, Franco Americans did not support their own. They were unwilling, for example, to act in unison in political matters. Suspicion of the "other" ran too high. The "other" could be someone of another nationality, or simply be a member of another Franco American parish, even a Franco American neighbor. These attitudes had been learned through a succession of generations enclosed within isolated communities.

Feeling forever attacked and conquered by outside forces, in the 1920s they were dealt a particularly demoralizing blow in the one area in which they were most confident, religion. In the *Sentinelle* affair, Franco Americans struggled against their Irish-controlled Roman Catholic hierarchy, demanding some degree of autonomy in their own parishes; the Pope excommunicated their leaders.

The Irish have been pitted against them ever since arriving in New England. Although they respect Irish success in church and secular politics, they tend to see the Irish as arrogant and brash. Franco Americans can, like the Irish, be articulate, witty, and colorful, but within the secure framework of home or parish, and usually in French.

Franco Americans have been "put down" since birth: first, by parents fearful of raising an arrogant child whose chances of fitting into a life of adversity, and eventually getting into heaven, would be diminished; and second, by religious teachers and priests for whom pride is thought to be the ultimate sin. They share the pervasive sense that because they have been born into a group whose chances of material and personal successes are problematic, they will be happier with their lot if they do not strive to rise above their lowly station in life. This upbringing discourages taking chances for the sake of future success. Those who do not dare to achieve the very best of which they are capable feel lasting bitterness. Toward those who have taught them excessive humility and caution, they harbor ambivalent feelings—both respect and resentment.

Collectively, Franco Americans spent much of their meager resources building a network of parish elementary schools, staffed by religious orders. Even though working-class Franco Americans did not put a high value on education, Franco Americans as a group have played active roles in founding 264 colleges, high schools, and primary schools (Woolfson, 1988). Today, less than 50 of these institutions are still in existence (Chartier, 1991). Those who could not afford to go to private Catholic colleges rarely went beyond high school. However, some young men of promise were subsidized by their parish priests to attend the classical colleges of Quebec. Franco Americans could be found at all strata of American society.

Thus, the religious upbringing of Franco Americans, coupled with a lack of education and worldly ambition, led them at an early age into the same mills where their parents had toiled before them. They were content to work for little return, having accepted, seemingly without question, that fallen man had to work by the sweat of his brow, but convinced that heaven would be reward enough for their lives of uncomplaining, dutiful labor.

## FAMILY PATTERNS

Family patterns have changed since World War II. It is vital to distinguish between prewar and postwar generations. Also, college-educated Franco Americans living in a large city or the suburbs are less likely than their high-school educated counterparts, living in the little Canadas of New England textile towns, to fall into the traditional family patterns attributed here to Franco Americans. However, among those who have not gone beyond high school and have remained in the little Canadas or in rural areas (some 20% of the population), it is fairly safe to assert that sex-specific roles are well defined, with very little sharing of tasks between husband and wife. Marriages are not companionate but oriented toward traditional roles and expectations. The husband's responsibilities are to exercise authority, to punish misbehavior, and to provide protection and economic support. The wife's responsibilities are to oversee the family's welfare, to manage the daily household activities, to plan leisure-time activities, and to rear and educate the children. Authority is almost always the man's prerogative, and although in recent times the father has been losing ground as the sole authority figure in the Franco American family, he still exercises most of the overt power (Chassé, 1975; Woolfson, 1983; Langelier & Langelier, 1996). In some instances of reported domestic violence and child abuse in Franco American homes in Vermont, a link to the traditional authoritarianism of the male parent was hypothesized: "Although alcohol has sometimes played a role in these incidents, there are indications that one factor in the attacks was the man's perception that his traditional authority as head of the household was being undermined" (Woolfson, 1983, p. 7).

The father is not only the authority figure and economic provider for the family, ideally he is also a moral leader who, in difficult times, provides the family with affection, attention, and support, and is responsible for creating a climate of security. According to Garigue (1968), "Men regard it as normal for their wives to depend on them and to trust in them" (p. 159). Such confidence stimulates a man's affection for his wife and his desire to protect her from, for example, any critical comments from other family members. A husband's affection should be expressed, above all, when his wife is weary or ill. Then he must show his love and make life easier for his wife and their family.

The mother is the heart of her family, and a kind of "sainthood" is ascribed to her (Benoit, 1935; Chassé, 1975). She is a powerful emotional force and a moral support for the entire family (French, 1976). She acts as a mediator in family relationships and prevents direct confrontation. As one therapist in our survey succinctly put it, she is the agent of "regression to the mean," either in the relationship between a harsh father and his children or as a rule reinforcer herself, when her husband is too lenient. She is expected to assist and to please her husband without challenging his authority. Although the father retains ultimate authority, the mother is usually responsible for discipline on a day to day basis. She exercises influence by covert persuasion, especially persuasion that will increase her husband's acceptance of her children's unorthodox behavior. This strategy has probably had greater impact on final decision making than has been generally acknowledged in sociological assessments of Franco American families.

Early marriage and the prompt assumption of parental responsibilities characterize the transition into young adulthood for less-educated Franco Americans, both in Louisiana and New England (Woolfson, 1990). The arrival of children is the most important step in the early marital life cycle. For the young women, childbirth—especially the arrival of the firstborn—is the *rite de passage* into adulthood. While children of either sex are welcome, male children are particularly desired and are, as a rule, more indulged (French, 1976).

After marriage the woman is likely to forsake her peer-group orientation for that of her new marital role, but the man "continues his peer-group membership all through his adult life, with such interests often superseding those of his immediate family" (French, 1976, p. 336).

Children are raised to be honest, loyal, and hardworking. Woolfson (1973), in a study of the value orientations of French Canadian and Franco American school children, writes, "They tend to value responsibility, self-control, and obedience" (p. 12). Franco American families emphasize conformity, respect for authority and institutions, family loyalty, religious principles, and self-control.

Upward mobility and acculturation are resulting in liberalization in third-generation families as they move to mixed neighborhoods and make friends with mainstream Americans. But child management by means of punishment rather than positive reinforcement is still generally the rule.

Parent–child relationship patterns among French Canadians have been studied by Garigue (1968), who finds that although children are oriented toward both parents, they reveal a preference for the mother. They see the father more as a manager, the mother more as a friend. Children feel confidence in and strive to ally themselves with their mothers. They treat their fathers with respect tempered by emotional distance and lack of spontaneity. It appears that Franco American patterns are similar. From the point of view of structural family therapy (Nichols & Schwartz, 1995), it could be said that fathers and mothers have enmeshed boundaries, with power apparently shared in relationship to the children. This is particularly true in matters in which problems cannot be solved by the exercise of paternal authority or maternal sentiment. Children have little or no power, and the boundaries between them and their father are rigid. Father has undisputed power to scold or otherwise punish those with lesser power.

Looking at the family from this perspective, we can describe the politics of four specific subsystems: mother–son, father–daughter, mother–daughter, and father–son. The first two cross-sex pairs are characterized by stronger ties than are the latter same-sex pairs. In dysfunctional families in which the marital coalition is relatively weak or absent, these cross-sex parent–child alliances are intense, and the possibility of emotional fusion is high. In addition to these parent–child subsystems, we must consider sibling relationships. These are generally characterized by friendship and mutual aid.

It is usually of therapeutic value to encourage awareness of individuality in parent–child relationships by sorting out the different roles within the family, such as the difference between what is expected of the eldest and the youngest, and by looking at actual differences between them, such as interests and special aptitudes. This process is also useful in improving the relationships between siblings.

Anger is not an acceptable emotion. Aggression within the family either is not allowed or, if it is vented, it is done only in controlled ways, such as participation in athletics. The controls are too rigid, and when anger eventually does erupt, it is often expressed in destructive ways, such as verbal or even physical abuse. Rage is vented at children by screaming and in some instances, spanking, but such conduct is regarded as weakness. Among adults, rage is more often expressed indirectly by prolonged silences or sometimes by pounding objects, slamming doors, and self-punishment. For women, expression of rage is a problem. There is no acceptable outlet. Coldness, withdrawal, and a martyred stance may be the indirect consequence of women's rage.

Feelings of intimacy and attachment tend to be expressed nonverbally. Love can be expressed by togetherness, for example, family reunions and gatherings. As one of our respondents said when describing the demonstration of affection among peers or among those of different generations, "We don't even have to speak to each other. Just being there, just a glance and we know we love each other." A more direct or verbal approach to feelings is avoided, with delicate subjects treated in a joking, offhand manner that belies their depth and sensitivity. According to another respondent, familial affection is often played down because of general sexual anxieties that have long been common in Franco American families. Guilt feelings about sex seem to derive from rigid religious teachings.

The rigidity of the moral code tends to interfere with warm and affectionate expressions of feeling among family members. Such blocking and consequent painful shyness in some individuals may lead us to overlook their genuine sensitivity, tenderness, nurturing warmth, and longing for love.

Family rituals play an important role in traditional Franco American culture. They center around church attendance, parish activities, and family gatherings. Among the most significant are Sunday mass; church weddings; *de rigueur* baptisms; large wakes; Christmas midnight mass followed by *le Réveillon*, an all-night festivity; and New Year's Day gatherings. Also customary are Sundays with extended family and leisure time, and holidays spent with family instead of friends.

Tensions are generated when the younger, more acculturated generation does not pay much attention to these rituals. A family member who does not obey the unwritten rules brings on criticism, derision, and scorn. Regular visits to the older, high-status members of the family hierarchy can, however, placate the family critics.

Older, rural Franco Americans suffer from the impact of culture change. A very strong tradition among French Canadian farmers has been the passing on of the family farm from generation to generation. For the last two decades, "their own children, unable to keep up with inflation or to compete with the large agri-industrial corporations sell the farm. . . . The sudden changes in lifestyle that result from selling the family farm have adversely affected inter-generational family relationships" (Woolfson, 1983, p. 14).

Although the elderly are now often sent to nursing homes, for many it is a last resort. As Esman (1985) points out, "We Cajuns just don't do things that way [use nursing homes] if we don't have to. The old people should be at home if they can. It's alright if you have no other way to take care of them, but we can take care of our mothers ourselves and that's how it should be" (p. 41). Aging brings considerable status, more so than in the dominant American culture, to both men and women. However, as French (1976) says, "If both grandparents survive, it is the female who has the higher status. Most social and religious events, as well as Sunday after-Mass visits, require a stay with *mémère* (a corruption of *grand-mère* or grandmother). Grandmothers are revered and respected as repositories of knowledge about the entire family kin-ship network" (p. 343). After the death of grandparents, kinship ties through-out the family often weaken. Yet the memory of a stay with *mémère* could be the source of inspiration in times of crisis. In a family therapy session, a 55-year-old mother reminded her five children that if *mémère* were still alive, they would listen to her advice to stop fighting immediately. This was a thera-peutic turning point in siblings relationships.

In the past, to counterbalance the dispersal of the children in large fami-lies, where some stayed in Canada and others migrated to the United States, many families made systematic efforts to maintain kinship ties (extending even to third cousins) to foster loyalty among immediate household members and to encourage frequent visiting and mutual assistance among relatives (Barkan, 1980). Today, except for the rural and lower-income families, for whom the family remains the major focus of social activities, the network of extended family relationships is scattered and usually limited to weddings and funerals.

There is disagreement among mental health professionals concerning the role of religion and, more specifically, the influence of the parish priest on the Franco American family. Some respondents report the priest to be no more than a figurehead. Others report that the parish priest is still consulted. The truth appears to lie somewhere in the middle. A *Washington Post*–ABC News national survey (Goodstein, 1995) during Pope John Paul II's visit to the United States showed that large majorities of American Catholics said they believe it is possible to disregard the church's teachings on abortion, premarital sex, birth control, and divorce, and still be a "good Catholic." Although there is no eth-nic data from this survey, it is probably safe to state, from clinical experience, that younger Franco Americans would have responded with the majorities. Certainly, religious teachings still affect most Franco Americans, regardless of their religious involvement, and breaks with the faith leave scars. It is likely that even if the Church's influence has waned, its historical impact is deeply embedded in today's Franco Americans, for example, in feelings of guilt and inferiority, and in values that seem almost old-world-order: compliance and hard work. Also, Franco Americans are grappling with the contemporary issues of sexual abuse of their children by priests, scandals that rocked the Church about pedophiles, and abusive nuns in orphanages.

Because Catholicism, especially French Canadian Catholicism, has traditionally opposed intermarriage and divorce, Franco Americans have married among their own. However, in the 1940s a trend began, so that now 50% or more of Franco Americans marry outside of their own ethnic group, although usually within the Church (Dugas, 1976). Those who intermarry tend to wed members of the other Catholic minority groups, such as Italian, Irish, and Polish. The intermarriage trend continues to dilute to concentration of Franco American families and communities.

Divorce is increasing among Franco Americans and parallels the national rate. These emerging changes in marital patterns cause confusion and conflict among Franco Americans who, like every other group, must rethink their traditional expectations.

The elderly revere the past and are deeply attached to and proud of their French language, culture, and religion. The middle aged are less committed to their traditional culture and often feel guilt, shame, and/or ambivalence about their ethnic background. The young tend to ignore their ethnic history. Those who do know it object to cultural discrimination, but they usually object only within the privacy of their own families or within official Franco American organizations. Little is done about the complaints. Many respondents reported that the younger generation is generally ignorant not only of Franco American history and tradition but also of past and present discrimination. Young Franco Americans today, except for some who live in rural areas, are becoming assimilated into American society. Many young Franco Americans do not want to be associated with an ethnic group, and they do not identify with more strident separatist cousins in Quebec. They rather identify with the historical theme of the melting pot in the United States. Most have very little interest in tracing roots; they do not teach their children ethnic self-awareness or promote the French language in households. Inferiority complexes continue to haunt many as they seem ill at ease with their roots, whether in therapy or at work.

These strong signs of assimilation contrast with opinions that Franco Americans are "more ethnocentric than Americans" (Gardner & Lambert, 1972) and "the most inassimilable of all [ethnic] groups in New England" (Gunther, 1947). They suggest, rather, the possible impending death of Franco Americans as an important ethnic group (Dugas, 1976).

Certain recent trends, such as bilingual education, as well as the founding of new societies devoted to the study and preservation of Franco American culture, point to a possible reemergence of Franco American ethnicity. The last three decades of the history of Franco Americans are described by Chartier (1991) as "ethnicity found again," characterized by continuity, authentic ideological diversity, and new manifestations of ethnic life. He states: "Certain analysts even talk about a renaissance that had started around 1970, whereas others see in the life of the group unexpected last gasps before complete assimilation" (p. 323).[5]

## FAMILY THERAPY

Franco Americans have a history of self-help and of accepting advice from kinship networks or the local priest rather than from outsiders, who are viewed with suspicion and mistrust. Frequently clannish, most are reluctant to acknowledge the need to turn to mental health workers and resent any implication that they should do so. Personal problems, especially family issues, are considered too intimate and private for a stranger (therapist). Thus they operate according to a familiar blue-collar ethic: Work the situation out as best you can—then try to be tolerant.

The first and second generation perceive therapy as a fearful experience, a violation of "pride" in being able to manage their own affairs. As Woolfson (1975) observes, "Recourse to outside aid, be it the Church or the social agency, is an indication that the family cannot handle its own affairs. It is a defeat only accepted as a last resort" (p. 13). Needless to say, there are not enthusiastic self-referrals for therapy services, and the mere thought of such a step brings to the surface hidden fears of violating the sacredness of family secrets.

Mrs. R., a 77-year-old mother of seven children who all lived within a few miles of her home, was referred following hospital discharge for a psychotic episode. Although she was compliant for her medication protocol, she refused forcefully for several sessions to have any family member other than her husband present.

---- ◦ ----

In addition, the experiences of poverty and low education foster an outlook in which spending money for tangibles that gratify is preferred to spending money for therapy, which shows no visible gain.

A major depressive episode may have to occur before a Franco American family or individual seeks help, and since therapy is a last resort, the therapist can expect to find neither hope, nor motivation, nor a sophistication about self or others. Franco Americans can be engaged in therapy but are usually very slow about revealing themselves to the therapist and exhibit obvious fear of being found out. Therefore, they proceed in a very tentative manner, with family attitudes favoring the withholding of information. Therapeutic interventions can take a long time and at times may be impossible.

The therapist can encounter resistance based solely on credentials. One respondent articulated this problem: "The social status that comes with the years of formal education and the Ph.D. or M.D. title can also act as an additional inhibiting factor, making the distance between counselor and patient abysmal in the Franco American's view." Therefore, it is important that the therapist explore concerns and check out whether differences are a problem.

Therapy may be influenced by historical experience with confession, as exemplified by a quotation from Jack Kerouac:

> "Very well, that's all? Well then, say your rosary and fifteen Hail Mary's."
> "Yes, my father."
> The gracious slide door slides. Gerard is facing the good happy wood, he runs out and hurries lightfoot to the altar, fit to sing—
> It's all over! It was nothing! He's pure again! (1963, p. 49)

The Franco American projects the fantasy of the powerful parish priest onto the therapist, especially one with religious credibility, who may use it as a chance to give advice and solve problems but who must also attempt to help the client work through this mistaken attribution. Such clerical transference is predictable and often continues throughout the therapy.

The therapist preferred by Franco Americans may be male, the same age or older, married, Catholic, and also Franco American. According to Anderson and Stewart (1983), "Therapists from a similar background often have many more clues about the problems a family is likely to be encountering and about the ways they will find acceptable for coming to terms with them. Further, they may be more likely to be able to quickly discriminate what kinds of behavior are pathological versus those that are simply variations of particular cultural or subcultural patterns" (p. 133). Yet the therapist has to be open to the risks of his or her own possible blind spots. But, if the clients feel too negative about being Franco American, they may not want to admit their ethnicity or to associate with other Franco Americans (Paradis, 1980).

Since French is the primary language for first-generation Franco Americans, these individuals may limit their choice of therapist to the parish priest or a sympathetic lay counselor. Subtle misunderstandings between the therapist and the family may easily produce cross-cultural and intrafamily confusion. As Woolfson (1975) points out, "The therapist must be sensitive to the fact that many Franco-Vermonters speak English as a second language with what appears ease and comprehension. But one cannot assume that there is near native control. If an ongoing process of translation is taking place, then there are many chances for misunderstanding" (p.15).

For instance, I was recently called upon to see a family struggling with a major break of communication between a 61-year-old alcoholic father who had relied most of his life on his more educated wife to understand English when necessary and his 17-year-old son, the youngest, who spoke only a few words of French and wanted more social independence from the family. The mother was depressed and had given up on her role as a mediator and translator between both of them. An unspoken underlying issue was the rejection of the father's traditional value, especially the value of individual sacrifice for the family (Searles, 1982).

This population is most commonly referred for family therapy because of a child with school problems or an acting-out teenager, perhaps involved in drug abuse. The family is guarded or cautious about going into sensitive family issues and requests help only for the offspring. The child's disruption is seen as a blow to parental control. The father is usually extremely hesitant about approaching a clinic, but once there, he cooperates and is important in the therapeutic process. Gurman and Kniskern (1978) found that "the father plays a major role in the efficacy of family therapy initiated because of a child or adolescent identified patient" (p. 884). However, this is a difficult experience, for the father sees himself as the key authority figure, family rule maker, and breadwinner. Particularly in low-income families, parents have a hard time accepting a child's interpretation of what is happening. Parents, and especially the father, are afraid of either losing control or losing a position of authority within the family. On the other hand, if the mother lacks interest in the process of therapy, it will flounder. Mothers are truly the key to the family's psychological life and the gate through which any intruder must enter (Napier & Whitaker, 1978).

Alcoholism is typically associated with strong denial. Franco Americans are no different from other groups in this regard. Only when the client is intensely stressed does drug rehabilitation become an option.

Most family therapy referrals are made because of depression from death, divorce, or anxiety associated with separation or fears. Cross-cultural coupling frequently becomes the basis of conflict. A genogram helps to highlight the larger context of the multigenerational family system and is a useful step in the assessment process (Guerin, Fay, Burden, & Kautto, 1987).

The most common defense mechanisms used by Franco Americans are denial, displacement, sublimation, and rationalization. Directly observed is the blaming of others for personal inadequacies and failures, the tendency to scapegoat outsiders, the assumption of a martyred stance, and the explaining away of tyrannical or oppressive behavior by citing the authority of the Church's restrictive edicts. There seems to be a tendency to believe that problems are a passing phase and to deny that significant family problems have long-range effects.

Taboo areas for discussion in family or therapeutic encounters have been incest, homosexuality, leaving the Catholic Church, and disparagement of the deceased. Needless to say, the process of family therapy is hindered by unspoken rules and unconscious rigidities and denial. For example, in one family therapy case where the primary issue was grief over the father's death, the family could not bear to think of him realistically. He had been idealized (as elderly members are), and the distortions that they were collusively holding allowed them to not face problems with themselves and others. In addition, past abuse by priests and nuns, now coming to prominence in lawsuits and publications, is finally being slowly revealed in treatment.

Taking into account the Franco American family's pessimistic outlook and lack of enthusiasm, the therapist's ability to establish rapport becomes paramount. Empathy, warmth, and genuineness, sometimes referred to as the client-centered therapeutic triad (Raskin & Rogers, 1989), are the key to motivating a family's return for the second interview. This triad addresses the best of the hidden qualities within the families that seek help. Appropriate self-disclosure by the therapist may also help build a relationship with the family (Yalom, 1995; Ivey & Simek-Downing, 1980). In addition, the provision of definite structure in early sessions decreases anxiety. Intensive brief therapy usually can be regarded as solidly launched in the fourth or fifth session—when the therapist is certain that the Franco American's qualities of persistence, endurance, and iron tenacity have been invested into the therapeutic relationship.

A sensible strategy, one that makes use of what would otherwise be obstacles, is to frame therapeutic tasks as ways to "fulfill our duty," be it as spouse, parent, church member, or therapy participant. Duty is the supreme value. Therefore, if the therapist defines problem-solving sessions and homework tasks as "duties," then they shall be done! Unambiguous assignments, such as family meetings at home for discussion of problems, will be carried out. Therefore, direct advice, positive reinforcement, and therapeutic consistency work well, with a cognitive approach to depression being effective. The following case illustrates these points.

Mr. and Mrs. Noir, a college-educated Franco American couple in their 30s, had been married for 11 years. Mrs. Noir made the initial contact and described the problem as Mr. Noir's moods. During the first session, Mrs. Noir described her husband's condition, with only occasional acknowledgment by him. Mr. Noir's "moods" appeared to be moderate to severe depression. At times he thought of suicide.

The evaluation included an individual session with Mr. Noir in which he seemed more willing to discuss the family problems. He expressed general pessimism about life and the inevitable badness of relationships. He described his father as passive and withdrawn and his mother as domineering and overly concerned with appearances. He could not recall ever seeing his parents argue.

Mrs. Noir said that she was happy, yet presented a worldview that was strikingly negative. She said her mother was a sad person but very much in control of the family. Her alcoholic father worked long hours and was distant from the family. She could remember very few, if any, expressions of conflict between her parents.

Initially the therapy required the establishment of a warm and supportive atmosphere. Confrontation and/or attempts at insightful exploration seemed inappropriate, considering their lack of experience and understanding of conflict resolution. Each felt that they had very little impact on each other or on the wider world. A didactic approach was used: The therapist focused on the cognitive aspects of their demoralization. He taught them to recognize repetitious self-reproaches that only led them into blind alleys. He taught them to "stop [those] thoughts" and to intentionally shift their attentions to recognizing and planning more constructive behaviors (Beck & Young, 1985). For example, Mr. Noir took on the responsibility to take his wife out "on the town" to a place that he picked out, at least once a week. The therapist emphasized the responsibility and duty of each family member to practice these constructive behaviors in order to maintain a truly warm and supportive family. Gradually, they were able to change their cognitive behaviors, and their morale was improved.

———————— ᪥ ————————

In crisis situations (and most families are first seen in an advanced stage of crisis), it is important that therapists create early on a collaborative climate in which problems can be explored in less defensive or polarized ways. Franco Americans will then probably respond best to planned change and behavior-change approaches with the teaching of concrete conflict-resolution problem-solving skills and role playing.

Paradoxical remarks in the form of a warm and sincere skepticism about a rigid family's ability to change may also work. The therapist can say, "You're doing the very best you can. Therefore I wonder if you are able to change." The family is likely to "resist" by coming up with a new way to change the status quo.

Since communication patterns and problems in Franco American families are fairly obvious, the therapist can work to enhance communication of positive and constructive messages in the early sessions. This enhances awareness of positive emotional bonding within the system.

A Franco American daughter was leaving home to live with a Jewish boyfriend and to go to college. Everyone in her family disapproved—she was breaking all of the rules—and she felt cut off. A meeting of the daughter and her four brothers was arranged (she was not willing to invite her parents). The focus of the meeting was not her defection, not confrontation, but a general discussion of how in the past, during difficult times, they had still found ways to help each other.

———————— ᪥ ————————

They wanted to think of themselves as a warm and supportive family, and this was the basis for the conduct of the session. To have focused on her defection constructively would have required skills in conflict resolution that the family did not have.

Particularly strong ties exist between the dyads, mother–son (Sorrell, 1981) and father–daughter. Instructing family members to listen to one another and distinguish between thoughts and feelings (Kerr & Bowen, 1988) is helpful in encouraging more constructive contact between father and son and mother and daughter.

In addition, since many tend to rely on nonassertive, passive–aggressive behaviors as outlets for hostility, self-assertion must be stressed and practiced. They must learn to recognize when they are angry and practice self-assertion. Emotional re-education is a must to sustain long-term change, including anger management and guilt reduction.

The Franco American's ego is blocked by an overly dominant superego, and some basic transactional analysis explanations often integrate well into their worldview. Understandably the use of unstructured experiential exercises for ventilation is not helpful; they feel threatened and confused. Modeling, both verbal and nonverbal, of appropriate ways to express emotion is helpful. Some therapists report that humor and hyperbole are helpful in facilitating the awareness of personality problems such as nonassertiveness, repression of hostility, and paranoia. Humor can be useful as well in dealing with intimacy issues and taboo areas such as anger toward parental figures or disobedience to Church dogma. Considering Franco Americans' tendency to take themselves and life too seriously, to lose perspective, and to be pessimistic, it may be very helpful to illustrate a situation to the point of absurdity. This "may often help [them] gain perspective on their overly intense involvement in a rigid position and reduce what was threatening and serious to triviality" (Carter & Orfanidis-McGoldrick, 1976, p. 200).

One particular caution about working with the family is their tremendous need to protect the mother from any negative comments by other family members. This is, of course, homeostasis maintained by the mother herself. She may shrewdly assume a martyred role that intensifies guilt in family members. The therapist must avoid becoming an agent in this maneuver by embarrassing or criticizing her. On the contrary, in order to transform the family system, the therapist may intervene to unbalance the system by forming a coalition with the mother against the other members. However, as Haley (1976) points out, those who were criticized soon should be praised to recreate balance.

In working with the whole or extended family, it seems to be more productive to focus on issues that harmonize with the value of having a warm and supportive family (e.g., finding how family members are attempting to help each other and making plans for future support). Approaches that rely on the stimulation of open conflict, such as network therapy, could be disastrous (Pearce, 1980). Franco Americans avoid conflict at all costs and use obvious (and effective) delaying techniques. One caution, however, is that the levels of power in the family organization must be recognized and accepted by the therapist. When the hierarchy is confused or when some members are vying for power in the family (a previously absent father trying to reestablish himself, or a parentified child establishing dominance over siblings), use family genogram techniques to map the levels and pockets of influence. Grandparents, especially grandmothers (the key parental advisers) are often a bridge among family members. It seems likely that the more the therapist works with the parents to put them back in charge, the better the results they will get within the entire network.

## CONCLUSION

In summary, therapy with Franco American families has a predictable profile: It begins with crisis and moves slowly as change is resisted by covert defensive maneuvers. The therapist, by appealing to the Franco Americans' sense of duty and their desire to have a warm and supportive family, will in time be able to engage clients in cooperative problem solving, emotional reeducation, and the relearning of coping strategies.

Therapeutic success with Franco American families will be tangible behavioral change rather than insight or psychic restructuring, although the latter are increasingly valued by the younger generation of clients.

## ACKNOWLEDGMENTS

Special thanks to the respondents to my survey for their invaluable contributions, and to Pamela Langelier, Claire Quintal, Armand Quintal, Madeleine Giguère, Eleanor Wilson, and Peter Woolfson for assistance in the preparation of this chapter.

## NOTES

1. In this chapter, the term "Franco American" refers to the descendants of French Canadian immigrants.
2. This section is written by Claire Quintal, Institut Français, Assumption College, Worcester, Massachusetts.
3. According to Pierre Anctil (1979), of the 2,225,000 descendants of Francophone Canadians living in New England and New York, some 200,000 are of Acadian stock. They are the French peoples of what are today Nova Scotia, New Brunswick, and Prince Edward Island. There are sizable French populations in California, with 1.3 million who claim some French ancestry. In the Midwest, Michigan has close to one million, and in the far West, Texas has 500,000.
4. According to 1991 U.S. Census, 1,702,176 persons reported they speak French, and French is the third most frequently spoken language in the United States, after English and Spanish. Maine has the highest number of French-speaking people. The

Census also reports that more than 13 million persons declared themselves to be of "French ancestry." In two New England states, Connecticut and Vermont, the "French" are the second leading ancestry group. However, French ceased to be a functional language in many communities with large populations of Franco Americans. There are very few social services and health providers who have proficiency in French.
5. My translation.

## REFERENCES

Anctil, P. (1979). *A Franco American bibliography, New England*. Bedford, NH: National Materials Development Center.

Anderson, C. M., & Stewart, S. (1983). *Mastering resistance: A practical guide to family therapy*. New York: Guilford Press.

Barkan, E. R. (1980). French Canadians. In S. Thernstrom, A. Orlov, & O. Handlin (Eds.), *Harvard encyclopedia of American ethnic groups* (pp. 388–401). Cambridge, MA: Harvard University Press.

Beck, A. T., & Young, J. E. (1985). Depression. In Barlow, D. H. (Ed.), *Clinical handbook of psychological disorders* (pp. 206–244). New York: Guilford Press.

Benoit, J. (1935). *L'âme Franco-Americaine*. Montreal: Editions Albert Levesque.

Carter, E., & Orfanidis-McGoldrick, M. (1976). Family therapy with one person and the family therapist's own Family. In P. J. Guerin (Ed.), *Family therapy* (pp. 193–219). New York: Gardner Press.

Chartier, A. (1991). *Histoire des Franco-Américains de la nouvelle Angleterre 1775–1990*. Sillery, Québec: Les Editions du Septentrion.

Chassé, P. (1975). *The family*. Unpublished manuscript, Franco-American Ethnic Heritage Studies Program, Assumption College, Worcester, MA.

Dugas, D. G. (1976). Franco-American language maintenance efforts in New England: Realities and issues. *Identité Culturelle et Francophonie dans les Ameriques, 1,* 44–57.

Esman, M. R. (1985). *Henderson, Louisiana: Cultural adaptation in a Cajun community*. New York: Holt, Rinehart & Winston.

French, L. (1976). The Franco-American working class family. In C. H. Mindel & R. W. Habenstein (Eds.), *Ethnic families in America* (pp. 323–346). New York: Elsevier.

Gardner, R. C., & Lambert, W. (1972). *Attitudes and motivation*. Rowley, MA: Newbury House.

Garigue, P. (1968). The French Canadian families. In B. R. Blisher (Ed.), *Canadian society: Sociological perspectives* (3rd ed., pp. 151–169). Toronto: Macmillan of Canada.

Goodstein, L. (1995, October 5). U.S. Catholics: Church out of touch. Poll finds gulf on religious issues. *The Washington Post,* p. 9.

Guerin, P. J., Fay, L. F., Burden, S. L., & Kautto, J. G. (1987). *The evaluation and treatment of marital conflict: A four-stage approach*. New York: Basic Books.

Gunther, J. (1947). *Inside U.S.A.* New York: Harper.

Gurman, A. S., & Kniskern, D. P. (1978). Research on marital and family therapy: Progress, Perspective and Prospect. In S. L. Garfield & A. E. Bergin (Eds.), *Handbook of psychotherapy and behavior change* (2nd ed., pp. 817–901). New York: Wiley.

Haley, J. (1976). *Problem-solving therapy*. San Francisco: Jossey-Bass.

Ivey, A. E., & Simek-Downing, I. (1980). *Counseling and psychotherapy*. Englewood Cliffs, NJ: Prentice-Hall.

Kerouac, J. (1963). *Visions of Gerard* (2nd ed.). New York: McGraw-Hill.

Kerr, M. E., & Bowen, M. (1988). *Family evaluation*. New York: Norton.

Langelier, R. (1982). French-Canadian families. In M. McGoldrick, J. K. Pearce, & J. Giordano (Eds.), *Ethnicity and family therapy* (1st ed., pp. 229–246). New York: Guilford Press.

Langelier, R., & Langelier, P. (1996). *Making marriage work: Fifty years of celebration or emotional separation*. Manuscript submitted for publication.

McGoldrick, M., Garcia-Preto, N., Moore-Hines, P., & Lee, E. (1991). Ethnicity and women. In M. McGoldrick, C. Anderson, & F. Walsh (Eds.), *Women in families: A framework for family therapy* (pp. 169–199). New York: Norton.

Napier, A. Y., & Whitaker, C. (1978). *The family crucible*. New York: Harper & Row.

Nichols, M. P., & Schwartz, R. C. (1995). *Family therapy concepts and methods* (3rd ed.). Boston, MA: Allyn & Bacon.

Paradis, F. (1980). Counseling the culturally different. *The Franco American Resource Opportunity Group Forum, University of Maine, 8*(1).

Pearce, J. K. (1980). Ethnicity and family therapy: An introduction. In J. K. Pearce & I. J. Friedman (Eds.), *Family therapy: Combining psychodynamics and family systems approaches* (pp. 93–116). New York: Grune & Stratton.

Raskin, N. J., & Rogers, C. R. (1989). Person-centered therapy. In R. J. Corsini & D. Wedding (Eds.), *Current psychotherapies* (4th ed., pp. 155–197). Itasca, IL: F. E. Peacock.

Searles, J. (1982). *Immigrants from the north*. Bath, ME: Hyde School.

Sorrell, R. S. (1981). La famille of Jack Kerouac: Ethnicity and the Franco-American family. *Journal of Psychoanalytic Anthropology, 4*(2), 199–222.

U.S. Bureau of the Census. (1991). *1991 census of population*. Washington, DC: U.S. Government Printing Office.

Woolfson, P. (1973). *Value orientations of French-Canadian and Franco-American school children in border communities in Quebec and Vermont*. Unpublished manuscript, Department of Anthropology, University of Vermont, Burlington.

Woolfson, P. (1975). Traditional French-Canadian family life patterns and their implications for social services in Vermont. In M. Giguère (Ed.), *A Franco-American overview* (Vol. 2, pp. 193–198). Bedford, NH: National Materials Developmental Center, French and Portuguese.

Woolfson, P. (1983). The Franco-Americans of Northern Vermont: Cultural factors for consideration by health and social service providers. In P. Woolfson & A. J. Senécal (Eds.), *The French in Vermont: Some current views* (Occasional Papers Series, No. 6). Burlington: The Center for Research on Vermont.

Woolfson, P. (1988). Cross-cultural families: The Franco-Americans. In E. Rathbone-

McCuan & B. Havens (Eds.), *North American elders* (pp. 271–281). New York: Greenwood Press.

Woolfson, P. (1990). The aging Franco-American and the impact on acculturation. *Ethnic Groups, 8,* 181–199.

Yalom, I. D. (1995). *The theory and practice of group psychotherapy* (4th ed.). New York: Basic Books.

# CHAPTER 34

# German Families

## Hinda Winawer
## Norbert A. Wetzel

Research about specific aspects of contemporary German American family life is sparse. We present, based on clinical teaching, interviews, and personal experience, our views of the relationship of German American history and culture to the therapeutic context. There is great diversity among German Americans related to region of origin, time of immigration, economic class, and other factors that contribute to the uniqueness of the story of every individual and every family. We have sought, therefore, to highlight common elements within the German American experience that may provide the culturally sensitive therapist with a guide for inquiry, understanding, and empathy in work with families of German heritage.

Our view of German American families is not a paradigm or a prescription. We offer a touchstone for ethnically sensitive inquiry with individual families of German heritage within the diverse and complex nature of life in the United States.

German Americans are the largest and one of the oldest immigrant groups in the United States. For many, this is a surprising statement. Although they have a rich cultural history in this country and are visible as a distinct group in selected areas, in contemporary U.S. society, at least on a national scale, German Americans have blended with the dominant, White Anglo-Saxon culture. The relative invisibility of the German American culture in the United States and the reasons for it are an important aspect of German American ethnic identity.

At the opening of a workshop devoted to family therapy and ethnicity, participants introduced themselves by identifying their ethnic backgrounds. One man, a German American, said that he had never shared that information in a professional or social context. He then related how, during his childhood, aspects of the German culture had disappeared, particularly in church, where English songs and hymns replaced the German texts he had known so well as a small child. He had learned to suppress his "Germanness."

The reluctance to claim a German heritage is not unusual. It is also not surprising. In the media, there is little with which German Americans can identify positively. Films that address war crimes by Germans (e.g., *Holocaust*, *Schindler's List*, *Shoah*) and reruns of World War II films recall negative, painful associations to the homeland. In the early television era, Germans were often portrayed as evil, incompetent, or mad, or were simply not represented as an ethnic group at all (Shenton & Brown, 1976). Consequently, German Americans may be torn between claiming a heritage that is regarded as unpopular in some settings or denying a part of themselves, the ethnic dimension of their personal history.

The low ethnic profile of German Americans nationally contrasts sharply to their actual numbers and impact on U.S. culture. Many German American contributions to American life have become virtual symbols of popular culture: frankfurters, hamburgers, the covered (Conestoga) wagon, school "gym" activities, and kindergarten, to name just a few. Families with a German American ethnic background, for reasons of their special history both in Europe and here in the New World, have blended into what may now be considered the dominant, White culture. An outsider, such as a therapist, may find it difficult to recognize the specific German heritage in a family's ethnic culture. The family members themselves may have ambivalent feelings toward, or may not be aware of, their family's ethnic tradition. However, work with German American families that probes into constructs of meaning and self-image may reveal how deeply they are influenced by a German heritage; it is reflected in their basic assumptions and in the subtle style of communication between family members, even if they have not strongly identified as German.

## ORIGINS AND DEMOGRAPHY

### The Early Immigrants: Their Settlement and Contributions

Although there were German settlers as early as 1607 in Jamestown (Furer, 1973), the "official" beginning of German immigration to the New World is marked by the arrival of the *Concord*, "the German *Mayflower*," in 1683. Those settlers founded, under the leadership of Franz Daniel Pastorius, Deutschstadt (Germantown), Pennsylvania, the first German settlement in the colonies. Although small German settlements were established throughout the 18th century, Pennsylvania continued to lead as a home for Germans. In 1790, 33% of Pennsylvania's population was German. Among the many accomplishments of colonial Germans were improved farming methods, the rapid establishment of schools, a flourishing press, and the first bible in America. Technological contributions included the first paper mill and glassmaking factory, as well as the famous Conestoga wagon, now a symbol of American pioneer history.

Germans played a central role in colonial history. At the Continental Congress in 1776, Pennsylvania cast the decisive 13th vote in favor of independence from Great Britain. In the Revolutionary War, Germans were not only soldiers, but also influential generals (Muhlenberg, von Steuben). The heroic Molly Pitcher, a familiar historical figure to school children, was also German.

In the next century, Cincinnati became a leading German American city. Between 1850 and 1900, Germans were never fewer than one-quarter of all foreign-born Americans. Many lived in the Upper Mississippi and Ohio Valleys, mostly in Ohio, Illinois, Wisconsin, and Missouri. Contributions of 19th-century Germans were leadership in farming, business, industry, education, science, medicine, and music. Emphasis on participation in sports and public family recreation were German practices that have become part of the American tradition. During the Civil War, many newly immigrated Germans, especially a group of intellectual refugees, led by Carl Schurz, inspired and helped organize the antislavery efforts of the Union.

In the 20th century, immigration declined. The greatest numbers of Americans of German background were in the large cities of the Midwest, particularly in Wisconsin. New York, however, from the turn of the century until 1970, led other states as a home for German Americans. The last group identified collectively as immigrants from Germany were those who sought refuge from Nazi Germany. Predominantly, although not exclusively Jewish, these Germans included many outstanding contributors to the arts and sciences (e.g., Mann, Tillich, Brecht, Weill, Fromm, and Erikson). Individual German Americans have been honored heroes (e.g., Eisenhower and Pershing, and others such as Babe Ruth and Lou Gehrig) who remain forever in the heart of our collective memory as a nation.

## Perspectives on a Hidden Culture

In the United States in 1990, there were 58 million Americans of German ancestry. They surpass the English (32 million) and the Irish (39 million (Roberts, 1995). Despite their numerical strength, German Americans seem to blend with their Anglo-Saxon cousins as part of the dominant culture (Conzen, 1980; Hall, 1976). With the exception of regions that are centers of German culture (e.g., Wisconsin and others) and enclaves of special groups of Germanic heritage, such as the Amish and Mennonites, signs of German life are barely visible as distinctly different from the majority culture. In the East, which has a high German population, one can discern only traces of German culture. Aside from the long history of immigration, consideration of the following interrelated phenomena may be helpful in our understanding of the experience of German Americans as a less visible ethnic group in the United States:

(1) diversity among German immigrants; (2) intermarriage and assimilation; and (3) the two world wars of the 20th century, in which Germany was the primary enemy.

## Diversity

Germans in America are a heterogeneous group. Germans referred to in this chapter are those "born in Imperial Germany, the various states that coalesced to form it in 1871 and the governments that succeeded it after 1918" (Conzen, 1980, p. 405). We include, therefore, Swiss Germans, Austrians, and Alsatians, who have shared in what is generally considered the German culture, even though they have different political histories. The dimensions and diverse characteristics of German culture in Europe (not unlike the Balkan cultures) were defined by region rather than by political boundaries.

To study the cultural, national, and familial history of German-speaking people, one must consider that the various regional groups have their own rituals and customs, idiosyncrasies of family life, and values. The immigrants, as well, varied with respect to regional origin, occupation, and religion. We can, therefore, talk about a cultural unity of the immigrating Germans only in a limited sense. Until the mid-19th century, the identity of the families of German immigrants in the United States was determined more by the culture (and religion) of the area from which they originated than by their common German heritage. This might, in part, explain the plurality of present-day German American family cultures.

In addition, Germans were divided by religious differences. The basic religious division originated in the Reformation of the early 16th century. For several centuries different German regions were, for political reasons, either Catholic or Protestant. The religious affiliation of the German immigrants is important because Catholicism and Protestantism have different values and traditions that specifically affect the lives and cultures of families. Catholic Germans tend to be more tradition oriented and guided by the authority of the Church. Protestants put more emphasis on individual responsibility and conscience.

In the New World, religion was central to the family life of early settlers; it formed a bond among them as a group and between them and the fatherland. The relationship among religion, culture, and language gradually became less important as Germans became Americanized. By 1916, only 11% of the German Catholic parishes used the mother tongue exclusively. Protestant churches, particularly Lutherans, continued to use German in services and other church activities. However, most Protestant denominations were unable to retain a pure ethnic character.

Although most Germans were Catholics or Protestants, there were minority groups (i.e., Anabaptists) that, for religious reasons, had a different ethnic experience, although they are linguistically and culturally German (Smith, 1950). Similarly, German Jews in the New World identified with both their Jewish and their German heritages (Goren, 1980). In Europe, German-speaking Jews had made notable contributions in science, philosophy, and the arts (e.g., Freud, Marx, Kafka, Mendelssohn, and Heine). However, their experience as Jews and as Germans in the United States warrants separate, more extensive consideration in view of the complex cultural heritage, the history of the Jews in Germany, and the Holocaust.

## Assimilation

Assimilation is a complex phenomenon: "The very size of the German immigration, its religious, socioeconomic, and cultural heterogeneity, its skills, time of arrival and settlement patterns all combined to ensure a gradual process of acculturation and assimilation" (Conzen, 1980, p. 406). The process of assimilation was, at times, externally imposed as part of rivalries among ethnic groups. For example, soon after the establishment of the new nation, competition began between the Germans and the English. Benjamin Franklin predicted a clash between German Americans and Anglo Americans, who feared that Germans might become the dominant culture. Franklin believed that the English would absorb the Germans or be absorbed by them; a stable cultural pluralism could not exist. Several generations later in the *New York Tribune*, Horace Greeley advocated the forced assimilation of all German groups. Views of this kind prompted state legislatures to institute educational programs designed to anglicize German children (Billigmeier, 1974).

German organizations gradually accommodated to the non-German environment simply to survive. Non-Germans were admitted into German American societies. Their transactions were soon conducted in English. There was, nevertheless, still a flourishing ethnic press and a highly developed network of clubs and organizations. But the experience of German American ethnicity was to change dramatically when the United States entered World War I.

## The Two World Wars

The two world wars had a profound impact on the fate of the German culture in the United States. Xenophobia during World War I was intense. German Americans were in a loyalty conflict between an emotional connection to a fatherland, which had become internationally disdained as aggressive, and their dedication to a nation where they had flourished but in which they now experienced discrimination. "Loyalty to the Kaiser or the Flag" became a familiar expression, often used to challenge their authenticity as U.S. citizens. Nationwide suppression of German language and culture became pervasive. A general "climate of harassment" led to "a ban on German-composed music, the renaming of persons, foods, and towns, vandalism, tarring and feathering, arrests for unpatriotic utterances, and even a lynching in Collinsville, Illinois in April 1918. Public burnings of German books were frequent" (Conzen, 1980, pp. 422–423). This suppression of cultural identity appears in discussions with clients of German heritage. For example, an older, working-class couple who had immigrated in the early part of this century described how the German American club they attended was under constant FBI surveillance during World War I. This period was followed hardly more than a decade later by the Nazi era. Glazer and Moynihan (1970) describe the impact of World War II on Germans in New York City: "The German American Bund was never a major force in [New York], but it did exist. The revulsion against Nazism extended indiscriminately to things German. Thereafter, German Americans, as shocked by the Nazis as any, were disinclined to make over much of their national origins" (p. 312).

Another client, an academician, reports having been repeatedly embarrassed during his childhood because of his German heritage. Strong anti-German feelings during World War I and discomfort about German ethnicity were widespread. World War II left German Americans with few positive cultural ties with which they could identify. Germans had committed atrocious crimes, and Germany had become the outcast among the nations of the world. The concept of a German national character became associated with the enslavement and genocide of millions of people: Jews, gypsies, and homosexuals, among others. Germans who were congenitally handicapped, the developmentally disabled, and the mentally ill were also murdered. One woman, now in her 80's recounted how, during World War II, she was advised, in great confidence, by her family physician: Without explicit reference to the possible consequences, he told her never to mention that her daughter's hip deformity was congenital but to insist that it was the result of an accident. Writings have emerged that indicate that the ordinary, even the most isolated Germans were aware of the nature and scope of Nazi crimes (Elon, 1996; Goldhagen, 1996). One's Germanic roots, therefore were toned down and experienced only carefully and secretly. For those Germans who lived through World War II, and for many members of subsequent generations, knowledge of war crimes became the subject of family secrets. It is not unusual to uncover, in the immediate or extended family, someone who had fought in the war, been a member of the Nazi party, or witnessed or heard stories about persecution. Ethnic origin for German Americans may, therefore, be associated with a profound loss of ethnic identity and pride. Indeed, many older adults in the United States may wonder about their elementary education which, with few exceptions, depicted the early settlers as largely English; Germans, although great in number, did not figure prominently.

In the process of what we call the "globalization" of the economies, cultures, and histories of, at least, the Western nations after World War II, a new type of German American family has evolved that shows quite different characteristics. As part of the intense cultural and commercial exchange between Germany and the United States, German professional families, university students, and experts of one field or another immigrate or reside for years in this country with their families. They often identify with their German background while they are open to and curious about U.S. culture. The commitment of these families to acculturate in the United States may be more ambiguous. They may feel more validated in their interest in retaining the language and customs of their German background. Modern communications and intercontinental travel allow these families to stay connected with relatives in Europe. The less conflicted identification with their ethnic heritage is made possible by the positive relationship between the United States and Germany in the last 50 years and provides a context that supports a more open and direct acknowledgment and expression of the German culture.

## CHARACTERISTICS OF THE GERMAN NATIONAL HERITAGE

It is difficult to determine specific aspects of the "national character" that immigrants brought from Germany. Many German American families are aware of some facets of their cultural heritage. If immigration occurred within recent generations, older members are often knowledgeable about history, have a sense of past events, and can recall names and facts that are part of their German background. An appreciation for history and tradition is central to the German legacy. German Americans have the capacity to look at themselves, study their own backgrounds, and scrutinize their past.

### Proximity, Space, and Structure

Understanding German cultural and familial heritage may be enhanced by examining external factors. Geographically situated in the middle of Western Europe, Germany was confined within borders that allowed for little natural expansion. People learned to live together peacefully within a small area. Explosive forces from within (internal friction, rivalries, overpopulation, lack of natural resources) or enemies from outside (against which there was little natural protection) could endanger survival. Indeed, the quest for *Lebensraum* (space for living) is a theme of German national and familial history (and still may be a salient issue for current immigrants). Available space had to be used intensively. German society was, therefore, highly structured. Living in proximity, people developed a need for clear, at times, rigid boundaries; complex social hierarchies helped to define personal territory. To this day, in Germany, the boundary that designates the interface between family unit and surrounding society is rather well defined. The transition between inside and outside the family is regulated, and there are formalities to be respected when entering a German house. The homes of middle-class families are usually surrounded by fences or bushes that delineate the property between houses. In Germany, "yards tend to be well fenced; but fenced or not, they are sacred" (Hall, 1966, p. 135). Similarly, the friendship patterns of middle-class families are clearly regulated (Salamon, 1977). There is a distinction between acquaintances, neighbors, and colleagues with whom one socializes, and personal friends with whom more open and intimate relationships exist. For recent immigrants, therefore, social interactional styles in the United States may seem freeing and relaxed; for some, adaptation may be uncomfortable and feel dystonic. In social intercourse, the use of *Sie* (the formal "you") and *Du* (the familiar "you") symbolizes the importance ascribed to proximity and distance. Boundaries help protect the family's space. Privacy is highly valued. German politicians, for example, do not involve their families in public life. The family's inner circle is protected against intrusions from the outside that might endanger members' well-being. Conflicts and emotional upheavals that are experienced as embarrassing can be contained within the family sphere "where they belong." Inside the family, physical space is also clearly structured. In the cool, Central European climate, houses are solidly constructed. The doors within contemporary German homes are usually closed. At the dinner table, everyone takes an assigned place. Similarly, in the New World, German homes were noted for their construction, effective heating systems, and suitability for productive indoor life (Billigmeier, 1974).

## Emotional Restraint, Sentimentality, and *Gemütlichkeit*

Another characteristic trait of the German heritage is the polarity of emotional restraint and sentimentality. Affection, anger, and emotion in general do not get expressed easily. What might be experienced as too explosive is contained by boundaries, structure, and emotional control. In the Germanic style of handling emotions, one is not encouraged to show emotions openly or to display affection, grief, or anger in public. Passions get repressed or sublimated in work or art. The work of Thomas Mann, one of the most "German" writers (Hatfield, 1951), is an example of an immensely rich human experience contained in a highly artful form, similar to the often intense, powerful music of the German masters. But there is a very acceptable expression of emotion within the culture: the tradition of *Gemütlichkeit*.

*Gemütlichkeit*, still found in homes of first- and second-generation German Americans, provides a contrast to emotional restraint. There is no word in the English language that accurately renders the meaning of *Gemüt* (disposition, temper, heart) or *Gemütlichkeit* (geniality, comfort, warmth). German Americans introduced it to the New World as their way of making themselves feel "at home": the experience of familiarity, emotional closeness, and fun.

# GERMAN AMERICAN VALUES

## Family Life

Among the diverse German immigrant groups, family life was highly valued. The family was considered the place of mutual support and strength in times of crisis. Loyalty was first to the family. Often, particularly in rural areas, work and family life were integrated just as in the German "household family" of the 16th–18th centuries (Weber-Kellermann, 1977; Billigmeier, 1974). Even today, under different circumstances, the relationships among members of German American extended family systems are strong and well organized through visits, calls, or letters. German American families live apart from their extended families, and the blurring of boundaries between nuclear and extended families that we see in other cultures is rare in German American family systems. Yet, there are emotional attachments and strong feelings. Children are expected to love their parents and to take care of them in their old age.

## Work

The work ethic, manifested in a respect for thoroughness, solid craftsmanship, and attention to detail, was transplanted from the fatherland to the New World. Other Americans admired German settlers' skills, diligence, and industriousness, particularly in farming (in 1870, Germans constituted 33% of all foreign-born farmers). The Germans, among all immigrant groups, made the most important contributions to the introduction of new methods of agricultural production (Billigmeier, 1974). Germans were also noted for their technical abilities. "Skilled technicians, engineers and scientists were drawn into American industrial enterprises, large and small, in every major field of manufacturing in every region of the country. Their contribution to the industrial development of the United States is extraordinary" (Billigmeier, 1974, p. 94).

Whether they inherited the tradition from their colonial ancestors or brought it through recent immigration, German Americans are likely to value a strong work ethic. Success in work is a source of pride and self-esteem. The exploration of occupational responsibilities should, therefore, be an integral part of therapy.

## Education

The emphasis on education is the heritage of all German groups in the New World. Since the colonial period, Germans have made lasting contributions to education. In 1714, German American Christopher Dock introduced the essential fixture of every American classroom, the blackboard, and published the first pedagogy work in the United States in 1750. The intellectually oriented

"Forty-Eighters" (political refugees of the failed revolution of 1848), critical of educational standards in the United States, spearheaded school reform; they spread knowledge about European pedagogical theories. During this time, German secular and religious schools appeared throughout the United States. Institutions, such as the German American Teachers' Seminary in Milwaukee, were founded to maintain high standards of education (Conzen, 1980). The cornerstone of early childhood education in this country, the *Kindergarten*, was first developed in Wisconsin by Margaretha Schurz, wife of the famous Carl Schurz. German American parents underwent hardships and were willing to sacrifice in order to give their children a "good" education. Children, in turn, were expected to work hard and do well in school.

## FAMILY PATTERNS

Certain "typical" role and relationship definitions may still be discernible among German American subgroups. Family patterns differ, however, according to time of immigration, region of origin, economic class, religious affiliation, and extent to which the German culture has been supported in the area of settlement.

## Men and Women

In German American families, as in others, one cannot underestimate the importance of the difference in gender-determined roles (Hare-Mustin, 1987), or of gender as a central aspect of family organization (Goldner, 1985). Before the social injustices inherent in ascribed gender roles were given voice, the role definitions of men and women in German American families were virtually unchallenged. Women worked hard and had no economic power. Historically, when the ethnic character of German American families was more clearly recognizable, their family structure and the complementarity of roles of men and women reflected the legacy from the homeland. The husband/father was the head of the household and the leader of the family. The wife took his name, adopted his family and friends, and gained his social status. The early Pennsylvanian German Americans (now called Pennsylvania Dutch) assumed that a male-dominated social order was proper, and that women had responsibilities in certain areas, which were called *kinner, kich, 'n karrich* (children, kitchen, and church), a phrase not unknown in modern Germany. The husband ran the farm, operated the mill, and concerned himself with economic enterprise (Parsons, 1976). As his forebear and European counterpart, the German American father is described as sentimental and stern. Underneath the self-controlled, reserved, at times unduly strict and stubborn attitude, lay hidden intense emotions and sentiments, often experienced as overwhelming and potentially destructive. To this day, we hear about German American fathers and grandfathers, known for their use of corporal punishment as a means of discipline. Rational and somewhat distant, the husband/father was less available to the children than their mother. He was to be a diligent worker and provide the material needs for his family. It was his right to make the major decisions or to ratify the common decisions of the couple.

German American women were expected to be hardworking, dutiful, and subservient, and were respected for these qualities. Among the early-Pennsylvania Germans, a wife's contribution was highly valued by her husband. She was cook, seamstress, nurse, laundress, baker, teacher, cloth maker, and supervisor of household production. Her role was indispensable in this early rural economy, and she was both frugal and dutiful (Parsons, 1976). German American women helped with harvesting and strenuous farmwork. The home-oriented roles of women were highly adaptive for those with "family businesses" in both rural and urban settings (Weber-Kellermann, 1977; Kletzien, 1975).

In German American families of the late 19th and early 20th century, the wife's main task was still the housework. A clean house and the neat appearance of husband and children were her responsibilities and source of pride. Above all, it was her "chore" to raise the children, with whom she was more involved than was her husband. In many ways, wives and mothers were the emotional power-center of the family, although for outside appearances, the leadership of fathers and husbands was not challenged. German American women are described as emotionally more open and available than their husbands.

## Marital Complementarity

The marital relationship and the division of "labor" between the parents tended to solidify the complementarity of a rational, dominant leader and an emotional, submissive nurturer. Apparently reserved emotionally, the father could be quite sentimental. Mothers could also be seen as capable of effectively leading the family. The specific familial as well as class context may determine how each of the partners develops attitudes and behavior patterns that correspond to their roles. One of the tasks in therapy with distinctly German American families is, therefore, to help them gain greater flexibility of role patterns and to increase the spectrum of acceptable responses toward each other. From a systemic perspective, we must consider not only the typical polar and complementary relationship of both marital partners, but also the entire family structure. The once common German American "patriarchal" family structure is rare today and would have to be viewed in relation to economic conditions, societal issues, and the impact of the feminist movement, which has afforded a greater variety of experience to many men and women.

## Parents and Children

Historically, in families with distinct German ethnic identity, infants and young children were raised with structure, limits on spatial exploration, and precise schedules. Individual family idiosyncrasies notwithstanding, it is not unusual to encounter German families that do not characteristically encourage open expression of emotions. The overall family climate may be more favorable to tasks than to overt nurturance and emotions. Disagreements between parents and children are settled through the decisions of the parents, without a lengthy period of verbalized anger, accusations, and mutual compromising. Children are rewarded less for airing feelings than for politeness in verbal expression, appropriate table manners, or fulfillment of their household chores.

## Life Cycle Issues

German American families may have difficulties with making the transition from a family with small children, who need to obey their parents, to a family with teenagers, who are being asked for age-appropriate cooperation, and who need a different kind of guidance. Fathers, in particular, may be unprepared when challenged in their authority by their adolescent offspring.

One encounters in practice and literature (Koomen, 1974; Devereux, 1962) descriptions reminiscent of German fathers of renowned figures such as Mozart (Hildesheimer, 1982), Kafka (Kafka, 1954), Beethoven (Solomon, 1977) or of Thomas Mann (Heilbut, 1996) himself. These men are described as unreachable, authoritarian, and without apparent vulnerability. Beethoven's father was physically abusive, partially due to his alcoholism. Descriptions of a "stern, feared, tyrannical" father, usually contrasted with a "warm, loving, subservient" mother somewhere in the family background are common among German American families in therapy and in the German culture (Glaser, 1976; Willi, 1982).

Domestic violence exists, of course, in all cultures (Levinson, 1989) and it is essential to investigate physical abuse in working with families and couples (Goldner, Penn, Sheinberg, & Walker, 1990) whatever the ethnic heritage. It is unclear, however, to what extent German American families have a significantly higher number of authoritarian or physically violent fathers/husbands than do other ethnic groups. The patriarchal family, in turn, would have to be viewed in relation to the socioeconomic conditions of the period in question. The fathers of Victorian bourgeois families around the turn of the century may be significantly different from their counterparts in agrarian household families of the 17th to early 19th centuries or from working class fathers of that era.

From our practice, we cannot determine whether physical violence or corporal punishment is characteristic of American families of German background, though curiosity about descriptions of strict fathers or grandfathers has on occasion revealed stories of abuse. This complex question warrants further exploration taking societal variables into account. There may be also differences due to the regional and religious diversity among German American families and, of course, due to the time of immigration.

It may be that studies of the characteristics of an "authoritarian personality" in general (Adorno, Frenkel-Brunswik, Levinson, & Nevitt, 1950; Mitscherlich, 1973; Erikson, 1950, 1962) and the family histories of Adolf Hitler (Stierlin, 1977; Langer, 1972) and D. P. Schreber (Schatzman, 1976; Israels, 1989; Lothane, 1992) in particular have been generalized in an attempt to contribute to an understanding of Germany's militarism, international aggression and the incomprehensible acts of the Holocaust during the first half of the 20th century (Dicks, 1950). Although characteristics such as an interest in militarism have been said to prevail regardless of migration (Sowell, 1994), specific research does not seem to support the idea that German fathers before World War II were more authoritarian than their American counterparts (Koomen, 1974).

Culturally sensitive clinicians may want to pay special attention to the adolescent phase in the life cycle of German American families, particularly when exploring the family background of fathers with a German ethnic origin. Having experienced the traditional emotional restraint and the often authoritarian features of the fathers in previous generations, the men in modern German American families often consciously decide to be more emotionally open and involved with their children.

Nevertheless, parents and children in German American families, to this day, seem to rarely talk openly about the struggles of increasing autonomy for the children and the pain of the separation process. If this phase of development is inadequately handled, the children may leave home and become emotionally cutoff (Bowen, 1978) from their parents, forsaking an extended family network. The process of individuation and continuing relatedness (Stierlin, Rücker-Embden, Wetzel, & Wirsching, 1980) in German families can have an either–or quality to it. Parents or children may give up their contact with each other altogether rather than experience the conflict of negotiating differences.

With ethnic German families, therapists may have to reopen the intrafamilial dialogue. Empathy must support all "sides" of the adolescent struggle: Fathers, who have not had the emotional education to engage in emotional challenges and to share their inner world, will require support. Examination of their entrenched positions may yield alternative descriptions of mothers' roles as well. For example, a woman viewed as "overinvolved " with her adolescent son may be considered as protecting both father and son from their feared confrontation. Her burdensome position may not only be unnecessary, but it also may hinder her own development. Adolescent sons and daughters need to be guided in a delicate balance that combines challenge with respect in the struggle for individuation within the ongoing familial relationship.

Often, higher education is valued in the family, which will make it less likely that the children will be unable to leave at all. In that instance, however, the transition into adulthood can be abrupt and without open sharing of the concomitant feelings.

## CONDUCTING THERAPY WITH FAMILIES OF GERMAN HERITAGE

The history and vicissitudes of the German cultural heritage in German American families and the subtle presence of the ethnic background in many contemporary German American families make it difficult to summarize the features of the German cultural tradition that bear on these families' attitudes toward and experience with therapy. The impressions presented here may help therapists organize their own inquiry.

### Entering Therapy

For German families, coming to therapy violates a tacit rule: "Do it yourself." German Americans, therefore, come for treatment when they feel they have no alternative: The marriage is on the verge of collapse and divorce is impending, or there is a symptom that impedes the family's functioning. Seeking outside help is often connected with a sense of failure: Hard work, responsible behavior, and conscientiousness have not been good enough. One second-generation German American mother remarked, "I would take my child to therapy only after I had done everything in my power and left no stone unturned in trying to solve the problem in the family." The therapist who bypasses this phenomenon in the initial moments of therapy risks shutting him- or herself out of the family (Winawer-Steiner, 1979). It may be helpful to take some time to track the decision-making process involved in coming to therapy. The therapist may enter the family by exploring how they chose to begin therapy, whether the decision is syntonic with the family's values, essentially pursuing an inquiry that can reveal the work the family may have already done not only in its effort to resolve the problem, but also in the decision to consider treatment.

### The Initial Interview

A stranger does not enter the family abruptly. During the initial interview, there is often an air of emotion, as illustrated in this vignette.

When Mrs. Gruenewald finished explaining her view of her daughter's acting-out behavior, the family fell silent. The children sat motionless, alternately staring at the floor, each other, or their father. Mr. Gruenewald shifted from one uncomfortable posture to another and sighed intermittently. Questions from the therapist were answered monosyllabically by the children. The mother seemed anxious. The therapist eventually remarked that the couple had raised discerning, loyal children, not easily convinced that a stranger should be allowed into the family. Not until the children's caution was viewed as protective of the family unit did the father begin to acknowledge that bringing his family to therapy was an arduous decision.

———————— ❧ ————————

The therapist who is accustomed to an expressive interactional style need not be discouraged by this apparently labored beginning. The Germanic style of forming relationships is generally more structured and includes a sequence of steps over time. The joining process is gradual and proceeds through certain stages, but once established, relationships are intense and lasting.

## Reaction to Therapy

Once the therapist is invited into the family, German Americans are responsible about therapy and take it seriously. Therapy is a task that requires serious attention. Of course, this does not mean that German families respond to the therapist's interventions better than do others.

## Therapeutic Styles

In a culture in which people are sensitive to clear, although at times subtle, hierarchies of power and authority, the therapeutic stance to which a German American family is likely to be most responsive would be one not only of empathy, but also of authority. The therapist is viewed as the expert. For recent immigrants, for example, the automatic use of first names for adults might be considered unprofessional or disrespectful, as would therapeutic styles that emphasize physical contact beyond a handshake.

## The Family in Treatment

A German family, as any other, brings to therapy a confluence of events, feelings, beliefs, and social conditions that is unique to them. We have limited our discussion to one dimension, complementarity of marital and parental roles, which has provided a useful point of departure for exploring the distinctive organization of individual German families. In traditional German American families gender-role complementarity (fathers provide for the family, and mothers are involved with household and children) and the dutiful adherence to the work ethic can be observed in therapy. Exploration of the belief system about role definitions over generations can enhance the work of therapy.

Fathers rarely complain about their roles. As one man of German descent, who had always held down two jobs, put it, "The first third of my life I worked for my mother, the second third for my wife and my children, now I want to enjoy myself." He intended now to work only one job. This sense of duty and responsibility for the family can grow so strong and all-encompassing that it drives people into untenable situations.

Mr. F., a successful lawyer, as was his father, regularly overworked to the point of exhaustion. Only in a severe depression could he grant himself some rest. Although his wife stated that she was willing to work, both could not, in fact, tolerate her contributing to the family income. That would have contradicted their understanding of what was expected of him.

---

In such a rigidly complementary system, it may be counterproductive to directly challenge the ethnic values. More effective would be a perspective that acknowledges the values of work and duty and allows respectful exploration of the complementarity of roles. We can also view the strong work ethic of German American fathers as an asset to the process of therapy. The seriousness and work orientation of German American fathers may render them amenable, for example, to instrumental models of therapy that utilize directives. Although changes in role may be unfamiliar, the notion of working on a given task is not. The German American father's understanding of his function in the family can facilitate a readiness to follow the therapist's directives. Similarly, mothers in German American families, as in other ethnic groups, have been socialized to withhold expression of dissatisfaction with their roles. It is not unusual to meet a wife who has adhered to her subservient role for years, containing enormous rage. Her awakening may be the shift that brings the family to therapy. If a way out of her submissive position is not negotiable, covert defiance of the father's authority may be manifested in subtle undermining, generally through the children. On the surface, however, it might appear as though the father were in control, and the effort to maintain this appearance is highly collusive and well entrenched in the family's modus operandi. It can be difficult, therefore, to overcome this polarization of roles.

Karen and Peter Hoffman came to therapy because 3 weeks earlier, after 8 years of marriage, Karen announced that she was leaving. Peter was bewildered. He had no idea that there had been any problem in the marriage and could not understand her present motives. Stuck in their complementary roles and confined by their emotional restraint, both spouses had been unable to communicate effectively. Karen revealed that she had felt dominated by and subservient to Peter throughout the years of their marriage. Through many tears, she explained that she had never thought of telling Peter how she felt.

---

Within the context of these fixed roles, a mother's expressiveness may be daunting for the father in his efforts to be more emotionally engaged with his wife or with the children. Supporting an increase in a father's contact with the children, for example, may be a slow and difficult process. Because he respects the knowledge and authority of the therapist, and because he is work-oriented, the father is likely to assume this challenge. Acknowledging the mother's position and enlisting her support with reassurance that she will not be sacrificed through isolation from her husband and children is essential for the process of change. Without the therapist's support, the mother may understandably undermine the father's involvement with the children, if she feels that they will be unprotected and her position not respected. It is essential to consider the mother's voice as the emotional center of the family, as it is necessary to realize that her contribution to the emotional work of the family may be the only role she feels is valued. Her collaboration is important and difficult work and can be treated as such with recognition and/or specific tasks. Timely exploration of the implications of change for her own growth may be the first support she has gotten as an individual within the family arena.

In treating families of German American heritage, we may be struck by the apparent lack of expression of feelings, despite the severity of problems. It is difficult to decide whether this is an indication of the individual family's need for privacy and emotional restraint or their cultural training within the family system.

In the Strumpf family, the parents had gone through enormous hassles to have their 16-year-old daughter treated for scoliosis and to have her wear a brace. Not long after, the daughter refused to wear the brace and got caught smoking marijuana. Despite the stress on everybody, the family's conversation centered around logistical, medical, and legal issues. None of the accompanying emotions were shared. Explorations into the family of origin of both parents revealed their German heritage of self-sufficient, hardworking, performance-oriented ancestors, who left little space for emotional issues.

—————————— ✎ ——————————

The therapist's most important asset is the awareness that the greater the emotional restraint within the family, the more explosive the underlying feelings (as symbolized by the daughter's acting out). Here, the turning point was the therapist's acknowledgment of the parents for having put aside their disappointment in their daughter in order to work harder at taking care of her.

## Ethnic Heritage as a Therapeutic Issue

The therapist who is interested in multigenerational issues will discover in work with German American families that it takes a while for family members to discuss the family's memory of the German culture. The need to be cautious about their German background creates, in some families, depending on their ages of immigration or experiences in this country during World Wars I and II, uneasiness about their ethnic identity. As a result, attitudes toward their German heritage may be ambivalent or unexplored. The ambivalence might also be directed toward the therapist who belongs to a different ethnic group. Exploration of a German American family's background might stir up the therapist's forgotten memories and hidden prejudices. The therapist might have to learn to accept his or her own suppressed German American heritage. On the other hand, therapists with different ethnic backgrounds will have to deal with their own stereotypes about German Americans. Clients are usually quite able to sense the negative, judgmental attitude behind their therapist's friendly facade. Ethnic stereotypes will invariably be communicated to the family. It is better to recognize one's own limitations as a therapist and to discuss openly whether treatment with a therapist of different ethnic background might be better. Jewish therapists, in particular, in work with recent immigrants and their families, need to be careful not to overestimate their tolerance in view of the pain of Jewish–German history.

German Americans as an ethnic group have, by and large, experienced a diminished visibility of their own culture. Highly assimilated Germans, whose families have intermarried, may have to be guided to articulate the specifics of their ethnic origins. In constructing a genogram, for example, generalized responses to inquiries about ethnicity are not uncommon for essentially "dominant culture" families: "Oh, our background is mixed, you know, English, Irish, German, maybe some French."

Careful questioning may reveal a grandfather described as a "stubborn Prussian" who "was actually kind of hard on my mother." The therapist must beware that, for many Germans, the negative stereotypes have also been transmitted multigenerationally. Pursuing an inquiry beyond one-dimensional constructs ("stubborn Prussian") that have been frozen in the family history can yield alternative descriptions. In a quiet family on the brink of divorce, a generally taciturn father answered questions about his grandfather in the presence of his young-adult children. He was able to reflect on how the grandfather's tenacity was not only painful, but also valuable: "My grandfather was actually more stable than my flamboyant father, and with his darn stubbornness, he did have a heck of a knack at teaching us some object lessons." Asked whether the grandfather was tough through and through, he thought a moment, and answered that the grandfather did indeed have a "soft side" and that you "knew that he cared; he just didn't show it."

Here the exploration of ethnic phenomena and history bring all family members within a hair's breadth of a new view of the speaker—the quiet, undemonstrative father—who was then asked how he thought his children saw him, like a father or grandfather. In most parts of the country, it is hard for Germans to find an ethnic community. Newer immigrants are culturally isolated and may be attracted to assimilate to the relatively unstructured, loose, casual style of life in the United States, as compared with the regulated, clearly delineated nature of contemporary German society. The same freedom, however, may create difficulties with respect to more flexible work environments, which can produce feelings of insecurity because of the sharp contrast to the German workplace which, while more rigid structurally, is also more predictable. These issues, in combination with the natural stresses of migration (Sluzki, 1979; Rogler, 1994), may be relevant to understanding family dilemmas. The ethnically sensitive therapist might, therefore, be particularly attentive to signs of loss, not only as part of the immigration process, but also as related to an ethnic legacy that may have been suppressed, distorted, or forgotten. Examining how the family has dealt with their less visible ethnicity may prove useful.

Some recent clinical experiences with poor families of German descent have revealed a sense of failure in a society organized around deprecation and oppression of people of color (West, 1994; Pinderhughes, 1989). German Americans' sense of failure in poverty has an added dimension: They are not integrated into the dominant White culture, but they also have no strong ethnic identity or national spiritual leaders who would speak for them. From a cultural perspective, their plight may be considered another casualty in a racist society, an issue that warrants further exploration.

Intergenerational work with German Americans from a family-therapy perspective, genograms, coaching, family voyages, and guiding through operational mourning have been effective in coping with loss in the family context (Bowen, 1978; Paul & Paul, 1986). A review of the actual history and contributions of this ethnic group can be an important intervention, particularly for German Americans who are ignorant of their rich legacy in this country.

## CONCLUSION

Therapists who work with German American families need to be aware of the myriad of social forces that evolve the characteristics of particular German American family systems over time. Not the least of these characteristics is the irony of the loss of their distinctive culture in most parts of the present-day United States, on the one hand, and the enormity and richness of German America at the foundations of U.S. society on the other. The authors hope that these reflections stimulate the observations of colleagues and lead to applications in clinical practice and further study. We further hope that we have presented no "typical" German American family structure. We have sought, rather, to respect the historical and social complexity of its ethnic context. We have offered information that can make a difference in the practitioner's development of a contextually aware therapeutic collaboration with the unique individuals in families of German heritage in the United States.

## REFERENCES

Adorno, T. W., Frenkel-Brunswik, E., Levinson, D., & Nevitt, S. R. (1950). *The authoritarian personality*. New York: Harper.

Billigmeier, R. H. (1974). *Americans from Germany: A study in cultural diversity*. Belmont, CA: Wadsworth.

Bowen, M. (1978). *Family therapy in clinical practice*. Northvale, NJ: Jason Aronson.

Conzen, K. N. (1980). Germans. In S. Thernstrom, A. Orlov, & O. Handlin (Eds.), *Harvard encyclopedia of American ethnic groups* (pp. 405–425). Cambridge, MA: Harvard University Press.

Devereux, E. C., Bronfenbrenner, U., & Suci, G. J. (1962). Patterns of parent behavior in the United States of America and the Federal Republic of Germany: A cross-national comparison. *International Social Science Journal, 14*, 488–506.

Dicks, H. V. (1950). Personality traits and national socialist ideology. *Human Relations, 3*(2), 111–154.

Elon, A. (1996, March 24). The Jew who fought to stay German. *The New York Times Magazine*, pp. 52–55.

Erikson, E. H. (1950). *Childhood and society*. New York: Norton.

Erikson, E. H. (1962). *Young man Luther: A study in psychoanalysis and history*. New York: Norton.

Furer, H. B. (Ed.). (1973). *The Germans in America 1607–1970*. Dobbs Ferry, NY: Oceana.

Glaser, H. (1976). *Sigmund Freud's Zwanzigstes Jahrhundert*. München, Germany: C. Hanser.

Glazer, N., & Moynihan, D. P. (1970) *Beyond the melting pot*. Cambridge, MA: MIT Press.

Goldhagen, D. J. (1996, March 17). Week in review: The people's holocaust. *The New York Times*, p. 15.

Goldner, V. (1985). Feminism and family therapy. *Family Process, 24*, 31–47.

Goldner, V., Penn, P., Sheinberg, M., & Walker, G. (1990). Love and violence: Gender paradoxes in volatile attachments. *Family Process, 29*(4), 343–364.

Goren, A. A. (1980). Jews. In S. Thernstrom, A. Orlov, & O. Handlin (Eds.), *Harvard encyclopedia of American ethnic groups* (pp. 571–598). Cambridge, MA: Harvard University Press.

Hall, E. T (1966). Proxemics in a cross-cultural context: Germans, English, and French. In E. Hall (Ed.), *The hidden dimension*. Garden City, NY: Doubleday.

Hall, E. T. (1976). *Beyond culture*. Garden City, NY: Anchor Books.

Hare-Mustin, R. T. (1987) The problem of gender in family therapy theory. *Family Process, 26*, 15–28.

Hatfield, H. (1951). *Thomas Mann*. Norfolk, CT: New Direction Books.

Heilbut, A. (1996). *Thomas Mann: Eros and literature.* New York: Knopf.

Hildesheimer, W. (1982). *Mozart.* New York: Farrar, Straus, Giroux.

Israels, H. (1989). *Schreber: Father and son.* Madison, CT: International Universities Press.

Kafka, F. (1954). *Dearest father.* New York: Schocken Books.

Kletzien, H. H. (1975). *New Holstein.* New Holstein, WI: New Holstein Reporter Press.

Koomen, W. (1974). A Note on the authoritarian German family. *Journal of Marriage and the Family, 35,* 634–636.

Langer, W. (1972). *The mind of Adolf Hitler: The secret war-time report.* New York: Basic Books.

Levinson, D. (1989). *Family violence in cross cultural perspective.* Newbury Park, CA: Sage.

Lothane, Z. (1992). *In defense of Schreber: Soul murder and psychiatry.* Hillsdale, NJ: Analytic Press.

Mitscherlich, A. (1973). *Society without the father: A contribution to social psychology.* Northvale, NJ: Jason Aronson.

Parsons, W. T. (1976). *Pennsylvania Dutch.* Boston: Twayne.

Paul, N., & Paul, B. (1986). *A marital puzzle.* New York: Gardner Press.

Pinderhughes, E. (1989). *Understanding race, ethnicity and power.* New York: The Free Press.

Roberts, S. (1995). *Who are we: A portrait of America based on latest U.S. census.* New York: Times Books.

Rogler, L. H. (1994). International migration: A framework for directing research. *American Psychologist, 49,* 701–708.

Salamon, S. (1977). Family bonds and friendship bonds, Japan and West Germany. *Journal of Marriage and the Family, 38,* 807–820.

Schatzman, M. (1976). *Soul murder: Persecution in the family.* Harmondsworth, UK: Penguin Books.

Shenton, J. P., & Brown, G. (Eds.). (1976). *Ethnic groups in American life.* New York: Arno.

Sluzki, C. (1979). Migration and family conflict. *Family Process, 18*(4), 379–390.

Smith, C. H. (1950). *The story of the Mennonites.* Newton, KS: Mennonite Publication Office.

Solomon, M. (1977). *Beethoven.* New York: Schirmer Books.

Sowell, T. (1981). *Ethnic America: A history.* New York: Basic Books.

Sowell, T. (1994). *Race and culture: A world view.* New York: Basic Books.

Stierlin, H. (1977). *Adolf Hitler: A family perspective.* New York: Psychohistory Press.

Stierlin, H., Rücker-Embden, I., Wetzel, N., & Wirsching, M. (1980). *The first interview with the family.* New York: Brunner/ Mazel.

Weber-Kellermann, I. (1977). *Die Deutsche Familie: Versuch einer Sozialgeschichte.* Frankfurt, Germany: Suhrkamp.

West, C. (1994). *Race matters.* New York: Vintage Books.

Willi, J. (1982). *Couples in collusion.* Northvale, NJ: Jason Aronson.

Winawer-Steiner, H. (1979). Getting started in family therapy: A preliminary guide for therapist, supervisor and administrator. In M. Dinoff & D. Jacobson (Eds.), *Neglected problems in community health* (pp. 154–174). University, AL: University of Alabama Press.

CHAPTER 35

# Greek Families

Sam J. Tsemberis
Spyros D. Orfanos

Immigrant Greek families in the process of acculturation face enormous economic, social, and psychological challenges. Family members are required to adapt to the host culture by making fundamental changes in family organization, marital relations, and parent–child interactions. When working with Greek American families, clinicians who are familiar with Greek culture and Greek heritage will better understand the meaning of demands placed upon these families in the United States. To contribute to this essential need for understanding, in this chapter we address issues encountered by first-generation Greek immigrant families who face the greatest degree of upheaval and discontinuity in their daily lives, with an emphasis on those who seek family therapy.

## BRIEF HISTORY OF IMMIGRATION

There have been two major waves of Greek immigration to the United States. These are broadly divided into the "old immigrants," who arrived at the turn of the century (1890–1920), and the "new immigrants," who arrived after the Immigration Act of 1965 (Moskos, 1989). Today there are an estimated 1.5–3 million Greeks in the living United States (Georgakas, 1994). The first cohort began leaving Greece in the late 19th century and comprised primarily peasant farmers from the Peloponnisos (the Southern peninsula of the Greek mainland). Major crop failures and the promises of prosperity in the New World resulted in a mass exodus of over 400,000 Greeks, mostly young men. These early immigrants initially had hopes of working abroad for a few years, returning home, buying land, and improving their lot and that of their families. Most women did not work outside the home, except in the family business. Since women's place in Greek culture has traditionally been defined in terms of their relationships to men, it follows that if a man's wife, daughter, or sister had to

517

work, it reflected poorly on his ability to provide and protect them from foreign influence (Dubisch, 1991; Moskos, 1989).

The story of a young man named Chris Tsakonas from the village of Zoupena, a few miles southeast of Sparta, is illustrative. In 1873, Tsakonas arrived in the United States and worked as a candy peddler in New York City. After a few years, he went back to Greece and returned to New York accompanied by a small group of young men, who, in turn, brought more relatives and friends. Tsakonas developed a chain of candy and fruit stores and aided fellow villagers to come to America (Dickson, 1991).

Many Greeks identified with Tsakonas's success and his altruistic assistance of fellow immigrants. A small percentage of Greek women also immigrated, usually accompanying husbands, siblings, or other relatives. These initial immigrants set up the supports and pathways for the subsequent stream of immigrants. Eventually they grew to a national community numbering approximately 400,000 (Moskos, 1989).

The second major wave of Greek immigrants began to arrive after the passage of the Immigration Act of 1965. These were mainly entire families, better-educated and more skilled than the first cohort. They contemplated returning to Greece to become proprietors of businesses rather than to buy land. They also hoped that their children would graduate from the American educational system and then enter professional life in Greece.

A smaller cohort of Greek immigrants arrived in the years between these two larger waves between the end of World War II and the mid-1960s (Gavaki, 1991). This group consisted overwhelmingly of permanent settlers. Leaving Greece after the destruction and poverty resulting from World War II and 4 years of a devastating civil war that followed were entire families, illegal immigrants, and "import" brides and bridegrooms (Moskos, 1989). This group arrived with few skills, low education, and without financial resources.

## FAMILY AND COMMUNITY

The basic social unit in Greece is the family (*ikoyenia*), which has strong patriarchial control and deeply binding extended kinships including godparents (*koumbari*) and affines (*simpetheri*) (Sant Cassia & Bada, 1992). The overarching value of a family is to defend its *philotimo* (love of honor). Families are organized hierarchically, and members interact in highly cohesive (usually enmeshed) ways. Because the family is the central social unit, needs of the individual are not focused on the same way as they are in American families, and every member is expected to defer to the greater needs of the family.

First-generation Greek families rely on extended family and kin as well as on community institutions such as the Church and hometown-based civic organizations (*topika somatia*) for support. The church is used to meet both social and spiritual needs. Parishioners sometimes seek counseling from their priests.

Perceptive priests not trained in pastoral counseling may provide spiritual or moral guidance but will refer families for therapy to qualified practitioners.

Many Greek Americans see a major problem with the Greek Orthodox Church's role in preserving and reinforcing the subordinate place of Greek women in the community. The only roles permitted women in the church is membership within the *Philoptochos*, or the Friends of the Poor Society. The mission of the *Philoptochos* is to preserve the faith, educate the young, and help the less fortunate. Its fund-raising activities provide the church with significant financial contributions. Women, however, are not given any leadership or power and remain relegated to the roles of fund-raiser or caretaker (Clamar, 1987).

Similarly, in the *topika somatia*, the women organize charitable work whereas the men tend to focus on community business and politics. The goals of such civic organizations promote Greek culture, provide opportunities for immigrants to meet with and help one another, and raise funds for the home region in Greece.

## MARITAL SUBSYSTEM

The present day roles of the husband and wife in Greek marriages are very traditional and have sociohistorical roots dating back to ancient times (Lacey, 1984). Greek marriages today remain traditional even as immigrants acculturate. Some Greek marriages today follow a pattern that is remarkably similar to that of the first wave of Greek immigrants. The men immigrate to the United States first. When they feel sufficiently secure in their jobs or businesses, they attend to the needs of the extended family by sending money back to their village in Greece and then marry (Salutos, 1964).

It should be noted that there is no Greek word for dating. In fact, there are very few culturally sanctioned courting rituals in Greek culture. There is, thus, little opportunity for prospective husbands and wives to develop open and direct communication. When one asks an American couple if they love each other, it is usually understood that one is asking about a set of behaviors that include being intimate, sharing feelings openly, and doing things together. If a Greek couple is asked the same question, it is usually interpreted that one is asking about another set of behaviors that includes whether the husband is a good provider and whether the wife is faithful and obedient to him and to her children (Vassiliou & Vassiliou, 1973; Zinovieff, 1991).

The traditional Greek cultural expectation is that a wife is not to make many demands of her husband and is to give love without expecting reciprocity. It is also expected that interpersonal conflicts will be resolved without discussion, usually through the wife's submission to the husband's wishes. For generations, Greek men in America have sought prospective brides through relatives or close friends, who either arrange a marriage (*proxenia*) or send for brides from Greece. In marriages like the latter, the couple engages in little or no courtship, and the husbands are often much older than their wives. Young women often live with their husbands' families for the first few years after immigrating and marrying. Left without the support of their own families, it is common for such immigrant brides to feel lonely and isolated.

In traditional marriages, the roles of the husband and wife are very rigidly defined. Any departure from expected social norms—for example a public display of superiority by the wife—puts her at risk for severe reproach, including physical abuse (Koos et al., 1994). Even though women (wives, daughters, or sisters) are not supposed to compete with, correct, or grow impatient with men (husbands, sons, or brothers), men may scold, quarrel with, or reprimand women (Vassiliou, 1970). It is thus very difficult to intervene in cases of spouse abuse in highly enmeshed first-generation families because the woman reporting the abuse may be accused of betraying her family.

## THE SUBSYSTEM OF CHILDREN

The traditional Greek mother is entrusted with the care of the children and the maintenance of the Greek language, customs, and values in the family. The father typically remains aloof and emotionally volatile, taking responsibility for the family's economic stability. In social situations, where action often symbolizes life, the mother and children defer to the head of the house (the father or oldest son). Yet in the home, where family issues are decided, the father and the children look to the mother for guidance. Children are expected to be respectful and obedient to their elders regardless of the content of the communication, simply because "*I* (the adult) said so." Children are trained to pay attention to the *person* who is communicating a message rather than to the *content* of the message. This focus on the hierarchical organization of social relationships can have a negative impact on a child's abilities to cope effectively in American mainstream culture, where attention must be paid to the content of a communication (Rotheram-Borus & Tsemberis, 1989).

Children who emigrate with their Greek parents face a host of challenges. Because they master American customs and the English language more rapidly than their parents, they are placed in excessively responsible roles, serving as cultural liaisons and language translators for their parents. For these same reasons, children are placed in awkward positions of power and may routinely witness signs of parental helplessness, which can be very frightening for them. These role reversals can damage the fragile structure of a family in transition, leaving parents feeling helpless and children very anxious (Alvarez, 1995).

Greeks also have a hierarchical orientation toward the values of achievement and work (Scourby, 1984). Achievement motivation is high in all "new" immigrants. For Greeks, this motivation is composed of a complex socio-psychological set of attributions about fate and God, as well as beliefs regarding the efficacy of work, family structure, community norms, and fables (Marinou-Mohring, 1986). Hines (1973) reported that mothers of boys high in achievement showed great warmth and had high levels of aspiration for their sons. The Greek mother is very nurturing and extremely ambitious for her son. Is it surprising that Greek sons develop high achievement motivation? In Greek families, as with *Oedipus*, the son is not expected to succeed his father, but to exceed him. This complex relationship is related to the power differences between husbands and wives in patriarchial families. The strong alliance between a mother and her male child may be construed as an effort to develop an alliance that will offset her disadvantaged position with her husband and possibly improve her situation when her son is older and has more power (Firestone, 1972; Tsemberis, 1991).

The daughters, neglected in these family dances and left alone, generally perform better in school. As the girls continue to perform well and achieve academically, the traditional family may insist that the daughter marry rather than pursue a career. Tensions may develop between daughters and fathers— daughters who are acculturating and embracing the independence offered by American culture, and fathers who retain their belief that daughters must be protected.

In the school setting, education and achievement are strongly emphasized (Orfanos & Tsemberis, 1987). Children are expected to learn and do well in school, while parents often work long hours and are unavailable and unable to offer their children the assistance they may need. If teachers inform parents of their children's academic or behavioral difficulties, then parents often react with reprisals toward the children. The parents are likely to attribute their children's school problems to laziness or lack of effort and to pressure the children to work harder. In such a family context, children learn to keep problems they are experiencing at school to themselves.

Children who attend Greek parochial schools encounter additional challenges. These children yearn to be accepted by teachers and peers in the American school as well as in their Greek parochial school. Displaying social skills that are considered "cool" or that demonstrate social competence and improve a child's popularity with their American peers may be regarded as disrespectful or serve to isolate them from their Greek friends or family. The pressure of excelling in these mutually exclusive cultural norms may be a source of confusion and distress for Greek youngsters (Rotheram-Borus & Tsemberis, 1989).

Parents, especially fathers, may be quickly angered by their children's abandonment of Greek traditions. Similarly, children may be increasingly embarrassed by their ethnic parents. Attachments to family members and family customs are neglected by the second generation, and such neglect compels threatened parents to increase their efforts to revive traditions. This intergenerational struggle leads both parents and children to feel frustrated, angry, confused, and ultimately, to experience a sadness for an unspoken loss.

Children and their parents often lack the support to cope with these adjustments. The parents misinterpret their children's striving for independence and assimilation as insolence, and the children are then at risk for disciplinary action, which often includes physical punishment.

Individualism within the family is absent in Greek life. Indeed, *there is no Greek word for privacy*. Children learn to keep secrets if they want privacy. There are few boundaries between children and parents or extended family members; thus, if a family member is disturbed, children are at risk for boundary violations such as physical or sexual abuse. The threat of abuse is also exacerbated because immigrant families are often isolated.

Similarly, because of the high level of cohesiveness in Greek families, issues related to separation–individuation, described in American culture as a normal adolescent and young adult developmental stage, evoke profound feelings of guilt, fear, or shame among young Greeks. Consequently, the quest for autonomy or individuality is fraught with difficulty in Greek families.

## FAMILIES WHO SEEK THERAPY

Family therapy can be well suited for Greek Americans because their primary social unit is the family and, thus, they have an intuitive understanding of systems and the fact that every family member plays a significant role. However, participation in any type of psychotherapy is considered stigmatizing for first-generation Greeks, and they must be either persuaded or mandated to seek counseling.

In the context of the consulting room, it is difficult for the therapist to bring into family members' awareness any dysfunctional patterns that they may observe. Fortunately, family therapy has the advantage of allowing the therapist to develop interventions to heal painful or dysfunctional patterns without requiring insight from clients.

The clinical observations summarized here are drawn from S. J. T.' s experiences working as a family therapist in a counseling center in Astoria, New York, from 1981–1991. Astoria, a working-class community, attracted large numbers of Greek immigrants in the 1960s. By the mid-1980s, there was a population of approximately 150,000 Greek immigrants living in Astoria. It is a lively immigrant enclave with plazas, *kafenia* (coffee houses), restaurants, churches, *topika somatia*, and sports clubs (Drucker, 1993). Today it remains one of the largest Greek communities outside of Greece.

It was almost always the mother who initially contacted the counseling center to request services. During the brief intake process, it was usually evident that she understood the complexity of the presenting problem within the family system. For example, she saw that her child's maladaptive behavior in school was actually a symptom of her marital conflict.

The majority (68%) of clients were nuclear families that sought services for a child with school-related behavior problems, or with a learning disability. In most cases, the family participated in therapy as a direct result of a guidance counselor's insistence. There were several court-mandated cases, usually involving allegations or findings of child physical abuse, and a small number of cases involving child sexual abuse.

The families that were mandated to participate in therapy as a result of allegations of physical abuse were among the most difficult to treat. Parents would express outrage that they were required to attend counseling sessions for the manner in which they reared their children. A "smack once in a while" was behavior that they condoned and believed to be consistent with effective child-rearing practices. The therapist had to make it clear to the family that although the father might regard discipline as a private matter, in the United States there are rules and consequences for using particular forms of punishment. In this way, the therapist could allow for other forms of discipline to be explored and discussed.

It is important to discuss with such parents the feelings of outrage and humiliation that they experienced during the court hearings. Even though there were significant language barriers, the Astoria parents understood very well that they were being treated as inadequate caretakers. The courtroom was often the scene of terrible cross-cultural misunderstanding. The parents' (mostly fathers') impassioned rebuttals and denial of the importance of the allegations served to fuel suspicions of legal guardians and judges that these Greek parents might indeed be dangerous.

A common initial impression in therapy is that men are not as competent as women in negotiating the therapeutic milieu. The therapist working with Greek parents must move gingerly in validating the mother's assessment to avoid alienating the father and must subtly maneuver to protect the father's self esteem even while challenging his behavior, so he does not feel exposed and abandon therapy. Marital disagreements concerning child-rearing practices are often symptomatic of other problems, but it is wise for the therapist to remain focused on the child-related problem until a therapeutic alliance is established.

Typically, there is little communication between a Greek husband and wife, and the father is somewhat distant from his children. In his view, the long hours he works are for the benefit of his family, and this contribution entitles him to a great deal of respect as a reliable, competent provider. He may be perplexed to discover that the less he sees his family, the less they appreciate him. He may begin to feel increasingly estranged. The mother might protect him from hearing their children's disappointments, their embarrassment about his ethnic ways, and from his more conservative, less acculturated customs. It is important for the therapist to indicate to the father that he or she empathizes with his feeling misunderstood and isolated before he or she challenges him to change the manner in which he communicates with other family members.

Greek women generally acculturate more rapidly than men to the more democratic American culture, and assimilation serves women better than remaining close to traditional Greek cultural morays. Among lower-middle-class women, the internalization of American core values (e.g., equality and independence) has been associated with psychological health, whereas the adoption of these American values among men of the same socioeconomic status is experienced as a loss of power and can result in psychological distress (Papajohn & Spiegel, 1971).

Children acculturate more quickly than their parents. This is unsettling for power relations in traditional Greek families where the parents believe they are to be in charge. To deal with this shift in power relations, Greek parents with authoritarian values may use a number of culturally sanctioned child-rearing methods. Some parents use deception and sarcasm to ensure that children are prepared for a treacherous world. Using such phrases as "Shame on you" (*dropi*) and "What will people say?" (*ti tha ley o cosmos*) emphasize the importance of a person's standing in the community and introduces the child to the importance of *philotimo*. As these phrases become instruments of socialization, the children may be shamed into changing unacceptable behaviors (e.g., little girls are forbidden to directly express powerful emotions, such as anger). Another method is for parents to falsely ascribe control or power over their children to people in socially sanctioned roles (e.g., "Behave yourself or the doctor will get angry"). Parents may fabricate a social reality in which others are described as jealous or as potential threats. This precludes development of the ability to cooperate with others beyond the in-group (Triandis, 1972) or family circle.

One of the most frequently encountered family dynamics in counseling these families concerns the issue of separation and family boundaries. This issue is especially problematic in families with adolescents. Greek immigrant parents expect their adolescents to keep early curfews, to refrain from dating, and to maintain close ties with the church. Yet, family boundaries need to become more flexible to accommodate the increasing demands for independence made by adolescents at this stage (Ackerman, 1980). This task is particularly difficult for Greek immigrant families because the adolescents are simultaneously acculturating and increasing their autonomy. Both parents and adolescents experience a great deal of discontinuity between the old and new family organization and old and new culture. The parents experience their children's changes as a potential loss of family life as they knew it and a rejection of their customs and values.

A majority of families begin therapy with somatic complaints as the presenting problem. Traditional families may attribute emotional and psychological problems to "nerves" or mask them as physical problems such as headaches, dizziness, stomach aches, and so on (Samouilidis, 1978). Psychological interpretations of physical complaints by the therapist are unwelcome in the early stages of counseling, especially if the therapist is not Greek American. The family's initial stance with the therapist is one of mistrust and a mixture of insecurity and rebelliousness toward his or her authority (Samouilidis, 1978).

## SINGLE PARENTS AND GAY AND LESBIAN FAMILIES

The second largest group of Greek families seeking services at the Astoria counseling center (23%) was single working mothers and their young children. For the most part, the estranged husbands and fathers provided little or no financial, let alone emotional, support to these families. The women lived either alone with their children or in their mothers' homes. Their mothers were mostly supportive yet highly critical. They wanted their daughters to remarry yet they discouraged dating. The stigma of divorce was still very strong in the Greek American community and the prospects for remarrying in this group were discouraging.

Single mothers also experience the conflicts arising from the clash between American and Greek cultures. In traditional Greek culture, fulfillment comes by serving others—family, in particular—whereas in American culture, fulfillment comes from getting a good education, building a career, and serving one's own needs. These opposing value systems can create a psychological split that leaves women feeling ashamed and guilty for not fulfilling their mothers' expectations, or angry and frustrated for abandoning their own pursuits. One of the most helpful interventions for these women was the formation of a women's mutual support group that met at the counseling center.

Gay and lesbian couples or families did not seek services at the counseling center. Because alternative lifestyles are usually stigmatized in the Greek community, members of these and other minority groups tend to seek services outside the community.

## THE ROLE OF THE THERAPIST

The first task of the therapist is to ensure that each member of the family feels understood. During the first session, the therapist should display culturally sensitive behaviors that reassure the family that they are not sitting with a complete outsider *(xenos)* (Stagoll, 1981). The therapist should be respectful of the lineal relationship values and the traditional hierarchical family organization (Primpas-Welts, 1982). In the early stages of therapy, the therapist can be hierarchical and prescribe behavioral changes. At the same time, however, he or she must indicate to the rapidly acculturating children and adolescents that the issues they are facing are familiar and important. If the therapist is uncertain about Greek customs and culture, then he or she can begin the session by conducting an ethnographic interview in which the family members are treated as experts and the therapist seeks to be enlightened by them. Inquiries can begin with cultural customs and lead to questions regarding the family's patterns.

The therapist should remain sensitive to the English-language fluency of each member and select one person to translate when there are wide discrepancies in comprehension among members. In cases where the therapist speaks Greek, she or he should observe the power struggles surrounding which language will be spoken in the session or at what point family members switch from one language to another. Spatial arrangements and organization, such as where people sit during the session, and all others forms of nonverbal communication should be noted, because they also provide clues regarding alliances, boundaries, and conflicts. The technique of asking family members to change seats in order to physically define subsystem alliances is often useful for establishing distinctly defined boundaries among family members.

To reduce any stigma related to the presenting problem, the therapist can reframe psychological or psychiatric symptoms as being health-related or stress-related problems (Stagoll, 1981). It is useful to proceed with interventions or prescriptions to effect measurable or observable behavior changes. Small, consistent successes inspire trust in the therapist and a belief in the process of change. The therapist should emphasize that therapy is short term and might even suggest an exact number of sessions to be attended.

During initial sessions with these families, the therapist often encounters what Goldner (1985) has called the "clinical paradox." Goldner (1985) and Hare-Mustin (1978) observed that family therapists erroneously conceptualize the parental subsystem as equal, whereas in reality, men and women do not have equal power. This is especially true for Greek families, where the women are not expected to disagree with their men in public, especially in the presence of an outsider. The Greek mother thus often finds herself in a difficult situation. She is expected to be a medium through which the father speaks, but she often disagrees with him. For example, it may be clear to the mother and to the therapist that the child's raucous behavior in school is a response to the father's overly strict discipline and beatings. School becomes the only place where the child is free to act his or her age. Feeling helpless to change the father's behavior, the mother resorts to protecting the child as best she can. Her protection and tacit disagreement with her husband activates his anger and compounds his efforts to maintain control, and he becomes increasingly intolerant of the child's behavior.

Conducting a full assessment ultimately serves to join families. A full assessment includes drawing a genogram, evaluating the hierarchical and cohesion relation–power dimensions, determining the individual life stage of members and the family's life cycle, inquiring about each members' economic and educational status, and determining the family's level of acculturation. It is important to remember that family members who have lived in the United

States for the same period of time may be at different stages of acculturation or may have very different feelings about the process.

Because gender roles are rigidly defined in Greek culture, the gender of the therapist will be a powerful determinant in the interactions among the family members. Male and female therapists will be perceived as having different kinds of power. Generally, it is more likely that Greek parents will be impressed by a formal, conservative manner. If speaking Greek with the family, the therapist should use the plural form of "you."

The therapist must acknowledge the importance of the family's cultural continuity while introducing the positive aspects of acculturation. Unless this process is handled in a sensitive manner, the male members of the family may experience any request for change as a demand to relinquish power. They are more likely to cooperate if, in the session, they can understand that they stand to gain increased familial intimacy by relinquishing their stereotypical authoritarian roles. Women will look to the therapist for the support and validation that has long been missing in their relationships with their husbands and parents. Women may eventually feel safe enough to express themselves directly, without fear of reprimand or reprisal, even after the session is over. Unlike families of other cultures where a period of productive dialogue may have existed that has recently become dysfunctional, Greek husbands and wives usually have not developed such an intimate dialogue. The therapist's task is therefore to assist the family in developing new patterns of communicative behaviors.

The therapeutic process with first-generation Greek immigrant families can serve as a powerfully condensed, successful acculturation experience. In most cases, the therapist is more acculturated than the parents and can provide them with valuable guidance. The children must be able to express their concerns, knowing that the therapist understands the demands of the Greek *and* American worlds. The women must feel supported and encouraged to develop their newly felt independence, whereas the men must feel that the therapist understands the value of maintaining some stability in the rapidly changing culture. In the security of such a therapeutic milieu, family members will feel free to express themselves and take the necessary steps to meet their needs in the new cultural context.

## REFERENCES

Ackerman, N. J. (1980). The family with adolescents. In E. A. Carter & M. McGoldrick (Eds.), *The family life cycle: A framework for family therapy* (pp. 147–170). New York: Gardner.

Alvarez, L. (1995, October 1). Interpreting new worlds for parents. *New York Times,* pp. B29, B36.

Clamar, A. (1987, August). *The changing Greek-American woman and the unchanging Greek Orthodox Church.* Paper presented at the Conference of Women, Haifa University, Haifa, Israel.

Dickson, P. (1991). The Greek pilgrims: Tsakonas and his Tsintzinians. In D. Georgakas & C. Moskos (Eds.), *New directions of Greek American studies* (pp. 35–54). New York: Pella.

Drucker, S. (1993, Spring). Immigration, media development and public space: The transformation of social life from Greece to a Greek community in New York. *Hofstra Horizons,* 12–16.

Dubisch, J. (1991). Gender, kinship, and religion: "Reconstructing" the anthropology of Greece. In P. Loizos & E. Papataxiarchis (Eds.), *Contested identities: Gender and kinship in modern Greece* (pp. 24–46). Princeton, NJ: Princeton University Press.

Firestone, S. (1972). *The dialectic of sex.* New York: Bantam Books.

Gavaki, E. (1991). Greek immigration to Quebec: The process and the settlement. *Journal of the Hellenic Diaspora,* 17(1), 69–89.

Georgakas, D. (1994, October). *The disappeared Greeks of the first generation.* Paper presented at City University of New York Seminar on the Modern Greek State, City University of New York.

Goldner, V. (1985). Feminism and family therapy. *Family Process, 24,* 31–48.

Hare-Mustin, R. R. T. (1978). A feminist approach to family therapy. *Family Process, 17,* 181–194.

Hines, G. H. (1973). The persistence of Greek achievement motivation across time and culture. *International Journal of Psychology, 8,* 285–288.

Koos, M. P., Goodman, L. A., Browne, A., Fitzgerald, L. F., Keita, G., & Russo, N. (1994). *No safe haven: Male violence against women at home, at work, and in the community.* Washington, DC: American Psychological Association.

Lacey, W. K. (1984). *The family in classical Greece.* Ithaca, NY: Cornell University Press.

Marinou-Mohring, P. (1986, September). *Life, my daughter, is not the way you have it in your books: Why Greek immigrants did well in the United States.* Paper presented at the meeting of the Greek American Behavioral Sciences Institute, New York.

Moskos, C. C. (1989). *Greek Americans: Struggle and success* (2nd ed.). Englewood Cliffs, NJ: Prentice Hall.

Orfanos, S. D., & Tsemberis, S. (1987). A needs assessment of Greek American schools. In S. D. Orfanos, H. J. Psomiades, & J. Spiridakis (Eds.), *Education and Greek Americans: Process and prospects* (pp. 185–203). New York: Pella.

Papajohn, J., & Spiegel, J. (1971). The relationship of culture value orientation change and Rorschach indicies of psychological development. *Journal of Cross-Cultural Psychology,* 2(3), 257–272.

Primpas-Welts, E. (1982). Greek families. In M. McGoldrick, J. K. Pearce, & J. Giordano (Eds.), *Ethnicity and family therapy* (1st ed., pp. 269–288). New York: Guilford Press.

Rotheram-Borus, M. J., & Tsemberis, S. (1989). Social competency training programs in ethnically diverse communities. In L. A. Bond & B. E. Compass (Eds.), *Primary prevention and promotion in the schools* (pp. 297–318). Newbury Park, CA: Sage.

Salutos, T. (1964). *The Greeks in the United States.* Cambridge, MA: Harvard University Press.

Samouilidis, L. (1978). Vicissitudes in working with Greek patients. *American Journal of Psychoanalysis, 38,* 223–233.

Sant Cassia, P., & Bada, C. (1992). *The making of the modern Greek family.* Cambridge, England: Cambridge University Press.

Scourby, A. (1984). *The Greek Americans.* Boston: Twayne.

Stagoll, B. (1981). Therapy with Greek families living in Australia. *International Journal of Family Therapy, 3,* 167–179.

Triandis, H. (1972). *The analysis of subjective culture.* New York: Wiley.

Tsemberis, S. (1991, August). *Mediterranean men: Myths and machismo.* Paper presented at the annual meeting of the American Psychological Association, San Francisco, CA.

Vassiliou, G. (1970). Milieu specificity in family therapy. In N. W. Ackerman, J. Lieb, & J. Pearce (Eds.), *Family therapy in transition* (pp. 81–88). Boston: Little, Brown.

Vassiliou, G., & Vassiliou, V. (1973). The implicative meaning of the Greek concept of *philotimo. Journal of Cross-Cultural Psychology, 4,* 326–341.

Zinovieff, G. (1970). Hunters and hunted: *Kamaki* and the ambiguities of sexual predation in a Greek town. In P. Loizos & E. Papataxiarchis (Eds.), *Contested identities: Gender and kinship in modern Greece* (pp. 203–220). Princeton, NJ: Princeton University Press.

CHAPTER 36

# Hungarian Families

## Debra Smith

*If the earth is the hat of God, Hungary is the flower on it.*
—Hungarian Children's Song (cited in Lengyel, 1965)

This chapter will provide an introduction to the rich tapestry that represents the Hungarian people and a beginning context for therapists working with Hungarian clients. The tapestry is richly woven, with contrasts that range from despair to elation, from darkness to light, from Eastern to Western values, from romantic gypsies to rational scientists, from ecstasy to mournfulness. Throughout the tapestry run the threads of individualism, spirit, and the will to survive that has sustained this solitary and indomitable culture for over 11 centuries, despite a history of continuous misfortune and oppression.

## HISTORICAL SETTING

The Hungarians are descendants of the Magyars of Central Asia, who are renowned from time immemorial as great horsemen and ferocious warriors. A negative perception of the Magyars represents them as raping, plundering, and murdering horsemen, reputedly distant cousins of Attila the Hun. They appeared in the heart of Europe and terrorized the "civilized" West en route to their chosen homeland in the Carpathian Basin. So formidable were the Magyar warriors, according to this perception, that their arrival signaled to many that the end of the world was at hand (Sisa, 1990).

Their own folktales represent the Magyars as a peaceful, nomadic people who were trying to avoid the more warlike tribes that pushed westward in the great migrations of the late eighth and ninth centuries (Volgyes, 1982). Although some historians depict the Magyars as a people of European origin, the best-known theory of the Magyar's origin is the Finno-Ugrian (Turcik) theory, which places their homeland on both sides of the southern Urals, a low mountain range that separates Europe from Asia (Sisa, 1990). Like their neighbors, the Magyars have a history of ethnic intermingling; however, if they could be linked to any other Asiatic race, it would be the Mongols (Volgyes, 1982).

The facts of their origins may be lost in time, but the stirring folktale of their beginnings, related in Kate Seredy's book *The White Stag* (1939), illustrates the strong tendency toward romance and drama that is a consistent Hungarian character trait: One morning, as the story goes, a white stag appeared in front of Magyar hunters and they began to follow it. The white stag led them westward to a fertile countryside across the Carpathian Mountains, which later became known as Hungary (Volgyes, 1982).

The first of many invasions suffered by the Hungarian empire took place in 1241. This invasion, by the Mongols, so depleted Hungary that immigration into Hungary, mostly by Germans, became necessary in order to rebuild the country. Over the ensuing 200 years, however, Hungary emerged as a significant power in Central and Eastern Europe. In fact, during the reign of King Matthias (1457–1490), the royal court of Buda soon emerged as the most important center of East Central Europe during the Renaissance (Vardy, 1985).

Subsequent invasion by the Ottoman Turks after the death of King Matthias, led to a period of rule that lasted for over 150 years, until the invasion by the Austrian Hapsburgs. The Hapsburg rule, following the Hungarian Revolution of 1848, signaled the end of feudalism and the transformation of the Hungarian Empire into the dualistic state of Austria-Hungary in 1867. Although Hungarian nationalism was once again repressed, Hungarian Jews enjoyed a greater degree of religious freedom during this period.

Hungary's alliance with the losing Central Powers in World War I, along with the terms of the Treaty of Trianon, had drastic effects. As a result of the Treaty of Trianon, Hungary lost three-fourths of its territory and two-thirds of its population (Sisa, 1990). Additionally, Hungary's early experience with Communism after World War I, and again during and after World War II, are noteworthy in that Communism influenced almost all aspects of Hungarian life until very recently, when Hungary moved away from authoritarianism and more toward a mixture of capitalist and communist economic policies known as "goulash communism" (Vardy, 1990). In 1990, Hungary became the first East-Central European country to receive full membership in the Council of Europe, the main consultative association of European democracies (Karoly Nagy, personal communication, August 1994).

Hungary's fertile land and her location at the crossroads of Europe have historically cast her in the role of protector of the Christian world from Asian invaders. As such, Hungary has constantly struggled with outside forces that were either invading, occupying, or oppressing her. This constant struggle for survival has contributed to the traits of individualism, resiliency, resourcefulness, adaptability, and a love of freedom, while at the same time contributing to an ever-present fear of extermination (Sisa, 1990).

The strong will of the Hungarian people to survive is apparent throughout history. It is well expressed in Seredy's book *The Singing Tree* (1939), when she likens the Hungarians to whispering trees:

> Whispering trees . . . they have weathered many storms. Some of them are broken and almost dead, but new shoots are springing up from their roots every year. Those roots grow deep in the soil, deeper than the trees are tall. No one could kill them without destroying the very soil they grow in; what they stand for lives in the hearts of all Hungarians. Nothing could kill that without destroying the country. (p. 39)

## IMMIGRATION

Hungarian immigration to the United States can be divided into four major waves, the first of which followed the Revolution of 1848. Approximately 4,000 of these well-educated political refugees journeyed to North America. Although few of these well-educated "forty-niners" planned to settle here, most of them did (Vardy, 1985).

The 50 years between the end of America's Civil War and World War I was the period of the greatest mass migration in world history. Approximately 1.7 million Hungarian citizens emigrated to the United States, settling primarily in the Northeast, and another 8,000 Hungarians went to Canada. A different type of immigrant, the economic immigrant, constituted this second wave (Vardy, 1990).

Unlike the political refugees of the previous wave, these turn-of-the-century immigrants were peasants and unskilled industrial workers descended from peasant families, so called "birds of passage," because they planned to make their fortunes in America and then return to the *O Kontri* (Hungary) and create a better and more satisfying life for themselves and their families. Like the first wave of Hungarian immigrants, they too remained (Varga, 1988; Vardy, 1990).

The decision of the United States to close its doors to mass immigration during and after World War I resulted in a major decrease of Hungarian immigration. Still, some Hungarians did enter the United States illegally through Canada and Mexico (Vardy, 1990). The majority of these immigrants, motivated to leave their homeland for political and economic reasons resulting from World War I, came from the ranks of the skilled workers and technical intelligentsia. Although they were still outnumbered by the peasants by a rate of three or four to one, by the 1930s their ranks were swelled by some of the country's most highly educated intellectuals, who fled for political reasons and due to the rise in anti-Semitism (Vardy, 1990).

Post-World War II conditions in Hungary led to a resurgence of Hungarian immigration to North America. This fourth wave of immigrants came from all levels of Hungarian society and included former inmates of German concentration camps, and later, a large number of refugees of the Hungarian Revolution of 1956 (Vardy, 1990). Since the 1960s, there have only been a very small number of political and economic immigrants entering North America from Hungary.

## SOCIAL STRUCTURE: FRATERNAL ORGANIZATIONS

Fraternal organizations (called fraternals) played a key role in the socialization and assimilation process of the Hungarian immigrant at the turn of the century. In fact, the fraternals, along with churches, were known as the "twin pillars of Magyar America" (Vardy, 1985).

The fraternals initially appeared in the late 1890s. Their function was primarily to take care of the injured immigrant workers or to assume burial responsibilities for those who died in the many industrial accidents (Vardy, 1990). Later, the fraternals expanded their domain to include the dual functions of social clubs as well as insurance companies. The fraternals had no equivalent in Hungary, where the extended family and the communities of each village cared for their own elderly, sick, or destitute (Vardy, 1985).

A typical fraternal could consist of 25–30 newly arrived male immigrants who lived together in a *burdos* house (boarding house). A sense of belonging, friendship, community, and personal connection were all benefits of belonging to a fraternal organization. In fact, in the small scattered settlements, those organizations provided the only form of group activity (Vardy, 1985).

Prior to World War I, hundreds of fraternals were organized. Their leaders, along with the clergy, became part of the Hungarian "ethnic elite" and served as the bridge between the immigrant communities and the mainstream American society (Vardy, 1985).

For the first time in their long history, Hungarian peasants seized the opportunity to organize and run their own associations and to prove to themselves and to others that they were able to handle complex social undertakings. In fact, the evolution of the fraternal organizations mirrors well the process of adaptation of the Hungarian immigrants to American life (Vardy, 1985).

However, transient membership, money problems, arguments among leaders, widespread abuse of sick benefits by the members, and class issues between the general membership and the educated immigrant-elite fraternal leaders finally led to the downfall of the fraternal organizations (Vardy, 1985).

## RELIGION

The most significant social and psychological support systems of the Hungarian Americans during the age of immigration, aside from the fraternals, were the immigrants' religious organizations. Although the religious life of the local

Hungarian village church was separate from the social life that centered on the village inn, in America the functions of church and inn were consolidated (Vardy, 1990). This union speeded up the modernization and assimilation process of the immigrants, although perhaps a bit at the expense of their religiosity (Vardy, 1985).

Clergymen played a significant role by representing the immigrants' interests in American society, while the church itself represented a portion of the *O Kontri* in an alien world. It served as a comfortable haven and gathering place, where the newcomers could carry on their own traditions and rituals in their native tongue and be with people who felt like them, spoke like them, and faced similar social and personal problems. Hungarian immigrants wanted to be attached to their church because it provided a link with their children, in that the Hungarian language spoken there served to keep them from becoming strangers in the parental home (Vardy, 1985).

The Hungarian American churches became instrumental in merging religiosity with patriotism and in perpetuating Hungarian patriotic feelings among the immigrants. As these churches became the centers of the social, cultural, and national life of the immigrants, so their clergy became their social, cultural, and national leaders and, as such, exerted a tremendous influence on the general course of Hungarian American life as well as Hungarian American family life (Vardy, 1990). This was particularly true for the Protestant churches, whose history was more intimately connected with Hungarian national traditions than that of the much more universalist Hungarian Catholic Church or that of the more assimilated Hungarian Jews (Vardy, 1985).

The "preemancipation" of the Hungarian Jews under the Hapsburg empire was a precursor to the full assimilation and absorption of native Hungarian Jewry. In 1869 the Jewish religion was declared an equal denomination, marking the beginning of the meteoric rise of Jewish talent in Hungary.

Scarcely 50 years later, following World War I, a dark shadow was cast on the relations between Jews and Gentiles in Hungary. In fact, the introduction of the *numerus clasus* (quota system) limited the admission of Jewish students to universities to 6%, then the exact ratio of Jews in Hungary's population. Although Hungarian Jewry suffered terrible losses during the Holocaust, Hungary has remained virtually the last bastion of Jewry in Central Europe.

Although Hungarian Jews were perhaps the earliest immigrants from Hungary (starting as early as the 1850s and 1860s), and although they have played a most significant part in Hungarian American cultural life, their synagogues and other religious organizations did not retain their Hungarian national characteristics for very long. This may have been due, in part, to several factors: the precedent set by their full emancipation (under the Hapsburgs) and subsequent rapid assimilation into Hungarian culture; as immigrants, their active involvement in American industry; and their eagerness to learn English for business purposes (Vardy, 1985).

While Hungarian American churches still serve as important focal points for many of the social and cultural activities of those who live in or close to large Hungarian American communities, their future does not seem to be promising, as most of the Hungarian American communities are now in the process of dissolution. However, their impact on the lives of the immigrants and their descendants for nearly a century will always be remembered (Vardy, 1985).

## LANGUAGE

If fear of physical and cultural extermination is a recurrent neurosis of the Hungarians, a sense of isolation is a more or less permanent trait of the Hungarian people. The obstacles of the Hungarian language contribute in a major way to the solitude of the Hungarian spirit (Parsons, 1992).

The Hungarians exemplify a people who have gone through a gradual and partial ethnic transformation, but who have done so without losing their original language. The Hungarians' language, called Magyar, is basically identical with that of their forebears and is the only "alien tongue" in its geographic region (Lengyel, 1965).

Magyar is phonetic, precise, and musical and is particularly adapted to poetry and the expression of fine shades of meaning; however, the many seductive beauties of Hungarian literature, particularly lyric poetry (Hungary's special métier), are a closed book to the world at large—a private cultural affair of which translation is almost always a travesty (Parsons, 1992; Volgyes, 1982). Thus, the Hungarian writer is much more isolated than his Western colleague. There are periods when national destiny suppresses every personal note, historical moments when the unity of the Hungarian nation, the meaning of its existence, and the sense of its vocation, survive only in literature (Sisa, 1990). It is ironic, therefore, that the Hungarian language "is at one and the same time [our] softest cradle and [our] most solid coffin" (cited in Parsons, 1992, p. 37).

## INTERPERSONAL RELATIONSHIPS: THE SIB SYSTEM

In Hungarian the word "family" has two meanings. Although the primary meaning refers to the nuclear family, a second definition refers to the "sib," an informal network of aunts, uncles, cousins and godparents whose key function was mutual aid (Kosa, 1957). All sib members are called "relatives" whether or not they are blood relations. In fact, blood ties were often superceded by ties of intermarriage, godparentship, or personal affections (Kosa, 1957).

In spite of these loose blood relationships, the sib was strongly linked by an unwritten code of customs and mutual obligations regulating the whole range of family life, including the rituals of marriage, burial, and birthday celebrations. The essential element, however, was the moral obligation to help each other in every way: money, labor, and moral support (Kosa, 1957).

Ivan Boszormenyi-Nagy, a Hungarian American who was one of the originators of the family therapy movement in the United States, has developed several concepts related to multigenerational family functioning, namely the concepts of ledger and legacy. These will be illustrated in the case examples to follow at the conclusion of this chapter. The "ledger" refers to what has been given and what is owed to family members, while "legacy" is something that is passed down through generations in families. It is perhaps not surprising that Dr. Nagy came up with this framework for describing family members' ethical obligations and loyalties, given the supreme value Hungarians place on one family member's ethical responsibility to another. The "sib" epitomizes this "ledger," because it is organized by customary cooperation rather than any single leadership. Traditionally, opinions of a successful, wise, or older member carried special weight. But he or she had no authority over families other than his or her own. The customs, etiquette, and genealogy of the sib system made up a notable part of every child's education, thus effectively sustaining the family system for centuries (Kosa, 1957).

The sib system was the main protective system of the immigrants, with sibs often financing part or all of the cost of a relative's passage to North America. Although the first generation of immigrants typically maintained strong connections to the sib, this connection was much less intense by the second generation. In fact, people usually left the sib after the death of their parents, thus hastening the assimilative process (Kosa, 1957).

## THE FAMILY SYSTEM

Hungarian families have characteristic structural and behavioral patterns and roles. These family patterns vary according to several factors, including circumstances surrounding immigration, religious affiliation, socioeconomic status, educational level, degree of language and cultural maintenance, and the ethnic network in the community of residence.

Regardless of economic class or profession, most Hungarians have inherited or brought with them a powerful work ethic, the drive to succeed, and a belief in solid family life, with gender roles following traditional lines (Vardy, 1990). The traditional family in Hungarian culture was patriarchal and regulated by ancient customs, with each family member having a defined role (Kosa, 1957). The father's role continues to be that of the wise family leader. It is expected that he will act with care and dignity, and possess not only factual knowledge, but wisdom and common sense for the practical matters of daily life. Particularly in financial matters, the father is to have the final word. Wives, adult children, and sib members are often consulted for important decisions, a safety measure against the abuse of parental authority (Kosa, 1957). The high expectations put upon the Hungarian father can often cause frustration, which may get expressed in outbursts of temper. However, domestic abuse and child abuse are no more prevalent than in other ethnic groups, according to August Molnar (personal communication, October 1994), President of the American Hungarian Foundation in New Brunswick, New Jersey.

As sociologist Karoly Nagy has described it, the role of the wife and mother in Hungarian families has always been a strong one, with the realm of her influence extending beyond household decisions. Mothers are generally the major disciplinarians within the family, but the final word on important family decisions remains with the father (Karoly Nagy, personal communication, August 1994). This can cause conflict when there is dissension over the disciplining of the children.

It would seem that while Hungarian women are influential in the larger spheres such as the political, business, and community arenas, their influence within the home is more clearly confined to child-rearing decisions and domestic tasks. Even then, the ultimate veto power for domestic decisions still rests with the father. This may be particularly frustrating for contemporary Hungarian women (as well as women within other ethnic groups) who have been encouraged by their families to achieve educationally and to aspire to careers.

It is vital, then, for the therapist to support women around the roles where they have more freedom and more power, while simultaneously taking into account the traditional patriarchal family structure that is the reality of their daily lives. It is equally necessary for the therapist to help female clients acknowledge and come to terms with the losses engendered by challenging women's traditional role in the larger culture and within their own families.

Traditionally it has been the responsibility of parents and extended family members to "guide, educate and supervise the children and, in general, to prepare them for adult life" (Kosa, 1957). In contemporary Hungarian society, boys and girls are treated equally in terms of being encouraged to achieve and to aspire to careers. In fact, there is typically a great deal of pressure put upon children to get a good education and be "successful" (Karoly Nagy, personal communication, August 1994). In turn, the children's duty is to follow, respect, and revere the older generation, and not do anything to disgrace the family (Kosa, 1957).

Elders play a very important role in keeping the Hungarian family intact. Elders are to be respected, and there is a feeling of responsibility toward the older generation. Upholding tradition and keeping the family close is important. This is particularly so because of the ever-present fear of extermination that has been a part of Hungary's history. Maintaining the religion and culture are key protective devices for keeping children out of trouble (Karoly Nagy, personal communication, August 1994). It can be surmised that the long history of ethnic mixing in the Hungarian culture is at least in part responsible for the general attitude of tolerance toward ethnic/religious intermarriages. Individual Hungarian families may find intermarriage a cause of particular concern, however.

Achievement at school, the selection of an occupation, and particularly the marriage of the children have historically been the main concerns of the family. However, parental supervision is exerted and obedience rendered in a way that does not stifle the will of the child: "The family education has aimed not to suppress, but rather to unfold this emotional life, and every major event of family life has typically been accompanied by a free display of emotions, kisses and tears" (Kosa, 1957, p. 51).

Emotions tend to be freely expressed in Hungarian families, particularly affectionate emotions, which are even exhibited before strangers or in public places. Parental control is easily accepted by children because it is generally surrounded by an affectionate atmosphere and seems to produce children who are self-assured rather than submissive individuals (Kosa, 1957).

## CHARACTERISTICS OF THE HUNGARIAN NATIONAL HERITAGE

Emotionality, romanticism, pessimism, isolation, and a duality of identification between Eastern and Western values are common Hungarian characteristics. According to an old proverb, Hungarians are happiest when they are in tears. Hungarians want music at weddings and at funerals, and much of that music is mournful tunes (Lengyel, 1965). Hungarian culture has always appealed more to emotions than to logic (Volgyes, 1982). It is a culture of extremes, plunging into despair one moment, soaring to heights of happiness the next: "Oh, these Hungarians! If they have the slightest problem they think it's a national tragedy, and cry and are distraught! But if they have the slightest cause to celebrate, they don their holiday garments, throw big celebrations, and are ecstatically happy! (Volgyes, 1982, p. 82).

The heritage of the Hungarian as romantic and emotional has been perpetuated throughout the Western world. Because of this tendency to indulge in emotionality, Hungarians may not always use the most practical ways and means of achieving their purposes. They may find refuge in an irrational world of dreams and it has been said that dreaming "impossible dreams" is a typically Hungarian trait (Sisa, 1990). The Hungarian's preferred mode of activity, then, "tends to be irregular, similar to a passing ardor or to the sudden flare up of a 'szalmalang' (fire) which soon dies down" (Sisa, 1990, p. 363).

Although Hungarians are generally an emotional people, certain negative emotions are not always expressed openly. For example, it is considered "shameful" to express conflicts, anger, or pain out in the open, possibly out of a sense of needing to preserve family loyalty. In contrast to negative emotions, Hungarians tend to be more free in their expression of affection, even in public places (Kosa, 1957).

Holding grudges is a time-honored tradition among Hungarians and stems in part from the village culture that is so ingrained in their heritage. While an outright vendetta is not a part of this culture, turning the other cheek, albeit begrudgingly, is very much so (Karoly Nagy, personal communication, August 1994).

The Hungarian's sense of inner despair and pessimism is often reflected in violent outbursts of temper as well as in Hungary's high suicide rate, the highest in the world, with an annual incidence of 45 per 100,000 (Carson & Butcher, 1991). One could surmise from Emile Durkheim's (1951) seminal work on suicide that the constant breakdown of social norms in Hungarian culture would contribute to this rate.

The author Arthur Koestler, one of the best known Hungarians outside his country of origin, remarked: "To be Hungarian is a collective neurosis" (cited in Parsons, 1992, p. 37). Indeed, Hungarians are a people with their roots in the East who have allied themselves with Western Christian culture (Sisa, 1990). In fact, Bela Bartok, Hungary's leading contemporary composer has said, "We want to realize a synthesis of East and West. Our origins and geographic location have predestined us to such a role, for Hungary is at the same time the westernmost point of the East and a bastion of the West" (cited in Sisa, 1990, p. 363).

Her location at the crossroads of religions, cultures, and powers has always placed Hungary in a position to be the defender of the West. Looking back through history, although Hungary's struggles have been praised in the West, she has seldom been aided in her proverbial role as the "Bastion of Christiandom and a vanguard of liberty" (Sisa, 1990). In fact, Hungary's feelings of abandonment by the West have been keenly felt throughout history and is a popular literary theme of Hungarian writers. Hungary's greatest poet, Sandor Petofi, has also lamented about the isolation of her people, calling them "the most orphaned nation in the world in his poem "Life or Death" (Sisa, 1990).

## CASE EXAMPLES

The following cases highlight some of the more prominent cultural traits of the Hungarian people, namely, emotionalism, romanticism, high parental expectations, and authoritarian methods of discipline. Therapeutic interventions that have proven effective with Hungarian families are detailed within the context of each case.

*An Acting Out Child*

Stephen and Theresa Szell, both in their 20s, were referred to me for treatment by their pediatrician. They were unable to successfully discipline 4-year-old David, who had violent tantrums in response to any limit setting imposed by his parents. Recently, when sent to his room for hitting his 2-year-old sister, David broke the window and was cut by some of the glass fragments. Although openly defiant to both his parents, David's preschool teacher reported that he was a model student.

Mr. Szell, with much questioning, reluctantly expressed his high expectations for his son's behavior, reflecting the cultural norms of his Hungarian background. When questioned about his own parents' methods of discipline, he recounted his father's history of physical discipline accompanied by emotional outbursts, what Boszormenyi-Nagy would call a "legacy," a concept referring to specific expectations that are rooted in the family and affect the offspring for generations to come (Boszormenyi-Nagy & Ulrich, 1981). For example, Stephen explained that his own father had been effective in getting him "into shape" by means of physical punishment and emotional harangues. He assured me that he would never even have thought about talking back to his father. Tantrums, even in the very young, were not tolerated. He felt that physical punishment, such as smacking, was the most effective means of discipline and could not imagine why it was so ineffective with David.

Theresa, on the contrary, felt very strongly about not disciplining her children by physical means. However, she was hesitant to confront her husband directly about her displeasure with his authoritarian philosophy and methods of discipline. On the few occasions that she attended sessions alone, she was able to voice her concerns. She would then return home and tell her husband what the "doctor" had suggested. Relying on the Hungarians' traditional deference to authority figures, Mrs. Szell hoped the doctor's words would help to effect a change in her husband's behavior. The therapist, on the other hand, worked hard in sessions with her to empower her to voice her own concerns and to make her own suggestions to her husband for disciplining David. Her suggestions were supported by the therapist during joint sessions.

The therapist was able to join with Mrs. Szell as the mother of a 5-year-old herself and with Mr. Szell as a "fellow Hungarian" who well knew the methods of discipline and the climate of emotionalism so common in Hungarian families. The therapist was then able to challenge some of the long-established beliefs held by each of them regarding the parent–child relationship and to educate them about discipline techniques that were more age-appropriate.

A non-Hungarian therapist, however, cannot rely on camaraderie or informality in engaging a Hungarian family. In fact, any attempt at becoming part of the Hungarian family system will be rebuffed. The only recourse, then, is formality, in keeping with the respect that most Hungarians accord authority figures.

A substantial part of the treatment centered around exploring, particularly with Mr. Szell, the romanticized notion of the kind father who in his wisdom guides his son to maturity. This relationship is juxtaposed against the realities of parenting a 4-year-old who is strong willed and exerting his independence in all arenas of life. Through the coaching process, Mr. Szell began to reinforce David's positive behaviors, no matter how small, and to develop a better rapport with both his children.

―――――――――― ◆ ――――――――――

## An Angry Husband

Ivan and Martha were referred for treatment by Martha's internist. She had begun to experience anxiety attacks over the past 6 months and found them to be more frequent as time went on.

Ivan, a 40-year-old engineer, and Martha, a 37-year-old teacher, had been married for 15 years and had two children, ages 10 and 8. Martha's anxiety attacks were affecting the couple's relationship to the degree that Ivan was considering leaving.

Ivan and Martha reported a history of marital conflict, with Ivan openly sharing the fact that he had always had a "bad temper" and that Martha and the children were frightened of his unpredictable outbursts. Martha observed that when Ivan was drinking, he was less able to curb his volatile temper. (Ivan's drinking was atypical of Hungarian society, in which, generally, alcohol is used more as a food than to get drunk or reduce tension.) Although Ivan felt powerless to stop his own outbursts of temper, he felt strongly that Martha, with concentrated effort, could stop her anxiety attacks if she would only try harder.

Ivan related that his parents, although still married, had a history of conflict in their relationship, with his father exhibiting a volatile temper toward his wife and all of the children while they were growing up. Boszormenyi-Nagy's theory of multigenerational family functioning was illustrated by Ivan, whose father's unapproachability left him with no way of dealing with his father's "ledger," to which his whole life had been subordinated (Boszormenyi-Nagy & Ulrich, 1981). The fact that Ivan had been unable to connect with his father caused him emotional pain and motivated him to have a different, closer relationship with his own children.

Work with Ivan initially revolved around getting him to acknowledge his fear of his temper and what it felt like to be so out of control. He reluctantly agreed to accept a referral to a local men's group whose focus was on examining imbalance of power in relationships and learning to express anger in ways that are not abusive. Positive changes have occurred in Ivan's relationships with his wife and children as a result of his participation in the group.

As Martha explored in sessions the events surrounding the onset of her anxiety attacks, she began to see the relationship between the evolution of her symptoms and the escalation of Ivan's abusive behavior toward her and the children. For Martha, who came from a very close-knit family, so typical in Hungarian culture, being together and sharing activities as a family were of paramount importance. Additionally, the loving relationship between Martha's parents was not mirrored in her own marriage, nor did she even have the freedom to express her feelings of disappointment and anger in the face of her husband's violent and unpredictable temper. Although Martha's symptoms did keep Ivan close by, he was angry about being there, so she won a pyrrhic victory.

Martha was unable at first to openly express her disappointment at the lack of romance in her relationship with Ivan, because her family of origin, although close knit, found negative emotions difficult to express to strangers. She also felt that expressing her anger at Ivan for his outbursts toward her and their children might cause him to use physical force, or, even more important to her, might initiate a marital separation. Because family closeness was of paramount importance to Martha, she repressed her anger, finding ultimately that anxiety attacks ensued. With growing trust in the therapist and great courage, she faced these important issues and explored her complicated feelings regarding abandonment, should she get better and be less dependent. As Ivan was able to acknowledge his sadness about his relationship with his father not meeting his needs, as a child or as an adult, and worked on his issues in his men's group, he was able to move toward a more positive and less authoritarian role with Martha and his children. As Ivan's behavior changed, Martha's symptoms slowly abated, although they do flare up on the occasions when there is tension within the family.

---------- ◆ ----------

## CONCLUSION

Over the past 11 centuries, the Hungarian people have survived repeated invasions, threats to their national identity, and forced assimilation. Despite how the winds of history have blown, the fire of the Hungarian spirit continues to burn steadily, a glowing tribute to their eternal will to survive. The words of the Hungarian poet Sandor Remenyik (1990) sum up perfectly the indomitable spirit of his people:

> Here in time's depths lurk many forms of death,
> And much may come to pass; but none so clever
> Lives under Heaven as can build a coffin
> To bury us forever!
> On poet-lips, the tree of Magyar speech
> Shall sprout anew in buds and branches vernal;
> Indomitable force in floods shall sing:
> Our spirit lives eternal. (quoted in Sisa, p. 363)

### DEDICATION AND ACKNOWLEDGMENTS

This chapter is dedicated to the memory of my Hungarian American father, Henry Weinberger. Special thanks to Dr. Barbara Wright, my friend and mentor, for all her help.

# REFERENCES

Boszormenyi-Nagy, I., & Ulrich, D. (1981). Contextual family therapy. In A. Gurman & D. Kniskern (Eds.), *Handbook of family therapy* (pp. 159–186). New York: Brunner/Mazel.

Carson, R., & Butcher, J. (1991). *Abnormal psychology and modern life* (9th ed.). New York: HarperCollins.

Durkheim, E. (1951). *Suicide: A study in sociology.* New York: The Free Press.

Kosa, J. (1957). *The land of choice: The Hungarians in Canada.* Toronto, Canada: University of Toronto Press.

Lengyel, E. (1965). *The land and people of Hungary.* New York: Lippincott.

Parsons, N. (1992). *Hippocrene's insider's guide to Hungary.* New York: Hippocrene Books.

Seredy, K. (1937). *The white stag.* New York: Penguin Books.

Seredy, K. (1939). *The singing tree.* New York: Penguin Books.

Sisa, S. (1990). *The spirit of Hungary: A panorama of Hungarian history and culture.* Toronto, Canada: Rakoczi Foundation.

Vardy, S. (1985). *The Hungarian Americans.* Boston: Twayne.

Vardy, S. (1990). *The Hungarian Americans: The Hungarian experience in North America.* New York: Chelsea House.

Varga, Y. (1988). *Children of Ellis Island.* New Brunswick, NJ: I. H. Printing Co.

Volgyes, I. (1982). *Hungary: A nation of contradictions.* Boulder, CO: Westview Press.

# CHAPTER 37

# Irish Families

## Monica McGoldrick

*But I, being poor, have only my dreams;*
*I have spread my dreams under your feet;*
*Tread softly because you tread on my dreams.*
—W. B. YEATS

Yeats's poem expresses several key Irish themes: the history of oppression and poverty, the importance of the dream in Irish imagination, the importance of relationships, and the sense of interpersonal vulnerability. In this chapter I have tried to be sensitive to the Irish fear of being judged negatively, and at the same time I felt I had to move past our tendency to cover over negative issues by joking about or denying them. By no means do I wish to add to the negative stereotyping of the Irish, which has plagued us for centuries. Discussing Irish characteristics honestly may leave some Irish feeling exposed and vulnerable, but it will also, I hope, be reassuring by giving voice to experiences that have often not been validated.

The Irish diaspora since the mid-1800s has meant that although there are currently only about 5 million people living in Ireland itself, there are about 70 million people throughout the world with some Irish heritage (Robinson, 1994); of these more than half, or about 40 million, are in the United States (Watts, 1988; Miller & Wagner, 1995; Kennedy, 1983; Kearney, 1990).

Discussion here will focus on families that were traditionally Irish Catholic, who generally formed a group apart from the Protestant Irish in culture and values (Biddle, 1976). Indeed, a very large group of Irish Protestants also immigrated to the United States. For centuries the British controlled Ireland, turning Protestant against Catholic under a series of codes called the Penal Laws. Catholics could not attend school or serve in the military or civil service. By converting to Protestantism a man could disinherit all his brothers. A Protestant landowner lost all his civil rights by marrying a Catholic, and the rare Catholic Irishman who owned land was limited in how much profit he could make from it and forced by law to divide the land among all his children rather than let the land remain whole (Ignatiev, 1995).

By 1776 the Irish comprised at least 10% of the U.S. population (Miller & Wagner, 1995). Their descendants included Davey Crockett and Presidents Jackson, Buchanan, and Wilson. Most of these immigrants were actually Scotch Irish (Jackson, 1993; Leyburn, 1962), who had been planted by the British in Northern Ireland in the 1600s with the hope that they would "bite the wild Irish into submission to British authority," as King James I, himself a Scot, put it (Jackson, 1993). These Protestant Irish immigrated to the United States, especially in the 1700s and 1800s, and now number about 22 million Americans. They have not tended to think of themselves as "Irish"; they have had the lowest rate of endogamous marriage of any ethnic group in the United States and, indeed, have tended to eschew any sense of ethnic identity (Fallows, 1979). Separating the Catholic Irish from the Protestant Irish is, however, like most cultural categorizations, an oversimplification, because the Protestant Irish (Anglo Irish) have influenced "Catholic" Irish culture profoundly. Many of those most often claimed as Irishmen were actually Protestant Irish: Yeats, Shaw, Wilde, Swift, Beckett, O'Casey, Synge, Lady Gregory, Douglas Hyde (the first President of Ireland), Wolfe Tone, Emmet, Constance Markiewicz, Maude Gonne, and Charles Stewart Parnell.

Many traditional Irish characteristics may best be understood in relation to the geography and history of Ireland. A small island (about the size of New Jersey) located at the extreme western point of Europe in the North Atlantic, Ireland has much rainfall and few natural resources. For many centuries this "marginal" country was dominated, oppressed, and exploited by the British. Irish history includes starvation, humiliation, and heartbreak, on the one hand, and a remarkable adaptive ability to transform pain through humor, fierce rebellious spirit, and courage to survive, on the other.

The Irish are a people of paradoxes. They have a tremendous flair for bravado, but inwardly tend to assume that anything that goes wrong is the result of their sins. They are good-humored, charming, hospitable, and gregarious without being intimate. They love a good time, which includes teasing, verbal word play, and sparring, yet they revel in tragedy. Although always joking, they seem to struggle always against loneliness, depression, and silence, believing intensely that life will break your heart one day. Although they are known for fighting against all odds, the Irish also have had a strong sense of human powerlessness in relation to nature. As a legacy of their heritage, perhaps, they may place great value on conformity and respectability, and yet tend toward eccentricity and subversion. They have tended to be compliant and accepting of authoritarian structures, yet their history is full of rebels and fighters. They often feel profound shame about, and responsibility for, what goes wrong, yet they characteristically deny or project blame outward. They are clannish and place great stock in loyalty to their own, yet they often cut off relationships totally.

The Irish have been shown to have a high tolerance for nonrealistic thinking compared to many other groups (Wylan & Mintz, 1976; Zborowski, 1969). Although often viewed as a weakness, their ability to weave dreams was undoubtedly crucial to their survival and may indeed be one of their most creative assets. Historically, the Irish have valued fantasy and dreaming more, perhaps, than any other Western European culture. Even third-generation Irish in the United States were shown to turn frustrations into compensatory fantasy more than others (Stein, 1971). In contrast to British and Jewish families, for example, who may value the pursuit of truth, clarification of feelings does not necessarily make the Irish feel better. Thus, therapy aimed at opening up family feelings will often be unsuccessful.

Because the Irish have such difficulty dealing directly with differences and conflicts, feelings tend to be submerged, leading each party to feel betrayed by the "disloyalty" of the other (McGoldrick, 1982; Diner, 1983). Total loyalty is expected, but unlike other loyalty-demanding groups such as the Italians or Arabs, the demand for it is almost never articulated. Much is left unexpressed, especially hurts and conflicts, which may linger unspoken for years. Problems may go unacknowledged for so long that families may reach the point where it is almost too late to help them pull back from the extremes of buried pain and resentment, though no one may know exactly what the issue is.

Their basic belief is that problems are a private matter between themselves and God, and they have therefore been unlikely to seek or expect any help when they have trouble (McGoldrick, 1982; Sanua, 1960; Zborowski, 1969; Zola, 1966), although this pattern is luckily changing in recent times (Cleary & Demone, 1988). The Irish are embarrassed to have a problem and ashamed to let anyone, especially a family member, know about it. Zborowski (1969), one of the key early researchers of ethnic differences in response to pain, focused his discussion of the Irish on their preference for suffering alone. Similarly, their traditional solution to marital problems was silent withdrawal, distance, or separation (McGoldrick, 1982) and for problems in family business, to define separate spheres of operation for different family members (McGoldrick & Troast, 1993). Indeed, learning how to separate without cut-off and bitterness has been shown to make a major difference in Irish couple relationships (Murphy, 1988).

## THE IRISH IN HISTORICAL CONTEXT

For centuries extreme poverty prevailed in Ireland. By the 19th century, rapid population increase, continual subdivision of the land, and exorbitantly high rents contributed to the overdependence of the Irish on potatoes, which had become almost their only food, leaving them extremely vulnerable to the frequent failures of potato crops. Such a failure was the major precipitant of the massive Irish immigration in the 1840s that led more than a million Irish peasants to immigrate in less than two decades (Scally, 1995; Miller & Wagner, 1995; Miller, 1985; Kennedy, 1983). Indeed, there was plenty of grain raised in Ireland during the years of the famine, which could have fed the whole population, but the British controlled the crops and chose to export it, while the peasants died by the millions (Kinealy, 1995; Bayor & Meagher, 1996). Indeed, the British leader of famine relief said the great evil was "not the physical evil of the famine, but the moral evil of the selfish, perverse, and turbulent character of the Irish people" (Miller & Wagner, 1995, p. 29). *The London Times* declared that Ireland's catastrophe was "a great blessing" offering the "valuable opportunity for settling" once and for all "the vexed question of Irish . . . discontent" (Miller & Wagner, 1995, p. 29).

No other country has given up a greater proportion of its population to the United States. And no other country has sent such a large percentage of single women as immigrants (Diner, 1983; Nolan, 1989; Rossiter, 1993). According to the 1990 Census, there are about 39 million Irish in the United States and even now about 30% more women than men. In recent decades there was a new wave of immigrants from Ireland, many of whom came to the United States illegally, with little hope of changing their status. Like other groups of illegal immigrants, they had to rely on an informal work network and remain invisible within the larger society (Aroian, 1993).

Although many Irish Americans continued to demonstrate concern for the fate of Ireland, the majority of 19th-century Irish immigrants thought of themselves more as political exiles of British oppression than as immigrants seeking adventure or economic opportunity (Foster, 1988; Miller, 1985; Kearney, 1990). They moved away from the history of oppression and suffering and by the second generation thought of themselves primarily as Americans. Indeed, though they started out on the side of the oppressed in the United States and positively inclined toward abolition, having been treated as an inferior race in their own country, they soon learned that they could define themselves as of the race of the dominant group in relation to people of color and generally moved toward this redefinition of themselves as quickly as they could (Ignatiev, 1995). Their experience varied much by the region in which they lived (Clark, 1988), but in general they adapted and flourished in the United States. They began to intermarry with other ethnic groups, although mostly with other Roman Catholics. Their Irishness was a sentimental part of their lives, and often they knew little of their heritage. Still, the Irish seem to have retained their cultural characteristics longer than most other ethnic groups (Greeley, 1977, 1981; Greeley & McCready, 1975), probably because assimilation did not require them to give up their language. Their values permitted the Irish to accommodate to U.S. society without giving up their deeply rooted culture, and Catholic schools run primarily by Irish nuns and priests transmitted Irish cultural values to generations of Irish American children.

# THE CHURCH

For the Irish in the United States, just as in Ireland, the Catholic Church was their primary cultural force and national unifier, with the Church being valued even more than the family. The role of the church goes deep into Irish history. Early missionaries to Ireland, such has St. Patrick, had established a strong Church, that developed a cultivated religious tradition and even the main source of high culture for continental Europe from the 8th to the 10th centuries (Cahill, 1995). Later, amid the struggles with the British, religious loyalty became closely tied with the Irish desire to recover their land and heritage. Even in the United States, the parish rather than the neighborhood defined the Irish community for generations. Unfortunately, the Irish Church was dominated by Jansenism, a mystical movement with a grim theology, which had been expelled from France. The Jansenists emphasized the evil and untrustworthy instincts of human beings. The Irish Roman Catholic Church, isolated from external influences, became rigid, authoritarian, and moralistic. Through this rigid Church, the Irish tended to absorb the belief that human beings were by nature evil and deserved to suffer for their sins.

The changes brought to the Roman Catholic Church by Vatican II were profound, for the first time giving people the option of deciding many issues for themselves. This development was very stressful for many Irish Catholics, who were raised with the security that there was a clear, definite source of authority in their lives. Once anything about the Church could change, their whole foundation was shaken (Wills, 1971). Irish Catholics tend to struggle harder than many other groups to make sense of their religion and to fit its rules and strictures into their lives. Even those who have left the Church may have intense feelings about religious issues. More than other ethnic groups, the Irish struggled with their sense of sin and guilt. The Church demanded absolute obedience to its rules, and Irish Catholics followed the rules of the Church and its priests without question. This, of course, has changed in recent years, although the underlying rigidity has been harder to overcome. Indeed, the Irish sense of their own sinfulness and inadequacy often lasts long after they have the trappings of success, an internalization of the 500 years of foreign occupation and the contempt with which they were viewed by their oppressors. This history has also played deeply in their anxiety about what others think of them (Miller, 1985).

When the Irish do seek help, they are apt to view therapy as similar to Catholic confession—an occasion in which to tell their "sins" and receive a "penance." They are embarrassed to have to come to therapy, and until recently have usually done so only at the suggestion of a third party, such as a school, doctor, or court. A recent Boston study of ethnic groups indicates that although the Irish were the least likely to report problems, they were the most likely to seek help for problems they did acknowledge, especially alcohol problems (Cleary & Demone, 1988).

## SILENCE, BLARNEY, MYSTIFICATION, AND HUMOR

Although they have very highly developed verbal skills, the Irish may be at a loss to describe their own inner feelings, whether of love, sadness, or anger. But they do love to talk. Language and poetry have always been highly valued by the Irish and closely associated with their love of dream and fantasy. For many centuries the Irish used their words to enrich a dismal reality. Indeed, they have more expressions for coloring reality with exaggeration and humor than any other ethnic group: blarney, malarkey, the gift of gab, blather, hooey, palaver, shenanigans, to name just a few. For the many centuries that they lived under the control of the British, clear speech could have meant their death. Their tradition of verbal obfuscation is a typical adaptive strategy for oppressed peoples, but the Irish raised this ability to a high art. They have come to place great value on complex, even convoluted, mystification and double entendre in their language. African Americans have a similarly rich and colorful language, which was also an adaptation to oppression. But their "double language" does not entail such ambiguity, perhaps because, unlike the Irish, they could always distinguish each other from their oppressors. For the Irish, one often could not tell whom to trust by looking at them.

Indeed, verbal talent has been the greatest Irish natural resource. For 2,000 years the poet has been the most highly valued member of Irish society, wit its greatest art form, and satire its most penetrating mode of attack. In ancient times, poets were the only citizens allowed to move freely around Ireland, and by their spiritual power over the Irish imagination they, like the Church, contributed to the cultural unity of the country. Even today writers are the only members of Irish society exempt from paying taxes! The splendor of the ancient epics, in striking contrast to the relative simplicity of life indicated by archaelogical remains, indicates that the Irish have always used creative imagination to elaborate where the gifts of this world were lacking (Chadwick, 1970).

The therapist may have difficulty discerning an Irish family's needs, because members seem at the same time extremely articulate, yet unable to express their inner emotions. The inexpressiveness of the Irish in therapy may not be so much a sign of active resistance, as blocking off of their emotions even from themselves. The Irish may also fear being "pinned down" and may use mystifying language to avoid it. Their affinity for verbal innuendo, ambiguity and metaphor is what the English call "talking Irish," referring to their way of communicating and not communicating at the same time.

Pugnacity rather than romance was a traditional theme of Irish tales, and occasionally the entire struggle was determined by those whose skill in verbal attack and ridicule was greater (Evans, 1957). Although the Irish have a well-deserved reputation for bravery and resourcefulness, even against great odds, in fighting their enemies, the terms "the fighting Irish" and the "wild Irish temper" do not refer to the direct expression of anger within the family. Fighting was encouraged only against outsiders and for a just and moral cause, particularly religion or politics. Wit and sarcasm have long been the most powerful means of attack. Except under the guise of wit, ridicule, sarcasm, or other indirect humorous expression, hostility, pain, and anger in the family are generally dealt with by a silent build up of resentments, often culminating in cutting off the relationship without a word—a form of social excommunication for interpersonal wrongdoing.

Humor is the greatest resource of the Irish for dealing with life's problem. It offers a primary avenue for expression of forbidden feelings and allows for sharing of misfortune, while its indirectness softens the sting of an attack. Irish joking often has the same mystifying and double-binding character as other Irish verbal expression—it may be difficult for listeners to know whether to laugh along or whether they are the butt of the joke themselves. Although humor is the greatest resource of the Irish, in personal relationships it can be experienced as a way to distance, avoid pain, or put the other on guard. Unfortunately, the Irish ability to joke, tease, and ridicule with humor can at times leave family members frozen in emotional isolation from each other, unable to become intimate.

## ALCOHOL USE

Alcohol abuse has generally been tolerated as "a good man's weakness." Ireland's damp climate, which has forced people to be confined indoors, might be enough to make anyone seek to repress physical sensations with alcohol. In any event, using alcohol to achieve an altered state of consciousness has been a major cultural ritual, and alcohol has been seen as a solution to many problems (Bales, 1962). It dulls the pain, keeps out the cold, cures the fever, eases the grief, enlivens the celebration, allows them all manner of expression, and even cures a hangover—"a hair of the dog that bit you" (Stivers, 1976). As one early group of ethnicity researchers put it, "It is remarkable that the Irish can find an outlet for so many forms of psychic conflict in this single form of escape" (Roberts & Myers, 1954, p. 762).

The Irish tend to use alcohol differently from some other cultures (Ablon, 1980; Johnson, 1991; Kaufman, 1988). Italians, for example, tend to drink primarily while eating, whereas the Irish do the opposite. They often avoid drink when eating, because food diminishes the effect of the alcohol. A very high percentage of the Irish never drink. In Ireland children have for a long time actually been encouraged to "take the pledge," which meant to promise they would never touch alcohol. In Italy, by contrast, virtually every adult drinks regularly at mealtime. Children are gradually inducted into this practice as they mature. As Dermot Walsh (1987) the premier Irish researcher has commented, "It may be that the Irish wherever they are have higher proportions of abstainers and of heavy drinkers than the British or Americans" (p. 118).

The Irish in Ireland still spend 13% of their personal expenditures on alcohol, the highest percentage in Western Europe (Walsh, 1987). Not only do the Irish celebrate almost every conceivable occasion with alcohol, but they also have often showed more interest in drink than in food (Bales, 1962). Indeed, their lack of attention to cuisine, even when they have ample resources, which has been the source of many stereotypic jokes directed at the Irish, is undoubtedly a result of generations of near starvation. In fact, fasting has been regarded with almost superstitious awe by the Irish for centuries (Scherman, 1981), and outsiders have remarked on their sense of embarrassment at enjoying good food. One could contrast this with the African American attention to familiar food cooked in special ways as a means of maintaining their culture against such great odds (Darden & Darden, 1978).

Traditionally, the pub rather than the family table was the center of Irish life, a fact that had profound implications for the family system. Considerable alcohol use was tolerated, especially by men, without being seen as troublesome. Alcohol abuse has thus been a serious problem for the Irish and the cause of much family disruption. Irish women are much less likely to be drinkers than Irish men, but they do drink more than women from other ethnic groups (Johnson, 1991), usually quietly, "sipping sherry," often at home and alone (Corrigan, 1980; Corrigan & Butler, 1991). When their drinking does get out of hand, it is considered extremely embarrassing for the family for various reasons, including the fact that women are supposed to be the strong ones in the family. But it does appear that drinking may serve as a rebellion against the constraints of gender roles (Bepko & Krestan, 1983; Teahan, 1987). The male alcoholic cycle in an Irish family may correspond to the religious cycle of sin, shame, guilt, and repentance, allowing brief periods of emotional contact without threatening the rigid distances usually maintained within the family. The partner and counterpart of the "no good drunk" is, of course, the "sainted Irish mother," and when she drinks, she may be seeking to break out of the constraints of this impossible role.

The therapy for alcohol problems with Irish families is too complex to cover in this chapter. Therapists should be cautioned to take a detailed alcohol history, even if the family does not present alcoholism as an issue, and to appreciate the degree to which the family may tolerate heavy drinking without labeling it a problem. The expressive difficulties for which the alcohol serves as a facilitator can be extreme, and they cannot be overcome quickly. Helping families integrate into their lives without alcohol the behaviors their drinking allowed is especially important for the Irish, who tend to have rigid emotional splits between what is allowed and what is considered intolerable. The structure of Alcoholics Anonymous (AA) is an excellent fit with Irish values, because it replicates the Irish reliance on a spiritual framework and the social functions of the pub as a communal hub away from the family. Indeed, the very idea of "anonymity" in AA, of openness with strangers as opposed to family, is an excellent fit with Irish practices of telling much more to a companion in a bar than one would ever share with intimate family members. The practice of anonymity, which works so well for the Irish, would be a great obstacle for cultures such as Hispanic or Italian, in which people's relationships depend completely on their "personalism" or personal connectedness. That same openness with their family might be highly embarrassing for the Irish.

## SUFFERING, SHAME, AND GUILT

The Irish sense of individual shame and guilt often leads them to assume that their suffering is deserved and, conversely, they may feel uneasy if things go too well for too long. They find virtue and sanctity in suffering silently and alone, or in "offering up" their pain to God "in imitation of Christ." The few studies we have of ethnic differences in response to physical pain suggest that the Irish show minimization, confusion, and inaccuracy in describing their pain, have high pain tolerance, and are likely to suffer in silence. Compared to other European groups, they are less likely to seek medical help, even when they obviously need it (Sanua, 1960; Zborowski, 1969; Zola, 1966; Tursky & Sternbach, 1967; Sternbach & Tursky, 1965), and they are less able to communicate with each other or their child about a child's illness (Fitzpatrick & Barry, 1990).

When the Irish do admit something is wrong, they are unlikely to be exaggerating. Given their traditionally low expectations for happiness in this life, they may also not expect that much change is possible. Trying to talk the Irish out of their sense of guilt and the need to suffer is a futile effort, because they believe that sooner or later they will have to pay for their sins. Unlike Jews, for whom the very experience of shared suffering is meaningful, the Irish believe in suffering alone (Zborowski, 1969). Certain strategies may, however, help them limit their guilt and suffering, such as ritualizing it within restricted time intervals (McGoldrick, 1982; McGoldrick & Pearce, 1981).

## DEATH AND THE FAMILY LIFE CYCLE

Helping the Irish deal with loss may be one of the most useful therapeutic activities (McGoldrick et al., 1988). Because of their tendency to turn pain inward, the Irish may suffer silently with it for years, perhaps blaming themselves for situations they could not change. Indeed, they often make merry at funerals, which are considered the most important life cycle transitions (McGoldrick, 1989). Such customs undoubtedly relate to their belief that this world is generally full of suffering, and death brings release to a better afterlife. There is often much joking, drinking, and storytelling, and the worst thing one could have is a boring funeral.

Interestingly, the Irish are perhaps the only culture to have a ritual around emigration, which was referred to as an "American wake," and for which all the rites of death rituals were observed, including the custom of staying with the departing person all night before the departure, just as they "waked" the corpse with all-night vigils from time of death until burial (Metress, 1990). Like the wake for the dead, the "American wake" involved public participation allowing the family and community to grieve over the loss. Attendance reaffirmed family and group ties. At the same time, one could ritualistically rejoice at the rebirth to a new state, because death and emigration freed one forever from the stark hopelessness of poverty (Metress, 1990). Public involvement acknowledged the altered relationships that both death and emigration brought about. These were of concern not only to the individual but also to the group as a whole. The high level of public participation in both wakes and emigration rituals reaffirmed the cohesiveness of the family and demonstrated the importance of social networks. The peculiar mix of celebration and sorrow that marked Irish wakes stood as testimony to the deprivation suffered by the living and the freedom enjoyed by the departed. The "American wake" reflecting Irish life, Irish death customs, and Irish ways of dealing with loss, was unique to Ireland. This ritual illustrates how profoundly the Irish react to the pain of loss, and suggests how important it is to address it in therapy.

## FAMILY PATTERNS

Traditionally, fathers in Irish families have been shadowy or absent figures, and husbands dealt with wives primarily by avoidance (McGoldrick, 1982; McGoldrick, Garcia-Preto, Hines, & Lee, 1989). An early study of psychiatric patients suggested that Irish men tend to view women as the main source of anxiety and power, while others, Italians, for example, usually focus on the husband (Opler & Singer, 1957; Singer & Opler, 1956). Although acculturation for many cultural groups has placed great strain on their traditional family ties and structure, it may be that life in America actually strengthened the Irish family by offering men more options to succeed in work and greater flexibility for relationships within the family.

Irish women have enjoyed comparatively more role flexibility than women in many other cultures. For example, unlike other ethnic groups, the rate of immigration of Irish women was higher than that of Irish men (Kennedy, 1983; Diner, 1983; Miller, 1985). Irish families often paid as much attention to the education of their daughters as their sons, and there has been a large representation of Irish women in professional and white-collar jobs (Blessing, 1980).

Traditionally, Irish women found their social life primarily through the Church, which, by its veneration of the Virgin Mary, reflected the Irish view of women as independent and dominant (Kennedy, 1983), while keeping them obedient to male domination as well. The Irish mother's reputation was for ruling the family with an iron fist, while at the same time being the unquestioning transmitter of rigid Church authority, even though this patriarchal authority did so little for her. It is remarkable that the Irish Catholic Church, which has been so vehement against divorce and abortion, has not a word to say about wife and child beating, rape, or incest, surely much more destructive phenomena in our society. Indeed, Ireland is a country in which 95% of the population is Roman Catholic, divorce was constitutionally forbidden until 1996, abortion is constitutionally restricted, 70% of married women are homemakers, and the Supreme Court has ruled that women's unpaid work does not entitle them to part ownership of the family home. It is also truly one of those typically Irish paradoxes that this same country in 1990 elected as its president a feminist lawyer, Mary Robinson, whose career had been marked by campaigns to legalize contraception, divorce, homosexuality, and freedom of information on abortion. And this president has had a remarkable tenure in Ireland, speaking out, empowering the Irish, strengthening their self confidence, and making remarkable strides to lift Irish women out of many of their fatalistic beliefs (McCafferty, 1992). As Imelda Colgan McCarthy (1992) has described it, Irish women have always featured prominently in myth as mother/wife, goddess/hag, and queen/warrior. And although there has been much pressure to write women out of history except in their role as mother in the home, the times are changing and expanding the awareness of the multifaceted roles women can and should have, drawing from mythology and legend and bringing these roles into reality.

The Irish did have a surprising number of female heroines and rulers such as the wild, self-willed Queen Maeve. The Irish never had a cult of romantic love (Chadwick, 1970; Power, 1993) and, indeed, have generally considered women to be morally superior to men. The Irish wife was often thought of as the brains, the manager, the savings bank, and the realist. Women tended to think of men as needing to be carefully handled or manipulated. Women bore their responsibilities and burdens stoically, "offering them up." Family researcher Theodore Lidz (1968) described the pattern thus:

> The Irish American child may grow up influenced by the mother's tendency to treat her husband like a grown-up child, pretending to believe the fabricated tales he tells her and admiring his ability to tell them; and while she seems to defer to her husband's authority, she holds the family reins tightly in her own hands, at the same time ceding to the Church a superordinate authority which must not be questioned. (p. 52)

Although Irish mothers have provided outstanding female role models of strong-minded, commanding, indomitable women, the stereotype of the "sainted Irish mother" is not totally positive (Rudd, 1984; McGoldrick, 1982, 1991; Diner, 1983; McKenna, 1979; Scheper-Hughes, 1979). She might be sanctimonious, preoccupied with the categories of right and wrong and with what the neighbors think, consciously withholding praise from her children for fear it would give them "a swelled head." Of course, this pattern makes sense in a culture with such a long history of foreign domination, in which she sought control through whatever means were available to her, and felt the need to keep her family in line to minimize the risk of their being singled out for further oppression. Sons might be pampered and protected much longer than daughters, and in traditional Irish families were called "boys" way into adulthood, probably largely because of their economic oppression, which made it hard for them to become self-supporting. A very high percentage of Irish men never married at all, and those who did were sometimes thought of as "married bachelors," more loyal to their mothers than to their wives (Connery, 1970). The Irish for a long time had the latest age and lowest rate of marriage of any nation in the world (Kennedy, 1983).

A surprising number of Irish songs relate to the intensely bound, almost romantic mother–son tie that developed in this context. The famous Irish ballad *Mother Machree*, for example, emphasizes directly that the son can never replace his tie to his mother with any other:

> There's a spot in me heart which no colleen may own,
> There's a depth in me soul never sounded or known,
> There's a place in my memory, my life that you fill
> No one can take it, no one ever will.

The mother–son bond may have no equal in intensity in Irish family relationships, even marriage. Sons may separate from their mothers with great difficulty, if at all, and their wives may be expected to go along with whatever is demanded by the mother-in-law.

What are we to make of these stereotypes of the Irish mother, who seems to be to blame for all sorts of problems—contempt for her husband, spoiling her sons and binding them in a love from which they will never be free, while teaching her daughters to rely only on themselves, become overresponsible, and repeat these skewed patterns? We must take into account the very ancient tradition of Irish women, celebrated as formidable, tenacious, and powerful rulers ever since the time of ancient Irish legends (MacCurtain & O'Corrain, 1978). This tradition must be combined with awareness of the 900-year history of Irish oppression, which was focused especially on Irish men, who were systematically deprived of any sense of power and, to blot out what was happening to them, often turned to drink, which became institutionalized in the culture as an acceptable form of escape. Women were forced to run their families, and it is no wonder they turned to their sons with the dreams their beaten down husbands could not fulfill. They turned to their daughters to carry on with and after them. For solace they turned to the Church, which, in its veneration of the Virgin Mary, reflected a view of women as independent. Yet for various political and historical reasons, the church had adopted a stance of particularly rigid asceticism, sexual repression, and glorification of self-mortification, while always being identified with salvation and liberation of the Irish from British domination (McGoldrick & Pearce, 1981; McGoldrick 1982, 1991; McGoldrick et al., 1989; Messinger, 1971).

Because of their difficulty in dealing with feelings, the Irish have trouble in close relationships, especially marriage. The Irish place less emphasis on marriage than do many other cultures. Romance in marriage was not a central concept, and partners have tended to resign themselves fairly frequently to an emotionally distant relationship. Irish distancing may be baffling or frustrating to someone from a culture that takes for granted more intense interactions, and it naturally presents difficulties for contemporary Irish who marry into more expressive groups. While the Irish may see distancing as merely the best temporary solution to interpersonal problems, others may see it as abandonment.

Given the rigid traditions of Irish Catholicism, sex has, perhaps not surprisingly, been referred to as "the lack of the Irish" (Messinger, 1971). A book entitled *Irish Erotic Art* (Cork, 1995) turns out to be a book filled with empty pages. Because of severe sanctions against sexual expression, the Irish also often avoid tenderness, affection, and intimacy. Members of Irish families may become isolated from each other emotionally, and when there are problems, the family atmosphere may become sullen, dour, and puritanically rigid. Indeed, the Irish jig even caricatures the repression of bodily experience: Only the feet of the dancer's body move, while the rest of the body remains as motionless as possible. This contrasts sharply with Greek or Brazilian dancing, in which physical suppleness and contact between dancers reflect very different attitudes toward the body and toward physical relationships between people.

Traditionally, the first recourse for help with problems was the Church. Irish priests, themselves trained to suppress their physical experience and to take vows of celibacy from adolescence, were not always the best counselors on matters of intimacy. The Church considered celibacy to be the highest state one could attain, and an enormous number of Irish men and women remained unmarried. Marriage was considered "permission to sin." Sex was for the purpose of procreation. Divorce and affairs have always been less common among the Irish, although pregnancy prior to marriage has not been uncommon, because a moment of "sin and weakness" was less unacceptable than planning to have sex and taking precautions against pregnancy.

Homosexuality was strictly considered sinful, yet, because the Irish leave so much unsaid, many families have had gay or lesbian members who were quite accepted by the family with their partners, as long as they made no reference to their sexuality. Everyone knew, but nothing was said. When families are confronted more directly with the homosexuality of one of their members, there is usually much discomfort or even a cut off. However, over time, family members can be coached to reconnect, and, perhaps because the Irish believe in "doing the right thing," Irish families are often able to move to connections and acceptance that includes this knowledge, just as they have been doing in relation to divorce, abortion, and pregnancy outside of marriage. Brendan Fay, a devout Catholic and one of the founders of the Irish Lesbian and Gay Organization (ILGO) established in 1990 in New York City, has said that as Irish gays and lesbians began to recover from invisibility, they discovered a "monster" in the prejudicial response from families and Church to their wish to participate in the St. Patrick's Day parade. They drew on their spirituality as they committed themselves to move beyond feeling ashamed of who they were. And they have persisted in their political efforts on behalf of those who will come after them (Menchin, 1993). This spiritual approach is characteristic of the Irish turning to their internal strength, which has helped them survive for centuries, and is a crucial resource for therapy with any Irish family.

## IRISH MOTHERS

Sons and daughters rarely dare to voice their resentment, being both guilty and admiring of their mothers' stoic self-sacrifice. Clinically, it is important to be nonblaming when we see mothers who are overly central in a family and dote on their sons, while being more demanding of their daughters. At the same time we must question with them and their families the patterns they are perpetuating.

Interestingly, the Irish have traditionally allowed more room for women not to be mothers than many other cultures in which women without a family might have no role or status at all. They are the only group in which the emigration of women to the United States far surpassed that of men. In the United States, as in Ireland, Irish women continued to be reluctant about marrying. They have enjoyed a comparatively open range of economic options in domestic work, nursing, and schoolteaching. And this, along with the high rate of desertion of Irish men from their families, augmented female family authority. There has long been a respected role for the unmarried "Auntie Mame," the feisty, independent, funny, and important contributor to family well-being. Clinically, we can strengthen women by underscoring and validating this appreciation for roles beyond mothering, helping single women see themselves as part of a long tradition within Irish families.

Irish women have generally had little expectation of or interest in being taken care of by a man. Their hopes have been articulated much less in romantic terms than in aspirations for self-sufficiency (Diner, 1983). They have always remained reluctant about the prospect of giving up their freedom and economic independence for marriage and family responsibilities. An Irish woman is likely to try to do it all herself and never ask for help. She may not expect to rely on a partner for either intimacy or contributing his share of the burdens of family life. This reflects, of course, a common gender assumption, but also a specifically Irish tendency not to articulate needs and feelings and to assume that if you are really loved, the other will know your feelings without having to be told. Often asking gentle questions about the assumed roles of men and women in the family can be an important first step in enabling them to change lopsided and dysfunctional gender patterns. However, therapists must always be careful that they do not unwittingly increase the Irish client's sense of guilt by subtle questioning that suggests they have done something wrong.

## CHILDREN

The Irish tend to view people moralistically as good or bad, strong or weak. The family often designates a good child and a bad one, and they may ignore aspects of a child's behavior that do not fit their designated roles. In one Irish American family, for example, the mother always spoke about her three children as "My Denny, Poor Betty, and That Kathleen."

Ridicule, belittling, and shaming have played a major role in child discipline (Barrabee & von Mering, 1953; Spiegel, 1971a, 1971b). In families where alcohol is abused, discipline is often inconsistent and harsh. However, in many families Irish mothers ruled so well that a mere look or even the thought of her disapproval would be enough to keep children in line.

Children in Irish American families are generally raised to be polite, respectable, obedient, and well behaved. Typical familial injunctions would be, "What will the neighbors think?", "Don't make a scene," "That's a sin," or "You'll go to hell." Irish parents may rarely praise their children, fuss over them, or make them the center of attention for fear of spoiling them (Barrabee & von Mering, 1953). This strict and restrained attitude toward children may be very hard for a therapist from a more expressive culture to understand, just as it may be difficult for the Irish to understand other groups' permissiveness and encouragement of children to "show off" their talents. Beyond the mother–son tie, family members tend to stick to their own sex and generation in forming relationships.

## EXTENDED FAMILY

Extended family relationships among the Irish are often not close, although families may get together for "duty visits" on holidays and act jovial and "clannish." Family members tend not to rely on one another as a source of support, and when they have a problem, they may even see it as an added burden and embarrassment for the family to find out. The sense of emotional isolation in Irish relationships is frequently a factor in symptom development and has important implications for therapy. While siblings may meet for holidays out of a sense of loyalty, there is often a feeling of emotional isolation. Though the family may act pleasant and humorous, any emotional exposure to outsiders may be felt as a severe breach of family rules. Older, unmarried relatives may be totally out of contact or may form isolated units of siblings or parent and child, who maintain almost no communication with other parts of the family. Typically, one extended family member (usually a woman) is of central importance for the family. It may be essential to get permission of this matriarch, most often a grandmother or senior maiden aunt, if therapeutic progress is to be made.

The Irish have a tremendous respect for personal boundaries, are enormously sensitive to each other's right to privacy, and will make strong efforts not to impose or intrude on one another. In older age they tend to have a more independent, active view of themselves than the elderly of some other ethnic backgrounds (Cohler & Lieberman, 1979).

## IRISH AMERICANS IN THERAPY

When the Irish go for therapy, they will probably not look their best. They may view therapy as being like confession, in which you tell your sins and seek forgiveness. They may not understand their feelings and will certainly be embarrassed to admit them. This creates a dilemma for the therapist, since, on the one hand, family members fear he or she will see through them, which is very embarrassing, or, on the other hand, that he or she will not understand what is really bothering them and they might have to explain it, which is highly embarrassing as well. Irish clients often take a one-down position, seeing authority as vested in the therapist.

As a general rule, structured therapy, focused specifically on the presenting problem, will be the least threatening and most helpful to Irish clients. Suggestions for opening communication that preserve the boundaries of individual privacy, such as Bowen therapy, will be preferable to bringing the entire family drama into a therapy session. Whereas large family sessions that draw on the resources of the whole family may be supportive for some groups, for the Irish they may raise the anxiety to a toxic level, leading to denial and embarrassed humor, to cover over their sense of humiliation. It is often more fruitful to meet with smaller subgroups of the family, at least in the initial stages.

The Irish will probably respond more readily to a fairly structured, problem focused (especially child-focused) approach. Brief, goal-oriented therapy with a specific plan and a right and wrong way clearly spelled out (such as behavior modification) would be likely to have appeal. Vague, introspective, open-ended emotive therapy might be experienced as very threatening. Therapy oriented toward uncovering hidden psychological problems is likely to increase their anxiety and their conviction that they are bad and deserve to suffer. The Irish may be more effectively helped by the somewhat mysterious, paradoxical, and humorous techniques of which they themselves are such masters. Perhaps it is not surprising that some of the most well-known therapists of Irish extraction, Bill O'Hanlon, Steve Gilligan, Phil Guerin, Tom Fogarty, and Betty Carter, for example, espouse more positive, humorful orientations to therapy. These methods encourage clients to change without dwelling on their negative feelings, and organize therapy around building on a positive connotation and a more hopeful vision of their lives.

One of the most creative therapy approaches in recent years, "The Fifth Province Model," developed by three Dublin therapists—Nollaig Byrne, Imelda Colgan McCarthy, and Philip Kearney—evolved specifically out of thinking about Irish history and has, not surprisingly, great merit for therapists dealing with Irish Americans (McCarthy & Byrne, 1988, 1995; McCarthy, in press). This model seeks intentionally to draw clinical attention away from polarizing conversations and into the realm of ambiguities, that unique place in Celtic mythology where all contradictions can coexist. "The Fifth Province," a magical place that included the other four Irish provinces of Munster, Connaught, Leinster, and Ulster, is a place of imagination and possibility, where ambiguities and contradictions can be contained, where ancient Celtic chieftans came to resolve their conflicts through dialogue with druid priests. In their therapy, they develop multiple stories, offer metaphors and Irish folktales as interventions, and intentionally expand narratives beyond "logical" linear discourse. Furthermore, they use the political metaphor of colonization as a framework for their whole therapy, scrutinizing carefully the potential role of therapy itself to "colonize" or oppress clients, as the Irish themselves had been colonized.

Whereas clients from other backgrounds may be quick to demand that plans be made to suit their convenience or that the therapist solve their problems, the Irish may have enormous difficulty with such self-assertions. Nevertheless, the Irish can be very gratifying to work with because of their extremely strong sense of loyalty and their willingness to follow through on therapeutic suggestions. They are also apt to accept the therapist readily; they may not question credentials, even when it may be in their best interests to do so. Unfortunately, their responsiveness can become a hazard when it produces compliance without real collaboration in the change process. The therapist must help them develop a genuine investment in the process of change and not rely on their politeness, sense of responsibility, and obligation to duty.

Small changes may be registered as large gains in the family, in spite of the many aspects of family relating that remain unaltered. Because of their ability to compartmentalize, they may change, yet have many levels on which they have not connected the therapy with their lives. Therapy, like their religion, their dreams, and and their prayers, becomes a new "therapeutic reality," one not necessarily integrated with their other spiritual or healing resources. The therapist can become an authority, who, like the priest, gives instructions that are to be followed.

Irish families also probably prefer therapists to keep a friendly distance. A sense of humor can be a great asset, provided the therapist remains serious and businesslike at the same time. Any personality style too loud or idiosyncratic is likely to make the family extremely uncomfortable. A therapist who swears, for example, is likely to be viewed as crude or sacrilegious.

Although family members may fail to see the need for the father's presence, it is important for the therapist to involve him in therapy. Although Irish men will often find a woman therapist intimidating, the strong role of Irish women may mean they are more comfortable with a woman therapist than are families from most other "traditional" cultures.

In working with the Irish, the therapist must often read between the lines, whether of blustering or of muted compliance, to ferret out what is really troubling them; then the Irish sense of loyalty, humor, and responsibility become the best clinical resources. Given the Irish embarrassment about their feelings on the one hand, and their wish to be responsive to suggestions on the other, tasks that can be carried out at home may promote communication more successfully than directly confronting family members in therapy. It may help to give tasks that focus on presenting symptoms, structuring family interactions at home to address maladaptive family communication problems, rather than unmasking them directly in sessions. There are many advantages to doing this. It fits with the Irish expectation of doing penance for their sins, provides structure within which to organize their behavior, spells out a right and wrong way, and spares them public exposure in therapy. This clarity is important to those who fear doing wrong. It also provides a sense of success early in therapy, which may be especially important for the Irish, who are preoccupied with feeling they are bad and have done wrong. When the Irish do engage emotionally in therapy, they may be seeking forgiveness or absolution, which can be a trap, since granting absolution keeps the client in a one-down position. Attempts at self-justification and tales told to show how it was someone else's fault tend to be a coverup for many layered levels of self recrimination.

The Irish family's sense of isolation can be so great that a therapist may not realize how much it means to them just to have a safe, accepting place to talk to each other about thoughts and feelings. At the same time, the use of nonverbal techniques such as touching exercises, psychodrama, or structural techniques to increase anxiety, may be highly threatening. Efforts to help them reconnect may do a lot to lessen their feelings of emotional isolation. However, this work requires respect for personal boundaries, for the family's need to preserve a degree of distance, and for leaving certain things unspoken.

In general, positive connotation, giving a caring interpretation to behavior, is of much more use than traditional psychodynamic interpretations for Irish clients, who are likely to blame themselves for whatever goes wrong and be fatalistic about internal change. Structuring the distance and intimacy will increase the family's sense of control over their feelings. The Irish may respond extremely well to Bowen Coaching, because of its emphasis on working out relationships in private, and on personal responsibility for change. The Irish are, indeed, excellent candidates for such therapy and may continue working to change relationships on their own, long after the therapy is over, because of the way it provides them with a method for reworking relationships they may have found overwhelming and confusing in the past.

One young woman, whose father had been a successful journalist and the rebel of his family, had great difficulty establishing a relationship with her sole surviving aunt, who was the principal upholder of "Irish Catholic values" for the family. This aunt had been the spinster sister who remained home to care for her aging parents until their deaths. She had built up a lifetime of unspoken resentments about her role, in spite of the secondary gains of being a martyr, similar to the heroine of *Final Payments* by Mary Gordon (1981). The aunt never missed sending cards for birthdays or Christmas, but when the niece attempted to make more personal contact, she resisted it strongly, agreeing to meet only rarely and for short visits, limiting discussion strictly to the topics she chose. Initially the niece was quite put off by this behavior, describing her aunt as "a prune with doilies on the chairs." She was annoyed that her "open-hearted" approaches were rebuffed for no apparent reason. However, the young woman persisted. It took several years of letters and gradually more personal phone calls before she was able to learn enough about the family background to realize that the resentment she was experiencing had been carried down in the family for several generations. This aunt was the unappreciated and over-burdened spinster, who stayed home and resentfully cared for her parents, while her brothers got the glory. She had become the repository of unforgotten slights, "offering up" her family burdens in her prayers for the family's return to the Church. Church rules had been used in the service of bolstering her self-righteous indignation, which covered her sense of betrayal and hurt that her efforts on behalf of the family had never been reciprocated or appreciated.

---

In families such as this the work obviously proceeds slowly. However, the long-term benefit of each pursuit to family members is often powerful in overcoming their painful sense of isolation and vulnerability.

## CONCLUSION

Do not expect the Irish to enjoy therapy or feel relieved by having a cathartic heart-to-heart discussion. The therapist working with an Irish family must be content with limited changes. Families may not wish to move beyond the initial presenting problem, and it is important for the therapist not to pressure them into further work. Attempting to get spouses to deal with marital issues after a child-focused problem has been solved, for example, will probably make them feel guilty and incompetent (Hines, Garcia-Preto, McGoldrick, Almeida, & Weltman, in press). It is better to reinforce the changes that the family members do make and to let them return for therapy later at their own initiative. Even if the therapist perceives that there are emotional blocks in the family that are still causing pain, it is important not to push the matter. Because of the lack of immediate feedback about therapeutic progress from the family, the therapist may be surprised to learn that their Irish families have continued therapeutic work on their own. Their deep sense of personal responsibility is, in fact, their greatest personal resource in therapy. They often do continue efforts started in therapy, although they may not openly admit either fault or their resolve to remedy it.

## REFERENCES

Ablon, J. (1980). The significance of cultural patterning for the "alcoholic family." *Family Process, 19*(2), 127–144.

Aroian, K. (1993). Mental health risks and problems encountered by illegal immigrants. *Issues in Mental Health Nursing, 14,* 379–397.

Bales, R. F. (1962). Attitudes toward drinking in Irish Culture. In D. Pittman & C. Snyder (Eds.), *Society, culture and drinking patterns.* New York: Wiley.

Barrabee, P., & von Mering, O. (1953). Ethnic variations in mental stress in families with psychotic children. *Social Problems, 1,* 48–53.

Bayor, R. H., & Meagher, T. J. (Eds.). *The New York Irish.* Baltimore: Johns Hopkins University Press.

Bepko, C., & Krestan, J. (1983). *The responsibility trap.* New York: Harper.

Biddle, E.H. (1976). The American Catholic Irish family. In C. Mindel & R. Halberstein (Eds.), *Ethnic families in America.* New York: Elsevier.

Blessing, P. J. (1980). Irish. In S. Thernstorm, A. Orlov, & O. Handlin (Eds.), *The Harvard encyclopedia of American ethnic groups.* Cambridge, MA: Harvard University Press.

Cahill, T. (1995). *How the Irish saved civilization.* New York: Doubleday.

Chadwick, N. (1970). *The Celts.* London: Penguin.

Clark, D. (1988). *Hibernia America: The Irish and regional cultures.* New York: Greenwood Press.

Cleary, P. D., & Demone, H. W. (1988, December). Health and social service needs in a Northeastern metropolitan area: Ethnic group differences. *Journal of Sociology and Social Welfare, 15*(4), 63–76.

Cohler, B. J., & Lieberman, M. A. (1979). Personality change across the second half of life: Findings from a study of Irish, Italian, and Polish-American women. In D. E. Gelfand & A. J. Kutzik (Eds.), *Ethnicity and aging*. New York: Springer.

Connery, D. S. (1970). *The Irish*. New York: Simon & Schuster.

Cork, S. O. M. (1995). *Irish erotic art*. New York: St. Martin's Press.

Corrigan, E. M. (1980). *Alcoholic women in treatment*. New York: Oxford University Press.

Corrigan, E. M., & Butler, S. (1991, March). Irish alcoholic women in treatment: Early findings. *International Journal of the Addictions, 26*(3), 281–292.

Darden, N. J., & Darden, C. (1978). *Spoonbread and strawberry wine*. New York: Fawcett Crest.

Diner, H. R. (1983). *Erin's daughters in America*. Baltimore: Johns Hopkins University Press.

Evans, E. E. (1957). *Irish folkways*. London: Routledge & Kegan Paul.

Fallows, M. A. (1979). *Irish Americans: Identity and assimilation*. Englewood Cliffs, NJ: Prentice-Hall.

Fitzpatrick, C., & Barry, C. (1990). Cultural differences in family communication about Duchenne muscular dystrophy. *Developmental Medicine and Child Neurology, 32*(11), 967–973.

Foster, R. F. (1988). *Modern Ireland 1600–1972*. New York: Penguin.

Gordon, M. (1981). *Final payments*. New York: Ballantine.

Greeley, A. M. (1977). *The American Catholic*. New York: Basic Books.

Greeley, A. M. (1981). *The Irish Americans*. New York: Harper & Row.

Greeley, A. M., & McCready, W. (1975). The transmission of cultural heritages: The Case of Irish and Italians. In N. Glazer & D. Moynihan (Eds.), *Ethnicity: The theory and experience*. Cambridge, MA: Harvard University Press.

Hines, P. M., Garcia-Preto, N., McGoldrick, M., Almeida, R., & Weltman, S. (in press). Intergenerational relationships in cultural perspective. In M. McGoldrick (Ed.), *Re-visioning family therapy in multicultural perspective*. New York: Guilford Press.

Ignatiev, N. (1995). *How the Irish became white*. New York: Routledge.

Jackson, C. (1993). *A social history of the Scotch Irish*. New York: Madison Books.

Johnson, P. B. (1991). Reaction expectancies of ethnic drinking differences. *Psychology of Addictive Behaviors, 5*(1), 36–40.

Kaufman, E., & Borders, L. (1988). Ethnic family differences in adolescent substance use. *Journal of Chemical Dependency Treatment, 1*(2), 99–121.

Kearney, R. (1990). *Migrations: The Irish at home and abroad*. Dublin: Wolfhound Press.

Kennedy, R. E. (1983). *The Irish: Marriage, immigration and fertility*. Berkeley: University of California Press.

Kinealy, C. (1995). *This great calamity: The Irish famine 1845–52*. Boulder, CO: Roberts Rinehart.

Leyburn, J. G. (1962). *The Scotch-Irish: A social history*. Chapel Hill: University of North Carolina Press.

Lidz, T. (1968). *The person*. New York: Basic Books.

MacCurtain, M., & O'Corrain, D. (Eds.). (1978). *Women in Irish society: The historical dimension*. Dublin: Arlen House.

McCafferty, N. (1992, May/June). Ireland: Ironic yarns from a "slightly constitutional" country. *Ms Magazine*, pp. 16–19.

McCarthy, I. C. (1992). Out of myth into history: A hope for Irish women in the 1990s, *Journal of Feminist Family Therapy*, 4(3/4).

McCarthy, I. C. (in press). Abusing norms: Welfare families and a Fifth Province stance. *Human Systems*, 5(4).

McCarthy, I. C., & Byrne, N. O. (1988). Mis-taken love: Conversations on the problem of incest in an Irish context. *Family Process*, 27(2), 181–199.

McCarthy, I. C., & Byrne, N. O. (1995). A spell in the Fifth Privince: Its between meself, herself, yerself and yer two imaginary friends. In S. Friedman (Ed.), *The reflecting team in action: Collaborative practice in family therapy* (pp. 119–142). New York: Guilford Press.

McGoldrick, M. (1982). Irish families. In M. McGoldrick, J. K. Pearce, & J. Giordano (Eds.), *Ethnicity and family therapy* (1st ed., pp. 310–339). New York: Guilford Press.

McGoldrick, M. (1989). Ethnicity and the family life cycle. In B. Carter & M. McGoldrick (Eds.), *The changing family life cycle*. Boston: Allyn & Bacon.

McGoldrick, M. (1991). Irish mothers: Ethnicity and mothers. *Journal of Feminist Family Therapy*, 2(2), 1–8.

McGoldrick, M., Almeida, R., Hines, P. M., Garcia-Preto, N., Rosen, E., & Lee, E. (1988). Mourning in different cultures. In F. Walsh & M. McGoldrick (Eds.), *Living beyond loss*. New York: Norton.

McGoldrick, M., Garcia-Preto, N., Hines, P., & Lee, E. (1989). Ethnicity and women. In M. McGoldrick, C. Anderson, & F. Walsh (Eds.), *Women in families*. New York: Norton.

McGoldrick, M., & Troast, J. (1993). Ethnicity and family business. *Journal of Family Business*, VI(3), 283–300.

McGoldrick, M., & Pearce, J. K. (1981). Family therapy with Irish Americans. *Family Process*, 20, 223–241.

McKenna, A. (1979). Attitudes of Irish mothers to child rearing. *Journal of Comparative Family Studies*, 10(2), 227–251.

Menchin, S. (1993, March 22). Break in the clouds. *The New Yorker*.

Messinger, J. C. (1971, February). Sexuality: The lack of the Irish. *Psychology Today*, pp. 41–44.

Metress, E. (1990). The American wake of Ireland: Symbolic death ritual. *Omega—Journal of Death and Dying*, 21(2), 147–153.

Miller, K. A. (1985). *Emigrants and exiles: Ireland and the Irish exodus to North America*. New York: Oxford University Press.

Miller, K., & Wagner, P. (1995). *Out of Ireland: The story of the Irish emigration to America*. Washington, DC: Elliott & Clark.

Murphy, M. W. (1988). Separating with dignity within the Irish value system. *Mediation Quarterly*, 22, 91–98.

Nolan, J. (1989). *Ourselves alone: Women's emigration from Ireland 1885–1920*. Lexington: Kentucky University Press.

Opler, M. K., & Singer, J. L. (1957). Ethnic differences in behavior and psychpathology: Italian and Irish. *International Journal of Social Psychiatry*, 1, 11–17.

Power, P. C. (1993). *Sex and marriage in Ancient Ireland*. Dublin: Mercier Press.

Roberts, B., & Myers, J. K. (1954). Religion, national origin, immigration and mental illness. *American Journal of Psychiatry, 110,* 759–764.

Robinson, M. (1994). Inaugural speech. In K. Donovan, A. Norman Jeffares, & B. Kennelly (Eds.), *Ireland's women.* New York: Norton.

Rossiter, A. (1993). Bringing the margins into the centre: A review of aspects of Irish women's emigration from a British perspective. In A. Smyth (Ed.), *Irish women's studies reader.* Dublin: Attic Press.

Rudd, J. M.(1984). *Irish American families: The mother child dyad.* Doctoral thesis, Smith College School for Social Work, Northampton, MA.

Sanua, V. D. (1960). Sociocultural factors in responses to stressful life situations: The behavior of aged amputees as an example. *Journal of Health and Human Behavior, 1,* 17–24.

Scally, R. J. (1995). *The end of hidden Ireland: Rebellion, famine, and emigration.* New York: Oxford University Press.

Scheper-Hughes, N. D. (1979). *Saints, scholars, and schizophrenics.* Berkeley: University of California Press.

Scherman, K. (1981). *The flowering of Ireland: Saints, scholars and kings.* Boston: Little, Brown.

Singer, J., & Opler, M. K. (1956). Contrasting patterns of fantasy and motility in Irish and Italian Schizophrenics. *Journal of Abnormal and Social Psychology, 53,* 42–47.

Spiegel, J. (1971a) Cultural strain, family role patterns, and intrapsychic conflict. In J. G. Howells (Ed.), *Theory and practice of family psychiatry.* New York: Brunner/Mazel.

Spiegel, J. (1971b). *Transactions: The interplay between individual, family and society* (J. Papajohn, Ed.). New York: Science House.

Stein, R. F. (1971). *Disturbed youth and ethnic family patterns.* Albany: State University of New York Press.

Sternbach, R. A., & Tursky, B. (1965). Ethnic differences among housewives in psychophysical and skin potential responses to electric shock. *Psychophysiology, 1*(3), 241–246.

Stivers, R. (1976). *The hair of the dog: Irish drinking and American stereotype.* University Park, PA: Pennsylvania State University Press.

Teahan, J. E. (1987, July). Alcohol expectancies, values, and drinking of Irish and U.S. collegians. *International Journal of the Addictions, 22*(7), 621–638.

Tursky, B., & Sternbach, R. A. (1967). Further physiological correlates of ethnic differences in response to shock. *Psychophysiology, 4*(1), 67–74.

Walsh, D. (1987), Alcohol and Ireland. *British Journal of Addiction, 82,* 118–120.

Watts, J. F. (1988). *The Irish Americans.* New York: Chelsea House.

Wills, G. (1971). *Bare ruined choirs.* Garden City, NY: Doubleday.

Wylan, L., & Mintz, N. (1976). Ethnic differences in family attitudes toward psychotic manifestations with implications for treatment programmes. *International Journal of Social Psychiatry, 22,* 86–95.

Zborowski, M. (1969). *People in pain.* San Francisco: Jossey-Bass.

Zola, I. K. (1966). Culture and symptoms: An analysis of patients' presenting complaints. *American Sociological Review, 5,* 141–155.

# CHAPTER 38

# Italian Families

## Joe Giordano
## Monica McGoldrick

For Italians, family has been the thread that has provided not only continuity in all situations, but also training to cope with a difficult world. *La via vecchia* (the old way), revered by Italians, symbolizes a value system organized primarily around protecting the family. While all cultures value the family, for Italians, family is an all-consuming ideal (Gambino, 1974; Ianni & Reuss-Ianni, 1972; Johnson, 1985; Mangione & Morreale, 1992). Luigi Barzini (1965), in his book *The Italians*, states that the family is the first source of power among Italians. He continues, "The family extracts everybody's first loyalty. It must be defended, enriched, made powerful, and feared. . . . Its honor must not be tarnished. All wrongs done to it must be avenged. All enemies must be kept at bay and the dangerous ones deprived of power . . ." (p. 193).

Family continues to provide a strong sense of security and identity for many second- and third-generation Italian Americans, although there are others for whom it stifles individual needs and desires for success (Messina, 1994; Riotta-Sirey, Patti, & Mann, 1985; Rolle, 1980).

What is generally referred to as "Italian" by most people in the United States is not representative of all Italian culture. It applies primarily to those who trace their ancestry to the southern section of Italy, commonly known as the Mezzogiorno, who constituted the vast majority of Italian immigrants to the United States. By virtue of geography and economy, Southern Italians have developed different customs, lifestyles, nuances in language, and food preferences from their Northern Italian neighbors.

Because of industrialization, Northern Italians have had the benefit of a thriving economy and a relatively prosperous existence. In contrast, Southern Italians, who have relied on farming for their livelihood, have tended to be poorer, less educated, and somewhat more fatalistic in their outlook on life. As one research team has described it, "The Northerner is a modern capitalist who seeks wealth as a means of acquiring the material objects he wants; the

Southerner seeks wealth as a means of commanding obedience and respect from others. While the North has accepted the modern ethic that power follows wealth, the South clings to the medieval tradition that wealth comes from power" (Ianni & Reuss-Ianni, 1972, p. 16). Poverty and the hope of a better life led to a large-scale Italian migration to the United States in the late 19th and 20th centuries; almost four million came from Southern Italy between 1880 and 1920 (Nelli, 1980).

## HISTORICAL BACKGROUND: ITS IMPACT ON CORE VALUES

Historically, Italy has served as a crossroads from Western to Eastern Europe because it occupies a strategic location on the Mediterranean Sea. It was considered desirable to be in possession of "the boot," as Italy was called, so the country was continually beset by invaders throughout the Middle Ages and into the Renaissance. When foreign armies invaded, Southern Italians could ultimately count only on their own townspeople. Against a backdrop of impinging hostile forces, Italians came to rely primarily on their families and on internal resources.

Value was placed on the personality traits that would provide a cushion against external instability. Adaptability and stoicism became ethnic trademarks. Rather than attempting to alter the course of events, Italians took pride in their ability to cope with difficult situations. Resilience became more than an attitude; it became a way of life. To counter the harshness and fatalism in their daily lives, Italians mastered the ability to fully savor the present, particularly with family gatherings and community festivals. Pleasure from food and eating became central to daily life, with food considered a primary source of emotional and physical solace (Femminella & Quadagno, 1976; Yans-McLaughlin, 1980; Mangione & Morreale, 1992).

### The Immigrants

Between 1900 and 1910, more than two million Italians, mostly peasants from southern Italy, immigrated to the United States to escape poverty and find a better life. The clash of cultures was enormous. Italian cultural attitudes contrasted strongly with dominant American values that emphasized individualism, independence, and personal achievement over group affiliation.

Most of the immigrants preferred urban living, settling primarily in "Little Italies" in cities throughout the mid-Atlantic States and New England. This pattern was largely influenced by the importance they placed on family, neighborhood connections, and relationships in which children would feel obligated to remain close to aging parents (Johnson, 1985; Ragucci, 1981).

Italians took pride in home ownership, not wanting to rent, which would leave them dependent on outsiders. The home was a symbol of the family, not of status, and the family table was at its center. Once they were settled in the New World, Italians tended not to move or travel. Many spent their whole lives in the same neighborhood, never even visiting other parts of the city or town.

Immigrant children often clashed with, or grew distant from, their parents. In America, parental identity was weaker and peer pressure often stronger than in Italy. Some women worked. Socializing networks, including schools, settlement houses, and clubs, existed outside one's immediate neighborhood, while popular culture promoted the values of the dominant society that were antithetical to the Italian American family.

But in the New World, prejudice against Italians grew as their presence increased. Italians were considered inferior, dangerous, uneducated, violent, and criminal. These images have become part of American folklore through the popular media's fascination with the Mafia mystique and movies such as *The Godfather* and *Prizzi's Honor*.

Although the Mafia is comprised almost exclusively of Italian Americans, relatively few belong to it. Yet the Mafia stereotype remains pervasive. A national survey (Response Analysis Corporation, 1989) indicates that three out of four Americans believe that most Italian Americans are connected in some way with organized crime.

Helmreich (1991) points out that historically the term "mafia," has an additional, more benign meaning among Italians:

> It was an adjective used to describe someone who commanded respect, who knew how to "take care of things" without running to the authorities. It referred to an individual who had both power and dignity while also inspiring fear. He was, most importantly, a person whom one could approach when in need. Thus, such a term might be applied to a family patriarch who had no connection with the organization known as the Mafia. (p. 48)

## Religion

In addition to having been at odds with the dominant American values, Italians have also encountered the hostility of the Irish, who dominated the Catholic Church in the United States and ran the parochial schools where Italians frequently sent their children. As Nelli (1980) states, "Italians in America found the Church a cold, remote, puritanical institution, controlled and often staffed, even in Italian neighborhoods, by the Irish. Even devout Italians resented the Irish domination of the local church and early demanded their own priests" (p. 553).

Far from the asceticism of the Irish Catholic Church, Italians prize church rituals more for their pageantry, spectacle, and value in fostering family celebrations and rites of passage than for their religious significance. For most

Italians, God is viewed a more as a benign friend of the family and the Church as a source of ritual and drama, in striking contrast to the Irish dire warnings about the Day of Judgment and emphasis on the Church's authority. However, because the Church represents tradition, family, and community, Italians still tend to support it.

## Achievement, Work, and Education

The disdain Italian immigrants had for spatial mobility was paralleled in their negative view of upward social mobility. The first-generation Italian immigrant interpreted the "American Dream" as the opportunity to obtain steady work and provide food and shelter for the family. Working as a domestic in someone else's home was frowned upon as a usurpation of family loyalty. Italians scrupulously avoided even appearing to exploit friends. Mutual trust was not to be jeopardized under any circumstances. Unwilling to work for outsiders, Italians often started family businesses, which, naturally, added to family solidarity.

Italians have viewed educational training as secondary to the security, affection, and the sense of relatedness the family had to offer. A popular saying in Southern Italy was "Do not make your child better than you are." The term *buon educato* did not refer to a formal education, but to an education in how to act morally and properly within the community. Schools were seen as a waste of time because they did not teach practical learning (La Gumina, 1982; Mangione & Morreale, 1992).

Attitudes toward education, once viewed by the first and second generation as a "threat to family values," have changed, and education is now embraced by the third and fourth generations. For example, in 1980 Italian American students at the City University of New York constituted the largest White ethnic group (Perrone, 1987). However, the value of staying close to family and neighborhood was also evident in another study, which indicated that more than 80% of Italian American students lived at home (Blumberg & Lavin, 1987).

It is not uncommon to hear college-educated Italian Americans express anger at their parents for not giving them enough support and guidance, which has left them feeling quite insecure. A middle-aged professional client said, "I got a strong message to succeed, but my home was void of anything related to learning. There were no books in my house. My parents didn't know how to guide me. When I told my mother I was accepted to a doctoral program she said, 'That's nice. What are you having for supper?' I wanted so much for them to share in my own joy."

In working-class and poorer families, negative attitudes toward education persist. In some large cities, Italian American youngsters have the highest high school dropout rates among White ethnic groups (Calandra Institute, 1990).

By the 1980s, Italian Americans had attained a kind of critical mass in terms of affluence, education, and "political clout." In three generations, they had "made it" from poor illiterate peasants to middle-class Americans (Giordano, 1986; Hall, 1983; Spadaro, in press).

## FAMILY PATTERNS AND ROLES

There is virtually no such thing as a separate nuclear family in Italian culture. Among immigrant and first-generation families, social interactions were guided by *l'ordine della famiglia*, an unwritten but all-demanding complex code of obligations regulating relationships within and outside the family (Gambino, 1974). Within this code family comes first, and members are expected to stay physically and psychologically close, coming together in a crisis and taking care of family members who are vulnerable. Getting married and having children serves to strengthen and expand the family.

Family members must never do anything to hurt (disgrace) the family. They must neither take advantage of other family members nor talk about the family to outsiders. Occasionally, secrets are maintained among family members to protect personal boundaries. Two individuals can maintain a closeness with each other but at the same time distance themselves from others in the family. (This neutralizing the family's engulfing nature may appear dysfunctional to the therapist.) Open expression of emotion is acceptable only within the family.

Third- and fourth-generation Italian Americans often are confused by the family's secrets and alliances and sometimes rebel against these dynamics, causing intergenerational conflicts (Papajohn & Spiegel, 1975); or they may find themselves "going along" with the family "to keep peace." However, they are often surprised to repeat as parents the behavior they rejected in their own families (Santo, 1984). This is often expressed by giving children a "double message." While encouraging their children to "get a good education," they will also convey another strong, more subtle message: "Do not leave the family. Do not attend school out of state."

For many upwardly mobile third- and fourth-generation Italian Americans, there is often an acute conflict between familial solidarity and America's emphasis on autonomy and individualization. And despite their rise into the middle class and the professions, Italian Americans often verbalize a sense of inferiority and lack of acceptance with their success. This conflict may engender conscious and unconscious feelings of shame, self-hatred, and identity confusion (Giordano, 1994; Rolle, 1980; Riotta-Sirey, Patti, & Mann, 1985).

The following discussion outlines traditional Italian family roles. Although clearly undergoing change, therapists can judge for themselves the extent to which these patterns apply to any particular Italian American family.

## The Father

Traditionally, the father has been the undisputed head of the household, often authoritarian and rigid in his rule setting and guidelines for behavior. His role has been to provide for and protect the family, and he has tended to be viewed as the family sage who could (and should) provide the right solutions to any problem. Family members cater to his desires, particularly around food. The father protects and coddles his daughters, teaches his sons to be like him, and demands ultimate respect from his wife and children.

In keeping with the cultural emphasis on food, Italian men pay a great deal of attention to whether their wives can cook as well as their mothers, and women take great pride in their culinary skills. One Italian patient stated that his marriage almost broke up during the first 2 years, until he got his mother to teach his non-Italian wife how to cook. The changing role of women in our society may naturally place great strain on Italian men who were raised in a traditional context.

## The Mother

In a traditional Italian family, the mother promotes emotional sustenance and is revered. Although her husband's needs take precedence over her own, she has a considerable amount of control within the home, running the household and taking pride in her domestic abilities. Sons perceive their mothers as all-powerful, and daughters see them as difficult role models to emulate. The mother acts as a buffer between her husband and her sons and is permitted to express her feelings in public—a luxury denied fathers (Michaud, 1990; Messina, 1994).

Marital intimacy is not a high priority (Aronson, 1979). The mutual support and complementarity of roles between husband and wife relate to their obligations to the entire family of at least three generations, not to marital sharing of emotions. Given this heritage, young couples of Italian background may not have models within their extended families for resolving martial issues through negotiation and role flexibility, as is encouraged in most marital therapy.

## Gender Issues

For many young Italian Americans, ethnic ambivalence is expressed in heterosexual relationships. In ethnotherapy groups—run to help Italian Americans explore their ethnic identity (Giordano & Riotta-Sirey, 1981; Riotta-Sirey et al., 1985)—members of each sex attribute to the other gender negative stereotypes. Men's perceptions of women reflect a wish for the traditional role (women as mothers, cooks) and anger at both old behaviors (smothering or controlling) and new, more assertive roles as women become educated professionals. Women verbalize a greater resentment and anger toward traditional male domination and assumed superiority. They naturally express indignance about their unequal status in the family.

Although wishing to hold on to the positive aspects of their Italian American identity, women clearly no longer want to be subjected to an unequal status. But men, although intellectually acknowledging that domination is not an acceptable way to relate to women, generally have been slow to change their behavior. This conflict over traditional gender roles is one of many reasons why both Italian American men and women are seeking out relationships with non-Italians in greater numbers than ever before. More than 80% of Italian Americans are marrying persons of a different ethnicity (Alba, 1985; Crohn, 1995).

## Children

There is a marked role differentiation between sons and daughters in Italian families. Sons are given much greater latitude prior to marriage. Indeed, a bit of acting out is expected, even subtly encouraged, as a measure of manliness. Sexual proficiency is especially important, not only to fulfill the masculine image, but also to exemplify a sense of mastery in interpersonal relations—a core Italian value.

Although cultivating social skills has been considered important for girls as well, they have been more restricted than their brothers and boy cousins. Daughters have been given more guidance and supervision and, in particular, have been taught to eschew personal achievement in favor of respect and service to their parents and brothers. Frequently, young Italian women say that their adult status was not really accepted by their parents, even after career and marital success, until they produced children themselves.

Children's needs do not govern family goals or direction. Parents have little involvement in the personal problems of their children, who are expected to take responsibility for their lives outside the home. From a very young age, children are talked to and expected to act like adults, and in ways that are pleasing to adults. Cross-sex ties are strongest, particularly the mother–son bond, and daughters are expected to take care of sick or aging parents.

Generally speaking, Italian children have shown less conflict about accepting their ethnic background than have other ethnic groups, but they have shown more conflict about upwardly mobile aspirations, which their families can find threatening. This contrasts with many other groups, in which children are more likely to feel anxious that they will *not* live up to their parents' ambitions for upward mobility.

## Extended Family

The extended family plays a central role in all aspects of Italian family life, including decision making. Members of the extended family often live in the same neighborhood. Family members are expected not only to work hard, but also to enjoy life and share food, music, and companionship with loved ones. Respect for and taking care of older family members is a strong norm. In working with these families, it is essential to learn the location and level of contact with relatives.

The family code also governs relationships outside the family. Family members should owe nothing to those outside the family, be unconcerned with the activities and behavior of "outsiders," and show respect—but not trust—for outside authority.

## Life Cycle Issues

There is virtually no such thing as a separate nuclear family unit in Italian culture. Throughout the life cycle, they think of relationships from an extremely inclusive perspective, and their primary life cycle difficulties have to do with stages involving separation, in particular "launching" and death. Indeed, it has been said that there is no such thing as launching in an Italian family, that the parents just send their children out far enough to find partners who are then brought into the family circle, which then is expanded. The network of significant others is usually large, including aunts, uncles, cousins, *gumbares* (old friends and neighbors), as well as godparents, who assume a role of great importance in child rearing.

Unlike the British, who raise children to be independent and self-sufficient above all else, and who think themselves failures if their children do not leave home on schedule, Italians raise their children to be mutually supportive and to contribute to the family. Separation from the family is not desired, expected, or easily accepted. The other most difficult life cycle phase is that involving death of a family member. Because separation is the most painful experience for Italian families, generally they deal with death emotionally, with much expression of feeling and profound experiences of pain and loss. Most intense may be the pain of the loss of a mother, or a mother's pain over the loss of her child.

It is not unusual for parents and grandparents to maintain daily contact. In one example, the father for years went to his mother's house next door for dinner each night before coming home to his nuclear family. Generally, each family member has a well-delineated role that dictates both the pattern and frequency of contact with various other family members.

## Acculturation

Integration into U.S. life has not been without its price for Italians. It has been accompanied by a confusion of identity that has left second- and third-generation Italian Americans feeling not quite American and certainly not Italian in the sense of the traditions described earlier. For example, second-generation Italian Americans often find that sticking close to home is not heavily rewarded in the United States, and they begin to question the tremendous allegiance to family. In fact, they may be in continuous conflict with other family members, who feel neglected or abandoned by them and may simultaneously experience an internal bewilderment—or even despair—as a result of the mixed messages they are receiving from their families and society.

The second generation may have the greatest problem developing a positive sense of identity, since they are most vulnerable to internalizing negative images that the larger culture has about them. To accommodate to the dominant society, this group often has denied a good portion of their Italian heritage. The result has sometimes been a discomfort with signs and symbols of ethnicity, such as names, styles of dress, and language. By the third generation, family ties have generally loosened, reflecting values shared by the larger culture. In-group solidarity has diminished, however, and Italian Americans may indeed feel a void or sense of personal anomie.

A shift in family roles has gone hand in hand with the breakdown of family ties. In the transition from the first to the second generation, Italian fathers may lose their high status and power in decision making; however, this loss, which is actually the product of shifting cultural values, is often experienced by the Italian man as a loss of self-esteem. As he begins to share power with his wife, the Italian husband is likely to feel that the discrepancy between present attitudes and those prevailing in his father's time results from his personal failure to command the proper respect. Thus, he may exhibit an increase in defensiveness and insecurity regarding his "maleness," which is often manifested clinically as depression.

By the third generation, most Italian Americans have, at least to a degree, accommodated to the prevailing norms and have adopted the customs, lifestyles, and language of the larger culture. They often have looser connections with nuclear and extended family members, may have moved to a different neighborhood, married a non-Italian, and developed relationships with many non-Italians. Ironically, it is third-generation Italian Americans who sometimes embrace the very same aspects of culture their parents (second generation) rejected in their immigrant grandparents (first generation). Much of the tension about cultural identity has subsided, and they may be less conflicted about their Italian ethnicity than their parents.

## Implications for Family Therapy

Not surprisingly, Italian Americans have tended to turn to the family for help in solving problems, and not toward available mental health services (Cleary & Demone, 1988; Femminella, 1982; Rabkin & Struening, 1975). When they do seek help, the problem is likely to have reached a serious level, and they may feel shame about not being able to handle the difficulty themselves.

The therapist first needs to convey reassurance that the patient is not to blame—and to assume that any intervention to solve the problem(s) will involve the family. However, because everyone outside the family is mistrusted until proven trustworthy, gaining acceptance as an outsider involves not taking the family's initial mistrust personally.

In the early sessions, the therapist sometimes can build trust by honestly sharing common values. In fact, responding in this way makes the therapist seem warm and approachable. It is also helpful to curtail probing until trust is established. Some families interpret extensive questioning as a message that they are "not smart enough," rather than as a way to "get at the truth" or "gain insight." Once a therapist wins the family's trust, most of the therapy will revolve around helping family members establish new boundaries and reducing guilt and fear of separation.

For Italian American fathers, particularly, therapy may be threatening, because it implies they are incapable of remaining in control of their families. The father may appear open and direct, but will often find ways to elude and rationalize away a problem to "save face."

The therapist's first encounter with the family may be quite lively. Italian Americans often are very engaging and colorful speakers; when under stress, their expressiveness can become exaggerated. This may take the form of loud-pitched voices, elaborate gesturing, or arguments among family members. In early visits with an Italian family, as in any good evaluation, it is important to be alert to the differences between style and content.

The expressive intensity of the Italian family may be overpowering to a therapist from a more restrained culture in which, for example, powerful verbal expressions would be interpreted literally. For Italians, words are not meant literally. They give expression to the moment; their purpose is not logical or measured. Italian families can also be vague, giving overdetailed narratives on how a problem began and elaborating the emotional and physical sensations they are experiencing.

They are likely to spend a great deal of time discussing the emotional impact and the social context of the problem, as well as any physical sensations (Zola, 1966). They have been shown to have a lower pain threshold than other groups, reflecting their sensitivity to their immediate physical and emotional experience (Zborowski, 1964). They also tend to somatize and have much concern and awareness about the connections between their emotional and physical well-being.

Italians typically deny difficult problems; "hot" issues are not openly discussed. The therapist should attend to what is not being said, particularly since Italians do more sidestepping than most in the initial stage of therapy, which is an outgrowth of their unwillingness to expose private subjects to outsiders.

This presentation and the related "dancing" around issues fit into the Italian cultural context. Although Italians may talk readily about most life experiences, family members are ashamed about having to go outside the family for help. The implication is that if they had greater control over themselves, their impulses, their family, and so forth, these problems would never have developed to the point of needing an outsider.

If the family is in a "crisis," it is essential to avoid lengthy analysis and give members some response to their problem. Even a seemingly benign or insignificant suggestion might be sufficient to "hold" a family until more enduring interventions can be found. But it is best not to offer advice that undercuts a family's authority.

To Italian Americans, resolving a problem often means relieving stress without changing the family's equilibrium—in other words, "getting things back to normal." Because parents are more receptive to assistance for their children, joining the family around a child-focused problem can break through family resistance. Such intervention is best tolerated in the form of "advice" rather than "exploration." Third- and fourth-generation Italian Americans, who hope to find a healthy balance between individual needs and strong familial connections, are more likely to take risks in therapy.

Although Italian families may appear to talk openly and engagingly, even in the initial contact, sharing real family secrets is an entirely different matter. Italian families are full of "secrets," as the therapist will soon learn by asking a question that is out of bounds. The existence of secrets may be puzzling to the therapist since the family seems to talk openly about all kinds of issues, including sex, bodily functions, and hostility. The content of the secret is often not important. Secrets tend to be aimed more at preserving the boundaries of the system—clarifying who is inside and who is not. Therapists must deal delicately with secrets, being aware of the sense of betrayal families will feel if the boundaries are crossed. The content of secrets is often not important to the therapy, and the therapist is advised to proceed on the assumption that the secret is a boundary-keeping maneuver until clinical evidence indicates otherwise. Pushing the family to tell its secrets will usually only heighten mistrust and resistance. In general, therapists must adjust the depth and range of topics addressed to the degree of their closeness with family members and not press with questions that might jeopardize their position with the family.

The method developed by Italian psychiatrist Mara Selvini Palazzoli (Selvini Palazzoli, Cirillo, Selvini, & Sorrentino, 1989) for working with very rigid families revolves around getting the parents into collusion with the therapists to "keep a secret to the grave," excluding everyone else in the entire family from information about the therapeutic suggestions. The power of secrets as boundary markers in Italian families makes this ritual an extraordinarily good strategy with them. In general, Selvini Palazzoli considers a family member's offer to reveal a secret as one of the major "snares" in family therapy.

As therapy proceeds, the therapist should constantly find ways to reinforce the family's problem-solving abilities. It's important to affirm values of protection, loyalty, respect, and identity, as well as attributes of hard work, warmth, and spontaneity. Even when the extended family does not exist or is dysfunctional, such values may be integral to members' personal and group identity. Labeling Italian Americans' intense involvement with each other as "intrusive and inappropriate" (much less "pathological") and quickly intervening to change this behavior without also communicating that the involvement is a positive expression of the family's caring, probably only increase the family's anxiety and resistance.

The therapeutic ideals of the dominant society—individuation, mastery over problems, and economic advancement—are not particularly compatible with Italian core values, and Italians may not take as an inalienable right their ability to master the problems they confront. The most they may expect is to get a portion of their needs met through their own personal attributes, and it is understandable why they often choose indirect methods (cunning, guile, or cleverness) to achieve a measure of personal efficacy and power. This tendency does not necessarily indicate a sociopathic inclination, but rather a reflection of a historically successful method of obtaining rewards. Rather than trying to eliminate these behaviors, treatment might be geared toward utilizing them in a socially appropriate manner. For third- and fourth-generation families, a frequent challenge is to help members gain greater self-differentiation, without causing others pain or cutting off relationships. Usually these individuals want closeness to family as well as autonomy.

Therapists would do best to encourage Italian Americans to negotiate their individuality within the family, even though this is a painful process and not easily accomplished. Because of the deep meaning of family to Italians, the price they pay for emotional disconnection is high. They are usually relieved and grateful to find ways to become reconnected to their families without becoming engulfed. Coaching family members usually involves encouraging them to space out family contacts, while advocating a high degree of emotional expressiveness when they are with their families. Clients need to be prepared at each step of differentiation to deal with their families' intense reactions, which include feelings of betrayal, abandonment, and rejection.

Yet, even a suggestion of separation or distancing may be a "red flag" for an Italian American family. Normal separations related to life cycle changes—a job promotion or getting married—can become sources of conflict, leading parents to "hold back" feelings of pride in their children's accomplishments. Their children, in turn, may become confused and angry at the parents for their lack of enthuiasm for their success.

The intense feelings surrounding separation and individuality are further complicated when a family is dealing with the issue of homosexuality. Italian American attitudes toward the recognition and acceptance of homosexuality are far below that of the general public. Despite the fact that there are many gay people who are of Italian American heritage, the subject is avoided because it is abhorrent to most Italian Americans. A gay family member may therefore refuse to deal with this issue, because of fear of being cut off by the family or causing its members hurt and shame. At the same time, Italian American loyalty to the group can create enormous emotional conflict for the gay person torn between loyalty to family and to the gay community. This may lead the family to open its hearts to the gay member rather than accept the even more painful alternative of separation and loss.

The therapist often must learn to differentiate between intense closeness and pathological enmeshment in Italian American families. Reframing the issue as a problem of uncompromising and unyielding "boundaries" may be important but the therapist must make clear that he or she is not challenging their desire to stay close.

In the final phase of treatment, the therapist will be presented with the therapeutic issue of how to extricate him- or herself from the system. Families may attempt to "absorb" therapists and make them auxiliary family members. Somehow the therapist must find ways to avoid becoming sucked into the system as a member, while being sufficiently engaging to maintain respect and connection. The special techniques developed by the Milan Group in Italy seem particularly well suited to the "enmeshment" of Italian American families as well (Selvini Palazzoli et al., 1989). They maintain connection by meeting generally with the family as a whole and distance by using the stance of doctor/consultant, who asks questions and then gives an evaluation and a prescription. The group places much emphasis on keeping out of the family process, using a team, a one-way window, and videotaping as tools for this. Their focus is on gathering information about the evolutionary connections among family members that are rigidifying the family process, impeding flexibility, and prohibiting further family development. They aim for an intervention that is dramatic enough to create new motion in the family and yet leave the therapists out of the actual changes. They take great pains to keep their focus and interventions on the family as a whole, a factor of special importance with Italian families. By carefully addressing themselves to the family's myths and values, as well as to their systemic interdependencies, the Milan Group tries to push the family toward a new pattern.

Bowen systems therapy (1978) also focuses on understanding and shifting the family process while staying out of the system, but avoids dramatic interventions, which could prevent the engagement necessary for Italian families to make use of Bowen's approach. However, the Bowen model appears to be the treatment of choice with Italians who have already distanced from their families, since its primary focus is differentiation through personalized connectedness. An important problem for Italian Americans who move away from their families is the loneliness and isolation they may feel, despite success by "mainstream" criteria—money, education, social status. Often, young Italian Americans seek therapy to support their separating from their families in attempts at pseudoindependence. Therapists may mistakenly foster this by emphasizing the individual experience over the need to maintain interpersonal connectedness. The family context is so deeply rooted for Italians that other structures will usually be shallow and inadequate by comparison.

## CONCLUSION

Although several striking departures from American customs have been outlined, it may be most constructive to consider these ethnic proclivities as potential strengths, rather than as impediments to therapy. For most Italian Americans, the core values that have endured are likely to persist. Foremost among these is the primacy of personal relationships, particularly close relationships with family and friends, enjoyment of home life, and respect for parental authority within the home. These strengths have enormous potential for the therapist to enlist in family treatment.

## REFERENCES

Alba, R. (1985). *Italian Americans: Into the twilight of ethnicity.* Englewood Cliffs, NJ: Prentice-Hall.

Aronson, S. (1979). Rankings of intimacy of social behaviors by Italians and Americans. *Psychological Reports, 44,* 1149–1150.

Barzini, L. (1964). *The Italians.* New York: Atheneum.

Blumberg, A., & Lavin, D. (1987). Italian-American students in the City University of New York: A socio-economic and education profile. In R. Gambino (Ed.), *Italian-American studies at City University of New York: Report and recommendations* (p. 85). New York: City University of New York Press.

Bowen, M. (1978). *The use of family therapy in clinical practice.* New York: Aronson.

Calandra Institute. (1990). *Education achievement level of Italian-American students in New York City public schools.* New York: Author.

Cleary, P., & Demone, H. (1988). Health and social service needs in a Northeastern metropolitan area: Ethnic group differences. *Journal of Sociology and Social Welfare, 15*(4), 63–76.

Crohn, J. (1995). *Mixed matches—How to create successful interracial, interethnic and interfaith marriages.* New York: Fawcett Columbine.

Femminella, F. (1982). Social psychiatry in the Italian American community. In R. Caporale (Ed.), *Italian Americans through generations.* New York: American Italian Historical Association.

Femminella, F., & Quadagno, J. (1976). The Italian American family. In C. Mindel & R. Habenstein (Eds.), *Ethnic families in America* (pp. 61–88). New York. Elsevier.

Gambino, R. (1974). *Blood of my blood: The dilemma of Italian-Americans.* New York: Doubleday.

Giordano, J. (1986). *The Italian American catalog.* New York: Doubleday.

Giordano, J. (1994, June 13). The shame we share in secret. *Newsday,* p. 25.

Giordano, J., & Riotta-Sirey, A. (1981). *An Italian-American identity.* Unpublished manuscript, Institute for American Pluralism, American Jewish Committee, New York.

Hall, S. (1983, May 15). Italian-Americans coming into their own. *New York Times Magazine,* pp. 15, 28–57.

Helmreich, W. (1991). *The things they say behind your back.* New Brunswick, NJ: Transaction Publishers.

Ianni, P. A., & Reuss-Ianni, E. (1972). *A family business: Kinship and social control in organized crime.* New York: Russell Sage.

Johnson, C. (1985). *Growing up and growing old in Italian-American families.* New Brunswick, NJ: Rutgers University Press.

La Gumina, S. (1988). *From steerage to suburb.* New York: Center for Migration Studies.

Mangione, J., & Morreale, B. (1992). *La storia: Five centuries of the Italian American experience.* New York: HarperCollins.

Messina, E. (1994). Life-span development and Italian-American women. In J. Krase & J. DeSena (Eds.), *Italian-Americans in a multicultural society* (pp. 74–87). New York: American Historical Society.

Michaud, T. G. (1990). Italian mothers: Ethnicity and mothers. *Journal of Feminist Family Therapy, 2*(2), 53–58.

Nelli, H. S. (1980). Italians. In S. Thernstrom, A. Orlov, & O. Handlin (Eds.), *The Harvard encyclopedia of American ethnic groups* (pp. 545–560). Cambridge, MA: Harvard University Press.

Papajohn, J., & Spiegel, J. (1975). *Transactions in families.* San Francisco: Jossey-Bass.

Perrone, J. (1987). Italian-American students at CUNY: A psychoeducational profile. In R. Gambino (Ed.), *Italian-American studies and Italian-Americans at City University of New York: Report and recommendations* (p. 92). New York: City University of New York Press.

Rabkin, J., & Struening, E. (1975). *Ethnicity, social class and mental illness in New York City: A social area analysis of five ethnic groups* (Working Paper No. 17). New York: American Jewish Committee.

Ragucci, A. T. (1981). Italian Americans. In A. Hargood (Ed.), *Ethnicity and medical care* (pp. 211–263). Cambridge, MA: Harvard University Press.

Response Analysis Corporation. (1989). *Americans of Italian descent: A study of public images, beliefs and misperceptions.* Princeton, NJ: Order of the Sons of Italy.

Riotta-Sirey, A., Patti, A., & Mann. L. (1985). *Ethnotherapy—An exploration of Italian-American identity.* New York: National Institute for Psychotherapists.

Rolle, A. (1980). *The Italian American: Troubled roots.* New York: Free Press.

Santo, L. (1984). *Parental identity: Harmonizing ethnic traditions and contemporary values.* New York: American Jewish Committee.

Selvini Palazzoli, M., Cirillo, S., Selvini, M. & Sorrentino, M. (1989). *Family games.* New York: Norton.

Spadaro, T. (in press). *Myths and realities: The evolution of an Italian American identity.*

Yans-McLaughlin, V. (1980). *Family and community.* Urbana: University of Illinois Press.

Zborowski, M. (1964). *People in pain.* San Francisco: Jossey-Bass.

Zola, I. K. (1966). Culture and symptoms—An analysis of patients' presenting complaints. *American Sociological Review, 5,* 615–630.

CHAPTER 39

# Portuguese Families

## Zarita A. Araújo

To work successfully with Portuguese families, the therapist must be aware of
the interwoven effects of history, geography, politics, and the immigration
experience. These factors shape four major dynamics present in Portuguese
immigrant families: fear of loss, fatalism toward life, ambivalence toward authority, and a drive for financial independence. Therapists should also recognize the characteristics of the three separate waves of Portuguese immigration
to the United States. After a family immigrates, one can identify three acculturation stages: honeymoon, anger and loss, and negotiation and acceptance.
These three stages can powerfully inform the therapeutic approach. Finally,
to develop trust and rapport, the therapist needs to understand four distinctive cultural values: *honra* (honor), *respeito* (respect), *bondade* (goodness), and
*confiança* (trust).

## HISTORY, POLITICS, AND GEOGRAPHY

Portugal went from being a great nation in the 15th century, with a spirit of
adventure and scientific nautical knowledge, to a country in financial crisis in
the 20th century. As a result, more than 1.5 million Portuguese immigrants
currently are living in the United States. A great majority are from rural Azores,
some from the mainland, and fewer from the Madeira islands. They have settled
mainly in New England, California, and Hawaii.

The Azores is an archipelago of nine volcanic islands in the North Atlantic about 800 miles west of Lisbon. They were discovered in the early 1400s
and later settled by continental Portuguese and various European populations.
The Azoreans often felt at a disadvantage in relation to the mainland (Marques,
1975; Moitoza, 1982). They felt oppressed by the centralized government in
the mainland, although they were not colonized.

The Crusades during the 15th century led Portugal to the discovery and colonization of South America (Brazil), Asia (Goa, Damão, Dio, Macau, and Timor) and Africa (Guinea-Bissau, Angola, Mozambique, Cape Verdean Islands). After several centuries of development as a colonial empire, Portugal's monarchy fell. A republic was established in the early 1900s.

Portugal was then embroiled in a civil uprising between the monarchists and the republicans for 15 years. This political instability drove the country into the hands of a fascist government led by Antonio de Oliveira Salazar in 1925 (Marques,1975). He implemented strict tax policies and a secret police (PIDE), which often tortured or killed citizens. Poverty was rampant in some parts of Portugal. Landowners paid no more than a bottle of wine, some food, and a few cents for a day's labor until as late as 1974.

Portugal's African colonies fought for years for their sovereignty. Eventually the army itself led a revolution and on April 25, 1974 overthrew the fascist government. The colonies won their independence, but the Azoreans did not benefit as rapidly as the mainland from the ensuing economic and social reforms. In 1975, an Azorean independence movement was created which successfully pressured the Portuguese government to establish an autonomous government (Handler,1976).

By this time Portuguese had become one of the most widely spoken languages in the world. However, it is important for clinicians to be aware that all Portuguese speaking countries are not the same. Indeed, there may be tensions between Brazilians, Azoreans, Angolans, Goans, and mainland Portuguese that have deep roots in the history of Portugal's colonization and exploitation of other countries.

## IMMIGRATION TO THE UNITED STATES

Portuguese immigration has occurred in three major waves. Each wave has a particular set of socioeconomic characteristics precipitating the influx of immigrants to America. The first wave of Portuguese immigration to the United States in the early 1830s was motivated by a need for Portuguese whalers in the waters of New England, California, and Hawaii. These immigrants were males who left their families in Portugal and visited them sporadically. Wives and children who remained in Portugal were supported by older males and extended family networks. The women were responsible for house and child-rearing duties, and the men left in Portugal were responsible for earning money to support the family. These extended families were crucial for the emotional and financial survival of families in Portugal.

The second wave of immigration began in the late 19th century and continued until 1974. It began when entire families from the Azores and Madeira settled as agrarian workers in California, Hawaii, and New England. As the need for industrial manpower increased in the United States, Portuguese families began to work in textile and leather factories (Handler, 1976). Many of these first- and second-generation immigrant families returned to Portugal during the depression years. Their children resumed life in the United States as the economy began to recover. Natural disasters, such as volcanic eruptions in the Azores in 1957 and political instability surrounding the guerrilla war in Africa, led to further immigration to the United States.

These families were often separated from their extended families back in Portugal. They felt vulnerable and became more rigid in their values without the support from the village and their family members. They settled in communities in the United States already populated with Portuguese people from their home towns. The values of the second wave of immigrants reflected those of an insular group from an agrarian Catholic tradition. They coped with the stresses of a strange country and new religious and political forces by isolating themselves and turning inward.

Azoreans had not only lived in fear of volcanic eruptions, but also suffered from political oppression during the fascist regime (McGill, 1980). For them, trust had consistently been broken by laws that encouraged citizens to betray others to the secret police in exchange for material rewards (Riegelhaupt, 1979). Laws prevented people from meeting in groups to express their grievances. Often, local civil servants were informants for the secret police, creating an environment of fear throughout Portugal (Riegelhaupt, 1979). Jobs or bank loans were mainly exchanged for personal favors (*cunha*). Portuguese peasants learned not to trust others but to seek solutions to their economic problems through individual effort.

When settling in the United States, many families attempted to maintain a familiar lifestyle with extended family members living next door. However families lost the ability to help each other as they had back in their rural towns because they had to work two jobs to make ends meet and had no time to care for each other (Moitoza, 1982). The structure of the family changed as women began working outside the home and children needed to take on adult roles. Men, feeling the loss of economic power and of their traditional role as the sole providers, often became depressed and rigid or gave up trying to participate in family life at all. Women were faced with raising their children alone, helping their husbands to cope with their losses, and working full time outside the home (McGill, 1980). These stresses further isolated immigrant families as they became suspicious of outsiders and politely avoided any disclosure that might jeopardize the family's honor.

The third major immigration wave, which began in 1974, consists of three major groups. One group, a mixture of unskilled laborers and the children of the Azorean bourgeoisie, came predominantly from the Azores where they feared a communist takeover. A second strand, the *Retornados*, were forced out of the former colonies and returned to Portugal. There they could not find jobs and immigrated once again to Brazil or other European countries before arriving in the United States. These *Retornados,* who have histories of repeated immigration before settling in the United States, differ from the first-time immigrants coming from the Azores. They are more prepared for urban life, learning English, and asserting themselves in the job market. This self-confident attitude toward life makes them more trusting and better prepared to seek mental health services. The third strand came from the Azores during the 1980s, following severe earthquakes, and from the North of Portugal, in response to financial problems.

The most recent wave is distinct for its mixture of classes and its urban background. These families appear to be less isolated, and the women seem to have gained more economic and social mobility, changing the traditional family structure. The men seem more willing to compromise as providers and child caretakers. However, they still show symptoms of depression, self-medicated with alcohol. Although this group of immigrants is more open to the challenges of urbanization, they still carry a distrust for therapists and authority.

## POSTIMMIGRATION STAGES

In my practice I have noticed that most Portuguese immigrants go through three distinct stages of acculturation. At first the immigrant falls in love with the United States, a period I called the *honeymoon* stage. The houses look beautiful, the cars and the appliances are bigger, and people dress in brighter colors. Parents may be tolerant of their children's attempts to try out different aspects of the culture, such as loud music and nontraditional clothes. Later, as immigrants become frustrated that their dreams are not coming true, they become more aware of the difficulties with finding jobs, language barriers, and the inability to have their Portuguese education recognized. This marks the second stage of *anger and loss.* Parents and children may no longer be spending time together because, once again, their overriding priority is to survive financially. They start to idealize their homeland culture, beliefs, and language, and become critical of earlier immigrants for having adapted to American ways too readily. Parents yearning for the familiar may be very guarded about having their children socialize outside of the family. As a result of children learning English, while parents continue to speak Portuguese, communication is sometimes limited to negative commands and answers.

As families continue to survive, they begin to integrate components of the new culture with the old, entering a third stage of acculturation: *negotiation and acceptance.* In this stage, parents might be fluent in English or at least speak broken English, allowing better communication between parent and child. These families will register their children in Portuguese cultural activities such as the *Rancho folclórico* (folk dancing group) and encourage participation in mainstream activities such as summer programs, day care, and preschool enrollment instead of family day care. Parents in this stage will allow their children to disagree openly with authority (new) as long as they show respect (old).

## FEAR OF LOSS, FATALISM, AMBIVALENCE TOWARD AUTHORITY, AND STRIVING FOR FINANCIAL SECURITY

There are four dynamics that will influence the personality of many Portuguese immigrants. These dynamics have geographic, historical, and political roots. The first dynamic is the *fear of loss*. Historically, the Portuguese have always been aware of having lost an empire. This historical trauma is an undercurrent of everyday Portuguese life as evidenced by feelings that investments or belongings could be easily lost at any time. The 50 years of fascism also accentuated this fear of loss. People could not trust friends, coworkers, or authorities. An expression of an opinion considered unacceptable by the government would have lead to denunciation and imprisonment, severing contact with one's family and loved ones.

The experience of immigration presents several major losses. Immigrants leave their homeland, wishing to return, but knowing that it may never be possible. The dynamics of the family change, and there are new demands on women and children due to language, cultural, and financial issues. This loss is felt most by the adult men who feel that they have lost power in the family, as discussed earlier.

The second major dynamic is the sense of fatalism carried by the immigrant families. Although Portuguese families have happy celebrations and are playful, they also live under a cloud of sadness and intense feelings of hopelessness. Throughout history, the mainland was constantly occupied by different invaders, creating a feeling of hopelessness and inability to protect their land and their families. In the Azores, there is an especially profound sense of fatalism due to the effects of both human history and nature (Moitoza, 1982; McGill, 1980). Historically, the Azores were a target for rapacious pirates. Some of the islands have expressions of fear and dismay that refer to warnings announcing the pirates' arrival so that women could seek refuge. The constant threat of earthquakes and storms also led to a sense of helplessness. This feeling of having little control over external forces is called *destino*, which Portuguese hoped they could overcome by respecting others and following directions from authority.

Often this wish to have more control over life is expressed through a deep ambivalent feeling toward authority, the third major dynamic. The Portuguese will seek a cure with one clinician and, without notice, will search for others to help them with the same problem. It is out of politeness that the client will not inform the clinician of their concerns or dissatisfaction, so, possibly, they will maintain parallel relationships with different kinds of providers. This is an important feature for clinicians to acknowledge when providing treatment to Portuguese families.

The fourth dynamic is the drive for financial security. The Portuguese will work at two jobs trying to be good providers. Children will also work alongside their parents rather than attend school. Portuguese believe that schooling is for the rich and the aristocratic; the way out of poverty is to buy land or immigrate.

This dream of financial security often leads Portuguese immigrant families into difficult family situations. The father becomes an outsider, the mother still keeps the house and handles child care while working a full-time job. The children are asked to perform adult tasks. Slowly, the family is faced with great role confusion and with little time to address it. The goal is to earn money to pay bills, buy a house, cover traveling expenses, or send money to family members in Portugal. Often, the children's education is interrupted so that the family can keep up with their financial goals. This strong financial commitment is observed in other ethnic groups, but rarely to the point of sacrificing schooling. Unlike Jewish, Asian, and Haitian immigrants—who view academia as a source of pride and an investment in the future—the Portuguese focus on the financial dream of the present, working multiple jobs and long hours.

## INITIAL STAGES OF WORK WITH A PORTUGUESE FAMILY

Four key values—*honra* (honor), *respeito* (respect), *bondade* (goodness), and *confiança* (trust)—are extremely helpful when intervening with Portuguese families. The clinician should work closely with the referral source to engage the family and to get past their embarrassment at needing treatment. They are likely to experience a referral as violating their *honra*, which for the Portuguese comes before everything. A family may respond by denying the problem, blaming the symptom carrier, then blaming other family members, friends, and finally the referral source. Another strong value with deep roots in a fascist country is *respeito*. Respecting others is a wonderful gift that gets passed from generation to generation. However, in Portuguese culture it becomes at times a hierarchical, unilateral dynamic: the younger should respect the older by not questioning; the weaker should respect the stronger by following orders.

Portuguese families generally show respect toward authority figures such as bosses, parents, doctors, and teachers. They may not agree with them but never let them know. The respect for authority may be perceived by clinicians as a sign of agreement. Most clients will show little discomfort through their body language when not comfortable with sessions. A similar attitude toward authority may be observed in the Asian and Latino cultures, where families might be smiling and compliant but not agreeing with the request.

The third value, *bondade*, is to act generously, such as sacrificing the self for the sake of others. Catholicism seems to have greatly influenced this value through the concept of sacrifice. Immigrant parents express this sacrifice by working at two jobs so they can provide for their children. *Bondade* is also described as the ability to forgive others although they may be inflicting or have inflicted suffering. The clinician will have to show empathy for the person's willingness to suffer for the sake of others.

The fourth value, *confiança*, is a sense of connectedness and trust. For example, *confiança* exists when the therapeutic alliance is established, and the family can comfortably joke or talk about their ambivalent feelings when seeking treatment.

The following case illustrates the four values:

Rui, a 13-year-old, first-generation Luso American boy, was referred to me a few years ago by his eighth-grade special education teacher. He was having sudden outbursts of anger at peers and his teacher. Rui's parents immigrated from the Azores in 1978 as older teenagers and both had had previous marriages. Rui was a product of his mother's first marriage. He never lived with his biological father, who returned to Portugal before his birth. His mother and step-father lived together since Rui was 4 years old. Both parents were working two jobs. Rui either was cared for by the neighbors or stayed home watching television until one of the parents came home to feed him.

At first, Senhora Rita showed reluctance at having a Portuguese therapist meet with her son. After several notes from the teacher, translated into Portuguese, the mother gave permission for her son to be seen. I met with Rui for about three sessions and assigned him the homework of being the family historian. Rui became more interactive with his parents, allowing me to connect with his mother. I scheduled the first family session at their home. Senhor Manuel reluctantly joined the session. We discussed his reluctance, the fact that he had adopted Rui, and his difficulties adapting to a new world. The following sessions were tenuous, I never knew when the parents were going to disappear from therapy. However, tensions began to ease as I began providing the family with concrete ways of clarifying their roles. The couple stated that they missed having time together. The father became very depressed during the sessions; he was feeling powerless in his family and at his work. The turning point in the family treatment was when the father was able to verbalize his sadness and losses due to immigration. This was facilitated by the increase in communication between father, mother, and son. Rui became less depressed and started to do better in school. The couple worked on their relationship and each agreed to give up his or her second job. Throughout the 11 sessions, I consulted with Rui's teacher on a weekly basis and coached her on the concepts of *honra*, *respeito*, *bondade*, and *confiança*. Also, I met with Rui for 15 minutes at school and addressed his impulsivity by using relaxation and paradoxical techniques.

It is not surprising that Senhor Manuel and Senhora Rita initially did not want a Portuguese therapist and informed the teacher that they spoke English.

This referral was an embarrassment for the parents. They had already created some turmoil in their community when they moved in together and married. Their *honra* was once again put in jeopardy by Rui's problems, especially for the mother who was his biological parent. When the teacher suggested that Rui be seen, the parents were ambivalent, wanting to help their son, but not wanting their honor to be hurt. When the mother gave permission she was clearly showing respect toward authority by letting the teacher know she was compliant, but she was also ambivalent. She said that the father might get very upset and prevent her from meeting with us. This externalization is common among the Portuguese when feeling vulnerable to an authority figure. It was important for the teacher and me to accept and acknowledge the ambivalence. Initially, when I met with Rui, I shared stories about my own difficulties with school when I was a child in Portugal. With these stories I shared information that allowed him to react and identify with my experiences. This made him feel safe and helped me to develop trust and rapport with him (*confiança*). He was asked to interview his parents about their experiences at school and with their own parents and advised to report their answers to me, but only with their approval. All of a sudden Rui became important in the family for a positive behavior—chronicling the family history—and communication developed between the members of this very busy family, who had had little time for each other. This intervention stimulated Rui's parents' curiosity about me. When I called to inquire about the interviews and how school was going, the mother seemed angry. I offered to meet with the whole family at their home in the evening and asked for the mother's help in the meeting with her husband. I addressed Senhor Manuel first in the session by mentioning the fact that his wife had told me that he did not want to be in the session. This intervention worked extremely well by showing respect and focusing on him. Senhor Manuel began to smile at all the attention given to him and stated, "I am too busy working in two jobs, so that my son can have a good future. He is not respecting us and the teacher. At his age I was responsible for feeding all the farm animals, and I could not go to school. I am working like a dog, no education!!!" I told him that he was the only one who could teach his son about the country life.

A crisis occurred when Rui stopped coming to family sessions because they were "boring." Although his parents found it very threatening, I reframed it as a reflection of the fact that now they were in charge of the family and Rui was feeling safe. He was giving permission for his father to take responsibility for his own serious depression. Rui's behavior at school began to improve; he started to joke more with his parents—a sign of trust or *confiança*. As the family overcame feelings of embarrassment and anger for being referred and having outsiders involved with them, a therapeutic alliance developed through the expression of *confiança*. This implied a certain intimacy, reflected in the comments made by the parents about pictures in my office and the fact that I wore different looking clothes for a Portuguese woman. Earlier on, they had noticed all those things, but, out of respect for an unknown authority, they would not comment on my personal belongings. This feeling of connectedness led to our sharing a few jokes. The couple began to work on their relationship and the fact they were losing each other as they were trying to succeed with their immigration dream.

———————— ❧ ————————

## PORTUGUESE FAMILIES

Moitoza (1982) describes the Portuguese family as having a "patriarchal structure, yet much internal and external facilitation and negotiation is handled by the female/wife/mother" (p. 416). Although the family structure has changed with the most recent immigration wave, this definition still holds in regard to the nuclear family. Often, Portuguese families stay together for the sake of their honor. This value can be a strength when all members are willing to work out the family issues or a major weakness when it is too rigid and forces family members to become the enablers of a dysfunctional individual or family dynamic.

For instance, immigrant parents, in general, use corporal punishments instead of words to assure respect for them as authority figures. It is common for the mother to inform the father of a child's misbehaving, or at least threaten to tell him. The father, complying with his duties for the sake of the family honor, spanks the children. However, at times the mother feels bad and is not consistent with seeking help from a father who may on occasion have spanked the children too hard. The mother may never explain her concerns to the father, so as not to upset him, but she will keep threatening the child with the father's spanking. The child is never clear when the father is actually told about a transgression. The child is then always afraid or disengages from the family.

The authority in the Portuguese immigrant family goes from father to mother to the oldest child. If a son is close in age to an oldest daughter, he, not she, may take over the family affairs with the outside world. When preadolescent girls challenge this vertical hierarchy, the family's reaction may be dramatic. She may act out sexually with boys from non-Portuguese backgrounds and from other races. This can devastate a family that believes it is important to respect others but never to mix with them. Also, sexuality is permissible only after marriage for both sexes. Again, when a child breaks the rules, not only is there an individual loss for the parents but also a fear of loss of respect, especially if it is a girl. The community is much less forgiving of girls' acting out behaviors, than the boys'.

The concept of spending "quality time" with children as discussed among professionals in this country is unnatural and not understood by new immigrants. They define quality time as providing basic living needs, good manners, respect for authority, and the capability of children to help the parents in the gender specific chores. Girls will help with house tasks, shopping, and creating arts and crafts. The boys will help the father with hobbies around the house, fixing their cars, or at second jobs.

Portuguese families take pride in how their homes look to others. It is common to see patios covered by grape vines and families eating outdoors. Often this is one of the most gratifying experiences for families to share. In particular men who suffer from depression will often improve if they have the task to help family members growing a garden.

## TREATING PORTUGUESE FAMILIES

The fear of losing the family in combination with grieving the loss of the homeland leads Portuguese families to isolate themselves. It usually takes at least 5 years for families to show some acceptance of the new situation and become less rigid with child-rearing issues. This is when referrals for family treatment, made by the school and court systems, may be effective. Women carry enormous covert power in the family's decision making. They are good readers of the needs of the family and its individuals. They worry about the future and often have developed great leadership skills in coaching their husbands on family decisions such as immigration. The first contact by the clinician should be made to the wife, showing the clinician's respect for her role in the family as the parent in charge of the emotional well-being of her child. She is also the primary source of information regarding how the clinician can best show respect toward her husband.

Some Americans believe that Portuguese men are more *macho* than American men or other non-Latino men. Portuguese men show their honor by providing financial and physical security for their families; women show honor by providing care and understanding, by being loyal to the husband, and by becoming mediators between traditional family roles and the outside Anglo American culture. Thus, while the responsibility of decision making in the family mostly lies with the woman, conflicts arise when the man feels he cannot demonstrate *honra* and feels a loss of *respeito.*

In therapy with Portuguese families, it can be helpful to approach delicate subjects by using open-ended statements. Instead of asking if a client is sexually active, one might ask, "How is your intimate life with your husband?" Although younger woman seem more at ease discussing topics covering sexuality with men, this subject is still taboo. Among the majority of the immigrant population, sex should only take place within marriage. Often, rural Portuguese women will refer to sex as "when we were playing" or "when my husband was serving himself." For these women sex is a duty as good wives. They may speak to other women about sexual pleasure in their marriages, but probably will not discuss the topic with their husbands.

Therapists must remember that rural women still "want" their husbands to be perceived as the ones who carry the power for the sake of the *honra*. This *honra* gets defined through a form of communication called *mexericos*—heavily opinionated and judgmental gossip through daily casual conversations at work and other social events. Often clients are so fearful of such gossip that they will avoid being seen walking to a mental health center. They fear that they will be blamed for the illness, breaking down their *honra* and *respeito*. It is important to assure clients of the confidentiality of the visits.

Often *clinical depression* is expressed for women through somatic symptoms and for men through alcohol abuse. It is important to distinguish *clinical* melancholia from *cultural* melancholia or *marasmo*. *Marasmo* is a common syndrome in the Azores. It is a state of mind with significant loss of energy and a feeling of hopelessness. These symptoms are also observed with clinical melancholia, making the differential diagnosis difficult. The *marasmo* is a condition common among men and women who live on islands and feel constricted by nature and the surrounding ocean. The clinical melancholia is mostly experienced by women.

Depression is most acceptable and expected after a major loss or trauma. This mourning process, at first, should focus on the community and the individual's reaction to the community expectations. Often, individuals are judged on the level of love and respect for the lost ones if they show a greater level of personal sacrifice. A clinical approach is augmented when the therapist is aware of and helps the client prepare for community reactions (i.e., negative *mexericos*). For instance, a young woman, presented with depression after her husband was murdered. I encouraged her to take care of herself and be aware of her individual strengths. However she became suicidal and improved only after I suggested a strategy to work around the community expectations of how she should behave as a widow. The community did not want her to become independent and develop new relationships, but rather to wear black, which she hated. I advised her to begin to ask for recommendations from her mother and her husband's family and friends for how long she should wear black, and discuss with them how it made her even more depressed. This allowed her to develop support among her family, so they could protect her from the negative *mexericos* if she decided to stop wearing black.

It is common for the agrarian and fishing populations to seek help from folk doctors such as *curandeiros, espiritualistas,* or other religious healers who provide *Healing Masses.* It is important to explore with clients other forms of treatment and to understand them in order to use these healers as "cotherapists." At times, it is appropriate to ask the family to retain the *curandeiro*'s approval for therapy to proceed.

## CONCLUSION

Engaging Portuguese families in treatment at first might seem an impossible task. We are asking families to discuss matters that traditionally are only discussed among the adults and not in front of the children. We are asking people to gather in groups, when 20 years ago this might have lead to imprisonment in their native country. We are asking families not to keep secrets, when they have long used secrecy as a way to keep their honor. Using the four concepts of *honra, respeito, bondade,* and *confiança* helps integrate traditional values with the new actions of therapy. Most often, therapeutic contacts must begin with efforts to engage the mother, who can then help bring in other family members including the father. Home visits may be an important tool to reach out to the family. Therapeutic strategies involving homework and managing community reactions may help augment usual approaches of individual empowerment. When rapport is established, the clinician has an opportunity to encounter the humor, spirit of survival, and loyalty that unifies the Portuguese immigrant family and inspires all of us facing a rapidly changing society.

## ACKNOWLEDGMENTS

My sincere thanks to Richard Lane, Ana Araújo, Lourdes Barros, Denise Moretto, David McGill, Harvey Daniels, and Monica McGoldrick.

## REFERENCES

Handler, M. (1976). *Azorians in America: Migration and change reconsidered.* Unpublished manuscript, Brown University, Providence, Rhode Island.
Marques, O. A. (1975). *História de Portugal* (Vol. 3). Lisboa, Portugal: Editora Palas.
McGill, D. (1980). *Ethnicity training for a community mental health center staff: Portuguese-American ethnicity and mental health in Fall River, Massachusetts.* Doctoral dissertation, Massachusetts School of Professional Psychology, Boston.
Moitoza, E. (1982). Portuguese families. In M. McGoldrick, J. K. Pearce, & J. Giordano (Eds.), *Ethnicity and family therapy* (1st ed., pp. 412–437). New York: Guilford Press.
Riegelhaupt, J. (1979). Peasants and politics in Salazar's Portugal: The corporate state and village "non politics." In L. Graham & H. Mackler (Eds.), *Contemporary Portugal: The revolution and its antecedents* (pp. 168–190). Austin: University of Texas.

# CHAPTER 40

# Scandinavian Families: Plain and Simple

Beth M. Erickson
Jette Sinkjaer Simon

Scandinavia is not a single monolithic culture. Rather, it is comprised of five countries: Denmark, Sweden, Norway, Finland, and Iceland. In addition, Greenland and the Faeroe Islands both have independent governments but are still under the Danish crown. It often is described as a family of nations, and one frequently hears the phrase "Nordic family," because of the kinship between the countries. The degree of similarity among these countries is extraordinary when one considers that the population of Scandinavia is 22.5 million, and that these people are scattered far and wide over lands separated by the Baltic and North Seas and the Atlantic Ocean. At one time, all five Nordic countries were united under one crown. In addition, 95% of her people are at least nominally Lutheran. Furthermore, despite their clear differences in grammar, usage, and vocabulary, close linguistic ties between the countries allow Danes, Swedes, and Norwegians to understand each other, even when speaking their own languages.

Yet, despite the affinity between the countries, there exists a friendly sibling rivalry, especially between Norway and Sweden, as if to remind everyone that the countries are not a homogeneous whole. Their rivalry is evidenced in the nursery rhyme, "Ten thousand Swedes ran through the weeds chased by one Norwegian," or in the typical joke, "The Swedes are proud of their new zoo. They built a fence around Norway" (Strangland, 1979, p. 17).

Bonds that are closer still between the countries are discouraged by the fact that, although Nordic people have a strong sense of kinship, they also passionately cherish their individualism and national independence. For example, Norway, Sweden, and Denmark have constitutional monarchies, whereas the others have elected presidents as heads of state. Finlanders are even reluctant to be called Scandinavians or to be considered the fifth Scandinavian state. Such distinctions, then, require that both similarities and differences between the countries be borne in mind by treating clinicians, making effective treatment for Scandinavians not a "one size fits all" approach.

The first known written references to Scandinavia were made in the first century A.D. by the Roman encyclopedist Pliny the Elder (Mead, 1985). Traditionalists tend to think of Scandinavia as the trio of ancient countries of Norway, Sweden, and Denmark. Therefore, for purposes of parsimony, this discussion will emphasize those countries.

## OVERVIEW

What does it mean to be Scandinavian? The very act of writing about oneself and one's own culture and country would make most Scandinavians, who stress reservedness, feel uncomfortable. Doing so betrays a cultural legacy centered around twin implicit ethics: "Don't think you're so special" and "Keep to yourself." Despite this, the authors, both full-blooded Scandinavians, will set aside their culturally induced shyness, ignore the warnings that the cardinal sin is to take oneself too seriously, and press on with the task. Scandinavians are nothing if not rational and practical!

This chapter will attempt to discern whether it is possible to see and to identify elements that are specifically and essentially Scandinavian. Its central focus will be to address what non-Scandinavian therapists need to know in order to act as cultural interpreters of one Scandinavian to another, and of Scandinavians to entirely different ethnic groups. We will seek to answer three questions: What are the systematic commonalities, modes of thought, feeling, and social behavior that distinguish Scandinavians from others? How are these commonalities evident in the individuals and families who present for psychotherapy? What does this mean for the treatment we provide?

## THE IMMIGRANT EXPERIENCE FOR SCANDINAVIANS

Perhaps what made the Scandinavian American experience different from that of other immigrants was the centrality of the church in helping bridge their experience between worlds, while providing a unifying force for both the family and for the community. Because 95% of Scandinavians are at least nominally Lutheran, and because Lutheranism historically was the state religion, there must have been an immediate sense of kinship on entering a Lutheran church in this country. To Scandinavian emigrants, then, the Lutheran church has served an important unifying and identity-building function, as well as clarifying and upholding society's mores.

When J. S. S. emigrated to Washington, D.C., from Denmark in 1989, she experienced all of the disorientation that any immigrant does, despite her having lived outside Denmark two other times in her adult life. Yet, she did not complain or even talk much about her difficulties. Her father's voice often echoed in her head: "Don't think you're so special. There are a lot of other immigrants out there who are worse off." This ethic, implanted as a child, combined with typical Scandinavian reserve and stoicism to shape her reaction to life in her new country.

Because we Scandinavians come from a culture where people are extremely adaptive, perhaps it is easier for us to adjust to the immigrant experience than it is for others. We move around and assimilate with relative ease. However, even while we assimilate with others' ways, we still silently believe that our own ways are best. Illustrating this trait is a coffee mug that reads, "You can always tell a Norwegian, but you can't tell 'em much."

Furthermore, because we tend to be so resilient, people can develop an expectation that we *should* be. Then, when we do have difficulty, either people do not notice our struggle, or they—and even we—take for granted that we will continue to function in the same ways as we always have, and even demand that we do so. This can lead to enormous conflict and stress that, because of our stoicism, we are loathe to discuss. This often yields weakened immune systems that result in psychosomatic symptoms and diseases as our emotions are sent underground to fester and erupt later in more socially acceptable ways.

## A PORTRAIT OF SCANDINAVIAN PEOPLE

Perhaps more so than in countries with more temperate weather conditions and less rugged topography, Scandinavians' most significant identifying characteristics can be seen as developing in response to the climate and geography of their countries.

Scandinavian life is geared to two seasons. Because of the countries' proximity to the Arctic Circle, day-to-day life for Scandinavians for the majority of the year is hard. In winter, people must become inured to extreme cold, short days, and long nights. For example, half of Norway is above the Arctic Circle, so the sun sets on approximately November 25th and does not reappear again for 2 months, and then only for 4 minutes a day in spring (Mead, 1985). In addition, the weather can become so cold that an unprotected individual outdoors can freeze to death in a matter of minutes. Therefore, Scandinavians spend long periods of time isolated by gloom and cold.

How have these factors affected our value systems? They have left us with a curious mixture of heartiness because life is so hard, an expectation of and tolerance for isolation because of being home-bound in the gloom and cold of winter, commingled with interdependence with others because sometimes life itself depends on it. Independence within the group is highly prized, but leaving the group often is met with great ambivalence because this is seen as a threat. But, in keeping with our taciturn manner and our cultural code of modesty and humility, there is an unwillingness to talk to anyone about these conditions. According to Anderson (1986), in his tongue-in-cheek description of Scandinavian mores, "We're good neighbors, [but] we aren't always trying to get everybody together for a block meeting to discuss neighborhood problems. We think neighbors should already know what the problems are" (p. 35).

Children grow up in an environment where everyone deeply mourns the decline of the sun in autumn. "For Scandinavians, sunshine is synonymous with life—something to be cherished, pursued, and exploited" (Mead, 1985, p. 83). In summer, as soon as the sun returns, Scandinavians take every conceivable opportunity to celebrate and to luxuriate in the sun, like human squirrels storing it up for the winter. There is a saying, "In Finland, the sun is king and the queen is silence" (Sodergren, 1993, p. 57).

Topography also is a factor shaping the sense of isolation that marks the Scandinavian psyche. For example, Norway always has been a poor country, with the greater part of its terrain being stark and rugged. One of the largest and most mountainous in Europe, it is the least developed Scandinavian country, with less than 3% of the land under cultivation (Mead, 1985). This is in contrast to Denmark, which has 70% arable land. Norwegians are isolated because of rugged mountains, glaciers, forests, the imprisoning world of the fjords, and the long, dark winters. And although all Scandinavians value self-reliance, because of her challenging environment, Norwegians put a premium on it. For example, whereas Denmark and Sweden currently are members of the European Union, in November 1994 Norway once again voted not to join. Isolation likewise characterizes the psyche of Denmark's people, but for different reasons. It is a tiny country, comprised primarily of islands whose seclusion is compounded because few bridges connect the islands. Ferries at one time being the only means of transportation between the islands, each developed their own dialect, thus making communication even between two Danes difficult. Therefore, unlike Swedes and Norwegians, who are still able to understand one another within and between countries, Danes are separated even from their own fellow citizens.

Darkness and seclusion haunt more than the land in Scandinavia; they infect her peoples' moods. These factors have given rise to a strict boundary between the private and the public in Scandinavian culture that often can be difficult for those of other ethnic groups to understand. This spawns two particular, interrelated personality traits that are typical among Scandinavians: reserve and shyness.

Typically, it takes a long, long time to get to know Scandinavians; and the farther away you get from big cities, the more of a challenge it is. This is due to the desire for social autonomy and a positive attitude toward loneliness. Among most Americans, the cultural norm is that shyness is negative; shy people are thought of as being afraid, less competent, less intelligent, and less socially desirable. However, this is not the view of Scandinavians. To us, shyness is a positive trait; shy people often are viewed as sensitive, reflective, and nonpushy (Daun, 1989). This behavior often is misinterpreted by non-Scandinavians as introversion, withdrawal, and anxiety; however, we believe it is attributable to less willingness to communicate.

Communication styles among Scandinavians reflect this positive valence on aloofness. Scandinavians tend to ask few questions in conversation that could be viewed as intrusive, to avoid deep and elaborate discussions outside the family and close circle of friends, and generally to seem passive in conversation. When it comes to conflict, the Scandinavian languages do not even possess a rich vocabulary for aggressive words. This reflects the conscious avoidance of conflict by holding back aggressiveness and by stressing instead practical solutions. The fact that open conflict in other parts of the world may be traced to strong emotions and aggressiveness is probably the ultimate proof to Scandinavians of the superiority of our model (Daun, 1989)! Swedes tend to be in favor of agreement and consensus. Swedish management styles are typified by approaching subordinate employees with a desire to avoid confrontation and open conflict. This same desire can be put to good use in mediation and negotiation in management, and in enhancing those skills useful for healthy family functioning, provided people also learn adaptive skills for managing conflict when it does arise.

We have a strong preference for practical solutions, rational arguments, facts, and concreteness, as opposed to emotions and speculative imagination. The effectiveness of planning and the ability to negotiate, to compromise, and ultimately to agree, can be attributed to our practical natures. All of this can be tied to the hostile forces of nature with which we must contend regularly. In order to survive, Scandinavians have been forced to find practical solutions. "One implication of this same reasoning could be that basic, continuous activity in old, rural Sweden gave little room for relaxation, pleasure, and joyful conversation. . . . There are no institutions like the English pub or the southern European Tavern" (Daun, 1989, p. 8). In addition, the church strongly emphasized that one must feel guilty for experiencing too much pleasure. Pleasure was permissible for short breaks or as a way of regaining the strength needed for work. In summary, the message is that comfort is sinful as well as impractical.

This emphasis on the practical gave rise to an ethic about honesty. The truth is told in very precise, unexaggerated ways. Daun (1989) refers to a European value system study done in the early 1980s, in which it was found, among other results, that lying is considered bad by a majority of Swedes (60%), whereas the figure for the rest of Europe is about 25%.

Although on the positive side these traits give rise to a comfort with silence and with being alone, on the negative side they spawn a tendency toward conflict avoidance that can cause logjams in relationships, feelings of deep isolation, melancholy, and, at times, depression. Ironically, for a culture that stresses independence, all of these can be seen as potentially working against the process of individuation and self-actualization. These values that shape personality traits can be seen as contributors to the tendency among Scandinavians toward somewhat higher rates of depression, alcoholism, suicide, marital infidelity, and the existential angst that cradled the ruminations of the great Danish philosopher Kierkegaard. On the positive side, these attributes help Scandinavians develop strong wills, stoicism that borders on resignation, and a sense of rugged independence. For example, less local anesthetic is used on Norwegians during minor surgical procedures than is common among the rest of Americans (Midelfort & Midelfort, 1982). When B. M. E.'s Norwegian mother died of cancer, she endured the disease in seven different sites in her body before it succeeded in taking her life. Truly, if there were only one word that captures the essence of Scandinavians, it undoubtedly would be "stoic."

The following example illustrates how strict and yet unconscious adherence to Scandinavian values can become problematic for people and for their intimate relationships.

Suzanne, a 41-year-old bank vice president of Scandinavian ancestry, sought therapy with B. M. E. when the relationship in which she was currently involved was on the verge of collapse. Divorced for 10 years, she had been in this on-again, off-again relationship for 8 years. When Suzanne and Ted began treatment, she frequently wept spontaneously and profusely during sessions; yet, the only word which she knew to identify her feelings was "frustrated."

Realizing that she virtually was bound and gagged in the expression of emotions—hers and Ted's—the therapist began to explore the rules of Suzanne's family of origin. Together, they generated the following list, which can be seen as both typifying and enforcing typical Scandinavian values:

1. Be hardworking.
2. Be caring for other people.
3. Be strong, strong-willed, and strong on the outside.
4. Show that you can deal with things externally, even if you have feelings internally.
5. It is preferable if people get along.
6. Getting angry is not getting along.
7. Keep hurt, sadness, and so forth, way inside.
8. It is okay to show good feelings.
9. But showing good feelings in an obvious way is never done; it has to be done subtly.

Before we could finish making the list, quiet tears began to roll down Suzanne's cheeks. When asked to talk about her tears, she spoke of several elements of her difficulty that were rooted in her ethnicity, although she was unaware of the connection. First, she described how difficult it is to feel compelled to be strong on the outside, even when she does not feel that way. Then she went on to discuss how, when she finally does express emotions, they come out very different from what she intends. She then described her isolation because of her inability to express herself, or to get herself understood. But perhaps the crowning statement was fear of her parents' judgment if she conducted herself any differently. It is worthy of note that when a successful woman in her 40s with a highly responsible job is still afraid of her parents' displeasure, her individuation and her ability to make affective connections have been compromised severely.

In summary, the reader will note Suzanne's conflict about reconciling her partner's requests, that soon became demands, for emotional intimacy with the prescriptions and proscriptions from her Scandinavian heritage. Identifying these conflicts and helping the client to do so as well suggests multiple places where therapeutic intervention is indicated and possible.

## CORE SOCIAL VALUES AMONG SCANDINAVIANS

The socialist ideal that society is more important than the individual pervades Scandinavian life. Scandinavians, perhaps more than other groups, have caught on to the paradox that in structure there is freedom, provided it is not authoritarian order. We believe that, in general, people and society are perfectible, if only the "right" rules are set. Hence, there tend to be many rules that are followed fastidiously. The Norwegian American humorist, storyteller, and radio personality, Garrison Keillor (1995), who lived for a time in Denmark, refers to this as "the tidy secret of Danish freedom," which he summarizes as "Do as you must, be as you wish."

In addition, although Scandinavia is a law-making society in which a great deal of respect for authority pervades, paradoxically, there is a natural suspicion about it. It is accepted that respect for authority is what maximizes one's freedoms, and yet, there is the typically pragmatic Scandinavian acceptance of the fact that laws are made by humans who are capable of error. So a companion belief is that rules are made to be broken—or at least bent.

Democracy, egalitarianism, nonviolence, and tolerance are fundamental values for Scandinavians. We advocate balance and moderation. We believe in social welfare and collective responsibility for making society work. These beliefs undoubtedly were embryonic to the contributions to the world of the eminent Scandinavian statesmen Vice-President Walter Mondale and Secretaries General of the United Nations Dag Hammarskjold and Trygve Lie. These ethics moreover explain why the King of Denmark also wore an arm band with the Star of David in support of the Jews in Nazi Germany, and why Sweden remained neutral during World War II.

These beliefs translate in daily life among Scandinavians to the staunch egalitarian value that people are neither better nor worse than anyone else, even while acknowledging, for example, that the other person might incidentally have more money or lower status. Hansen (1970) calls this "sanctioned egalitarianism" (cited in Borish, 1991, p. 222), which implies that the "cardinal sin is to appear to take oneself too seriously and to indicate thereby that one has an inflated view of one's own worth" (p. 222). Individuals who take themselves too seriously and/or place themselves on a pedestal will be chastised by joking and sarcasm. Garrison Keillor, who extols the virtues of typical Scandinavian modesty that borders on feelings of inferiority, is the personification of this self-effacing ethic.

This value not to think you are so special plays out in gender roles as well. Marriages and families tend to be egalitarian, with everyone taking a share of household tasks. Laws regarding equal pay for men and women in public service were enacted as early as 1919. In 1973, every woman was given the right to abortion up to the end of the first trimester. If an individual displays what to Scandinavians is pretentious behavior, he or she will be punished. For example, a certain teacher at a Danish university, who often was interviewed for television and newspapers, stated that no one would comment on her interviews the next day. This illustrates the norm that when you have been too visible, your peers will make sure that you become invisible again, because you should not believe that you are more clever than the rest. The operation of this principle can be seen in daily life when one compliments a Scandinavian, who then usually feels compelled to discount the comment by self-deprecation.

The Danish Norwegian writer Aksel Sandemose captured some of the negative roles that govern relationships in Scandinavia. Referring to these 10 negative commandments as "The Law of Jante," he actually detailed a cultural code of humility that has become part of Scandinavian folk culture (1936). These canons are variations on the Scandinavian theme, "You should not believe that you are somebody." In essence, the Law of Jante is a reminder of our insignificance, and is a set of rules on how to be first in line to be second. "Don't be different" is really the underlying message, and the mood behind this code of conduct is concealed envy, fueled by a deep sense of personal insecurity (Borish, 1991). To be outstanding is to risk banishment, and being ostracized from society and from family is a terrible fate.

"The same leveling principle that so effectively limits the inappropriate individual exercise of power can have another, more troubling, effect. It can work to keep talented people in 'their place' and to discourage the development of their individuality" (Borish, 1991, p. 317). It also can translate to peer groups who want their members to fit in, no matter the cost. Thus, people often are expected to surrender their autonomy and demand that their children do the same, out of fear that they might become independent personalities. This really is the other and darker side of egalitarianism.

Democracy and egalitarianism are fundamental values to Scandinavians. Comparatively few people suffer hardship, and the number of very wealthy people is limited. For example, a Swedish cabinet minister in 1984 was paid only about double the salary of a factory worker (Mead, 1985). However, this is not at all to deny that Scandinavian society possesses its own internal system of social class. At issue here is not the existence of class divisions, but how the people themselves perceive and evaluate them. What is important is that their extent is continually minimized and challenged by the presence of the democratic egalitarian idea, which is given frequent expression in daily life (Borish, 1991).

There is a preference for orderliness that can translate to regimentation and an obsession with neatness. Louis Anderson, the humorous observer of Scandinavian life, invented a Scandinavian deity, the "Goddess of Compulsive Neatness," whom he depicted ironing shoe laces (1986). As Ingmar Bergman's films graphically portray, Scandinavians also can be expected to be modest, unemotional, ponderous, and philosophical; to keep to ourselves; and, as a possible result, to have difficulty with either physical or emotional closeness. We expect precision, are hard and often silent workers, and often have difficulty accepting outsiders because we believe in our heart of hearts that we have, should be, and are enough in ourselves.

## SNAPSHOT OF A TYPICAL SCANDINAVIAN FAMILY

Given these salient features of Scandinavian life, what kinds of families can clinicians expect to see in the treatment room? First of all, many who need help will have great difficulty availing themselves of it. Scandinavians' idea of therapy typically is doing arts and crafts using skills cultivated during our long winter months of isolation and boredom. Consistent with our overall behavior, we even amuse ourselves in ways that reward isolation and silence. The non-Scandinavian therapist needs to bear in mind that the most important job recognition for us comes from our own families. Yet, families rarely are obvious in their acknowledgment. This is a culture whose central ethic stresses figuring it out for yourself and keeping it to yourself.

Even in arguments, Scandinavians do not believe in confrontation. Yet, we are strong people with strong wills. Our predominant communication style is, again according to Anderson, "Like all Scandinavian-American communication, it's a hint inside a nuance inside a suggestion, and it's up to you to figure out what it means" (1986, p. 150). Reasons or motivations are entombed in the sort of silence that only Scandinavian Americans, especially rural ones, can create.

Because of all of these factors, when Scandinavians do present for treatment, therapists are likely to see families who are more disengaged than enmeshed; who resist talking about their problems; who have great difficulty in expressing emotions; whose fights usually are not overt; who stress independence and figuring concerns out on one's own without calling attention to oneself; who, although practical, will not resist a philosophical, even existential focus, provided feelings are downplayed, at least initially.

Often families with adolescents who are engaging in their typical struggle for autonomy will present for treatment. This occurs when parents attempt to control their children because of the shame that acting-out children bring to the family by drawing attention to themselves and to the family. This expectation of conformity, of course, often generates cycles of more rebellion and more family shame. Even families in which no disturbance is evident maintain a great deal of space between each other, emotionally and literally. When Scandinavian couples present for treatment, difficulty with establishing an emotionally intimate connection usually is the basis of their dysfunction. And couples in a "mixed marriage" who present for treatment may be expected to seek therapy because of a difficulty with reconciling what appear to be incompatible styles of intimacy, emotional expression, and conflict resolution.

## THE ROLE OF THE THERAPIST WITH SCANDINAVIANS

What does this mean regarding the role of the therapist with Scandinavian families or families with Scandinavian members? First and foremost, it involves understanding and respecting several caveats. Because Scandinavians emphasize egalitarianism and because of their subtle but discernible oppositional core deriving from suspicion of authority the therapist cannot be the leader easily. And although most Scandinavians know on some level that their lives are played out on the edge of depression, most of them are loath to admit it or to seek help for it. They expect to be able to work it out themselves. This suggests that when Scandinavian families do present for treatment, their problems likely will appear—at least to the family—to be intractable. To summarize, to work effectively with Scandinavians, therapists must be able to lead without being obvious, lest clients feel compelled to remind them not to think they are so special; keep order in sessions without being authoritarian because this invites rebellion among egalitarian Scandinavians; call up appropriate emotions without leaving clients feeling ashamed by emotional displays that make them feel denuded; learn to discern and help family members acknowledge the extremely subtle evidences of emotion that tend to typify Scandinavians' affective interactions and connections; gently help families speak the unspeakable, thereby breaking their isolation and countering their tendency to somatize.

## SCANDINAVIANS AND SOCIAL CHANGE

Could it be that Scandinavia leads the rest of the world in the quest for the ideal society? Sociologists have pondered and argued this question for at least half a century. And not without good reason. According to Mead (1985), as far back as the Viking era, from 800 to 1050 A.D., there is evidence of a greater degree of equality than that apparent with other peoples of that time. For example, Viking men could have rights to land without paying dues or levies to an overlord. Women could own land and manage property. Divorce could be obtained easily and without shame. Today's Vikings have gone far beyond these basic rights to create an even more egalitarian society. Scandinavian countries are fertile ground for the development of democracy and gender and class equity.

An expression of the balance principle is indulgence of dissenting points of view. This underlying tolerance can be seen in issues that involve individual lifestyles, politics, education, and religion. Many modern Scandinavian couples are more concerned with the quality of their relationship than with its legal status. However, for them, equality often is relative to practical issues such as child care, household duties, vacation choices, and the like, rather than to emotional intimacy. One general trend is illustrated by the fact that, even though more and more people currently are returning to marriage, there are now more single than married adults in Denmark, which can be explained by the relatively large number of people living together without benefit of papers. Another trend is that a greater number of women than ever before are deciding to have children without the presence or long-term participation of any male partner (Borish, 1991).

There is a strong feminist sentiment in Scandinavia, and its influence is felt in the lives and experiences of women who would never think of calling themselves feminists. For example, Scandinavian women have been conspicuously successful in the political arena. In the mid-1980s, the proportion of women in the various Nordic parliaments was 31% for Finland, 28% for Sweden, 26% for Norway, 24% for Denmark, and 15% for Iceland (Mead, 1985). By 1994 in Denmark, out of 20 ministers in the Parliament, 7 are women. In 1983, Norway's labor party decided that at least 40% of each sex must be nominated in all party elections. The Prime Minister of Norway currently is a woman, as is the President of Iceland. And men are much more involved in household responsibilities in Scandinavia than tend to be in the United States.

Class and status divisions are very real in Scandinavian society, but in all the countries there is an attempt to try to minimize them.

> An ongoing public critique of power that uses skepticism, humor, and irony as its chief weapons creates an atmosphere not at all conducive to the raw exercise of power. A formal political system in which as many as sixteen political parties contend for the right to attempt to govern is a further indication of strongly democratic and antiauthoritarian sentiment. (Borish, 1991, p. 238)

Another area where egalitarianism can be observed is in the treatment of gay and lesbian couples. In Denmark, for example, they are allowed to form registered partnerships that give them most of the rights of married heterosexuals. And in 1995, Denmark passed a law allowing gay and lesbian immigrants to bring their partners into the country to live as couples.

In addition, Scandinavian governments have placed an emphasis on child welfare in modern times. This is evident especially in Sweden. For example, it is against the law to spank a child—even one's own (Berlin, 1994). This also is apparent in Sweden's parent-leave programs, in which 15 months of paid leave can be shared between parents when a child enters the family, and in the state-subsidized day-care centers and state-approved "child-minders" (Mead, 1985). These social programs are funded by what most Americans would consider to be astronomically high taxes. Compared to the tax rate of 31.6% in the United States, Scandinavia has the highest tax burden in Western Europe: Denmark, 58.6%; Sweden, 56.2%; Norway, 55.2%; and Finland, 54.0% ("Compare and Contrast," 1995, p. 23).

## SCANDINAVIANS AND EMOTIONS

Scandinavians are nothing if not reserved, so people often experience a great deal of loneliness even inside their marriages and families. Because the overall message Scandinavians give themselves and each other is "Don't talk about it," communication can be unclear and equivocal, and affective constriction is the corollary. The key therapeutic task is to learn when and how to ask Scandinavian families to break their unspoken rule prohibiting the expression of emotions and learn to share.

Anger for Scandinavians can be precarious for their relationships. Expected to be stoic and taciturn, Scandinavians use silence as a way to fight; emotional expression in general is to be quashed. This means the expression of anger and outright arguments are experienced as psychically dangerous. And, in that people are forced to live cooped up indoors with each other for over half the year, anger could run amock and be downright harmful. Furthermore, because of the centrality of experiencing and expressing the emotions that accompany a loss, Scandinavians are highly susceptible to losses becoming unresolved and to people becoming symptomatic as a result.

Peter was a 14-year-old Norwegian boy referred to J. S. S. by his high school teacher. Within the 4 months before referral, he had begun to leave school in the middle of the day, and, with increasing frequency, was spending his days at home with his mother. He was the oldest of three, having two younger sisters. The family had moved from Norway to the United States 2 years earlier because of the father's career, which left him extremely busy and part of the family only on weekends. Mother was a homemaker.

During the first interview with mother and son, it became clear that both shared a deep longing for Norway. Despite the fact that the decision to move had seemed like the parents' mutual decision, the emphasis had been on how profitable the move would be for the father. Both mother and son described a deep feeling of helplessness and sadness. In the same way that the son had withdrawn more and more from social life, so had the mother. This was in contrast to the daughters and the father, who were increasingly more involved outside the home.

As might be expected with Scandinavians, the mother and son's pain had never been talked about; they felt they could not impose their struggles on the others. Each, in his or her own way, had tried to control these feelings with the predictable effect of increasing disconnectedness from the rest of the family and from the community. When the lack of dialogue and intimacy no longer could be converted into practical problems and solutions, and with increasing pressure from the school to address this issue, the family finally and reluctantly decided to see a therapist.

In the second meeting, the therapist shared the story of her own immigrant experience, and in many ways, her story resonated with their own. The family realized that in times of difficulty, they did not turn to each other for guidance and support. Instead, their tendency was to be silent. Hearing the therapist's story, they could see how it mirrored their own and began to accept it as permission to begin expressing their own. With that, they slowly began to feel connected again, and the feeling of deep loneliness slowly dissolved as the dialogue between them continued.

--------- ◆ ---------

## EFFECTIVE THERAPEUTIC APPROACHES
## WITH SCANDINAVIANS

Certain therapeutic approaches can be expected to work better than others with Scandinavians. In general, because Scandinavians are a pragmatic people, solution-focused approaches may work effectively. However, therapists need to be indirect in working with these clients. Again, Anderson's tongue-in-cheek observation of Scandinavians is instructive. He writes, "Our concept of 'sharing' does not include telling strangers the details of our sexual dysfunctions, dependencies, and adolescent traumas. We do not blab anything you tell us— whether it is a secret or not" (1986, p. 50). Therapy that emphasizes a total-reality focus may be experienced by Scandinavians as shaming, exposing them to humiliation for having called attention to themselves. Because of their tolerance for loneliness, therapeutic approaches that deal with existential issues can be expected to work well. Although waxing philosophic sometimes might be considered frivolous, if therapists can help clients see pragmatic reasons to think philosophically, they will concede and ponder spiritual questions, such as searching for meaning in their lives in general or from specific experiences. In short, perhaps the best way to work with Scandinavian clients is for therapists to allow them to figure out as much for themselves as they can, with guidance. This allows them to maintain their dignity, independence, and sense of control of their lives. Otherwise, their oppositional approach to authority may intervene to block therapists' attempts to help.

## CONCLUSION

Although writing about Danes specifically, the metaphor developed by Danish writer Karen Blixen captures the essence of all Scandinavian people. She says, "The Danish character is like dough without leavening. All the ingredients that supply the taste and nourishment are there, but the element that makes the dough able to change, to rise, has been left out" (cited in Borish, 1991, p. 320). When people present for psychotherapy, it is the therapist's mandate and challenge to supply the yeast in a way that families will knead it into their interactions to create the conditions required for everyone's growth and development.

## REFERENCES

Anderson, J. L. (1986). *Scandinavian humor and other myths.* Minneapolis: Nordbook.
Berlin, P. (1994). *The xenophobe's guide to the Swedes.* London: Ravette Books.
Borish, S. (1991). *The land of the living.* Nevada City, CA: Blue Dolphin Press.
Compare and contrast Western Europe's tax burden. (1995, February 16). *New York Times,* p. 23.
Daun, A. (1989). *Swedish mentality.* New York: Swedish Information Service.
Hansen, J. (1970). Democracy and egalitarianism. In S. Borish (Ed.), *The land of the living* (pp. 222–249). Nevada City, CA: Blue Dolphin Press.
Keillor, G. (1995, February 16). The tidy secret of Danish freedom. *New York Times,* p. 23.
Mead, W. (1985). *Scandinavia.* Amsterdam: Time–Life Books.
Midelfort, C., & Midelfort, C. (1982). Norwegian families. In M. McGoldrick, J. K. Pearce, & J. Giordano (Eds.), *Ethnicity and family therapy* (1st ed., pp. 438–456). New York: Guilford Press.
Sandemose, A. (1936). *A refugee crosses his track.* New York: Knopf.
Sodergren, E. (1993). Chambers of consciousness. In W. R. Mead (Ed.), *An experience of Finland* (pp. 54–66). London: Hurst & Company.
Strangland, E. (1979). *Norwegian jokes.* Sioux Falls, SD: Norse Press.

# PART VIII

# JEWISH FAMILIES

# CHAPTER 41

# Jewish Families: An Overview

## Elliott J. Rosen
## Susan F. Weltman

Recent data suggest that there are approximately 5.5 million Americans who identify themselves as being Jewish, nearly 45% of the world's Jewish population (Singer & Seldin, 1994). This figure has fluctuated only a minor degree since the first edition of *Ethnicity and Family Therapy* appeared 14 years ago.

Jews historically have perceived themselves not only as coreligionists, but as part of a cultural–ethnic–national body. Their fundamental membership was bestowed by birth rather than by belief or practice. This may be more true today than ever before, given that a significant proportion of the American Jewish population is not affiliated with a synagogue or other institution representing the Jewish community (Cohen & Rosen, 1992).

Declaring one's Jewishness has always been an acceptable criterion for membership in the Jewish community, and conversion to the Jewish faith assures complete access to membership. Born Jews who might not otherwise identify themselves as such are often counted by communities in census figures (Goldstein, 1993). In fact, if all individuals currently living in a household with at least one Jew are included as part of a "comprehensive Jewish population," the total Jewish population rises to 8.1 million (Goldstein, 1993).

A small proportion of American Jews are descendants of Sephardic (Spanish) Jews who trace their origins in the New World back to the mid-17th century. The first organized Jewish community in the United States was established in 1677 by Sephardim in Newport, Rhode Island (Diner, 1992). Recent immigration from South and Central America has added to the numbers of Sephardim in North America. The proportion of the Jewish community descended from Western European (primarily German) Jews who immigrated to the United States in the middle of the 19th century has become about equal to that of the Sephardim. These German Jewish immigrants, many of whom established themselves as the scions of large American business empires, were once a powerful force in American Jewish affairs as founders of communal and synagogue organizations (Faber, 1992). In recent years, however, their descendants have tended to blend into the mainstream of American Jewish life.

Within the last three decades nearly 300,000 Jews from the former Soviet Union have emigrated to the United States, the largest immigrant group to enter the country in 70 years (Gold, 1994). They have been greeted with some ambivalence by the American Jewish community: Although there is sympathy for their escape from oppression, there has been the feeling that if they were genuinely seeking Jewish roots (rather than an easier economic life), they would have gone to Israel.

Unlike Eastern European Jews who migrated to the New World from 1881 to 1924, recent immigrants from the former Soviet Union are highly educated professionals who have marginally identified as Jews. The American expectation of reliance on the individual and nuclear family, rather than the State and the extended family, is a difficult adjustment for many of these new immigrants to make.

Along with this large, new immigrant group have come other smaller groups, primarily from Eastern Europe and South Africa. Perhaps the most visible of these contingents are Jews who have recently emigrated from Israel. Israelis who come to the United States have emigrated largely for economic and "quality-of-life" reasons. They frequently have the expressed (but often unrealized) intention of returning to their homes and do not define themselves as immigrants. Israelis tend to congregate in insular neighborhoods, and they are unlikely to affiliate with synagogues or become involved in communal organizations. They do, however, fiercely identify themselves as Jews and are likely to further define themselves as "different" from their American counterparts.

The majority of American Jews have their roots in Eastern Europe. They are second-, third- and fourth-generation descendants of immigrants who came to this country from the turn of the century until World War II. Seventy-five percent congregate in large cities, primarily on the East and West Coasts (Goldstein, 1993), with California and New York having by far the largest percentage population today; over 2.5 million Jews live in these two states, nearly half the total number of American Jews.

Only 48% of Jews hold formal membership in synagogues or temples (Cohen & Rosen, 1992). The three main branches of Judaism in the United States are Orthodox, Conservative, and Reform, as well as a growing number of "Reconstructionists," the small fourth branch whose religious observance places them somewhere between Conservative and Reform. Orthodox claims the most fidelity to traditional religious practice and Reform the least. A significant number of American Jews identify as secular (nonreligious) although retaining a "Jewish identity," thus creating a wide array of possible Jewish commitments.

The Jewish Americans whose parents and/or grandparents came to this country from Eastern Europe in the early part of the century have made the most visible "Jewish mark" upon society through literature, art, music, and religion, and they are the group most likely to seek therapy. Thus the focus of this chapter will be on the characteristics associated with this group.

## CENTRALITY OF THE FAMILY

The family's centrality cannot be underestimated in looking at Jewish cultural dynamics. Jewish "familism" stems primarily from the idea that it is a violation of God's law not to marry. The first commandment in the Torah is, "You shall be fruitful and multiply." Currently, this value is reflected most vividly in Orthodox Jewish families. They explicitly follow the teachings of the Talmud, the traditional compendium of Jewish law, and see bachelorhood (and birth control) as unacceptable.[1] Marriage and raising children—establishing a family—have been the core of Jewish tradition. Historically, asceticism was viewed negatively, and celibacy was absolutely condemned.

At least three other factors account for the unusually strong Jewish emphasis on marriage: (1) the child-focused nature of the Jewish family, with children and grandchildren considered the very essence of life's meaning; (2) the powerful forces of suffering and discrimination, which imbue the family with the quality of "haven and refuge" when all other social institutions cannot be trusted; and (3) the strong connection Jews feel to previous generations and to the obligation to preserve their heritage.

The spiraling Jewish divorce rate, the ubiquity of later marriages, and the phenomenon of more people remaining single directly threaten this important concept of the value of family. A family that recently presented in treatment struggled with their eldest son's having "come out" as gay. Both parents were deeply distressed by this information and were virtually inconsolable, despite their son's and the therapist's attempts to help them deal with it. Only in the third session, when the son stated strongly that he and his lover had every intention of adopting children and establishing a family, were his parents able to begin listening to him.[2]

The importance of family has commonly been expressed in popular images of the Jewish man as a good father, husband, and provider and the Jewish woman as a devoted wife and mother of intelligent children. The pressure on Jewish women to find a husband and their mothers' investment in that task has been popularized in movies, television, and jokes. Pressure is also exerted upon men, but that on women remains greater. Perhaps this is because of the assumption that sons will achieve success, and an automatic by-product of that success will be a good marriage. For women, marriage is seen as a prelude to childbearing, which increases the urgency parents express about their daughters' marrying. The importance of maintaining a marriage may make it more difficult for families to acknowledge the presence of even severe problems, such as domestic violence or substance abuse.

After marriage, connections and obligations to the extended family continue to be important. Young Jewish couples typically spend much time defining the boundaries, connections, and obligations between themselves and their families, perhaps even more than couples of other ethnic backgrounds. Some young Jewish individuals and couples feel that they will always be children who, in their parents' view, will need to be cared for, financially and otherwise. Their elders' expectation of geographical as well as emotional closeness can seem stifling.

Living far away is not an acceptable excuse for failing to fulfill family obligations. One family stopped speaking to several family members who had not returned from a European vacation to attend an uncle's funeral. Another East Coast family had not communicated for some time with family members on the West Coast because the latter had not flown in for a Bar Mitzvah. To non-Jews this tendency toward cutoffs in response to a perceived breach of commitment may appear extreme. Yet it reinforces the powerful value of family connectedness, which is frequently the source of much joy as well as pain in Jewish families.

## INTERMARRIAGE

Intermarriage traditionally has been perceived as the most flagrant breach of family togetherness, and total emotional cutoffs once were common in such circumstances. However, there are fewer reports of such behavior today, except in ultra-Orthodox communities, where the ultimate example is families who "sit *shiva*" (i.e., formally mourn) for a child who intermarries. Today even the most liberal and assimilated Jewish families remain highly sensitive to intermarriage, which may be perceived as a betrayal of family and community. Even among families initially willing to accept the inevitability of a child's intermarriage, it is not uncommon for intergenerational conflict to arise at a later point, particularly around the birth of grandchildren.

Some families who have a distant, even hostile, attitude toward organized religion and Jewish institutions still nearly decompensate in the face of a child's prospective intermarriage. Even a non-Jewish partner's willingness to convert to Judaism may not alter the feelings of betrayal that "marrying out" awakens. A family recently seen by one of the authors illustrates the intensity of this issue:

The life of the Goldens had centered for years around the physical and mental illnesses of their youngest son, Sam, who was hospitalized on an adolescent inpatient unit due to "fainting spells" without organic basis. The mother felt unable to work and the family was struggling financially. Their older son was doing well academically and was involved in Jewish organizational activities. Sam and his family responded well to treatment. His parents had formed a stronger alliance; they felt more able to deal with Sam's problems, and Mrs. Golden was looking for work. In the last session, the parents sheepishly asked if they could raise something "personal." The therapist wondered aloud about what could be more personal than what they had discussed the past month. They then questioned whether they were living in the right neighborhood since Sam was Bar Mitzvah age and might begin dating non-Jewish girls. They were reminded that they had been working on developing a place within the family for Sam, rather than placing him in the controlling center. They agreed that they needed to continue this work in outpatient treatment.

Many Jewish organizations, including some synagogues, have developed outreach programs designed to maintain ties with those who have "married out" and thus increase the chances of children being raised Jewish. With more traditional institutions allowing access to the intermarried, and thus legitimizing these unions, it is now possible for families who heretofore had imagined their children as hopelessly lost to see possibilities for inclusion. Not that the stigma is completely removed, but the climate for acceptance has certainly been enhanced.

## DIVORCE

Divorce, too, is often seen as a violation of family togetherness. Jewish parents frequently personalize a child's divorce; more than one client has reported a parent's response to his or her marriage's end as being: "How could you do this to me?"

Recently, the Jewish divorce rate, once considered low in relation to other ethnic groups, has grown to about that of the general population. The marriage survival rate for intermarried couples and for unaffiliated and/or secular Jews, compared to religiously observant Jews, is even lower (Goldstein, 1993).

There is an added dimension to Jewish divorce that needs to be considered. In traditional families there is the expectation that the couple arrange for a writ of Jewish divorce (a *get*) as well as a civil divorce. Jewish law does not permit a woman to initiate obtaining a *get*. This creates obvious difficulties and may be an issue around which divorcing couples—as well as their respective families—can triangulate.

In traditional religious families, divorce can contribute to an alienation from Judaism. Ritual ceremonies in the home and synagogue are frequently family-centered, and certain roles are gender specific. For example, women traditionally light the Sabbath-eve candles, while men recite the sanctification blessings over the wine. At the end of a marriage, a uniquely "Jewish loss" may be reinforced by the absence of a man to recite certain blessings, or a woman to perform certain obligations. This is attenuated by many communities willingness to forego the gender-relatedness of many tasks, but it has not disappeared altogether.

## CHOSENNESS AND SUFFERING AS A SHARED VALUE

Historically, Jews have been persecuted so often that they tend to be on their guard, anticipating attack while paradoxically assuring themselves that they are God's "chosen people." In Jewish folk tradition, this notion of "chosenness" has had a cruel double meaning: Although Jews may have been especially chosen by God, they have undergone such travail that this special status has come to mean that suffering is a basic part of life. Suffering may even reinforce the notion of superiority by virtue of the burden of oppression. A well-known Yiddish saying, *Shver zu zein a yid* ("It's tough to be a Jew"), while often accompanied by a resigned sigh, also more subtly suggests that one wears the burden of that suffering with pride.

The prevalence and impact of anti-Semitic persecution cannot be underestimated when assessing the nature of the American Jewish character. No nation in which Jews have lived has been free of this phenomenon. For many Jews, the first social distinction they experience is between themselves and non-Jews. It is fairly common for Jews to attribute prejudice to those who treat them unfairly or harshly. In many cases, of course, this is hardly fantasy. Although many contemporary Jews eschew the notion that anti-Semitism is a powerful force in their lives, they nonetheless often react strongly to news accounts of bias incidents and to personal instances of perceived anti-Semitism.

One result of seeing suffering as an everyday occurrence is that enjoyment for its own sake, or the carefree expression of feelings, is sometimes questioned. A couple struggling over a morning routine with their young children agreed that they both found it difficult if the children were particularly silly when they were trying to get them dressed. Both noted that getting ready was "serious business" in their families of origin. As the husband remarked: "My mother always said: 'If you sing in the morning, you'll cry at night.'"

Not surprisingly, hypochondriasis is a common Jewish syndrome. Zborowski's classic study *People in Pain* (1969) reflects the experience of therapists who work with Jewish families and is reinforced in contemporary Jewish literature.[3] Jews who complain about their symptoms often do so with a resigned sigh that signifies that they hardly expected better treatment from life. The importance of finding the "right" doctor or specialist may preoccupy a Jewish family faced with serious illness, but the likelihood that they will be satisfied is slim. Often Jews manifest ambivalent attitudes toward the medical (and, by extension, the mental health) community. On the one hand, physicians are idealized and seen as having nearly magical powers; on the other, they are vilified for falling short of the family's expectations. As one popular joke has it: "Jews don't die a natural death . . . they're killed by the last doctor they saw."

The centrality of suffering for the Jewish family is underscored as Holocaust survivors and their children share their experiences. Many otherwise unaffiliated Jews have found themselves seeking information and desiring a closer connection with this cataclysmic event, as well as with their Jewish identity. A family seen by one of the authors reported a dramatic shift in their lives after one weekend experience. On a trip to Washington they visited the United States Holocaust Museum and then saw the movie *Schindler's List*, a powerful film about the Holocaust. They returned home, determined to reshape their family life to include an active Jewish component. Both parents had been raised in nonobservant families but now began a Friday evening Sabbath ritual, joined a local synagogue, planned a trip to Israel, and generally began reworking their priorities to incorporate these activities. A year later their commitment to this new way of life has deepened.

In some survivor families, issues of suffering and doubts about the right to joy and happiness are particularly pronounced. A daughter of concentration camp survivors reported, "No discomfort, disappointment, or difficulty seemed worthy of my parents' attention, considering their own experience in the war." She never felt the right to her own feelings because her parents' own suffering was so great. Any expression of her own seemed presumptuous.

In addition, secrets may abound in the families of survivors: complete families destroyed, but never mentioned; previous children who perished and remain as ghosts in present family functioning; and communities and/or extended families who vanished . . . all may never appear on conventional genograms. As one young woman pointed out, the parental message, "Be happy," took on a grotesque incongruity when coupled with her parents own history (Mostysser, 1975).

## INTELLECTUAL ACHIEVEMENT AND FINANCIAL SUCCESS

Success (and its public recognition) is vitally important to the Jewish family ethos. Jokes about "my son, the doctor" (now expanded to include "my daughter, the doctor"), while often used to ridicule status-seeking Jewish parents, reflect a central family value of education and professional achievement. In their seminal study of the *shtetl* (small town) of Eastern Europe, Zborowski and Herzog (1952) emphasized that learning was honored and earned one prestige, respect, authority, and status. Only recently have Jewish families come to value their daughters' intellectual and professional successes. Learning was portable, an advantage because Jews were constantly forced to be on the move. Discriminatory laws in Christian Europe closed many professions to Jews, which resulted in great respect for the "profession" of scholar.

The openness of American society and upward mobility contributed to Jews acquiring more conventional notions of success (i.e., in status and material terms). As one patient, a successful accountant remarked, "Most of my adult life, my mother introduced my brother and me as 'This is my son, Dr. Gelb, and this is Bobby.'" A child's status reflects favorably upon the family and parents. An economically struggling family expressed a preference for a non-Jewish therapist, with whom they believed they would feel less ashamed of their lack of financial success.

Today, in most Jewish families and communities, it is almost obligatory that children go to college; graduate and professional studies are often expected as well.[4] Parents may start worrying about their children's academic achievements in kindergarten, or even in preschool. In some communities Gentiles comment humorously that if you want to know which teacher your child should have, or what the school is not teaching, you should ask your Jewish neighbor.

Financial success is also highly valued in the Jewish family. Although Jewish attitudes toward money are often stereotypically portrayed, the historical reality is that, denied access to many crafts and professions, Jews tended to gravitate toward pursuits in which money was handled directly. It thus became symbolic of status; one of the tools of survival is liquidity: Money, jewelry, and other movables were accumulated (rather than land, which Jews could not own in most of Europe) so they could be taken along in flight.

Because success often means sacrificing attachment to family and community, these values are increasingly coming into conflict. Although this conflict has always created stress for Jewish men, who experience great family pressure to succeed, there is now increased stress for women, who also find themselves experiencing a tension between their roles as parents and partners. It may be difficult for Jewish couples who feel themselves locked into professional roles to make choices contrary to the strong pull of public status associated with their professional lives.

In some Jewish families, almost no one feels he or she can truly meet the high standards for success. For example, families may go to great lengths to deny or hide the fact that their child is unable to excel academically. In addition, expectations often are implicit and unspoken, and therefore can never really be met.

A family seen by one of the authors denied the seriousness of their son's learning disabilities. This interfered with getting him all the help that was available, kept him feeling that he was disappointing his family, and prevented his parents from getting the emotional support they needed. They could not acknowledge their son's skills and strengths in nonacademic areas, and he developed a bitter relationship with his siblings, who seemed to succeed so effortlessly.

Given the demands of the Jewish family system for success and achievement, it is easy to feel a failure no matter how much one accomplishes. As in the earlier example, this may lead to competition and sibling rivalry that interferes with family intimacy. A vicious cycle may develop in which family members devalue each other in order to bolster individual self-esteem.

Giving and receiving play an extremely important role in the Jewish family. The Jewish view of justice comes from a belief that humankind is made in the image of God and, therefore, man was created to do God's will—to make the world a more just place (Lipset, 1990). In the *shtetl* and in Jewish religious thought, valuable things such as material goods, wealth, and learning were seen as finite and attainable. They were acquired not only for the pleasure of ownership, but also because they made it possible to help weaker, poorer, and more vulnerable families (Zborowski & Herzog, 1952). Even wealthy families had a strong identification with the poor and disadvantaged, in part because their own status in society was so marginal. Thus, the perception of the poor as morally inferior was never a Jewish view.

## VERBAL EXPRESSION OF FEELINGS

Being verbal, which is highly valued, is a by-product of an educational system in which men studied the Torah and Talmud by utilizing complex academic methodologies. The student's task was to examine various interpretations and understand the intent of the ancient arguments and articulate them. A youngster capable of this was held in the highest regard.

In today's Jewish families, children's opinions remain highly valued; it is not unusual for parents to take great pride in the contributions their children make to solving a family problem. There is a less clear-cut boundary between parents and children than in many other ethnic groups.

Cynicism and criticism are frequently used in Jewish families to get family members to react and respond. To an outsider, this may appear as anger or hostility. However, such expressions or criticism may actually be ways of showing caring. Thus, the therapist can often positively reframe these verbal attacks, shifting the family to a more productive, positive direction. For example, in one family seen by one of us, the wife was extremely critical of her husband's earning ability. Although it initially appeared that her concerns were totally materialistic, it ultimately became clear that her real concern was her husband's health problems and how they had interfered with his ability to get ahead in his job.

## FAMILY PATTERNS

## Men in Jewish Families

In the *shtetl* of Eastern Europe, families prayed that their offspring would be boys, for the study of Torah, considered life's quintessence, was the lofty pursuit of men alone. Tevye's whimsical lament in *Fiddler on the Roof,* that "If I Were a Rich Man," he would sit in the synagogue all day and study the holy books, was a longing shared by many men in the traditional Jewish community.

Few men achieved the status Tevye desired. The works of Yiddish writers such as Isaac Bashevis Singer contain hints that men who did sometimes were privately scorned as drains upon the family and community. To express such an attitude publicly, however, was considered sacrilegious.

In America, success outside the family has sometimes been achieved at the cost of devaluing the husband/father in family life, when the mother exercised most authority. Although the father's role might be peripheral within the home, the family and Jewish community continued to pay obeisance to his achievements, for it was *his* public persona that accounted for the family's status.

These dynamics are weaker today. The impact of feminism means that many Jewish women no longer see themselves as dependent upon men for status. Vestiges remain however, particularly in the not uncommon case in which a wife has decided to abandon a career to raise children.

Tom and Barb Gruen came to treatment because of increasing marital conflict. Barb had been a senior editor of a top-flight publishing house but left reluctantly (but happily) after the birth of their first child. Tom, a successful attorney, had recently won two well-publicized cases that brought him a measure of fame.

The Gruens found themselves thrust into a world of highly visible "fast-track" couples as a result of Tom's success. Barb was miserable, Tom ecstatic; she felt that her own parents' marriage had been re-created and that she was on the verge of becoming "lonely, isolated, and irrelevant" like her own mother.

Tom, on the other hand, was thrilled with his newfound fame and income. Unlike his father, whom his mother consistently berated as a "failure," Tom had finally "made it." His complaint was that he suddenly felt excluded from the lives of his children and family because Barb had taken over all the decision making, leaving him feeling powerless at home. An explosion over a daughter's school conference that Barb arranged without informing him, and a dinner party with old friends that she planned without his knowledge, precipitated their seeking therapy.

---------------- ❧ ----------------

Tom's situation illustrates the paradox of the Jewish man who, having achieved position and prestige outside the home, may feel unappreciated or ignored within the family. This may raise problems of self-esteem for men who see themselves as impotent in the face of powerful wives and demanding children. Among Jewish men, banter about powerlessness in the face of strong wives is quite common, although frequently coupled with a more subtle acknowledgment that competent wives make their lives possible.

The public status and financial support provided by Jewish men have been more valued than emotional succor and interpersonal skills. Paradoxically, the lack of these qualities in a husband/father is often one of the complaints of Jewish women in treatment. Moreover, in the wake of feminism, many Jewish men have begun to embrace the nurturing qualities of father/husband and face the difficult task of balancing professional success with personal gratification.

## Women in Jewish Families

The Eastern European Jewish community was a male-oriented culture in which women were regarded as subordinate, and observant men greeted each day by offering thanks to God "that Thou hast not made me a woman," as part of the morning worship service. A woman's role was to serve as a helpmate—or complement—to her husband. Women's domain was traditionally the home, and they were limited in their ability to participate fully in religious observance due to both family obligations and religious injunctions.

Since the early 1970s, Jewish feminists have begun asserting themselves, participating in many previously proscribed religious rituals. As women have studied Torah, they have found scriptural justification for increased involvement in ritual practice. Since 1972 there have been women rabbis in Reform congregations; Conservative synagogues have accepted women as rabbis since 1985, and Reconstructionists even longer (Schneider, 1985).

Women have also been developing or rediscovering rituals to satisfy their particular needs. Among these is the celebration of *Rosh Chodesh*, the first day of each Hebrew month, which was celebrated by women in ancient times and linked to the menstrual cycle. Today, in some communities, women gather for this monthly celebratory event.

Jewish women in the 1960s and 1970s who chose to pursue careers, often to the dismay of their mothers, had role models within their families. Their grandmothers, who came to America from Eastern Europe, usually had to work out of economic necessity. Jewish women were among the leaders of labor unions formed in the early 20th century. Thus, many young Jewish women are looking to their foremothers for inspiration and guidance about how to combine work, family, and commitment to the larger community.

Since marriage, home, and family are vitally important, and since Jews place a high value on academic achievement and financial success, it is a small wonder that present-day Jewish women struggle with the competing demands of family and career. The two-career family can be stressful, and the pressures experienced sometimes lead families to enter treatment.

Jewish women also are delaying marriage, a general American trend over the last 30 years. There remains, however, a great deal of pressure on Jewish women to marry, given the emphasis on family and continuity. This has made it difficult for more ritually observant single women to find a place for themselves in the Jewish community. In addition, the current statistics on life span indicate that women live longer than men, so that three out of four women can expect to be widowed (Schneider, 1985). Only recently has the organized Jewish community begun to recognize the needs of these women.

## Marriage

In Eastern Europe, a "good" marriage meant a balance of learning, *yikhus* (pedigree or lineage), and money on the part of both the bride and groom's families (Zborowski & Herzog, 1952). Today, Jews still tend to have a high rate of marriage and only a slightly lower rate of divorce than the general population.[5] Parental anxiety about their children's marriage is proverbial: Giving one's child in marriage is still considered a primary obligation, and the failure of one's children to marry is experienced as a painful rejection and a bitter disappointment.

Jack, a 41-year-old single physician, relates that until he reached age 40 his parents seemed enormously gratified with his professional accomplishments and financial success. "It seemed that my two sisters' marriages and children had made it possible for my parents to allow me a more unconventional choice of remaining unmarried and pursuing my career." However, after his 40th birthday, Jack found that the message had changed, and the demands and expectations that he marry and raise children became intense. He invited them to come to therapy with him to discuss the problem. Both parents felt that they had been patient with their son while he established himself, but that now "time was running out" and they expected him to get married. They were anguished at his decision to remain single, and both felt betrayed ("But we were so patient!") and wondered where they had failed as parents.

———————— ⤚ ————————

The centrality of family demands that children marry. Only when this obligation is discharged is one free to enjoy the rewards and the *naches* (joys) of parenthood. An 88-year-old woman visited by one of us in a hospice explained her resilience and longevity as a function of her need to make sure her 69-year-old widowed daughter was married before she herself died.

Despite the impact of feminism, the pressure upon Jewish women to find the "right" mate remains strong. In preparing for the future, Jewish women are encouraged to do all that is necessary to ensure the best possible match, including choosing the best schools and the appropriate workplace for meeting a mate, and giving careful attention to their physical appearance.

Jewish women traditionally have been encouraged to find men capable of financially supporting them. In recent years, a growing number of Jewish women have initially sought the perquisites of a professional career, only to decide to stop work after marriage or the birth of children; they may then look to their husbands to bear the family's financial burden. Consequently, couples may struggle to find a balance between new societal expectations of equality and the pull toward traditional roles:

Mark and Jayne, a young couple with a 1-year-old son, came for therapy because of escalating conflict and anger that had begun shortly before the birth of their son. They had met as lawyers when both were considered rising stars. Jayne became pregnant after 5 years of marriage and left work; she was presently undecided about when—or if—she would return, since she was enjoying raising their son, wanted a large family, and stated that this was more valuable work than she could ever do in a law office. Mark declared that he felt betrayed, that the entire burden of supporting his family fell upon him alone—a situation he resented. Jayne was quite straightforward in her belief that, whether he was the sole wage earner or not, Mark would commit no more or less effort to his work. Furthermore, she argued, since there was little likelihood of their sharing equally in child rearing, she ought to do the job fully and properly. To his angry retort that she was a JAP (Jewish American princess), she replied that he knew in his heart that a good Jewish man supported his family: His father had done it, her father had done it, and why should he expect that they would be different?

## Sexuality

The Talmud recognizes both female and male sexual needs and instructs men to attend to their wives' sexual desires. In traditional Orthodox practice, sex is not discussed openly, and there is a great value placed upon sexual modesty, particularly for women. They are considered ritually untouchable during their menses; before sexual relations can be resumed, a wife must go to the *mikveh* (ritual bath), where her immersion purifies her and allows her once again to be sexually available. Today the *mikveh* and other sexual regulations are practiced primarily by more observant Jews, although some Jewish feminists have an interest in revitalizing some of the rituals.

Although the ultimate goal of intercourse is procreation, sexual relations between husband and wife are considered sanctified and encouraged as a necessary, and even pleasurable, activity. A woman's inability to conceive or bear children, as well as sexual incompatibility, are mentioned in the Talmud as grounds for divorce.

Both sex and marriage have long been the source of much humor with a

Jewish twist. It is not uncommon for Jews (and non-Jews) to revel in jokes that mock the controlling (or frigid) Jewish woman. The ubiquity of this humor, and its seeming acceptability among Jews themselves—and even Jewish women—has led many to infer that the depicted stereotypes reflect reality. However, long before ethnic humor became the norm for Blacks, Hispanics and others, as it has in recent years, male "Borscht Belt" comics mocked their wives and mothers—although not necessarily themselves—with impunity. Given that laughter has always been the refuge for those who see themselves as "one down," this self-deprecatory humor was an acceptable part of American Jewish folk life for generations.

## Children and the Parent–Child Relationship

In the traditional Jewish community, having children was seen as a religious and social obligation. Children complete a blessed marriage and are viewed as an extension of the parents' worth (Zborowski & Herzog, 1952). The changing mores toward later marriage, delay of childbearing, smaller families, and couples choosing not to have children, have put enormous pressure on many family relationships.

Jewish couples have a relatively high rate of infertility, which may be related to the delay in having children because of demands of education and career (Della Pergola, 1980). Because of their strong commitment to family, Jewish couples often adopt if they have fertility problems. The issues surrounding infertility and adoption (including the fact that the adopted child is unlikely to be born Jewish) may lead couples into therapy (Gold, 1988).

In the traditional Jewish nuclear family, the mother is considered the nurturer of the entire family, including the father. She continually outdoes herself in caring for others, foregoing satisfaction of her personal needs for the benefit of her family. No sacrifice is too great, especially for the sake of her children. They, in turn, may feel overwhelmed by guilt because there is no way to repay her efforts adequately.

A young married daughter who decides to postpone childbearing to pursue a career may well feel that her behavior is a betrayal of her mother. The daughter's decision not only threatens her mother's familistic values, but also rejects the traditional obligations between generations. The requirement of "giving parents a grandchild" transcends mere individual choice. In very few cultures do mothers see adult children postponing having children as a personal affront. Some couples report that the decision to have a child was based, in part, on the desire to gratify one of their mothers.

Traditionally, the Jewish mother has been viewed as her children's primary educator, inculcating in them the values of education and achievement. Many generations of highly successful Jewish doctors, lawyers, and social workers testify to the efficacy of her methods. Since she is merely the instrument of their success, her enjoyment must be vicarious, and her implicit mission is to work primarily for the development of others.

The Jewish mother's ambivalence regarding her role may aggravate her relationship with her daughter(s); she may communicate this ambivalence by unclear or unstated expectations regarding a woman's role in life. Jewish daughters increasingly have felt the need to be the "Super Mom." Not only should they be well educated, have a good professional job, and be a help to their spouses, but they should also be active in the community and know everything about their children's schools. A Jewish woman may say of her mother, "I don't know what she expects of me. I've never been able to figure out how to please her." Some experts suggest that these unstated demands may contribute to the disproportionate rate of anorexia and other eating disorders in Jewish girls (Schneider, 1985).

The conflict between a Jewish mother and her son(s) conversely results not from her ambivalence regarding her own or his role, but rather from disappointment in his failure to meet her expectations. As a male client said recently, "I know what I have to do to please my mother; I'm just tired of doing it." Another stated, "I've decided to go to law school, even though it's going to please my mother."

Jews tend to rear children through reasoning, explanation, and rationality, and Jewish parents have tended to be permissive, overprotective, and concerned about their children's happiness, at times at the expense of their own (Sanua, 1978). However, they also have fostered greater independence in their children compared with both Irish and Italian families (McClelland, DeCharms, & Rindlisbacher, 1955). Children are viewed as people with drives that require controls and opportunities for expression. The parental task is to create outlets for them, rather than to shape behavior. Punishment is considered only as a method of diverting behavior into new channels.

Children's obligations generally proceed from their role as extensions of their parents. Through the child's success, parents are validated; through their defects and wrongdoings, they are disgraced and shamed. One couple came into therapy in conflict with their son, who had recently graduated from a prestigious college but had difficulty making career decisions. He found a job at a neighborhood gas station, seeing this as a temporary solution to being financially dependent on his parents. However, they felt they would be publicly embarrassed and preferred to support him; they could not understand his wish for financial independence if it risked public humiliation.

Judaism sees children's duties to parents as rooted in religious principles, not the least of which is the commandment to honor one's father and mother. This concept results in a plethora of "shoulds" and "musts" that are an aspect of the family ethos. Performing the *mitzvah* (commandment) of filial obligation also provides opportunity for both personal and spiritual rewards.

Parents' sacrifice, suffering, and solicitude generate filial indebtedness, which the children return through good manners and respect. For example, a son was traditionally referred to as "our *Kaddish*"; the implication was that he knew that he would have the responsibility of reciting *Kaddish* (the memorial prayer) for his parents upon their deaths. In common usage, however, it also implied comfort and dependence: A parent who reminded a child that he was "my *Kaddish*" reinforced that son's obligation for his parents' emotional succor and physical care. Today, young Jewish women are also expressing a feeling of obligation to say *Kaddish*, with some interesting implications for religious observance and family relationships (Reguer, 1983). A related concept is that of *naches* (literally, "satisfaction" or "pleasure" in Yiddish), something Jewish children learn early on that they are expected to provide their parents. It can be delivered via achievement, financial success, marriage, and/or grandchildren. Failure to provide parents with some *naches* is considered cause for much guilt. Of course, there can never really be enough of this valued psychic commodity.

## LIFE CYCLE RITUALS

The ritual circumcision (*bris*) of a Jewish baby boy is a nearly universally observed rite. Special ceremonies for naming female infants have also become more common. Jewish families may no longer use traditional ceremonies but simply have a party to celebrate the child's birth, leaving the circumcision, which substitutes for a ritual *bris*, to medical personnel and the "naming," if done at all, to grandparents or other relatives. Even in these instances, families often desire that the ceremony have religious meaning. Children are traditionally named for a recently deceased relative, although in families of Sephardic background, children are often named for living relatives. Obviously, the choice of a name is seldom simple! In the process of Americanization, other rituals have also been abandoned, transformed, and rediscovered.

It can be extremely difficult to strike a balance between a commitment to Jewish tradition and the desire to make independent decisions. The recent phenomenon of the younger generation's return to religious observance leaves some parents uncomfortable with their adult children practicing rituals with which they are unfamiliar.

Stuart and Jean, both in their 20s, came seeking guidance as to how to deal with their parents, who were disturbed that the young couple had become Orthodox. Enormous conflicts had developed around holidays, food, child rearing, money, and extended family. While the therapist might have immediately labeled this as merely an example of two people who had not adequately differentiated from their families of origin, it was suggested instead that both bring their parents in, and that they work together on the problem. It became apparent that both families found their children's choice unpalatable.

For Stuart's parents, mental health professionals from Orthodox, Old Country backgrounds, this choice represented everything they had fought to leave. They were convinced that their son's religious observance was an attempt to put them in their place and distance from them, and that it was Jean who was responsible for "turning Stuart against them."

Jean's parents, longtime liberals and wealthy pillars of a Reform Temple, were scandalized that their daughter and son-in-law identified themselves with "those primitive, reactionary Jews" who represented everything they found embarrassing.

The first phase of family work involved a number of meetings with the young couple and their parents to encourage communication among the families. The goal was to educate the parents about why their children had chosen their lifestyle. This forced Stuart and Jean to reflect clearly on their choices and helped them to understand, and thus clarify, why these choices made their parents so uncomfortable. The second, much longer phase of treatment was couple therapy with Stuart and Jean, focusing on their need to take the necessary steps to individuate from their families while staying emotionally connected.

## The Bar and Bat Mitzvah

An important rite of passage occurs with the Bar and Bat Mitzvah, when a child reaches 13 years of age.[6] The ceremony's significance is the child's being called to recite blessings over the Torah at a regular synagogue service, thus establishing him- or herself as an adult worshiper. There is great variation in how a daughter's Bat Mitzvah is celebrated. In some very Orthodox congregations, girls are accorded no special ritual at all. In many, there is a Bat Mitzvah, with the typical ceremony being limited to a few English or Hebrew readings and no specific ritual participation. In other non-Orthodox but more traditional synagogues, girls may be afforded somewhat greater participation but nevertheless not be considered as having the same status as a male contemporary. However, the last two decades have seen a tremendous growth of the inclusion of women in synagogue ritual in all but the most traditional places. In most Conservative, Reconstructionist, and Reform synagogues and temples, the Bat and Bar Mitzvah are afforded equal importance.

The Bar and Bat Mitzvah are the only life cycle events that do not mark the leaving or entry of a family member. Nevertheless, this is a powerful moment in the family's life and may involve such issues as loved ones who are ill praying to stay alive at least until that day, families on the verge of breaking up deciding to wait until after that day, and long-neglected and distant relatives once again being invited back into the family circle. Recently there has also been a strong movement toward inclusion of handicapped children, who are given special training so that they can partake of this important rite of passage.

## Death and Mourning

The contemporary Jewish community views death as an ending of this life, rather than as a beginning of another. Several aspects of the Jewish rituals around death are unusual in the context of mainstream American life and should be noted by the therapist working with Jewish families (Rosen, 1991). We will note a few of the more typical aspects of the ritual and refer the reader to the excellent text *The Jewish Way in Death and Mourning* (Lamm, 1969) for a complete presentation.

Jews commonly bury their dead at the earliest possible time, which is historically within 24 hours. "Sitting *shiva*," which does not begin until after the burial, extends for 7 days and involves mourning in the home and visits by family and friends. *Kaddish*, a memorial prayer, is traditionally said daily for the year after burial of a parent or spouse and on the anniversary of the death.[7] Eleven months following death, the family reconvenes at the cemetery for the "unveiling" or dedication of the tombstone, which also marks the end of the mourning period.

Major family life cycle events may be stressful, but they also are times during which the family is most amenable to change; thus they are potential moments for therapeutic intervention. Friedman (1988) and Imber-Black (1991) suggest that the therapist should try to maximize the potential of the rituals to promote family strengths and relationships.

## FAMILY THERAPY WITH JEWISH AMERICAN FAMILIES: SOME FINAL OBSERVATIONS

The chapter on Jewish families in the first edition of *Ethnicity and Family Therapy* noted that Jews are major consumers of psychotherapy (Herz & Rosen, 1982). This remains true; many Americans continue to perceive psychotherapy as a "Jewish profession." This is undoubtedly connected to the historical roots of therapy and the important role played by Sigmund Freud. Freud's own identity as a Jew and the peculiar connections between Talmudic scholasticism and psychoanalysis have been extensively discussed (Yerushalmi, 1989; Rice, 1990). The Jewish predilection for verbal facility, multiple meanings, and intellectual pursuits may make Jews somewhat more comfortable with individually oriented, psychoanalytically focused therapies. However, there is no evidence to suggest that they will resist a systems approach to family problems. To the contrary, Jewish families generally are more respectful of therapy than other ethnic groups (Rosen & Weltman, 1995).

It is important to recall the oft-repeated Yiddish saying, "Where there are two Jews, you'll find three opinions." This proverb also characterizes the experience of many family therapists who work with Jewish families; their opinionated natures often make such families frustrating, but also challenging. Non-Jewish therapists may feel intimidated when working with Jewish clientele whose verbal facility, intellectualizations, cynicism, and intensity sometimes make progress slow and illusory. Jewish therapists report difficulties related to their own conflicted ethnic or religious identity, more (or less) traditional outlook than the families they treat, and beliefs about how Jewish families "ought" to behave. Jewish families are unique among cultural groups because they constitute a curious mix of both religious and ethnic identity, although some may affirm neither.

Jewish American identity is a paradox: Historically freer than ever, Jewish Americans remain strongly bound by the expectations of previous generations.[8] Although Jews have been in the forefront of liberal causes for decades, the perception of Jewish affluence casts them as belonging to a power elite. No therapist can entertain the naive belief that Jews are a homogenous group whose behavior is predictable. Although Jewish families may present particularly confounding problems, they are seldom dull.

## NOTES

1. Orthodox rabbinic authorities are often called upon by couples to allow exceptions to traditional strictures on birth control when physical or emotional health might be threatened by pregnancy, and such exceptions are not uncommon.
2. Family therapy colleagues indicated that Jewish families seem to be initially more distraught about a child' coming out than other ethnic groups, although ultimately they tended to be more accepting (Rosen & Weltman, 1995).
3. In the novels of Philip Roth and Bernard Malamud, for example, illness—and complaints about illness—are common images in their portrayal of Jewish families.
4. The 1990 U.S. Census revealed that 52.7% of Jews had completed college and pursued graduate studies, as compared to 20.5% of the total U.S. White adult population (Goldstein, 1993).
5. There are no definite figures on divorce among Jews but the 1990 U.S. Census data suggest "that divorce has become relatively common among American Jews" (Goldstein, 1993).
6. The age of Bar and Bat Mitzvah differs slightly for boys and girls in different communities; in more observant communities, girls celebrate the rite at 12 or 12½.
7. Actual mourning periods for various relatives differ somewhat, but generally "a year" is considered the overall time for formal mourning.
8. There has never been a time or place in diaspora Jewish history when Jews have been less threatened by anti-Semitism or freer to abandon their faith and community altogether than in 20th-century America.

## REFERENCES

Cohen, R., & Rosen, S. (1992). *Organizational affiliations of American Jews: A research report.* New York: American Jewish Committee.

Della Pergola, S. (1980). Patterns of American Jewish identity. *Demography, 17,* 261–273.

Diner, H. R. (1992). *A time for gathering: The second migration, 1820–1880.* Baltimore: Johns Hopkins University Press.

Faber, E. (1992). *A time for planting: The first migration, 1654–1820.* Baltimore: Johns Hopkins University Press.

Friedman, E. H. (1988). Systems and ceremonies: A family view of rites of passage. In E. Carter & M. McGoldrick (Eds.), *The changing family life cycle* (pp. 119–147). New York: Gardner Press.

Gold, M. (1988). *And Hannah wept.* Philadelphia: Jewish Publication Society.

Gold, S. (1994). Soviet Jews in the United States. In D. Singer & R. Seldin (Eds.), *American Jewish yearbook, 1994* (pp. 3–57). New York: American Jewish Committee.

Goldstein, S. (1993). *Profile of American Jewry: Insights from the 1990 national Jewish population survey.* New York: Center for Jewish Studies, City University of New York.

Herz, F., & Rosen, E. (1982). Jewish families. In M. McGoldrick, J. K. Pearce, & J. Giordano (Eds.), *Ethnicity and family therapy* (1st ed., pp. 365–392). New York: Guilford Press.

Imber-Black, E. (1991). Rituals and the healing process. In F. Walsh, & M. McGoldrick (Eds.), *Living beyond loss* (pp. 207–223). New York: Norton.

Lamm, M. (1969). *The Jewish way in death and mourning.* New York: Jonathan David.

Lipset, M. S. (1990). *American pluralism and the Jewish community.* New Brunswick, NJ: Transaction Publishers.

McClelland, D. C., Decharms, R., & Rindlisbacher, A. (1955). *Religions and other sources of parental attitudes towards independence training.* In D. C. McClelland (Ed.), *Studies in motivation.* New York: Appleton-Century-Crofts.

Mostysser, T. (1975). The weight of the past—*Reminiscences of a survivor's child. Response, 8,* 3–32.

Reguer, S. (1983). Kaddish from the "wrong" side of the *Mehitzah.* In S. Heschel (Ed.), *On being a Jewish feminist* (pp. 177–181). New York: Schocken Books.

Rice, E. (1990). *Freud and Moses: The long journey home.* Albany: State University of New York Press.

Rosen, E. (1991). Mourning in other cultures. In F. Walsh & M. McGoldrick (Eds.), *Living beyond loss* (pp. 194–200). New York: Norton.

Rosen, E., & Weltman, S. (1995). [Unpublished survey of family therapists' observations of Jewish families in treatment.]

Sanua, V. D. (1978). The contemporary Jewish family: A review of the social science literature. In G. Babis (Ed.), *Serving the Jewish family.* New York: KTAV.

Schneider, S. W. (1985). *Jewish and female: A guide and sourcebook for today's Jewish woman.* New York: Simon & Schuster.

Singer, D., & Seldin, R. (1994). *American Jewish yearbook, 1994.* New York: American Jewish Committee.

Yerushalmi, J. F. (1989). Freud on the historical novel: From the manuscript draft (1934) of *Moses and Monotheism. International Journal of Psycho-Analysis, 70,* 375–395.

Zborowski, M. (1969). *People in pain.* San Francisco: Jossey-Bass.

Zborowski, M., & Herzog, E. (1952). *Life is with people.* New York: Schocken Books.

# CHAPTER 42

# Soviet Jewish Families

## Irene Feigin

## CULTURAL BACKGROUND AND ETHNIC IDENTITY

Soviet Jewish immigrants comprise a new group that only began to arrive in the United States in the mid-1970s, when mass emigration from the former U.S.S.R. first became possible. Their cultural background deserves special attention, since their experiences and sense of cultural belonging do not always coincide with their ethnic identity.

In the United States, Soviet Jews often call themselves Russians, partly for simplicity, but also for reasons of cultural self-definition and to acknowledge their being part of the Soviet population under totalitarianism. But it would be simplistic to attribute their limited knowledge of Jewish culture and their general lack of eagerness to learn about it, as well as their widespread atheism, exclusively to Soviet rule and anti-Semitism.

Even before the Revolution, Russian culture deeply influenced many Jews who wanted to identify with their country's mainstream. After 1917, Soviet Jews enjoyed a brief period of equality, and many believed that the era of Russian anti-Semitism had passed forever. Inspired by greater opportunities, many young Jews enthusiastically rejected their own ethnic and cultural identity in favor of internationalism. They left their *shtetls* (villages where Jews lived) in search of the knowledge and education traditionally prized in Jewish culture, and also refused to speak Yiddish, which was seen as a symbol of self-isolation and backwardness.

Looking back during the 1980s, one observer noted: "Members of non-Jewish pre-revolutionary educated strata were either expelled, . . . killed, or excluded from bureaucratic and professional positions. . . . the educational level of non-Jews in the country was abysmally low. Jews were in an ideal position to take on white-collar and professional work" (Zaslavsky & Brym, 1983). Soviet Jews thus became active participants in building a new society and in performing crucial functions in government, sciences, and industry in the transition to an industrial society.

The tragedy of the German invasion in 1941 and the Holocaust, as well as subsequent official Soviet anti-Semitism, contributed to the vanishing of Jewish culture. The intense experience of the war raised the Soviet people's self-respect and produced much popular sentiment that the future would bring an end to political oppression. Therefore, to consolidate its own position, the Stalinist leadership needed a focus for its "divide and conquer" policies. Many Jewish intellectual leaders, writers, actors, well-known doctors, and scientists were accused of espionage and proclaimed traitors. Soviet Jewry became the scapegoat of nationwide rage and a target for demonization and possible subsequent annihilation.

State-sponsored anti-Semitism and the perception of Jews as enemies were endorsed by many strata of Soviet society after the Stalin era, leaving scars of fear and humiliation that influenced Soviet Jews' behavior. This hostile environment led to such traits as reliance on ethnic networks rather than official lines of hierarchy, alienation from the state, an attitude of "laying low," and the overprotection of children.

Since the Soviet Union's Jewish population was very diverse, immigrants from different regions exhibited quite varied cultural traits. Immigrants from Russia proper, who typically came from such major cities as Moscow and St. Petersburg, were raised with the traditions of Russian culture. Usually highly educated, they actively participated in social and intellectual movements for change and identified themselves with the Russian intelligentsia, whose humanist values stressed the common good over individualism and encouraged public service.

Other Jewish immigrants came from the Ukraine and Byelorussia, areas of the former Pale of Settlement (where the czars permitted Jews to reside before the Revolution). A higher percentage of this group were workers and craftsmen than was the case among other Russian Jewish immigrants. Jewish culture still is very much alive in these families, their structure, and their values.

The older generation has not entirely forgotten Yiddish and distinguishes between the Jewish and "non-Jewish" worlds. Jewishness for them is largely of day-to-day interest and, sometimes, practice, since they were exposed to everyday anti-Semitism from the local population. Many immigrants from Ukraine and Byelorussia had relatives who were murdered during the Holocaust.

## FAMILY CHARACTERISTICS

Most Jewish immigrants are urban and offspring of two parents who are professionals. The ordeals of history, economic difficulties, and the intrusion of the Soviet state into family life affected them greatly.

Because of Soviet cities' shortage of housing, many families lived in communal apartments, where several households shared a few rooms. Even for those fortunate enough to have a separate apartment, three generations of an extended family often lived together. Consequently, almost all Russian urban families had only one or two children. Frequently, two generations of adults cared for a single child. These living conditions strengthened family ties, individual adaptability, and a tolerance of personal discomfort. But they also allowed for little privacy and resulted in blurred family boundaries and enmeshment.

Despite its slogans, the Soviet government did little to promote the young adults' financial and professional well-being. In the former U.S.S.R., key positions usually were occupied by older men who were close to retirement age. Parents were forced to offer financial help to their adult children, who often shared their parents' apartments. As a result of this dependency, there was frequent parent–child conflict, as well as alliances of grandparents and grandchildren.

All parents have great expectations of their children. Should they be disappointed, parental guilt and dissatisfaction with offspring often result. Elaborate care and worry for children and the desire to protect them from the humiliation of anti-Semitism sometimes left Soviet Jewish families quite isolated, leading to socialization and other problems that necessitate therapy.

Alcoholism is a notorious Russian problem that affects various societal strata. Russian and Soviet governments traditionally were tolerant of excessive drinking and failed adequately to address or acknowledge the problem's scope. The Russian population always felt pity and sympathy toward a drunken man and sometimes was even suspicious of people who did not drink. Difficult day-to-day living conditions, the sense of the uselessness of individual effort and initiative, and political oppression, all contributed to alcoholism in Soviet society. The atmosphere of tolerance and acceptance of drinking makes it difficult to admit a need for treatment.

Alcoholism rates in Soviet Jewish families are low, despite the overall strong Russian cultural influence, and they remain so after immigration. The traditional Jewish values of intellectual achievement, financial success, and strong family ties apparently are among factors that explain the difference between the two cultures. Jewish families from Russia tend not to use alcohol to relieve tension; instead, they seek support and compassion through verbal expression of their emotional discomfort.

## THE FAMILY IN TRANSITION

The great majority of families likely to enter therapy recently have immigrated to the United States. Because many Soviet Jews came from a long-term totalitarian country, professionals tend to view their adaptation process in political terms, which reduces myriad problems to one: adaptation to life in a free country. These researchers have concluded that nearly all difficulties experienced by Soviet Jewish immigrants arise from their "adaptation to freedom"

(Goldstein, 1984) or even from peculiar *Homo Sovieticus* characteristics (Halberstadt & Mandel, 1989), which connotes dependency, an emphasis on collectivism, feelings of insecurity and inadequacy, and hunger for admiration. Consequently, the emotional effects of cultural transition and the uprooting of the family structure and functioning, which are common for all immigrants, have been underestimated.

According to other studies, Soviet Jews' problems in the United States are rooted in a family structure that discourages children's separation and autonomy (Hulewat, 1981). This explanation also ignores the drama of immigration itself, which is laden with loss, disruption, and new challenges (Aroian, 1990). In fact, Soviet Jewish immigrant families undoubtedly endure similar types of adjustment conflicts and crises as other immigrants (Sluzki, 1979; Landau, 1982).

Therapists working with Soviet Jewish immigrant families, should identify accurately the beginning of the transition period so as to understand the causes and content of family crises and the dynamics of their symptoms. Due to the Soviet Union's collapse, the traumatic processes of migration and family uprooting often preceded actual immigration to the United States:

Alex, a 10-year-old boy, was referred for excessive truancy, rudeness, and fighting at school, as well as lying and fighting with his 16-year-old brother at home. The family, which consisted of a divorced Jewish mother and her two sons, lived in the United States a year before entering therapy, but their real migration had begun 3 years earlier when this half-Jewish, half-Armenian family was forced to flee from the anti-Armenian violence in Azerbaidzhan, where they had lived in very comfortable circumstances. When the father chose not to follow his wife and children, the parents divorced. The mother and her two sons left behind almost all their possessions and arrived in Moscow, where they rented one room in a two-bedroom apartment.

All this coincided with Alex's starting school. The mother felt depressed and guilty, especially toward her younger son, for whom she was unable to provide the necessary support and structure, while his older brother became his sibling's disciplinarian.

––––––––– ❧ –––––––––

In addition to political and ethnic violence in some Soviet republics, the Chernobyl catastrophe prompted many to abandon their apartments and belongings in Kiev and other Ukrainian cities, or to send their children far from the region that was affected by radiation if they could do so.

Nina, a 14-year-old girl from Kiev, was referred by her parents after she made several suicide attempts. After the breakdown of the Chernobyl plant, she was sent away to her paternal grandmother, who lived in Azerbaidzhan, together with the son of her father's coworker, for about a year. She did not go to school regularly there. Nina found out that her father's coworker also was his mistress, and told her mother about this, which resulted in her parents' divorce.

Nina emigrated with her mother and grandparents within a year, while her father remained in Kiev and worked in a high-radioactivity zone near the Chernobyl plant. His wife later discovered that he had a cancer, apparently as a result of his being exposed to radiation. Nina's mother sponsored his arrival to the United States, where the parents reunited. The grandparents strongly opposed this reunification, because they believed that their daughter should not forgive him for his adultery. The father's arrival coincided with the beginning of the daughter's suicidal behavior.

This case demonstrates how a family's preimmigration uprooting marked a turning point in its current dynamics.

## SOME ASPECTS OF FAMILY THERAPY

Typically, Soviet Jewish immigrant families view therapy as a last resort and enter it only when all other family resources are exhausted. By then, children usually exhibit signs of severe disturbance, including drug use, suicide attempts, and violent behavior at home. In response, family members' predominant emotions are despair, guilt, and depression. Most parents who enter therapy expect that their children will be given medication that will stop undesirable behavior. Because of the biological model of emotional disorders promoted by Soviet psychiatry, as well as its discriminatory and, in some cases, persecutory character, the idea of "talking to a stranger" appears foreign. The family invariably expects the therapist to take care of a "sick" child. Therefore, it is important to bring the entire family to sessions. We believe that the therapist should be persistent and firm from the beginning; otherwise, other family members may never appear.

It also is important for the therapist to establish a therapeutic alliance with the family. This often is difficult, because Soviet families usually have an ambiguous attitude toward authority and solve their problems with the support of friends, generally not trusting outsiders. Finally, Western cultural values that are implicit in family therapy differ strongly from those of Soviet Jewish families: The contrasts include individual versus group responsibility; independence versus mutual dependency; and self-reliance and individualism versus dependence on support systems and collectivism. For an American professional, these value differences can be a serious obstacle to understanding Soviet Jewish families (in addition to the language barrier). Most therapists and social workers who work with this group are employed by various Jewish communal organizations, and thus are likely to interpret the problem of adjustment as one of acculturation, a nontherapeutic issue. Professionals unfamiliar with Soviet

Jewish culture assume that their clients are merely the victims of governmental anti-Semitism, a view that assumes obedience and passivity on the part of family members and renders worthless many positive aspects of their previous experiences. As the family resists this attitude, the therapist is likely to see its behavior as manipulative. He or she should guard against quick conclusions about family structure and the desirable evolution thereof. Thus, a therapist who notes a grandmother's excessive power and attempts to weaken the bonds between her and her grandchild, or who attempts to disengage one spouse from his or her parents, can quickly lose the family in treatment. If, instead, he or she relates to the grandparents as experts who are able to help the parents to take charge of their child's behavior, the outcome can be promising.

The therapist also should actively initiate and facilitate communication, encouraging and modeling open exchanges, thus discouraging Soviet Jewish families' tendency to speak to each other through the therapist.

Since Soviet Jewish families usually enter therapy when a situation is out of control, intense feelings often are expressed, with anger often the dominant emotion. It is important for the therapist to support the family's emotions, but not to become absorbed in them and lose control over the therapeutic process. Frequent stormy expressions of feelings should not inhibit the therapist, who might understand that these outbursts often express clients' sense of helplessness.

Therapy with a Soviet Jewish family often involves an attempt by a child, parent, or grandparent to reveal a secret in the absence of other family members, or to talk about it with the therapist individually. This tendency is rooted in an old tradition of protecting family members from "too much knowledge" and keeping children safe from the dangerous realities of the adult world. The therapist ought to remain on guard against this dynamic and encourage family members to discuss together important information.

As with most immigrant families, financial pressures play a major role in many Soviet Jewish families' day-to-day life; they may largely guide members' behavior. Yet the therapist often meets with a determined avoidance of these issues, exploration of which can be very fruitful for understanding a family's struggles, as well as clarifying its structure. For example, college students might continue to live at home not because of separation problems, but because of the higher expense of living on campus.

## CONCLUSION

Soviet Jewish immigrants are very diverse, coming from a geographic and cultural background that ranges from Central Asia to the Baltics. Thus, generalizations about this group are of limited validity. Yet with the given that each family is unique, we have tried to outline some issues pertinent to family therapy with Soviet Jews, including their ambiguous attitudes toward their identity, therapists' unwarranted interpretations of their adjustment process, the up-rooting that often preceded actual emigration from the Soviet Union, the perception of therapy as a last resort, and the hopelessness and devastation often expressed in therapy.

## REFERENCES

Aroian, K. J. (1990). A model of psychological adaptation to migration and resettlement. *Nursing Research, 39,* 5–10.

Goldstein, E. (1984). Homo sovieticus in transition. *Journal of the American Academy of Psychoanalysis, 12,* 116–126.

Halberstadt, A., & Mandel, L. (1989). Group therapy with Soviet immigrants. In D. A. Halperin (Ed.), *Group psychodynamics: New paradigms and new perspectives.* Chicago: Year Book Medical Publishers.

Hulewat, P. (1981). Dynamics of the Soviet Jewish family: Its impact on clinical practice for the Jewish family agency. *Journal of Jewish Communal Service, 58,* 53–60.

Landau, J. (1982). Therapy with families in cultural transition. In M. McGoldrick, J. K. Pearce, & J. Giordano (Eds.), *Ethnicity and family therapy* (1st. ed., pp. 552–572). New York: Guilford Press.

Sluzki, C. E. (1979). Migration and family conflict. *Family Process, 18,* 379–390.

Zaslavsky, V., & Brym, R. J. (1983). *Soviet-Jewish emigration and Soviet nationality policy.* New York: St. Martin's Press.

# CHAPTER 43

# Israeli Families

## Eva Fogelman

In the United States, every Jewish immigrant group was made to feel not entirely welcome by its predecessors. Israeli families in the late 20th century also have encountered stigmatization and even neglect, which has affected their self-esteem.

Israeli immigrants, however, have differed from most of their predecessors in one important respect: They have not been escaping persecution. Israelis who have immigrated for economic or personal reasons have not been perceived as requiring this level of communal support. Indeed, their very presence in America has been questioned by many American Jews, who see them as people who ought to be in Israel, fighting and maintaining the homeland and the Zionist dream.

The stigma against them was reinforced in 1976 by the late Prime Minister Yitzhak Rabin, who, during a television interview, called *yordim*[1] "the leftovers of weaklings." The phrase "stuck" for a generation.

Twelve years later, Moshe Shokeid noted, "The Israeli experience represents a dramatic turn in Jewish history, as well as in the components of personal Jewish identity which sharply separate Israelis and other Jews. Nevertheless, the *yordim* are the first generation of Jews in thousands of years who have voluntarily chosen to leave the land of Israel for life in the Diaspora" (Shokeid, 1988, p. 210).

Israelis, like other immigrants, are subjected to many stereotypes. In New York, the typical Israeli was perceived in the 1970s and 1980s as a taxicab driver or, more recently, as driving a moving van—someone aggressive, sometimes dishonest, and too ashamed to go back.

In the 1990s, these stereotypes persist, but American Jews' attitude toward Israeli Americans changed to greater acceptance. Israeli consulates are more open to helping *yordim*. In 1991, even Rabin came full circle when he was quoted as saying, "What I said then [1976] doesn't apply today. . . . The Israelis living abroad are an integral part of the Jewish community and there is no point talking about ostracism" (cited in Rosen, 1993, p. 3).

## DEFINITION AND DEMOGRAPHICS

Defining the Israeli American population is itself a thorny issue. One fairly clear-cut definition is a person who was born in Israel and now resides in America. But what about someone who lived many years in Israel, but was born elsewhere, or children of Israelis who have American citizenship but are considered Israelis by themselves or by others?

The 1990 National Jewish Population Survey estimates that 65,000 Israeli-born Jews reside in the United States. If one counts households where Hebrew is spoken, the population is 144,000, or under 3% of the current Jewish population of 5.5 million. Most live in New York, Los Angeles, and Miami. They range from academicians and professionals to small and large entrepreneurs and skilled laborers. Israeli American women who work part- or full-time are concentrated in the teaching and social service professions.

## MOTIVATIONS TO IMMIGRATE TO THE UNITED STATES

Most Israeli Americans immigrate to further their education, improve their economic status, or reunite with their families.

Psychological factors influence why some Israelis, and not others, choose to leave their native land. The immigrant may be the "black sheep" in the family, a non-Orthodox member of an ultra-Orthodox family, an Orthodox child in a secular family, a gay or lesbian who feels ostracized, someone who has not lived up to parental expectations, or a single person in search of a mate. He or she also may be the motivated member who hopes to "make it" in the "Promised Land" of America.

Some have felt isolated in Israeli society for political or ideological reasons. As one man said, "It feels worse to be alienated among your own than in a country of total strangers." For still others, a move to the United States can serve as an escape from intimate problems, or to join a loved one who refuses to establish roots in Israel.

When a family is involved, the husband usually is the prime mover, with his wife and children reluctantly following. The motivating forces need be examined in the context of the family dynamics.

## FAMILY ADJUSTMENT

Recent studies of Israeli families in Los Angeles (Gold, 1992) show that most have adapted economically and educationally to life in America. Yet, they also struggle with a stigmatized immigrant status, ambivalence, and cultural marginality. They have difficulty enjoying material success because they are ambivalent about remaining here, miss their family still in Israel, and no longer belong to a close-knit community.

Understanding three themes about Israeli American family dynamics is critical to successful therapeutic intervention.

## The Sojourner Theme

Israeli Americans often are, to use Siu's (1952) useful concept, "sojourners": people who never make their new country their emotional home. Although they do not recreate Israeli society in the United States, they share the sojourners' yearning to return to their native land. Family conflicts manifest themselves around issues of staying or returning.

Teenagers may act out family ambivalence and guilt at having left Israel by deciding to return to Israel for an education or to serve in the army. This move sometimes intensifies intrafamily conflict.

Other dynamics are set in motion when an Israeli couple has American-born children, or offspring who were young when the parents emigrated and thus have no ties to Israeli society. The entire family mirrors the alienation that the parents feel in America. Communication can become constricted because parents and children lack a common language. Americanized children may feel that their parents cannot relate to them and their needs (e.g., fathers who assist with Little League baseball teams), and may decide to marry a non-Jew, creating a family crisis. Parents may be overwhelmed with guilt for leaving Israel, feel shame within their American and Israeli peer groups, and question whether it was worth the financial gains or other benefits to have immigrated to the United States.

Judah and Sylvia met while both pursued doctorates at an Ivy League college. He came from a prominent Israeli diplomatic family and lived outside of Israel on and off during his childhood; she was raised in a Jewishly committed family that emigrated to the United States from Eastern Europe.

While still graduate students, they had a son. When Judah completed his studies, he was eager to move to Israel and start a career. Despite her Zionist ideology, Sylvia was unable to leave her elderly father behind and felt that Israel would be too provincial for her cosmopolitan tastes.

Judah felt heartbroken, humiliated, and betrayed; he thought he had married a Jewishly and Zionistically committed woman who understood him and shared his ideals.

During couple therapy, it became clear that Sylvia had married a status symbol. For her, the marriage had become passionless, and Judah's decision to return to Israel gave her the chance to end it. Their child's need for nurturing and attention detracted from intimacy, which they did little to enhance since he was conceived in order to unite them as a couple.

The therapy included assignments to go away together for a weekend without their child, and to set aside one evening a week to "date" in order to renew romance. After several months, Sylvia agreed to go to Israel, provided that Judah later would consider a temporary position in America.

Years later, the couple spent a few years in the United States and then faced another decision about staying or returning to Israel. Although Sylvia was hesitant to return to Israel, she now had stronger positive feelings toward her successful husband, and the decision did not become a crisis. Twenty years later, the marriage endures.

––––––––––––  ✍  ––––––––––––

## The First- and Second-Generation Conflict

Many Israeli parents have difficulty transmitting an "Israeli identity"—speaking Hebrew, celebrating Jewish holidays as national/cultural rather than religious occasions, and presenting Jewish history of the Biblical and modern Zionist period. For example, *Yom Hazicharon*, Remembrance Day for the fallen soldiers, the "holiest," most sacred Israeli national holiday is not on the calendar of most Jewish institutions.

Children in Israeli American families may feel alienated from their Jewish American peers who celebrate Jewish culture more around synagogue and religious life rather than national holidays. The parents' longing to return to an idealized Israeli society may also diminish the second generation's feeling of belonging in American society and fitting into a peer group. If members of the second generation suffer from alienation and not belonging to a peer group, they may engage in extreme measures to adapt, and thus create family conflicts.

After World War II, Jacob and Mila, both from Lodz, Poland, met in a German displaced-persons camp and married. Mila was the sole survivor of her family, except for a few cousins in the United States. Jacob had one brother in Israel and one in America: All his other relatives were murdered. Jacob was in the Vilna Ghetto and then escaped into the woods; he was not in a concentration camp.

To fulfill their Zionist dream, they headed for Palestine after the war. Jacob fought in the Israeli War of Independence and the 1956 Sinai War.

They came to the United States for economic reasons and to be reunited with family members. Their 40-year-old son attended my group for children of Holocaust survivors upon completing a drug rehabilitation program. Leonard was 10 when he arrived in the United States with his parents and younger sister. As an adult, he only remembered a word or two of Hebrew and never had been back to Israel. When his relatives from there visited, he could not communicate with them because he didn't know Hebrew or Yiddish. Leonard has a fragmented self.

Jacob was the sole breadwinner; Mila stayed home, took care of the children, and never became integrated into either American society or the community of other survivors.

Although the family was not religious, Leonard was placed in an Orthodox *yeshiva*, where he never fit in. After Leonard was enrolled in a public school that had many minority-group students, he often was beaten and feared for his life.

To obtain protection, Leonard became a gang member, began taking and dealing in drugs, and could not concentrate on his schoolwork. His family denied his problem and became victims of Leonard's wrath. The resulting victim–oppressor family dynamic seemed almost a repetition of Nazi Holocaust psychodynamics.

At age 45, Leonard is living with his parents after having been in jail, in several rehabilitation programs, and living with several women who took care of him. He continues to persecute his aged parents, one of whom has been close to death several times. In recent years, Leonard has expressed an interest in going to Israel but cannot afford to.

Family therapy has focused on breaking the victim–oppressor equilibrium. Jacob and Mila were validated for their fears of being harmed by Leonard, who is dependent, insecure, and alienated. Both parents were made aware of their enabling role and how their helping Leonard started with Mila's alienation as a new immigrant. Not being independent, she fostered his dependency on her whenever he got into trouble in school, with the law, or with peers. When the Israeli American mother is isolated, family relations can take extreme forms, such as overdependence on a child to be the link to the outside world or enmeshed family relations.

———————— ᘓ ————————

## Economic Failure

Conflicts often erupt in Israeli American families when the "American dream" is not realized.

If one spouse was the prime mover for the immigration, the sometimes reluctant mate may assume the role of mourner. If economic comfort and other personal goals are thwarted, the marital conflict may intensify because there is no way to go back. It is common for a child to become the identified patient by "acting out" in an attempt to bring the family together.

Abraham, an Israeli, was referred to me for couple therapy with his American wife Batya, or Betty. Abraham had started drinking, had a temper that was out of control, and his wife feared for his well-being (particularly related to his heart problems), and for her own safety. This was a second marriage for Abraham and a first for Batya. Abraham and his younger sister had survived the Nazi occupation of Belgium in hiding. They were brought to Israel by Youth Aliyah with the assistance of family friends who had searched for them after the war. Abraham's parents were deported to concentration camps and did not survive; an aunt and some young cousins survived and emigrated to America after liberation. Abraham and his sister were raised on a *kibbutz* in Israel.

After his army service, Abraham married a woman who lived on a different *kibbutz* and fathered four children. The *kibbutz* gave him space and time for his creative work as an artist.

Abraham's marriage was not satisfying, and he left his wife and four children when a patron invited him to the United States to continue his artistic work. He never regarded his move to the United States as permanent; he was hoping to spend half a year in America and half a year in Israel. After a year or so, Abraham's relationship with the patron soured, and he was left to struggle as a poor artist. He felt awkward returning to the *kibbutz* because he was divorced and felt he no longer had a home.

In the meantime, he met an American woman who started helping to promote his artwork, and he felt a renewed sense of hope that his art career would enable him to live in both the United States and Israel. When Abraham married the American woman, he found that she wanted a suburban lifestyle and could not devote as much time to his art career. His hopes took a backseat as he struggled with odd jobs to pay the mortgage. Around the same time, in 1982, some 13 years ago, his son was killed protecting Israel's borders. Since that time, Abraham has not been able to resume his artwork in a serious manner. He blamed his lack of productivity on all sorts of external reasons and bemoaned the fact that he left Israel. He felt that there was no way to return, particularly since his American wife had a job that she enjoyed and in which she thrived, and she would not be able to be the breadwinner in Israel.

During couple therapy, the children (who came to the United States for brief or extended periods of time) joined some of the sessions. They had all felt abandoned by their father, resentful that he had left Israel, and were disappointed that he kept bemoaning his failure and was not successful. Israelis in Israel feel that if someone leaves Israel for the "Golden Land," at least they should "make it."

Family therapy sessions have focused on communication between Abraham and his children, and the children's articulation to Batya of their appreciation for the home they have in America because of her love and warmth. Now in their 20s, the children have accepted their father's decision to divorce their mother and have come to perceive him as a real person rather than retain the image of who they wanted him to become in America. Abraham still bemoans his lack of success in America and his mistake in leaving Israel.

---  ◈  ---

## CONCLUSION

The Israeli American family's adaptation is complicated by lack of acceptance by the existing American Jewish community.

Israeli families in therapy often overemphasize their sojourner status as a means of denying difficult family problems and dealing with their distrust. An American Jewish therapist may evoke their rage toward those who ostracized and did not help them, whereas a non-Jewish clinician may not understand the Israeli, and evoke his or her mistrust of Israelis of the outside world in general. An Israeli therapist may know people with whom the client is acquainted; the client thus may feel the therapist cannot be trusted to keep the family secrets. To foster trust, the therapist should raise issues at the onset of treatment so an alliance can begin.

Some of the intergenerational problems Israeli Americans face (e.g., drug abuse) lie beyond Israeli parents' experience; they often are accustomed to close-knit family ties and to a simpler life. Feelings of great guilt and shame further alienate the parents from peers and family in America and in Israel. In family therapy, these feelings need to be addressed directly to alleviate them.

Despite its traditional egalitarian pathos, Israel has remained a male-dominated society. Men have the role of providers; women that of caring for the family needs and maintaining social ties. When the male fails in his role, therapy can help him reestablish his position as an authority figure and enable other family members to acknowledge his positive attributes.

The family unit takes on an inordinate significance for Israelis, who for the most part do not feel integrated into American society. Although the family therapist's role is to focus on internal family conflicts and dynamics, he or she also is a bridge to the outside world. This involves helping the family integrate its identity and acculturate into American society. Most Israelis also face the challenge of integrating Israeli and Jewish identity. The former is largely nationally and culturally based; Jewish identity is largely historical and religious.

## NOTE

1. *Yordim* are Israeli Jews who "descend" from the "higher" place of Israel to the *diaspora*, as opposed to *olim*, who ascend from the *diaspora* to Israel. *Aliya* (immigration to Israel) is viewed as ascending to a higher place. *Yerida* (emigration) has, in contrast, a pejorative connotation.

## REFERENCES

Gold, S. (1992). *Israelis in Los Angeles: Pilot study report.* Los Angeles: Susan and David Wilstein Institute of Jewish Policy Studies.
Rosen, S. (1993). *The Israeli corner of the American Jewish community.* New York: American Jewish Committee.

Shokeid, M. (1988). *Children of circumstances: Israeli emigrants in New York*. Ithaca, NY: Cornell University Press.

Siu, P. C. P. (1952). The sojourner. *American Journal of Sociology, 58*, 34–44.

## SUGGESTED READINGS

Cohen, S. M. (1986). Israeli emigres and the New York Federation: A case study in ambivalent policymaking for "Jewish communal deviants." *Contemporary Jewry, 7*, 155–165.

Cohen, Y., & Tyree, A. (1994). Palestinian and Jewish Israeli-born immigrants in the United States. *International Migration Review, 28*(2), 243–255.

Elias, N., & Blanton, J. (1987). Dimensions of ethnic identity in Israeli Jewish families living in the United States. *Psychological Reports, 60*, 367–375.

Freedman, M., & Korazim, J. (1986). Israelis in the New York area labor market. *Contemporary Jewry, 7*, 141–153.

Gold, S. (1994). Israeli immigrants in the United States: The question of community. *Qualitative Sociology, 17*(4), 325–363.

Gold, S. (1994). Patterns of economic cooperation among Israeli immigrants in Los Angeles. *International Migration Review, 28*(105), 114–135.

Gold, S. (1995). Gender and social capital among Israelis in Los Angeles. *Diaspora., 4*(3), 267–301.

Kass, D., & Lipset, S. M. (1979). Israelis in exile. *Commentary, 68*(5), 68–72.

Kass, D., & Lipset, S. M. (1982). Jewish immigration to the United States from 1967 to the present: Israelis and others. In M. Sklare (Ed.), *Understanding American Jewry* (pp. 272–294). New Brunswick, NJ: Transaction Books.

Levi, L. G. (1986). Israelis in New York and the Federation of Jewish Philanthropies: A study of anomie and reconnection. *Contemporary Jewry, 7*, 167–180.

Peleg, M. (1989). The relationship of separation from love objects, and a severed national ideology, to depression, among Israeli immigrants in the United States. I. *Journal of Psychology and Judaism, 13*(4), 189–223.

Peleg, M. (1990). The relationship of separation from love objects, and a severed national ideology, to depression, among Israeli immigrants in the United States. II. *Journal of Psychology and Judaism, 14*(1), 5–48.

Ritterband, P. (1986). Israelis in New York. *Contemporary Jewry, 7*, 113–126.

Shokeid, M. (1993). One-night-stand ethnicity: The malaise of Israeli-Americans. *Israel Social Science Research, 8*(2), 23–50.

Thernstrom, S., Orlov, A., & Handlin, O. (Eds.). (1980). *Harvard encyclopedia of American ethnic groups*. Cambridge, MA: Harvard University Press.

Yanover, Y. (1992, September 18). Israelis living in North America are upset that their children are adopting American values. *Baltimore Jewish Times*, pp. 52–53, 114–117.

# PART IX

# SLAVIC FAMILIES

CHAPTER 44

# Slavic Families:
# An Overview

Phyllis P. Marganoff
John Folwarski

Legend has it that three brothers looking for land to colonize stopped in the vast plain now known as Poland. One brother, Czech, went south and became the father of the Southern Slavs (Serbs, Croats, Slovenes, Macedonians, and Bulgarians). Another, Rus, went east and was the father of the Eastern Slavs (Russians, Belarusians, Carpatho Rusyns and Ukrainians). The third, Lech, stayed and became the ancestor of all Polish people and the other groups that constitute the Western Slavs (Poles, Czechs, and Slovaks). Some eastern countries still refer to Poland as Lechistan (Chorzempa, 1993), and Russia and the Czech Republic bear the obvious imprint of the other brothers.

Centuries later, most Westerners are ignorant of the geography, history, and traditions of this area. During the period when an "Iron Curtain" separated Eastern and Western Europe, it was easy to think of all peoples behind the Iron Curtain as Communists and alike. Now, at the end of the era of Soviet domination of Central and Eastern Europe, as war in the Balkans has raged, our confusion and lack of understanding of the Slavs is daily reinforced by media reports of territorial occupations, border changes, and ethnic cleansing in the former Yugoslavia. And we cannot make sense of who these people are, or why they are fighting.

Slavic immigrants to the United States have suffered from this ignorance. In movies, for example, Slavic Americans have always been portrayed stereotypically as "physically strong, hardworking, brutal, crude, sexual, inarticulate, stubborn, amoral, clannish, violent, intemperate" (Gladsky, 1992, p. 138). To truly understand them requires familiarity with their past history and present circumstances. Even then, if the Westerner "is not willing to feel with his whole being, he cannot hope to understand" (Kaplan, 1993, p. xv). The Western mind cannot comprehend because it would never occur "to a citizen of the West . . . that he could be beaten with whips as a practical measure either of investigation or of punishment" (Kaplan, 1993, p. xvi).

## FAMILY STRUCTURE

It is dishearteningly beyond the scope of this chapter to provide more than a brief overview of Slavic American families. There is sparse research available on Slavs, and a review of it reveals almost nothing about family life. Material written in English primarily addresses political, economic, and religious issues related to power and dominance congruent with the patriarchal model. National literature and poetry are for the most part untranslated and thus unavailable to the English speaker.

The Slavic people emerged in Central Europe at the crossroads of Europe and Asia. This fact is central in shaping who they are, and its impact cannot be overestimated. Historically, the Slavs have been subjected to East–West tensions. Originally a peaceful, pastoral people, they experienced conquest by the Turks and have been pulled into different spheres because of their allegiance to either Roman Catholicism, Byzantine Catholicism, Eastern Orthodoxy (Russian, Greek, Serbian, or Bulgarian), or Islam. They coexist, but not always peacefully.

Gimbutas (1971) describes a form of familial and community organization that has ancient origins and was found at one time in all Slavic groups. The family was patriarchal, patrilineal, and joint (communal), with women having greatly inferior status. This form still exists to a slight degree in the former Yugoslavia, Bulgaria, and Belarus. Serbo-Croatian language has two words for it: *zadruga*, meaning "joint family, home of several brothers and their families"; or *druzina*, meaning "community." Members of the *zadruga* are called "comrade." In Croatian, *zadruga* means "united" or "undivided brothers." In parts of Bulgaria, the word "household" referred to both the *zadruga* (community) and its members "and Bulgaria was the country that, in the 10th century, proposed something called the Bogomil Heresy—a radical system of belief that tried to abolish all hierarchy and inequality in the church, including the inequalities between men and women" (Hoffman, 1993, p. 352).

In Russia, a distinction is made between the large generic family and the small paternal family. The center of the community is the hearth, the house in which the head of the community lives with his immediate family. It is one large room with a hearth sunk into the ground. Historically, here members of the *zadruga* congregated in their leisure time and took one or all of their meals together. The other houses, actually sleeping quarters, were arranged in a semicircle around the hearth. In 1897, it was reported that in Belarus, in the Minsk area, the father would build his sons separate huts, one for each new family, but the land, stock, and tools were owned collectively, and everyone would eat and work together. Each family individually owned only clothes and other small items. The whole community had one patronymic, given at baptism, which was the name of the founder of the *zadruga*. The father or grandfather was at the top of the hierarchy.

The "housemother" supervised the women's work. She had charge of the kitchen, food, cows, pigs, clothing, weaving, and spinning, and was responsible for relationships among the women in the family and for assigning their tasks. Generally the wife of the father or grandfather, she derived her power from him and lost it when he died or was replaced. She was the mediator between the housefather and the rest of the family, but she herself never became the head of a *zadruga* or community.

At home, the father was a judge, seeing that all duties in the family were fulfilled, and settling problems and quarrels. The sons formed the family council. The position of women, lowly in all Slavic groups, was most menial in Russia, where the *zadruga* was "cruelly patriarchal" (Gimbutas, 1971, p. 135) and the housefather was allowed to beat his own wife and children and even to commit incest with his sons' wives. In the 1800s, the *zadruga* disappeared in the Western Slavic groups but in the East and South Slavic areas it was strong through the turn of the century (Gimbutas, 1971).

About 12 different groups of Slavic peoples have immigrated to the United States. Space permits only a brief explication of who they are. The two largest Slavic immigrant groups are the Poles and the Slovaks. They will be discussed in subsequent chapters, as will the Czechs and the Russians; Soviet Jews were discussed in Chapter 42.

## THE EASTERN SLAVS

The largest of the Eastern Slav groups, the Russians, will be discussed later. Other Eastern Slav groups include the Ukrainians, Belarusians, and Carpatho Rusyns.

### The Ukrainians

The Ukrainians are distinguished primarily by language and religion, and the Ukrainian language is classified as East Slavic, and religious affiliation is split between the Ukrainian Catholic and Eastern Orthodox Church. The name "Ukrainian" as a national or ethnic designation was not widely used in Europe until the second quarter of the 20th century, so arrivals to the United States from Ukrainian ethnolinguistic territories called themselves something other than Ukrainian. The ethnic identity of Ukrainians is stronger than that of some of the other Slavic groups. Ukrainian language continues to be taught at home and used in in churches, schools, and fraternal and social organizations. There are Ukrainian-language newspapers and radio programs. Ukrainian Americans have created a self-sustaining community. Ukrainian ethnic identity is further reinforced by the larger society, whose ignorance of the differences between Poles, Russians, and Ukrainians obliges Ukrainians to explain these differences. Ukrainian Americans as a group seem more cohesive than many other Slavic American groups.

## The Belarusians

Arriving in the United States between 1880 and 1914, the Belarusians had little sense of national group identity and joined existing Polish or Russian American communities. Post-World War I immigrants felt a more distinct identity, and since that time a Belarusian American community has developed. Post-World War II immigrant professionals, artisans, and skilled workers raised in Soviet Belarussia arrived fully aware of their Belarusian identity. They speak Belarusian and worship in one of a small number of Belarusian Orthodox Churches. The community has a few newspapers, and since 1945 distinctly Belarusian organizations have been formed, including the Belarusian American Youth Organization, which has folk dance ensembles, sports groups, and sponsors seminars on Belarusian culture. Ethnic identity is not as strong as that of some of the Slavic groups.

## The Carpatho Rusyns

Ruthenia was part of the Polish Lithuanian Commonwealth from the 14th through the 17th centuries. Carpatho Rusyns have always lived as a minority group in regions ruled by others, at times in Hungary, and at times in Czechoslovakia, never having their own state. Carpatho Rusyns now reside in the Ukraine and Slovakia. In Europe, most call themselves Ukrainian, but in the United States maintain themselves as a distinct ethnic group. It is estimated that in the 1970s 618,000 Carpatho Rusyns were living in the United States, mostly in the Northeastern industrial centers.

Carpatho Rusyns are mostly Eastern Christians, belonging to either the Byzantine Rite (Greek) Catholic Church or one of several Eastern Orthodox churches (Thernstrom, Orlov, & Handlin, 1980, p. 203). Although community life is organized around the church calendar and festivals, and ethnic identity depends largely on the individual's relation to the church, the church has not helped the Carpatho Rusyn community to preserve its integrity or its heritage. People who converted to orthodoxy began to think of themselves as Russian rather than Rusyn. There is one full-fledged ethnic church, the American Carpatho Rusyn Orthodox Greek Catholic Church, which encourages the preservation of the unique characteristics of the Carpatho Rusyns. The Roman

Catholic Church hierarchy, which had jurisdiction over the Carpatho Rusyns, has been antagonistic to and suspicious of them. When Byzantine Catholic priests arrived from the homeland to serve the Carpatho Rusyns, Roman Catholic bishops refused to accept them. Eventually many converted to Russian Orthodoxy, thus further confusing students of ethnicity.

## THE WESTERN SLAVS

Poles, Slovaks, and Czechs will be discussed in depth in subsequent chapters. They adhere to Roman Catholic or Protestant faiths and use the Latin alphabet.

## THE SOUTHERN SLAVS

The Southern Slavs include Serbs, Croats, Slovenes, and Bulgarians. The name Yugoslavia means "Land of the Southern Slavs," and it represented a 19th-century idea of cultural and political unification for these peoples. "Here the battle between Communism and capitalism is merely one dimension of a struggle that pits Catholicism against Orthodoxy, Rome against Constantinople, the legacy of Hapsburg Austria–Hungary against that of Ottoman Turkey—in other words, West against East, the ultimate historical and cultural conflict" (Kaplan, 1993, p. 7). The South Slavic languages are so similar that, with varying degrees of ease, their speakers can understand one another. The Roman Catholic Croats use the Latin alphabet for spoken language. The Orthodox Serbs use the Cyrillic alphabet for spoken Serb. Except for the difference in alphabets, Serbo-Croatian or Croato-Serbian, the literary language of the Serbs and Croatians is "virtually identical" (Thernstrom et al., 1980, p. 916). Referring to the current war in the Balkans, *The New York Times* ("The Week in Review," 1995) called it "fratricidal rivalry between people who are ethnically indistinguishable" (p. 6). This suggests that the sibling bond shared among the Slavic peoples may hold clues to understanding the turmoil in Eastern Europe. Bank and Kahn (1982) observed that perceptions of sameness and difference are very significant to sibling relationships, facilitating closeness or distance. They noted that siblings usually "organize themselves into emotionally significant pairs, either positive or negative, in the service of love or hate" (p. 50). The concept of polarized rejection and rigidly differentiated relationships seems to apply to the family of Slavic peoples and particularly to the Southern Slavs.

### The Serbs

Largest of the national groups of the former Yugoslavia, Serbs use the Cyrillic alphabet, follow the Orthodox religion, and focus community life around the church parish in the United States. These three "badges of ethnicity" have alienated the Serbian Americans from their Slovene and Croatian neighbors, just as in the homeland. Serbs still use the Julian or Old Style calendar for religious observances. Traditions of music and chanting of poetry have survived in this country and have been revitalized by recent immigrants. The *krsna slava*, or family patron saint's day, is a uniquely Serbian celebration. The male head of the household, along with the priest, conducts this celebration. The *kum* and *kuma* (godfather and godmother) play a very important role in Serbian family life. They are so connected with the families of their godchildren that intermarriage between these families is restricted. The closeness engendered by these connections has deepened cohesion in the Serbian American community.

Serbs arrived in the United States as early as 1815, settling in California. They joined the California Gold Rush and prospered as businessmen, opening restaurants, saloons, hotels, and coffeehouses. The majority of Serbian immigrants came between 1900 and 1912. Refugees from poverty, they were young men who intended to earn money quickly in American factories and mines and then return home to improve their circumstances in the homeland. Serbian patriarchal values did not permit women to immigrate on their own. They came for arranged marriages or to join relatives. After World War II, Serbian patriotic organizations in the United States brought many Serbian refugees to this country. Unfortunately, when they arrived they were found to "hate each other" (Thernstrom et al., 1980, p. 924). Due to their hostility, there was much discord among Serb emigré groups. Serbian Americans are concentrated in the industrial Northeast, the industrial Midwest, Arizona, and California.

## The Croats

The second largest ethnic group in the former Yugoslavia, and the largest group of Southern Slavs to settle in the United States, the Croats are Roman Catholic, use the Latin alphabet, and speak a distinct language, properly called Croatian. Prior to 1880, Croatian immigrants came from the Adriatic coast and settled in California and around New Orleans. After 1880, the Croatian immigrants were part of the flood from Eastern Europe and established themselves around Cleveland and Pittsburgh, settling around the three institutions that were important to them: the fraternal association, the saloon, and the boardinghouse. The saloon served as the community center, with the saloon keeper functioning as banker, interpreter, and legal adviser to his patrons. The boardinghouse was an extension of the traditional community organization, the *zadruga*, which existed in some form in all Slavic groups. Croatian community life did not revolve around the church, as it did for some other Slavic groups, and Croats organized ethnic parishes more slowly than others did. Newer immigrants are competent in English, and use of the Croatian language is not a requirement for ethnic identity; but interest in the Croatian language was revived with the immigration of large numbers of women in the 20th century, who have not learned English.

## The Slovenes

A small but ethnically and linguistically distinct national group, 95% of Slovenes are Roman Catholic and the remainder are Lutheran. Located in the northwestern part of the former Yugoslavia, the Republic of Slovenia was established in 1945. Prior to 1918, the Slovene homeland was under the control of the Austro Hungarian Empire. Slovene men came to the United States at the turn of the century seeking to better themselves economically and then return to the homeland. They found work in mines, factories, and the lumber industry. Slovene women, in contrast to Serbian and Croat women, came as employees of Slovene tavern owners, who paid for their passage in return for agreement to work as waitresses for a certain period. Most of them married soon after arrival, but this was not required, as it was for Serbian and Croat women who came specifically to marry. Cleveland, by the 1890s, was (and still is) the largest and most vital center of Slovene American life. For Slovenes, as for other Slavs, the boardinghouse and the tavern, run by married Slovene women, were the focus of life outside the factory or mine. Slovenes also developed ethnic churches and schools, and the Slovene language was (and still is) taught. Descendents of turn-of-the-century immigrants have not regarded fluency in the language as a requirement of Slovene identity, but the presence of more recent immigrants who are native speakers has kept the language alive in the community. A Slovene newspaper, still published three times a week in Cleveland, has a largely postwar immigrant readership. Contact between Slovene Americans and the homeland has been encouraged by the Slovene government, resulting in a revitalized sense of belonging to the Slovene community.

## The Bulgarians

The Bulgarians originated in Bulgaria and Macedonia (today located in the south of the former Yugoslavia and northern Greece). Approximately 50,000 single men, mostly peasants, immigrated between 1900 and 1910. From 1919 to 1939, Bulgarian immigrants were mostly the wives and children of the men who had come earlier. Most Bulgarian Americans live in Detroit, with others concentrated in Indiana, New York, and Los Angeles.

The Bulgarian boardinghouse (*boort*) and coffeehouse (*kafené*) had unique features. Typically the *boort* owner rented two large rooms to as many as 12 men, who would use one room as sleeping quarters and one as a living area. They often did their own cooking to save money. The *kafené* owner/operator was Bulgarian, usually better educated than the factory workers. This was the place to find Bulgarian drinks and snacks, the company of other Bulgarians, and help with legal, insurance, employment, and real estate matters. Bulgarian family life was traditional, patriarchal, and cohesive. Mail-order brides were carefully arranged by family members and usually resulted in successful marriages. Children lived with or near their parents. Most Bulgarians married Bulgarians or others with Balkan backgrounds. The Bulgarian Orthodox Church, which is affiliated with the Orthodox Church in America, remains a central focus of life for Bulgarian Americans (Thernstrom et al., 1980, p. 188).

## CONCLUSION

Immigration of all the Slavic peoples to the United States followed a general pattern. Small numbers entered the American continent prior to 1880 and made distinctive contributions. Czechs were tobacco growers in the Colonies, Poles fought in the American Revolution, Russians participated in the California Gold Rush, and Croats ran the oyster industry in New Orleans. However, their presence was not strongly felt in the dominant culture.

All that changed between 1880 and 1914, when poor economic conditions in Central and Eastern Europe caused a flood of illiterate or semiliterate, landless Slavic peasants to immigrate to the United States. They came in response to letters from former neighbors telling of the opportunities in this land of plenty and had a huge impact on the United States economy. Working for the lowest wages, they spoke languages unintelligible to English speakers. Living together in ethnic enclaves, all were grouped together in the minds of Anglo Americans as Slavs or "Polacks." They stuck together because they feared, expected, and received ridicule, and experienced bigotry and brutality. They recreated the institutions of the homeland, including fraternal insurance societies, cultural organizations, music and dance societies, and their own newspapers in the major mining and industrial centers of America. They organized around their churches. Recent Slavic immigrants of higher socioeconomic and educational status gravitated to the established ethnic communities but had little in common with the earlier arrivals. Yet they have brought about a renewed interest in ethnic roots and revitalized churches, schools, ethnic theater, and musical groups. Many Americans know little about these new ethnic groups, who are often survivors of the trauma of war and life in a repressive Communist society. They are employed in education, the arts, and the sciences, and have started new businesses to serve the emigré communities of which they are a part.

These groups are distinctly different from one another, although the differences seem subtle or unnoticeable to the uninformed. A useful model for understanding how crucial it is for each Slavic group to differentiate its own uniqueness, even to the point of war, is to think about issues of sibling differentiation in a family. Distinctions that may seem small, unimportant, even irrelevant to outsiders are, for siblings, the basis for their claim to their inheritance and identity. Accomplishments, religion, language, property, and ancestors of all kinds become badges of belonging. In families, as in distinct ethnic groups, the need for togetherness and the simultaneous need for separateness can trigger ageless rivalries, in which the favorite daughter or son, as well as other siblings, can lose sight of the treasures of their common inheritance in their struggle to be special or powerful. Fear of loss (which was certainly the experience of the descendants of all three mythic brothers) keeps the focus on conflict and can disenfranchise the family or group, limiting options for personal or group power needed for health. The illusion of the togetherness of the peoples of the Soviet bloc was just that for 70 years. Slavic families in Europe and North America are now reinventing themselves. Family therapy and theory can help promote that process.

## ACKNOWLEDGMENTS

Our thanks to Helen Greven, L.C.S.W., Ph.D., for reading this and the Polish Families chapter; and to Danielle P. Marganoff, who kept us laughing.

## REFERENCES

Bank, S., & Kahn, M. (1982). *The sibling bond*. New York: Basic Books.

Chorzempa, R. (1993). *Korzenie Polskie: Polish roots*. Baltimore: Genealogical.

Gimbutas, M. (1971). *The Slavs*. New York: Praeger.

Gladsky, T. (1992). *Princes, peasants, and other Polish selves: Ethnicity in American literature*. Amherst: University of Massachusetts Press.

Hoffman, E. (1993). *Exit into history*. New York: Penguin.

Kaplan, R. (1993). *Balkan ghosts*. New York: St. Martin's Press.

Thernstrom, S., Orlov, A., & Handlin, O. (Eds.). (1980). *Harvard encyclopedia of American ethnic groups*. Cambridge, MA: Harvard University Press.

The week in review. (1995, September 3). *New York Times*, p. 6.

# CHAPTER 45

# Polish Families

John Folwarski
Phyllis P. Marganoff

## THE POLISH PEOPLE IN CONTEXT

Poland's boundaries have been threatened throughout history. Attack and occupation by foreign armies and the partition of Poland among its three neighbors—Russia, Prussia and Austria–Hungary—resulted in its disappearance from the map of Europe for 125 years. The Polish Republic arose again in the aftermath of World War I and existed for 20 years, until it was destroyed in World War II.

The election of the Cardinal of Krakow to the papacy in 1978 placed the international spotlight on Poland. The new Pope's visit to his homeland in 1979 was the "final breach in the wall behind which [the Poles] had been kept since 1945" (Zamoyski 1988, p. 389). By 1980, the Polish trade unions had begun the process that led 10 years later to the dissolution of the Polish Communist Party and the election of Lech Walesa as President. Polish emigrés around the world watched events in Poland, including large numbers of new, politically active immigrants who had left the country as the Communist influence waned.

## IMMIGRATION

The first Poles in the New World were glassblowers and craftsmen who came to the Jamestown Colony in 1608. Poles were invited to settle in New Holland around 1658. During the 18th century, small groups of wealthy Polish gentry immigrated to settle in the colonies. Until about 1875, the Polish tragedy of lost statehood was viewed sympathetically in the United States. Nobles who had lost titles came as political exiles and were seen as romantic, exotic figures.

Americans were inspired by the Polish struggles for independence from their Russian, Prussian, and Austrian occupiers.

Between 1870 and 1914, over 3 million illiterate, landless Polish peasants immigrated to the United States from the Russian, Prussian, and Austrian sections of the former Poland. The majority settled in large cities, clustered in neighborhoods called *Polonia* that were organized around the Catholic Church. The Polish language was spoken, and patterns of family and village life were replicated; simultaneously, enormous pressure was exerted on the new arrivals to become Americanized.

The particular discrimination and bigotry to which Polish and other Slavic immigrants were subjected are well documented. Since Poland did not exist, the immigrants' official documents often indicated they were of Russian, Prussian, or Austrian origin, which created a problem for descendants researching their roots. Also, people who had embarked together as neighbors in Poland (Jews, Poles, Lithuanians, Byelorussians) became necessarily attached to their distinct national group with its own cultural life immediately upon arrival. Similarities were ignored, differences emphasized, and common origins obscured. Polish Americans at this time "were among the most disadvantaged of immigrants . . . 'the white niggers' of the northern states" (Davies, 1992, p. 258). Their very survival depended on the support of their church and the fraternal and mutual-aid societies of their ethnic community. For these reasons, "the identity of Pole and Catholic was even more exclusive than at home; . . . Polish nationalism of the narrow, intolerant ethnic variety was even more widespread than in Poland" (Davies, 1992, p. 258).

More recent Polish immigrants have been professionals and intellectuals with a notably higher cultural and educational status than previous groups. Following World War II, from 1945 to 1960, they were people who were displaced by the war, Jews of Polish origin, and couples of mixed marriages in which one spouse was Jewish. They were "invited" by the Polish Government to emigrate, to give up their Polish citizenship, and they left Poland with great bitterness. The Poland they departed from was not the Poland in the memories of the Polish Americans. They left a country devastated by World War II. Destruction of Poland and its people was second in Hitler's mind only to destruction of the Jews.

After Solidarity's suppression by the Polish Communist government in 1980, new immigrants arrived who had grown up in the Communist People's Republic of Poland. They were accustomed to a society in which consumer goods were scarce, and opposition to authority was the main tool of survival. These immigrants had little in common with the older residents of Polonia, beyond Catholicism and the Polish language. They revitalized Polish American communities as they opened new businesses, filled the churches (especially for Polish masses), sent their children to parochial school, and opened new secular Polish schools.

A therapist who wishes to be effectively sensitive to the Polish American family's values, beliefs, and experience will locate the family on this immigration time line. The following cases reflect the experiences of families who came from Poland at different periods.

## The Ramirez Family

Joann Ramirez recently separated from Barry Ramirez. She came to therapy for help in adjusting to the separation. Joann is the younger of two daughters of Alex Zukowski, whose parents were born in Poland and were part of the great wave of immigration between 1870 and 1914. The family is typical of Polish immigrant families of that time. Of eight siblings, all but Alex remained in Polonia. Joann's father was an alcoholic, and she characterizes his siblings as heavy drinkers, too. Alex moved to a distant community and had infrequent contact with his family of origin, so Joann is effectively cut off from her father's family. The last time she saw them was at his funeral. Although unaware of her Polish roots, Joann has unconsciously followed the pattern of a good Polish wife. She remained married to a man with addiction problems, worked long hours as a nurse, and provided good meals and a good home. She is an example of someone who presents for therapy without any clear indicators of her ethnicity. Therapy could be helpful to Joann by placing her within her ethnic context, allowing her to better understand herself, her father, and his family, and to make conscious some of the hidden rules that govern her feelings and behavior. In doing so, she could discover hidden resources for defining herself and extend her options for self-empowerment.

———————— ∾ ————————

## The Szych Family

Marion Malinowski, his wife, Dominika, their daughter, Maria, and her husband, Stanislav Szych, immigrated in 1961, when the Polish Communist government encouraged Polish Jews, Poles who acknowledged Jewish ancestry, and those in mixed marriages to leave the country and renounce their Polish citizenship. Because of the continuing anti-Semitism in Poland, many felt they had no choice but to leave, although most were patriotic Poles whose families had lived in Poland for centuries, and believed they belonged there.

Marion Mittelman was a member of a Jewish merchant family in Warsaw. Dominika Olshevski was a Polish Catholic who hid him from the Nazis. After the war, despite disapproval of the remaining members of both families, they married. Maria, their daughter, was born in 1943. Marion changed his surname to Malinowski to make life easier for his family in postwar Poland, and Maria was raised as a practicing Catholic. In her teens she gave up her faith, and in her early 20s married a Polish Jew named Stanislav Isaac Szych. Stanislav's name was originally Wertman (a Jewish name), but he also had changed it to make life easier. In 1961, due to enduring anti-Semitism, Maria, her husband, and her parents came to the United States. Dissatisfied, they returned to Poland after 6 months, but inhospitable conditions in Poland forced them to bitterly renounce their Polish citizenship and return to the United States, where Maria gave birth to twins, Jurek (Jerry) and Grzegorz (Greg). Here, both Marion and Stanislav resumed their original Jewish names "because it was easier in this country to be Jewish than to be Polish."

The identity confusion of this family in terms of ethnicity is manifested in the way the twins describe themselves. When asked, "Are you Polish (or Jewish)?", Jerry answers, "That's a long story." He says he was always aware that, being Polish, he had to prove that he was not stupid by excelling in school. At times he would say he was Jewish to avoid the "dumb Polack" stereotype.

Greg says, "I wear a necklace on which there is a Polish Eagle and a Torah. There is supposed to be a crucifix, but for me it is a Torah." Regretting that he was not raised Jewish, Greg has begun studying Torah and is an observant Jew. Jerry is less clear. He identifies as neither Catholic nor Jewish, yet when he prays each night, as taught by his grandmother, he makes the Sign of the Cross. Both men married Jewish women. Maria says the family has always felt isolated because they have nothing in common with Polish Americans who arrived earlier in this century. They have experienced prejudice from Jews for their Polishness and from Poles because of their Jewishness.

❧

### The Pietrowski Family

Dr. Anna Pietrowski, age 35, a psychiatrist, and Mateusz, age 37, an engineer, and their two daughters, ages 15 and 13, immigrated in 1982. When asked if the interview could be videotaped, Anna became visibly anxious, refused, and apologized, saying that having lived under the Communist regime, she feared taping. When she talked about leaving Poland, Anna wept. She said that coming to this country felt like being in the middle of the ocean, unable to swim. "I did not feel equal to any American despite my education. I would drive around, taking my children to school, and ask myself, 'What am I doing here?' I felt like an outsider . . . part of my identity was lost. When I came here, I didn't understand, and then I learned . . . that in this country Polish ancestry is treated as much worse than Irish or Italian."

❧

## SHAME

Shame is a central dimension of the experience of the Polish American family. When a Polish family comes into therapy, it is likely that the therapist will be dealing with a shame-based system. There is the shame of being Polish, of belonging to an ethnic group that is regarded by the dominant culture as moronic. For Polish Americans, the election of a Pole to the Papacy gave a boost to their self-esteem. For non-Poles, it was an opportunity for a Polish joke. Shame in the Polish family is also rooted historically in the complex social class structure of Poland. Strong measures of family social control were used to prevent deviation that might lower the family's reputation in the community, and fear of being shamed extended to the whole household. Family members who disgraced their kin were rejected and, in extreme cases, legally disowned. The status struggle was so important that all behavior was scrutinized and through gossip, the status level of the family was raised or lowered. The reputation of individual family members added to or detracted from the status of the entire family and revolved around efficiency, competency, property, personality, looks, and behavior. Evaluation of status was a constant, ongoing process for all members of the community (Lopata, 1975).

Therapists need to know that Poles are very class conscious, and are ambivalent about upward mobility, despite their hunger for status and social recognition. This conflict has complex roots in the history of Polish class structure and stratifications, and in the influence of French culture, manners, and habits on the *déclassé szlachta* (nobility). It has been noted that "Poland is [still] a Francophile culture" (Hoffman, 1989, p. 12). The high style of the French nobility matched the values of the noble ethos of Old Poland. The importance of noble birth, for example, remains central in the Polish psyche. "Lineage gives a solidity, . . . it implies a moral uprightness and the dignity of not having to prove yourself, of being somebody to begin with" (Hoffman, 1989, p. 44). However, "having class" is different than rising in class. For countless Polish peasants and their descendants, money, power, and position have always been suspicious, if not immoral, attributes. Polish families are then in a double bind of encouraging success while being ashamed of it.

Most Polish Americans experience their Polishness as a major problem. The extent to which they will admit it is another matter. Poles' ambivalence toward their own ethnicity is a product of history. "It comes from many invasions, partitions, occupations, and border shifts that have changed, sometimes overnight, the national identity of large numbers of Poles" (Gladsky, 1992, p. 3). Polishness has been brutalized by historical events, distorted by the media and literature, and ridiculed by countless Polish jokes. Whether a descendent of prince or peasant, regardless of education or socioeconomic level, Poles in the United States continue to be afflicted by "unresolved problems of social belonging" (Gladsky, 1992, p. 287), view their own ethnicity as "a prison" (Gladsky, 1992 p. 148), something shameful to be hidden.

Although such shame is a factor for other ethnic groups, it remains for most Poles an unacknowledged focus of discontent, yet is rarely the focus of therapy. The question, "How do you feel about being Polish?" elicits responses such as: "How did you know I was Polish?" (name change); "What's that got to do with anything?"; "Is this therapy or are you taking a survey?"; and "You've got to be kidding!" Defensiveness, a nationally necessary historical stance, has become a personality trait.

## ALCOHOLISM

Steven (1982, p. 13) notes, "It is impossible to visit Poland and not be struck by the inordinately heavy drinking among all sections of society. . . . Those used to Western social drinking habits need a strong constitution to match the serious drinking of the Poles." Poles say defensively that heavy drinking has always been a part of their culture, that vodka is even more deeply enshrined in the Polish tradition than it is in the Russian. Morawski (1992) notes that the attitude in Poland has evolved from the idea that alcoholism is a moral fault to viewing it as a serious illness, but the underlying, abiding attitude for Poles is that drinking is a natural and positive part of life. The hardworking, hard-drinking Pole is the "salt of the earth." An old Polish proverb captures the tone: "*Maciek zmarl, lezy na desce / A pil by jesce* (Maciek died and he lies on a plank, but he'd still like a drink") (Knab, 1993, p. 262).

What happens, then, when alcohol moves to alcoholism, when drinking becomes a major social problem, when the salt, so to speak, has lost its savor? Tryzno, Pedagogic, Grodziak-Sobczy, Prawn, and Marowski (1989, p. 268) note that in Poland alcoholism is "one of the two major causes of divorce," the other being marital infidelity, and that 21.3% of Polish children are raised in alcoholic families. Violence in alcoholic families is two to three times greater than in the general population. He points out that much more is not reflected in statistics, because Poles consider outside help an attack on the family "which, in spite of disputes, confrontations, and injuries, proves itself resistant to outside influences" (p. 268).

Resistance to acknowledging or recognizing alcohol as directly related to family problems is stronger in Polish families than in many other ethnic groups. This attitude is replicated in the United States. Drinking is accepted as a norm (there are more bars than churches in Polonia) and, in conjunction with the dictum "Do not shame your family!" contributes to the denial that is so centrally a part of progressive alcohol dependence and the family's enabling role. Therapists can be seen as "outside influences," as accusers, not as helpers, and there is resistance not only to giving up alcohol, but also to exposing the family to shame. One nondrinking Polish woman, whose husband was ordered to treatment for drinking on the job, said, "I know most Poles drink, but why can't he stop?" When asked what she thought, she replied, "It goes way back to the *szlachta* (nobility) who forced peasants to drink. They paid them vodka instead of money, so now everyone does it." Resistance to acknowledging alcoholism takes many forms; some of them are ethnic.

## NAMES

Polish families seeking treatment are sometimes readily identifiable by their names. However, therapists will discover the Polish roots of many only by doing a three- or four-generational genogram. Even then the names may not reveal Polish origins, because many have Anglicized their names to hide their Polishness.

Tom Suchomski worked for years as a therapist at a clinic with a colleague named John Mason. There were many occasions to remark on the Polishness of Suchomski: the usual jokes and comments about Polish ineptitude, such as when the Polish ship arrived 3 days late for the parade of tall ships in New York Harbor on July Fourth. After Tom moved on to private practice, a man named Bill Mason came to him for therapy, presenting with alcohol problems and job losses. Tom asked about the family, but never about ethnicity. The following exchange occurred months into treatment.

BILL: What my father said was law. He hit us a lot, but its funny, . . . he never once swore.

TOM: I have to tell you that sounds very Polish. I was just looking at a picture of a Polish saint (Stanislaw Kostka). The caption on the painting was, "The young saint is here shown fainting after having heard one of the guests swear."

BILL: Well, that's funny, because I'm Polish.

Bill checked with his father, and was told that their name had been Maciejewski. Bill then said that his older brother was John Mason, Tom's former colleague. For 10 years, John Mason knew Tom was Polish, remarked on it, but never once indicated that he was also Polish.

According to Lopata (1975), changing one's name is a major form of reaction against negative self-image. The data she has collected suggest that Poles change their names more than any other ethnic group. In the United States, the quintessentially recognizable Polish name ending is undoubtedly -ski. Centuries ago, -ski was a sign of nobility (Chorzempa, 1993), but now the stereotype is just the opposite. A Polish American college professor relates feeling very guilty at the birth of his daughter, and thinking, "Sorry, Anne, I really hate to saddle you with my last name." For the first time, he consciously wished he had changed it. Therapists working with Polish families would do well to spend time on names, to ask what a client knows about the meaning of his or her name, where it came from, who had it and who did not, and so on. Most Poles will know and have stories about it, and when they do not, it will still matter. To Shakespeare's question, "What's in a name?", we answer in this case, "Plenty."

## ETHNIC RELATIONS

Complex historical factors have led to Poles having a reputation for biased attitudes toward other minorities, and they have met with more than their share of bias from others. The largest and most uneducated group of Polish immigrants arrived in the United States at a time of strong antiforeign sentiment. They economically threatened other minorities by displacing them from the lowest paying jobs. Polish clergy suffered serious discrimination from the predominantly Irish hierarchy of the U.S. Roman Catholic Church in achieving higher clerical ranks. The assassination of President McKinley by a Polish immigrant further intensified prejudice. By early 1900, "Polack" had become a negative epithet. Poles in Chicago were found to have "one of the lowest ethnic group prestige ranks (aside from Appalachian)" (Sanders & Morawska, 1975, p. 76). Polish jokes, of course, are the most visible, personally hurtful, and most resented form of discriminatory attitude. A therapist working with Poles must be sensitive to the tenacity and depth of conflictual Polish ethnic self-consciousness.

The negative attitudes held by Poles toward others are also rooted in history. Subjected to Russian, Prussian, and Austrian domination, Poles have been understandably uneasy about foreigners. Stanislawa (Stella) Krawczyk believed she could never get married as punishment for having had "an affair with a man of a different race." When asked what race, she replied, "German." It has been noted that Poles have been biased toward other Slavs. While religious differences between Orthodox and Roman Catholics intensified prejudices, even when they belonged to the same church, there was hostility between them. Research has shown that Poles have the same negative attitudes toward African Americans as held by other American ethnic groups. Polish immigrants adopt "native" hostile attitudes to those lower on the social hierarchy to make themselves feel "more American" and less rejected.

The mutual antipathy between Poles and Polish Jews deserves special mention. Few subjects are more sensitive in Polish circles today than Poland's relations with her Jewish minority (Steven, 1982). Hoffman (1989, p. 33) remembers her mother's warning, "There is an anti-Semite in every Pole." At a dinner party, the authors were told by a Jewish American that "everyone's allowed one prejudice; mine is Poles."

Much of the hostility between the two groups relates to Polish collaboration, or the perception of such collaboration, with the Nazis. "Blood and ashes of the Holocaust have fused Poland and the Jewish people. It is not in our power to free ourselves" (Czapska, p. 53, cited in Hertz, 1988, p. 5). The issue of the Holocaust has the kind of volcanic power found in American Black–White race relations and certain other universal traumas. The wounds run deep, and transformation needs to be just as deep, personally and culturally. Conceivably, some of the rancor held by Poles toward Jews comes from the seeming impossibility of withstanding the shame of being accused of some "unforgivable sin" (a familiar concept in Polish Catholic culture) as collaborating with the Nazis. There are countless and profound variations in individual, family, and group experience of this monumental face-off. Some deal with it by avoidance. For others, who attempt direct confrontation, it can be difficult, if not impossible, to see history, the other, or the self, through the enormous, mesmerizing, and blinding light of the event called the Holocaust. Pointing out the historical fact that Hitler set out to systematically obliterate all of Poland (both Jewish and Catholic), recounting the many stories of mutual heroism of both groups, or the fact that "penalties in Poland for helping Jews were the most Draconian in occupied Europe. . . . automatically punishable by the death of entire families" (Bartoszewski, 1991, p. 28) for a Pole seems hopelessly reductionistic or feebly apologetic, and for a Jew may seem condescendingly gratuitous.

In Poland after the Holocaust, the word "Jew" was heavily loaded. The much cherished old image of the Jewish innkeeper as the wise man of the village, as one of the recognized authorities on history and culture as well as business, was no longer available. Mickiewicz, Poland's most illustrious poet, viewed Israel as the older brother of the Poles. It was the Holocaust that placed the stigma of Cain and Abel on the brotherhood.

When treating Polish or Polish Jewish families, therapists should be aware of the complexity of the issue. It may present in the therapist's office directly in mixed marriages, indirectly as an underlying source of conflict, or obliquely as "cultural camouflage" (Friedman, 1982, p. 500). Or it may erupt in strange and confusing ways. For example, when a client's Polish American mother died, he made arrangements honoring her wish to be cremated. No one from the extended family attended the memorial service. When he questioned a family member, she answered simply, "It's just too much like the Holocaust."

To come to terms with their past, Poles, (and perhaps Polish Jews) must confront their Polish Jewish past. For emigré descendants assimilated into the United States at different times, this issue will have different meanings and varying intensities. For all, we are suggesting an attitudinal starting point in the forgotten fact that Poland, between the 13th and 16th centuries, protected by Polish kings, gradually became home and haven for 75% of the world's Jews.

In Poland, Jewish faith, thought, and culture flourished unsurpassed. We suggest looking at connections rather than differences. For Polish Americans and Polish Jewish Americans seeking to accept or find their ethnic identity, some of the connections include a common origin and history and a need for a homeland. Both view themselves as children of the Covenant. Both have suffered *diaspora* not once but many times. Each has greatly enriched the cultural history of the other. Each may be able to exist without the other, but that would, indeed, in the language of family therapy, be a major cutoff. This is what is happening in Poland today. Conditions there are not the same as conditions here. Emigré descendants of Poles and Polish Jews may be in the best position to contribute to resolution.

## RELIGION: THE CATHOLIC CHURCH

The Roman Catholic belief system has played such an influential role in the history of Poland that being Polish is synonymous with being Catholic. Polish Catholics have a strong predilection for mystical piety and self-abnegation as spiritual ideals. The lives of saints are regarded as models for living, and the Blessed Virgin Mary the epitome of a meaningful life. Faith is shown by steadfast adherence to the church, even to the point of martyrdom. Faithful parishioners support and participate in social services. A good Polish Catholic behaves uprightly in the community and school, works hard, and accepts his or her lot in life as the "will of God."

Both educated and uneducated immigrants were nourished in this tradition through the vast system of parochial education and the role of the parish priest. The chief purpose of education is teaching "faith and morals." The goal of child rearing is to raise good Catholics. Children are to be obedient and respectful of parents. The goal of marital sex is procreation, and spouses are to fulfill the obligations of the sacrament of matrimony and have many children. Marriage is forever; divorce is forbidden. Frequent attendance at Mass and the other sacraments is expected. The religious vows of "poverty, chastity, and obedience" also govern secular life. Through the system of parochial education, monastic choices become family values. Catholicism is conservative, particularly on the subject of sexuality and gender roles. Poles are not likely to be open to discussions on whether God is female, or homosexuality is a matter of choice.

There is, however, a vast gulf between religious ideals and practice. As Polish Americans became educated, upwardly mobile, and left Polonia, family values and religious values became viewed as "quaint and old-fashioned." Those who leave Polonia and attend secular schools are believed to have "lost their faith." Their children are seen as "disrespectful and disobedient," and their divorce rates are almost equal to the larger population.

## EMOTIONAL PROCESS AND PATTERNS

"American Poles tended to risk marriage on the basis of close ethnicity rather than on the idea of romantic love" (Sanders & Morawska, 1975, p. 160). Marriage is considered a socially accepted institution, not a love affair or an equal relationship between partners. Becoming a couple through marriage is probably the central life cycle stage of the Polish family. The Polish wedding traditionally went on for 2 or 3 days. It is the family's opportunity to demonstrate its social standing in the community, and it is not unusual for families to spend lavishly for a wedding extravaganza.

Historically, Polish couples were organized in a patriarchal system, and they still tend to be characterized by a traditional assignment of gender roles. During the immigration process, however, women gained a large measure of autonomy, because they were left in Poland to function as heads of the household while the men came to the United States to establish themselves. Once here, the women continued to exercise authority in the home, because the men were away working most of the time. But the belief that men should have complete authority over women remained. Although it is currently estimated that 50–75% of women in families in the United States are working outside the home, the Polish American woman continues to be solely responsible for housekeeping and child care.

Traditional Polish patriarchal family culture expected children to follow parents' orders without question and continuously contribute to the family's material well-being. In the second and third generations, young people flatly refuse to turn over earnings to their parents, and in some cases parents sue or disown them. The expectation of the immigrant generation that their children would take care of them, as was done in Poland, has been unfulfilled. As the upwardly mobile younger generation has moved to the suburbs, leaving their parents living in the old neighborhoods among Blacks and Latinos with whom they have conflictual relationships, the elderly parents have felt abandoned.

The issue of children "leaving home" emotionally as well as geographically is a toxic one in Polish American families. Children of all ages are expected to be grateful for whatever sacrifices their parents make for them, and at the same time are taught to have few expectations about what their parents will do for them. The expectation continues that children should be responsible for their parents' care, and for maintaining a viable relationship through ongoing contact. Those who leave home are often simply ignored and treated as nonmembers, left out of the family information loop, off guest lists for weddings and family parties, and so on, especially when intermarriage occurs outside the Polish American community to Catholics or to non-Catholics.

# EXPRESSION OF FEELINGS

Traditional Polish patterns of courtship, marriage, and child rearing did not include open expression of affection (Sanders & Morawska, 1975). The Polish American family today continues to value stoicism and strongly inhibits feelings and expressions of need for emotional connectedness. Mondykowski (1982) discusses problems that Polish Americans have expressing a need to be cared for. Children are expected to conceal their anxieties and needs from their parents, and "take care of themselves." Polish Americans "fear dependency [because] . . . being taken care of implies weakness and inability to pull their own weight. Feelings of need are not seen as normal, and are often connected with shame and humiliation" (Mondykowski, 1982, p. 403). Intense expressions of anger in Polish families are often a cover for anxiety that is not allowed expression, as it "implies a need for emotional reassurance and support that violates the value of stoicism" (pp. 402–403).

The prohibition of expression of feelings of pain and sadness complicates and attenuates the process of dying, and mourning after death occurs. The history of the Polish American family is full of experiences of loss and loss denied. There is the loss of language, home, and culture, the loss of a "Polish self," which is part of the immigration experience. There is loss from cutoffs that happen in Polish families because of the concern for status and the importance of disconnecting from family members who shame the family. Often when someone in a family is very ill, members of the extended family will avoid inquiring about the patient's condition. Instead there is ongoing tension that every time the phone rings, it is bringing bad news, which must be borne stoically.

When it comes to conflict and conflict resolution, Poles are stubborn and have a national and individual reluctance to yield or compromise. Within the family, tempers flare and violence, alcohol abuse, or both often ensue, or a "cold war" state is achieved. Poles are notorious for holding grudges. A combination of persistence and stubbornness operates to prevent dialogue in which both parties in a conflict can be heard. Disagreements become contests of will. In the words of one family member, a dispute is resolved "only when a son backs off and realizes he's talking to his father." There is no way for mutual empathy to develop as a route to problem solving. Personal positions get expressed in unequivocal terms. A vicious cycle of attack and defense begins, and problems are left unresolved to go underground, where they remain as deeply held resentments.

This inability to negotiate to achieve mutually satisfying goals probably is both a contributing cause and an effect of the pervasive use and abuse of alcohol in the Polish American culture. The heavy drinking functions to allow the expression of weakness through crying or losing control. If individuals are drunk, they can disclaim responsibility for their words and actions (Mondy-kowski, 1982). When Poles perceive that they are affronted, they might silently cut you off for years, or they might look for an occasion to spit in your eye. An atmosphere of cordial respect may surround both proceedings.

## POLISH AMERICANS IN THERAPY

Poles go to medical doctors only as a last resort. They are suspicious of the motives of health-care providers, believing that they "just want to make money, and what you don't know won't hurt you." They will suffer great pain, often for years, before seeking medical attention. It is not uncommon to then find that they are terminally ill. Poles typically do not complain about pain, because "What good will it do?" They also are likely to resist taking medication in favor of natural remedies, unless they have opportunities to medicate themselves. An interpreter who currently aids Polish arrivals reports antibiotics are now so readily available in Poland, due to loose regulatory standards, that the Polish people believe there is a pill to cure everything and immigrants come with large caches of antibiotics (S. Dobosz, personal communication, September 17, 1994).

Resistance to help from a "mental health doctor" is even stronger. Admitting to a mental health problem in the family is taboo. Even when a priest recommends that a family seek help, they rarely do. Usually a concerned employer is the motivator for therapy and then only because job performance is being affected. Sometimes therapy is sought when an "acting-out" problem threatens family control. Mental illness is not only feared for itself, but also for the shame and guilt it is perceived to bring to the family.

Let us return to Stanislawa (Stella) Krawczyk, the woman who stayed single because she once had an affair with a German. Stella had a "nervous breakdown," fearful that she had "lost Jesus." In therapy, her concern was that she was "bringing shame to the family" and she did not want to take medicine prescribed by a psychiatrist. Her sister sent Catholic parishioners to persuade Stella to return to the faith, urged Stella's employer to forbid her to return to work without medication, covertly obtained and sneaked medication into Stella's juice. Stella's sister's husband threatened to choke her for "talking religion." Anxiety about psychiatric illness, threats to control, the possibility of shame, and the primacy of Catholicism are ethnic facets of this case. The family would not join in treatment, nor did Stella want them to.

---- ❧ ----

Bowen (1978) observed that one-to-one relationships are the hallmark of a differentiated person. In such a relationship, two people "can relate personally to each other about each other, without talking about a third person (triangling) and without talking about impersonal things" (p. 540). Lerner (1989, p. 18) calls this "emotional connectedness" with "more self." People with "more self" can know and express a balanced view of their strengths and weaknesses, clearly state their beliefs, values, and priorities, and behave congruently. They stay emotionally connected with significant others in situations of high anxiety, speak rather than remaining silent, take an "I" position on difficult or toxic issues, acknowledge differences, and permit others to do so.

Looking at these criteria, Polish Americans rarely have, and even more rarely express, a balanced view of their strengths and weaknesses. Expressing a view of one's strengths is seen as "bragging," and admitting to weakness can bring shame on the individual and family. Most Poles do not stay emotionally connected with significant others when tension rises. It is much more likely that they will cut off or at the least distance into ritualized contact. In addition, they are likely to remain silent, drink, or shout, rather than take an "I" position on difficult or toxic issues.

Finally, Poles will not readily acknowledge differences or allow others to do so, because obedience (to parents, the church, the "rules") does not permit it. In the Polish community, gossip can be seen as a means of lowering anxiety between a conflictual twosome. Distance or cutoff seems the preferred way Poles handle messy, powerful feelings. Given the intimate connection between being Polish and being Catholic, we suggest that a powerful triangle for Poles is comprised of this threesome: the individual, the institution of the church, and the concept of God. This may be viewed as a fixed triangle that has existed for centuries. Fusion of the Polish self with Church dogma leaves little room for the option of a differentiated self.

## CONCLUSION

Poles are deeply religious people, also deeply opinionated and judgmental, strongly united, yet divided and isolated. They are constitutionally defensive, fiercely loyal, inveterately ceremonial. Poles with "true grit" can be educated but cannot show off, be upper class, but not let it go to their heads, and be wealthy, provided they contribute to church, community, and family. Poles place great store in hard work, loyalty to church and parents, courtesy at all times despite adversity, and devotion to style and good manners. Above all, be true to one's roots, be "the salt of the earth." Finally, Poles take pride in being long-suffering. For Polish Americans, as we have discussed, success in all of these traditional Polish endeavors can still leave them disconnected from the larger culture and from themselves, because of a shame-based disavowal of their ethnic heritage. To the extent that being Polish necessarily also means being Catholic, Poles not on good terms with the traditional Church can be even more conflicted. In the context of therapy, they can be difficult to engage, but once committed to personal or family change, are likely to keep working at it long after the therapist loses connection.

Ethnicity and religion, perhaps not unlike terror or parental bonding, can run deep in the marrow of the bones. Assisting Poles to revisit their ethnic roots can be for them a way of going home, not again, but for the first time. Ameliorating what Gladsky called "the loneliness of the long-distance ethnic" (1992, p. 249) is no small achievement. Being "somebody to begin with" (Hoffman, 1989, p. 44) cannot happen if the beginning needs to be hidden. Poland has survived as a powerful and positive factor in the configuration of modern Europe and is currently redefining itself. One young Polish college student, a recent immigrant, said of her (our) homeland: "Everything is different. You won't believe it. *Now* is *best* time to go to Poland." Perhaps she is right.

## REFERENCES

Bartoszewski, W. (1991). *The convent at Auschwitz.* New York: George Braziller.
Bowen, M. (1978). *Family therapy in clinical practice.* New York: Jason Aronson.
Chorzempa, R. (1993). *Polish roots.* Baltimore: Genealogical Publishing.
Davies, N. (1992). *Heart of Europe: A short history of Poland* (rev. ed.). New York: Oxford University Press.
Friedman, E. (1982). The myth of the shiksa. In M. McGoldrick, J. K. Pearce, & J. Giordano (Eds.), *Ethnicity and family therapy* (1st ed., pp. 499–526). New York: Guilford Press.
Gladsky, T. (1992). *Princes, peasants and other Polish selves: Ethnicity in American literature.* Amherst: University of Massachusetts Press.
Hertz, A. (1988). *The Jews in Polish culture.* Evanston, IL: Northwestern University Press.
Hoffman, E. (1989). *Lost in translation.* New York: Dutton.
Knab, S. H. (1993). *Polish customs, traditions, and folklore.* New York: Hippocrene Books.
Lerner, H. (1989). *The dance of intimacy.* New York: Harper & Row.
Lopata, H. Z. (1975). The Polish-American family. In C. H. Mindel & R. W. Habenstein (Eds.), *Ethnic families in America: Patterns and variations* (pp. 15–40). New York: Elsevier.
Mondykowski, S. (1982). Polish families. In M. McGoldrick, J. K. Pearce, & J. Giordano (Eds.), *Ethnicity and family therapy* (1st ed., pp. 393–411). New York: Guilford Press.
Morawski, J. (1992). The odyssey of the Polish alcohol system. In H. Klingemann, J. Takala, & G. Hunt (Eds.), *Cure, care, or control: Alcoholism treatment in sixteen countries.* New York: State University of New York Press.
Sanders, I., & Morawska, E. (1975). *Polish American community life: A survey of research.* New York: Polish Institute of Arts and Sciences in America.
Steven, S. (1982). *The Poles.* New York: Macmillan.
Tryzno, W., Pedagogic, M., Grvdziak-Sobczy, E., Prawn, N., & Marowski, J. (1989). The role of the family in alcohol education and alcohol abuse in Poland. *Medical Law, 8,* 267–273.
Zamoyski, A. (1988). *The Polish way.* New York: Franklin Watts.

# CHAPTER 46

# Slovak Families

## Suzanne Kerr

*In the old country the Slovaks had been an oppressed minority from the
beginning of time, a simple, unwarlike people, a nation of peasants and
shepherds whom the centuries had taught patience and humility. In
America they were all this and more, foreigners in a strange land,
ignorant of its language and customs, fearful of authority in whatever
guise.*

—THOMAS BELL (1976, p. 419)

By the early 1920s, over 600,000 Slovaks had settled in the United States. Today
they number about 2,000,000, yet little is known of them and little is heard
about Slovaks in the arts or sciences, in politics or business—or in the therapist's
office.

Slovaks are descendants of Slavic tribes who migrated to Central and
Eastern Europe by 500 A.D. Because they were without a written language until
the eighth century A.D., much of their history was left unrecorded. From arche-
typal evidence and Slavic terminology, Gimbutas (1971), a Slavic anthropologist, surmises that early Slavs lived as seminomadic farmers in an extended
family system. The patriarch and his immediate family slept in the large, central room with the hearth. At other times during the day, the central room
served as the living space for all members of the extended family where meals
and recreational activities took place. Small sleeping quarters for other family
units were arranged in a semicircle outside the central room, and all items in
the confines of the community were considered jointly owned by the whole
family, not owned by an individual family member. Joint families formed
alliances with other families, then tribes, who frequently viewed other tribes
as alien and oppositional forces (Capek, 1906).

Once a singular ethnic group in Central Europe, the Slavs were dispersed
and segmented into national minority groups by stronger, larger and/or more
predatory tribes from both the East and West. Germanic tribes scattered them
"to the four winds" (Pearson, 1983). Asiatic horsemen (Huns and Goths,

673

Avars and Magyars, and Mongols) further displaced Slavic inhabitants until three fluid, yet distinct Slav groups emerged: (1) the Eastern Slavs—Russians, Ukrainians, and Belarusians most influenced by the East; (2) the Northern Slavs—Slovaks, Czechs, and Poles most influenced by the West; and (3) the Southern Slavs—Bulgarians, Serbs, Croats, Slovenes, and Macedonians, culturally segmented and conflicted groups influenced by both East and West (Krader, 1968).

The Slovaks have been classified as Northern Slav, yet when they immigrated to the United States (1880–1920), Slovaks traditionally thought of themselves as belonging to the property where they lived, and perhaps to a particular village or county. They were far less aware of political entities such as empire, state, or ethnic group (Stein, 1980). The early immigrant Slovak men and boys worked as laborers in coal mines and steel mills because family plots of land in the old country were not large and fertile enough for a family's sustenance.

"We are not Magyars. We are not Czechs. We are Slovaks." (First-generation female)

Slovakia is geographically located between Poland and Hungary (north to south) and the Czech Republic and the Ukraine (east to west); included in the terrain are dense forests, with portions of the Carpathian Mountains and Danube River.

Slovaks are most readily identified with Czechs in "Czechoslovakia." As a nation, Czechoslovakia was a relatively short and unhappy union conceived in the United States and Versailles after World War I (Pearson, 1983). Its formation occurred after the majority of Slovak immigrants arrived in this country.

From a historical perspective, Slovakia's principal political tie is with Hungary. For about a millennium, from approximately the 10th century A.D. to World War I, Slovaks were subjugated by Magyar feudal domination. Magyars, the fierce Asiatic horsemen who settled in Hungary, overwhelmed the agrarian Slovaks. Although part of the Hungarian empire, Slovaks were largely excluded from its socioeconomic system (except as peasant laborers). As a result, they developed a way of life geared for hardship and domination by others, emphasizing survival through tenacity, hard work, physical strength, and family loyalty. Unlike other ethnic groups, such as the Czechs, who fared better under the Austrian Hapsburgs, Slovak survival efforts were all-consuming and opportunities to advance culturally, intellectually, and/or politically were missed. In 1848, with the breakup of the Hungarian feudal system, the harsh yet stable economic world of the Slovaks ground to a halt, leading to the eventual emigration of more than 20% of the population (Stolarik, 1989).

## FAMILIES

"In my family, I noticed we have a different viewpoint about family relation. . . . Slovak families are tighter knit and have closer relationships . . .
not like families in isolation with everyone having their own room and
toys . . . they don't learn to understand each other." (Third-generation
female)

Much of what was previously described as early Slavic tribal life is relevant to
Slovaks today: the extended family's cohesiveness, the concept of "family" as
the paramount emotional center and authority in experiencing life, individual
wishes subsumed by family needs and desires, and the distrust and alienation
of those outside the family circle.

Slovaks acquired a view of life common to peasant societies: Resources
are scarce and always will be, and no one (i.e., peasant) has the power to change
the system. (For more on peasant societies, see Foster, 1965). Each individual
and family must sacrifice wants and desires for all to survive. For one individual
or family to gain means another must suffer.

"If you get more land, I will spit on it. If my cow dies, yours should die
too. If you get a goose and I get a goose, then that is fair." (Grandfather,
quoted by first-generation male)

Out of the peasant scenario comes the only negative trait to which Slovaks readily admit: envy; they begrudge each other's successes. An individual
must have the mutual consent of the family before distinguishing him- or
herself in any way, and conversely, the family is held culpable by the community for nonconformist members. To aspire to become a doctor or scholar may
be to risk perpetual scorn and even abandonment (H. F. Stein, personal communication, February 24, 1995).

Besides envy, Slovak families are emphatic about being problem-free.
What goes on behind the hallowed walls of the "home" is no one's business,
so that no priests, neighbors, or therapists are privy to "family secrets." Thus,
when gleaning information from a Slovak family, the therapist must move
carefully and thoughtfully, seeking to demonstrate how family secrets, information, and values can be used constructively and not only pathologically. The
therapist may lose an opportunity to establish trust if he or she is seen as an
external authority bent on discovering and destroying the family stronghold
(H. F. Stein, personal communication, February 24, 1995).

Traditionally, Slovak families are patriarchal in structure. However, mothers generally wield greater subtle authority in an atmosphere rife with power-
based alliances (Stein, 1980).

"My sister Annie used to run with motorcycle gangs. My father would beat her as punishment until one day she came home pregnant and he kicked her out. Three years later Annie showed up with her baby, but I made her leave because she was upsetting Mother." (Third-generation first-born male)

The therapist needs to establish him- or herself as an authority and a powerful resource. To do so, he or she must understand the power configuration of the family, be aware of the influence of one's own gender, and hypothesize the extent to which this Slovak family or individual will extend trust (C. Cobb-Nettleton, personal communication, February 27, 1995).

## CHILDREN

"Keep them tired, hungry, and poor or watch them be stubborn, willful, and defiant." (Second-generation female)

Slovak children are raised primarily by their mother, and sometimes also by the eldest daughter. While growing up, children learn the meaning of life by being heavily involved in religion, with 85% being practicing Catholics (both Latin and Byzantine Rites), and with Lutherans being the largest minority.

Traditionally, both Slovak Catholic and Protestant children are taught that their own wills and desires are evil and need curbing, and that they are weak and require protection from their own fragility. "Authority," "power," and "goodness" are thought to be alien to the innate child; they are divined from God, who is perceived to be distant and remote to those on earth (H. F. Stein, personal communication, February 24, 1995). By submitting to authority and adhering to its rules in a dark and sinful world, one may achieve rewards: a good family life on earth and riches in heaven (whatever one wants and does not get in this life).

The Slavic child-rearing practice of swaddling is designed to instill in the infant a sense of limits and respect for authority. The newborn is placed in a soft pillowcase-like bundle. Straps are tied around the outside of the bundle to further restrict the baby's arms and legs. Until 6 months of age, the infant is freed only for feeding and bathing, not necessarily when it cries, but when mother is ready (Stein, 1978).

Slovak siblings are socialized to think they are equals and to share possessions. The depth of sibling relationships vary: Some are close; others have a veneer of civility that masks hidden resentment. Birth order and gender help determine what a child means to the family and frequently causes hostility among siblings. The eldest daughter has a unique identification with her mother as heiress of the domicile responsibilities of hearth and home. The eldest son will inherit the family home and is generally taught to carry the weight of responsibility. Younger children experience the same harsh disciplinary standards as older children, yet at the same time, are more likely to be coddled and indulged with food. Slovak child-rearing practices frequently establish permanent dependency needs, particularly for younger children.

> "My mother always said she loved us all equally. I don't know. My baby brother (age 42) always got special treatment. He lived on pastries and mother was always nagging him to eat more. To this day he acts like a spoiled 6-year-old." (Second-generation female)

## COUPLES

> "Do you know the commercial about the husband giving his wife diamonds on their anniversary because they love each other so much? No Slovak ever did that." (Second-generation male)

The husband–wife relationship for Slovak couples is traditionally weak (in comparison with family-of-origin loyalties and pressures) and often the focal point for each partner's general hostilities. Historically, marriage was based on economic security, not a personal relationship, and was arranged through parental influence. The family of origin held dominance over the nuclear family in setting priorities and rules of households, while more frequently than not, first- and second-generation Slovaks (along with third-generation children) lived under the same roof.

Men frequently compensate for lack of marital intimacy at their fraternal lodges (organizations originally established to handle immigrant needs). "Drinking sprees," whether at the lodge, at home, or elsewhere, provide physical and emotional numbing as a sanctioned "cure" of all problems. The easing of pain or anxiety, whether chemically induced or as a learned process, can authentically allow the Slovak family/individual to respond with, "We are happy and have no problems" (C. Cobb-Nettleton, personal communication, February 27, 1995).

## SLOVAK FAMILIES TODAY

What has been described thus far provides a common Slovak base from which Slovak American families are moving in varying stages of acculturation. Intermarriage, which introduces new patterns, has provided Slovak Americans new possibilities for experiencing life. First-generation Slovak Americans generally married other Slovak Americans, while the second generation tended to marry other Slavs of the same religious background. Third-generation Slovak Americans further chose from Irish and Germans mates of the same religious background (M. M. Stolarik, personal communication, January 1995).

Many Slovak American parents today are concerned about their teenagers' desire to adopt dominant cultural values, such as spending leisure time with friends, desiring expensive clothes and electronic devices, having personal goals and ambitions, and moving away from home, all of which are at variance with Slovak culture. A therapist can assist families and individuals by helping them to negotiate within a framework that integrates the old and new.

Mary and George were desperate about their 16-year-old son, Michael, whom they feared they were on the verge of "losing." Michael wanted a job so that he could have clothes and spending money on par with his schoolmates. The mere idea of money earned for personal use was considered defiant by Mary and George. The therapist used the conflict as an opportunity for the family to discuss the meaning of money. Michael talked about its importance in being "accepted" at school, but how he was "torn" because spending money on unnecessary things felt like he no longer had any values. George talked about losing his job if the factory closed. The family decided to "give" one-third of the income to Michael to do with as he pleased. The balance would go into a savings account, the use of which would be renegotiated by the family in 2 years' time.

———————— ❧ ————————

Slovak families readily "adopt" outsiders as family members, which can be used as an important link for the therapist. Requirements include respect for Slovak values and adherence to family rules. The association of "Czech" with "Slovak" culture generally is considered an insult to Slovaks. (If your aunt visited Prague recently, keep it to yourself.) Slovaks also are not "Slovene," a Slavic group out of the former Yugoslavia. An open mind and nonjudgmental attitude toward Slovaks is paramount in gaining their trust; just do not expect them to reciprocate with an open mind and nonjudgmental attitude toward the therapist!

### ACKNOWLEDGMENTS

Many thanks to Carol Cobb-Nettleton, Jo-Ann Krestan, M. Mark Stolarik, Howard F. Stein, the Michael Stretanski family, and the Slovak Heritage Society of Wilkes-Barre, Pennsylvania, for their invaluable contributions to this effort.

### REFERENCES

Bell, T. (1976). *Out of this furnace.* Pittsburgh: University of Pittsburgh Press.
Capek, T. (1906). *The Slovaks of Hungary.* New York: Knickerbocker Press.

Foster, G. (1965). Peasant society and the image of the limited good. *American Anthropologist, 67,* 293–315.

Gimbutas, M. (1971). *The Slavs.* New York: Praeger.

Krader, L. (1968). *Formation of the state.* Englewood Cliffs, NJ: Prentice-Hall.

Pearson, R. (1983). *National minorities in Eastern Europe, 1848–1945.* London: Macmillan.

Stein, H. F. (1980). *An ethno-historic study of Slovak-American identity.* New York: Arno Press.

Stein, H. F. (1978). The Slovak-American "swaddling ethos": Homeostat for family dynamics and cultural continuity. *Family Process, 17*(1), 31–45.

Stolarik, M. M. (1989). *Immigration and urbanization: The Slovak experience, 1870–1918.* New York: AMS Press.

CHAPTER 47

# Russian Families

## Leonid Althausen

Much has been written recently about issues related to the psychosocial adaptation of Russian Jewish immigrants. But little has been said about the ethnic Russian emigrés, partially because all immigrants from Russia are seen as "Russians," a perception that conceals nuances of ethnic difference. Although ethnic Russians share with their Jewish countrymen many characteristics common to immigrants from the former U.S.S.R., they have distinct concerns of their own. This chapter is an attempt to begin to increase understanding of this population.

## EMIGRATION

Russians are well known for their attachment to their country of birth (Smith, 1987), which they call *rodina* (motherland) or, even more affectionately, *Rossiya-matushka* (little mother-Russia). In tsarist times, the Emperor of All Russias was referred to as *Tsar-batyushka* (little father). During the Soviet era (1918–1991), the state itself assumed the "parental" role of providing for its citizens the perquisites of a welfare system, as long as they conformed to its dictates. Thus, for many Russians, relocation to a foreign country has the unwelcome connotation of abandoning one's family and home.

Despite their country's difficult history, Russians have seldom chosen to emigrate (unlike the Jews, who, because of the pervasive anti-Semitism, did not always feel at home in Russia), partially because of this attachment. Those who left usually did so only as a last resort, forced to embark on this course by extreme circumstances. The 1917 Revolution sent hundreds of thousands of Russians into exile in Western Europe and America (the first wave of Russian emigration) where, surrounded by the few family heirlooms salvaged from the revolution, they spent the rest of their days in nostalgic contemplation of the past, hoping to reclaim their lost motherland some day (du Plessix Gray, 1990;

680

Nabokov, 1989).[1] After World War II, many Russians, displaced by the war and left stranded in the West, chose not to return home for fear of being persecuted by Stalin as "betrayers of the motherland" (the second wave of Russian emigration).

Under the Communist regime, emigration was banned for all but a few ethnic Russians, who managed to emigrate either by defecting or by marrying Jews (one of the few ethnic minorities allowed to emigrate). These emigrés were denounced as "pariahs," stripped of their Soviet citizenship, and never allowed to return.

Since 1991, when the ban on emigration was lifted, thousands of Russians, displaced by the economic and social upheavals of the post-Soviet era, have come to the West in search of a better life (Aslund, 1995; Gerasimov, 1994; Handelman, 1995).[2] This current wave of Russian emigrés largely consists of members of the intelligentsia, the educated, professional class whose forerunners are best-known in the West through the works of Anton Chekhov (such as *Uncle Vanya*). Mistrusted by the lower classes because of its sophistication and erudition and feared by the ruling class for its liberal ideals, the intelligentsia always has been alienated from the rest of the Russian society (Smith, 1987). This alienation brought its members closer together.

In Soviet times, intimate social networks of friends that resembled extended families gathered around kitchen tables (the Russian family hearth) for soulful discussions of everything from politics to spirituality. In the atmosphere of fear and mistrust that characterized over 70 years of Soviet rule, such networks were a vital source of emotional and intellectual support. Since financial success and professional achievement were "tainted" because they required affiliation either with the criminal element or the oppressive Communist apparatus, dedication to friends became a treasured value.

With the Communist regime's demise and the introduction of a market-type economy, the old intimate networks have given way under the pressure of competition and social stratification. Work commitments now consume the time previously devoted to friendship, and the new disparities in income level and social status have led to estrangement between even close friends (Stanley, 1995). These lifestyle changes have caused many Russian immigrants to feel uprooted even before they leave their native land.

## FAMILY CHARACTERISTICS

Today's Russian family values and loyalties have formed in response to the prevailing conditions of economic scarcity and political oppression. In such conditions, the extended family's combined resources, including grandparents, relatives, and friends, often were necessary to cope with the privations of Soviet life. In this dance of survival, every family member had a role to play.

Grandparents often provided care for the young, financial help, and even housing. In return, adult children were expected to assume responsibility when their parents became frail or sick (Althausen, 1993).

Friends provided much-needed emotional support. With one-child families predominating, close friends often became substitute brothers and sisters (Smith, 1987). They were privy to the family's secrets, celebrated its successes, shared its sorrows, took part in negotiating various family conflicts, and provided advice.

Women had the lion's share of responsibility for raising the family, for men often were either absent or disabled, due to the combined effect of three devastating wars (1914–1918; 1918–1920; 1941–1945), Stalin's terror (1936–1953), and widespread alcoholism (Conquest, 1973; Smith, 1987). Even in dual-career families, women usually performed most of the domestic tasks, including child rearing. However, the prevalent (if tacit) Russian convention still equates femininity with weakness and therefore demands that women act helpless and vulnerable. In reality, Russian husbands often are considered by their wives to be weak, passive, and infantile (du Plessix Gray, 1990).

Children represented the family's hope for the future and were seen as symbols of innocence, in contrast to the society's widespread cynicism (Smith, 1987). They were considered to be weak and were overprotected, especially from any emotional conflict, and were often indulged at home, while parents expected schools and kindergartens to provide structure and set limits.[3]

# SUFFERING

For Russians, suffering is not only a natural part of life, but it also has a certain redemptive value (Smith, 1987; Dostoyevsky, 1869/1950). In the Russian lexicon of psychological pain, arguably the most important word is *toska*, which connotes melancholy, depression, yearning, anguish, pangs of love, ennui, weariness, tedium, boredom, and nostalgia all rolled into one. However, the word does not always have negative connotations; almost any thinking individual was expected to have this malaise to some degree.

Russians do not always accept such American values as maintaining a "positive mental attitude" (although they often perceive its possible merits), or the belief that a rational solution to life's problems can be found (McPhee, 1994). What we Americans may sometimes perceive as a "depressed mood," in a Russian client's mind could be only a normal case of *toska*.

This melancholy strain in the Russian psyche, traditionally ascribed to the country's cold winters and its vast, open spaces that seem to separate and swallow individuals (Erikson, 1963), has been augmented by its history of totalitarian oppression, including the infamous purges of the Stalin era (1936–1953), during which most families lived in fear that a family member (usually the father) might be denounced as an "enemy of the people" and taken away by the secret police, never to be seen again. In order to save themselves from such a fate, many citizens were coerced (or chose) to denounce their friends and even family members; the normal fabric of human relations was destroyed (Conquest, 1991). The family's emotional pain from this collective trauma, which may have been denied for decades, but which often becomes apparent when the family is asked to provide its history, should be approached carefully lest the family become overwhelmed and leave treatment.

## PRIVACY

Russians usually are reluctant to discuss emotional suffering with outsiders, whether laypeople or mental health professionals (du Plessix-Gray, 1990). There is usually a great deal of shame involved in divulging the family's private matters. This reluctance partly stems from the old Russian tradition of keeping psychological and other family issues private. Under Soviet rule, crowded living conditions and the intrusive "Big Brother" atmosphere allowed very little privacy, which only increased Russians' appetite for it (Specter, 1995).

But even within the family circle, suffering often is not expressed, for fear that it might somehow jeopardize the individual's physical health and even the family's survival. Historically, individuals and families were expected to be "strong" and not to crumble in the face of the vagaries of Soviet/Russian life.

## DRINKING

Perhaps no other cultural stereotype about Russians is as pervasive as their alleged love of drinking. In a nation that keeps its suffering to itself, and where neither antidepressant medication nor psychotherapy has yet taken root, vodka is widely regarded as *the* remedy for a range of physical and emotional problems. Drinking is also associated with conviviality (Smith, 1987), which makes it especially hard to confront the family's denial around it. (Popular belief has it that one only has a drinking problem when one drinks in solitude.) Often the wife will tolerate her husband's "tippling" as long as he maintains his family responsibilities. One must add that heavy drinking and its attendant social ills, such as domestic violence, are far less common among the intelligentsia than among the working classes.

## RELIGION

Religion has always been an important value for Russians. Even during the Soviet era, when attendance of religious services could have dire consequences and the privacy of confession was frequently violated (because of the Church's collaboration with the Communist regime), Orthodox Christianity remained, for many Russians, an abiding spiritual resource. For Russian immigrants, the church offers a spiritual link to *rodina*, as well as access to pastoral counseling, which some immigrants might choose as an alternative or an adjunct to psychotherapy.

## PSYCHOLOGICAL ADAPTATION

Apart from the normal losses common to migration and the specific losses experienced by Jewish immigrants from the former Soviet Union, there are particular issues of adaptation that are specific to ethnic Russians.

Although emigration is no longer banned, psychologically it may still elicit feelings of shame for leaving *rodina* and the extended family. Unlike the Russian Jewish immigrants to this country who, because of their refugee status, are allowed to bring in their elderly parents and kin, most Russian migrants cannot do so until after they have gained their U.S. citizenship, which takes at least 5 years. Separation from parents and kin often becomes permanent.

Another issue is alienation from the rest of the Russian-speaking immigrant community. As mentioned previously, Americans usually perceive all immigrants from the former Soviet Union as "the Russians." Since the majority are Jewish, the ethnic Russians may become "lost in the shuffle." They do not always receive the attention and resettlement resources given to their Jewish countrymen by the local Jewish community. For many Russian Jews, emigration provides an opportunity to confirm their ethnic identity by joining the local Jewish community, but ethnic Russians may lack such a clearly defined host community.[4] This lack may amplify not only their sense of loss but also the feelings of alienation and uprootedness they experienced back in the old country.

## ASPECTS OF FAMILY THERAPY

Because of the cultural norms outlined earlier and the negative stereotypes associated with Soviet psychiatry (see Chapter 42, this volume), Russians are often wary of therapy and have shameful feelings about "resorting" to it. In the interest of establishing an alliance with the family, it may sometimes be necessary to deemphasize the "mental health" aspect of work by using appropriate euphemisms that are more acceptable culturally.

After Yuri, a 4-year-old preschooler, was teased by his classmates about his "funny language" (Russian), he refused to speak Russian to his parents and would only communicate with them in English. The family was reluctant to have Yuri work with a psychotherapist, but had no objections to hiring "a tutor" who helped the child reconnect emotionally with his native language.

As with other immigrant groups (Aroian, 1990), Russian immigrants' psychological adaptation will be contingent on the dual tasks of mastering the new culture and resolving grief over the loss of the old one. In this light, it is important to begin by acknowledging the family's achievement in picking themselves up and transplanting themselves to the New World. Such an acknowledgment would set the "right" tone by communicating to the family the therapist's confidence in their ability to resolve their problems.

It also is helpful to keep in mind that the word "therapist" (*terapevt*) in Russian means "physician," so the family may unconsciously expect a therapist to provide a "prescription," whether in the form of advice or a directive to make its suffering go away. This gives the therapist a natural opportunity to assign tasks to help the family "do it" on their own. Such an approach, aimed at empowering the family, is in keeping with the Russian family's tendency to resolve problems on its own.

Galya and Nikolay, a professional couple in their 30s, came to the clinic seeking help around their 6-year-old daughter, Marina's, school-avoidance behavior. The couple, who had arrived a year prior to treatment, had both left their respective extended families back in Russia, but were reluctant to discuss feelings related to that, preferring to focus on the daughter's problems. A subsequent meeting with Marina established that the child was very concerned about her parents, who would lock themselves in their room when reading letters from Russia. They later explained that they did not wish to "upset" the child with the emotional pain that the letters elicited in them. The therapist suggested that the couple's emotional reaction seemed perfectly normal, in the circumstances, and asked them to include Marina in the reminiscing/letter reading. The couple agreed to do so only when assured that "it will be good for your daughter." The assignment proved helpful in resolving the impasse that had led to the child's symptoms.

This family came to treatment around the child's problems, but the actual issue turned out to be their difficulty mourning the loss of their home country. The family was given "permission" and a directive, to grieve together at home, which assured the child that they were "all right." By giving the family the home assignment, the therapist demonstrated respect for the family's boundaries and implied a confidence that it could successfully handle the emotional crisis.

In working with Russian immigrant families, one should keep in mind some notable differences in cultural values and expectations regarding gender roles. Russian women often are expected to "play second fiddle," and families expect the husband to be the head of family, although in many cases, the decision maker might be the wife. Therapists must use diplomacy and care in any moves to rebalance gender roles. Such moves are, of course, easier once the family has adjusted to the prevalent cultural values of their new country.

## CONCLUSIONS

We have discussed some of the concerns of ethnic Russian immigrants that have an impact on therapy. Their experience of uprootedness begins prior to leaving Russia, with the disintegration of old support networks. Their adaptation in the host country is accompanied by complex feelings about their history, separation from their native land, and separation from their kin. In work with this population, the therapist should be careful to respect the family's boundaries and its cultural imperative to solve problems on its own.

## ACKNOWLEDGMENT

Special thanks to Janice Rogovin.

## NOTES

1. Subsequent generations of Russian Americans had to contend with the dichotomy between the endearing images of the old Russia, handed down to them with their family lore, and the "Evil Empire" stereotype that characterized the American perception of that country throughout the Cold War years (1945–1990). Many resolved this conflict by pursuing the enduring values of Russian art, literature, and religious tradition.
2. These emigrés should be distinguished from the Russian "evangelical" migrants, members of various non-Orthodox religious sects who are admitted to this country as refugees. A discussion of these refugees, who maintain an autonomous, self-contained, religious lifestyle, is well beyond the scope of this chapter.
3. Russian immigrant parents are often disappointed when schools in this country do not set limits and expect the parents themselves to do this for their children. Russian students in the American schools, therefore, may act out as a way of asking for limits that are not provided at home (West, 1979).
4. As suggested previously, the potential role of the Russian Orthodox church in filling this gap could be invaluable.

## REFERENCES

Althausen, L. (1993). Journey of separation: Elderly Russian immigrants and their adult children in the health care setting. *Social Work in Health Care, 19*(1), 61–75.

Aroian, K. J. (1990). A model of psychological adaptation to migration and resettlement. *Nursing Research, 39*(1), 5–10.

Aslund, A. (1995). *How Russia became a market economy.* Washington, DC: Brookings Institution.

Conquest, R. (1973). *The great terror.* New York: Macmillan.

Conquest, R. (1991). *Stalin: Breaker of nations.* New York: Viking.

Dostoyevsky, F. (1950). *Notes from the underground.* New York: Modern Library. (Original work published 1869)

du Plessix Gray, F. (1990, February 19). Reflections: Soviet women. *The New Yorker,* pp. 48–81.

Erikson, E. (1963). *Childhood and society.* New York: Norton.

Gerasimov, G. (1994, December 17). A death wish is haunting Russia. *New York Times,* p. A-23.

Handelman, S. (1995). *Comrade criminal: Russia's new mafiya.* New Haven, CT: Yale University Press.

McPhee, J. (1994). *The ransom of Russian art.* New York: Farrar, Straus & Giroux.

Nabokov, V. (1989). *Speak, memory.* New York: Vintage Books.

Smith, H. (1987). *The Russians.* New York: Ballantine.

Specter, M. (1995, July 8). Gay Russians are "free" now but still stay in fearful closet. *New York Times,* pp. 1–4.

Stanley, A. (1995, January 1). A toast! To the good things about bad times. *New York Times,* p. D-1.

West, C. T. (1979). Adolescent immigrants from the Soviet Union. *Jewish Education, 47,* 27–32.

# CHAPTER 48

# Czech Families

## Jo-Ann Krestan

When we think of that part of central Europe that is now the Czech Republic, we think of Bohemian crystal and Pilsner beer; Freud and Kafka; *avant garde* literature; and the Romany gypsies, so many of whom perished with the Jews in Hitler's death camps. In our minds we see heavy industry powered by fossil fuels contrasting with bucolic countrysides dotted with willow trees, white swans on the rivers, geese in the barnyard, and castles brooding over the landscape.

Czechs are originally Western Slavs, whose language is Serbian, Polish, and Slovak. They preferred to be called Bohemians until World War I. I will refer to Bohemians and Czechs interchangeably throughout this chapter. Bohemian social and political history is rich, complex and, as Václav Havel, their first freely elected president in a thousand years, said in 1990, "driven by hope." The hope was the hope of autonomy for the Czechs, and that dream finally culminated in the formation of an independent Czech Republic in 1993, after centuries of suffering foreign rule.

A man in his 80s from Prague encapsulates the confusing political and social history of the Czechs in this way: "I was born in Austro-Hungary, I grew up in Czechoslovakia, suffered from the Germans and spent forty years in a colony of Russia—without ever leaving Prague!" (cited in Abercrombie, 1993, p. 37).

In his lifetime, this man has lived under four different governments without ever leaving home. Imagine a jigsaw puzzle of Central Europe with the pieces reconfigured multiple times over the centuries. The homeland of the Czech people is a piece reshaped dozens of times. It gets larger; it gets smaller; it spreads around the edges of other territories; it conserves its existence, nestled between larger pieces. Still, ethnic identity and culture are preserved under multiple rules. Like Native American nations who continue to preserve tribal governments within the borders of states to whose laws they are still subject, the Czechs creatively carved out semiautonomy, not once but several times under foreign domination.

## HISTORY

The Czechs have occupied the homelands of Bohemia, Moravia, and Silesia since the fifth century. The richness of the lands and their location made Bohemia an almost constant target of foreign conquest. The Bohemians, although remaining in the same geographical area, needed to maintain their identity under different rules. In the ninth century, Moravia dominated, extending the borders of the Great Moravian Empire to include Bohemia, southern Poland, and northern Hungary. The Czechs, or Bohemians, retained their own monarchy within the Moravian empire. When the Holy Roman Empire succeeded the Great Moravian Empire, the Germans claimed Bohemia and Moravia as part of the Holy Roman Empire, and Hungary and the Magyars took Slovakia.

Charles I, the monarch of this independent kingdom of Bohemia, was crowned Holy Roman Emperor in 1355, thus ruling the entire empire. Charles I presided over the Czechs' golden era of prosperity and cultural vitality. Not only did architecture and art prosper, but Charles University, the first Central European university, was founded in 1348 in Prague. It remains one of the greatest learning centers of Europe. Charles also penned the Golden Bulls, documents establishing the rules of succession for the Bohemian monarchy, thus perpetuating independence for Bohemia within the Holy Roman Empire. A Bohemian monarchy under Moravian rule and an independent Bohemian monarchy under the Holy Roman empire set a precedent of autonomous Czech government.

Religion is a critical part of the history of Bohemia. Until the early 1400s, the Bohemian intellectuals were largely Protestant. When the Czechs elected a Catholic Hapsburg to the Bohemian throne, the Hapsburgs imposed Catholicism. Jan Hus, a priest and professor, led a popular attack on the clergy, advocating not only reform of the Roman Church, but also the liberation of Bohemia. As Hus gained followers, the Hapsburgs started to persecute the Protestants. Hus was burned at the stake for heresy in 1414. The Hussite Wars lasted for more than 100 years.

The Hapsburgs definitively defeated the Czechs during the Thirty Years' War. Over 36,000 families, essentially all of the Protestant intelligentsia, fled to Protestant countries rather than submit to Catholicism. A small but vital group of them set sail for America.

The Hapsburgs established German as the official language and Catholicism as the State religion. Bohemian remained the language of peasants until the mid-1800s, when the Czechs resuscitated their determination to revive their ancestral culture and language, and the desire for Czech autonomy continued. The first Czech dictionary was published as part of this cultural reawakening.

During World War I, Czech patriots in the United States and abroad helped defeat the Austro-Hungarian empire, in league with Slovak immigrants seeking independence for Slovakia. In 1918, together they pledged to support the allies. An independent Czechoslovak state was formed at the close of World War I. Although Czechs and Slovaks were to have an equal voice in governing, Czechs outnumbered Slovaks two to one. The alliance was always uneasy.

In 1939, Hitler marched into Bohemia and annexed all the land once controlled by the Holy Roman Empire. The Nazi occupation ended only with Hitler's defeat and only with the cooperation of the Russians. Stalin allied with Czechoslovak leaders to create a new Czech state and, in return, secured a large Communist presence in postwar Czechoslovakia. As the leading literary figure of the resistance, novelist Milan Kundera, puts it in the novel that prompted the Czech government to revoke his citizenship, "And so it happened that in February 1948 the Communists took power not in bloodshed and violence, but to the cheers of about half the population. And please note: the half that cheered was the more dynamic, the more intelligent, the better half" (1980, p. 8).

The communist presence was to become a consuming one and ushered in a repressive Communist regime. Czechoslovak intellectuals were arrested for alleged political crimes and sent to forced labor camps. The oppression eased after Stalin's death in 1953 but was not thoroughly challenged until 1968, during the period of reforms called the Prague Spring. Dubcek, head of the Czech Communist Party and a Slovak, further lifted restrictions such as censorship of the press and the media. The Soviet Union was not happy with Dubcek's reforms, and in August 1968, the communists invaded Czechoslovakia to put an end to them.

In 1990 the first free elections were held in over a thousand years. Václav Havel, a Czech, was elected president of Czechoslovakia and Dubcek, a Slovak, was elected Speaker of Parliament. By 1993 the Czechs and Slovaks, artificially unified after World War I, were formally separated into two independent republics. Both Havel and Dubcek opposed their separation.

## PATTERNS OF IMMIGRATION

The Czechs were the first Slavs to reach the United States. Small numbers came for religious reasons during our Colonial period. From the mid-1800s until World War I, over 100,000 Czechs immigrated for economic reasons. The first of these immigrants were peasants, largely from the wooded pasturelands of Southern Bohemia. Reminded of the climate they had left behind, and driven by the dream of landownership, they were drawn to the Midwest, where they settled in Wisconsin, Nebraska, Minnesota, Iowa, Kansas, and Texas. These Czechs homesteaded the great prairies, first living in sod houses, then clearing the forest for building materials. They were the first large Slavic farming population in the

United States, working ceaselessly until they owned their own land. Bohemian women were reputed to be able to grow food even in the poorest soil.

The next wave of immigrants was largely comprised of skilled workers who settled in urban centers. Chicago became the third largest Czech city in the world, after Prague and Vienna. Cleveland and New York also drew thousands of Czechs. By 1924, when the United States established immigration quotas, over half a million Czechs had come to America. In 1948, and again in 1968, there were smaller, predominantly political migrations to the United States.

## EARLY SETTLEMENT

Unlike so many immigrants who came singly, the Bohemians initially came in family groups, or the men were followed by their wives in very short order. The first settlers have been described as highly intelligent. Czechs came to this country with a 97% literacy rate and more savings than other immigrant groups. They were proud of the nobility from which many of them were descended, and fiercely proud of being Bohemian.

The Czech farmers of the Upper Plains and Midwest were among our early pioneers. Their rich grain harvest built the great breweries of Pilsen and Budweiser. Czechs were known for loving their beer. Since they came from an advanced, industrialized economy, Czechs were also highly skilled workmen. The next wave of immigrants found skilled manufacturing and mechanical jobs in the large urban centers of Chicago, Cleveland, and New York, and also became entrepreneurs. Cigars and pearl buttons were two of their largest manufacturing interests.

The Czechs did not assimilate quickly, either in the city or the country, but formed their own neighborhoods that in many ways replicated the villages of Bohemia. Always prizing education, they learned English but retained the Czech language. In a manner reminiscent of their history of dual monarchies and relative autonomy within larger empires, the Czechs bought proportionately more war bonds during World War I than other foreign-born groups, while still retaining a strong ethnic identity and resisting assimilation. Until World War I, they married primarily within their groups.

Every settlement had a Czech society of some kind—a church, an amateur band, and a tavern—and the active community life before World War I revolved around these groups. The earliest organizations were fraternal benevolent societies that provided life and health insurance benefits, and *sokols*, or gymnastic societies. Community, color, and beauty were important. Garden plots replaced lawns in front of their houses, with riotous crowds of tall perennials. And music—there was always music. A saying, *Co Cech, to muzikant*

(If he's a Czech, he's a musician), expresses their love of music and dance. Every village had its own band of self-taught musicians.

Bohemians were extremely emotional people and yielded easily to melancholy and depression. Their emotionality finds expression in their music, from operettas such as *Vagabond King* by Rudolf Friml to the *New World Symphony* by Dvořvák. Polkas were actually created by the Czechs in honor of the Poles. If one listens to Slavonic dances or some of Dvořváks' violin concertos, one hears the same haunting undercurrents of strangeness and melancholy that have been described in their character. In *My Antonia*, Willa Cather's (1918) famous novel of a Bohemian homesteading family, Cather vividly depicts Antonia's father sadly fingering his violin and then committing suicide, unable to reconcile himself to the new way of life on the plains.

The largest wave of immigration had been completed by World War I. After World War I, native-born Czechs increasingly outnumbered immigrants. By 1940 a movement away from agriculture was apparent, and by 1970, white-collar jobs were held by approximately half of third-generation Czech Americans. The numbers of Czech Americans employed as blue-collar or service workers also declined with each subsequent generation.

## PRAVDA VITEZI

My Bohemian aunt always said, "A Czech will die for a cause." She was referring to the strong spirit of the Czech people. *Pravda vitezi* translates, "The truth will win." The motto captures the Czech history of free thought and opposition politics. Czechs are usually highly individualistic, love to argue among themselves, and are actually fairly divisive, except when adversity unifies them in rebellion against foreign rule.

Religion was always controversial. Most of the immigrants were nominally Catholic when they arrived. However, given their legacy of Jan Hus's dissent and their association of the Catholic Church with the cruelty and repression of the Germans, it is perhaps not surprising that one-half to two-thirds of them shortly left the Catholic Church. Free-thought societies and societies promoting faith in reason, science, and the individual conscience became a broad-based, organized movement among the Czechs in America. The free-thought societies were largely anticlerical. Communities could sometimes be polarized into Catholic and free-thinking camps. Later, Czech socialists played an important role in American politics. Not surprisingly, the most powerful Czech Americans in the 1860s and 1870s were journalists and newspaper editors. The Czech community supported special-interest papers for women, agriculture, poultry farmers, and others. The *Women's Gazette* in Chicago flourished from 1894 to 1947 as a feminist journal.

## FAMILY AND CHARACTER

Czechs valued independence in their children, who grew up to be exceptionally self-reliant and mature. Families, particularly farm families, pulled together as a unit. Men were willing to do housework. Women were independent and self-reliant, and could work the fields alongside the men. More than one generation often lived in the same household. Their values were democratic and pluralistic, imbued with work and thrift ethics. The Czechs were typically among the last to receive government assistance, even during the Great Depression. Education was prized and children established tremendously good school-attendance records. Record numbers of them went on to college. Czechs consider themselves peace loving, brave, generous, hardworking, and intelligent. They have also been prone to see themselves as somewhat backward.

Many Czechs went on to prominence in the United States. One of the biggest Czech entrepreneurs was Ray Kroc, the founder of the McDonald's fast-food chain. Czech Americans were prominent in science and scholarship. The first curator of the Smithsonian Museum of Physical Anthropology was Czech. The *sokols* (gymnastic societies) also flourished in the early settlements, and when we think today of superior physical abilities, one of the first great Czechs to come to mind is the tennis player, Martina Navratilova. The Czechs are also a cultured people. Think of Václav Havel, the recent Czech president and playwright; Milan Kundera, the great novelist in exile; and Milos Forman, the movie director.

Havel, a passionate champion of a multicultural civic society writes, "I am in favor of a political system based on the citizen, and recognizing all his fundamental civil and human rights in their universal validity, and equally applied, that is, no member of a single race, a single nation, a single sex, or a single religion may be endowed with basic rights that are any different from anyone else's" (1991, p. 49).

## SUGGESTIONS FOR FAMILY THERAPY

The Czechs are justifiably proud people with rich cultural and intellectual traditions. One must acknowledge and honor that pride when working with them. Therapy with Czech families might best be approached through reason. It is extremely important to demonstrate respect for their intellectuality and their rich cultural history. Eastern Europeans can easily be confused with one another. Even though Czechoslovakia was one country from after World War I until 1993, most Czechs would be offended if you considered them Slovak. They consider themselves more cultured than their Slovak neighbors. Second- and third-generation Czechs may still refer to themselves as Bohemian in order to make this distinction.

Because Czechs have traditionally fought on religious grounds, it is important to find out what the family's framework of belief is, despite the folk wisdom of never mentioning religion or politics. Introduce controversial content areas such as politics and religion, and let them talk about their beliefs. Introducing such topics into conversation is a good way for the family therapist to get some sense of the family's identity. Always find out when the family emigrated to America. The economic immigration of the 1800s and early 1900s was very different from the largely politically motivated immigrations in 1948 and 1968.

Education is extraordinarily important to Czech Americans. The therapist can assign useful reading to Czech families, explain the ideas behind family therapy, and discuss the readings with them. Approach the therapy seriously, as if it is work. Talk, listen, play chess with them (!!), and, by all means, ask for a piece of their apple strudel. Czech women are wonderful gardeners and cooks. The therapist can gain entry to their emotional life through appreciating music, dance, and theater.

Assess for depression and alcoholism, which occur frequently and seems to be syntonic with their family life. The work ethic that was so important in first- and second-generation Czechs may be weakening in newer generations. As in other ethnic groups, the strain between the relative degrees of acculturation in different generations may produce conflict. Traditionally, for example, three generations might live together in one household when the first generation grew old. With a higher incidence of Czechs intermarrying with other groups and moving away from the family, such three-generational accommodation is somewhat less likely to occur and may be a point of conflict. Ask directly about what the family considers appropriate roles for men and women. Often you will find that working hard and saving money are family endeavors, and everyone pulls their weight, regardless of gender. The Czech family replicates Czech history in that family members are highly individualistic while remaining tightly bound within the family structure, just as Bohemia maintained an individual culture while under the larger authority of foreign rule.

When working with a Czech family, it is critical to respect their tremendous pride in self-sufficiency and to treat them as collaborators in the therapeutic endeavor rather than as recipients of help. Czech stoicism hides tremendous emotionality and deep grief for their losses. They are a sentimental people. They have endured hardship for centuries and know how to endure. They do not admit a need for assistance easily.

"I remember many times that my father was in pain, but he would not show it. He had such calcification in his shoulder from bursitis that you could hear it cracking, but rather than take an anti-inflammatory drug, he did exercises with his arms, reaching as high as he could to release the shoulder muscle from the calcification deposits while grimacing in pain, but never making a sound. I didn't know then that his stoicism was central to his identity because I knew little of ethnic backgrounds. I did know that he was ferociously proud of being a man."

Finally, money is an issue to Czechs. They have worked hard to own their own land, their own houses and businesses. They have saved for the future. Therapy must not be frivolous or a luxury or they will not think it is worth paying for. Therapy should be hard work that will benefit the family. Doing therapy with Czech American families, however, can be extremely rewarding because once you convince them intellectually of the worth of the endeavor, they will make a commitment to what they will see as self-improvement. They love to learn.

## REFERENCES

Abercrombie, T. (1993, September). The velvet divorce. *National Geographic*, pp. 2–37.

Cather, W. (1918). *My Antonia*. New York: Houghton Mifflin.

Havel, V. (1990, March 5). The revolution has just begun. *Time*, pp. 14–15.

Havel, V. (1991, December 5). On home. *New York Review of Books*.

Kundera, M. (1980). *The book of laughter and forgetting*. New York: Penguin.

## SUGGESTED READINGS

Bollag, B. (1992, December 17). Milan Kundera's mixed feelings. *The New York Times*, p. C-18.

Chada, J. (1981). *The Czechs in the United States*. Chicago, IL: SVU Press (The Czechoslovak Society of Art and Sciences, Inc.), Chicago State University.

Johnson Freeze, K. (1980). Czechs. In S. Thernstrom, A. Orlov, & O. Handlin (Eds.), *Harvard encyclopedia of American ethnic groups* (pp. 261–272). Cambridge, MA: Harvard University Press.

Havel, V. (1994, August 1). Post-modernism, the search for universal laws. *Vital Speeches of the Day, 60*(20), 613.

Moquin, W. (Ed.). (1971). *Makers of America—The new immigrants 1904–1913*. Chicago, IL: Encyclopedia Britannica Educational Corporation.

Radio Free Europe. (1970). *The Czech and Slovak self-image and the Czech and Slovak image of the Americans, Germans, Russians, and Chinese* [Monograph]. Munich, Germany: Audience and Public Opinion Research Department.

Sakson-Ford, S. (1989). *The Czech Americans*. New York: Chelsea House.

Severo, R. (1992, November 9). Alexander Dubcek, 70, dies in Prague. *The New York Times*, p. B-8.

# Author Index

Abad, V., 193, 195, *197*
Abercrombie, T., 688, *695*
Ablon, J., 550, *563*
Abudabbeh, N., 334, 341, *346*
Ackerman, N. J., 524, *527*
Adams, W., 348, *363*
Adorno, T. W., 508, *515*
Agoncillo, R. A., 324, *329*
Agpalo, R., 325, *330*
Ahmad, I., 414, *420*
Akbar, N., 67, 68, *81*
Alba, R., 428, *439*, 573, *580*
Alba, R. D., 5, *25*
Aleman, J., 100, *110*
Alers, J. O., 190, *199*
Al-Hibri, A., 414, 417, *420*
Alibhai-Brown, Y., 19, *25*
Allen, J., 451, *466*
Allman, T. D., 148, *153*
Almeida, R., 5, *25*, 67, *82*, 108, *110*, 395,
     399, 403, *420*, *421*, 563, *564*, *565*
Alpert, M., 193, *198*
Al-Qaradawi, Y., 115, *128*
Al-Qazzaz, A., 337, *346*
Althausen, L., 682, *686*
Alvarez, L., 520, *527*
Alvarez, R., 190, *198*
Amand, M., *111*
Amaro, N., 157, *166*
American Psychiatric Association, 288,
     *292*
Anctil, P., 492, *493*
Anderson, C. M., 487, *493*
Anderson, J. L., 598, 603, 607, *608*
Angelou, M., 1, 8, *25*
Anthony, E. J., 304, *304*
Aponte, H., 77, 79, *81*, 105, *110*, 194, *197*
Appathurai, C., 320, *323*

Araki, N. K., 273, *278*
Araneta, E. G., 326, 327, *330*
Arasteh, A. R., 349, 350, 353, 354, *363*
Arce, C. H., 170, 174, 178, *181*
Arkoun, M., 415, *420*
Arnalde, M., 160, *168*
Aroian, K. J., 547, *563*, 634, *637*, 685, *687*
Aronson, S., 572, *580*
Arredondo, P., 216, *224*
Asante, M., 67, *81*
Asian American Health Forum, 227, 228,
     *247*, 249, *266*
Askari, H., 348, *363*
Aslund, A., 681, *687*
Atkeson, P., 325, *330*
Attneave, C., 32, 33, 35, 37, 38, 39, 40, 41, *43*
Auth, J., 170, *182*
Axtell, J., 47, *54*, 462, *466*
Ayakar, K., 402, *420*

Bada, C., 518, *529*
Badillo-Ghali, S., 183, 193, *197*
Baffoun, A., 414, *421*
Bahar, E., 319, *323*
Bailey, A., 473, 474, *476*
Bakalian, A., 378, 381, 382, 383, 384, 385,
     386, *391*
Baldwin, G. B., 348, *363*
Baldwin, J., 67, *81*
Bales, R. F., 550, 551, *563*
Balsameda, L., 155, *166*
Bank, S., 653, *657*
Banks, J., 429, 430, 431, *439*
Banks, J. A., 4, *25*
Banuazizi, A., 349, *363*
Baptiste, D., 133, *138*
Barakat, H., 338, 339, 340, *346*
Barkan, E. R., 484, *493*

Barker, P., 93, *95*
Barrabee, P., 558, *563*
Barry, C., 552, *564*
Bartoszewski, W., 666, *672*
Barzini, L., 567, *580*
Basch, L., 170, *182*
Bateson, M. C., 361, *363*
Bayor, R. H., 544, 547, *563*
Bean, F. D., 145, *153*
Beatty, L., 67, *82*
Becerra, R. M., 178, *180*
Beck, A. T., 490, *493*
Beck, L., 340, *346*
Behar, R., 165, *166*
Bell, D., 16, *26*
Bell, T., 673, *678*
Benet, N., 37, *43*
Benoit, J., 481, *493*
Bensussen, G., 172, *182*
Bepko, C., 551, *563*
Bergin, A., 75, *81*
Berkhoffer, R., 31, 32, *43*
Berkman, L. F., 172, *180*
Berlin, P., 606, *608*
Berman, P., 432, *439*
Bernal, G., 157, 158, 159, 160, 161, 162, *166*, 220, *224*
Bernal, M., 160, *166*
Bernstein, R., 433, *439*
Berry, G., 67, *82*
Berry, J. W., 400, *421*
Best, T., 87, *95*
Bettelheim, B., 380, 387, *391*
Biddle, E. H., 544, *563*
Bill, J. A., 347, 348, *363*
Billigmeier, R. H., 500, 503, 504, *515*
Billingsley, A., 67, 68, 70, 74, 76, *82*
Bingham, M. W., 403, *421*
Bitterman, B., 144, *153*
Black, C. V., 58, 59, *65*
Blanc-Szanton, C., 170, *182*
Blessing, P. J., 553, *563*
Bloom, A., 6, *26*
Blumberg, A., 570, *580*
Boas, F., 182, *197*
Boehnlein, J. K., *305*
Bograd, M., 108, *110*
Boncy, M., *111*
Booth, J., 214, 215, 216, *224*
Borders, L., *564*
Borish, S., 602, 603, 605, 608, *608*
Boscolo, L., 311, *315*
Boszormenyi-Nagy, I., 540, 541, *543*

Bourne, P., 255, *266*
Bowen, M., 93, *95*, 491, *494*, 508, 514, *515*, 579, *580*, 670, *672*
Boyajian, L., 380, 386, *391*
Boyce, E., 193, 195, *197*, 357, *363*
Boyd-Franklin, N., 5, *26*, 59, 64, *65*, 67, 68, 70, 74, 76, 77, *82*, 100, 105, *110*, 131, *138*, 193, *197*
Brayboy, T. L., 190, *199*
Brice, J., 106, *110*
Brice-Baker, J., 93, *95*
Brimelow, P., 431, *439*
Brody, R. A., 158, *167*
Bronfenbrenner, U., *515*
Brookheiser, R., 430, *439*
Brown, B., 66, *82*
Brown, G., 497, *516*
Brown, T., 301, *304*
Browne, A., *528*
Brudner-White, L., 176, *180*
Brutus, M. L., *111*
Bryce-LaPorte, R. S., 88, *95*
Brym, R. J., 631, *637*
Buchanan-Stafford, S., 101, *110*
Bui, A., *305*
Bulatao, J., 325, 326, *330*
Bumiller, E., 403, *421*
Burden, S. L., 488, *493*
Burnam, M. A., 170, *180*
Bush, G., 437, *439*
Bustamante, J. A., 159, *167*, 170, 173, *180*
Butcher, J., 539, *543*
Butler, S., 551, *564*
Byrne, N. O., 560, *565*

Cahill, T., 548, *563*
Calandra Institute, 570, *580*
Calvert, P., 144, 150, *153*
Calvert, S., 144, 150, *153*
Calvin, J., 471, *476*
Capek, T., 673, *678*
Carey, J. C., 400, *422*
Carini-Giordano, M., 439, *440*
Carmichael, J., 336, *346*
Carson, R., 539, *543*
Carter, E., 491, *493*
Carter, E. A., 161, *167*
Carter, R. T., 4, *26*, 435, *440*
Carvalho, J. A. M., 202, *213*
Castro, F., 156, *167*
Cather, W., 692, *695*
Cecchin, G., 311, *315*
Centers for Disease Control, 103, *111*

Chadwick, N., 549, 554, *563*
Chai, A., 282, *292*
Chan, C. S., 320, *323*
Chandrasekhar, S., 397, *421*
Chanes, J., 430, *440*
Chang, C. F., 256, *267*
Chang, W., 255, *266*
Charles, C., 102, *111*
Chartier, A., 480, 485, *493*
Chassagne, R., 98, 100, *111*
Chassé, P., 481, *493*
Chasteen, J. C., 143, *153*
Chavez, L. R., 173, *181*
Cherry, K., 273, *278*
Chien, C. P., 301, *304*
Chinn, T. H., 251, *266*
Chorzempa, R., 649, *657*, 664, *672*
Choy, B.-Y., 281, *292*
Choy, P., 251, *266*
Cirillo, S., 577, *581*
Clamar, A., 519, *528*
Clark, D., 547, *563*
Cleary, P. D., 546, 548, *563*, 575, *580*
Cobas, J., 157, 161, *167*
Cobbs, P., 9, *26*, 93, *95*
Cohen, R., 611, 612, *629*
Cohler, B. J., 304, *304*, 559, *564*
Coleman, H. L. K., 170, *181*
Collins, E. F., 319, *323*
Comas-Díaz, L., 5, *26*, 171, *180*, 183, 187, 190, 191, *197*
Comer, J., 70, *82*
Condon, M. E., 289, *293*
Connery, D. S., 555, *564*
Conover, T., 216, 218, *224*
Conquest, R., 682, 683, *687*
Conzen, K. N., 498, 499, 500, 501, 505, *515*
Cooney, R. S., 161, *167*
Cooper, M. H., 413, *421*
Cork, S. O. M., 556, *564*
Corliss, R., 47, *54*
Corrigan, E. M., 551, *564*
Covell, A. C., 289, *292*
Crohn, J., 2, 19, *26*, 573, *580*
Cummings, J. T., 348, *363*
Curtin, P., 58, *65*

Dagirmanjian, S., 390, *391*
Da Matta, R., 202, 203, *212*
Danieli, Y., 314, *315*
Daniels, R., 272, *278*
Darden, C., 551, *564*

Darden, N. J., 551, *564*
Daun, A., 599, *608*
Davies, N., 659, *672*
Davis, L. E., 94, *95*
Davis, M. P., 173, *180*
DeCharms, R., 625, *630*
De La Cancela, V., 187, *197*
Delgado, M., 185, 190, *197*
Della Pergola, S., 624, *630*
Demone, H. W., 546, 548, *563*, 575, *580*
Denton, N. A., 144, *153*
Der Nersessian, S., 377, 378, *391*
Desrosiers, P., 107, *111*
Desvarieux, M., 103, 104, *111*
Deutsch, M., 66, *82*
Devereux, E. C., 507, *515*
DeWind, J., *111*
De Young, C. D., *198*
Dhruvarajan, V., 401, *421*
Díaz-Guerrero, R., 175, *180*
Dicks, H. V., 508, *515*
Dickson, P., 518, *528*
Diner, H. R., 546, 547, 553, 555, 558, *564*, 611, *630*
Doepel, D., 313, *315*
Doi, T., 274, 275, *278*
Dominquez, V., 87, *95*
Donaldson, S., 409, 410, *421*
Dorris, M., 7, 8, *26*
Dostoyevsky, F., 682, *687*
Drachman, D., 216, *224*
Draguns, J. G., 107, *111*
Drucker, S., 522, *528*
Duany, J., 157, 161, *167*
Dubisch, J., 517, *528*
DuBray, W., 33, 41, *43*
Dugas, D. G., 485, *493*
Duninage, G., *96*
du Plessix Gray, F., 680, 682, 683, *687*
Durkheim, E., 539, *543*
Duster, M. C., 295, *304*
Dynes, W., 409, 410, *421*

Ebihara, M., 308, *315*
Egeland, J. A., 448, 449, *450*
Eggers, M. L., 147, *153*, 191, *198*
Eisenberg, L., 301, *305*
Elon, A., 501, *515*
Enchautegui, N., 157, *166*
Erdrich, L., 7, 8, *26*
Erickson, G. D., 174, *180*
Erikson, E. H., 508, *515*, 682, *687*

Ernst, R., 68, *82*
Eron, J., 387, 390, *391*
Escobar, J. I., 170, *180*
Escudero, M., 325, *330*
Esman, M. R., 484, *493*
Esposito, J. L., 339, 340, *346*
Evans, E. E., 549, *564*

Faber, E., 612, *630*
Fagan, R. R., 158, *167*
Falicov, C. J., 5, 18, *26*, 141, 144, *153*, 169,
    171, 172, 174, 175, 176, *180*, 220,
    *224*, 292, *292*
Falicov, Y. M., 141, *153*, 169, *180*
Fallows, J., 324, *330*
Fallows, M. A., 545, *564*
Farmer, P., 98, 103, *111*
Fay, L. F., 488, *493*
Femminella, F., 568, 575, 580, *581*
Fernandes, F., 202, *212*
Fernandez, C. C., 192, *197*
Fernandez, M., 256, *267*
Fernandez-Mendez, E., 183, *197*
Fernea, E., 338, *346*
Firestone, S., 521, *528*
Fischer, D. H., 462, *466*
Fishman, C., 328, *330*
Fitzgerald, L. F., *528*
Fitzpatrick, C., 552, *564*
Fitzpatrick, J. P., 185, 187, 192, *197*
Flaskerud, J., 234, *247*, 327, *330*
Fleck, J., 295, *305*
Flomenhaft, K., *198*
Fôlha de São Paulo, 200, *212*
Foner, P. S., 156, *167*
Foster, G., 675, *679*
Foster, R. F., 547, *564*
Fouron, G., *111*
Frank, O., 469, *476*
Franklin, A. J., 69, *82*, 435, *440*
Franklin, J., 200, 201, *212*
Frazier, E. F., 66, *82*
French, L., 481, 482, 484, *493*
Frenkel-Brunswik, E., 508, *515*
Freyberg, J., 304, *304*
Friedman, E., 436, *440*, 666, *672*
Friedman, E. H., 628, *630*
Friedman, L., 453, *466*
Friere, P., 6, *26*
Frieze, R., 296, *304*
Fung, D., 237, *248*
Furer, H. B., 497, *515*
Fusco, C., 13, *26*, 156, 166, *167*

Gable, R. W., 350, 351, *363*
Gambino, R., 567, 571, *581*
Gandhi, M. K., 395, *421*
Garcia, C., 155, *167*
Garcia, M., 216, 217, 218, 219, 220, 221, *224*
Garcia-Preto, N., 2, 19, *26*, 67, 70, *82, 83*,
    152, 153, *153*, 187, 188, 189, 193,
    *197, 198*, 204, *212*, 220, *224*, 399,
    *421, 422*, 477, *494*, 553, 563, *564*,
    565
Garcia-Remis, M., 190, *198*
Garcia Vasquez, J., 150, *154*
Gardner, R. C., 485, *493*
Garigue, P., 481, 482, *493*
Garrison, V., 190, *198*
Garvey, M., 87, *95*
Gary, L., 67, *82*
Garza-Guerrero, A. C., 170, *180*
Gastil, R. D., 350, *363*
Gavaki, E., 518, *528*
Gaw, A., 256, 258, *266*
Georgakas, D., 517, *528*
Gerasimov, G., 681, *687*
Gerson, R., 71, *83*, 93, *96*, 194, *198*
Gerton, J., 170, *181*
Gibran, J., 364, *375*
Gibran, K., 364, 365, *375*
Gilman, S., 430, *440*
Gimbutas, M., 650, 651, *657*, 673, *679*
Giordano, J., 9, 23, *26*, 439, *440*, 571, 572,
    *581*
Giordano, M. A., 23, *26*
Gladsky, T., 649, *657*, 662, 672, *672*
Glantz, O., 88, *95*
Glaser, H., 507, *515*
Glazer, N., 501, *515*
Gleason, P., 451, *466*
Glenn, E. N., 250, *266*, 273, *278*
Goddard, L. L., 67, *83*
Gold, M., 624, *630*
Gold, S., 612, *630*, 639, *644*
Golden, J. M., 295, *304*
Goldfajn, D. S., 212, *212*
Goldhagen, D. J., 501, *515*
Goldner, V., 505, 507, *515*, 526, *528*
Goldstein, E., 634, *637*
Goldstein, S., 611, 612, 615, 629, *630*
Gong-Guy, E., 295, 303, *305*
Gonzales, E., 173, *180*
Gonzales-Mandri, F., 166, *167*
Gonzalez, D., 142, *153*
Gonzalez, J., 193, *198*
Good, B., 301, *305*

Good, B. J., 359, 360, *363*
Good, M.-J. D., *363*
Goodman, L. A., *528*
Goodstein, L., 484, *493*
Good Tracks, J., 37, *43*
Gopaul-McNicol, S., 5, *26*, 60, 64, *65*, 85, 89, 91, 92, 93, 94, *95*, 105, *111*
Gordon, M., 435, *440*, 562, *564*
Gordon, P., 254, *267*, 325, *330*
Goren, A. A., 500, *515*
Greeley, A., 1, *26*, 435, *440*
Greeley, A. M., 547, *564*
Green, R.-J., 5, 22, *27*
Greenblatt, S., 69, *84*
Greene, B., 5, *26*
Grier, W., 93, *95*
Griffin, K., 141, *153*
Griffith, J., 170, *180*
Grigorian, H., 380, 386, *391*
Grinberg, L., 170, *180*
Grinberg, R., 170, *180*
Gross, S. H., 403, *421*
Grupo Areito, 165, *167*
Grvdziak-Sobczy, E., 663, *672*
Guerin, P. J., 194, *198*, 488, *493*
Guerney, B. G., Jr., 80, *83*
Guerrero, M. C., 324, *329*
Guest, P., 317, *323*
Gune, R., 400, *421*
Gunn, P. A., 36, *43*
Gunther, J., 485, *493*
Gurman, A. S., 488, *494*
Guroian, V., 382, *391*
Guterson, D., 270, *278*
Gutierrez, M., 157, 159, 161, 162, *166*

Haas, W. S., 349, *363*
Hacker, A., 16, *26*
Hakken, J., 144, *153*
Halberstadt, A., 634, *637*
Haley, J., 273, *278*, 491, *494*
Hall, E. T., 498, 503, *515*
Hall, R. C. W., 295, *306*
Hall, S., 571, *581*
Hammerschlag, C., 42, *43*
Handelman, S., 681, *687*
Handler, M., 584, 585, *594*
Handlin, O., 430, *440*, *441*, 451, *466*, 652, *657*
Hane, M., 269, *278*
Hanna, N., 159, 160, *168*
Hansen, J., 602, *608*
Hardy, K. V., 4, *27*
Hardy-Fanta, C., 193, *198*

Hare-Mustin, R. T., 505, *515*, 526, *528*
Harris, D., 301, *304*
Harris, M., 311, *315*
Hartman, A., 174, *180*
Hassan, R., 365, 372, 373, *375*
Hatfield, H., 503, *515*
Haule, J., *96*
Havel, V., 688, 693, *695*
Hays, H., 69, *82*
Healy, J., 365, *375*
Heilbut, A., 507, *516*
Helmreich, W., 569, *581*
Henderson, L., 67, *82*
Henriques, F., 90, 92, *95*
Henry, F., 89, 90, *95*
Herman, J., 432, *440*
Hernandez, M., 223, *224*
Herrera, J., 179, *181*
Herring, R., 39, *43*
Herrnstein, R. J., 136, *138*
Hertz, A., 666, *672*
Hervis, O., 290, *294*
Herz, F., 628, *630*
Herzog, E., 617, 619, 622, 624, *630*
Hildesheimer, W., 507, *516*
Hill, R., 67, 68, 76, *82*
Hillel, J., 107, *111*
Hillier Parks, S., 172, *181*
Hills, H., 70, *82*
Hines, G. H., 521, *528*
Hines, P. M., 64, *65*, 67, 69, 70, 73, 76, 81, *82*, *83*, 399, 402, 410, *421*, *422*, 553, 563, *564*, *565*
Hinnels, J. R., 399, *421*
Hirayama, H., 274, *278*
Hirayama, K. K., 274, *278*
Ho, M. K., 5, *26*, 171, *181*, 239, 240, 243, 244, 245, *247*, 259, *266*
Hoffman, E., 650, *657*, 662, 665, *672*, *672*
Hong, G., 246, *247*
Honorat, J. J., 99, *111*
Honychurch, L., 61, *65*
Hopkins, J. W., 150, *153*
Horii, J. M., 273, *278*
Hosakawa, B., 272, *279*
Hostetler, J. A., 442, 445, 446, 447, 448, *450*
Hostetter, A. M., 448, 449, *450*
Hough, R. L., 170, *180*
Hourani, A., 333, 337, *346*
Hsu, F. L. K., 231, *247*
Hsu, J., 253, *267*
Hu, L. T., 234, *247*
Huang, K., 301, *304*

Hugg, L., 68, *82*
Hughes, C., 319, *323*
Hulewat, P., 634, *637*
Hurbon, L., 98, *111*
Hurh, W.-M., 283, *292*
Hutnik, N., 411, *421*
Hyer, S., 50, *54*

Iacocca, L., 437, *440*
Ianni, P. A., 567, 568, *581*
Ichioka, Y., 272, *279*
Iga, M., 237, *248*
Ignatiev, N., 14, 15, *26*, 433, *440*, 545, 547, *564*
Imber-Black, E., 628, *630*
Inclan, J., 223, *224*
Israels, H., 508, *516*
Ivey, A. E., 489, *494*
Izbudak, M., 348, *363*

Ja, D., 230, *247*
Jablensky, A., 256, *267*
Jackson, C., 545, *564*
Jackson, P. A., 320, *323*
Jalali, B., 357, *363*
Jamieson, D., 4, *26*
Janelli, D. Y., 284, *293*
Janelli, R. L., 284, *293*
Jean-Gilles, M., 100, *110*
Jeffers, S., 40, *44*
Jiobu, R. M., 411, *421*
Johnson, C., 567, 569, *581*
Johnson, P. B., 550, 551, *564*
Johnson, W., *111*
Jones, A., 80, *82*
Jones, R., 67, *82*
Jones, W., Jr., 295, *305*
Jordan, J., 277, *279*
Jornet, B., *96*
Jung, M., 276, *279*

Kafka, F., 507, *516*
Kahn, M., 653, *657*
Kamaraju, S., 398, *422*
Kanin, G., 429, *440*
Kantrowitz, F., 208, *212*
Kaplan, D. M., *198*
Kaplan, R., 649, 650, 653, *657*
Karno, M., 170, *180*
Karnow, S., 233, *247*
Karrer, B. M., 4, *27*
Katz, J. H., 15, *26*, 434, *440*
Kaufman, E., 550, *564*

Kautto, J. G., 488, *493*
Kayal, J., 365, 368, 369, 370, 371, 372, *375*
Kayal, P., 365, 368, 369, 370, 371, 372, *375*
Kearney, R., 544, 547, *564*
Keddie, N., 340, *346*
Keefe, S., 174, *181*
Keillor, G., 601, *608*
Keita, G., *528*
Kennedy, R. E., 544, 547, 553, 554, 555, *564*
Kent, M., 67, *83*
Keopraseuth, K., *305*
Kerouac, J., 478, 487, *494*
Kerr, M. E., 491, *494*
Kesselman, M., 193, *198*
Khalid, M., 368, *375*
Khalidi, U., 415, *421*
Khan, B., 410, *421*
Kiesling, R., 107, *111*
Kiev, A., 173, *181*
Kilonzo, G., *96*
Kim, A.-S., 281, *293*
Kim, B.-L. C., 282, 283, 284, 286, 287, 289, 290, *293*
Kim, C., 282, *293*
Kim, D. S., 282, *293*
Kim, J. Y., 98, 103, *111*
Kim, K. C., 283, 286, *292*
Kim, L., 288, *293*
Kim, S., 239, 245, *247*
Kim, S. C., 290, *293*
Kim, Y.-C., 281, *293*
Kinealy, C., 547, *564*
Kinzie, D., 254, *267*, 312, *315*
Kinzie, J. D., 295, 303, 304, *305*
Kitano, H. L., 268, 269, 271, 272, 274, *279*
Klein, J., 9, *26*, 430, *440*
Kleinman, A., 254, 256, *266*, *267*, 301, *305*, 312, *315*
Kletzien, H. H., 506, *516*
Knab, S. H., 663, *672*
Knight, G., 160, *166*
Kniskern, D. P., 488, *494*
Ko, H. Y., 276, *279*
Kolenda, P., 406, *421*
Kooman, W., 507, 508, *516*
Koos, M. P., 520, *528*
Korean Overseas Information Service, 286, *293*
Korin, E. C., 152, *153*, 173, *181*, 210, *212*
Kosa, J., 535, 536, 537, 538, 539, *543*
Kosmin, B., 433, 438, *440*
Kottak, C. P., 204, 205, *212*

Krader, L., 674, *679*
Krauss, C., 150, *153*
Kraybill, D. B., 442, *450*
Krestan, J., 551, *563*
Krishna, A., 400, *421*
Krugman, S., 314, *315*
Kundera, M., 690, *695*
Kuo, W. H., 276, *279*
Kurtines, W., 159, 160, 162, 165, *168*, 290, *294*
Kutsche, P., 175, *181*

Lacey, W. K., 519, *528*
LaDue, R., 34, *44*
La Fromboise, T., 33, *44*, 170, *181*
Laguerre, M. S., 97, 101, *111*
La Gumina, S., 570, *581*
Lai, M., 251, *266*
Laird, J., 174, *180*
Lam, J., 237, *248*
Lambert, W., 485, *493*
Lamm, M., 628, *630*
Lamphere, L., 161, *167*
Landau, J., 137, *138*, 232, *247*, 634, *637*
Lang, M., 217, *224*
Langelier, P., 481, *494*
Langelier, R., 477, 481, *494*
Langer, W., 508, *516*
Langsley, D. G., *198*
Lapuz, L., 327, *330*
Larmer, B., 63, *65*
Laroche, A., *111*
Larsen, J., 75, *82*
Lateef, S., 415, *421*
Lau, A., 277, *279*
Lavelle, J., 304, *305*, 312, *315*
Lavin, D., 570, *580*
Lee, E., 5, *26*, 70, *83*, 232, 235, 238, 243, 244, 246, *247*, 259, 261, 263, *266*, *267*, 295, 303, *305*, *422*, 477, *494*, 553, *565*
Lengyel, E., 530, 535, 538, *543*
Leonard, K. B., 399, 401, *421*
Lerner, H., 671, *672*
Leung, P. K., *305*
Leung, P. L., 295, *305*
Levine, I., 432, *440*
Levinson, D., 507, 508, *515*, *516*
Levy, J., 35, *44*
Lewis, J., 67, *82*
Lewis, S., 101, *110*
Lewter, N., 75, *83*
Leyburn, J. G., 545, *564*

Liautaud, B., *111*
Lidz, T., 554, *564*
Lieberman, M. A., 559, *564*
Limansubroto, C., 321, *323*
Lin, K., 255, 256, *267*, 295, 303, *305*
Lin, M., 257, 258, *267*
Lin, T., 257, 258, *267*
Lipset, M. S., 619, *630*
Liu, W., 256, *267*
Lo, B. L., 169, *182*
Looney, J., 67, *82*
Lopata, H. Z., 662, 664, *672*
Lorde, A., 1, *26*
Lothane, Z., 508, *516*
Lott, J., 324, 325, *330*
Lovejoy, P. E., 58, *65*
Lowenthal, D., 92, *95*
Lund, T., 387, 390, *391*
Lynch, O., 398, *422*

MacCurtain, M., 555, *564*
Machtka, P., *198*
MacMahon-Herrera, E., 194, *198*
Maingot, A., 57, *65*
Malayala, S., 398, *422*
Maldonado-Sierra, E., 188, *198*
Maloney, S., 37, *43*
Mandel, L., 634, *637*
Mangione, J., 567, 568, 570, *581*
Mann, L., 567, 571, *581*
Mann, T., 67, *83*
Manson, S., 295, 304, *305*
Marcos, L., 193, *198*
Margolis, M., 200, 201, 206, *212*
Marie, A., *305*
Marín, G., 160, *167*
Marinou-Mohring, P., 521, *528*
Markowitz, L., 433, *440*
Marowski, J., 663, *672*
Marques, O. A., 583, 584, *594*
Marris, P., 170, *181*
Marsella, A., 254, 255, *267*, 325, *330*
Massey, D. S., 144, 145, 146, 147, *153*, 191, *198*
Masuda, M., 295, *305*
Mathurin, J., *111*
Matsushima, N. M., 234, *247*
Matthiessen, P., 31, *44*
Maxim, K., 69, *82*
Mayer, E., 433, 438, *440*
Mbiti, J., 129, *138*
Mbiti, J. S., 67, 74, *82*
McAdoo, H. P., 5, *26*, 67, 70, *82*, *83*

McAdoo, J. L., 67, *83*
McCafferty, N., 554, *565*
McCarthy, I. C., 554, 560, *565*
McClelland, D.C., 625, *630*
McCready, W., 547, *564*
McGill, C., 244, *247*
McGill, D., 171, *181*, 451, *466*, 585, 587, *594*
McGoldrick, M., 2, 5, 19, 22, *26*, 67, 70,
　　71, *82*, *83*, 93, *96*, 161, *167*, 194,
　　*198*, 206, *212*, 235, 236, 237, *247*,
　　260, *267*, 398, 399, 408, *421*, *422*,
　　437, *440*, 477, *494*, 546, 552, 553,
　　555, 556, 563, *564*, *565*
McIntosh, P., 15, *27*, 434, *440*
McKenna, A., 555, *565*
McKenna, R. B., 365, *375*
McKenzie-Pollock, L., 311, *315*
McKinney, H., 234, *247*, 277, *279*, 289, *293*
McLaughlin, D., 50, *54*
McPhee, J., 682, *687*
Mead, W., 596, 597, 598, 603, 605, 606, *608*
Meagher, T. J., 544, 547, *563*
Meinhardt, K., 170, *182*
Melendez, E., 184, 190, *198*
Menchin, S., 557, *565*
Mernissi, F., 414, 415, *422*
Messina, E., 567, 572, *581*
Messinger, J. C., 556, *565*
Metress, E., 553, *565*
Michaud, T. G., 572, *581*
Middelton-Moz, J., 52, *54*
Midelfort, C., 600, *608*
Miller, C., 204, 205, *212*
Miller, D., 379, 380, 384, 385, *391*
Miller, K., 544, 545, 547, *565*
Miller, K. A., 547, 548, 553, *565*
Miller, L. T., 379, 380, 384, 385, *391*
Mintz, B. R., 282, *293*
Mintz, N., 546, *566*
Minuchin, S., 72, 80, *83*, 105, *111*, 174,
　　*181*, 328, *330*
Mirkin, M. P., 4, *27*
Misumi, D. M., 412, *422*
Mitchell, H., 75, *83*
Mitscherlich, A., 508, *516*
Mitter, S. S., 399, 403, *422*
Mizio, E., 186, 192, 193, 194, *198*
Mock, M., 276, *279*
Mohatt, G., 33, *44*
Moitoza, E., 583, 585, 587, 591, *594*
Moll, L. C., 179, *181*
Mollica, R. F., 304, *305*, 312, *315*
Mondykowski, S., 669, 670, *672*

Montague, A., 19, *25*
Montalvo, B., 80, *83*
Montes Mozo, S., 150, *154*
Moore, L., 216, *224*, 305
Moore-Hines, P., 105, *111*, 477, *494*
Moradi, R., *363*
Morawska, E., 665, 668, 669, *672*
Marawski, J., 663, *672*
Morejon, N., 166, *167*
Moretto, D., 200, 201, *212*
Morishima, J., 258, *267*, 301, *305*
Morreale, B., 567, 568, 570, *581*
Moser, R. J., 173, *181*
Moses, K., 63, *65*
Moskos, C. C., 518, *528*
Mostysser, T., 617, *630*
Moynihan, D. P., 66, *83*, 501, *515*
Mozo, M., 150, *154*
Muecke, M. A., 295, *305*
Mura, D., 272, *279*
Murguia, E., 144, *154*
Murphy, M. W., 546, *565*
Murray, C., 136, *138*
Myers, J. K., 550, *566*
Myrdal, G., 433, *440*

Nabokov, P., 37, *44*
Nabokov, V., 681, *687*
Nagata, D. K., 276, *279*
Nahm, A. C., 281, *293*
Naidoo, J., 416, *422*
Nakano, M., 270, 273, *279*
Namias, J., 462, *466*
Nanda, S., 398, 409, 412, *422*
Napier, A. Y., 488, *494*
National Science Foundation, 348, *363*
Ndase, N., *96*
Neki, J., 93, *96*
Nelli, H. S., 568, 569, *581*
Nevitt, S. R., 508, *515*
New, L. K., 49, *54*
Nguyen, S. D., 295, *305*
Nichols, M. P., 482, *494*
Niiya, B., 269, 270, 271, *279*
Nobles, W., 67, 68, 74, *83*
Nolan, J., 547, *565*
Novak, M., 432, *440*
Novas, H., 146, 147, 148, 149, *154*, 191,
　　*198*
Nuckolls, C. W., 406, *422*
Nwadiora, E., 137, *138*
Nydell, M. K., 334, 337, *346*
Nyrop, R. F., 352, 355, *363*

O'Corrain, D., 555, *564*
O'Hare, W., 67, *83*
Okada, J., 271, *279*
O'Leary, T. J., 158, *167*
Oliner, P., 469, *476*
Oliner, S., 469, *476*
Olsen, V., 468, *476*
O'Mara, J., 4, *26*
Opler, M. K., 553, *565, 566*
Orfanidis-McGoldrick, M., 491, *493*
Orfanos, S. D., 521, *528*
Orjuela, E., 216, *224*
Orlov, A., 430, *441*, 451, *466*, 652, *657*
Ortiz, F., 159, 160, 165, *167*
Ortiz, V., 170, *181*
Otero-Sabogal, R., *167*

Padilla, A. M., 173, *181*, 190, *198*
Palazzoli, M. S., 311, *315*
Pamphile, M., *111*
Pane, F. R., 183, *198*
Paniagua, F. A., 239, *247*
Papademetrius, D. G., 397, *422*
Papajohn, J., 185, 186, *198*, 454, *466*, 524, *528*, 571, *581*
Papanek, H., 407, *422*
Pape, J. W., 103, 104, *111*
Paradis, F., 487, *494*
Pare, D. A., 277, *279*
Parry, H. H., 57, *65*
Parsons, N., 535, 539, *543*
Parsons, W. T., 505, 506, *516*
Patai, R., 365, 366, 368, 369, 371, 372, 373, *375*
Patti, A., 567, 571, *581*
Paul, B., 514, *516*
Paul, N., 514, *516*
Payne, M., 91, *96*
Pean, V., *111*
Pearce, J. K., 453, *466*, 491, *494*, 552, 556, *565*
Pearson, R., 673, 674, *679*
Pedagogic, M., 663, *672*
Penn, P., 507, *515*
Pera, G., 433, *440*
Pérez-Firmat, G., 155, 165, *167*
Pérez-Stable, E. J., 148, *154, 167*
Pérez-Stable, M., 156, *167*
Perez-Vidal, A., 290, *294*
Perlmutter, P., 430, *440*
Perrone, J., 570, *581*
Petsonk, J., 19, *27*
Piazza, T., 433, *441*

Pickwell, S. M., 173, *181*
Piercy, F., 318, *323*
Pilisuk, M., 172, *181*
Pinderhughes, E., 4, *27*, 59, *65*, 70, *83*, 125, *128*, 435, 436, *440*, 514, *516*
Pinkney, A., 68, *83*
Pittman, F. S., 193, *198*
Pliskin, K. L., 359, *363*
Polacca, M., 32, 33, 41, *44*
Pollard, K., 67, *83*
Portes, A., 157, *166*, 170, *181*
Power, P. C., 554, *565*
Prata, G., 311, *315*
Prawn, N., 663, *672*
Pressler, M., 469, *476*
Price, M., 67, *82*
Primpas-Welts, E., 525, *528*
Procter, E. K., 94, *95*
Puerto Rican Congress of New Jersey, 186, *198*

Quadagno, J., 568, *580*
Queralt, M., 159, 160, *167*
Quintero, R. M., 192, *197*

Rabkin, J., 191, *198*, 575, *581*
Ragucci, A. T., 569, *581*
Ramana, K. V., 398, *422*
Rambaut, R. G., 170, *181*
Ramirez, O., 174, 178, *181*
Ramirez, R., 176, *181*
Ramos, J., 195, *197*
Ramu, G. N., 401, *422*
Rashad, A., 112, 113, *128*
Raskin, N. J., 489, *494*
Rath, B., *305*
Red Horse, J., 34, 35, *44*
Rege, M., 414, *422*
Reguer, S., 626, *630*
Reimers, C. W., 145, *154*
Reischauer, E., 273, 274, 275, *279*
Remsen, J., 19, *27*
Response Analysis Corporation, 569, *581*
Reuss-Ianni, E., 567, 568, *581*
Reza, R., 179, *181*
Rice, E., 628, *630*
Richman, P., 69, *82*
Riegelhaupt, J., 585, *594*
Riley, C., *305*
Rindlisbacher, A., 625, *630*
Riotta-Sirey, A., 9, *26*, 567, 571, 572, *581*
Risech, F., 166, *167*

Rizvi, S. A. A., 416, *422*
Roberts, B., 550, *566*
Roberts, S., 3, 4, *27*, 427, *440*, 498, *516*
Robinson, M., 544, *566*
Rodriguez, C., 203, *213*
Rodriguez, C. E., 144, *154*, 191, *199*
Rodriguez, E. E., 190, *199*
Rodriguez, P., 216, 217, 218, 219, 220, 221, *224*
Rogers, C. R., 489, *494*
Rogg, E. M., 161, *167*
Rogier, L., 220, *224*
Rogler, L. H., 514, *516*
Rohrbaugh, M., 437, *440*
Roland, A., 175, *181*, 402, *422*
Rolle, A., 567, 571, *581*
Rosen, E., *422*, 565, 628, 629, *630*
Rosen, S., 611, 612, *629*, 638, *644*
Rosman, B. L., 80, *83*
Rossiter, A., 547, *566*
Rothenberg, A., 186, *199*
Rotheram-Borus, M. J., 520, 521, *528*
Rouse, R., 170, 172, 173, *181*
Royse, D., 67, *83*
Rubin, L., 461, *466*
Rücker-Embden, I., 508, *516*
Rudd, J. M., 555, *566*
Rueda, R. S., 179, *181*
Ruiz, R. A., 190, *198*
Rumbaut, D. R., 159, *167*
Rumbaut, R. G., 159, *167*, 173, *181*
Russo, N., *528*

Saba, G. W., 4, *27*
Sabogal, F., *167*
Sack, W., 304, *305*
Sacks, D., 200, 206, 207, *213*
Sager, C., 190, *199*
Saijwani, V., 413, *422*
Salamon, S., 503, *516*
Salutos, T., 519, *528*
Samouilidis, L., 524, 525, *529*
Sanchez-Korrol, V., 190, *199*
Sandemose, A., 602, *608*
Sanders, I., 665, 668, 669, *672*
Sanford, M., 92, *96*
Santa Cruz, A., 159, *167*
Sant Cassia, 518, *529*
Santisan, D., 290, *294*
Santo, L., 571, *581*
Sanua, V. D., 546, 552, *566*, 625, *630*
Sartorius, N., 256, *267*
Scally, R. J., 547, *566*

Scanzoni, J. H., 69, *83*
Schatzman, M., 508, *516*
Scheper-Hughes, N. D., 319, *323*, 555, *566*
Scherman, K., 551, *566*
Schiller, N. G., 99, *111*, 170, *182*
Schleshinger, A., 6, *27*
Schlesinger, B., 89, *96*
Schmitt, A., 410, *422*
Schneider, M., 320, *323*
Schneider, S. W., 19, *27*, 621, 622, 625, *630*
Scopetta, N. A., *168*
Schumer, F., 80, *83*
Schwartz, R. C., 482, *494*
Schwarz, B., 6, *27*
Scopetta, M., 160, *168*
Scourby, A., 520, *529*
Seagull, A., 80, *82*
Searles, J., 488, *494*
Segal, R., 58, 59, 64, *65*
Seldin, R., 611, *630*
Selvini, M., 577, *581*
Selvini Palazzoli, M., 577, 579, *581*
Seredy, K., 531, 532, *543*
Shabbas, A., 337, *346*
Shapiro, E., 156, 159, 161, 166, *167*, *168*
Sharabi, H., 338, *346*
Sharpe, J., 39, *421*
Sheinberg, M., 507, *515*
Sheler, J., 433, 435, *440*
Shenton, J. P., 497, *516*
Sherlock, P., 57, *65*
Shokeid, M., 638, *645*
Shon, S., 230, *247*
Shorris, E., 60, *65*, 144, 146, 148, 150, *154*, 173, *182*
Shuval, J. T., 170, *182*
Simek-Downing, I., 489, *494*
Simons, R., 319, *323*
Singer, D., 430, *441*, 611, *630*
Singer, J., 553, *566*
Singer, J. L., 553, *565*
Sisa, S., 530, 531, 535, 538, 539, 542, *543*
Siu, P. C. P., 640, *645*
Skidmore, T., 215, *224*
Sluzki, C. E., 172, *182*, 187, *199*, 211, *213*, 514, *516*, 634, *637*
Smith, C. H., 500, *516*
Smith, D., *305*
Smith, H., 681, 682, 683, *687*
Smith, P., 215, *224*
Smith, R., 89, *96*
Sniderman, P., 433, *441*
Sodergren, E., 598, *608*

Sodowsky, G. R., 400, *422*
Soekandar, A., 321, *323*
Sofer, J., 410, *422*
Soldevilla, E., 327, *330*
Solomon, M., 507, *516*
Sorrell, R. S., 491, *494*
Sorrentino, M., 577, *581*
Soto, I. M., 97, *111*
Sowell, T., 88, *96*, 461, *466*, 508, *516*
Spadaro, T., 571, *582*
Specter, M., 683, *687*
Spiegel, J., 185, 186, *198*, 454, *466*, 524,
    *528*, 558, *566*, 571, *581*
Spielberg, S., 430, *441*
Stagoll, B., 525, 526, *529*
Staino, K., 66, *83*
Stanley, A., 681, *687*
Staples, R., 67, 68, 71, 76, *83*
Stein, H. F., 674, 675, 676, *679*
Stein, K., 301, *304*
Stein, R. F., 546, *566*
Sternbach, R. A., 552, *566*
Steven, S., 663, 665, *672*
Stevens, E., 187, *199*
Stevenson, M., 320, *323*
Stewart, S., 487, *493*
Stierlin, H., 508, *516*
Stivers, R., 550, *566*
Stolarik, M. M., 674, *679*
Strand, P. J., 295, *305*
Strangland, E., 595, *608*
Struening, E. L., 191, *198*, 575, *581*
Suci, G. J., *515*
Sue, D., 301, *305*
Sue, D. W., 234, 246, *247, 248*
Sue, S., 234, 239, *247, 248*, 258, *267*, 277,
    *279*, 289, 290, *293*, 301, *305*
Sung, B. L., 250, *267*
Sustento-Seneriches, J., 326, 327, *330*
Suzuki, K., 177, *182*
Swierenga, R., 470, 471, *476*
Szapocznik, J., 159, 160, 162, 165, *168*,
    290, *294*
Szasz, C. M., 48, 50, 51, *54*

Tafoya, T., 33, 36, *44*
Takaki, R., 269, 270, 271, 273, *279*
Tamura, T., 277, *279*
Tan, F., 237, *248*
Tanaka, M. J., 276, *279*
Tashima, N., 234, *247*
Tataki, R., 5, 6, 7, *27*, 429, 430, 431, *441*
Tazuma, L., 295, *305*

Teahan, J. E., 551, *566*
Teller, C. H., 170, 173, *180, 182*
Telles, E. E., 144, *154*, 202, 203, 211, *213*
Terkel, S., 434, *441*
Thernstrom, S., 430, 431, 435, *441*, 451,
    *466*, 652, 653, 654, 656, *657*
Thiederman, S., 4, *27*
Thomas, A., *111*
Thomas, F., *111*
Thomas, H., 156, *168*
Thomas, R., 4, *27*
Thurow, L., 16, *27*
Tibrewal, C. S., 399, 401, *421*
Tidewell, B., 67, *83*
Tienda, M., 145, *153*
Tinker, J. N., 274, *279*
Tomas, P., 191, *199*
Tomm, K., 177, *182*
Tompar-Tiu, A., 326, 327, *330*
Torres, M., 166, *168*
Torrey, E., 173, *182*
Tremble, B., 320, *323*
Trent, R. D., 188, *198*
Triandis, H., 524, *529*
Trimble, J., 33, *44*
Troast, J., 546, *565*
Troiden, R. R., 320, *323*
Troyano, A., 155, 166, *168*
Truss, C., 159, *168*
Tryzno, W., 663, *672*
Tsemberis, S., 520, 521, *528, 529*
Tseng, W. S., 253, 254, *267*
Tulchin, J. S., 143, *153*
Turner, G., 67, *83*
Turner, J. E., 170, *182*
Turnier, L., 107, *111*
Tursky, B., 552, *566*

Uba, L., 5, *27*, 227, 233, 234, *248*
Uchendu, V. C., 130, 131, 134, *138*
Ueda, R., 86, *96*
Ulrich, D., 540, 541, *543*
Urcuyo, L., 193, *198*
U.S. Bureau of the Census, 32, *44*, 129,
    *138*, 141, 146, 147, *154*, 191, *199*,
    283, *294*, 461, *466*, 492, *494*
U.S. Department of Commerce, 397, *422*

Vaidyanathan, P., 416, *422*
Valle, R., 172, *182*
Vandi, A., 67, *81*
VanOss Marín, B., *167*
Vardy, S., 531, 532, 533, 534, 535, 536, *543*

Varga, Y., 532, *543*
Vasquez, G., 150, *154*
Vasquez, L. P., 179, *181*
Vassiliou, G., 519, 520, *529*
Vassiliou, V., 519, *529*
Vega, W. A., 169, 170, 174, 175, *182*
Vermeulen, M., 436, *441*
Vicente, M., 415, *423*
Vignes, A. J., 295, *306*
Visram, R., 396, *423*
Volgyes, I., 530, 531, 535, 538, *543*
von Mering, O., 558, *563*
Vreeland, M. M., 350, *363*

Wagenheim, K., 184, *199*
Wagenheim, O. J., 184, *199*
Wagner, P., 544, 545, 547, *565*
Walker, G., 507, *515*
Walker, T., 214, 215, 216, *224*
Walsh, D., 550, 551, *566*
Warheit, G., 170, *182*
Watts, J. F., 544, *566*
Watts-Jones, D., 108, *111*
Waxenberg, B. R., 190, *199*
Weber-Kellermann, I., 504, 506, *516*
Weltman, S., 67, *82*, 399, *421*, 563, *564*,
    628, 629, *630*
West, A., 157, *168*
West, C. T., 514, *516*, 686, *687*
Westermeyer, J., 233, *248*, 304, *306*, 311, *315*
Westridge Young Writers Workshop, 273,
    *280*
Wetzel, N., 508, *516*
Whitaker, C., 488, *494*
Whitaker, M., 434, *441*
White, J., 67, 68, *83*
White, M., 177, *182*, 275, 276, *280*
Whiting, B., 432, *441*
Wilber, D. N., 351, *363*
Willi, J., 507, *516*
Williams, C. L., 311, *315*

Williams, R., 416, *422*
Willie, C., 69, *84*
Wills, G., 548, *566*
Wilson, M., 70, *84*
Wilson, P., 89, 90, *95*
Winawer-Steiner, H., 509, *516*
Wirsching, M., 508, *516*
Wishile, S. M., 173, *181*
Wong, M. G., 250, 251, *267*
Wood, C., 202, *213*
Woolfson, P., 480, 481, 482, 484, 486, 487,
    *494, 495*
Wright, L., 438, *441*
Wylan, L., 546, *566*
Wyshak, G., 304, *305*, 312, *315*

Yalom, I. D., 489, *495*
Yamamoto, J., 237, *248*, 301, *304*
Yang, E. S., 282, *294*
Yans-McLaughlin, V., 568, *582*
Yap, P. M., 255, *267*
Ybarra, L., 175, *182*
Yerushalmi, J. F., 628, *630*
Yinger, J., 144, *154*
Yoshihara, N., 233, *247*
Young, J. E., 490, *493*
Yu, A., 277, *280*
Yu, E., 256, *267*

Zamichow, N., 170, *182*
Zamoyski, A., 658, *672*
Zane, N., 239, *248*, 277, *279*, 290, *293*
Zaslavsky, V., 631, *637*
Zborowski, M., 9, *27*, 454, *466*, 546, 552,
    *566*, 576, *582*, 616, 617, 619, 622,
    624, *630*
Zinovieff, G., 519, *529*
Ziv, T. A., 169, *182*
Zola, I. K., 9, *27*, 546, 552, *566*, 576, *582*
Zonis, M., 349, *363*
Zorn, E., 434, *441*

# Subject Index

Acculturation theory, 170
Achievement (*see* Work values)
Adolescence, 108–109, 122, 207, 208, 275, 276, 407, 456, 508, 509
Adoption, 151, 186
Adultery, 90, 297
African American Muslims, 112–128
African Americans, 66–84
  attitude to treatment, 78, 79
  couple relationships, 70
  family therapy considerations, 77–81
  gender roles, 69, 70
  kinship bonds, 68, 70–72
  mental health services utilization, 78, 79
  multisystem treatment approach, 77, 78
  Muslim families, 112–128
  parent–child systems, 72
  racism against, 433–435
  three-generation system, 72–74
Aggression, 186, 483 (*see also individual ethnic groups*)
Ahimsa, 395
AIDS, Haitians, 103–105
Alcoholics Anonymous, 551, 552
Alcohol abuse, 550–522, 663, 664 (*see also individual ethnic groups*)
"Alternation theory," 170, 172
*Amae*, 275, 277
American Indians (*see* Native Americans)
"American wake," 553
Amish, 442–450
  family and community structure, 444–446
  life cycle transitions, 446–448
  mental illness, 448, 449
  "parallel lives" of, 447, 448
  spousal role conflicts, 444
  therapeutic guidelines, 449, 450

*Amok*, 256, 319, 320
*Amor propio*, 329
Anger, 368, 369, 483, 606
Anglo Americans, 451–466
  attitude to treatment, 452
  adolescents, 456
  children, 454–456
  couple relationship, 457–459
  family therapy theory, 459, 460
  hyperindividualism, 451
  regional cultures, 462–465
  work values, 454
Anti-Semitism, 430, 616, 631, 632
Arab Christians, 336, 337
Arabs, 333–346
  attitude to treatment, 341, 342
  children, 340, 341
  couple therapy, 344, 345
  family structure, 338
  marriage, 339, 340
  mental health problems, 341, 342
  religion, 335–337
  therapy strategies, 342–344
Armenians, 376–391
  attitude to treatment, 387
  children, 386
  church and politics, 381, 382
  family structure, 384–387
  family therapy, 387–390
  Genocide of 1915, 378, 379
  sexual mores, 386
  stereotypes, 384
  "survivor syndrome," 380, 381
Arranged marriages, 408, 416
Asians, 227–248
  attitude to treatment, 242
  culturally relevant treatment, 239–246
  family characteristics, 230–235

Asians (*continued*)
  migration stress, 235–237
  psychopathology, 233, 234
"Astronaut families," 252
*Ataques*, 189
Authoritarianism, 508
Azoreans, 583–586

*Bahala na*, 325, 329
Bar and Bat mitzvah, 627
Barbadians, 62
*Barrio* churches, 172, 173
*Bayanihan*, 328
Bedouins, 338
Belarusians, 652
Bicultural marriage (*see* Intermarriage)
"Boat people," 99
Bohemians, 688
*Bondade*, 588, 589
*Boon-soo*, 288, 289
Brazilians, 150, 200–213
  attitudes toward therapy, 206, 207
  cultural values, 203–205
  "different but united" value, 203
  sex roles, 204
Bulgarians, 655, 656

Calvinism, 467, 471–473
Cambodians, 307–315
  refugee experience, 309–314
  social values, 308
  treatment model, 310–312
Carpatho Rusyns, 652, 653
Caste system, India, 396–399
Catholicism, 172, 173, 484, 485, 548
Central Americans, 149, 150, 214–224
  acculturation, 219–223
  migration experience, 218, 219
  refugee experience, 216–223
  treatment considerations, 216–218, 223
*Chae-myun*, 289, 290
*Chi*, 257, 258
Chicanos (*see* Mexican Americans)
Child discipline/child rearing
  African Americans, 79, 80
  Arabs, 340, 341
  Germans, 507, 508
  Greeks, 523
  Haitians, 106
  Iranians, 354, 355
  Irish, 558
  Jamaicans, 90, 91
  Puerto Ricans, 188, 189

Children (*see under specific ethnic group*)
Chinese Americans, 249–267
  assessment, 259–263
  contemporary family structure, 253, 254
  diversity, 249
  mental health problems, 254–259
  migration history, 250–252, 259, 260
  role reversal stress, 261
  support system, 262
  traditional family structure, 252, 253
  treatment strategies, 263–265
  work and financial stress, 261, 262
*Choteo*, 160
"Clinical paradox," 526
Clitorectomy, 136
*Compadrazgo*, 186
*Compadres*, 151, 186
*Confiança*, 588–590
Confucianism, 296
"Conspiracy of silence," as a coping
    method, 242
Coparents, 186, 187
Coptic Orthodox, 337
Corporal punishment (*see* Child disci-
    pline/child rearing)
Costa Rica, 149, 214, 215
Croats, 654, 655
Cubans, 147, 148, 155–168
  clinical considerations, 161–164
  cultural traits, 159–161
  family role, 159
  migration, 147, 148, 157–159
  "one-and-a-half" generation, 160–161
  social supports, 161
Culture and Migration Dialogue tech-
    nique, 223
*Curanderos*, 173
Czechs, 688–695
  cultural characteristics, 693
  family characteristics, 693
  family therapy, 693–695
  immigration patterns, 690–692
  Slovak relationship, 693, 694

Danes, 595–608 (*see also* Scandinavians)
*Dar um jeitinho*, 204, 211*n*7
Death customs, 373, 374, 408, 409, 552,
    553, 628
*Dekasegi*, 270
*Delicadeza*, 325
Depression (*see also individual ethnic groups*)
  Amish, 449
  Asians, 234

Brazilian adolescents, 208
Central Americans, 218
Chinese, 254, 255
French Canadians, 489, 490
Haitians, 107
Iranians, 359
Japanese, 276
Pilipinos, 326
Portuguese, 593
Vietnamese, 303, 304
*Destino*, 587
*Dharma*, 396, 402
Divorce (*see also individual ethnic groups*)
    Arab countries, 340
    Indian Hindu society, 402, 403
    Iranians, 354
    Jews, 615, 616
    Lebanese, 372, 373
"Doctor shopping," 360
Domestic violence, 507, 508
Double-standard, 90, 187, 386
*Druzina*, 650
Dutch, 467–476
    family relationships, 473–476
    immigration, 469–471
    religion, 471–473

Eastern Rite Catholics, 337
Eastern Slavs, 651–653
Educational values, 504, 505, 521, 570, 571, 617–619
Elderly, 484, 459
Emotional expressivity (*see also individual ethnic groups*)
    Czechs, 692
    Germans, 503, 511, 512
    Hungarians, 538, 539
    Italians, 576
    Jews, 619
    Koreans, 287–289
    Mexicans, 176
    Poles, 669
    Scandinavians, 599–601, 606, 607
Endogamy, 339, 372
"Enmeshment" issues, 579
*Enryo*, 274, 275
*Envidia*, 173
*Espiritistas*, 161
Externalization technique, 177, 178
Extramarital affairs, 90, 187

Face-saving, 289
*Familie-ziekte*, 473, 474

*Familismo*, 159, 175
Family characteristics (*see under specific ethnic group*)
Family intermediary, 179
Family network (*see* "Sib" system)
Family-of-origin work, 210
Family "secret"
    Asians, 242
    Italians, 577
    Jamaicans, 93
    Slovaks, 675
    Soviet Jews, 636
Fatalism, 350, 387
Father–son relationship, 274
Father's role (*see also individual ethnic groups*)
    African Americans, 69
    French Canadians, 481, 488
    Germans, 507, 508
    Greeks, 521
    Haitians, 108
    Iranians, 351–353
    Italians, 572
    Jamaicans, 91
    Puerto Ricans, 188, 189
"The Fifth Province Model," 560
Folk-healing (*see* Traditional medicine)
Food customs, 61, 367, 368 (*see also individual ethnic groups*)
French Canadians, 477–495
    assimilation, 485, 486
    attitudes toward therapy, 486, 487
    family patterns, 480–486
    family therapy, 486–492
    intermarriage, 485
    language, 479
    religion, 484, 485, 487
    sex roles, 480, 481

*Gemütlichkeit*, 503
Gender roles (*see under specific ethnic group*)
Genital retraction disorder, 256
Genocide, 34, 378–381
Genogram, 71, 93, 94, 322
German Americans, 496–515
    assimilation, 500
    attitude to therapy, 509, 510
    authoritarianism, 508
    diversity, 499, 500
    family patterns, 505–509
    family therapy, 509–514
    gender roles, 505, 506, 510, 511

German Americans (*continued*)
  low ethnic profile, 497–499, 512, 513
  national heritage characteristics, 502, 503
  values, 504, 505
  work ethic, 504, 511
Gift-giving, Asians, 239, 246, 277, 291, 292
Godparents, 151, 178
*Gosei*, 272
Grandmothers, African Americans, 72, 73
Grandparent's role, American Indians, 36
Greek Americans, 517–529
  acculturation, 524
  child discipline practices, 523
  children, 520–523
  family boundaries, 524
  family structure, 518, 519
  gender roles, 519, 520, 526
  homosexuality, 525
  marital subsystem, 519, 520
  therapist's role, 525–527
Grief (*see* Mourning)
*Guignon*, 102
Guilt, 372, 552

*Hahn*, 288
Haitians, 97–111
  AIDS, 103–105
  attitudes toward mental health, 106, 107
  childrearing practices, 106
  family relationships, 100
  father's role, 108
  migration of, 99
  religion and spirituality, 101, 102
  symptomatology, 107, 108
*Hak-bul*, 286
*Harijans*, 398, 399
Healing rituals, 41, 42
*Hembrismo*, 187
*Hijab*, 116, 413–415
*Hijos de crianza*, 151, 186
*Hijra*, 409, 412
Hindus, 395–423 (*see also* Indians, Asians)
Hispanics, 142, 143 (*see also* Latinos)
*Hiya*, 325, 329
Holocaust experience, 45–54, 666
Holocaust survivors, 617
Home visits, 193, 194
Homosexuality (*see also individual ethnic groups*)
  Amish, 446
  Armenian attitudes, 386

Indonesians, 320
Irish, 556, 557
Muslim prohibitions, 123, 409, 410
Nigerian taboo, 134
Scandinavians, 605, 606
Honduras, 149, 214, 215
Honor, 371, 372
*Honra*, 583, 588–590, 592, 593
*Housom*, 386
Hungarians, 530–543
  cultural heritage, 538, 539
  emotionality, 538, 539
  family system, 536–538
  fraternal organizations, 533
  immigration, 532, 533
  Magyar language, 535
  religion, 533–535
  "sib" system, 535, 536
  suicide rate, 539
*Hwa-byung*, 288
Hypochondriasis, 616, 617

In-law relationships, 36, 285, 286, 353, 404
Indians (*see* Native Americans)
Indians, Asian, 395–423
  acculturation process, 400–402
  caste system, 396
  Christians, 411, 412
  communication patterns, 407
  gender roles, 401–408, 414–417
  homosexuality, 409–412
  life cycle, 402–408
  Muslim families, 412–417
  perception of treatment, 417, 418
  religious values, 397–400
  sibling roles, 406
  treatment issues, 417–419
Indigenous healing (*see* Traditional medicine)
Indirect communication, 274, 308, 319
*Indirectas*, 176
Individualism
  Anglo Americans, 451, 452
  Armenians, 377
  Cuban values, 160
  Greek culture view, 522
  Iranians, 349, 350
Indonesians, 316–323
  diversity, 317, 318
  family relationships, 318
  gender roles, 320
  homosexuality, 320

shame in, 319, 320
therapeutic approaches, 321, 322
Infertility, Jewish couples, 624
Infidelity, 90, 187, 188
Intermarriage, 19, 20
  American Indians, 38, 39
  Asian Americans, 233
  European Americans, 438, 439
  Jamaicans, 89
  Japanese, 274
  Indian Muslims, 414
  Iranians, 361, 362
  Jews, 614, 615
  prohibitions, 19, 20
Interpreters
  Asians, 245
  Cambodians, 310, 311
  Koreans, 290
  Puerto Ricans, 193
  Vietnamese, 303
Interracial marriages, 434
Intimacy, 447, 448, 556
"Invisibility syndrome," 69
Iranians, 347–363
  child rearing, 354, 355
  cultural characteristics, 349–351
  family structure, 351–353, 355–359
  family therapy, 361, 362
  gender roles, 352, 356
  generation gap, 357, 358
  immigration, 347, 348, 357–359
  marriage, 353, 354
  treatment issues, 359, 360
Irish, 430, 433, 436, 544–566
  alcohol use, 550–552
  Catholic Church influences, 548
  children, 558
  family patterns, 553–559
  family therapy, 559–563
  gender roles, 553–556
  historical context, 544–547
  homosexuality, 556, 557
  mother's role, 555–558
  sexual expression, 556
  suffering and guilt, 552
  verbal skills, 549–550
Irish mothers, 555–558
Islam, 112–128, 334–336, 339, 340
Israeli Americans, 638–645
*Issei*, 272, 274
Italians, 430, 436, 438, 567–582
  acculturation, 574, 575
  "enmeshment" issues, 579

family patterns/roles, 571–580
family secrets of, 577
family therapy, 575–580
historical context, 568–571
homosexuality, 578, 579
Mafia stereotype, 569
religion, 569, 570
separation conflicts, 578, 579

Jamaicans, 85–96
  British influence, 88, 89
  childrearing attitudes, 90, 91
  class structure, 89–92
  family relationships, 89–92
  gender role paradoxes, 89, 90
  migration, 85–87
  support system, 86
  therapist's race impact, 94
Japanese Americans, 268–280
  communication in families, 274, 275
  gender roles, 272, 273
  family patterns, 272–276
  immigration, 268–272
  parenting, 275, 276
  psychological disorders, 276
  treatment considerations, 276–278
*Jeong*, 288
Jewish mother, 624, 625
Jews, 611–645
  divorce, 615, 616
  family patterns, 613, 614, 620–626
  family therapy, 628, 629, 635, 636
  intermarriage, 614, 615
  Israeli, 612, 638–645
  life cycle rituals, 626–628
  parent–child relationship, 624–626
  Polish, 665–667
  sexuality, 623, 624
  sojourner theme, 640, 641
  Soviet, 612, 631–637
  suffering as value, 616
*Jihad*, 336

*Kaddish*, 626, 628
*Kapulungan ng pamfamilia*, 328
*Karma*, 396, 398, 399, 406, 408, 409
*Ki*, 277
*Kibei*, 272
*Kindergarten*, 505
Kinship bonds, 68, 70–72, 365–367
Koreans, 281–294
  assessment, 290
  culture-bound syndromes, 288

Koreans (*continued*)
    family patterns/values, 283–287
    help-seeking, 289, 290
    immigration, 282, 283
    in-law relationships, 285, 286
    marriage customs, 284, 285
    parent–child relationships, 285, 286
    treatment considerations, 289–292

Language barrier, 193
Latinos, 141–154
Lebanese, 364–375
    anger expression, 368, 369
    family relationships, 365–369
    food/meal customs, 367–368
    independence in, 369–371
    marriage/divorce, 372, 373
    religion, 371
    sexual expression, 373
    therapy approach, 375
*Lebensraum*, 502
"Ledger" concept, 536, 541
"Legacy" concept, 536, 540
Lesbianism, 409, 410 (*see also*
    Homosexuality)
Liberation Theology, 202, 211*n*4
*Loas*, 102
Loneliness, Scandinavians, 606, 607

*Machismo*, 159, 176, 187, 192, 195
Mafia stereotype, 569
Magyars, 530, 531, 533, 535
*Mahinhin*, 328
*Malu*, 319, 320
*Marasmo*, 593
*Marianismo*, 187
"*Marielitos*," 148, 158
Marital infidelity, 90, 187
Maronites, 337
Maroons, 59, 88
Marriage (*see under specific ethnic group*)
"Melting pot," 431–433
Mental disorders, 233, 234, 254–259, 303,
    304, 326, 327 (*see also* Depression)
Mental health, 9, 10
"Mestizos," 143, 215
*Mexericos*, 593
Mexican Americans, 169–182
    alternation model, 170, 172
    emotional expressivity, 176
    family organization, 174–178
    gender roles, 175, 176
    historical context, 143, 144, 146

    migration/acculturation, 169–172
    religion, 172, 173
Milan Group, 579
*Millet*, 377, 378
*Mississippi Masala*, 398, 399, 402
*Moo-dang*, 289
Mothers-in-law, 404
Mother's role (*see also individual ethnic*
    *groups*)
    African Americans, 69
    French Canadians, 481, 491
    Greeks, 521
    Iranians, 352
    Irish, 556
    Italians, 572
    Jamaicans, 90
    Japanese, 275
    Jews, 624, 625
    Nigerians, 134
    Puerto Ricans, 188, 189
Mourning
    Asian Indians, 408, 409
    Iranians, 355
    Jews, 628
    Lebanese, 373
*Mulato/a*, 203, 209–210
Mulatto, 64
Multiculturalism, 5, 6
*Mushqaq*, 409
Music, 61, 692
Muslims
    African Americans, 112–128
    Arabs, 335, 336
    India/Pakistan, 409, 410

*Naches*, 626
*Narahati*, 359
Native American Church, 42
Native Americans, 31–54
    boarding-school system effects, 50–53
    communicative style, 37
    family structure/obligations, 35–37
    family therapy, 33, 37–39
    genocide, 34, 45–54
    historical perspective, 48–52
    missionary system effects, 49, 50
    time perception, 39, 40
"Nativist" movement, 431
Nicaraguans, 149, 150, 214–224
Nigerians, 129–138
    acculturation stress, 137
    gender roles, 133–135
    homosexuality taboo, 134

marriage customs, 130–134
racism effects on, 136
support group importance, 137
*Nirvana*, 398
*Nisei*, 272, 274
*No-No Boy* (Okada), 271
*Noon-chi*, 288, 289
Norwegians, 595–608

*Obeah*, 60, 92, 93
*Okpara*, 136

*Pakikibaka*, 328, 329
*Pakikisama*, 325, 329
Pakistani Muslims, 412–417
Paranoid ideation, 107, 108, 326
Parent–child relationship (*see* Child
    discipline/child rearing; Mother's
    role)
Patriarchy, 108, 129, 133, 338, 351–353
"Pennsylvania Dutch," 445, 505
Permissiveness, 275
"Personalism," 151, 160, 177, 185, 186,
    204, 205
*Philoptochos*, 519
*Philotimo*, 518, 524
Pilipinos, 324–330
    attitude toward mental illness, 327
    family therapy, 327–329
    mental illness expressions, 326
    values and psychodynamics, 325,
        326
"Pillars of Islam," 336
*Plaçage*, 100
Poles, 658–672
    alcoholism, 663, 664
    Catholicism, 667
    class consciousness, 662
    emotional expression, 669, 670
    ethnic relations, 665–667
    family patterns, 668
    family therapy, 670, 671
    name changes, 664, 665
    resistance to therapy, 670
    shame, 661–663
Polish Jews, 665–667
*Polonia*, 659
Polygamy, 119, 120, 297, 298, 339, 340,
    353, 354
Portuguese, 583–594
    acculturation stages, 586, 587
    cultural dynamics, 587, 588
    family structure, 591, 592

family therapy, 588–593
history and geography, 583, 584
key values, 583, 588–594
Posttraumatic stress disorder, 304, 312,
    313
*Pravda vitezi*, 692
Privacy issue, 370, 371, 522, 683
Problem-solving therapies, 160, 243, 244,
    290, 291, 559, 560
Psychoanalysis, 628
Psychodynamic family therapy, 459
Psychoeducational approach, 244, 290, 291
Psychopathology (*see* Mental disorders)
Psychosis, 234
Puerto Ricans, 183–199
    aggression control, 186
    attitude to therapy, 195–197
    culture shock, 191, 192
    demographics, 146, 147, 190, 191
    family structure, 186–188
    gender roles, 187, 188, 192, 195–197
    historical context, 183–185
    migration effects on family, 190–197
    parent–child relationship, 188, 189,
        192–197
    sexual behavior, 187
    spirituality, 185
    therapy issues, 192–197
*Purdah*, 407, 413–415
Puritans, 463, 464

Quakers, 464, 465
Qur'an, 335, 336, 339, 340, 409, 413

Racism, 14–16, 61–63, 433–435
*Racismo*, 173
*Raki*, 406
*Rasa malu*, 319, 320
Rastafarian religion, 60, 61
Reframing technique, 245, 290, 291
Refugee experience, 216–223, 309–314
Religion (*see under specific ethnic group*)
Resistance, 80, 487
*Respeito*, 205, 588, 589, 592
*Respeto*, 159, 175
*Retornados*, 585, 586
*Rodina*, 680, 684
Role reversals, 192, 236, 237, 261, 520, 524
Russian Jews (*see* Soviet Jews)
Russians, 680–687
    emigration, 680, 681
    family characteristics, 681, 682
    family therapy, 684–686

Russians (*continued*)
    gender roles, 685, 686
    psychological adaptation in U.S., 684,
       685
    religion, 683, 684
    suffering, 682, 683

Salvadorians, 149, 150, 214–224
Sansei, 272, 274, 276
*Sati*, 408, 409
Scandinavians, 595–608
    cultural characteristics, 597–601
    egalitarianism, 602, 603, 605, 606
    emotional reserve, 606, 607
    family characteristics, 603, 604
    gender roles, 602
    homosexuality, 605, 606
    stoicism of, 600, 606
    therapeutic approaches, 606, 608
    therapist's role, 604
Schizophrenia, 256, 326
Separation issues, 578, 579
Sephardic Jews, 611, 612
Serbs, 653, 654
Sex roles (*see under specific ethnic group*)
Sexuality
    Anglo Americans, 458
    Irish, 556
    Jews, 623, 624
    Portuguese, 592, 593
Shakti movement, 409
Shamans, 289
Shame, 319, 320, 371, 372, 552, 661–663
*Shariah*, 119, 120
Shyness, 319, 598, 599
"Sib" system, 535, 536
Silence, 37, 549
*Simpatia*, 175
Slavs, 649–657
Slovaks, 673–679
Slovenes, 655
Social class factors, 16, 17, 89–92, 436,
    437, 461, 462, 662
Social networks, 172
Social support (*see* Support systems)
"Sociotherapy," 328
"Sojourner" theme, 250, 270, 640, 641
Somatic complaints, 234, 254, 255, 359,
    524
South Americans, 150, 151
Southern Slavs, 653–656
Soviet Jews, 612, 631–637
Spiritists, 93, 190

Spirituality (*see under specific ethnic group*)
Structural family therapy, 276, 277, 559,
    560
Suffering, 552, 616, 617, 682, 683
Sufism, 349, 350
Suicide, 255, 256, 639
*Sungkan*, 319
*Sunni* Muslims, 114–116, 122–124, 339
Support systems (*see also individual ethnic
    groups*)
    African Americans, 74, 75
    Asian Americans, 237, 238
    Chinese, 262
    Cubans, 161
    Jamaicans, 86
    Lebanese, 366, 367
    Mexicans, 172
    Nigerians, 137
Survivor families, 617
Survivor syndrome, 380, 381
*Susto*, 173
Swedes, 595–608
Systems therapy, 459, 579, 580

*Taghdir*, 350
Team therapist approach, 80, 81
Termination phase, 246, 265
Therapeutic contracts, 452
Therapeutic relationship, 194, 208, 209,
    264, 489, 635, 636, 684, 685
Therapists
    advocacy role, 194
    bilingual model, Cambodians, 310, 311
    credentials of, 239, 241, 263, 487
    ethnicity of, impact, 94, 109, 110, 435,
       437, 513
    and family boundaries, Italians, 579
    gender impact, 94, 527
    indirect communication, 308, 319
    self-disclosure, 489
    stereotypes of clients, 513
    team approach, 80, 81
Three-generation system, 72–74
Time perception, 39, 40, 368
*Tinikling*, 329
*Topika somatia*, 518, 519
*Toska*, 682
Traditional medicine, 41, 42, 161, 173,
    257, 258
Transference, 487
Translators (*see* Interpreters)
Traumatic events, 217–223, 235, 236, 304,
    312, 313

Triangulation, 176
*Tullich*, 413

Ukranians, 651, 652
*Umircan*, 366
*Umma*, 338
*Ummat*, 127
"Untouchables," 398, 399
Uruguay, 150
*Utang nang loob*, 326, 329

Veiling, 116, 413–415
Vietnamese, 295–306
    family structure, 296–301
    gender roles, 297, 298, 300
    interpreter training, 303
    mental illness prevalence, 303, 304
    resistance to intervention, 301,
        302
    treatment considerations, 301–303
Virginity, 187
Voodoo practices, 101, 102

Witch doctors, 92
Women's liberation, 69 (*see also individual ethnic groups*)
Work values (*see also individual ethnic groups*)
    African Americans, 76, 77
    Anglo Americans, 454
    Asians, 237
    Chinese, 261, 262
    Germans, 504, 511
    Italians, 570, 571
    Jamaicans, 88
    Jews, 617–618
Working women, 69, 70, 525

*Yin* and *yang* imbalance, 257
*Yogi*, 398
*Yonsei*, 272, 274
*Yordim*, 638
*Yuutsu*, 276

*Zadruga*, 650, 651, 654